Advance praise for *Economic Theory and Community Development*...

This is a book for those who are seeking political economy alternatives both in academia and in wider communities. While providing a scholarly discussion of many heterodox (and orthodox) theories, Howard Richards shows that several already existing alternatives can work. They worked for a while in various countries such as Sweden during the social democratic era, and also today there are illuminating examples such as the Community Work Programme in South Africa. The book sets community against economy, especially as the latter is currently understood by mainstream economics. Richards argues not only that theory and practice must be consistent, but also that local community experiments can become the method of changing the 'basic social structure.' While Economic Theory and Community Development stresses the role of globalization, it sees the future of human survival and flourishing in terms of developing communities that respect and meet the needs of everyone in a generalizable manner. This book is a noteworthy contribution to the ongoing discussions about what will come after neoliberalism and what will make our global civilization sustainable.

– Heikki Patomaki, Professor of World Politics,
University of Helsinki

Strategies for economic development, besides being grounded in the varied realities that exist around the world, ought to have an ethical basis. This book with its underlying philosophy of unbounded organization provides guidance in the form of mental models, tools, and experiments. This is sorely needed at a time when the world needs to activate all available resources and optimize adaptive responses. Facing a global pandemic, wrestling with the climate crisis, and undoing the ravages of late-stage capitalism require that we widen the pool from which we draw knowledge. I highly recommend the perspectives of Richards and Andersson as an invaluable part of our conceptual exploration and purposeful change journey.

– Gillian Marcelle, economist,
CEO of Resilience Capital Ventures LLC

Since Rostow and Schultz, narrow calculations within an economic growth paradigm, culminating in a neoliberal straightjacket, have too long attempted to overrun other disciplines in the humanities and social sciences. The time has now come for economists to listen to voices outside their ivory tower, including those speaking from the world of informal economies. In this extraordinary contribution, Howard Richards and his collaborators build *two-way* bridges among academic disciplines that have too long attempted to claim epistemic hegemony in development thought and practice. More than that, the two-way bridges constructed in this book are solidly grounded in community development experience among the most disadvantaged victims of economic structures at work since colonial and post-colonial times. At a micro economic level, the poor "take the spoon in their own hands" and improve contextual conditions in their own communities and thereby learn that "it works."

It is essential that solidarity and cooperation prove themselves in a time when neoliberal competition and exploitation are the order of the day. This community approach may become recognized nationally and globally as a way toward an economic thought and practice that contributes to more fairness and equity in a world where the gap between rich and poor is only increasing. As an educator, I can only applaud this approach in lining up new ways to approach both theory and practice in economic development as *praxis*. When this and similar books in critical economy are included as compulsory reading in business and economic disciplines, one might hope that human rights and *human development* might widen the horizons of minds still stuck in coloniality.

– Magnus Haavelsrud, Norwegian University of Science and Technology, Trondheim

This book is just what many of our elders in government need to read in order to plan.

– Ela Gandhi, Gandhi Development Trust

Unbounded thinking is a powerful challenge to the crippling limitations of patriarchy. It enables us to break free of the reductionist, patriarchal worldview that rationalizes violence, denies our common humanity, blinds us to the positive possibilities of human diversity, and blocks practical action toward achieving the common good. Through unbounded thinking we can perceive the oneness of our human family; envision possibilities for equitable, just, and ecologically balanced economies; and become empowered to conduct politics toward a nonviolent social order that provides well-being for all and nurtures the human spirit

– Betty Reardon, Peace Education Chair, Columbia University (emerita)

Howard Richards' new book is a breath of fresh air at a time when we are bombarded with too much information that is either depressing or pointless. While he offers a radical critique of current economic theory and its concomitant version of "development," he also documents the success possible when things are done differently.

Richards, among other hats he wears, is a professional philosopher. So alongside a knowledgeable account of classical and recent texts in economics, the book refers to a wide range of recent and contemporary philosophers: Searle, Bhaskar, Barthes, and more. These are not only resources for his explication of how thinking works in our understanding of the world and the creation of culture; they also underscore the relevance of philosophy to action.

It is surely not surprising that human beings flourish when they work together for things that matter to them. What we need is to get rid of structures that prevent such flourishing. One hopes that Richards' clarity and passion will help to puncture the illusion of "economic reality" that has been holding the world captive.

– Eleanor M. Godway, Professor Emerita of Philosophy, Central Connecticut State University

This is an empowering book that helps educators to approach the field of economy, which is not considered relevant in the current curricula of secondary, tertiary level and teachers training, in spite of its importance in the quality of daily life of individuals and society as a whole.

For scholars committed to social change in formal and non-formal education, it offers a challenge to rethink yesterday's change strategies and teaching methodologies. For educators working with learners at all levels and in all kinds of settings, it is a storehouse of useable ideas and good practices that can help to rethink production, life and the relationship in between them.

The book articulates new ways of thinking and doing that are rooted in both recent on-the-ground experience and long-term historical understanding. It not only makes explicit the ideological defences of dysfunctional institutions that work as barriers to new alternatives, it also illustrates practical methods to build functional institutions and to help remove the existing obstacles to creating dynamic new outcomes.

Many paragraphs, short excerpts and also single phrases like "discourse coalition," "seeing as," or "imaginary world that holds the real world captive" cry out to be used to catalyse discussions leading to necessary conversations and transformative actions towards social change. The publication makes itself indispensable and irreplaceable.

– Alicia Cabezudo, Professor of Education,
National University of Rosario, Argentina

You give a voice to the heart of life. The heart of social structural life can think about itself and speak, thanks to your writing.

– Michael Britton, counseling psychologist

Economic Theory and Community Development

Why putting community first is essential to our survival

featuring South Africa's Community Work Programme

HOWARD RICHARDS
with the assistance of Gavin Andersson

Copyright © 2022 by Howard Richards and Gavin Andersson
All rights reserved under International and Pan American copyright conventions. No part of this book may be reproduced or utilized in any form, by electronic, mechanical, or other means, without the prior written permission of the publisher, except for brief quotations embodied in literary articles or reviews.

Published by Dignity Press
16 Northview Ct.
Lake Oswego, OR 97035
www.dignitypress.org

Cover image by Alta Oosthuizen

Book design by Christy Collins, Constellation Book Services,
www.constellationbookservices.com

ISBN: 978-1-952292-08-8 (paperback)
ISBN: 978-1-952292-09-5 (epub)

10 9 8 7 6 5 4 3 2 1

Contents

Foreword by Evelin Lindner		ix
Abbreviations		xii
A Note on Using the First-Person Plural		xiii
Introduction		1
1.	South Africa Now as a Land of Credible Threats and Incredible Promises	15
2.	Community as a Guiding Star for Navigating the Seas of Late Modernity in Neurath's Boat	43
3.	Economics as Social Structure	60
4.	Two Staggering Facts That Change Everything	87
5.	The Community Work Programme as a Sea Change in Public Policy	108
6.	India's Employment Guarantee as an Accumulation of Anomalies	142
7.	The Swedish Model as Programmed for Failure	178
8.	Neoliberal Economics as an Imaginary World That Holds the Real World Captive	228
9.	The Community Work Programme at Orange Farm as Community Development	273
10.	The Fiscal Crisis of the State as a Philosophical Problem: Part One	316
11.	The Fiscal Crisis of the State as a Philosophical Problem: Part Two	355
Index		401
About the Authors		443

Foreword by Evelin Lindner

This is an illuminating and crucially important book. It repays a careful study. It is lifesaving, for you and me, for us all, for humanity as a species.

How does it illuminate? It systematically guides the reader to see what economies are, what theories about economies are: they are social structures. I cannot explain this book's concept of social structure in the short space available here, yet I am confident that anyone who reads it will find it clear and convincing. It illuminates many widely held ideas about how the world works, ideas that surround us from morning to evening as they circulate in everyday conversation, in academic debates and in the media. It articulates them in novel and highly enlightening ways. It opens up the very horizons that we, as humankind, need to survive on Planet Earth. It offers more than just another perspective; its analysis reaches both deeper and higher than most others. It starts out with the "brute facts" of life and relates them to key texts in economic theory by Adam Smith, David Ricardo, Karl Marx, Leon Walras, Rosa Luxemburg, Alfred Marshall, John Maynard Keynes, Milton Friedman, Amartya Sen and many others.

The resulting improvements in our understanding of economics are no small matter. Should you work with building a culture of mutual caring, you certainly have noticed that economic issues confront us at every turn. Many of the decisions we make—I almost want to say all of the decisions we make—depend entirely or in part on our understanding of economic causes and economic effects. Our decisions and what we do are deeply entangled. What we do determines the future. What if our understanding of economic causes and effects is treacherous?

Chapter 8 can be read as a polemic against the currently dominant neoliberal model, yet what the book proposes is neither the complete rejection of neoliberalism nor a different one-size-fits-all economic model. The book's argument is at a very different level. It sends out a revolutionary call for something that is not economic at all, namely, community. This is because the important issues of life and survival, in the end, are psychological and ethical rather than economic *per se*. The book calls for unbounded organization. Unbounded organization—to anticipate briefly a central concept to be developed at length—means alignment for the common good across sectors. It means deploying an unlimited variety of economic practices while remaining firmly committed to the goals of dignity for all human beings and harmony with Planet Earth.

The book interweaves theoretical clarifications with extensive reports on important social innovations. We meet South Africa's Community Work Programme and learn how it uses public employment to catalyse community development. This work programme puts into practice some of the principles the authors of this book advocate. The theory of unbounded organization benefits from hands-on historical experience. Chapter 6 is devoted to the experience of India's Mahatma Gandhi National Rural Employment Guarantee Act, the world's largest public employment programme. Chapter 7 studies the rise and fall of the Swedish Model.

This book is urgently needed because humanity has reached a point where economies are out of control. When we read projections of the future, usually they start from current trends, and then they assume, as if it were obvious, that economic and technological forces are basically autonomous and will shape our future regardless of what we humans may think, feel or do. This book, in contrast, takes seriously the possibility that human beings might come to understand what an economy *is*, how economies have been historically constructed and how economies can be *changed*. This book is urgently needed as part of a paradigm shift that will change economics from the status it has now, namely, the status of inevitable fate. It will save us from economics as an inevitable fate that drives humanity toward social disintegration and ecological catastrophe against its will. It will open space for the status of what Gunnar Myrdal called a "created harmony".

In closing, let me say some words about this book's self-conscious use of language. Following in the footsteps of an earlier book by Catherine Hoppers and Howard Richards,[1] this book takes seriously John Searle's theory of speech acts. Talking is acting. Writing is acting. Choosing which word to use is ultimately an ethical choice. It is a matter of assuming responsibility for the consequences of one's acts. A related point is that, in our large and diverse human family, there are many different ways of speaking. If we had to wait to construct peace, justice and sustainability until everyone agreed on a single vocabulary with uniform definitions of its terms, we would wait forever. We would wait much longer than the time we still have left to change course before the disruption of the delicate balances of the biosphere makes the extinction of life inevitable. What we must do—the only thing

---

1. Catherine Hoppers and Howard Richards, *Rethinking Thinking* (Pretoria: University of South Africa, 2012).

we can do—is to practice mutual respect, honour intellectual differences, accept cultural diversity and simultaneously cooperate on a physical level to make sure that people receive the supplies of goods and services they need to live, even as our technologies and practices become greener every day.

It is a merit of this book that it tries to avoid what might be called an intellectual version of a dominator mindset. The book engages other thinkers in their own terms, understanding their words as they understood them. The authors of this book do not insist that there is only one right way to use a word or to define a concept. They are fully aware that this book cannot be more than a contribution to a centuries-long, ongoing dialogue in many voices. They are consciously aware that nobody can do better than express tentative judgments in words that are tentatively chosen because they appear to be the best way to express them here and now.

This does not mean that this book is vague. On the contrary. This book makes strongly felt points, at times passionately. It develops an overall viewpoint. That overall viewpoint has also been expressed in more philosophical terms in a trio of journal articles that complement each other.

> Howard Richards, 'On the Intransitive Objects of the Social (Or Human) Sciences', *Journal of Critical Realism*, vol. 17 (2018), pages 1–16.
>
> Howard Richards, 'Moral (and Ethical) Realism', *Journal of Critical Realism*, vol. 18 (2019), pages 285–302.
>
> Howard Richards, 'Moral Economy and Emancipation', *Journal of Critical Realism*, vol. 19 (2020), pages 146–158.

The book's viewpoint might be called a *cosmovision* or a metaphysic. It is a lifesaving metaphysic.

Abbreviations

ABC	Abastecimiento Basico Comunitario (Argentina)
ABCD	Asset-Based Community Development (Chicago, US)
ANC	African National Congress (South Africa)
APF	Anti-Privatisation Forum (South Africa)
CBO	Community-based organization
CDI	Centre for Democratising Information (South Africa)
CHAT	Cultural historical activity theory
COGTA	Cooperative Governance and Traditional Affairs (South Africa)
CPF	Community Policing Forum (South Africa)
CV	Curriculum vitae
CWP	Community Work Programme (South Africa)
EFF	Economic Freedom Fighters (South Africa)
EPWP	Expanded Public Works Programme (South Africa)
FIFA	Fédération Internationale de Football Association
GDP	Gross domestic product
ILO	International Labour Organization
IMF	International Monetary Fund
NABARD	National Bank for Agriculture and Rural Development (Argentina)
NDP	National Development Plan (South Africa)
NGO	Nongovernmental organization
NREGA	National Rural Employment Guarantee Act (India)
OECD	Organisation for Economic Co-operation and Development
PHP	People's Housing Process (South Africa)
RDP	Reconstruction and Development Programme (South Africa)
RHV	Dani Rodrik, Ricardo Hausmann and Andres Velasco, authors of One Economics, Many Recipes
SF1	Staggering Fact 1
SF2	Staggering Fact 2
TIPS	Trade and Industrial Policy Strategies (South Africa)
VEP	Victim Empowerment Programme (South Africa)

Foreword | xiii

A Note on Using the First-Person Plural

In this book, often (but not always) I write in the first-person plural. I do this not only because Gavin Andersson is my co-author but also because I feel that I am expressing thoughts that co-belong to others who have over the years produced them with me.

To the erudition and feedback of my partner, Carolyn, I owe whatever claim this book may have to adhering to academic standards of responsible scholarship. Others whose thoughts I cannot separate from my own include our colleagues and students during our thirty-seven years on the faculty at Earlham College. They include colleagues in the philosophy department and in the Peace and Global Studies Programme, most notably the programme's present director, Joanna Swanger. They also include economists. Many of the thoughts on the following pages I owe to pleasant conversations with Earlham economists I usually did not agree with. The benefits of those conversations are such that I recommend that the rest of the world indulge in similar pleasures. Others among the thoughts that follow are ones I would never have arrived at without the help of Earlham economists and sociologists I usually *did* agree with.

I have assimilated many ideas from my Oxford tutor Rom Harré; from my mentors in the study of education and moral development, Betty Reardon and Magnus Haavelsrud (and thus indirectly from Johan Galtung, whom I barely know personally); as well as from Ed Sullivan and Clive Beck at the University of Toronto, Sara Horowitz at the University of Buenos Aires, Lawrence Kohlberg at Harvard, and Kosheek Sewchurran at University of Cape Town. Many thanks also for what we (Carolyn and I) learned from our former colleagues at the Holy Cross Centre for Ecological Spirituality, Fathers Tom Berry and Steve Dunne and Sister Anne Lonergan.

When I write of South Africa's Community Work Programme, I identify with the small group of thoughtful committed citizens who initiated it, including Kate Philip (who reviewed earlier versions of the chapters that directly concern the CWP), Sidwell Moguthu, Nkere Skosana, and Gavin again. Since 2019, I have had the opportunity to create thoughts with Gillian Marcelle and with members of the newly founded Unbounded Academy—including Gert van der Westhuizen, Evelin Lindner, and Crain Soudien. These thoughts, too, have merged with whatever thoughts I call my own. Catherine Hoppers is both a member and a grandmother of the Unbounded Academy, since it grew out of the deliberations of fellows of a South African Research Chair in Development Education she held for ten years. Many of us are now collaborating in her new NGO based in Uganda, the Global Institute of Applied Governance in Science, Knowledge Systems and Innovations. This book is the third of the "taproot" series she started. The first two (*Rethinking Thinking* and *Following Foucault: The Trail of the Fox*) were prepared with the assistance of Na-iem Dollie.

Looking back farther, I cannot clearly distinguish my own thoughts in the late 1960s from those of the overlapping teams of young admirers of Paulo Freire at the Centre for Research and Development in Education (CIDE) and at the Ministry of Education of Chile, most memorably Juan-Eduardo Garcia-Huidobro, Jorge Zuleta and padre Patricio Cariola, S.J., and more recently Alicia Cabezudo and Raul Gonzalez. Before Carolyn and I moved to Chile in 1965, my tutors in community and union organizing were Cesar Chavez and Dolores Huerta. That was back in the days when United Farm Workers was a fledgling start-up in Delano, California. I was simultaneously the union's volunteer lawyer and the paid personal assistant to Robert Maynard Hutchins, who ran an all-star think tank over the mountains from Delano in Santa Barbara. Among the all-stars whose ideas I find hardest to separate from my own are Hutchins himself, Linus Pauling, Rexford Tugwell and Abba Lerner. Today, half a century later, the same can be said of many of the authors who publish in the *Journal of Critical Realism*.

It took a team also to create this book. Kudos are due to Carolyn Bond, Raff Carmen, Zuzana Lukay and Natascha Scott-Stokes for brilliant editing and to Catherine Bowman for crafting a fine index. An earlier version of the chapter on India was reviewed by Ela Gandhi. An earlier version of the chapter on Sweden was reviewed by Dean Björn Åstrand of Karlstad University. Malose Langa of Wits University is the principal author of chapter 9, a case study of the Community Work Programme on the ground on the south side of Johannesburg.

– Howard Richards

Introduction

This book aspires to contribute to solving humanity's most serious and fundamental problems. Its overall aim is to contribute to saving humanity and the biosphere.[1] Although the focus is on public employment programmes, at issue is whether it is possible to organize human life sustainably at all and whether it is possible to avoid further descent into social chaos. I introduce the book by outlining briefly here this book's premise, a few central concepts that make its approach unique, an introduction to critical realism, and the contents of each chapter.

OVERVIEW OF THE INTRODUCTION
1. Our Dominant Way of Thinking Is Flawed
2. A Few Central Concepts
3. An Introduction to Critical Realism
4. About Today's Basic Social Structure
5. A Little More on Critical Realism
6. The Chapters of This Book

1. Our Dominant Way of Thinking Is Flawed

This book's premise is that life (to name humanity and the biosphere with one word) is in danger and needs to be saved. This premise is perhaps obvious from the point of view of ecology and of the prevention of nuclear war, among others. What is less obvious is that life needs to be saved from humanity's dominant way of thinking. It is less obvious, and many will say it is not true, that the more people and their computers think in the current dominant ways, the deeper they think themselves into holes that are harder and harder to climb out of.

In seeing today's dominant way of thinking as counter-productive, my coauthors and I express a minority view, but we are not alone. Many agree with us that today's dominant way of thinking is orthodox liberal economics,

---

1. In this respect the present work can be regarded as a sequel to Catherine Hoppers and Howard Richards, *Rethinking Thinking* (Pretoria: University of South Africa, 2010).

and that life needs to be saved from it. A smaller number agree with us that life needs to be saved *from economics in general*—that the economic way of thinking that began in Europe in the eighteenth century is no longer compatible with the survival of the human species and the biosphere.

Shelves of university libraries are filled with books that demonstrate how the orthodox economics that dominates in schools and high-prestige journals is systematically misleading.[2] Other shelves are filled with books that offer heterodox alternatives.[3] It would be premature to draw a bright line—if indeed a bright line can be drawn—separating those who (like André Orléan[4] and many feminist and indigenous writers) agree with us that it is time to abandon the main premises of eighteenth-century European political economy, ethics and jurisprudence from those who (like Joseph Stiglitz[5]) agree with us that the reigning neoliberalism is bogus but nonetheless accept the bulk of standard theory. My view is that even if a bright line could be drawn, it would not be useful. Valuable practical advice can and should be drawn from diverse perspectives.

2. A Few Central Concepts

One of several central concepts of this book is the ethical principle that *we should share the surplus.* It is an ancient principle that, in early modern times Adam Smith, the father of modern economics, took great pains to deny—even though, as Amartya Sen points out, Smith founded both the 'ethical' and the 'engineering' traditions in economic theory.[6] Indeed, ever since Smith, economists have advocated the productive use of surpluses, as distinct from using them to profit from speculation or to wallow in luxury.[7] Moreover, norms prescribing the sharing of surplus are present in one form or another in most of the cultures *Homo sapiens* has constructed—including modern Western economic culture, which has never completely separated itself from the European Judeo-Christian subsoil in which it grew and against

---

2. One example among many is Steve Keen, *Debunking Economics* (London: Zed Books, 2001). The book is constantly updated on its author's website.

3. Fred Lee, *A History of Heterodox Economics* (London: Routledge, 2005).

4. André Orléan, *L'Empire de la valeur* (Paris: Seuil, 2011).

5. Joseph Stiglitz, *Freefall: America, Free Markets, and the Sinking of the World Economy* (New York: Norton, 2010).

6. Amartya Sen, *On Ethics and Economics* (Oxford: Blackwell, 1987).

7. This is pointed out by several of the contributors to Hilary Putnam and Vivian Walsh, eds., *The End of Value-Free Economics* (London: Routledge, 2011).

which it rebelled. Ethics prescribing sharing survive today in most religions. Ideals like caring and stewardship are, implicitly at least, centrepieces of socialism and of responsible capitalism, perhaps most conspicuously in the ethical approach to the fourth industrial revolution advocated by Klaus Schwab and the World Economic Forum. Therefore, with regard to this principle, we think of ourselves not as proposing a new idea but as reviving an old one that never completely died out and whose time is now returning.

As an ethical proposition, 'we should share the surplus' is close to a tautology. It can be read as a remark on how the noun 'needs' functions in what Ludwig Wittgenstein called 'language games' and what Michel Foucault called 'discourse'. If needs should be met, and if sharing the surplus means that those who have more than they need ought to share with those who have less than they need, then *prima facie* and *ceteris paribus* it follows that we should share the surplus, whether 'we' refers to individuals, informal groups or institutions. Here the noun 'needs' should be read as setting agendas for conversations, not as naming foregone conclusions.

Sharing the surplus is similar to, but not the same as, the idea of capturing rents[8] in order to channel them for use in public purposes. It bears some similarities to, but is not the same as, using public funds to provide a universal basic income, as proposed by Guy Standing and others. We will argue that sharing the surplus—doing things like donating to nonprofits, volunteering, and in general moving resources from where they are not needed to where they are needed—can make it possible to provide dignified livelihoods for all, by which we mean meeting the needs of each and every human being in a brave new world where labour markets fail catastrophically to provide livelihoods with dignity for all.[9]

John Maynard Keynes famously advocated government spending and low interest rates as ways to bring unemployment down to tolerable levels, so that most if not all people could meet their needs by selling their labour power. Karl Marx famously proposed, or at least famously implied, that unemployment, along with the private appropriation of the social surplus, would end if workers owned the means of production. Oskar Lange, less famously, proposed that central planning could do what ideal markets in equilibrium would do if they existed, but do them more reliably, including

---

8. We mean "rents" as economists use the term. For more on how this usage differs from "rent" as what one pays the landlord, see the relevant articles on Wikipedia.

9. International Labor Office, *World Employment and Social Outlook: Trends 2020* (Geneva: ILO, January 20, 2020). This report is pre-Covid. Reports including effects of the pandemic are available from the same source.

providing employment for everybody.¹⁰ History has not been kind to any of these three proposals.¹¹ History has been even less kind to the orthodox approach of counting on capital accumulation and economic growth to produce full employment. Adam Smith's starting point for his theory of wages—the natural right of the worker to the product of his own work—simply has to give way to some other starting point in a world where human work is no longer the principal source of products.

The concept of sharing the surplus opens up other options. In this book we report at length on South Africa's Community Work Programme (CWP) as an operational example of dignity for all, financed by sharing. The Programme shows how local communities can plan work and allocate resources with neither price signals from markets nor command signals from central authorities. Social surplus can be shared by the government in ways that stimulate the mobilization of existing local community resources and private-sector surplus—in market ways, in nonmarket ways and in ways hard to classify as one or the other.

The proliferation of options—of which one (using public employment to catalyse community development) will be examined later in detail—leads to another central concept that makes this book unique: Gavin Andersson's concept of *unbounded organization* (UO).¹² For any given social problem the possible solutions are not one or two or any finite number. They are, in principle, infinite. Many old material practices have fallen into disuse and could be revived. Around the world thousands of alternatives are being practiced.¹³ Other alternatives have not yet been invented. There are possibilities for the future that we today cannot even imagine. But there is more to unbounded organization than infinite options. Like Bill Mollison's permaculture, unbounded organization starts with an ethical

---

10. Oskar Lange, 'On the Economic Theory of Socialism: Part One', *The Review of Economic Studies*, vol. 5 (1936), pp. 53–71.

11. Susan Woodward, *Socialist Unemployment* (Princeton, NJ: Princeton University Press, 1995). It would be arbitrary to cite one of the innumerable books on the failures of central planning, and dogmatic to do so without citing also literature on the benefits of planning well conceived and well implemented.

12. See www.unboundedorganization.org. Gavin Andersson and Howard Richards, *Unbounded Organizing in Community* (Lake Oswego, OR: World Dignity University Press, 2014); Gavin Andersson, *Unbounded Organization: Embracing the Societal Enterprise* (forthcoming). Additional references will be given later in this work.

13. Diverse contemporary material practices are described in the works of Jeremy Rifkin and of John McKnight and his coauthors; others will be mentioned in the course of this book; still others exist, notwithstanding their not being mentioned by us, Rifkin or McKnight.

commitment,[14] which is to work together across sectors for the common good. An example, described in detail in Andersson's doctoral thesis, is the successful construction of several million units of social housing in South Africa through the aligned efforts of the public sector, the private sector and a people's self-help housing movement.[15]

Another key concept of our approach, closely linked to the preceding two, is our *naturalist moral realism*, or *moral realism* for short. Moral realism stands opposed to the current dominant liberal ethic, reflected in the currently dominant social structure and in private law, and is allied with a number of ethical theories we will have occasion to mention. Partly inspired by the more general philosophy of critical realism, our version of moral realism can be introduced by mentioning two of its features.

First, naturalist moral realism underpins the ethical principle that human needs should be met in harmony with nature. Nature judges culture. We agree with Abraham Maslow that 'the "good" or healthy society would then be defined as one that permitted man's highest purposes to emerge by satisfying all his prepotent basic needs'.[16] We identify with Carol Gilligan when she says that practicing a care ethic requires attending to and responding to needs.[17] This aspect of naturalist moral realism can be called an ethic of solidarity.

Second, moral realism respects and shows deference[18] to people and to their existing morals that are actually practiced at a given time and place—except where there are good reasons to make exceptions. This aspect of moral realism can be called an ethic of dignity.

Realism holds that it is important to respect the existing morals practiced at a given time and place. Whatever improvements we may propose to better meet human needs or to harmonize more with nature, we must start with what is. We make history not on our own terms but on terms that previous history has dealt us. Previous history has dealt us a diverse world. Given that

---

14. Mollison's ethic has three parts: (1) Love the land. (2) Love the people. (3) Share the surplus.

15. Gavin Andersson, *Unbounded Governance: A Study of Popular Development Organization* (Darmstadt: Scholar's Press and More Books, 2018).

16. Abraham Maslow, 'A Theory of Human Motivation', *Psychological Review*, vol. 50 (1943), p. 396.

17. I have not found precisely this phrase in any of Gilligan's published writings. However, I have heard her say it twice, once in a summer school course at the Graduate School of Education at Harvard and once in a public lecture at the Ontario Institute for Studies in Education.

18. Howard Richards, 'Deference', *International Journal of Ethics*, vol. 74 (1964), pp. 135–142.

ecology and heterodox economics are telling us that it is not a sustainable world, then, in Paulo Freire's terminology, we need 'hinges' to connect what must be said with what people can understand. These 'hinges' become 'invasions' and 'banking' when the worldviews of the interlocutors are insulted or ignored. Further, as Aristotle noticed more than two millennia before Emile Durkheim, the result of wholesale sweeping away of existing norms is *anomie*. The conventional morals of a given time and place are usually better than anomie and its companion, social disintegration. Still further, it is not feasible to challenge the hegemony of the pathological autonomy of liberal ethics[19] by crafting a new, alternative moral of solidarity and dignity to which the bulk of humanity can sign on as convinced adherents. It is much more likely that a global consensus promoting social responsibility, respect for diversity, and solidarity will be achieved by discourse coalitions drawing on the moral codes of already existing cultures. For example, a Muslim, a capitalist, a socialist and a Hindu can agree that everybody ought to have pure drinking water and that desertification ought to be reversed, even though each frames in her or his own way the moral imperatives prescribing action to make pure drinking water available to everyone and to reverse desertification.[20] Discourse coalitions can be formed only if the dialogue begins with mutual respect.[21]

A concept of *community* figures in this book as economics' other. Economics is not community, and community is not economics. Obviously, I will make a case for using these words this way. My *démarche* would make no sense if 'economics' were defined as Lionel Robbins defines it, as 'the science which studies human behaviour as a relationship between ends and scarce means which have alternative uses'.[22] Nor would it make sense if 'community' were defined as Talcott Parsons defines it, as 'that collectivity the members of which share a common territorial area as their base of operations

---

19. Frédéric Vandenberghe, 'Realist Engagements in Critical Hermeneutics', ch. 4 in Margaret Archer and Andrea Maccarini, eds., *Engaging with the World* (London: Routledge, 2013), pp. 86–89. This article is the source of the notion of the pathological autonomy of liberal ethics.

20. Hoppers and Richards, *Rethinking Thinking*.

21. Among authors who have developed versions of moral realism, in addition to Maslow, Gilligan, Freire, Durkheim and Aristotle already mentioned, are John Dewey and Georges Canguilhem. See John Dewey and James Tufts, *Ethics* (New York: Henry Holt, 1908), and the updated synthesis of Canguilhem by his disciple Frederic Mathieu, *Les Valeurs de la vie* (N. p.: Read Books, 2014), Kindle. In my *Letters from Quebec* (San Francisco: International Scholars Press, 1995), I argue that Plato should be counted as an ecologist *avant la lettre* and as a realist.

22. Lionel Robbins, *Essay on the Nature and Significance of Economic Science* (London: Macmillan, 1935), p. 16.

for daily activities'.[23] If, on the other hand, one defines 'economics' as does André Orléan, starting with concepts of *relation marchande* and *séparation marchande,* or as Adam Smith does, starting with 'truck or barter'; and if one traces 'community' to its Latin and Greek roots, *communitatem* and *koinonia,* one is more likely to be sympathetic to treating economics and community as a binary polarity. One is also more likely to get excited about community development as a complement to economics that meets needs economics alone does not meet.

Another key concept in the book consists of a pair of what I call *Staggering Facts*. The first Staggering Fact is that capital accumulation has become so consequential for the continuation of human life that keeping it going (insofar as it is possible to do so) has become what Ellen Meiksins Wood calls a 'systemic imperative'.[24] The second Staggering Fact is the Keynesian point that there tends to be a chronic insufficiency of effective demand, a fact often associated with its Keynesian corollary that there tends to be a chronic weakness of the inducement to invest. Both Staggering Facts are treated in this book as consequences of what I call the *basic social structure,* among other names. Before saying more about the roles that Staggering Facts will play, however, it will be useful to introduce some of the main philosophical perspectives provided by first-wave (i.e., initial) critical realism.

3. An Introduction to Critical Realism

When our version of moral realism says there is a natural reality that social reality depends on and must conform to, it segues into expressing appreciation for Roy Bhaskar's efforts to, as he puts it, 'reclaim reality'.

In *A Realist Theory of Science*[25] Bhaskar shows that empiricism (which critical realists criticize as 'actualism' or 'irrealism') misunderstands causal laws, mistakenly identifying them with their empirical grounds. Thus, David Hume identified causality, to the extent that he believed in it at all, with the constant conjunction of observed events. John Stuart Mill, in his *Logic*, articulated five canons of induction (method of difference, method of agreement, joint method of agreement and difference, method of concomitant variation, method of residue) all designed to find causality in patterns

---

23. Talcott Parsons, *The Social System* (Glencoe, IL: The Free Press, 1951), p. 91.
24. Ellen Meiksins Wood, *Empire of Capital* (London: Verso, 2003).
25. Roy Bhaskar, *A Realist Theory of Science*, 1st ed. (Leeds: Harvester Press, 1975). Bhaskar builds on earlier work in the philosophy of science done by Rom Harré, Mary Hesse, Edward Madden and others.

of observed events. More recently, Carl Hempel identified explanation and prediction in science with the application of covering laws that (as in Hume) codify the constant conjunction of one type of observed event with another type of observed event. Bhaskar argues that, outside of astronomy, the constant conjunctions that empiricists mistakenly identify with causes occur mainly in meticulously controlled laboratory experiments contrived by human beings. The empiricist is therefore locked on the horns of a dilemma. One horn of the dilemma is the absurdity that the laws of nature are created by human beings when they create the artificial conditions under which constant conjunctions occur. The other horn of the dilemma is the truth: experiments enable scientists to identify the mode of operation of natural structures they do not produce; the natural structures are the generative mechanisms that produce the observed events.

We follow Bhaskar's suggestion that social structures (like markets) be treated as social science mechanism analogues of the structural generative mechanisms (also called causal powers) found in nature.[26] This book takes for granted that what Gustavo Marques calls 'mainstream philosophy of economics' (MPE)[27] is out of date and indefensible. Mainstream philosophy of economics asserts or assumes that economics should conform to a positivist ideal of an exact science.[28] In this book we will not refute either positivist or empiricist approaches to philosophy of science, because they have already been refuted by Bhaskar and others.

An important part of saying that the two Staggering Facts will be treated as consequences of something that will be called the "basic social structure" is Bhaskar's point that the identity of objects of scientific study is preserved when different scholars describe them with different words. Often much is gained, for example, when the causes of a chronic weakness of effective demand are described in different words and inscribed in different theoretical

---

26. Roy Bhaskar, *The Possibility of Naturalism*, 4th ed. (London: Routledge, 2014), p. 37 and implicitly passim, Kindle.

27. Gustavo Marques, *A Philosophical Framework for Rethinking Theoretical Economics and Philosophy of Economics* (London: World Economics Association, 2016). Marques quotes from an unpublished paper favouring exact economics in the positivist tradition by Nancy Cartwright at p. 54; he cites and disagrees with similar views throughout the book.

28. See Tony Lawson, *Essays on the Nature and State of Modern Economics* (London: Routledge, 2015), especially ch. 7; Richard Crockett, *Thinking the Unthinkable: Think Tanks and the Economic Counter-Revolution 1931–1983* (London: Fontana Press, 1995); Fred Lee, *A History of Heterodox Economics: Challenging the Mainstream in the Twentieth Century* (London: Routledge, 2009). Here we cite Lawson, Crockett and Lee for the proposition that the winning doctrines in economics are often determined at least as much by institutional power as by intellectual merit—*not* for the proposition that the winners are always advocates of exact science in the positivist tradition.

frameworks and studied by different disciplines—economics, sociology, ethics, history, law, politics, biology, psychology and others. Much is lost when a writer, for the sake of conceptual clarity, uses only one vocabulary. That single vocabulary never determines the identity or defines the causal powers of the intransitive[29] (in Bhaskar's terminology) objects that science is trying to understand. Using only one way of talking when the study of the intransitive objects in question (for example, inducements to invest) has already been enriched by several ways of talking about them (for example, those of Smith, Marx, Walras, Marshall, Keynes, von Hayek and Minsky) usually results in a net loss rather than a net gain for scientific understanding.

4. About Today's Basic Social Structure

Even though we will use several vocabularies, let me outline just one here: the vocabulary of social structure (sometimes called cultural structure). 'Social structure' can be defined as the material relations among social positions.[30] The positions (for example, of buyer and seller) are internally related to each other (for example, a seller can be a seller only if there is a buyer).[31] Social structures are established by constitutive rules; for example, the rules that constitute the language game of buying and selling constitute—i.e., create—the practice of commercial exchange, and similarly, the rules of chess constitute the game of chess).[32] Constitutive rules assign social status (for example, the status of owner to seller and then to buyer; the status of money to bits of paper).[33]

A social structure is called 'basic' if it governs the provision of the basic necessities of life, such as food.[34] For example, property ownership, buying and selling, and money are basic in modern society. Amartya Sen illustrated the causal powers of the cultural rules that constitute basic social structures

---

29. For more on intransitive, see: Howard Richards, 'On the Intransitive Objects of the Social (or Human) Sciences', *Journal of Critical Realism*, vol. 17 (1918), pp. 1–16

30. Douglas Porpora, *Reconstructing Sociology* (Cambridge, UK: Cambridge University Press, 2016, p. 98).

31. Tony Lawson, *The Nature of Social Reality* (London: Routledge, 2019), pp. 31–65, especially pp. 55 & 61. Lawson does not employ the word 'community' as we do.

32. Douglas Porpora, 'Cultural Rules and Material Relations', *Sociological Theory*, vol. 11 (1993), pp. 212–229. Porpora proposes the thesis that cultural rules constitute material relations.

33. John Searle, *The Construction of Social Reality* (New York: Free Press, 1995), pp. 43–51.

34. This idea is developed in Howard Richards, *Letters from Quebec* (San Francisco: International Scholars Press, 1995).

in his study of famines, where during every famine there was food available but poor people starved. Since they had no money to buy food, they were not legally entitled to eat.[35] Basic social structures usually have the force of law. In the famines Sen studied, material relations defined by culture and enforced by law provided that people with no money had no right to eat.

Accumulation, or profit, can be regarded as the dynamic that powers the basic social structure of modern society. Historically, our present situation grew out of earlier forms of market exchange that, over time, tended to produce a system driven by capital accumulation. This can be seen in Marx's account, in the opening pages of *Capital*, of how one form of exchange leads to another. It can also be seen in what Alfred Marshall meant by the law of substitution (more efficient production drives out less efficient production) and in what Eugen von Bohm Bawerk meant by the superior efficiency of roundabout production. All three theoretical approaches tend to show how accumulation evolves over time and how it favours those who accumulate the most.

The opening chapters of Marx's *Capital* are written as a timeless allegory of the metamorphosis of forms of value from simple exchange, where a certain amount of a commodity X is worth a certain amount of commodity Y, to selling in order to buy (selling a chicken at the fair and buying grain to take home and eat), to buying in order to sell (buying grain to sell later when its price goes up), to buying in order to produce in order to sell (buying labour power and other inputs, using them to produce commodities, selling the commodities), to buying in order to produce in order to sell for profit to 'accumulate accumulate. That is Moses and the prophets!' Profit is reinvested over and over for the sake of more and more profit in an endless cycle of accumulation. So it comes to pass that, to a large extent, the poor have employment if and only if people richer than themselves get richer than they already are—i.e., only if somebody makes a profit by hiring them.

Elsewhere Marx anticipates the further metamorphosis of forms of value into today's 'bankism' or 'financialization', where 'the 1 percent' dominate partly by using what he called 'fictitious capital',[36] i.e., capital that has no productive function in the real economy. Marx's texts often describe what tends to happen in history. It has happened not so much because people

---

35. Amartya Sen, *Poverty and Famines: An Essay on Entitlement and Deprivation* (Oxford: Oxford University Press, 1981).

36. http://michael-hudson.com/2010/07/from-marx-to-goldman-sachs-the-fictions-of-fictitious-capital1/.

consciously decided that such would be the course of history as because of the operation of the rules of what Wittgenstein might have called buying and selling language-games. It illustrates what is meant by the causal powers of the basic social structure.

5. A Little More on Critical Realism

Bhaskar's early contributions inform this book even when we do not use his language. Specifically, our version of moral realism relies more on the language of Maslow's and Gilligan's meeting needs and uses less of Jürgen Habermas's and Bhaskar's language of emancipation. But variations in language need not imply disagreement, for reasons Bhaskar himself brilliantly articulates. On Bhaskar's account, intransitive objects of any science exist and act independently of their descriptions. So also Habermas, in several of his contributions, argues that the moral growth of human beings happens mainly in face-to-face encounters on a human scale, in what he and others call the life-world (*Lebenswelt*). While we affirm community development, we do not think of ourselves as disagreeing with Habermas. We think of ourselves as affirming the importance of the life-world for moral growth under a different description. We agree with Bhaskar that the same reality (natural or social) can go on saving us or killing us independently of how we describe it, although it is also true that social realities are products of human action.

A realist theory of science goes together with moral realism. Conversely, the subjective theories of value of mainstream economics, which tend (as in Paul Samuelson's writings) to identify value with revealed preferences, go together with empiricist tendencies to separate 'is' from 'ought' in ways that deny that right and wrong can be distinguished by discerning human needs.

Scholars have often defined their overall aim as advancing scientific knowledge. They have pledged allegiance to what Max Weber called 'science as a vocation'. Critical realism as a school of thought deliberately goes a step further: Facts imply values. 'Is' implies 'ought'. Human emancipation is part and parcel of the purpose of doing science.[37] In Margaret Archer's terminology, science should contribute to constructive forms of morphogenesis (i.e., structural change, or change of social form).[38]

---

37. Roy Bhaskar, *Scientific Realism and Human Emancipation* (London: Routledge, 1986).
38. Margaret Archer, *Realist Social Theory: The Morphogenetic Approach* (Cambridge, UK: Cambridge University Press, 1995).

6. The Chapters of This Book

The first chapter of this book starts with an account of violence along with massive unemployment and extreme political confrontation in South Africa. The government's official cure was prescribed by the National Development Plan. The plan's academic advisors included famous academic economists from Harvard and Princeton: Dani Rodrik, Ricardo Haussman and Andres Velasco. The chapter points out that the plan can be no better than the science it relies on to link its prescriptions with its predicted results. A section on Nelson Mandela explains that when he gave up socialism, he preserved his ideals in the form of a new constitution that (on paper) guarantees many social rights.

Chapters 2, 3 and 4 explain why not just the science behind the plan but all orthodox economic science cannot possibly solve the problems of the poor, citing foundational texts by Smith, Ricardo, Marx, Walras and Keynes (mainly). What is needed instead is not a new economic theory or a new economic model but a new basic social structure.

Chapter 5 begins to outline the new (or revived old, or plural, unbounded and realistic) basic social structure recommended in the book and how to get there, albeit on a small scale. The invention of the Community Work Programme (CWP), motivated by South Africa's failure to make a large enough dent in poverty during the first twenty years of democracy (1994–2004), is treated as a theoretical breakthrough. In the CWP, work no longer depended on sales. Organizing the work no longer depended on price signals or on central plans. At the admittedly few sites where the CWP worked well and certainly not at all sites, unlike with cash grants, the upper levels of Maslow's hierarchy of needs, not just the lower levels, were attended to (a point elaborated further in chapter 9).

Chapter 6 shifts the scene to the world's largest public employment plan, the Mahatma Gandhi Rural Employment Guarantee in India. Once again, the hopeless contradictions of today's dominant thinking and dominant institutions are demonstrated in practice. Analysing the theoretical absurdities of the science supporting the dominant social structures opens the way to spelling out more details of how an unbounded moral realism can work. The ethics and law that establish the present world order logically imply that it cannot, in principle, reliably provide dignity for all—in spite of technologies coming on line that could produce a healthy green future for everyone.

Chapter 7 examines the history and logic of Swedish social democracy. While crediting its achievements, the chapter explains why that form of social democracy could succeed only under unusual conditions and is now over. Studying its principles and their inevitable failures shows how to amend them. Higher levels of institutional flexibility and moral responsibility can do what rigidity and liberal individualism cannot do. Examples from around the world that are working are given.

Chapter 8 is about neoliberal theory.

Chapter 9 is a detailed account of how the Community Work Programme operates on the ground in the district called Orange Farm on the South Side of Johannesburg.

Chapters 10 and 11 are about public finance. They examine the meanings of 'surplus' and 'economic rent'. It is about how to raise the money to pay for nonmarket employment (including activities like science, dance, sports, lifelong-learning and whatever makes life worth living) for everyone who needs it. The aim is both to finance the public sector better and to give it less to do through an unbounded approach in which all sectors, not just the government, align to serve the common good. The chapter also recounts some of the history that has led to the separation of human needs from the resources that should be available to meet them.

In the chapters that follow, we often take premises established in our own prior works as given, rather than repeating what we have written elsewhere even in abbreviated form.[39] In *Unbounded Organization: Embracing the Societal Enterprise* (forthcoming) Gavin Andersson proposes a general theory of unbounded organization. In *Looking Back to the Future: Conversations on Unbounded Organization* he imagines a South Africa where unbounded organization is practiced. *Unbounded Organizing in Community* by Gavin Andersson and Howard Richards is a practical guide to doing community development. In *Understanding the Global Economy* Howard Richards shows how causal explanations in economics assume as premises cultural norms derived from socially constructed realities. In *Gandhi and the Future of Economics* Howard Richards and Joanna Swanger imagine Mahatma Gandhi in dialogue with other major Indian intellectuals, including Jawaharlal Nehru, Vandana Shiva, Arundhati Roy, Jayaprakash Narayan, Tariq Ali, Amartya Sen and Manmohan Singh.

The same coauthors, in *Dilemmas of Social Democracies*, argue that social democracy is unsustainable because it is incompatible with the basic

---

39. We refrain from citing our prior writings here partly because they can be easily found on the internet or Research Gate and partly because we cite them elsewhere when we refer to specific ideas in them.

cultural structures of modern Western civilization. They hold that the revival of social democratic ideals will require, in Gramscian terms, intellectual and moral reform; or, in the terms of the early Swedish socialist leader Hjalmar Branting, *Uppfostran* (upliftment, or moral development); or, in their own terms, 'cultural resources' and 'ethical construction'. In *Following Foucault: The Trail of the Fox,* Howard Richards, in dialogue with Evelin Lindner and Catherine Hoppers, examines Foucault's writings and makes a case, often against Foucault, for moral authority legitimized by a realist ethical philosophy. In *Rethinking Thinking,* Catherine Hoppers and Howard Richards make a case for taking indigenous knowledge systems seriously.

To help the reader, and ourselves, to stay in touch with reality on the ground, in chapters 2 through 8 we insert from time to time brief quotations from participants in the CWP. We do not pretend that these 'voices from the CWP' come from a random or representative sample. We do attest that they are exact words (or English translations of exact words in an indigenous language) spoken by real people at real places and times. Our focus in this book is on CWP at its best because we believe that is what merits the attention of readers. We do not explore cases where CWP was mismanaged by implementing agents or government officials, but we do include a few citations from participants that illustrate potential pitfalls.

Some of these words from CWP participants were derived from a report, published in 2013 by CDI (Centre for Democratising Information), by Melani Prinsloo and her colleagues on focus groups they conducted with CWP participants.[40] Some quotations were taken from a section of the COGTA (Department of Cooperative Governance and Traditional Affairs) website in 2010 titled 'Voices from CWP,'[41] which also appeared in a booklet published by COGTA at the same time.

This book has at least one limitation that must be mentioned and perhaps two. First, some citations are more than a decade old. The book took more than a decade to write. We lacked time and energy to update all old cites. Second, the book is deliberately repetitive. From experience in community development we have learned to repeat key messages at least three times. We expect some readers to be peeved and others to be grateful.

---

40. Shamima Vawda et al., *The South African Community Capability Study: The Community Work Programme* (Centre for Democratising Information, 2013).
41. This section of the COGTA website no longer exists.

CHAPTER ONE

South Africa Now as a Land of Credible Threats and Incredible Promises

OVERVIEW OF THE CHAPTER

1. Methodological Remarks
2. Anger and Violence
3. The Economic Freedom Fighters
4. Mandela's Choices
5. The National Development Plan
6. Economic Theory, Community Development and South Africa's Community Work Programme

Consideration of the first five topics leads to an appreciation of the importance of the sixth.

1. Methodological Remarks

The brief discussion of constitutive rules in the introduction already hints at our sympathy with John Searle's account of the construction of social reality, which he reads as the creation of institutional facts out of brute facts. Brute facts (like pieces of paper with certain markings on them) are assigned social status (like the status of money). That social status makes them institutional facts.[1] The rules that turn brute facts into institutional facts Searle calls constitutive rules.

A constitutive rule takes the form of 'X counts as Y in context C'. To continue with Searle's example: certain brute facts in the form of pieces of paper count as money in certain historical contexts. Another example (our adaptation of Searle, not pure Searle) is the legal rules that constitute property rights; here it is members of the species *Homo sapiens* who are the brute facts assigned a social status—that of 'owner'. 'Owner' is an institutional fact.

---

1. John Searle, *The Construction of Social Reality* (New York: Free Press, 1995); Joshua Rust, *John Searle and the Construction of Social Reality* (London: Continuum, 2006).

The general acceptance of constitutive rules is the means by which cultural facts about meanings create material facts about social structure[2] and by which material relations are established among social positions. To revisit Sen's example presented in the introduction, it is a constitutive rule that establishes who, at some given time and place, has a legal or customary right to eat and who does not. Transposing this idea from the Anglophone idiom of Searle and Porpora into the Francophone idiom of Michel Foucault, at certain historical moments material practices and regimes of truth converge to form dispositifs (devices) of power/knowledge.[3]

A key purpose of this book is to contribute to rebuilding not only economic theory but also the basic social structure that (mainstream) economic theories presuppose. However, this effort begs for sympathy. The words available to us as building materials denote essentially contested concepts. They are words with long histories marked by socially violent and academically convoluted confrontations. We therefore find ourselves in a distressing situation not unlike that of seasick passengers on Neurath's boat.[4]

Otto Neurath likened scientific knowledge to a boat that must be repaired while at sea. The sailors must reconstruct the boat they are sailing on, so they can replace only one plank at a time. If they removed and replaced too many planks at once, the boat would sink. Similarly, we are constrained to work with mainstream thinking and the basic social structure as they are, even when we believe they are mistaken not just at a few points but *ab initio* (from the beginning).

Our situation, however, is even worse than that of Neurath's sailors because, much more than the history of physics that Neurath mainly had in mind as his boat, the history of economics is a history of the construction of social realities. We claim that economic theory did not arise just to understand its object of study, i.e., modern economic society; it arose as part of the social construction of its object of study. Adam Smith was not just a student of market exchange; he was an advocate and an architect of a society under construction whose most powerful institution would become market exchange organized by the rule of law.

Economics did not begin with Smith's political economy or as a science at all. Before it was a science, it was a moral and political movement in

---

2. Douglas Porpora, 'Cultural Rules and Material Relations', *Sociological Theory*, vol. 11 (1993), pp. 212–229.

3. See Michel Foucault, *La volonté de savoir* (Paris: Gallimard, 1976).

4. Willard van Orman Quine discusses Neurath's Boat in *Word and Object* (Cambridge, MA: MIT Press, 1960).

favour of what was called natural liberty.⁵ Preexisting social structures in the seventeenth and eighteenth centuries established what Foucault would call the historical conditions of the possibility of economics. These conditions were established only in Europe; economics as we know it became possible in the rest of the world only when its European conquerors brought European law and customs with them.⁶ Among the preexisting discourses that facilitated the emergence of the discourse on political economy in Western Europe were those of Roman law, the similar common law of England, eighteenth-century notions of natural rights and social contracts, Protestant theologies, several schools of ethics, and Newtonian mechanics.

Our plight now, in the twenty-first century, is that of passengers on Neurath's boat who wish they had some influence over the direction the boat is going but have good reason to doubt that they do. Today, an account of economic theory should—so we claim—offer ideas about where society is going and why, and about how to change economic theory's object of study: the basic social structure. It should give people hope that they can contribute to transforming economic society. It should propose a strategy for changing the course of history.

This book does indeed propose such a strategy, and it intends to encourage readers to believe they can make a difference. The strategy, which we call unbounded organization and ethical realism, hits the ground running by building on community development methods that already exist and are already achieving some success.

The discursive approach of this book starts from the premise that one will not get far in changing the linguistic side of discourse without changing its practical side. For this reason, this book includes many pages filled with brute facts. Otherwise put, if, in terms of Searle's story about how to construct social reality, the brute facts are where the institutional facts come from, and if we want to change the institutional fact that humanity is currently condemned to live under one or another regime organized to facilitate accumulation to the detriment of nature, then we would be wise to ground our search for change strategies at the brute-fact level.

Some might challenge our approach by claiming that there are no brute

---

5. This point is brought out in ch. 2 and in the discussion of Say's Law in ch. 9. It is fair to speculate that Adam Smith may have had a different view of natural liberty than did the people taken out of Africa as slaves at the time Smith was writing.

6. See Maria Mies, *Patriarchy and Accumulation on a World Scale* (London: Zed Books, 1986); Catherine Hoppers and Howard Richards, *Rethinking Thinking* (Pretoria: University of South Africa, 2012).

facts. For instance, while John Searle proposes a plausible vocabulary and viewpoint in which concepts like brute fact and basic fact are given reasonably clear, nuanced meanings, Martin Heidegger proposes an equally plausible vocabulary[7] expressing a quite different viewpoint. Most people would agree that every so-called brute fact is actually a description by some speaker speaking some language. It does not necessarily retain the same brute status when it figures as a fact in some other speech. Martin Heidegger goes further: To see something is already to interpret it;[8] that is, we cannot see without *Auslegung*—without interpretation, without reading. Even before we open our mouths to describe a fact and thus sully the fact's pristine bruteness with the cultural baggage of our language and our extempore choice of words, our eyes have already betrayed us.

Our defence, our appeal to the mercy of the court, as it were, is that we will do our best to ground our word choices in physical realities (ecology) and in the realities of people's lives (what they experience). To back up our defence we again call upon the author of *Reclaiming Reality*,[9] Roy Bhaskar, as a witness to make one key point that he qualifies at length elsewhere in his extensive writings. He testifies that, although it is true that every fact is a fact only under some description and only in the light of some way of seeing, it is also true that science can detect underlying causal powers that produce observed phenomena. So it is okay to repose some faith in a naturalist worldview (in an emergent-powers materialism neither wholly like nor wholly unlike Searle's naturalism) and at the same time agree with Heidegger that all seeing is *seeing as*. Roy Bhaskar's early work (known as 'first wave critical realism') was nothing if not a reconciliation of science and hermeneutics; we intend to stand barefoot on his shoulders and let our ankles be tickled by his long hair.

Having set out our methodology, we offer next a plausible description of facts about contemporary South Africa. While these facts may not be wholly brute, they are at least more brute and less institutional than—to cite an economic theory discussed later—Dani Rodrik's theory of economic growth.

---

7. Heidegger's plausible vocabulary is hard to translate, since so much of it depends on plays on words in German, such as *eigen, Eigentum, eigentlich.*

8. Martin Heidegger, *Sein und Zeit* (Tubingen: Max Niemeyer Verlag, 1986 (1926)), p. 149. Heidegger adds that every description is an interpretation.

9. Roy Bhaskar, *Reclaiming Reality* (London: Routledge, 1989).

2. Anger and Violence

A wave of violence swept across South Africa's poor townships starting in May 2008. In some places it was preceded by a history of protests dating back as far as 1996, just two years after democracy was established in the country. It was followed by even more protests, many of them violent, in the succeeding years. We focus on 2008 and 2009 because we have access to careful case studies of those years' violence at eight locations.[10]

Various incidents triggered the violence. Protests led to mass meetings and marches. Then came the burning of private and public buildings, and work stay-aways and deaths. Once the protests began, the police became a factor, either because of their absence or because their excessive violence led to running battles between youth and police. In most cases, there were attacks on foreigners and foreign-owned shops and dwellings, and in one case study (of Slovoview), the researchers found xenophobic violence to be the primary violence.[11]

A common trigger for the violence was real or alleged corruption; for example, in the town of Voortrekker in the province of Mpumulanga, the trigger was the disappearance of 150 thousand rands. Whatever the underlying structural causes may have been, the proximate cause of that violence was that money intended as prizes for winning athletes in a competition had disappeared. Somebody had stolen it.

In each case of violence studied, there was some form of broken trust or broken promise. For example, a protest organizer in Voortrekker asserted: 'That the houses were burnt down was the mistake of the premier. He promised to come but did not.'[12] Sometimes the violence was triggered by a faction in local politics mobilizing popular discontent to serve its own interests. A protestor at Kungcatsha described the discontent this way: 'People of this township are very patient, but this time they are very angry. They are sick and tired of waiting.'[13] Another described partisan and even

---

10. Karl von Holdt, Malosa Langa, Sepetla Molapo, Nomfundo Magapi, Kindeza Ngubeni, Jacob Dlamini, and Adèle Kirsten, *The Smoke That Calls: Insurgent Citizenship, Collective Violence, and the Struggle for a Place in the New South Afri*ca (Johannesburg: Centre for the Study of Violence and Reconciliation and Society, Work and Development Institute, 2011). One of the cases studied, Bokftontein in North West Province, was a case in which a result of the Community Work Programme (CWP) preceded by an Organization Workshop (OW) was 'the end of intra-community violence and the deliberate rejection of xenophobic violence' (p.3). The CWP, OWs, and the case of Bokfontein will be considered later in this book.

11. Ibid., p. 6.
12. Ibid., p. 15.
13. Ibid., p. 15.

self-serving mobilization: 'Some of the leaders were angry that they were no longer getting tenders, and then they decided to mobilize the community against the municipality.'[14]

Over and above the particular sparks that ignited particular conflagrations, three recurrent fact patterns stand out. The first pattern underlies the partisan mobilization of discontent and is well summarized by Karl von Holdt, author of one of the case study reports: 'Using the appropriation of state activities as a basis for accumulation, a thuggish local elite is able to rise through a combination of criminal, extra-legal and quasi-state activities.'[15] The protests frequently did not target the national government or the ruling African National Congress. Rather, they targeted the misdeeds of local authorities and then looked to higher authority to correct them.

The second pattern is the continuity of the ideas and repertory of the protest activities with those of the decades-long anti-apartheid struggle before 1994. A protestor in Azania said, 'The Freedom Charter says people shall govern, but now we are not governing, we are being governed.'[16] During the struggle against apartheid and again in 2008–2009, violence was preceded by peaceful protest in the form of mass meetings, marches, petitions and strikes. During both periods of protest, the burning of a public building—a library, a clinic, a community centre—was a symbolic disruption of oppressive authority. The report says, 'It is a symbolism that is well understood, both by community and by authorities, since it was central to the struggle against apartheid authority.'[17] Burning down the homes of local authorities perceived as corrupt in 2008–2009 was similar to the burning out of collaborators practiced in the 1980s. The protestors of the later era burned tyres and barricaded streets, as their predecessors had done. They engaged in *toyi toyi*, marching aggressively while singing struggle songs. Video footage of protestors at Voortrekker shows them chanting *Tambo, kumoshekile; bayasithengisa*—'Tambo, things are bad; we are being sold out'—referring to Oliver Tambo, who headed the African National Congress during the freedom struggle.

The third and most fundamental pattern is the contrast between the prosperity promised to the masses during the struggle against apartheid and their present reality of grinding poverty under democracy. Jacob Dlamini,

14. Ibid., p. 16.
15. Ibid., p. 21.
16. Ibid., p. 23.
17. Ibid., p. 27.

in his report on violence at Voortrekker, provides some detail: 'In Mpumalanga, as in the rest of South Africa, despite the ANC commitments to eliminating poverty and the expectations of the majority of black people, poverty and inequality have increased dramatically since 1994. For example, South Africa's Gini coefficient [a measure of inequality] moved ahead of Brazil's to become the world's worst among major countries: from 0.66 in 1993 to 0.70 in 2008. The income of the average African person fell as a percentage of the average white's from 13.5 percent (1995) to 13 percent (2008) (Development Policy Research Unit, 2009).'[18]

Young protestors in Azania Township responded angrily to the suggestion that, in protesting, they were being manipulated by the local elite. One said: 'It is an insult to my intelligence for people to think we are marching because someone has bought us liquor. We are not mindless. People, especially you who are educated, think we are marching because we bored. We are dealing with real issues here. Like today we don't have electricity. We have not had water for the whole week.'[19]

The violence of 2008 has recurred at different moments and places in the years since then. At times it takes the form of service-delivery protest, or xenophobic violence, or, as a daily painful reality, violence against women and children. Violence is an ongoing social reality for the vast majority of South Africa's people.

3. The Economic Freedom Fighters

We write here of a particular political party now (in 2019) active in South Africa. In the interim between when we write this and when someone reads this, this party as a specific movement may have waxed, waned or disappeared. But political movements that articulate and mobilize popular discontent will not disappear. They will recur as long as there is popular discontent and as long as there is politics.[20]

On July 26, 2013, on the sixtieth anniversary of Fidel Castro's unsuccessful storming of the Moncada Barracks in Havana, a radical movement

---

18. Ibid., p. 34.
19. Ibid., p. 23.
20. See the studies of groups that articulate and mobilise popular discontent in Ted Robert Gurr, *Why Men Rebel* (Princeton, NJ: Princeton University Press, 1970); and the references to 'leaderships' in Benedict Anderson, *Imagined Communities* (London: Verso, 2006), pp 160–161.

rolled out its founding manifesto in Soweto, South Africa.[21] They called themselves Economic Freedom Fighters (EFF), and they called their leader commander-in-chief. They cast themselves as the finishers of the unfinished revolution that had won democracy for South Africa. In their manifesto they state that political power without economic emancipation is meaningless:

> Concerning real economic transformation, the post-1994 democratic state has not achieved anything substantial owing to the fact that the economic-policy direction taken in the democratic-dawn years was not about fundamental transformation, but empowerment/enrichment meant to empower what could inherently be a few black aspirant capitalists, without the real transfer of wealth to the people as a whole.[22]

The Freedom Charter of 1955 had inspired much of the resistance to apartheid before the African National Congress (ANC) came to power in 1994. It continues to play an important role in South African politics. The Manifesto of the EFF reads the Freedom Charter radically. The Charter says that South Africa belongs to all who live in it. In the EFF Manifesto, that principle is read to imply public ownership of natural resources and key industries,[23] as well as nationalization of mines, banks and monopolies. It is also read to mean that the state should assure economic opportunities to all. The Charter also says that while the state should be in control of the commanding heights of the economy, 'people shall have equal rights to trade where they choose, to manufacture and to enter all trades, crafts, and professions'. Therefore, there will never be nationalization and state control of every sector of South Africa's economy.[24] However, says the Charter, 'there will be cooperatives and other kinds of common and collective ownership'.[25]

The EFF Manifesto goes on: 'The struggle for economic freedom is not a struggle against white people, but a struggle for the emancipation of the working class and for equal benefit of those who are not benefiting from

---

21. *Economic Freedom Fighters Founding Manifesto*, (http://effighters.org.za/documents/economic-freedom-fighters-founding-manifesto/).
22. Ibid., par. 16.
23. Ibid., par. 30.
24. Ibid., par. 31.
25. Ibid., par. 36.

the current economic realities.'[26] It declares that the EFF will be present at the barricades. It will be involved in mass movements and community protests.[27] From this it appears to be reasonable to anticipate that, in the future, successive waves of protest triggered by local issues will be joined and supported by militants of one or more national organizations with a definite ideology.

In its Manifesto the EFF self-identifies as leftist, anti-capitalist and anti-imperialist. It purports to draw inspiration from Karl Marx, Vladimir Lenin, Frantz Fanon and all those who over the centuries have struggled for the economic liberation of humanity. In 1992, Francis Fukuyama looked around the world and concluded that history was over;[28] from then on and into the indefinite future, all leftist ideologies would remain in the dustbin—defeated, disproven and discredited. The EFF Manifesto of 2013 says 'not anymore'. Not in South Africa.

However, the admiration of the EFF for nineteenth- and twentieth-century leftist revolutionaries appears to be more a matter of honouring the lives of heroes than one of advocating an economic model like that of the former Soviet Union. (When it comes to naming models, according to the EFF, South Africa can learn from the countries on an honour roll that includes Brazil, India, China, Singapore, South Korea, Hong Kong, Taiwan, Japan and Finland.) Much of the Manifesto is not so much about the choice of an economic model as it is about basic morality (which critics of the EFF are quick to charge its leadership with violating). It denounces the juicy perks of public officials, cronyism, sexism, silencing the truth for fear of losing your job, putting profit before people and self-serving venality.

It declares seven cardinal pillars of a strategic mission for economic freedom in our lifetime.[29] The seven cardinal pillars are (slightly simplified) as follows:

1. Expropriation of South Africa's land, without compensation, for redistribution in use. (Redistribution in use is later explained as granting permits to use land for up to twenty-five years for stated uses, presumably mainly as farmland.)

26. Ibid., par. 137.
27. Ibid., par. 33.
28. Francis Fukuyama, *The End of History and the Last Man* (New York: Free Press, 1992). Fukuyama made an exception for certain countries that were 'not yet' capitalist democracies. He described them as 'still in history'.
29. Other documents of the EFF movement available on its website spell out details.

2. Nationalization of mines, banks and other strategic sectors of the economy without compensation.
3. Building state and government capacity, which will lead to the abolition of tenders.
4. Free quality education, health care, houses and sanitation.
5. Massive protected industrial development, leading to jobs and adequate minimum wages for all.
6. Massive development of the African economy on the entire continent.
7. Open, accountable and corruption-free government.[30]

While the EFF's campaigns against corruption and its admiration for Asian developmental states are not especially radical, its first two cardinal pillars are undoubtedly radical. Not even five years after the party's launch, however, the call for the expropriation of land without compensation had won such a degree of support that the ruling ANC adopted the same position.

Were these pillars to become facts on the ground, they would lead to what Lewis Coser calls 'absolute conflict'.[31] In an absolute conflict, the parties do not acknowledge a common frame of reference for rationally negotiating a compromise or a mutually agreed-upon settlement. In the terminology of the ancient dialogues featuring Socrates and composed by Plato, there is no presiding logos (reason or plan) for making the outcome of the argument independent of the will of the arguers. Nothing enables the arguers to convince each other with reasons. Let us look at the two views of this issue.

In the first view, which is the EFF's discourse, the dispossessed have been cheated and have a right to take back what is theirs. The liberation movement had promised that a free South Africa would belong to all its citizens. Liberation came, but that promise was not kept. Therefore, the anger of the masses, articulated and mobilized by the EFF, is righteous.

Quite apart from the unkept promise made in the Charter, a number of arguments can be made in support of sharing property. One is that communal property is a desirable part of the cultural heritage of South Africa; it was suppressed through force of arms by European conquerors and should in some form be restored. According to that heritage, the land is sacred to the ancestors, while the living are stewards of it and use it (prefiguring the EFF's proposal to organize use without ownership) not only for themselves but

---

30. *EFF Manifesto*, par. 35.
31. Lewis Coser, *The Functions of Conflict* (Glencoe, IL: Free Press, 1956).

to improve it for those yet unborn.³² Africans did not know or practice the Roman law concept of dominium, imposed on them by colonialism and now enshrined in the rules of the World Trade Organization that are obligatory throughout the global economy.³³ This indeed is one of the constitutive rules of modernity spoken of earlier. The Africans did not accept modernization (read: marketization and immersion in the cash economy) willingly but had to be coerced—for example, by being forced to pay a tax in money, which in turn forced them to work in the mines or on farms to earn the money.³⁴

Throughout the world precapitalist and non–Roman law traditions express, in one way or another, the idea that the resources of the earth should be shared and used for the good of all.³⁵ Pope Francis I underscored this tradition when he wrote in 2013 of 'creating a new mentality that thinks in terms of community, of the priority of the life of all over the appropriation of property by some'. He continued: 'Solidarity is a spontaneous reaction of those who recognize the social function of property and universal purpose of property as realities prior to private property. The private possession of property is justified to the extent that it serves to take care of it and to use it to better serve the common good. Therefore, solidarity should be lived as a decision to return to the poor what belongs to them.'³⁶

There is, then, a convincing logic underpinning the EFF (and later the ANC) position about land expropriation. However, if we apply here Heidegger's insight that all seeing is *seeing as*, all seeing is interpretation,³⁷ then expropriating the commanding heights of the economy and using them to serve the good of all can not only be seen as justice for reasons such as those sketched above; it can also be seen as tyranny. In the first place, the social rule of private property is so ingrained in modernity that any diversion from it appears anarchic and destructive to the economy; indeed the

---

32. Mfuniselwa J. Bhengu, *Ubuntu: The Global Philosophy for Humankind* (Cape Town: Lotsha Publications, 2006).

33. Hoppers and Richards, *Rethinking Thinking*.

34. Maria Mies, *Patriarchy and Accumulation on a World Scale* (London: Zed Books, 1986).

35. For an Asian perspective see Howard Richards and Joanna Swanger, *Gandhi and the Future of Economics* (Lake Oswego, OR: World Dignity University Press, 2011). For a Latin American view see Gustavo Gutierrez, *A Theology of Liberation* (Maryknoll, NY: Orbis Books, 1988). In the posthumously published vol. 3 of *Capital* (various editions), Karl Marx speaks of 'gifts of nature' which should not belong to any individual because they were not created by anybody, and of 'gifts of history' which should not belong to anybody now living because they were created by the labour of people now dead.

36. Pope Francis I, *Evangelii Gaudium* (Rome: Tipografia Vaticana, 2013), pars. 188–89.

37. Martin Heidegger, *Sein und Zeit* (Tubingen: Max Niemeyer Verlag, 1986 (1926)), p. 149.

South African Banking Council issued a strongly worded condemnation of appropriation without compensation, noting that the entire banking system was underpinned by loans against land.

In the second view, in opposition to the EFF's stance, one can imagine the anger of men and women faced with expropriation of land they 'own' without compensation by an EFF-led government. Regardless of what happened during the past few hundred years, in their own memory and the fairly recent past, they bought their land with hard-earned money. They put their own sweat, blood and tears into farming it. These people, farmers and city dwellers alike, are not likely to see EFF government officials as saints who selflessly administer the land for the benefit of all. They are more likely to see them as twenty-first-century versions of the monarchs of old who stole whatever they wanted from their subjects until, thank God, modern republican constitutions were instituted to protect the people against having their property seized by their rulers. They are likely to see them as twenty-first-century versions of twentieth-century dictators who stripped citizens of all their rights. They will send a call around the world to show how the basic rules of the game are being flouted in South Africa. Solemn promises to protect property rights were part of the democratic transition and then became part of the Constitution. International law will support them, not least because South Africa has signed and ratified international treaties guaranteeing human rights that include property rights.

This brief analysis suggests that the radical pillars of the EFF Manifesto would indeed lead to absolute conflict. Even if the EFF as an organization proves ephemeral, similar thinking proposed by another organization would lead to absolute conflict, with no apparent common moral framework that could be a basis for negotiation, compromise or cooperation.

The facts are telling us that economic theory bears on questions more serious than the allocation of scarce resources among competing uses. It bears on meeting basic needs without which life cannot go on (what heterodox economists sometimes call 'provisioning'). It bears on creating social peace and on avoiding civil war.

In this book, we advocate for unbounded organization as a successor to conventional economic thinking and a contribution to management science. In the course of this text we will explore fully what we mean by 'unbounded organization'. For the moment, we mention two supporting lines of thought that count, among their benefits, the defusing of absolute conflict over property rights. The flexibility these lines of thought offer is to be contrasted with the rigidity of the juridical framework that has been decisive for the social construction of both economic society and the science that studies it. They suggest that there are superior alternatives to the conventional economic response given by South Africa's National Development Plan (NDP), which promises, though not credibly, economic growth as a path to defusing conflict by enriching all parties. Our hope is that these two lines of thought will help South Africa to step back from the brink of absolute conflict.

The first such line of thought is ethical realism. For a realist ethical philosophy, there are no absolute rights; therefore there can be no absolute moral conflict, as when one party claims to have an absolute right incompatible with an absolute right claimed by the other party. The nonexistence of absolute rights entails that anyone who claims to have such rights is mistaken.

Rights talk is often recommended for good, practical reasons, one such good reason being the observed empirical fact that the security of property rights keeps the wheels of industry turning and the ploughs of agriculture churning.[38] However, the very fact that rights talk is recommended for good practical reasons implies that there can be good practical reasons for backing off from rights talk when it leads to absolute conflict. By the same token, there can also be good reasons for modifying property rights. Once we start having rational conversations about the social functions of property, we can take into account empirical evidence supporting the idea that property rights usually work better when they are more widely distributed, when more of them are common, and when more of them are public.[39] For a realist, a pragmatic compromise is not a second-best solution that falls short of the ideal; pragmatic compromise is the ideal.

The second line of thought consists of whatever improves social theory and transformative practice. As things now stand, the poor people of South Africa are urged to be patient because help is on its way in the form of social and economic development. They are told that their eventual prosperity will be delayed or will not come at all if they frighten away investors. They are admonished not to listen to populists. Behind such pleas to the poor lies a faith, widespread among governing elites, in the teachings of mainstream liberal economics. But if it is the case—and we will argue that it is the

---

38. Theodore Panayatou makes rational arguments for the ecological benefits of secure property rights in his *Green Markets: The Economics of Sustainable Development,* a copublication of the Harvard Institute for International Development and the Institute for Contemporary Studies (San Francisco, 1993).

39. See Richard Wilkinson and Kate Pickett, *The Spirit Level: Why More Equal Societies Almost Always Do Better* (London: Allen Lane, 2009) and other works by the same authors.

case—that mainstream liberal economics does not work for the poor, then the faith elites have placed in it is erroneous, and the grounds for asking the poor to be patient lack credibility.

Stepping back from the brink of absolute conflict calls for a more believable story. We offer our unbounded approach as one such story. We believe it contributes to building better social theory and more effective practices that will, in turn, contribute to defusing violence. The spectre of absolute conflict will fade away to the extent that better science leads to better practical results that demonstrate sincerity and meet needs.

Related to the topic of how the absolute conflict inherent in talk of absolute rights might be defused are a pair of questions. The first is whether government control of the commanding heights of land, banking and industry would or could lead to the results desired. The second is whether the absence of government control of the commanding heights of the economy would or could lead to the results desired. One of the aims of this book is, in G. W. F. Hegel's terms, to *aufheben* these twin questions (raise them to a higher level, taking seriously Albert Einstein's warning that our main problems cannot be solved at the same level of thinking as the thinking that caused them).

If economic theory, like any scientific theory, is about which causes produce which effects, then questions about what will work to achieve the results desired are questions about economic theory. They are questions for empirical research and theoretical reflection. The framing of the research and the interpretation of the results are embedded in the theory.

A first observation concerning the question economic theory should answer—the question of what will work—concerns the claim in the EFF Manifesto that, according to heterodox economists,[40] nations that have successfully developed have succeeded because of state-led industrialization and because of protection of key home industries. We observe that there is no nation that has successfully developed, certainly not the countries named in the manifesto: Brazil, India, China, Singapore, South Korea, Hong Kong, Taiwan, Japan and Finland. In fact, the modern world system is in crisis everywhere in the world. Further, there is certainly no relevant model for successful development if one thinks not of industrializing using yesterday's

---

40. The founding manifesto does not name any heterodox economists, but it may refer to the MERG report, proposals made from time to time by COSATU, and other technical studies that have been attacked and shelved in South Africa. See Matthew Kentridge, *Turning the Tanker: The Economic Policy Debate in South Africa* (Johannesburg: Centre for Policy Studies, 1993); and Hein Marais, *South Africa Pushed to the Limit: The Political Economy of Change* (London: Zed Books, 2011).

technologies but of achieving social justice in harmony with nature, using tomorrow's technologies.

A second observation concerning the question of what will work is that the ANC leaders during the freedom struggle believed that socialism (in some generic sense of that capacious term) would work, but by the time they became the government they had for the most part changed their minds. This second observation leads to our next topic, which is why the ANC backed away from a socialist reading of the Freedom Charter.

4. Mandela's Choices

According to his authorized biography, at some point in 1992 Nelson Mandela called together his inner circle and said to them: 'Chaps, we have to choose. We either keep nationalization and get no investment, or we modify our own attitude and get investment.'[41] A logical first response to this statement would be to say that Mandela was wrong: South Africa did not have to choose.

South Africa already had a large public sector, built largely by Afrikaners as a counterweight to Anglo economic supremacy, and if it had any difficulty in accessing international capital markets, such difficulty was because of moral condemnation of apartheid, not because financial institutions refused to lend to government-owned enterprises or to buy their bonds. Brazil's state-run Petrobras has had no problems raising investment funds in capital markets or partnering with private-sector petroleum giants like British Petroleum. Indeed, Brazil's experience in establishing a plastics industry was the opposite of what Mandela appears to assert: private capital was not willing to take the plunge until public capital had put up most of the money and assumed most of the risk.[42]

To be sure, ideological prejudice exists. When the American retail giant Walmart acquired the Chilean supermarket chain Lider, all products made in Cuba or Venezuela disappeared from Lider's shelves. But for the most part, business is business. When an enterprise in any sector is profitable enough to pay the cost of capital at market rates, it can acquire capital.

This is especially true today, when the world is awash in accumulated funds unable to find productive use in the real economy. Today enormous

---

41. Nelson Mandela quoted in Anthony Sampson, *Mandela: The Authorized Biography* (New York: Alfred A. Knopf, 1999), p. 429.
42. This and other similar experiences are documented in Cheryl Payer, *The World Bank: A Critical Analysis* (New York: Monthly Review Press, 1982).

sums find no better use than speculating in the ups and downs of currencies and other paper and electronic fictions in what has become known as the global casino economy. Today what John Maynard Keynes called a 'liquidity trap' has become the stuff of everyday life—as is shown in European countries where central banks have lowered interest rates to zero and still there is a shortage of entrepreneurs brave enough to take out loans. An enterprise in any sector with real resources producing real products for real customers holds the aces when playing poker with global investors. And for every Walmart there is an employee-controlled pension fund or an investors' social responsibility fund somewhere in Europe or North America that positively prefers to invest in social and ecological progress and is happy to fund viable enterprises with worthy purposes in any sector.

Nevertheless, Mandela's conversion to accommodating liberalism is understandable, and when he backtracked on socialism, he did not backtrack on his ideals. Instead he became an ardent advocate of human rights, chairing the writing of a progressive constitution which guarantees a record thirty-five inalienable rights.

In 1990, when Mandela was released from jail, he told a cheering crowd in Cape Town during his first public appearance that he was still a loyal ANC member and that the Freedom Charter was still its programme. Two years later, he told his inner circle that they would have to modify their attitude to get investment. We can assume that what was going on in his mind from 1990 to 1992 was a gradual adjustment to a world and to an economic science that had changed while he was in prison. In 1993, he wrote as the first paragraph of an article he contributed to the American magazine Foreign Affairs:

> As the 1980s drew to a close, I could not see much of the world from my prison cell, but I knew it was changing. There was little doubt in my mind that this would have a profound effect on my country, on the southern African region, and on the continent of which I am proud to be a citizen. Although this process of global change is far from complete, it is clear that all nations will have boldly to recast their nets if they are to reap any benefit from international affairs in the post–Cold War era.[43]

---

43. Nelson Mandela, 'South Africa's Future Foreign Policy', *Foreign Affairs*, vol. 72 (1993), pp. 86–97.

In the article, Mandela spells out how South Africa would join the 'new world order'. By the early 1990s, the Soviet Union and the Eastern Bloc that might have supported a socialist South Africa had melted away. Social democracy was melting away in western Europe. In Sweden, which like the Soviet Union had faithfully supported the freedom struggle in South Africa, a conservative government had been elected after the world-famous Swedish model had proven to be unsustainable.[44] The proposition that socialism does not work appeared to have been demonstrated by historical experience. Neoliberal thinking was firmly entrenched in the governments of the world's major powers, including those seated at Moscow, Beijing and Hanoi.[45] It was entrenched in the International Monetary Fund and at the World Bank, as well as in the World Trade Organization, which would soon meet in South Africa with Mandela as host. The neoliberals had the power. South Africa was largely constrained to play by their rules; in particular, it needed the 850-million-dollar emergency loan that the ANC had secretly negotiated with the IMF.[46]

In addition to the de facto power of the new neoliberal world order, by the 1990s academic neoliberal economists had been generating intellectually powerful theories supported by persuasive empirical findings for half a century, in the process generating a dozen Nobel Memorial Prizes in Economic Science. It seemed reasonable to believe their claims that minimal government and maximum free markets would bring employment to the unemployed, reduce inequality, and lift the poor out of poverty.[47] Their superficially plausible theories had not yet been refuted by tragic historical experience in South Africa and the rest of the world. It is easy, then, to understand why in the early 1990s Nelson Mandela and other ANC leaders put their faith in somewhat nuanced neoliberal ideas. It was a necessary

---

44. See Assar Lindbeck et al., *Turning Sweden Around* (Cambridge, MA: MIT Press, 1994).

45. Two important influences in Mandela's conversion were his conversations with leaders from China and from Vietnam who told him of the acceptance of private enterprise in those Communist countries. 'They changed my views altogether', said Mandela (Sampson, *Mandela: The Authorized Biography*, pp. 210–211).

46. John Saul and Patrick Bond, in *South Africa: The Present as History* (Woodbridge, UK: James Currey, 2014), give details on the power-politics aspects of the imposition of neoliberalism on South Africa.

47. Such optimism is expressed in Milton Friedman's now classic neoliberal text *Capitalism and Freedom*, published by University of Chicago Press in 1962. Similar claims were made for a reform package proposed by the South Africa Foundation in 1996. We do not think they could be made today. The history of these issues in South Africa is reviewed by Hein Marais in *South Africa Pushed to the Limit*.

accommodation to the perceived realities of economic and political power. It was a defensible intellectual judgment.

We suggest that one reason for the persistence of such ideas today is that even though neoliberal economics is discredited, the well-known alternatives to it have also been discredited. As we write this book in 2019, experience and thought are still in flux. The implausibility of neoliberalism does not prompt a return to Soviet-style central planning. Nor does it mean reviving the Western European style of social democracy that was dying in the late eighties and early nineties even as democracy was being born in South Africa. Rather, at this point in history a reconsideration of premises common to all three (central planning, social democracy and neoliberalism) is called for. We are being asked to reconsider what Joseph Schumpeter in his *History of Economic Analysis* named the 'institutional frame' of economics.[48]

Today the physical realities of ecology and the social realities of deepening structural unemployment, underemployment and precarious employment are happening off the blackboards of mainstream liberal economics in a space different from the Cartesian space of its curves. The breaching of the natural boundaries of the biosphere makes daily more poignant Kenneth Boulding's remark that anyone who believes exponential growth can go on forever in a finite world is either a lunatic or an economist. The onward march of technologies such as robotics, 3-D printers and artificial photosynthesis is consigning mainstream ideas like 'full employment is normal', 'a natural rate of unemployment around five percent is normal', and 'investment (or growth or development) will bring an end to mass unemployment' to the same lunatic category as the beliefs of flat-earthers, holocaust deniers, and global-warming deniers.[49] But a call to reconsider the institutional frame need not imply a free pass for dissident economists. Nor is it a call to revive without amendment the economic beliefs held by Nelson Mandela and his colleagues when they first set foot on Robben Island.

---

48. Joseph Schumpeter, *History of Economic Analysis* (New York: Oxford University Press, 1954), p. 544.

49. Bernard Stiegler, *For a New Critique of Political Economy* (New York: Wiley, 2010); Jeremy Rifkin, *The Zero Marginal Cost Society* (New York: Palgrave Macmillan, 2014). Rifkin's point is not just that today's new technologies make human labour increasingly redundant. It is that in principle the tendency to replace humans with machines and electronics is infinite with no end in sight.

5. The National Development Plan

In February of 2010, President Jacob Zuma constituted a National Planning Commission to 'take a broad, cross-cutting, independent and critical view of South Africa, to help define the South Africa we seek to achieve in 20 years' time, and to map out a path to achieve those objectives'.[50] In June 2011, the Commission released a diagnostic report, and in November of that year, it submitted a draft plan. Many thousands of people from all walks of life discussed the draft in meetings held throughout the country. In August 2012, a widely owned revised version became South Africa's official National Development Plan (NDP). We comment on a few of its key statements.

> *The plan draws extensively on the notion of capabilities.*
> (NDP, Executive Summary)

The source of the notion of capabilities is Amartya Sen and his coauthors, Martha Nussbaum and Jean Dreze. Sen, Nussbaum and Dreze also emphasize pluralism—the idea that no one institution, in particular the market, and no two institutions, in particular the market and the state, can solve society's problems. Sen wrote of 'the mean streets and stunted lives that capitalism can generate, unless it is restrained and supplemented by other—often nonmarket—institutions'.[51] In this book we extend the idea of pluralism to the idea of unboundedness.

> *The fragility of South Africa's economy lies in the distorted pattern of ownership and economic exclusion created by apartheid policies.* (NDP, ch. 3, 'Economy and Employment')

We show in chapter 3 of this book that every economy is fragile. There may or may not be investment. There may or may not be buyers. There may be—and sooner or later there always are—new technologies producing new products or producing the same products more cheaply, thus making whatever a person, firm or nation has to sell unmarketable. The phrase 'community development', when associated with unbounded organization,

---

50. All quotations are from the plan itself and associated documents found at www.npconline.co.za.

51. Amartya Sen, 'Sraffa, Wittgenstein and Gramsci', *Journal of Economic Literature*, vol. 41 (2003), p. 1247. We will quote this line several times.

names ways to make people more secure in a world where purely economic relationships are always relationships at risk.[52]

> *Several studies, most notably Aghion and Fedderke, argued that profit margins are already very high in South Africa, even in the manufacturing sector. The high profits have not generated higher investment levels because many of these markets are highly concentrated with low levels of competition.* (NDP, ch. 15, 'Transforming Society and Uniting the Country')

This statement implies a dubious scientific assertion: that if manufacturing in South Africa were more competitive than it is, there would be more economic activity. This assertion relies on theories that regard competitive markets as normal and normal markets as tending toward full employment of all factors of production.

We argue that such theories have never accurately portrayed the real world of business, and that, in any case, they will be useless in a high-tech future. Instead of making business more competitive, a better approach is to make business contribute more to society by generating a larger social surplus, and then to transfer the surplus to create more livelihoods that do not depend on sales. To this end, instead of sending high-powered promoters of South Africa to scour Wall Street and the city of London to find new investors and convince them that new businesses in new niches can be new sources of profit in South Africa, it is better to work hand-in-glove with enterprises that are already in South Africa—develop more transparent and ethical relationships with, and expect more contributions to the common good from, businesses that already have an emotional attachment to this long-suffering country and that have already proven themselves to be profitable here.

> *South Africa's level of emissions will peak around 2025, and then stabilise. This transition will need to be achieved without hindering the country's pursuit of its socioeconomic objectives.* (NDP, ch. 5, 'Transition to a Low Carbon Economy')

---

52. See Ulrich Beck, *Risk Society: Towards a New Modernity* (London: Sage, 1992).

There is no more graphic or poignant illustration of the clash of social structure with physical necessity than the struggle of South Africa's planning commissioners to come to consensus on environmental policy. As the quote above reveals, their efforts ended in a nonconsensus prescribing an impossibility. As further evidence of the commissioners' split opinions, chapter 4 of the NDP calls for a new rail corridor to the Waterberg coal fields and for generating more coal-fired electricity. Stabilizing South Africa's carbon dioxide emissions by 2025 is too low an objective, despite the objective stated here to reduce emissions.

The carbon dioxide in the earth's atmosphere is already over 400 ppm, which is too high, and experts tell us it cannot be stabilized short of 500 ppm, which is much too high. Nobody should be surprised if even the too-low goal of 500 in 2025 is not achieved. And nobody should be surprised that whatever South Africa does will be ineffective, since success would require concerted global action that included the large economies.

None of this is the fault of the NDP. Nor is it the fault of the commissioners or the South African government. It is the fault of the logic and dynamics of the economy, which in turn is the fault of the basic social structure, which in turn is the fault of history. As history has turned out, although it is physically possible to save the biosphere and with it the human species, it is not, as things now stand, socially possible. In this book, we are proposing unbounded organization as an approach to making socially possible what is physically possible.

Society is constrained by a socially constructed reality called economic reality, and the current economic reality is that human needs are met by a system that either runs on profit or does not run at all. Specifically, the commissioners could not, even if they wanted to, shut down a large privately owned business that brings money into South Africa by exporting coal to Asia. They knew this. We quote them: 'Indeed, in the era of globalisation, is it possible for any government to be able to discipline capital?' (ch. 15, p. 477). The NDP's power, like the government's power, does not extend to reversing the dynamics driving the self-destruction of *Homo sapiens*.

A footnote in chapter 1 of the NDP, 'Key Drivers of Change', includes a quote from Dani Rodrik's book *One Economics, Many Recipes*[53]: "You don't understand; this reform will not work here because our entrepreneurs do not respond to price incentives," is not a valid argument. "You don't

---

53. Dani Rodrik, *One Economics, Many Recipes* (Princeton, NJ: Princeton University Press, 2007).

understand, this reform will not work here because credit constraints prevent our entrepreneurs from taking advantage of profit opportunities" or "because entrepreneurship is highly taxed at the margin", is a valid argument.' Rodrik's unabashedly neoclassical book was published in 2007, prior to the 2008 meltdown leading to the global recession that has continued. Paul Krugman, a Nobel Prize winner in economics, in his 2009 book, *The Return of Depression Economics*, argues that whatever may happen on a practical level, on the level of economic theory, the series of crises in the last few decades, culminating in the 2008 meltdown, demonstrates that on some key issues the neoclassicals were wrong and the neo-Keynesians are right.[54]

In this book we criticize Rodrik (and his coauthors, Andres Velasco and Ricardo Hausmann) in some detail. Although theirs is the only mainstream book we critique, we mean our critique to apply to other books of the same genre, which we call 'mainstream empirical studies'.[55] Such books compare the results of left-leaning and right-leaning economic policies. The weight of empirical evidence tends to favour right-leaning policies, in spite of the exceptional empirical counter-evidence cited by left-leaning economists. Our approach is to analyse the basic structural causes of the empirically observed relative success of, for example, lower wages, lower taxes on profits, less welfare and more austerity. Instead of concluding that right-leaning policies should as a general rule be adopted, we propose (and empirically illustrate the effectiveness of) transforming the basic social structure.

We hold that in the long run, and perhaps in the medium run, there can be no future for humanity or the biosphere without emancipation from the social structures that produce the anti-life results that are, unfortunately, currently observed. Emancipation so conceived does not require imposing on humanity an abstract totalitarian utopia. It does require an open-minded (unbounded) approach to economic theory, along with a psychologically effective and multicultural approach to ethics. A better theory will be capable of seeing—and a stronger ethics will be capable of actively supporting—the thousands of transformative social innovations already happening. Some achievements at some sites of South Africa's Community Work Programme are among them.

---

54. Paul Krugman, *The Return of Depression Economics* (New York: Norton, 2009).

55. Other books of the mainstream empirical studies genre include David Neumark and William Wascher, *Minimum Wages* (Cambridge, MA: MIT Press, 2008); Rudiger Dornbusch and Sebastian Edwards, eds., *The Macroeconomics of Populism in Latin America* (Chicago: University of Chicago Press, 1991); and Alberto Alesina, Carlo Favero and Francesco Giavazzi, *Austerity: When It Works and When It Doesn't* (Princeton, NJ: Princeton University Press, 2019).

While South Africa's planning commissioners cite Rodrik's hard-nosed, semi-standard economics, they also appeal to sentimental patriotism. The NDP begins with a picture of children putting their hands together in a gesture of solidarity. It continues with a long lyrical prose-poem vision that celebrates the traditional African value of *ubuntu*. The NDP calls for social cohesion across society. It calls on both business and labour to moderate narrow self-interest for the sake of the greater good. Integral parts of the Plan are more psychological than economic. Children are to learn social values in school—on this point we could not agree more. A 'Bill of Responsibilities' is included in the Plan as a tool to change behaviour.

Echoing the NDP, Adam Habib writes in an article on South Africa, 'The successful consolidation of democracy requires . . . an expanding economic system within which resources are made available for redistribution, so as to lead to an appreciable increase in the standard of living of the populace.'[56] The opinion that higher economic growth is an indispensable prerequisite to higher employment and lower poverty is not only the opinion of the NDP commissioners, their academic advisors and, presumably, the thousands who participated in the planning process. A recent survey of public policy debates, reported in the South African media, concluded that it is an opinion nobody denies. The surveyor was himself surprised to find that, even though South Africa had its Economic Freedom Fighters and its share of left-leaning politicians, labour leaders and intellectuals, nobody—or at least nobody visible in the media—was offering an alternative to the standard International Monetary Fund prescription of investment to create growth and growth to create employment.[57] This prescription is implicit on every page of the NDP.

Nevertheless, chapter 1 of the NDP confesses that prospects for high levels of growth are not good for the foreseeable future. Every year so far, growth has been less than the NDP target of at least five percent. It was 2.8 percent in 2010, 3.1 percent in 2011, 3.9 percent in 2012, 4.4 percent in 2013, 1.5 percent in 2014, 1.3 percent in 2015, 0.3 percent in 2016, 1.3 percent in 2017 and 1.8 percent in 2018.[58] As we discuss later, Thomas

---

56. Adam Habib, South Africa: 'The Rainbow Nation and the Prospects for Consolidating Democracy', *African Journal of Political Science/Revue Africaine de Science Politique*, vol. 2 (1997), p.19.

57. Keith Boyd, *Over the Rainbow: From Closed Circles to Virtuous Cycles* (Unpublished MBA Dissertation, University of Cape Town, 2016), p. 40.

58. Statistics South Africa Statistical Release P0441; and 'World Bank: South Africa Country at a Glance', www.Worldbank.org/en/country/SouthAfrica. These numbers would be lower if they were expressed in terms of GDP per capita, thus taking into account the growth of population.

Pikkety has made a convincing argument that, except for nations doing what he calls technological catch-up, slow growth will be the norm for the twenty-first century.[59]

In this book, we criticize the very concept of growth. With respect to growth, the famous words of Ludwig Wittgenstein apply: 'A picture held us captive. And we could not get outside it, for it lay in our language and language seemed to repeat it to us inexorably.'[60] Growth is commonly pictured as a larger pie to be sliced. We argue that there is no such pie and that if there were such a pie, there would be no one authorized to slice it. Instead of advocating no growth or degrowth, we advocate what we call governable growth.

We agree with the NDP's call for the wise use of rents from natural resources. Rent is a major part of surplus. To use surplus wisely is to use it to meet needs in harmony with nature. However, we propose a different vocabulary expressing a viewpoint that reworks theory in the light of brute facts and on-the-ground working alternatives. A first step must be to face the question of how to eliminate poverty and how to reduce inequality under conditions of slow or no growth. We put community development forward as a big part of the answer to this question, and we put community broadly understood as, in principle, a complete answer. Later steps include critiquing GDP as a measure of growth.

> *Citizens have a responsibility to dissuade leaders from taking narrow, short-sighted and populist positions.* (NDP, Overview)

The term 'populist' denotes a pattern of tragedy all too common in the twentieth century.[61] Leaders seen as demagogues by some and as progressives by others win political power by promising a welfare state. To win and to keep power, they mobilize the masses. Ever more popular participation in politics leads to ever more demands on the state. Taxes go up. Wages go up. Capital flees. The state has assumed more burdens than it can carry. The leaders have made more promises than they can keep. The people come

---

59. Thomas Piketty, *Capital in the Twenty-First Century* (Cambridge, MA: Belknap Press of Harvard University, 2014).

60. Ludwig Wittgenstein, *Philosophical Investigations* (Oxford: Blackwell, 1958), par. 115.

61. Rudiger Dornbusch and Sebastian Edwards, eds., *The Macroeconomics of Populism in Latin America* (Chicago: University of Chicago Press, 1991).

to feel that their leaders have betrayed them. The country is paralyzed by protests and strikes. Inflation makes wage increases illusory and business impossible. The dénouement is an authoritarian crackdown that persists until the authoritarian regime itself crumbles and the cycle begins again.

The NDP proposes in place of such a vicious cycle a virtuous circle. A social compact establishes the preconditions for economic growth. Economic growth makes it possible to fund a welfare state. The first principle of the social compact is the security of property rights, especially the property rights of the mine owners. With credible guarantees that there will be no nationalization, mine owners can invest with confidence. The requirement of a stable environment for economic growth is the reason why citizens have a responsibility to dissuade leaders from taking short-sighted populist positions. Populism chills growth because it chills confidence.

By the same token, as the NDP whispers and reality shouts, if economic growth leads not to welfare but to profits being taken out of South Africa and invested elsewhere, there will be no virtuous circle. Either populism or the socially irresponsible exercise of property rights can render the careful work of the commissioners vain.

In this context, we emphasize, the spectre of absolute conflict reappears. From a moral point of view, conservatives can argue that the legitimacy of any government depends on its respect for property rights. Progressives can argue that everyone who is born on this earth deserves a fair share of the gifts of nature (products of nobody's labour) and the gifts of history (products of the labour of nobody now living), and sooner rather than later; the dispossessed have already waited too long to receive their rightful inheritance. While the NDP appeals to citizens to resist populism, its anti-populist appeal relies only slightly on a moral defence of property rights. It appeals much more to the human longing to be part of a social whole with a common purpose.

The NDP will inevitably be reconsidered. The numbers the commissioners projected as objectives for tomorrow will inevitably be replaced, one by one, by numerical descriptions of yesterday. It will always be possible to argue that the plan would have worked if only the masses had been less populist and if only the classes had been more socially responsible.

This book argues instead that any such plan cannot possibly work in the absence of a practical method for transforming the basic social structure. Unbounded organization is such a practical method. We argue that some things that South Africa's Community Work Programme has been doing on the ground show how such a method works.

6. Economic Theory, Community Development and South Africa's Community Work Programme

At this point, as Robert Frost wrote, two paths diverge in the woods, and we take the one less travelled. The more common path—the path of Spain's Podemos party, of Jeremy Corbyn and Yanis Varoufakis, and of much of the South African left—calls a plan like the NDP neoliberal, even though its authors and its ideological mentors, Rodrik, Hausmann and Velasco, deny that they are neoliberals. And the common path of the left, quite rightly, calls for alternatives that are not neoliberal.

The problem, as we see it, is that these very alternatives have not worked in the past for reasons inherent in their basic structure. They are old and inadequate versions of democratic socialism. Typically, their goals in the South African context include nationalizing the mines, implementing the Freedom Charter, bringing the banking system or at least the Central Bank under democratic control, rebuilding a shattered welfare state, crafting an industrial policy where the state plays a leading role in accelerating development and so on. The political strategy for realising a not-neoliberal alternative usually calls for a broad-based coalition capable of achieving an electoral majority. It usually calls for exercising direct economic power through strikes, boycotts, cooperatives and worker-owned enterprises. It should be evident by now that this commonly travelled path regularly fails to arrive at its laudable goals.

Our less-travelled path treats the NDP and its mentors as a foil for rethinking basic economic theory and, moreover, as a foil for dissolving economic science altogether into a design science approach that does not separate constructing a world from understanding a world.[62] We view the failures so far of efforts to build democratic socialism as consequences of the basic cultural structure of modernity.[63] Changing policies, changing governments, changing who owns the means of production and changing economic models will not get *Homo sapiens* off the endangered species list unless such changes are accompanied by deeper intellectual and emotional changes that refocus humanity as a cultural animal. (We want to say 'spiritual animal', but we use that phrase only occasionally because for many it calls to mind exactly what we do not mean.)

---

62. Herbert Simon, *The Sciences of the Artificial*, 3rd ed. (Cambridge, MA: MIT Press, 1996). Unbounded organization can be viewed as a science and art of the artificial and also as practicing what Paulo Freire called 'cultural action'.

63. Howard Richards and Joanna Swanger, *The Dilemmas of Social Democracies* (Lanham, MD: Rowman and Littlefield, 2006).

At a practical level, we often agree with the common path. We agree with building an electoral majority, strikes, boycotts, cooperatives and worker-owned enterprises. We have participated in those activities, and we support them as long as they are accompanied by rethinking, redefining the problems, and unbounded organizing. We are intellectually convinced that the common path without rethinking, without doing what Fritz Schumacher called 'inner work' and without building a broad consensus will not work because we ourselves have experienced it as not working.

It is becoming more evident to more people every day that economic theory and community have to be rethought, or unthought, from the ground up. Our effort claims to be distinct from the many other rethinkings of economics on offer because (1) it reframes the issues in terms of social structure, and (2) it combines a conceptual study with an empirical study of a programme that (quite imperfectly) demonstrates in action some of the principles our rethinking advocates in theory. Unbounded organization, like Latin American *economia solidaria*, is a new theory that already has some practical achievements to its credit.

The empirical parts of this book examine one part of the public employment that South Africa's National Development Plan called for: the creation of a million new jobs in public employment by 2015 and two million by 2030. This was to be done principally through the Expanded Public Works Programme (EPWP), of which the Community Work Programme (CWP) is a part. The following are some of the reasons why the CWP at its best has demonstrated the idea of unbounded organization in terms of practical experience:

1. The CWP partly succeeded in decentralizing a huge national programme by empowering grassroots citizen participation and partnering with local partners in many ways.
2. In the absence of social validation of the efficiency of resource allocation through sales in markets, and in the absence of a command economy with a Gosplan, the CWP found innovative ways to distinguish useful work from useless work.
3. Earning a dignified livelihood does not depend on selling or on complying with the requirements of a regime of accumulation.
4. The CWP seeks, in addition to the usual multiplier effect as money spent on public works is respent by its recipients, an additional kind of multiplier effect. It uses community development to mobilize

resources complementary to those that can be mobilized through public budgets.
5. It has moved toward—though not yet to—an employment guarantee that would effectively insulate the right to a decent life from the vagaries of today's labour market and from the virtual certainty that future technologies will make most work obsolete.
6. It achieved outcomes in social cohesion, and in mental health and a psychological sense of well-being, not achieved by social grants or less innovative forms of public employment.

CHAPTER TWO
Community as a Guiding Star for Navigating the Seas of Late Modernity in Neurath's Boat

Community as a guiding star refers to the proposal, implicit in the title of this book, to complement economic theory and practice with community development. Navigating the seas of late modernity in Neurath's boat refers to the complexity encountered in rethinking and reconstructing today's basic ideas and institutions, which do not work and are not sustainable.[1]

OVERVIEW OF THE CHAPTER

1. One Plank at a Time: Questioning Mainstream Development Theory
2. Applying the Logic of the Social Construction of Reality to Its Reconstruction
3. A Biologist's View of History as the Selection of Moral Systems
4. Economy and Community: Community as Guiding Star
5. Words from Prominent Authors Supporting Our Novel Definition of Community
6. Talking Community Up versus Talking Community Down

1. One Plank at a Time: Questioning Mainstream Development Theory

South Africa's National Development Plan (NDP), while calling for national unity, admonishing the poor not to listen to populists, and pleading with the rich to invest in South Africa and not elsewhere, makes at least two promises dependent on cause-and-effect relationships. One promise is that if all South Africans behave as the NDP recommends, there will be growth. The other is that if South Africans follow the provisions in the

---

1. For a discussion of late modernity see Anthony Giddens, *Modernity and Self-Identity* (Stanford: Stanford University Press, 1991).

plan made possible by growth, poverty will be alleviated. Specifically, the planners projected eliminating extreme poverty in South Africa by 2030—presenting this not as a promise but as a target made reasonable if the plan is followed.

The text of the NDP recommends to its readers the book *One Economics, Many Recipes* by Dani Rodrik, a Turkish economist based at Princeton and Harvard. Ricardo Hausmann, the director of the Centre for Economic Development at Harvard, and Andres Velasco, professor of international development and finance at Harvard and minister of finance of Chile from 2006 to 2010, coauthored some of the chapters with Rodrik. A more mainstream trio would be hard to find, although Rodrik deviates from the mainstream in his positive assessment of some socialistic aspects (like public banking) of the causes of China's economic growth. We will sometimes refer to the ideas in that book as the Rodrik-Hausmann-Velasco (RHV) mainstream theory of development.

We would, if we could, offer constructive alternatives to nearly every concept expressed in Rodrik's book and to the worldview, ethics, and legal framework it silently presupposes. However, following the wisdom of the sailors on Neurath's boat, we are considering and replacing one plank of mainstream theory at a time. And the plank we choose to address first concerns mainstream development theory.

Mainstream development theory relies heavily on investments. We quote from RHV: 'The most important question in the short run for an economy stuck in low-activity equilibrium, is how to get entrepreneurs excited about investing in the home economy.'[2] We pair this with a quotation we nominate as one of the six most important sentences in John Maynard Keynes's *General Theory*: 'The weakness of the inducement to invest has been at all times the key to the economic problem.'[3] RHV spell out the basics of how to excite investors—in Keynes's terms, how to cope with the chronic weakness of the inducement to invest: promising that investors will be able to raise their profits, lower their risks, and keep wages and taxes low while accessing a skilled work force and publicly funded infrastructure; that they can bring less money into South Africa by having access to credit; and that they will be able to remove their profits from South Africa whenever

---

2. Dani Rodrik, *One Economics, Many Recipes* (Princeton, NJ: Princeton University Press, 2009), Kindle, location 731.

3. John Maynard Keynes, *The General Theory of Employment, Interest, and Money* (London and New York: Macmillan, 1936), pp. 347–348.

they wish. Enough said. We leave RHV now—we will come back to them later—in order to present the new thinking we propose.

♦ ♦ ♦

> 'I appreciate that they [CWP] look after the sick that cannot look after themselves. They have the welfare and love of the people at heart.'
>
> — CWP PARTICIPANT, RANDFONTEIN

2. Applying the Logic of the Social Construction of Reality to Its Reconstruction

We propose to understand the quotations from RHV and from Keynes as referring to consequences of what we propose to call the *basic social structure,* sometimes also called the *basic cultural structure*.[4] While acknowledging that the phrases we are proposing are novel, that we made them up,[5] we assert that they describe socially and historically constructed realities in existence at least since the seventeenth century in Europe. The basic social structure and the constructs that it comprises (for example, property law and contract law) generally arrived later on other continents as those regions were colonized by Europeans. These constructed realities have a fateful consequence wherever they have been introduced: the vital processes of life come to depend on investments, and 'our normal lot', to borrow a phrase from Keynes,[6] is that there are not enough of them.

As we saw in the introduction, what makes the basic social structure *basic* is that it governs the provisioning of people with the basic necessities of life, such as food and safety, and what makes it a *social structure* is that it is about material relations among social positions.[7] For instance, when RHV advise the poor nations of the world that to develop they must get

---

4. Howard Richards, *Letters from Quebec* (San Francisco: International Scholars Press, 1995); Howard Richards, *Understanding the Global Economy* (Santa Barbara, CA: Peace Education Books, 2004) (there is a PDF digital version online); Howard Richards and Joanna Swanger, *Dilemmas of Social Democracies* (Lanham, MD: Rowman and Littlefield, 2006).

5. We cannot truthfully say, following Peter Strawson, that the phrases we propose significantly refer because there exist language habits, conventions or rules that make it possible for them to refer. P.F. Strawson, 'On Referring', *Mind*, vol. 59 (1950), p. 329.

6. Keynes, *General Theory*, p. 203.

7. See Sen's study of famines, *Poverty and Famines: An Essay on Entitlement and Deprivation* (Oxford: Oxford University Press, 1981); see also Douglas Porpora, *Reconstructing Sociology* (Cambridge, UK: Cambridge University Press, 2015), p. 98.

investors excited about investing, they refer to the operative and material fact that investors occupy the social position of owners of capital. What makes the basic social structure *cultural* is that its existence and operation depend on the unique human capacity to invent cultures and pass them on through education. (Culture has given humans an evolutionary advantage over animals, who generally adapt to environmental challenges by strategies like mutation of DNA and natural selection.[8])

In Roy Bhaskar's terminology, the basic social structure is an intransitive object of social science.[9] At an ontological level, its identity and causal powers do not depend on how people name it. We are not inventing the basic social structure; we are naming it. Nor is it another name for capitalism; it is a name for capitalism's key prerequisites, namely, arms-length individualistic human relationships and the basic rules of markets. It is a name for key structural causes of the mass unemployment that public employment programmes now struggle to remedy.

Over the centuries, people have made the basic social structure by their actions, and not always intentionally. How did people make it? As we saw in the introduction and in more detail in chapter 1, John Searle argues that we socially construct social reality by assigning social status to brute facts, by collective intentionality, and by making up constitutive rules.[10] What we find so helpful about Searle's logic of the social construction of reality is that the same logic can be employed to deconstruct it and then to reconstruct it.

In other words, the social status of brute facts can be reassigned.

For example, Eva Peron attempted a reassignment of the social status of brute facts when she declared to her fellow Argentines, '¡Donde hay una necesidad hay un derecho!' (Where there is a need, there is a right!) The brute facts of hunger remained the same: human bodies were receiving insufficient calories, proteins and vitamins. But the social status of those brute facts changed; food became a right. So also, Jesus reassigned the social status of the brute facts of need when he declared eternal reward in heaven for those who meet the needs of others here on earth: because 'I was hungry and you gave me something to eat, I was thirsty and you gave me something to drink, I was a stranger and you invited me in, I needed

---

8. See Victor Turner, 'Body, Brain and Culture', *Performing Arts Journal*, vol. 10 (1986), pp. 26–34; and Douglas Porpora, 'Cultural Rules and Material Relations', *Sociological Theory*, vol. 11 (1993), pp. 212–229.

9. See Howard Richards, 'On the Intransitive Objects of the Social (or Human) Sciences', *Journal of Critical Realism*, vol. 17 (2018), pp. 1–16.

10. John Searle, *The Construction of Social Reality* (New York: Free Press, 1995), p. 13.

clothes and you clothed me, I was sick and you looked after me, I was in prison and you came to visit me.'[11]

Similarly, collective intentions can change.

For example, the official collective intentions of humanity changed with the ratification of the Universal Declaration of Human Rights of 1948. In chapter 6, on India's Mahatma Gandhi Rural Employment Guarantee Act, we suggest how humanity can move that collective intention from incredible promises to credible realities by practicing unbounded organization and moral realism.[12]

So also, constitutive rules can change.

For example, perhaps the most fateful of all constitutive rules, those that constitute property rights, could be, as Mahatma Gandhi proposed, changed on a small yet achievable scale by individuals who decide to administer their surplus for the benefit of the poor. As the Community Work Programme in South Africa demonstrates, the poor themselves often have a surplus to share in the form of time and caring. To cite two among innumerable possible examples:[13] (1) The prevailing cultural structure could reconstitute property by defining what is mine as belonging not only to me but also to those I can help with my surplus;[14] and (2) what Karl Marx called 'gifts of nature' (such as minerals in the ground) and 'gifts of history' (such as wealth accumulated by people no longer living and intellectual property created by deceased scientists) could be reconstituted (partly or wholly) as a common inheritance belonging to every child born.

As moral realists, we want to say with Plato[15] that the true architect of the *polis* is our needs, and the first and greatest need is food. And we want to say with Abraham Maslow[16] that humans also need safety, love, esteem,

---

11. Matthew 25: 35–36, New International Version.

12. Here we do not follow Searle. In Searle's opinion it was irresponsible to ratify the declaration of rights of 1948 without first providing adequate financing to pay for delivering the social rights promised.

13. Innumerable examples are provided by David Ellerman in his account of the history of how property rights became what they are today: *Property and Contract in Economics: The Case for Economic Democracy* (Oxford: Blackwell, 1992).

14. Thomas Aquinas, *Summa Theologica II*, question 32, article 5. Similarly, the Apostle Paul, who was a tent-maker, reports that after making enough tents to meet his own needs, he made more tents in order to have a surplus to share with the weak. Acts of the Apostles 20: 33–38.

15. In bk. 2 of *The Republic*.

16. Abraham Maslow, 'A Theory of Human Motivation', *Psychological Review*, vol. 50 (1943), pp 370–396. While we take from Maslow his summary of what was then known about human needs, his point that esteem and self-realization are just as much needs as food and safety, and his suggestion that society ought to be organized to meet human needs, we

self-esteem and self-actualization. It is no minor matter that the Community Work Programme at its best provides for these needs, while a guaranteed income for every citizen, consisting of a certain sum per month, does not. *Homo sapiens* evolved not only to succeed in eating and avoiding being eaten, but to eat and avoid being eaten in a particular way: the way of the ethical, language-using, social animal who lives in communities.

John Searle makes another key point. Humans have evolved not to be just any kind of ethical animal. We are *deontic ethical animals*, meaning that humans have a remarkable capacity for *deontic ethics*; that is, humans have adapted to environmental challenges over many thousands of years by being capable of doing things they do not want to do because they see those things *as their duty*. A classic example is the half-starved Eskimo hunter who trudges long distances carrying the seal he has just killed on his back without eating a bite of it until he arrives back at the igloo to share it with his kin.[17] If it were not for the human capacity for deontic ethics, many socially and historically constructed realities could not be constructed. There could be no families, schools, hospitals, business enterprises, banks, armies or governments.

> 'We are able to get money at the end, about R500. We then buy maize meal, rice and oil; then we are happy. The government helped us by giving us these jobs. Thank you.'
>
> – CWP PARTICIPANT, UMTHWALUME

3. A Biologist's View of History as the Selection of Moral Systems

David Sloan Wilson is one of the distinguished biologists who have studied the evolution of the human capacity to organize for the common good.[18] He holds that when it comes to human evolution, the units of Darwinian natural selection that prove either adaptive or not adaptive are not individual human bodies or groups of bodies but 'moral systems'.

---

do not believe in his hierarchy. See also Amitai Etzioni, 'Basic Human Needs, Alienation and Inauthenticity', *American Sociological Review*, vol. 33 (1968), pp. 870–885.

17. See the discussion of Eskimo ethics in Robert Wright, *Nonzero: The Logic of Human Destiny* (New York: Pantheon Books, 1999).

18. Among the others are C.H. Waddington, *The Ethical Animal* (London: George Allen and Unwin, 1960); and Richard Joyce, *The Evolution of Morality* (Cambridge, MA: MIT Press, 2006).

Wilson's view can be compared to Arnold Toynbee's view of history. Toynbee found that nations are unsatisfactory units of analysis for studying what happens in history. Instead he studied civilizations, which he defined as functional units held together by shared values. Civilizations (more precisely, the governing elites that lead civilizations) either succeed or fail at responding creatively to the existential challenges posed by the physical environment and by competing civilizations. Accordingly, they flourish, stagnate or die.

I would suggest that what Wilson calls a moral system Toynbee calls a civilization. I would also suggest that today's global economy is a moral system or a civilization in this sense. (Immanuel Wallerstein says it is now the only object of study for social science because there is nothing outside it.) I would further suggest that the global economy's shared values are those of the basic cultural structure; they are articulated, for example, in the economic, legal and ethical thinking of the World Trade Organization. Similarly, we can say that a key existential challenge confronting today's global economy (or moral system or civilization) is mass unemployment.

Francis Fukuyama tells us that history is about competition among what he calls *systems*[19] (I do not believe it distorts his meaning to call them *moral systems*) and that history is now over, since there is only one system left standing—the democratic capitalist one. (He accounts for the parts of the world that are not democratic capitalist by saying they are 'still in history'.) He says further that the one system left standing is in deep trouble, and we agree with him.

Not only biology but also the sciences that go even further back in time to the generation and persistence of heavy molecules, starting from hydrogen and helium, show that when things endure and/or reproduce themselves over long periods of time, there are causes for their endurance. In our view, capitalism is no exception.[20] Capitalism is homeostatic because when capital accumulation fails to move production, life itself is in jeopardy, so powerful forces are mobilized to restore conditions favourable for capital accumulation. This long-term view of capitalism is through the cosmological framework of unbounded organization and moral realism. It is not a cosmovision that entails that capitalism is all bad and deserves

---

19. Francis Fukuyama, *The End of History and the Last Man* (New York: Penguin, 1992).

20. We identify capitalism with the basic social structure not of all market societies but only of those whose dominant moving force is capital accumulation. No society is purely capitalist or purely anything; every real society is a mix.

to be abolished root and branch; it entails only that capitalism is what it is, and that it cannot successfully be reformed or transformed without our understanding what it is.

♦ ♦ ♦

Noma Indiya Nqolo is a co-coordinator at Randfontein.

> 'Most of the participants have changed. What they did mostly was to drink, steal and all of those things. Now most of the people have joined this project that keeps them busy. The crime rate has decreased.'

– CDI

4. Economy and Community: Community as Guiding Star

In my view of the history of philosophy, philosophers have always been what Paulo Freire called cultural activists and Antonio Gramsci called intellectual and moral reformers, working (often with a class bias) to adjust culture to its physical functions in the historical circumstances where they find themselves.[21] Behaving as cultural activists aspiring to be moral and intellectual reformers, we, as philosophers, now add another new plank for Neurath's boat alongside 'basic cultural structure' and 'assign to the brute facts of need the social status of rights' and other new planks already proposed for the consideration of the reader, since we cannot do any shipbuilding by ourselves.

The new plank is this: 'economy and community'. The conjunction 'and' indicates connection or addition. For two things to be connected, they must also be mutually exclusive. Therefore, the actual meaning of 'economy and community' is 'economy (or economics) is not community; community is not economy'. We think the reader will see why this is convenient as the book proceeds; for instance, it will help the reader to understand that 'the organization workshop made Bokfontein into a community'.

At the same time, for two things to be connected, they also must have something in common such that they can be in relationship. Therefore, the relationship between 'economy' and 'community' is also complementary. For example, Marx can be read as saying economy (labour) is the metabolism of society, and we can agree with him, even though we will also be

---

21. Howard Richards, *Letters from Quebec* (San Francisco: International Scholars Press, 1995).

noticing many other uses and nuances of the word 'economy'; and we can simultaneously adhere to Martin Luther King's complementary goal (adapted from Josiah Royce): 'If you cannot find the beloved community, create it.'

What is our purpose in defining community and economy as both complementary and mutually exclusive? It allows us to say that community and economy, while different, need each other. In other words, both are needed for humanity to get its act together. For, in our view, if humanity could get its act together, we as nations and as a species could use the fantastic new technologies now in the pipeline to meet everybody's needs in harmony with nature.[22]

We do not presume to tell anyone else how to choose among the myriad uses of these two terms any more than we presume to tell Margaret Archer to mix 'cultural' and 'social' as we do, when, for her purposes, it is essential to keep them clearly distinct. Nevertheless, having chosen to treat the relationship between 'economy' and 'community' in the above way, we propose that today most people suffer from an overdose of economy and an underdose of community. Therefore, following Royce, King[23] and others, we proclaim 'community' as our 'guiding star' as we move forward toward a better world, in order to bring it in balance with economics. When evaluating any activity, we would ask, 'Are we building community?' Or, more cautiously, 'Are we building *good* community?'

This is not theory without practice. It draws on the practical experience of South Africa's Community Work Programme (CWP)[24]—not all of the CWP, and not a random sample, but at selected sites that illustrate what is possible when the CWP's founding ideals are conscientiously implemented. Those founding ideals include a mandate from the South African cabinet 'to use public employment to catalyse community development'.

We believe that our use of the word 'community', besides being successfully demonstrated in practical application, needs to comply with two

---

22. Peter Diamandis and Steven Kottler, *Abundance: The Future Is Better than You Think* (New York: Simon and Schuster, 2012).

23. We will refer several times to King's last book, *Where do We Go From Here: Community or Chaos?* (Boston: Beacon Press, 1967).

24. An introduction to the Community Works Programme can be found on the website of the International Labour Organization, ILO (accessed 29 January 2013). In the subsection 'Features' of the section 'ILO Newsroom', an article dated 27 July 2011 is titled 'South Africa and the ILO Team Up to Promote Public Employment and Community Work Programmes'. It begins, 'With an official unemployment rate of 25 percent, the South African government knows that employment creation cannot be left to the private sector alone. There is a huge gap between the jobs that are needed and the jobs that the market can generate. The State has the responsibility to fill that gap.'

more criteria to justify its usage. First, it needs to be succinct as well as clear. In particular, our meaning for 'community' has to make it easy to give reasonable answers to the question, 'Are we building (good) community?' It should help people tell the difference between what is and what is not community.

Second, our use of the term has to be sufficiently close to existing usage to make it valid for saying what we are trying to say. Mikhail Bakhtin said, quite rightly, that we never own the words we speak; we borrow them from languages we did not make and do not own. He would ask whether 'community' is 'a valid word to borrow' instead of whether it is 'a valid word to choose'. Chosen or borrowed, it does no good to define 'community' clearly if our definition does not designate anything anybody else calls community. In statistical research this second criterion is called 'construct validity'.

Others use the same words in other ways for other purposes. Alfred Marshall and John Maynard Keynes, for example, use 'the community' as a synonym for 'the public'. For them the price of a commodity tends to rise when 'the community' wants and is willing and able to pay for more of it. We do not object. We do humbly beg leave to use 'community' for other purposes.

To define community clearly, we start with the first definition of the word found in the *Oxford English Dictionary* (OED): 'The quality of appertaining to or being held by all in common, joint or common ownership, tenure, liability etc; as in *community of goods.*' This definition is illustrated by an old example from Jean Calvin's *Institutes of the Christian Religion*, written for the citizens of the city of Geneva in 1561. A different definition of community in the OED reads: 'The body of those having common or equal rights or rank, as distinguished from the privileged classes; the body of commons; the commonalty'; it is illustrated by a still older example, one from 1375. Themes from these two OED definitions—namely, holding in common, community of goods, equal rights or rank, people who form together 'a body'—run through other early and typical definitions.

We propose to synthesize these themes in one word that defines community: *sharing*. An example of its application is the ethical principle *share the surplus*. (Among the merits of this ethical principle is that it facilitates a creative response to an existential challenge faced by our civilization: mass unemployment.)

Further, in reviewing definitions of 'community', one cannot avoid the conclusion that community is what W. B. Gallie called an essentially contested concept.²⁵ The social role of the concept 'community' is not to bear a standard meaning everyone agrees on but to be a contested terrain. Over the years, different individuals and groups with different interests and passions have promoted different meanings for it, and they have tried to convince people to see community their way and not their opponents' way. To count a concept as essentially contested, however, there must be something that all parties agree the concept includes, which Gallie calls an 'exemplar'. An exemplar is what makes it possible to win the contest or to lose it by using a word wrongly, not just differently, and thus be condemned for talking to oneself in one's own private world.

In this book, we are generous in saying that we will not complain if others use words differently. Our opponents, however, may not be so generous. For this reason, we have taken Keynes's general theory as an exemplar of economic theory in order to avoid this book's being disconnected from what other people call economic theory. Similarly, we take John McKnight's work to be an exemplar of community development.²⁶

McKnight identified community with *caring* human relationships. Caring cannot be commodified. It cannot be managed by a bureaucracy. He often said, 'Medicare does not care.' Medicare is an agency of the US government that writes checks to reimburse certain medical expenses, following rules. The rules follow principles laid down by acts of Congress. A check arriving from Medicare is not the same as a family member, friend or caregiver coming to visit you at your bedside while you are ill. The check is not caring.²⁷ It is not community. Without checks written by bureaucracies, and without certain commodities found on the shelves of pharmacies, many patients now alive would be dead. But the checks and the commodities are not community.

Our definition of community, then, is *sharing and caring*. Taking Bakhtin's views into account, we realize that however we define the word, it will continue to evoke its relevant common meanings. We expect our short definition to be enriched and empowered by common meanings, similar to but not always exactly the same as our definition, such as those employed by the writers cited in the next section.

---

25. W. B. Gallie, Essentially Contested Concepts, *Proceedings of the Aristotelian Society*, n.s., vol. 56 (1955–1956), pp. 167–198.

26. See John McKnight, *The Careless Society: Community and its Counterfeits* (New York: Basic Books, 1995); and other works by the same author and his coauthor Jody Kretzmann.

27. For extensive discussions of what the word 'caring' means, see Nel Noddings, *Caring: A Relational Approach to Ethics and Moral Education* (Berkeley: University of California Press, 2013).

♦ ♦ ♦

Phumi Bombo is a teacher at the Gobelha primary school in Umthwalume in KwaZulu-Natal Province (chapter 4).

> 'Since we've had teacher assistants from CWP there is yet to be a fatal accident that involves a child from our school. The change is visible, and the learners are taken care of. When I am late or cannot come to school for whatever reason, I do so with the knowledge and confidence that I have left my learners with somebody who is capable of holding the reins until I can take over.'
>
> – CDI

5. Words from Prominent Authors Supporting Our Novel Definition of Community

Marx and Engels, in *The German Ideology*, called for real community ('In a real community the individuals obtain their freedom in and through their association').[28] Alex Honneth claims that all the early socialists, including Marx, proposed to correct the coldness and cruelty of market-based human relationships with community, understood not just as shared values and common aims but also as mutual responsibility and sympathy.[29]

The difference between community and economy was starkly drawn by Ferdinand Tönnies, who, writing in 1887, fostered a sociological vocabulary that distinguishes community (*Gemeinschaft*) from society, or economic society (*Gesellschaft*). He saw the former as more fundamental and historically earlier, the latter as more problematic and historically later. Tönnies wrote: 'Even learned scholars are scarcely ever able to free themselves from making judgments based on personal likes and dislikes, and to arrive at an impartial, strictly objective understanding of the physiology and pathology of social life. They admire the Roman Empire and its law; they deplore the decay of the family and of morality. They are unable to look further and train their sights upon the causal connection between the two phenomena.'

Notice that for Tönnies the admirers of modernity (*Gesellschaft*) and the admirers of Roman law are the same people. We quote these particular

---

28. Karl Marx and Friedrich Engels, *The German Ideology* (London: Lawrence and Wishart, 1974, 1845–46), p. 83.
29. Alex Honneth, The *Idea of Socialism* (Cambridge, UK: Polity Press, 2017).

lines from Tönnies because they support our view that economic theory in its standard forms lives, moves and has its being within the basic cultural structure of modernity, which in turn is built on seventeenth- and eighteenth-century conceptions of natural rights, which in turn derive from Roman law.[30]

We find support for our definition of community in Emile Durkheim's summary of what Tönnies meant by community (*Gemeinschaft*): 'Community is unity; community is cohesion; the whole is more real than the parts; community is the silent and spontaneous accord of minds that think and feel alike; its most perfect example is the family united by ties of blood, but community is not only family; it is also the unity of people who have long lived together in the same space and share common memories; it is a necessary consequence of a shared existence, of performing the same functions, sharing the same beliefs, and having the same needs.'[31]

While Tönnies can be read as a pessimist who lamented capitalist modernity more than he celebrated it, this book can be read as an exercise in optimism—as an antidote to pessimists like Zygmunt Bauman,[32] who describes the community-dissolving radical insecurity of contemporary life but does not prescribe and illustrate community development as a cure. We propose to prepare for a future when robots will do most of the work and most humans will be redundant in the labour market by learning how to do community development and how to fund it.

Once again, our argument is a proposal for a tautology, to be constructed by defining the terms so they become a tautology. If the objective is meeting human needs in harmony with nature, and if the economy (the *Gesellschaft*) at best succeeds only partially in doing so, then by definition finishing the job requires something that is not economy. If the economy is what we say it is, a form of life built on the constitutive rules of market exchange, then a guide to building not-economy (i.e., community) can be articulated as tempering the rules of market exchange.

---

30. For a similar view developed in more detail and at greater length, see Costas Douzinas, *The End of Human Rights* (Oxford: Hart Publishing, 2000).

31. Jean Aldous, Emile Durkheim and Ferdinand Tönnies, 'An Exchange Between Durkheim and Tönnies on the Nature of Social Relations', *American Journal of Sociology*, vol. 77 (1972), pp. 1191–1200. The above is a summary of Durkheim's summary.

32. Zygmunt Bauman, *Liquid Times: Living in an Age of Uncertainty* (Cambridge, UK: Polity Press, 2007). If we are unfair to Bauman by calling him a 'pessimist', even though in some of his works he expresses a certain optimism regarding the achievement of autonomy under contemporary conditions, it is because we are pessimists about autonomy.

We express tempering those rules in several possible ways,[33] citing traditional Roman legal maxims:

Temper *honeste vivere* with the relational subject.[34]
Temper *pacta sunt servanda* with unconditional love, contract with status.
Temper *suum cuique* with the social functions of property, trusteeship[35] and servant leadership.[36]
Temper *alterum non laedere* with an ethic of care and service to others.[37]

These statements, though mere words, refer to actual material relations of positions in material social structures. They refer to the homeless person with dirty blankets sleeping on the material cement of a material sidewalk. They refer to the flesh-and-blood secretary in Washington, DC, with a nine-to-five office job who volunteers after work at the Church of the Savior.[38]

When we complement economics with community, we stir old memories.[39] Maurice Blanchot wrote that we live 'at a time when even the ability to understand community seems to have been lost'.[40] He then asks, 'But isn't community outside intelligibility?' We follow Blanchot's question with a question of our own: 'If today we find community unintelligible, is it not because we have come to identify the intelligible with the economic?'

Samuel Bowles and Herbert Gintis chime in here, writing that while the intelligible has often in recent centuries been identified with the economic, today the image of a rational and therefore intelligible *Homo economicus* is becoming ever more tarnished, while it is becoming ever clearer that trust,

---

33. Marx famously expressed these ways as Freedom, Property, Equality and Bentham. Immanuel Kant in his *Rechstlehre* deduces them from one principle, *Freiheit,* also known as autonomy, regarded by Kant as the principle of all true morality, as opposed to heteronomy, the principle of all false morality.

34. Pierpaolo Donati and Margaret Archer, *The Relational Subject* (Cambridge, UK: Cambridge University Press).

35. Howard Richards and Joanna Swanger, *Gandhi and the Future of Economics* (Lake Oswego, OR: World Dignity University Press, 2011).

36. Robert Greenleaf, *Servant Leadership: A Journey into the Nature of Legitimate Power* (Mahwah, NJ: Paulist Press, 1977).

37. Matthew 25: 31–46.

38. Elizabeth O'Connor, *Call to Commitment: The Story of the Church of the Saviour* (New York: Harper and Row, 1963).

39. See David Minar and Scott Greer, *The Concept of Community* (New Brunswick: Transaction Publishers, 1969); Amitai Etzioni, 'Creating Good Communities and Good Societies', *Contemporary Sociology*, vol. 29 (2000), pp. 188–195.

40. Maurice Blanchot, *The Unavowable Community* (Barrytown, NY: Station Hill Press, 1998), p. 1.

generosity and collective problem-solving are indispensable. In fact, today, *social capital* is stealing the show. However, social capital, while a good idea, is certainly a bad term. 'Community' is a better term.[41]

◆ ◆ ◆

> 'I would like them to increase the sports because I would like to see the youth focusing more on sports. That helps a lot in health. They won't do bad things such as rape and other criminal activities.'
>
> — CWP PARTICIPANT, UMTHWALUME CDI

6. Talking Community Up versus Talking Community Down

In today's world, any effort to talk up community will sooner or later come across speakers who are talking community down. Margaret Somers, for example, hears 'community' as a right-wing weapon in a culture war waged to dismantle the achievements of post–World War II social democracy. Somers portrays community as a weapon flanked on one side (in positive conservative talk) by the discourses of subsidiarity, social capital, volunteerism and faith-based charity and on the other side (in negative conservative talk) by the discourses of welfare dependency, the road to serfdom, the decay of the ethic of individual responsibility and permissiveness.[42] In her view and the views of others who think similarly, the purposes of the rhetoric of community are to excuse the state from its duties to guarantee compliance with social human rights, to legitimize lower taxes, and to deny justice to the 99 percent while reducing them to relying on charity.

Roland Barthes, if he were alive, might say at this point that we have fallen in love with an unfaithful word, in this case, 'community'. Our being deceived in this way is inevitable because in power politics all beautiful words are sold to the highest bidder. We want to sidestep Barthes and reply to the Margaret Somerses of this world, who are legion, that what are today called culture wars—the wars where 'community' is drafted by right-wing culture warriors to fight the welfare state—are not what they appear to be. Their competing rhetorics, like Plato's flickering shadows on the walls of

---

41. Samuel Bowles and Herbert Gintis, 'Social Capital and Community Governance', *The Economic Journal*, vol. 112 (2002), p. F420.

42. Margaret Somers, 'Sociology and Economics', in George Steinmetz (ed.), *The Politics of Method in the Human Sciences* (Durham, NC: Duke University Press, 2005), pp. 263–65.

his cave, are illusions, not reality. The culture wars have little or no effect on which way history is going.

The reality is that the welfare state as we used to know it is in decline. *Pace* Margaret Somers, the welfare state is not in decline because people who are supposed to be friends of the left unwittingly speak the language of the right—saying 'community' when they should say 'solidarity'. *Pace* Robert Reich, social democracy is not in decline because control of the political process in all major countries has fallen into the hands of lobbyists for megabusinesses (like Disney, whose lobbyists have won for it an unending right to the exclusive use of Mickey Mouse). *Pace* Joseph Stiglitz, it is not in decline because today's global economy has been deliberately designed by powerful and secretive interests to lower wages and dismantle the social safety net. The welfare state is in decline because it is incompatible with the basic social structure. The factors Somers, Reich and Stiglitz emphasize exist and are important, but they are not decisive.

We are talking community up instead of down (following Roy Bhaskar's advice to treat social structure as the social science analogue of the generative structures that explain the phenomena studied by the natural sciences). And in our eyes—and the eyes of others who have concluded, however reluctantly, that, for structural reasons, social democracy in its previously existing forms is already dead in the water because of the fiscal crisis of the state—South Africa is taking a step forward, not backward, by calling on community development to supplement locally whatever the government can do with its budgets already deep in deficit and its national debt already unpayable.

The main event at a practical level consists of hundreds of such social innovations around the world struggling to create alternatives *that do work.* The culture wars are a sideshow with little or no power to influence who wins. The belligerents fight to promote or retard a decline and fall of cradle-to-grave social insurance that is already inevitable. It is inevitable because neoliberal economics reigns. It reigns partly because of the amazingly persistent and not surprisingly well-funded effort to create it and sell it. But it reigns mostly because the well-known alternatives to it do not work. Neither capitalism nor socialism nor communism nor fascism has worked in any of the versions so far tried. The main event at an intellectual level—the vision of the good you see, which blinds your eyes when you first emerge from Plato's cave—is the struggle between neoliberal economists and diverse congeries of heterodox scholars labouring to re-arm social democracy for a counterattack.

Admittedly, when this book jumps on the bandwagon of John McKnight's call for using community development to create caring communities, and when it treats unbounded organization coupled with moral realism *as a method* for structural transformation, *not as a substitute* for structural transformation, it is pressing into service polysemic and controversial terms ('community' and others) well-known for doing other work for other masters with other agendas. We have to accept that we may be giving those other masters some ammunition for attacking institutions that should be defended. Nevertheless, on balance, on tiptoe, holding our breath and opening our mouths, we have decided to recommend community development, unbounded organization, and moral realism to a world we see as dying from an overdose of economics, rigid jurisprudence, and subjective ethics.

In the next chapter we suggest a definition of economics as a series of intellectual edifices built on, in and by the partly functional and partly dysfunctional social structures Adam Smith called (interchangeably) natural liberty and perfect liberty. That definition will complete the mutually dependent but different duo of economy versus community.

CHAPTER THREE
Economics as Social Structure

Building on Searle's concept of constitutive rules, Porpora's concept of social structure and Heidegger's concept of *sehen als,* we regard social structure as material positions constituted by cultural rules. In this chapter, we examine economics as comprising socially and historically constructed material positions, especially the positions of buyer and seller. When John Maynard Keynes made the insufficiency of effective demand and of the inducement to invest central to his economic theory, he glimpsed but did not fully grasp some consequences of the basic social structure of modern market societies, namely, the freedom of buyers to *not* buy and the freedom of investors to *not* invest. This stands in contrast to the constellation of economic institutions in, for example, archaic societies whose basic social structure was culturally constituted by ceremony, myth and kinship. This contrast begins to show the usefulness of thinking of economics (some of the time) as social structure and as not-community.

OVERVIEW OF THE CHAPTER

1. Adam Smith: Facts and Ideals
2. The Dependence of the Economy on the Confidence of Investors and Entrepreneurs
3. Pure Economics: Leon Walras
4. The Basic Structure Does Not Work for the Poor: Low Wages
5. The Structural Sources of Instability (Keynes and Minsky)
6. Why the Dominant Social Structure Motivates Immense Productivity

1. Adam Smith: Facts and Ideals

We now turn to 'economy'. We will look at what Adam Smith meant by 'natural' economics and then at what Leon Walras called 'pure' economics (both of which we at times, for short, call simply 'economics'). These two terms, 'natural' and 'pure', will help us explain what we mean when we say economics is a science whose essence as well as object of study is a social structure defined by the constitutive rules of markets. Here we feel licensed by Bhaskar's approach to ontology to name or describe the same causally active, independently existing and sometimes existing social structure in different ways. Although one can describe the basic social structure using Roman law's maxims, Marx's satire and Hayek's extended order, we now call it the constitutive rules of markets. Robert Solow was singing our song, though singing it with other lyrics, when he wrote: 'Ever since Adam Smith, economists have been distinguished from lesser mortals by their understanding of and—I think one has to say—their admiration for the efficiency, anonymity, and subtlety of decentralized competitive markets as an instrument for the allocation of resources.'[1]

The words 'natural' (in Smith) and 'pure' (in Walras) help us to characterize the mental 'software' that people who are called economists use to process information. These words also pave the way for explaining what it means to transcend economics with unbounded organization or, what amounts to the same thing, with *economía solidaria*.[2]

For Adam Smith, the landlord *naturally* extracts from the tenant (Smith has in mind tenant farmers who rent from landowners) as much money as the tenant can pay: 'Rent, considered as the price paid for the use of land, is naturally the highest the tenant can afford to pay.' The hard bargain is natural. Smith admits that as an empirical matter there are some exceptions, yet he insists that the most the tenant can afford 'may still be considered as the natural rent of land, or the rent that it is naturally meant that land should for the most part be let'.[3]

For Smith, there is also a natural price of a commodity, a natural profit and a natural wage. The market price is supposed to gravitate around, and over time converge toward, the natural price. Competition is supposed to lower price to the cost of production: 'When the price of any commodity is neither more nor less than what is sufficient to pay the rent of the land,

---

1. Robert M. Solow, 'On Theories of Unemployment', *The American Economic Review,* vol. 70 (1980), p. 1.

2. Howard Richards, 'Un Concepto de Economía Solidaria: Organización Ilimitada', in Raúl González Meyer (ed.), *Ensayos sobre Economía Cooperativa, Solidaria y Autogestionaria* (Santiago: Forja Editores, 2017).

3. Adam Smith, *The Wealth of Nations* (various editions, first edition 1776, but most reprints are based on the 1789 edition). The quotations are from the beginning of bk. 1, ch. 11, 'On the Rent of Land'. The phrase 'naturally meant' recalls Smith's earlier work *Theory of the Moral Sentiments* (Cambridge, UK: Cambridge University Press, 2002; first edition 1759), where he argued that divine providence had designed humans to act from self-interest. The famous 'invisible hand' metaphor is found in part 4, ch. 1.

the wages of the labour, and the profits of the stock employed in raising, preparing, and bringing it to market, according to their natural rates, the commodity is then sold for what may be called its natural price.'[4]

Smith adds that although there may be exceptions in practice, natural price is the necessary result wherever there is 'perfect liberty'. This is a clue that, at bottom, his doctrine is ethical. A second clue is Smith's statement that when a product is sold at its natural price, it is sold for exactly what it is worth. In Smith's view, exactly what it is worth is what it cost the seller.

Smith is certainly not a reporter summarizing reams of data gathered by observing prices in markets. He is not a metaphysician deducing what pure reason decrees that prices must necessarily be. Smith is an advocate of perfect liberty. He is not only a commentator on what would happen if there were perfect liberty (a phrase he uses interchangeably with 'natural liberty'). As Gunnar Myrdal was an architect, not just a student, of social democracy, so Smith was an architect, not just a student, of free markets. Smith describes as natural and, in effect, *normative* a world of competition among individuals out to maximize their gains in free markets. But to say this is natural and normative and thus morally right is not to say anything about the effects it causes. It remains to be asked how this social structure answers the question Smith set out to answer in *Wealth of Nations*, namely, 'What causes wealth?'

As Smith states at the outset, the book's purpose is to explain the nature and causes of wealth, and it begins with an extended invidious distinction: Savages do not practice the division of labour, and they do not have wealth. Civilized people practice the division of labour and they do have wealth. Thus the division of labour is *seen as* the first and primary cause of wealth. But the division of labour in turn supposes exchange; it supposes buying and selling, a practice 'common to all men, and to be found in no other race of animals, which seem to know neither this nor any other species of contracts'.[5] But exchange on a large scale can take place only when the rules of the game being played are generally accepted. The civilization that makes possible the division of labour and therefore wealth turns out to depend on the constitutive rules of markets, as well as on the self-interested *Homo economicus* those rules presuppose and protect—the very rules and the very

---

4. Smith, *Wealth of Nations*, at the beginning of ch. 7 of bk. 1. The natural profit for Smith is that which will just induce the entrepreneur to stay in the business and not switch to some other trade.

5. Smith, *Wealth of Nations*, at the beginning of ch. 2 of bk. 1.

individualism Karl Marx satirizes as freedom, equality, property and Bentham.[6] Thus, for Smith, the moral question and the causal question have the same answer. That answer is the basic social structure.

Later, Smith complements his claim that the division of labour causes wealth with the claim that the accumulation of capital also causes wealth.[7] This cause of wealth was destined to wax fruitful and multiply. In our view—extending Smith's reasoning beyond where he himself takes it—when the legal framework and the practice of investing to produce to sell for the sake of capital accumulation became solidly established, the die was cast. It became inevitable, or nearly so, that in due time the people's daily bread would *depend* not only on the prior existence of a large stock of capital but also on ever-continuing accumulation. The absence of the latter causes unemployment and want.[8] In ways such as this, the historical evolution of social structures often brings consequences nobody intended.

◆ ◆ ◆

'It has really helped me because I no longer drink that much. I am able to stay at work and keep myself busy.'

— CWP PARTICIPANT, JOE MOROLONG LOCAL MUNICIPALITY,
NORTHERN CAPE PROVINCE

2. The Dependence of the Economy on the Confidence of Investors and Entrepreneurs

We turn again to Marx, simplifying a diagram he uses in the second volume of *Capital* to drive home the economy's dependence on ever-continuing capital accumulation. We do this to continue our triangulation[9] of the basic social structure and the dependence of the principal facts of economics on the positions established by the social structure. And we do it for another reason: to make the point that 'natural', or 'pure', economics cannot meet

---

6. Smith remarks at the end of his long digression on silver at the end of book 1 that the only encouragement industry requires is some tolerable security that it shall enjoy the fruits of its own labour, which amounts, we claim, to saying it needs the rule of law, i.e., the social structure that liberal civil codes or case law constitute and protect.

7. This can be inferred from *Wealth of Nations*, ch. 6 of book 1.

8. Smith anticipates this point when he writes that it is not the amount of the existing stock but 'the increase of the revenue and stock' that increases the demand for labour. *Wealth*, bk. 1, ch. 8.

9. See the Wikipedia article 'Triangulation (Social Sciences)'. https://en.wikipedia.org/wiki/Triangulation_(social_science)

human needs in harmony with nature. God loves you. Your mother loves you. The market does not.

Such considerations lead toward our conclusion that the crisis of the current world system cannot be remedied short of what we are proposing to call unbounded organization. Unbounded organization is a world-changing but in essence simple remedy: it consists of aligning across sectors to do what works to solve problems. We think Keynes's famous remark at the end of his preface to *General Theory* applies: the difficulty lies not in the new ideas but in escaping from the old ones.

There is nothing particularly Marxist about the point we are using his diagram to make. Marx simply provides a convenient graphic for displaying what everybody already knows: that to the extent that the institutions regarded as natural by Smith (and by most eighteenth-century philosophers and authors of declarations and constitutions) reign, production is for sale, and when entrepreneurs are not confident that they can expect profits, production slows down or stops.[10]

Capitalism persists through time for the same reason any resilient system persists: because it has built-in mechanisms for defending itself when it is perturbed. A strategy for changing it will not work if that strategy undermines the inducement to invest without organizing alternative ways to meet human needs. We believe there is a gap in theories of social change—a gap to be filled by considering capitalism's homeostatic mechanisms and alternatives for countering them.[11] If the morphogenesis of Margaret Archer,[12] and/or the structuration theory of Anthony Giddens,[13] and/or the *habitus* of Pierre Bourdieu[14] and/or the contradictions analysed by Marxist writers[15]

---

10. Marx uses diagrams like this several times in the second volume of *Capital*, which was edited by Friedrich Engels after his death and first published in German in 1885. It is available in English in a translation by Ben Fowkes published by Penguin classics in London in 1990.

11. We made what Rom Harré kindly called in an endorsement on the cover 'a splendid start' in Howard Richards and Joanna Swanger, *Dilemmas of Social Democracies* (Lanham, MD: Rowman and Littlefield, 2006), showing how basic structures stymied change in Spain, Sweden, Austria, South Africa, Indonesia and Venezuela and sketching a theory of 'cultural resources' as sources of alternative dynamics.

12. Margaret Archer, *Realist Social Theory: The Morphogenetic Approach* (Cambridge, UK: Cambridge University Press, 1995).

13. Anthony Giddens, *The Constitution of Society: Outline of a Theory of Structuration* (Oxford: Polity Press, 1984).

14. See Howard Richards, 'Pierre Bourdieu and the Crisis of Modernity', available online.

15. David Lockwood, 'Social Integration and System Integration', in George Zollschan and Walter Hirsch, *Explorations in Social Change* (Boston: Houghton Mifflin, 1964), pp. 244–257; David Harvey, *Seventeen Contradictions and the End of Capitalism* (Oxford: Oxford University Press, 2014).

adequately described the world as it really is, then changing capitalism would be easier than it really is.

$$M > C > \ldots\ldots P \ldots\ldots > C^* > M^*$$

In Marx's diagram, the investor or entrepreneur begins with M, money. With the money (M) the capitalist buys the commodities (C) necessary for production, including most notably the labour power of workers.

Marx's German word for commodities is *Waren*, a cognate of the English 'wares', things made to be bought and sold. The word 'wares' is famously employed in an English nursery rhyme about the innocent Simple Simon, who says to the pie man, 'Let me taste your wares', unaware that in a purely mercantile economy possessing money is a legal prerequisite to eating (a point developed in detail by Amartya Sen in his study of famines[16]). Having no penny, young Simon cannot acquire the pie and taste it. So also, in one of the cases studied by Sen, the enforced separation of the bodies of peasants from the food they need to stay alive is not because there is no rice. It is because flooding rained out the seasonal labour of transplanting rice seedlings on which they relied to earn money to buy rice.

The first phase of Marx's didactic diagram depicts strangers being transmuted into collaborators—although not necessarily into friends—by a contract, thus beginning to flesh out the defining of economics in terms of material positions constituted by cultural rules. André Orléan has epitomized the social structure that is economics in two words: *séparation marchande*.[17] Less academically and more poignantly, Viviane Forrester names it *l'horreur économique*.[18] Marx, Sen, Orléan and Forrester help us to adumbrate our sometimes useful contrast: community is not economics; economics is not community. Economics is separation. Community is unity. Economics accumulates. Community shares. In economics, people make commitments by contract.[19] In caring, people feel motivated to meet each other's needs even when they have no contractual obligation to do so.

---

16. Amartya Sen, *Poverty and Famines: An Essay on Entitlement and Deprivation* (Oxford: Clarendon Press, 1983).

17. André Orléan, *L'Empire de la valeur: Refonder l'économie* (Paris: Seuil, 2011). Starting at Kindle position 328 and continuing thereafter, Orléan finds *séparation marchande* to be the best name for the *rapport social* that constitutes *l'économie*.

18. Viviane Forrester, *L'Horreur économique* (Paris: Fayard, 1996).

19. Nancy Hartsock analyses at length the capitalist and patriarchal tendency to reduce human ties to contractual obligations in *Money, Sex and Power* (Boston: Northeastern University Press, 1983).

Once the entrepreneur has purchased the commodities (C) with money (M), he (or she) sets in motion the process of production (P). At the end of production, the entrepreneur has become the owner of commodities (other wares) with a greater value, designated as C*. The sale of C* results in M*, the quantity of money earned by the sale of C*. M* is greater than M, the quantity of money initially invested.

This graphic of the obvious[20] implies staggering consequences we cannot stress enough.[21] We recommend never losing sight of the dependence of the economy on the confidence of investors, and the dependence of *that* dependence on the social structure.[22] We briefly mention a few staggering consequences now.

Money is advanced for the purpose of producing some good or service to sell at a profit.[23] If money-seeking profit is not advanced, nothing happens.[24] The aim of the game is to make the difference M* minus M as large as possible. For that to happen, the difference C* minus C must be as large as possible; in other words, the aim is to maximize the difference between the selling price of the goods and the cost of making them. Costs must be kept down. Wages are a cost; therefore, the wage bill must be kept down,

---

20. Max Weber regarded Marx's account of capitalism as an analysis of ideal types. Max Weber, *The Methodology of the Social Sciences* (New York: Free Press, 1949), p. 103. Louis Althusser and Etienne Balibar, in their commentary on *Capital*, emphasize that Marx makes many simplifying assumptions. See their *Reading Capital*, abridged English edition (London: New Left Books, 1970). Complete French edition, *Lire le Capital* (Paris: François Maspero, 1968).

21. The diagram shows the essence of the logic and dynamic of accumulation. Once M has become the larger quantity M*, the process can be repeated. M* can become the even larger quantity of money M**. M** can be reinvested to produce M***, and so the accumulation of money can go on indefinitely.

22. What we have to say will be only a tiny addition to the huge existing literature on capital accumulation. Marx himself wrote in the first volume of *Capital*: "With the accumulation of capital there develops the specifically capitalist mode of production, and with the specifically capitalist form of production there develops the accumulation of capital. . . . Each accumulation becomes a means for making a new accumulation.' *Das Kapital* Erstes Buch, Kapitel 23, part 2, pars. 7–8 (our translation). Four basic sources are Rosa Luxemburg, *The Accumulation of Capital* (London: Routledge and Kegan Paul, 1951; original German 1913); Patrick Bond, Horman Chitonge and Arndt Hopfmann (eds.), *The Accumulation of Capital in Southern Africa* (Durban: University of KwaZulu-Natal, 2006); Samir Amin, *Accumulation on a World Scale* (New York: Monthly Review Press, 1974); Maria Mies, *Patriarchy and Accumulation on a World Scale* (London: Zed Books, 1986).

23. Today, in practice, the amount of money changing hands every day speculating in the 'casino economy' dwarfs the sums invested in the real economy producing goods and services. See Susan Strange, *Mad Money* (Manchester, UK: Manchester University Press, 1998). From Marx's perspective, this shortcut turning M into M* without P cannot possibly be sustainable because the only way to earn sustainable profits is to hire workers whose cost to the employer is less than the value of what they produce.

24. In Marx's vocabulary, there is no *Bewegung*, no movement. Money advanced is the impetus that sets everything else in motion; without it everything else stands still.

by limiting both hires and wages. If costs rise to the point where the spread C* minus C shrinks toward zero, causing the spread M* minus M to shrink toward zero, then no money-seeking profit is advanced. In that case, there is no employment and no production, and consequently (since nothing is produced) no consumption.

The resulting physical dependence of human life on the beliefs of investors that their investments will be profitable is what characterizes 'pure' capitalism. That dependence is alleviated to the extent that people have other ways of meeting their needs that do not depend on capitalism.[25] It is also alleviated to the extent that reformed capitalisms (stakeholder, creating shared value, social market economy, servant leadership . . . and others) move production to serve ethical social missions. They strive to meet human needs in harmony with nature. They seek to manage capital for the common good. They move toward becoming democratic post-capitalisms indistinguishable from democratic post-socialisms. Marx's diagram depicts a classic pure capitalism whose most essential characteristics are making a product that will sell, for the purpose of turning money into more money over and over again, by exploiting labour. Today everybody knows this pure form is being questioned and modified, but nobody believes it has disappeared.

Looking again at Marx's diagram, notice that both the left-hand side (the beginning) and the right-hand side (the end) consist of sales. In the beginning, the capitalist *buys* the labour power and other inputs needed to set in motion the production process. In the end, the capitalist *sells* the products. The legal rules that constitute exchange in markets must be in force, or the process will not work.[26] It follows that social change projects must be thought through very carefully, because any measures that shake confidence in the rule of law will (*cet. par.*) slow or stop production.

---

25. See José Luis Coraggio, *De la emergencia a la estrategia* (Buenos Aires: Espacio Editores, 2004). Coraggio recounts the experience of Argentines in improvising alternative survival strategies when their capitalist economy collapsed in 2001. He then recommends building alternatives to capitalism (such as worker-owned cooperatives) as a strategy for changing the system.

26. Max Weber is famous for the implausible claim that capitalism began with the protestant ethic of inner-worldly asceticism, but more often he made the more plausible claim that capitalism could begin only after or concurrently with the establishment of a rational legal order of the western Roman type. Without law, he pointed out, economic decisions could not be made because their consequences would not be *kalkulierbar*; in other words, without law, the future enforcement of property rights and contract compliance would be so uncertain that no investments could be made. See the section of Weber's *Economy and Society* on 'Meaning and Limits of Legal Authority for the Economy'.

The recommended answer to the question of how to meet human needs in harmony with nature is that there is no single answer. Rather, there are plural answers that amount to a world where nobody's needs go unmet because, when the contributions of one sector wane, the contributions of other sectors take up the slack. This is the recipe for getting started on unbounded organization. Wean society from its addiction to capital accumulation not by stopping capital accumulation but by starting everything else: nurture every way to meet needs that does *not* depend on capital accumulation. Plant a garden. Organize an ethical bank.[27] Pay for public hospitals with a tax on airline tickets.[28] Fund musicians with an endowment. Share child care. Pair a rich parish with a poor parish of the same denomination. Buy eggs from the neighbours who run a hatchery to make a living, not a fortune. Do free-cycling on the internet.[29] Volunteer. Share the surplus—voluntarily, by making nonprofits the owners of enterprises or by rethinking taxes along the lines Thomas Piketty suggests. This list has no end, but it does have footnotes and follow-ups.

In a world guided by unbounded organization and moral realism, the relative weight of the capitalist sector is small enough, and the capitalists are socially responsible enough, not to expose the country to the danger of being shut down by capital flight and disinvestment. The governors of nations can say to delegations of investors from elsewhere: 'You are welcome to join us in constructing our ethical commonwealth, but if you do not feel that you can make a normal profit[30] while protecting our spotted owls and respecting our union shops, that is okay, because we have other fish to fry on other grills, so let's have a good-bye drink at the airport VIP lounge and call the whole thing off.' Don't cry for me Argentina.

♦ ♦ ♦

Gogo Karlina Mvhendana is 91 years old and lives in Belfast, South Africa. She has been blind since 2004 and has no one to take care of her. CWP participants built her a one-room home with donations from people in the

---

27. See the section 'la différence Desjardins' on the website www.desjardins.com.

28. See the Bachelet Report, http://www.ilo.org/wcmsp5/groups/public/@dgreports/@dcomm/@publ/documents/publication/wcms_165750.pdf for a list of creative ways third-world countries finance welfare.

29. www.freecycle.org.

30. A normal profit is what Alfred Marshall called the supply price of business. It is a profit sufficient to motivate the entrepreneurs; it is similar to the amount Adam Smith says the landlord naturally allows the farmer. Anything above it is surplus, a.k.a. rent.

area. They helped her get groceries and also linked her to an eye specialist in nearby Hazyview. After a cataract operation she has regained sight in one eye.

> 'God has sent the CWP to assist me. I am so happy. I sometimes feel that I can walk to the river and go for a swim', she says.
>
> — COGTA

3. Pure Economics: Leon Walras

Nearly a century after Smith published *The Wealth of Nations* (1776) and nearly a decade after Marx published the first volume of *Capital* (1867), Leon Walras published his *Elements of Pure Economics* (1874 and 1876). *Pace* his protestations that he was separating economics from ethics, we suggest that for Walras, the point of writing about *pure* economics was to defend the social structure. For Walras, unlike Smith, this project was not a matter of being a glorious founding father of a new era; it was a matter of defending an entrenched but beleaguered capitalism in the tumultuous second half of the nineteenth century.

A *pure* economics, Walras writes, is an ideal economics: 'Thus in an ideal market we have ideal prices that stand in an exact relation to an ideal demand and supply. And so on.'[31] The method of pure economics is rational. It is mathematical, not empirical. If one asks the reason for knowing what ideal prices are, when the only prices ever found in markets are really existing prices, Walras answers, 'It is only with the aid of mathematics that we can understand what is meant by the condition of maximum utility.'[32] There could be no clearer confession that despite his explicit separation of what he thinks he is doing from ethics, the point and purpose of his project is his implicit definition of the good, i.e., 'the condition of maximum utility'.

Walras's whole theory rests on the theory of exchange, and what he says about the theory of exchange can be summed up as giving a proof (which can be given only in mathematics). In his own words, he offers 'a mathematical solution of the problem of the determination of current prices'.[33] Here the operative word is 'determination'. As in Smith, we will see that in Walras, 'determine' does not mean 'calculate what is'; it means 'calculate what ought to be'.

---

31. Leon Walras, *Elements of Pure Economics*, William Jaffe, tr. (London: Routledge, 2003), lesson 3, p. 71.
32. Ibid., p. 43.
33. Ibid., p. 35.

What could it mean to determine prices by an ideal and rational method that is not an empirical inquiry into the causes that in fact determine prices?[34] For Walras, it means calculating the simultaneous satisfaction of two conditions of market equilibrium. We have already mentioned the first: each party must attain maximum utility. The second is that markets must clear. That is, for each kind of good sold in the market, the aggregate demanded must equal the aggregate offered so that no goods remain unsold.

Walras's theory is profoundly and irremediably contradictory. On one hand, Walras insists—and needs to insist to make his theory coherent—on an amoral definition of utility. Thus, it makes no difference when calculating the *rareté* (scarcity value) that defines the utility, whether a buyer is buying potatoes to feed his child or arsenic to poison his wife. In either case, the more he buys of whatever he chooses to buy, the more his utility is maximized. A fire wall is built separating pure economics from ethics.[35] On the other hand, Walras does not hesitate—and if he did hesitate he would be conceding that his enterprise has little point or purpose—to prescribe how society ought to be organized.

If one asks why one should take the trouble to make elaborate mathematical calculations showing that there could, in principle, be a society where all parties to contracts of purchase and sale attained a maximum of whatever they wanted (which would be maximally efficient in the sense that no resources would be wasted producing goods that could not be sold; in other words, to calculate the possibility of a general equilibrium), an answer can be found in Walras's own words, paraphrased as follows: The economists prior to Walras were not giving a satisfactory answer to the socialists.[36] The economists of his time were trying to pass themselves off as one more species of natural scientists, doing what one might call (our suggestion, not Walras's) *impure* science.

While Adam Smith in 1776 might have gotten away with saying the market way of life is the right way of life because it is the natural way of life, in 1874 an appeal to nature was unacceptable. To reply to the socialists, the answer had to be that the higher level of civilization Europe had then

---

34. Among the diverse schools of economic thought, the Latin American structuralists have distinguished themselves by their efforts to determine empirically what in fact determines prices. Their answer tends to be 'the bargaining power of the parties'. See Armando di Filippo, *Latin American Structuralism and Economic Theory* (Santiago: Economic Commission for Latin America and the Caribbean, 2009).

35. Walras, *Elements of Pure Economics*, pp. 58–64.

36. Ibid., pp. 54–55.

attained was the product of human *reason and freedom*. Pure economics had to concern what society would be like if it corresponded to its ideal of rational individuals making free choices. We suggest that even though Walras says he is leaving the choice between individualism and communism, as well as the justification of property rights, to the separate subject of ethics (even while promising to come back to ethics with the fruits of purely mathematical economics later[37]), the point of writing about pure economics is to defend a social structure whose ideological centrepiece and juridical *Grundnorm* (basic norm) is free choice.

Indeed, at the end of *Elements*, where he discusses what ideal economics offers ethics, Walras does not hesitate to prescribe that when reality is in conflict with theory, it is reality that ought to change. He writes, for example: 'Freedom procures, within certain limits, the maximum of utility, and since the factors that interfere with freedom are obstacles to the attainment of this maximum, they should, without exception, be eliminated as completely as possible.'[38]

Here the operative word is 'should'. Taken literally, Walras is saying, or implying:

> 1. Whatever maximizes utility should be done. Freedom maximizes utility, and therefore whatever interferes with freedom *should* be eliminated.

Reading the same words somewhat differently, one can also detect sympathy for a second proposition:

> 2. Freedom is the criterion for distinguishing right from wrong. Free choice performatively establishes what should be, and therefore whatever interferes with freedom *should* be eliminated.

Let us briefly consider both propositions. Regarding the first proposition, we submit that 'maximizes utility' denotes the welfare optimum defined by

---

37. Calling his work purely mathematical should perhaps be qualified, because often after his mathematical analysis Walras will write in effect, 'And this is what happens in practice in competitive markets'. Then without reporting any empirical observations he outlines how, in principle, the *tatonnage* (groping by trial and error) of markets leads to the same result he gets by solving equations.

38. Walras, *Elements of Pure Economics*, p. 256.

the first theorem of welfare economics (the *Pareto optimum*, named after Walras's successor in the chair of political economy at Lausanne[39]). At a *Pareto optimum*, trading stops because there are no more exchanges that would benefit both parties.

We submit that what is denoted as 'freedom' here is the same basic cultural structure we have been triangulating by naming from diverse perspectives. There is precedent for using 'freedom' as a one-word summary of the basic social structure of the modern world. Immanuel Kant, in his *Metaphysical Elements of Justice* (*Rechtslehre*), deduces property rights and the other main principles of liberal justice from the single starting premise of freedom. He attributes validity everywhere and everywhen to each of Ulpian's maxims of Roman law on the basis of chains of reasoning that start in each case with freedom. Although Milton Friedman states in chapter 1 of *Capitalism and Freedom* that his ultimate goal is the freedom of the individual,[40] as the book progresses it becomes clear that by 'freedom' he is also referring to property rights and to the rules of the buying and selling game that constitute markets. One could cite other cases.

In this book we are running an alternative to the first proposition. Instead of 'maximum of utility' as what should be optimized, we say 'meeting human needs in harmony with nature'. Instead of 'freedom' as what is expected to cause the optimizing, we say 'unbounded organization'.

The second of Walras's propositions takes us to the heart of the revolution in ethics that took place in the eighteenth century. As Costas Douzinas has shown in detail, modern concepts of rights and of freedom required the replacement of God as a principle of authority.[41] In one form or another, in many early cultures and in the European Middle Ages—specifically, in the culture of Christian theology—to be good meant to be obedient. On Douzinas's account, God's will, or interpreting God's will, was the source of political legitimacy. In the eighteenth century (in a process that started earlier), however, free choice became the litmus test separating right from wrong. The consent of the governed became the source of political legitimacy. Rights limited the powers of governments and protected the powers of individuals. The rise of the market as an institution was the rise of buyers and sellers as decision makers.

---

39. See 'Pareto optimal' in Wikipedia.
40. Milton Friedman, *Capitalism and Freedom* (Chicago: University of Chicago Press, 1962), p.12.
41. Costas Douzinas, *The End of Rights* (Oxford: Hart, 2000).

The first theorem of welfare economics sees what has come to be called revealed preference as a measure of value; RHV (Rodrik, Hausmann and Velasco) and the South African National Development Plan made the centrepiece of development the growth of the gross national product (i.e., of sales, of people revealing their preferences by buying). Walras declared the elimination of obstacles to freedom as a moral imperative. All of the above remarks regarding Smith and Walras and Douzinas's account of the ethical revolution of early modernity concern the historical roots of today's orthodox economic theory. The ethical foundation of orthodoxy is now called 'choice' or 'revealed preference'.[42]

Although Walras eschews any labour theory of value, he agrees with Smith that free competition drives prices down to the cost of production.[43] But note this: when, if ever, the theoretical ideal of general equilibrium were reached, all businesses would operate *sans perte ni benefice* (with no loss and no profit). In the twenty-first century, Joseph Stiglitz echoes: 'After all, with transparent and competitive markets, profits are driven to zero.'[44]

On this point we agree with Walras and with Stiglitz and draw the conclusion that perfect free competition is a mathematical ideal that has never existed and would be a disaster if it ever did exist. There is a moral duty to share the surplus. Consequently, there is a moral duty—which may be the calling of some people though not necessarily everyone—to create surpluses to share. 'Sharing' includes paying taxes, donating to nonprofits and in any number of other ways moving resources from where they are not needed to where they are needed.

To be sure, entrepreneurs do not get nothing at all when Walrasian profits fall to zero; they still get some income falling in other categories.[45] Still, advocating fully competitive markets can serve only frivolous purposes, such as giving some people the psychological pleasure of imagining the monopoly capitalists defeated. If driving profits to zero is taken seriously and actually put into practice, it defeats more than one of the major ethical purposes of business. It defeats the purpose of generating a social surplus that

---

42. Kenneth Arrow makes this point in the opening pages of *Social Choice and Individual Values* (New Haven: Cowles Foundation, 1951). For Arrow, speaking for orthodoxy, voting and buying create value. All else is romanticism, tyranny, and/or invalid reasoning.

43. Walras, *Elements of Pure Economics*, pp. 225, 240, 243, 248, 271.

44. Joseph Stiglitz, *The Great Divide: Unequal Societies and What We Can Do About Them* (New York: Norton, 2015), p. 16.

45. No profit, for Walras, does not mean entrepreneurs literally get nothing. It means that whatever they get is reckoned as reward for their labour and as rents from resources they control, and not as profit. It also does not mean that the rate of interest will fall to zero.

can be used to fund serving the common good—especially the good of the millions rejected by the labour market, who need a decent livelihood with dignity too. George Richardson (echoing Schumpeter with a more precise demonstration) has persuasively argued that perfect competition would put an end to the ceaseless stream of innovation that has done so much to raise the living standards of so many. Under the conditions required for perfect free competition leading to general equilibrium, no entrepreneur could gain a competitive advantage by innovating, because all others would have the same information and opportunities.[46]

Apart from being a disaster if it ever happened, a world of fully competitive markets can never happen. Whether firms regard themselves as agents of their shareholders, recognize a moral responsibility to all stakeholders, embrace the concept of creating shared value or are (as Walras says monopolies should be) publicly owned; whether they are owned by the workers who work for them, are cooperatives owned by their customers, are state-owned though not monopolies like South African Airways, are owned by the endowments of charities or are autonomous parastatals like the Cape Town Port Authority, they all do financial accounting. They make thousands of big and small decisions every day whose rationality depends on thinking in terms of the bottom line. A bottom line of zero profit is not desired or expected. If zero profits were reported by all firms, the world would not know how to cope. A general equilibrium *sans perte ni benefice* can only be imaginary.[47]

Today, all of the great companies that dominate the world economy (most of which would be likely to persist even if a transformed social structure were to align them with the common good, whittle them down to size, take away their exorbitant privileges and make them governable)

---

46. G. B. Richardson, 'The Organization of Industry', *Economic Journal*, vol. 84 (1972), pp. 883–96.

47. Steve Keen gives another reason why a world of perfectly competitive markets can only be imaginary. The orthodox doctrine that prices are fixed where marginal cost equals marginal revenue has for several reasons no relevance to what happens in business. The normal case is increasing returns to scale. Score a point for Marx: in any normal industry, the larger firms will gobble up the smaller ones; the result will be an oligopoly or a monopoly where a tacit or explicit understanding keeps prices far above what they would be in perfect competition—commonly at a mark-up over costs. Steve Keen, *Debunking Economics* (London: Zed Books, 2001), p. 110. Michael Porter, previously cited and cited below, arrives at similar results with his famous doctrine of the five forces that enable firms to avoid the hell of perfect competition—bargaining power with suppliers, bargaining power with customers, barriers to entry, tacit understanding among players in the industry and common action against substitutes. This result is not essentially changed when Nike or Cadbury outsources to hundreds of tiny sweatshops in Indonesia or China.

have achieved solid niches in the market. They differentiate their products and/or control scarce resources that lower production costs and allow them to charge premium prices.[48] No, or virtually no, great successful business is in the position once described by the CEO of John Deere as 'commodity hell'. In commodity hell, a firm produces the same things numerous competitors also produce under similar conditions and with similar access to scarce resources. In commodity hell, the mathematical economic theory of Walras comes true, and nobody likes it.

As Adolf Berle and Gardiner Means showed in 1932 in *The Modern Corporation and Private Property*,[49] surplus, in the sense of a profit available to be distributed as a dividend to shareholders, is a moveable number. Management can always make a case for retaining earnings to retool or to pay some other allegedly essential expense. In the 1960s, Richard Cyert and James March showed that America's major corporations, with no known exceptions, enjoyed organizational slack,[50] defined as the surplus (the difference) left over when necessary payments are subtracted from total resources. They compared a large firm to a city or nation where diverse political factions with different interests and different ideologies contend for control of the slack. The company, considered as an abstract legal entity possessing a unified will, has discretion. It can pay higher wages than it has to pay, charge lower prices than it could charge, build new manufacturing facilities or launch new product lines it does not have to build or launch, acquire subsidiaries or spin off new independent corporate entities and so on. Who actually makes the decisions, for what reasons, for whose benefit and with what results is not a foregone conclusion. The ethical construction of more functional institutions by conscientious human beings is neither a certainty nor an impossibility.

In our view, the twenty-first-century ideal with regard to big profitable companies should be to generate surplus as a major part of the social mission of business. This does not mean maximizing surplus at any price, ignoring other aspects of social and environmental responsibility. We suggest defining 'surplus' as 'what is not needed' (a starting point for a longer discussion in chapters 10 and 11). This four-worder provides a functional orientation for creating resources that will move from where they are not needed to where

---

48. Michael Porter, *Competitive Advantage* (New York: Free Press, 1985), and follow-on books by the same author and the writings of the resource-based school.

49. New Brunswick, NJ: Transaction Publishers, 1991 (1932).

50. Richard Cyert and James March, *A Behavioral Theory of the Firm* (New York: Wiley-Blackwell, 1992 [1963]).

they are needed. The surplus should be shared. Of course. If there were no surplus, there would be none to share. Of course. For a realist, these two points are obvious.

Another part of the twenty-first-century ideal should be supporting the many private noncapitalist sectors that already produce goods and services and create employment—for instance, assuring them adequate health insurance and pensions. They are noncapitalist because they do not accumulate any considerable surplus. The people who work in those sectors—for example, the independent motel owners whose motels barely break even—are used to living that way. Unlike the executives of giant firms, they know how to do it.

♦ ♦ ♦

Nongenisolo Madlazi is the elected CWP supervisor for her village, Upper Mnyameni in Keiskammahoek in Eastern Cape. Of the seven people in her household, she is the only one who is working.

> 'The CWP has helped to chase away the hunger. In my house there was no furniture, and now I have furniture and there is food in the house. It has also warmed my heart because I have got respect in the village because of this project.'
>
> – COGTA

4. The Basic Structure Does Not Work for the Poor: Low Wages

Concerning one of the most important facts not yet discussed—a persistent tendency toward low wages—Marx agrees with Smith.[51] When the two look at commodity exchange where labour is a commodity, they see the same practices governed by the same norms leading to the same miserable results. Both give reasons that are still valid in the twenty-first century— and therefore make us question the optimism of South Africa's National Development Plan. Both find that a consequence of market exchange is, by and large, the poverty of the wage earner, although Smith draws some comfort from finding that British working people were less poor than working people elsewhere. Both detect an underlying causal mechanism that tends to drive down wages.

---

51. This point was not lost on Marx, who observed that Smith himself explained why, in a free market, in negotiations between employer and employee the employer commonly has the stronger bargaining position. *Das Kapital,* Erstes Buch, Kapitel 23, par. 6. Smith's general discussion showing why workers are usually the losers is in ch. 8 of bk. 1 of *The Wealth of Nations.*

In our view, even though in an open system like an economy, intervening variables often mask the causal powers of the basic structure, normally and in the long run the basic structure keeps wages low. That wages will be low follows from Smith's principle that prices in general, including wages (the price of labour) gravitate around and tend to converge on the natural price.[52] The natural price is the cost of production. Competition tends to push the prices that sellers can charge buyers down toward the cost of production of the item sold.

Classical economics was not deliberately designed to meet human needs in harmony with nature. It was deliberately designed to comply with the ideal of *limited government*. A founding myth of modern governments was a (fictitious) social contract obliging the government to respect the rights of 'the people'. The victorious 'Commons' in England and the victorious 'Third Estate' in France represented 'the people' in principle but were in fact made up of male property owners.[53] The natural liberty of classical economics grew in soil that revolutionary politics had ploughed. The point of the revolution was to tie the hands of the government and to put effective power in the hands of owners of private property.

Smith, Marx and other classical economists note that wages could be higher than usual in unusual circumstances, such as in the early days of the United States of America, where workers had the alternative of fleeing westward to the unsettled frontier, squatting and growing their own food. They taught that in the case of skilled and educated workers, the cost of production of a worker included the cost of acquiring skills and education. But in the case of the ordinary worker in eighteenth and early nineteenth century Europe—the kind of worker most observed and most discussed by classical economists such as Smith, Ricardo, Malthus, Marx and their French contemporaries and predecessors—the principal component of the cost of production of a worker was the cost of food. Smith implies that lack of market demand for labour stops the production of labour because children die or are never born, or because adults die as the result of wages being too low to buy sufficient food. He writes:

---

52. We omit the complications derived from the fact that the classical economists worked with a labour theory of value, while most contemporary economists tend to define the value of a thing as whatever a buyer is willing to pay for it.

53. Although many writers make this general point, Michel Foucault makes it particularly well. See his *Society Must Be Defended* (New York: Picador, 2003), especially the lectures at the end given in March 1976. The 'Glorious Revolution' in England actually happened at the end of the 17th century.

> The demand for men, like that for any commodity, necessarily regulates the production of men; quickens it when it advances too slowly and stops it when it advances too fast. It is this demand which regulates and determines the state of propagation in all the different countries of the world.[54]

David Ricardo makes a similar point with more explicit language:

> Labour, like all other things which are purchased and sold, and which may be increased or diminished in quantity, has its natural and its market price. The natural price of labour is that price which is necessary to enable the labourers, one with another, to subsist and to perpetuate their race, without either increase or diminution.[55]

Notice the reason why wages are low: because competitive markets drive down the price of labour to its cost of production, that is to say, to the price of food. When supply exceeds demand, production stops. The production of workers stops because working-class families cannot sell more labour power to buy more food. Unemployed workers cannot exist for long because lack of employment means lack of money, which means lack of food, which means life cannot continue.

Ricardo's expectation is that that poor people whose services could not be sold in the labour market would cease to exist. They would not be born, or if they were born, they would not survive. As Ricardo looked around him in early nineteenth-century England, what he saw confirmed his view. We do not see such confirmation today. Since today the poor do not cease to exist but somehow go on living, in twenty-first-century terms, Ricardo's expectation translates into teeming masses getting by on precarious and irregular ways to earn a little cash, government grants, charity and crime.

---

54. Smith, *Wealth of Nations*, bk. 1, ch. 8.

55. David Ricardo, *On the Principles of Political Economy and Taxation* (London: Macmillan, 1951). The lines quoted are the opening paragraph of ch. 5, 'On Wages'. We are not saying the views of Smith, Ricardo and Marx (and Thomas Malthus) were identical, only that they all expected wages to be low and that this expectation was valid given the institutional structure they studied and the facts they observed. In other texts the same authors qualify their views, acknowledging that the cost of production of a worker is not necessarily that of bare subsistence. It also includes a culturally determined minimum that varies from place to place. Smith also adds, with a logical inconsistency showing that his heart was in the right place, that employers often pay more than the minimum they could get away with paying because of 'common humanity'.

The ideas of Smith and Ricardo still echo in academic economics. Milton Friedman, for example, calls for 'price flexibility in correcting unemployment',[56] i.e., lowering wages to make it profitable for employers to hire. But our main point is not that today's neoliberals are using basically the same ideas used long ago by Smith and Ricardo but that such ideas are correct whoever uses them. They are consequences validly deduced from the basic social structure. They are made correct by the constitutive rules.[57] In the absence of exceptional circumstances, wherever the basic structure reigns and wherever deliberate steps are not successfully taken to modify the basic structure, life for the poor will be precarious and wages will be low.

John Maynard Keynes might be interpreted as writing a dissenting opinion. He says: 'Perhaps it will help to rebut the crude conclusion that a reduction of money-wages will increase employment "because it reduces the cost of production".'[58] In fact, Keynes is questioning the entire conceptual apparatus of classical economics. Entrepreneurs as a class, he argues, are mistaken when they think they can lower wages, hire more workers for the same money, produce greater quantities of the same products with that larger number of workers and then sell larger numbers of the same products at the same old prices, thus increasing their profits. On the contrary, effective demand is the sum of expected consumption and expected investment.[59] There is no other source for the demand to buy the products the entrepreneurs have to sell. When entrepreneurs lower consumption by lowering wages, then, given the probable values of other variables in play, they quite likely lose in sales whatever they gain by cutting wages.

Notice, by the way, that Keynes does not argue on the basis of induction from regularities observed. He does not deduce from existing theory a falsifiable hypothesis to be tested. He does not build a model and try to make it fit the data. He argues from accounting identities. He draws conclusions about what must happen when people buy and sell following the rules that constitute markets.

---

56. Milton Friedman, 'Interest Rates and the Demand for Money', *Journal of Law and Economics*, vol. 9 (1966), p. 71. See also Milton Friedman, *Capitalism and Freedom* (Chicago: University of Chicago Press, 1962), ch. 8, where Friedman argues in favour of wages being set by competitive markets and against unions.

57. The limitations imposed by the constitutive rules of the institutional framework are elaborated in Howard Richards and Joanna Swanger, *The Dilemmas of Social Democracies* (Lanham, MD: Rowman and Littlefield, 2006). See especially ch. 7, 'The Revenge of the Iron Law of Wages'.

58. John Maynard Keynes, *The General Theory of Employment, Interest, and Money* (London and New York: Macmillan, 1936), p. 261.

59. Ibid., p. 260.

In our view, Keynesian economics is best regarded as departing from natural, or pure, economics, which in some contexts for short we just call 'economics'. Keynes's argument that, in general, a high-wage economy might after all be viable is a projection of what could happen if the structure were changed. Keynesians advocate structure-challenging policies like government support for collective bargaining and minimum-wage laws. Contemporary post-Keynesians have not been asleep at the switch; they have constructive ideas to offer anyone who will listen.

We have argued in other works and will further argue in chapter 7 (on Sweden) that even though for several decades the Keynesian 'unnatural' and 'impure' economics of social democracy appeared to be the wave of the future, its success not only did not last, it could not last. Social democracy has been frustrated by the same basic cultural structure it has been trying to change. An example is what Samuel Bowles and Herbert Gintis call 'the exit power of capital'.[60] The solace for labour derived from Keynes's accounting identities does not quite work, because the sums added do not fully take into account capital's option to go elsewhere for the lower wages and then come back again to sell at higher prices. The basic social structure does not work that way; its naked workings, nakedly displayed in classical economic theory, still dominate.

♦ ♦ ♦

> 'About the taverns: since the introduction of curfews for them, where they are required by the metros to stop selling alcohol at a certain time, we now notice the level of crime decreasing. So as far as I'm concerned, the CWP and the patrollers are doing a fine job and must never stop.'
>
> — CWP PARTICIPANT, RANDFONTEIN

5. The Structural Sources of Instability (Keynes and Minsky)

The starting point for explaining *structural instability*, and for explaining *structural humiliation* in the next chapter, is Keynes's initial remarks on the insufficiency of effective demand,[61] seen as an encounter with the basic cultural structure of the modern world. That an encounter with the brute facts

---

60. Samuel Bowles and Herbert Gintis, *Democracy and Capitalism* (New York: Basic Books, 1986).

61. In chs. 2 and 3 of his *General Theory*.

of life in societies ruled mainly by markets motivated Keynes was suggested by Roy Bhaskar when he wrote that the mass unemployment of the 1930s provided the 'motor' for Keynes's demonstration of the theoretical possibility of market equilibrium with unemployment.[62] Mass unemployment was something big and brute. It was outside the range of phenomena the then-reigning economics was prepared to see.

Keynes associated the blind optimism of the orthodox economists of his time with their belief in Say's Law (exactly what that law is will be discussed in chapter 11).[63] It was being used in his time to give allegedly scientific support to the belief that any job seekers trying to find a buyer for their services could find one, provided they were willing to lower their wage to what a buyer wanted to pay. Very roughly, Say's Law says that for every seller there is a buyer.

In a footnote, Keynes quotes a line from Alfred Marshall that casts doubt on Say's Law:[64] 'But though men have the power to purchase, they may choose not to use it.' In other words, the rules of the game, the structure, provide freedom to buy or not buy. The material position of buyer includes the right to not play the game, to not buy. The position of seller grants a similar right to not sell. But if the seller happens to be a person who needs to sell something to earn a living, as was the case with those who died of famine in Sen's studies, and was the case with Ricardo's working-class infants who did not survive because there were no buyers for their parents' labour power, then Say's Law can be *seen as* verbal cleverness that conceals the failure of a culture to constitute a structure that functions to meet human needs.

Keynes goes on to quote with approval J. A. Hobson's comment on the line from Marshall: 'But he [Marshall] fails to grasp the critical importance of this fact [that buying is optional] and appears to limit its action to times of "crisis".'

That people may not buy is of enough critical importance that we are justified in calling it a staggering *structural* fact. A feature of the constitutive rules of the economic game is that there are losers. It is no specific nonbuyer's fault that many need to earn an income but find no buyers for

---

62. Roy Bhaskar, *A Realist Theory of Science* (London: Verso, 2008 (1975)), p. 246.
63. Keynes summarizes the conceptual defects that were preventing the economists from seeing the world as it is in three of their assumptions, each of which implies the other two. One of them is Say's Law expressed as follows: 'Supply creates its own demand in the sense that the aggregate demand price is equal to the aggregate supply price for all levels of employment.' *General Theory*, pp. 21–22.
64. Ibid., p. 19.

what they have to sell. It is the structure's fault. Too much economy. Not enough community.

Further, when acquiring the physical necessities of life and keeping the economic machine going depend on sales, cash sales are never enough. There must be credit and always more credit. In modern society, ever-increasing debt is needed to get things done, which implies that sooner or later debts must become unpayable. Hyman Minsky, building on Keynes and rescuing Keynes from his misinterpreters, has developed this point as the 'instability hypothesis'. Given that the capitalist system cannot function without generating unpayable debts, eventually the towers of illusion must come crashing down. All the king's horses and all the king's men cannot stabilize a system that cannot function unless people make promises they cannot keep.[65]

When a modern human being, i.e., an emancipated juridical subject capable of owning property and entering into contracts, is born destined to become an adult free to buy and sell, the consequences are positive and negative.[66] Like Si and Am, the two cats belonging to Aunt Sarah, they are Siamese if you please and also—here is where the mouse dies—Siamese if you don't please. *Homo economicus* is *free to buy* whatever he may choose to buy and can afford to buy. He is also *free not to buy* whatever he may choose not to buy. The existence of would-be sellers without buyers is a structural fact. It follows from the constitutive rules of markets.

We agree with Keynes that once the assumption that there will be a buyer for every seller collapses, all else changes. Economic theory changes. Common sense changes. We add that the illusion that poverty can be cured by educating the poor so they will all be qualified for jobs collapses. The naïve belief that economic development until every country is as rich as America or the UK or France will end poverty is now seen to be as illogical in theory as it is disproven by the observed facts. The belief that technical progress, with little or no ethical community development, will make technology more productive until all needs are met becomes unbelievable.

Keynes writes: 'The celebrated *optimism* of traditional economic theory, which has led to economists being looked on as Candides, who, having left this world for the cultivation of their gardens, teach that all is for the best in

---

65. See Hyman Minsky, *John Maynard Keynes* (New York: McGraw-Hill, 2008). See also other works by the same author and the work continuing Minsky's, being done at the University of Missouri at Kansas City and at the Levy Institute of Bard College.

66. See David Graeber, *Debt, the First 5000 Years* (London: Melville House, 2011); Viviane Forrester, *L'Horreur économique* (Paris: Fayard, 1996).

this best of all possible worlds ... is also to be traced, I think, to [economists] having neglected to take into account the drag on prosperity that can be exercised by an insufficiency of effective demand.'[67] Keynes also says that once classical economics is granted its premise that the chronic shortage of buyers found in the real world does not exist, 'all the rest follows: the social advantages of private and national thrift, the traditional attitude towards the rate of interest, the classical theory of unemployment, the quantity theory of money, the unqualified advantages of *laissez-faire* in respect of foreign trade, and much else which we shall have to question'.[68]

♦ ♦ ♦

> 'It [the CWP] has made my life better because my kids used to say, "Mom, it is better to eat poison because there is no purpose for me. I am just sitting and I do not even have money for bread. I do not go to school, and other kids are always having their lunch boxes". So this thing made me sad when I heard this child talk like this, that he'd rather take poison and die because there is no purpose for him to live.'
>
> — CWP PARTICIPANT, BUSHBUCKRIDGE CDI

6. Why the Dominant Social Structure Motivates Immense Productivity

There are other consequences of what Douzinas calls the revolution in ethics of early modernity. We are suggesting (again) that the same intransitive objects of social science can be described with different vocabularies and analysed with different conceptual schemes. Thus Karl Polanyi (we suggest) frames a sea change of the causal powers of the deep cultural structures as 'the Great Transformation' that made the 'Market Economy'. Alternatively, it could be called a transformation from Luxemburg's 'natural economies' or Braudel's 'material practices' embedded in matrices of social relations to what Friedrich von Hayek calls 'extended social order', which he praises for many of the same characteristics for which Polanyi deplores it. Wallerstein marshals many of the same facts under the name 'modern world-system', while Amin and Mies see everywhere 'accumulation on a world scale'.

We are also suggesting (again) that to save life we need ethical realism

---

67. Keynes, *General Theory*, p. 35.
68. Ibid., p. 21.

(which is by definition plural, working with and not against existing morals in existing cultures) or some better approach (if there is one) to socializing human beings. Modernity regards the inner lives of human beings as private. But people's inner private lives have public effects. For urgent practical reasons, moral education and spiritual disciplines are needed. Why? Because an out-of-control economy becomes inevitable whenever humans treat other humans not as sisters and brothers to serve but as buyers and sellers to outwit. The historic trend toward the dependence of everybody on investor confidence becomes unstoppable whenever what André Orléan calls *la séparation marchande* prevails.[69] Once the autonomous, self-interested self becomes the *adharmic*[70] substance of daily life, physical dependence on a regime of accumulation sooner or later follows. Or so we claim.

Now I want to make a third point. The historic transition from tribal to feudal (or, broadening the term, the ethic of a military, hierarchical nobility) to modern liberal market ethics has led to immense productivity, aided and abetted by science (which has its own cultures, distinct from economic systems and from religions). Smith, Durkheim, Weber and others have already told us why individualism goes also with the division of labour and the accumulation of capital. But there is something else to add. Without lack of appreciation for Joseph Schumpeter's classic accounts of innovation and the creative roles of entrepreneurs, to make my point I cite Janos Kornai.

Kornai compared the planned economies of Eastern Europe with the capitalist economies of the West during the decades immediately following World War II.[71] He found that in the East, in terms of cold logic and abstract mathematics, the plans were often plausible, although they were vulnerable to the criticism of Friedrich von Hayek and like-minded authors that the planners could not possibly gather and process the infinite amounts of information gathered and processed by innumerable decision makers

---

69. André Orléan, *L'Empire de la valeur* (Paris: Seuil, 2011), Kindle, position 328. This is not to deny Fernand Braudel's point that modernity began largely without the knowledge or participation of the common people—for example, with international financial transactions most people knew nothing about—and only later compelled the masses to conform to the norms it required.

70. *Adharmic*, without *dharma*, is Gandhi's term for the essence of modern Western ways of life in *Hind Swaraj*, published in 1909. See Howard Richards and Joanna Swanger, *Gandhi and the Future of Economics* (Lake Oswego, OR: Dignity Press, 2013).

71. Janos Kornai, *Economics of Shortage* (Amsterdam: North-Holland Publishing Company, 1990). Joseph Schumpeter makes similar points in his writings on business cycles.

in markets.⁷² According to the plans everything should have worked, and indeed some things did work; for example, capital formation was generally higher than in the West. But in many ways the plans did not work. Superficially, there was full employment, but there were shortages everywhere. As Richard Musgrave put the matter, 'The socialist trauma, corresponding to aggregate demand instability in the capitalist system, is that of imbalance between industrial sectors.'⁷³

In the West, on the other hand, says Kornai, the economic theories of J. B. Say, the liberals and the neoliberals were plainly wrong, and the people Schumpeter calls 'hitch economists'—himself, Malthus, Luxemburg, Sraffa, Keynes—were plainly right. In the West, virtually every industry was plagued by overproduction. Sales constantly lagged behind targets, threatening to fall behind producing the revenue needed just to break even. There were periodic recessions. Nobody could erase the memory of the Great Depression that was ended only by World War II. There were debt burdens that threatened to become unpayable, and frequently did become unpayable, leading to bankruptcies. The result? Facing competition from rivals, insufficient demand to absorb the industry's potential output and financial threats to its very survival, the capitalist firm was under pressure to *innovate* to secure as much as possible of the industry's demand for itself. Innovation drove growth, and growth added yet more excess capacity. A new factory had to be built when there was already more capacity than needed to meet existing demand. Why? Because otherwise, competitors would be the ones to build the new factory with the new, more efficient technology making the new, more attractive product. The firm would be reduced to making products so old-fashioned and/or so expensive that nobody would buy them. It would fail. To solve its problem, it added to everybody else's problem: overproduction. And thus it drove everyone else to innovate also.

In other words, a well-grounded *fear of failure* in the turbulent West produced ceaseless innovation. The West's insecurity proved more motivational than secure employment (not forgetting that the East had its own cruder and more primitive versions of fear and insecurity). The West succeeded so well in producing better, less expensive and more abundant

---

72. Friedrich von Hayek, *The Fatal Conceit* (Chicago: University of Chicago Press, 1988).

73. Richard Musgrave, *Fiscal Systems* (New Haven: Yale University Press, 1966), p. 30. Ludwig von Mises exaggerates this point, claiming that there can be no markets for producer's goods in a socialist system, and hence no rational decision-making.

products that refugees from the Soviet Union cried tears of joy when they arrived in New York City—not because they saw the Statue of Liberty or read the Constitution but because they visited a supermarket and saw rows and rows of shelves well-stocked with consumer goods.

The same *séparation marchande*—the same individualistic social structure that powerfully tends to inequality, exclusion and low wages, to denuded hillsides where forests used to be and to overwhelming nature with trash in dumps and plastic in oceans—also powerfully tends to generate a steady flow of new, better, cheaper and more abundant products. Let it be added that many innovations now in the pipeline are greener, doing more with less.

CHAPTER FOUR
Two Staggering Facts That Change Everything

OVERVIEW OF THE CHAPTER
1. Two Staggering Facts
2. Structural Humiliation
3. Thinking about Social Change Strategy
4. South Africa's Community Work Programme: Tomorrow's Solutions under Construction Today
5. Theoretical Appendix: John Maynard Keynes versus Milton Friedman

1. Two Staggering Facts

We can achieve a pretty good working grasp of how modern society works, as well as how to change it, if we keep two facts, which we consider staggering in nature, in mind:

Staggering Fact 1 (SF1): Production depends on profit—not entirely but to the degree that the dominant sector dominates.
Staggering Fact 2 (SF2): There is a chronic shortfall of effective demand.

To elaborate: Production depends on expectations of profit, while expectations of profit depend on expectations of sales. And, as John Maynard Keynes once put it: the weakness of the inducement to invest has always been *the* economic problem.[1] Of course. Profits depend on sales, while sales tend to lag because people keep some of their money instead of spending it. And there is no guarantee that there will be enough sales to justify a given investment, much less a guarantee that there will be enough sales to produce enough investments to produce full employment. There is even less guarantee that there will be employment for those no longer counted as unemployed because they have given up and left the work force—the excluded, the down and out.

---

1. John Maynard Keynes, *The General Theory of Employment, Interest, and Money* (London and New York: Macmillan, 1936), p. 304.

Indeed, it can be persuasively argued that there *is* a guarantee that there will *not* be enough sales.[2] The apparent evidence to the contrary is illusory—the sort of illusion to which positivist methodologies are prone. We refer to the counting of full employment in Switzerland in the 1960s as proof that there can be a market with stable full employment. The illusion is that there exists an independent Swiss economy with a separate labour market. It is an epistemological error to treat the Swiss economy as a separate unit of analysis when measuring unemployment, seeking to learn its causes. The illusion gets worse if one concludes that if every country adopted policies like those of Switzerland in the 1960s all the time, then every country could have full employment all the time.

In the light of our two Staggering Facts much can be understood, including the homeostatic nature of capitalism (its capacity to recover when perturbed),[3] the decline and fall of social democracy,[4] structural humiliation and structural frustration (discussed below), as well as the merits of unbounded organization and *economía solidaria* as effective social change strategies that can replace ineffective social change strategies.

These two Staggering Facts are generated by the underlying reality (the structure) that produces them as surely as the clashes of tectonic plates generate earthquakes. One convenient name, among many, for this underlying reality is the *basic social structure*. Sometimes that structure's invisibility, such that we call it 'underlying', is due not so much to financial transactions in distant banks appearing far from daily life[5] as it is to the structure's being so deeply ingrained that it is unconsciously assumed.

From a methodological point of view, there comes a point when so many facts fit together so well and have so many practical applications that it becomes unreasonable to object that an idea like the basic social structure (or the evolution of species) is arbitrary speculation. It becomes unreasonable to object, in the style of Karl Popper or Willard van Orman Quine, that it is just one of innumerable theories that can be spun to 'explain' the facts when the facts to be explained are already evident. Instead,

---

2. That insufficient sales are a mathematical certainty was persuasively argued, a quarter century before Keynes's theory of liquidity preference, by Rosa Luxemburg, *The Accumulation of Capital* (London: Routledge, 2008 (1913)).

3. See Howard Richards and Joanna Swanger, *Dilemmas of Social Democracies* (Lanham, MD: Rowman and Littlefield, 2006).

4. Ibid.

5. See Fernand Braudel, *Civilization and Capitalism: 15th–18th Century*, vol. 1 (Berkeley: University of California Press, 1992).

it becomes reasonable to conclude that the concept of the basic social (or cultural) structure has an ontological basis in the way things are, even though it makes no claim to be the only vocabulary suitable for describing it. It 'tells it like it is'.

Among the observable consequences of that basic social (or cultural) structure are the two facts we are highlighting. We call them staggering because of their astonishing breadth of application. In critical realist terms, they are intransitive objects of science.[6] The reason why the theory of evolution and our Staggering Facts tell it like it is, is that indeed that is the way it is—and continues to be while people talk about it in different ways. The word 'existential' is added regarding our Staggering Facts because in their case (as in the case of Durkheim's social facts) they were, over the course of history, created by human beings.

♦ ♦ ♦

Phindile Ntshangase is the Njoko community garden supervisor in Nongoma. She is an orphan looking after four siblings.

> 'When my mom died in 2008 I thought it was finished for my family. I felt helpless. I am really happy now that I am able to care for my siblings and myself. This has brought hope into my life. Every month I am saving R200 because I want to continue my nursing studies. As long as I am employed I will not be helpless.'
>
> – COGTA

2. Structural Humiliation

Humiliation is a psychological concept relevant to economic theory that is normal and inevitable, given the currently dominant basic social structure. By 'humiliation' we mean the abasement of pride, which creates mortification or leads to a state of being humbled. It is an emotion felt by a person whose social status has just decreased or whose existing low social status has just been publicly demonstrated.[7] This 'social status' way of thinking about humiliation is a construct derived from cross-cultural psychological research, especially that of Evelin Lindner.[8]

---

6. Howard Richards, 'On the Intransitive Objects of the Social (or Human) Sciences', *Journal of Critical Realism*, vol. 17 (2018), pp. 1–16.

7. These words are from Wikipedia's article on humiliation.

8. Evelin Lindner, *Humiliation and International Conflict* (Santa Barbara, CA: Praeger, 2006); and other works by the same author.

People are expected to stand on their own two feet and to pay their own way. They are expected to care for their children. They are expected to dress nicely. But to do so requires selling their labour, and selling requires buyers. It is one thing to be willing to work. It is another to find a buyer who will pay you for working. As things are, the basic social structure generates people who fail to sell their labour, or whatever they need to sell, and are therefore unable to maintain their social status and so are humiliated.[9]

Our starting point for building the concept of structural humiliation is Keynes's concept of liquidity preference as laid out in his *General Theory*. We could demonstrate the inevitability of structural humiliation by starting from the theories of any number of economists, since we argue that humiliation is a consequence of the basic social structure that all the orthodox and many heterodox economists presuppose and study. In choosing Keynes, we are moved in part by Roy Bhaskar's comment that the mass unemployment of the 1930s provided the 'motor' for Keynes's demonstration of the theoretical possibility of market equilibrium with unemployment.[10] Mass unemployment was something big, something structural. It was happening outside the range of phenomena classical economics was prepared to see. Ontology, *what is*, intruded on epistemology, the theory of knowledge. It forcibly reminded scholars of Heidegger's point that ontology should determine epistemology, not the other way about.

We read Keynes's initial remarks on the insufficiency of effective demand due to the liquidity preference, which appear in chapters 2 and 3 of *General Theory*, *as* an encounter with the basic cultural structure of the modern world. Simply put: nobody has to buy if she or he does not want to buy. As we saw in chapter 3, Keynes saw the defective lenses of classical economics as framed by Say's Law (the law that every seller, including of labour, will find a buyer), and he quoted Alfred Marshall in a footnote to affirm this.

Perhaps because he was born too soon to benefit from Bhaskar's critical realist philosophy of science, Keynes lets his illuminating insight into the social structure constituting SF2 slip out of focus in the next chapter in *General Theory*, which is chapter 4, on 'the choice of units'. He thinks he needs exact numbers to do causal analysis. He feels he must use differential calculus, which he eventually succeeds in doing, by defining dCw/dYw as the marginal propensity to consume. To make his definition of 'income' yield

---

9. We omit writing "labour-power" instead of "labour" just to make the text simpler, not to express disagreement with Marx's point.
10. Roy Bhaskar, *A Realist Theory of Science* (London: Verso, 2008 (1975)), p. 246.

the exact numbers he believes are required to tie causes to effects, he ties it to the rules defining income followed by the UK's Inland Revenue Service in the 1930s. He thus establishes his credentials as a scientist by conforming to the prevailing philosophy of science of his day. However, he does so after having said enough about the relationship of mass unemployment to the falsity of Say's Law[11] to identify what we call *structural humiliation*.

Even so, there is something else relevant to structural humiliation that Keynes may have glimpsed but did not grasp—an insight essential to our case for replacing the dominant liberal ethics with a realist ethics of sharing and caring. To set the stage for this point, we call on Adam Smith to testify that there is an essential connection between liberal individualist ethics and liberal economic theory. Consider this famous passage from *The Wealth of Nations*: 'It is not from the benevolence of the butcher, the brewer, or the baker, that we expect our dinner, but from their regard to their own interest. We address ourselves not to their humanity, but to their self-love and never talk to them of our own necessities but of their advantages.'[12]

Here and elsewhere, Smith is plainly aware that economic ideology has competitors that do address humanity and do talk of necessities. In constructing his economic theory, Smith argues against them. He makes arguments to discredit traditional notions like love of neighbour. He takes the trouble to answer people who believe in old community norms that make the members of communities responsible for meeting one another's needs. In fact, in his earlier work, *Theory of the Moral Sentiments* (1759), Smith goes to great pains to show that, contrary to traditional norms of kinship and religion, we are not, after all, our brother's or sister's keeper but rather are ordained by divine providence to pursue our own self-interest.[13] We take his repeated efforts to justify liberal ethics as evidence that he knew he needed them to underpin his economic theory. However, it can also be said that he never fully made up his own mind, and as a result a text from Smith can be found to cite on almost any side of any issue.

As Karl Polanyi and his collaborators and followers have shown, societies with noneconomic structures and ideologies are usually organized by norms

---

11. This was not the last of Keynes's great structural insights, nor was it the last time he mixed diverse methods and modes of argument.
12. Smith, *Wealth of Nations*, near the beginning of ch. 2, bk. 1.
13. For detailed studies of *The Theory of the Moral Sentiments*, of Smith's theology and of how Smith relates to the theological controversies of his day, see the works of Andres Monares: *Oikonomia, economía moderna, economías* (Santiago: Editorial Ayun, 2008); and *Reforma e ilustración, los teólogos que construyeron la modernidad* (Santiago: Editorial Ayun, 2012).

of reciprocity and redistribution.[14] The idea that one person's necessity implies a duty to aid that person that is binding upon other members of his or her clan or tribe, and the ideas that food security, security in old age, and other kinds of security can be achieved by reciprocity and redistribution are old and wise ideas. They do not die easily. Smith acknowledges their power when he argues against them. They made a promising but now frustrated comeback in the twentieth century in the form of the welfare state.

♦ ♦ ♦

> 'I also noticed that they like what they do because the cleaning people, they made a design with white stones which says CWP. That is good and nice.'
>
> — CWP PARTICIPANT, UMTHWALUME

3. Thinking about Social Change Strategy

In today's world, where the amount of specialized information available is so huge that nobody can assimilate it, traditional general worldviews providing overall orientation and guidance are challenged. They are hard to believe. They are also challenged because when they are believed, they often lead to intolerance and sectarian violence instead of to love of God and love of neighbour. There is a need for a general worldview that is easy to believe, is not intolerant or sectarian and is conceptually tied to a prosocial attitude. We offer one. We call it unbounded organization and connect it to moral realism.[15]

Our two staggering facts, SF1 and SF2, dramatically illustrate why bounded thinking connected to moral liberalism leads to ineffective social change strategies. They dramatically demonstrate why unbounded thinking, committed in principle to aligning across sectors for the common good and to seeing the number of possible solutions to any given problem as unlimited, is needed to craft effective social change strategies.

Unbounded thinking calls for a realist worldview that learns from what

---

14. Karl Polanyi et al. *Trade and Market in the Early Empires* (New York: Free Press, 1957); Richard Wilk and Lisa Cliggett, *Economies and Cultures: Foundations of Economic Anthropology* (Boulder, CO: Westview Press, 2009); George Dalton, 'Traditional Production in Primitive African Economies', *The Quarterly Journal of Economics*, vol. 76 (1962), pp. 360–378; Paul Bohannan and George Dalton, *Markets in Africa* (Evanston, IL: Northwestern University Press, 1965).

15. Howard Richards, 'Moral and Ethical Realism', *Journal of Critical Realism*, vol. 18 (2019), pp. 285–302.

science has to teach us. It places in parentheses the eighteenth-century founding mythologies of liberalism: social contract, self-evident truths, pure reason, natural liberty, et cetera. Notably, it does not reject liberal institutions because they have proved not to be the truths Immanuel Kant and Thomas Jefferson thought they were; instead it reframes them as eighteenth-century European culture gone global. Following the realist, naturalist, pragmatist philosopher John Dewey, from the standpoint of unbounded thinking, all institutions, regardless of their provenance, are treated as hypotheses to be (cautiously and carefully) evaluated and modified in light of their performance.[16]

Our realist worldview sees culture as the ecological niche of the human species.[17] It concurs with the worldview of the anthropologist James Boggs,[18] who works with culture somewhat as Weber works with *Gemeinhandel*. In Weber's terminology there has to be *community*, in an important sense of that polysemic and indispensable word, before there can be any human action at all, because human action supposes common understandings. Human action is social. It presupposes expectations about how others will interpret and react. Bicyclists in Weber's Germany pass each other on the right, presupposing one conventional norm, while, as Weber points out, in Britain they pass each other on the left, presupposing a different conventional norm.

One can make a similar point using another polysemic and indispensable word, "culture". Without culture, there is no humanity at all and therefore no human action and no human institutions. We say the same thing about morals and ethics. Moral and ethical norms are found in every culture. The existence of these norms is part of what the word "culture" designates. Without some morality or other, there is no humanity at all.[19]

In an essay on the concept of culture, Boggs regards culture as the flagship of anthropology as a discipline. It plays a role in anthropology similar to

---

16. John Dewey, *The Public and its Problems* (New York: Henry Holt, 1927); John Dewey and James Tufts, *Ethics* (New York: Henry Holt, 1908).

17. This idea was adumbrated in the 1970s by Rom Harré and his coauthors in several works that connect (1) an interpretive social science featuring explanations of human behaviour that rely on concepts of rules (or norms) with (2) a realist philosophy of natural science. This connection has been carried forward by Roy Bhaskar and Margaret Archer, among many others.

18. James Boggs, 'The Culture Concept as Theory, in Context', *Current Anthropology*, vol. 45 (2004), pp. 187–209.

19. The biologist C. H. Waddington, in *The Ethical Animal* (London: Allen and Unwin, 1966), is one of many authors who make this point. Some treat ethics, which is sometimes used as a synonym for morals and at other times used to refer to philosophic or theological thinking about morals, as an activity that exists in some cultures but not in others.

the role evolution plays in biology, tying the science together and making it what it is. Culture can be thought of as the ability to transmit innovative adaptations to the environment from one generation to another through upbringing. Culture gives the human species an evolutionary advantage over other species, which can only innovate by genetic means like mutation and natural selection.

In the twenty-first century, the anthropological concept of culture is compelling the rethinking or, according to Immanuel Wallerstein, the *unthinking* of the social sciences. Culture is becoming the new overarching theoretical framework. Anthropology is placing economic theory in a new light. Economic theory can now once again be seen as an elaboration of cultural rules that constitute material positions—in other words, as social structure.

Culture is a concept that links the natural sciences to the human sciences. Causal explanations in economics rely on premises derived from the basic cultural structure of modern society.[20] And culture is, in the light of biology, an adaptation. Thus, we connect the natural sciences with anthropology, anthropology with culture, culture with norms (or rules), rules with constitutive rules, constitutive rules with the particular rules that constitute markets.

The rules of markets organizing capital accumulation are the main driving force of the economy. This is SF1: Production is driven by profit.

It follows from bearing SF1 constantly in mind that an effective social change strategy will not undermine the main driving force of the economy unless and until it can offer other driving forces to replace it. It also follows, not as an immediate logical consequence but as a conclusion from due deliberation, that completely abolishing SF1 is neither possible nor desirable.

Here lies the beauty of social change strategies that are more constructive and less confrontational, like unbounded organization and *economía solidaria*. An effective social change strategy will be pluralist and ethical. It will mobilize ways to get the work of the world done that free humanity from having to comply with the requirements of one or another regime of accumulation. It will look to spiritual practices and the psychology of moral development for methods for making SF1 less dominant by making humans more driven by the higher needs identified by Maslow and the need

---

20. This is the burden of the argument in Howard Richards, *Understanding the Global Economy* (Santa Barbara, CA: Peace Education Books, 2004). A methodology that sees economics as working within the basic constitutive rules of modernity is applied to case studies in Richards and Swanger, *Dilemmas of Social Democracies*.

for meaning identified by Victor Frankl and relied upon for thousands of years by the world's great religions.

As Martin Luther and his namesake Martin Luther King Jr. emphasized, every job, every role in the economy, should be treated as a calling, a *Beruf*, a vocation. Thus leadership is *seen as* a matter of cultivating the best instincts of the led and of satisfying their thirst for meaningful lives. Such a culture shift will, we claim, make the capitalist or post-capitalist system, or any system, more ethically governable. As Peter Drucker suggests, it will add, to the necessity to earn profits, the pride in the constructive uses to which the profits are put after they are earned.[21] It will aim to achieve sustainability and justice while performing the social functions of profit as well as or better than they are performed now.

Thus, changes at the level of moral values, of cultural norms, of personal identity and its influence on motivation, of mental health and spiritual practices, can become changes at the level of social structure. Such changes influence the cultural rules that define material positions—for example, the position of owner. In terms of Amartya Sen's study of entitlement and famines, they influence who lives and who dies—this is one good reason for choosing to call them 'basic'. In terms of the purpose of production, they can make an organization mission-driven, treating profit as a means rather than an end. They can enlighten the criteria for deciding what to do with earnings after they are earned. They can include the excluded because they are humans with needs, whether or not they are human resources that can be tapped to make products that can be profitably sold.

Effective social change strategies will take into account that redistribution of income to move resources to where they are needed may slow or stop production. It may lead to not meeting needs that were being met before the redistribution—and not only because, for example, raising wages or raising taxes may make previously profitable businesses unprofitable. Production may slow or stop for political reasons (because the social change strategy has powerful enemies) even when production would be profitable. This is a reason for preferring consensus to conflict whenever possible. It is not, however, a reason for preferring the 'consensus' sociology of Talcott Parsons over the 'conflict' sociology of C. Wright Mills. Indeed, acknowledging the realities of conflict provides reasons for preferring consensus.[22]

---

21. Peter Drucker, 'Business Objectives and Survival Needs', *Journal of Business*, vol. 31 (1958), pp. 81–90.

22. Norbert Lechner, *La conflictiva y nunca acabada construcción del orden deseado*

Our reading of the realities of the twenty-first century and of human nature regards wide acceptance of an ethic of sharing the surplus as necessary and possible. It follows, if our reading is true to the facts, that zero-sum games should and could become less common and win-win solutions should and could become the norm.[23]

Bearing SF1 in mind also reminds us that just the unrealized threat of stopping production or moving production elsewhere can be a powerful bargaining chip. A well-known feature of SF1 is that major decisions to invest are often made by a few people who are in a position to threaten many others with unemployment or worse. Threats can be moves in high-stakes games—for example, games whose outcomes decide who pays taxes and how much. As James Buchanan and Gordon Tullock point out, when self-interested parties are bargaining in markets, they regularly misrepresent their true intentions. The name of their game is concealing preferences, not (as mainstream economics would too often have us believe) revealing preferences.[24]

The claim that human nature can be improved by moral education and can become less antisocial and more mission driven, where the mission serves the common good, is compatible with seeing the sordid side of the facts. Negotiation is frequently about bluffs and threats, in spite of the best efforts of professionals in the field to raise its moral level.[25] SF1 can serve as a reminder that effective work for change must synthesize Gandhi's first principle, *ahimsa* (treating every human being as a soul) with Aristotle and Plato's first virtue, *phronesis* (practical wisdom).

There is still more that can be concluded about effective social change strategies from considering our two staggering facts, SF1 and SF2. Such strategies are fundamental for avoiding the mistakes of the twentieth century in order to be effective in changing the course of history in the twenty-first.

The objective of meeting human needs in harmony with nature regularly clashes with the economy's overriding imperatives. One such imperative, due to SF1, is to keep alive expectations of profits, indeed, expectations of profits

---

(Santiago: FLACSO, 1984); (Madrid: Siglo XXI, 1988). This is one of the classics of the self-criticism of the Chilean left after the military coup of 1973.

23. Robert Wright, *Nonzero: The Logic of Human Destiny* (New York: Pantheon, 2000).

24. James Buchanan and Gordon Tullock, *The Calculus of Consent* (Ann Arbor, MI: University of Michigan Press, 1962).

25. Roger Fisher and William Ury, *Getting to Yes* (London: Penguin, 2011); John Paul Lederach, *The Little Book of Conflict Transformation* (New York: Simon and Schuster, 2003).

higher than the rate of interest and higher than gains from speculation in the global casino economy. As Keynes eloquently explains, nothing in the capitalist sector moves without 'confidence'.[26] The overriding imperative to sustain investor confidence tends to win out in the end, whatever other factors may be in play.[27] The imperative to assure investors that investing will be profitable and safe overrides all other imperatives—because meeting the basic needs of the people depends on it, at least insofar as the dominant system dominates. It follows that effective change must work for plural economies, where there is more than one way to assure that basic needs are met.

Keeping SF1 in mind helps to explain why humanity as a whole is now crashing hell-bent toward outcomes that are not in the interests of any human being. They include the destruction of the biosphere. They include replacing human labour with technology, which leads to mass unemployment with its sequels of violence, drugs and other antisocial escapes from reality. They include general insecurity. And they include authoritarian repression motivated by general insecurity. Why are we doing all these destructive things that serve nobody's interests? Because every government has learned from experience that pursuing social and ecological objectives clashes regularly with what it is forced to make its top priority: to get more investment to keep the GNP growing and to prevent the GNP from shrinking. We call this *structural frustration*.

To talk of structural frustration is to acknowledge that the world as it is now organized under SF1 and SF2 is ungovernable. Rational choices and ethical choices regularly clash with the overriding imperative of capital accumulation, and they regularly lose. To talk of structural transformation is to motivate another overriding imperative, which is to communicate these staggering facts to the public. A promising approach is to organize what Linda Hartling and Evelin Lindner call 'dignifying dialogues', or 'dignilogues'.[28] Such dialogues are necessary conversations. They are

---

26. Keynes, *General Theory*, ch. 12. In our view, this is a tautology. To the extent that the motive of production is not an expectation of capital accumulation, the system is not, strictly speaking, capitalist, although it can be called by a similar name like conscious capitalism. See, for instance, John Mackey and Rajendra Sisodia, *Conscious Capitalism* (Boston: Harvard Business Review Press, 2014). Keynes adds a twist: people invest not only because they expect a firm to be profitable but also because they think the value of their shares will increase because other people will regard them as a profitable investment. He emphasizes that investment is motivated not by profits but by the expectation of profits.

27. This point is illustrated by Richards and Swanger in *Dilemmas of Social Democracies* with case studies of Spain, Sweden, Austria and South Africa.

28. See www.humiliationstudies.org.

necessary to create and to popularize realistic change strategies for saving life (human and that of other living forms) from a mute, inglorious end, leaving a lonely Planet Earth to circle the sun shorn of the multitudinous creatures it formerly hosted.

An effective social change strategy will be educational. It will facilitate understanding SF1 and SF2. It will organize necessary conversations around how to govern SF1 and SF2 and around how to become independent of the necessity to please big investors at any cost. Learners will learn that effective social change transforms deep cultural structures that are often invisible because they are taken for granted as unquestionable common sense.

We repeat that the unbounded approach is basically very simple. Like the proposition that the surplus that is not needed should be shared with those who are in need, it is basically a series of tautologies:

- Do not set any *a priori* theoretical limits on social imagination.
- Align across sectors to do what works in practice.
- Embrace a realist ethic: Once it is accepted that the goal is to meet human needs in harmony with nature, it follows that people ought to act in ways that lead to meeting human needs in harmony with nature.
- Allow organization to be unbounded: 'We ... use the term "unbounded organisation" to refer to intersectoral collaboration, individuals linking between their "own" organisations, coalition-building, cross-cultural activities and involvement by all segments of society.'[29]

♦ ♦ ♦

Mzi Taelo is a principal at Diphalane Public School in Munsieville, Krugersdorp.

> 'We are grateful for the wonderful work being done by CWP. You cleaned our schools, helped to distribute books, organized kids in classrooms and made sure that kids were settled for the first week of January. You guys made it possible for effective teaching to take place on the first day when schools reopened. You work hard, you are committed and dedicated. We are truly blessed to have CWP in our community.'
>
> – CDI

---

29. Gavin Andersson, *Looking Back to the Future: Conversations on Unbounded Organisation*, Dark Roast Occasional Paper Series Number 12 (Cape Town: Isandla Institute, 2000), p. 4.

4. South Africa's Community Work Programme: Tomorrow's Solutions under Construction Today

We have been taking the position that the answer to the question whether there really is a chronic insufficiency of effective demand (endlessly debated by Keynesians and anti-Keynesians) is to be found at the level of what Roy Bhaskar called the intransitive objects of science. In Bhaskar's terms, the basic social (or cultural) structure, which generates SF1 and SF2, is existentially intransitive. That is to say, it is not a naturally occurring underlying generative mechanism but a socially constructed one.[30] There is indeed a chronic insufficiency of effective demand inherent in the basic social structure. It is a problem with no solution within economic theory, because any economic theory (by definition, in order to be counted as economic) presupposes the basic social structure.

An effective social change strategy is indispensable to (cautiously and carefully) transforming the basic social structure. We propose South Africa's Community Work Programme (CWP) as an example illustrating, in the admittedly few cases where its founding ideals are properly implemented, certain aspects of how to transform the basic structure.

The CWP has a mandate to use public employment to catalyse community development. Not at every site but at a few of its sites, the CWP exhibits, in limited but important ways, the implementation of its mandate. It exhibits transformation by community development.

For example: In Alexandria (affectionately called 'Alex'), a poor district of Johannesburg, as is unfortunately the case at too many locations on this planet, the majority of the young people are unemployed and unhappy. Many sink into drugs; into indiscriminate sex leading to AIDS and gender-based violence; into hustling suckers and mugging those who resist; and if they are female, roaming the streets looking for a man who will give them money for favours. But if you visit a certain old church building on the main avenue of Alex on a weekday afternoon, you will find twelve young CWP participants who are employed. They look happy.

They are practicing song-and-dance routines to music like 'Black Motion' by Imali and 'Babes Wodumo' by Wololo, as well as to oldies like 'Cat Daddy' and 'Bird Walk'. They had to audition to get into the troupe. Once they were in, they needed discipline and self-discipline to learn the steps and lines and do them right, as well as the self-discipline to show up

---

30. Howard Richards, 'On the Intransitive Objects of the Social (or Human) Sciences', *Journal of Critical Realism*, vol. 17 (2018), pp. 1–16.

for work, be on time, arrive sober and stay clean in more senses than one. Agreeing with those moral realists (like Andrew Sayer[31]) who find merit in Aristotelian virtue ethics as updated by Alasdair MacIntyre and Martha Nussbaum, I believe that discipline leads them to virtue and virtue leads them to happiness.

Expressing general agreement with Abraham Maslow, who said that 'the "good" or healthy society would then be defined as one that permitted man's highest purposes to emerge by satisfying all his prepotent basic needs',[32] I suggest that, whatever else may be going on in their lives, the young dancers' performances in public spaces, mostly schools, satisfy their need for recognition, which in turn tends to satisfy their need for self-esteem. Their paychecks give them the dignity denied to the millions who are structurally humiliated because they are rejected by labour markets, where for the structural reasons discussed above, supply perpetually exceeds demand. A little money in the pocket gives them food, drink and clothing they do not have to beg, borrow or steal for.

The services the dancers provide for the school children who are their main audiences are more than entertainment. They provide role models of drug-free youth who are having fun. They keep alive the hope that employment might be a real possibility after all for those children when they grow older.

But the main reason we call the song-and-dance troupe practicing in the old church in Alex an example of structural transformation is that it is an example of nonmarket livelihoods made possible by solidarity. A basic feature of the deep structure of legal entitlement in modern society, displayed by Amartya Sen in his explanatory critiques of famines, has been transformed: it is no longer necessary, *cet. par.*, to sell something to live. In the terminology of Wilber and Jameson, in the CWP, economic relations are being reembedded in social relations.[33]

♦ ♦ ♦

> 'I am a captain of the Mavusana soccer team, which helps to keep the youth active. So I think I'm doing my part in building the community.'
>
> — CWP PARTICIPANT, RANDFONTEIN CDI

---

31. Andrew Sayer, *Why Things Matter to People: Social Sciences, Values and Ethical Life* (Cambridge, UK: Cambridge University Press, 2011).

32. Abraham Maslow, 'A Theory of Human Motivation', *Psychological Review*, vol. 50 (1943), p. 395.

33. Charles Wilber and Kenneth Jameson, *An Inquiry into the Poverty of Economics* (Notre Dame, IN: Notre Dame University Press, 1983).

5. Theoretical Appendix: John Maynard Keynes versus Milton Friedman

The thesis of this appendix is that the most important aspect of Keynes's work is that he calls attention to two features of the basic structure, namely, the chronic insufficiency of effective demand and the chronic insufficiency of the inducement to invest, both of which are aspects of what we are calling Staggering Facts.[34] Keynes devotes about a third of his *General Theory* to each of these chronic insufficiencies. Obviously, if sales are chronically slow, then investment will be chronically slow too because the standard purpose of standard investments is producing some good or service and then selling it for a profit. Paul Krugman has argued that despite the endless theoretical debates and empirical studies after which liberals repeatedly claimed victory and declared Keynes dead and thrice buried, the financial crisis of 2008 ended the debates in favour of Keynes. Whatever the consequences of that crash may be in practice, at the level of theory they ended all doubt. There really is an SF2. There really is a chronic lack of sales, and there really is its corollary, a chronic weakness of the inducement to invest.[35]

SF1, on the other hand, is the dependence of production on profit. We have found it convenient (as in chapter 3) to explain it by citing Marx. SF1 is virtually identical to a virtual tautology of Marx: 'Where there is accumulation there is capitalism, and where there is capitalism there is accumulation.'

From a common-sense point of view, there is in fact a great deal of production that is not capitalist; for example, mothers produce milk for infants and give it to them for free. However, it is a tradition in economic theory (to be discussed in detail in a later chapter) to count as 'production' and as 'productive' only production for sale for money. SF1, therefore, from a common-sense viewpoint applies only to some production, while for some economists it applies, by definition, to all production, because what is not done for profit is, by definition, not productive.

This theoretical appendix concerns Milton Friedman, one of many economists who devoted enormous quantities of intellectual energy to burying Keynes and keeping him buried. The logic of the casket Friedman designs for Keynes is that when one cashes out Keynes's claims as quantitative predictions and then tests the predictions with empirical evidence, Keynes's

---

34. 'The weakness of the inducement to invest has been at all times the key to the economic problem.' Keynes, *General Theory*, pp. 347–8.

35. Paul Krugman, *The Return of Depression Economics* (New York: W.W. Norton, 2009).

claims are in general false. In particular, predictions deduced from Keynes's theories are false in certain empirical studies Friedman himself conducted.

Regarding the design of the casket, let it be said that one expects economics to make correct quantitative predictions of future events *only if* one has not read (or perhaps has read but not believed) writers like Roy Bhaskar, Tony Lawson and Friedrich von Hayek (for example, his Nobel lecture). Such writers point out—with impeccable logic that, in our view, trumps the casket Friedman designed for Keynes—that an economy is an open system and that its basic tendencies are regularly offset by any number of crosscurrents, some of which depend on unpredictable human choices.

Keynes himself goes back and forth between trying to formulate equations that yield the exact value of a dependent variable when the exact values of the independent variables are plugged into them, and being satisfied with approximations derived from business experience and common sense.[36] This gives the Friedmans of the world an opportunity to trap their prey: Keynes himself bought into the positivist epistemology of his day, thereby implicitly agreeing to be judged by whether predictions derived from his theory were confirmed by empirical tests. As noted in section 2 of this chapter, right after glimpsing the cultural structure (the ethical individualism and the law of contract) that made weakness of sales, persistent unemployment and frantic efforts of governments to please investors the stuff of everyday life in the modern world, Keynes immediately turned in his next chapter to proving his credentials as a scientist by quantifying his variables and writing a differential equation.

But there is the fact that Keynes goes back and forth. He remarks occasionally that he is writing about the social institutions prevailing at his time and place, not about truths valid everywhere and always. If this side of Keynes is true, then his work is not social physics. It should not be judged as if it were.

Nevertheless, Keynes was no Amartya Sen or Jean Dreze, who regarded the market as one option among many for provisioning a population. He wrote his theory (although not the philosophical and political implications of his theory) as if sales in markets were the only game in town. He begins his fifth chapter with the sweeping statement: 'All production is for the purpose of ultimately satisfying a consumer.' And in the next sentence, he explains that 'satisfying' means resulting in 'the purchase of the output

---

36. See, for example, his discussion of the wage-unit in ch. 6 and of the cost-unit in ch. 21.

by the ultimate consumer'. It could not be clearer that, contrary to what Lionel Robbins would have us believe, in Keynes's view, economics is not about any and every way to decide how best to assign scarce resources to alternative uses. It is about the buying and selling game. The rules of that game are the constitutive rules of markets. Production is for sale.

To be sure, Keynes as a human being does see a role for public employment that does not produce for sale, even though his *General Theory* and allied journal articles are about employment generated by investment for the purpose of producing goods for sale. More importantly, without going anthropological and doing a Polanyi, Keynes feels his way through an analysis of the standard economic process studied by the standard economic thinkers to a conclusion that changes everything: that process is just as likely to stop as it is to go.

Both the inducement to invest and effective demand are chronically unreliable. Keynes's pessimism about reliability resembles our larger point that commerce (whether or not it is capitalist) has no inherent tendency to feed the hungry or to heal the sick. If it does produce use values, a commercial social order does so only as a by-product of producing exchange values. One can, of course, argue that market exchange is the best way to produce use values—but that argument leads to Sen and Dreze and to unbounded organization because, obviously, sometimes market exchange is the best way and sometimes it is not.

Orthodox economics brings this obvious point in by the back door: first, by regarding markets as normal; second, by regarding alternatives to markets as made necessary by market failure; and third, by regarding efficiency in the public sector as measured by the extent to which it simulates markets.[37] Sen, Dreze and unbounded organization bring the same obvious point in by the front door: there is no initial prejudice either for or against markets; market failure is not a prerequisite to other options being considered.

Keynes is primarily an inside critic except for discussions such as his chapter 24 in *General Theory*, where he steps out of the role of economist and dons the robes of the social philosopher. Otherwise, he addresses his fellow economists and, for the most part, assumes their assumptions.

---

37. See, for examples, James Buchanan, *The Demand and Supply of Public Goods* (Chicago: Rand-McNally, 1968); Paul Samuelson, 'The Pure Theory of Public Expenditures', *Review of Economics and Statistics*, vol. 36 (1954), pp. 387–89; and Oskar Lange and Fred Taylor, *On the Economic Theory of Socialism* (Minneapolis: University of Minnesota Press, 1938).

Nevertheless, contrary to the teachings of the classical economists, for whom the level of employment is determined by employers bargaining with workers, Keynes sees the level of employment as determined by the level of output, which is determined by investment, which is determined by expectations—meaning expectations of sales at prices that cover costs and bring a profit. It thus becomes essential to Keynes's inquiry into employment levels to ask what motivates buyers to buy or not to buy. As Alvin Hansen noted in his review of *General Theory* when it was first published in 1936, for Keynes, the determinants of the level of output and therefore the level of employment are three:

1. the propensity to consume, i.e., the flip side of the liquidity preference, i.e., to what extent buyers will buy and to what extent they will not buy;
2. the marginal efficiency of capital, i.e., expected profitability, which depends on expectations of buyers buying; and
3. interest rates, which is the main area where central bank policies can hope to influence employment levels.

When one examines each of these three determinants, one finds that the causes of economic phenomena are, at bottom, psychological and cultural. In Hansen's words: 'The ultimate causal forces are therefore found outside of the price system, in the mores, customs, habits, and behaviour patterns of the people. The fundamental psychological factors are the psychological propensity to consume, the psychological expectation of future yield from capital assets, and the psychological attitude to liquidity. Psychological propensities, mores, and behaviour patterns are thus the root forces which lie back of and control consumption and investment.'[38]

Keynes, in *General Theory*, introduces the liquidity preference and defines it as a preference for holding onto cash (or assets similar to cash) instead of spending the cash to buy something.[39] He gives a list of psychological reasons why people often prefer having money over spending it. These are Keynes's own words, although I do not put them in quote marks and leave some out for simplicity and brevity:

---

38. Alvin Hansen, 'Mr. Keynes on Underemployment Equilibrium', *Journal of Political Economy*, vol. 44 (1936), p. 671.

39. Keynes further distinguishes a category of money not spent on consumption but not held in liquid form either, but rather held as illiquid assets one cannot immediately spend (*General Theory*, p. 166).

1. To build up a reserve against unforeseen contingencies.
2. To build up a reserve for foreseen future needs, such as old age, paying for the education of children.
3. To build up funds to enjoy consumption at a later date.
4. To enjoy a gradually increasing expenditure, i.e., instead of taking all one's enjoyment now.
5. To enjoy a sense of independence.
6. To secure a flexible sum of money for carrying out business projects.
7. To bequeath a fortune.
8. To satisfy pure miserliness.[40]

Keynes drew up additional lists of motives for not spending money that apply to central and local government and to business enterprises.[41]

This is perhaps enough paraphrasing of Keynes to support what I want to say, which is that, on the whole, Keynes was neither clear nor dogmatic about method. He only sometimes followed preconceived canons regarding what the scientific method is supposed to be. On the whole, he can be described (like Darwin and other great scientists) as trying to get a handle on the underlying causal powers of the generative mechanisms that in open systems tend to produce the phenomena observed.

Now let us consider a sample of Milton Friedman's rebuttals.

Early in his career, Milton Friedman carried out meticulous empirical examinations of hypotheses derived from Keynes's liquidity preference theory. He found that, contrary to Keynes's expectations, people often save about the same proportion of their incomes as their incomes go up, rather than saving larger proportions.[42] When Friedman studied in detail the spending patterns of dentists, he found that when they (or at least the dentists in the sample) are young, they tend to take out mortgages and banks tend to grant them loans on the assumption that as they advance in their careers, they will make more money. When they get older and actually do make more money, they tend to spend it at about the same rate as they spent it when they were young, and not to spend a smaller portion (and save more), as Keynes expected. Later, when he had become a tenured professor and a global celebrity, Friedman wrote:

---

40. Keynes, *General Theory*, pp. 107–8.
41. Ibid., pp. 108–9.
42. Milton Friedman, *A Theory of the Consumption Function* (Princeton, NJ: Princeton University Press, 1957). The consumption function and the liquidity preference go together, the former being a measure of how much of income is spent and the latter a measure of how much is not spent.

> One major strand of Keynesian analysis traces the implications of a particular empirical assumption about the demand for money—that its elasticity with respect to interest rates is very high, approaching infinity (in Keynes's own terms, liquidity preference is, if not absolute, approximately so). Such a situation would have very far-reaching implications: it would greatly limit the effectiveness of price flexibility in correcting unemployment; it would render changes in the quantity of money produced by open market operations impotent to affect economic conditions; it would make the effect of government deficits on income and employment independent of the way in which the deficits are financed. By now, there is wide agreement that conditions of near-absolute liquidity preference, if they occur at all, are very rare, so that this strand of Keynesian analysis has receded to the status of a theoretical curiosity.[43]

We could answer that attributing a doctrine of absolute liquidity preference to Keynes is an exaggeration. We could also say that the impotence of central banks, which Friedman in 1966 regarded as a false corollary and which Keynes was committed to asserting because it followed from his premises, has been recently observed. But we won't.

What we do want to say is that Friedman is following the precepts of his own (invalid) philosophy of science.[44] He is reading Keynes's book as if Keynes were, like Friedman, a latter-day Humean. That is to say, Friedman reads *General Theory* as a series of empirical assertions about alleged patterns of observed events. Or more likely, he reads it as a combination of such empirical assertions and philosophical speculation. He feels free to disregard the parts he reads *as* philosophical speculation. Only the testable assertions about patterns in observable data count as science. He then deduces testable hypotheses from the assertions he reads in Keynes and gathers data to test them. One might add that Friedman's political views quite likely led him to parse Keynes while looking for empirical claims likely to be false.

---

43. Milton Friedman, 'Interest Rates and the Demand for Money', *Journal of Law and Economics*, vol. 9 (1966), p. 71.

44. Milton Friedman, *Essays in Positive Economics* (Chicago: University of Chicago Press, 1953). Concepts, Friedman says, are nothing more than convenient filing folders for filing data. Science is entirely about which data 'predict to' which other data.

Our view, of course, is that what is important about Keynes is not the tip of the iceberg that Keynes tried to define in quantitative terms and measure—the preference for keeping money instead of spending it, known as the liquidity preference. What is important is the iceberg itself, which Keynes glimpsed but did not grasp: the historically and socially created social structure.

CHAPTER FIVE

The Community Work Programme as a Sea Change in Public Policy

OVERVIEW OF THE CHAPTER

1. South Africa's Second Economy Study
2. The CWP: A New Kind of Public Employment Programme
3. Activity Theory
4. Organization Workshops
5. Success of the Organization Workshop at Bokfontein
6. The Second Economy Strategy Discovers Organization Workshops
7. On the 'Community' in Community Development
8. Moral Values

1. South Africa's Second Economy Study

Many people have pointed out that South Africa's so-called second economy, the name given to the economic condition of South Africa's poorest, was misnamed.[1] South Africa has one economy, and that one economy includes some and excludes others. Nevertheless, the presidency initiated a Second Economy Study in 2008, and from September 29 to October 1, 2008, some seventy-seven civil servants and researchers met at a hotel near Pretoria to review the study. They also reported to each other on the anti-poverty programmes they were managing. They sought to understand *why* South Africa's economic and social policies were not having their intended impact on poverty and economic marginalization—why South Africa was losing and poverty was winning.[2]

---

1. For criticism of the second economy idea, see ch. 5 of John S. Saul and Patrick Bond, *South Africa: The Present as History* (London: James Currey, 2014).

2. The full name is the Second Economy Strategy Project Report, submitted to the authorities responsible for the Accelerated and Shared Growth Initiative of South Africa (AsgiSA). Our remarks are based on the presentations at the meetings mentioned. Revised versions of them can be read on the website of South Africa's Trade and Industrial Policy

Michael Alber, Barbara Tapela, Tim Hart and Mompati Baipeti reported on poverty alleviation among the nearly four million black individuals from nearly two million households practicing subsistence-oriented agriculture in the former homelands, the areas reserved for blacks under apartheid. The potential for poverty alleviation among this population appeared great; there was, in principle, underutilized capacity among this population that could be used to meet rising demand. Public funds had been spent generously to nudge commercial agriculture in the former homelands into the category of going concerns. Money was designated, for example, to jump-start the poultry business in Vhembe, a district made up of the former Venda and Gazankulu homelands at the northern end of Limpopo Province. The funds had supported small-scale broiler production based on buying chicks, raising them and then (mostly) selling the grown birds live to consumers and hawkers. The government had provided production training at the local agricultural college, as well as a quality control system to assure the viability of the chicks purchased, along with veterinary support, poultry expert support and free advertising on the radio.

The results? A survey of 9 individual and 7 group producers showed that the individual poultry projects did much better than the group poultry projects, but even with strong public support, all of the projects led to weak results.

Individual Enterprises (averages over the 9 cases studied):
- Own initial investment: 26,000 rands to build a capacity on residential land for 2,650 birds at a time (ca. 10 rands per bird)
  (The initial investment did not at first buy the capacity to fatten so many birds; it generated income that was then partly reinvested.)
- Annual production: 12,441 birds
- Annual net income per individual: 53,582 rands (R 5.71 per bird)

Group Projects (averages over the 7 cases studied)
- Initial investment, provided by pooling resources plus grant funding: 187,782 rands to build a capacity on

Strategies Institute (TIPS), www.tips.org.za, under the heading 'A Review of Second Economy Programmes'. Go to 'Focus Areas', then to 'Inequality and Economic Marginalisation', then to 'Strategy Project'.

tribal land of 1,586 birds at a time (ca. 118 rands per bird).

> (Each group began on average with 17 members, so the initial investment per participant was R 11,046; the initial investment then failed to generate income that could be re-invested).

- Annual production: 4,386 birds
- Annual net income per group: 14,738 rands (earning R 3.36 per bird)
- Annual net income per individual: 1,842 rands.[3]

> (Because of various deductions, the annual net income actually received by each participant was less than R 1,842; it was negligible.)

In short, the government's substantial investments succeeded in raising 9 individuals out of poverty and failed to raise 119 individuals out of poverty. Where do we get the number 119? By multiplying the number of groups (7) by their average initial membership (17). The success stories, apparently, were about the individuals who began with greater capital and with some residential land to put a henhouse on. It seems likely that their levels of cultural capital and motivation were also, on average, greater.

The team at the hotel near Pretoria reporting on the Vhembe project did not attempt to calculate how much the government spent to accomplish this result. Some might argue that the government support accomplished nothing because the 9 economically stronger individuals would have succeeded even without the programme, if not in poultry then in something else. We are not among them. We have no doubt that there was a causal relationship between their success and the government's backing them up with training, expertise and quality control of inputs.

The 9 successful individuals, each producing on average 12,441 birds annually, were collectively bringing nearly 112,000 birds a year to market. Now imagine that the government concluded from this and other studies that individual entrepreneurship works but group projects do not work and therefore it ought to provide resources to support 128 (119 + 9) successful individual broiler production operations in Vhembe. We say 'ought to' because if indeed many of the 119 were less business savvy than the 9,

---

3. The figure 1,842 is 14,738 divided by 8, not by 17, because on average 9 participants dropped out.

then bringing the 119 up to snuff might be in principle desirable but in practice impossible. However, assuming 128 successful broiler production operations in Vhembe were possible, they would be bringing approximately 1,592,448 (12,441 times 128) birds to market. No doubt there would be enough hungry people in Vhembe to eat all of that chicken. But this is not to say there would be enough chicken desirers in Vhembe rich enough to buy chicken at prices high enough to cover production costs and yield the producers a profit.

At the same time, the people of Vhembe able to buy chicken would be paying less per bird than they paid in earlier days, when local chicken sellers brought only 40,000 birds to market. This means that the original 9 would see their incomes fall as prices dropped due to increased supply. One would then have to ask whether the government would want to invest further to support the shipment of poultry out of Vhembe for sale elsewhere. This question is a forceful reminder of the fact that SF2, the chronic shortfall of effective demand, is a consequence of the basic social structure.

There would also be no particular reason to stop at 128 broiler producers and 1,592,448 birds per year. The government might subsidize into existence many more. At some point, the influence of this increased supply on the price the birds fetch in the market would become an issue, one that segues into other reports given at the same meeting.

Other reports told of programmes where government agencies and nonprofit organizations attempted to empower poor, small-scale producers to scale up their production in order to access larger and more distant markets—only to find that efficient large-scale production and distribution of most merchandise already existed. Kate Philip, the leading author of the Second Economy Strategy Project Report, summarized the key results in the following terms: Markets are already being supplied with maize meal, sunflower oil, flour, peanut butter, mango/litchi/orange juice, canned goods, bread, sugar, milk and dairy products, tea, beer, flour and more. They are supplied by the likes of Iwisa, Ace, White Star, Black Cat, Yum Yum, Nestlé, Procter and Gamble, Ceres, Pick n Pay, Albany, SASKO, Illovo, Tongaat-Hulett, Clover, Dairy Belle, Five Roses, South African Breweries and Premier Milling.[4] This is not surprising because wherever there is effective

---

4. 'Most manufactured or processed goods bought by poor people are mass-produced in the core economy, and are easily accessible even in the most remote *spaza* shops.' Kate Philip, 'Towards a Right to Work', a December 2010 research report available at www.tips.org.za, pp. 4–5.

demand, there is opportunity to make profits. People with more capital, more know-how and more experience than South Africa's poor were already making whatever consumers wanted and could pay for.[5]

Still other reports demonstrated that when NGOs and government try to help poor people insert themselves into the circle of suppliers to large and distant markets, the first barrier they run into is formality.[6] As Philip observed, transacting business across distances requires enforceable contracts. There must be invoices, delivery notes, receipts, bank accounts, a postal address, a telephone number, formal proof of ownership of assets to get credit, tax returns and balance sheets. Without these, auditors, the Revenue Service and distant large buyers do not regard the potential supplier as existing.[7]

A second barrier is scale. For example, marula oil, extracted from the nuts of the marula tree and a key ingredient in traditional African cosmetics, appeared to be a booming market niche not already fully occupied. But to become a supplier to Ceres (the corporation exporting marula oil to world markets), it was necessary to meet Ceres' volume requirements, which would have required coordination of the work of 4,000 women in 42 villages. Here are two more examples: The Spanish department store chain Il Corte Inglese bought 17,000 beaded bracelets in a single order from the South African supplier Gone Rural, which, in turn, buys from women's cooperatives. It took 200 beaders to make those bracelets. And Umgeni Products tried to buy 8,000 tons of sugar beans from small farmers. It could secure only 17.3 tons.

Caroline Skinner, senior researcher at African Centre for Cities, reported that surveys of the approximately one million hawkers who eke out a living on the streets of South Africa's cities highlighted needs for shelter from the elements, access to water, toilet facilities and places to store their goods.

---

5. In terms of theories to be discussed later, South African reality resembles the 'low level equilibrium' of John Maynard Keynes, where supply and demand converge at a point that leaves factors of production unemployed, more than it resembles the 'general equilibrium' of Leon Walras, where there is full employment. See John Maynard Keynes, *The General Theory of Employment, Interest, and Money* (London and New York: Macmillan, 1936), pp. 30, 236, 242–3;. Leon Walras, Éléments d'économie *politique pure* (Paris: Guillaumin, 1889), leçon 21 & leçon 25.

6. For another discussion of the formality barrier facing the poor, see Hernando De Soto, *The Other Path* (New York: HarperCollins, 1989).

7. Some experiences reported at the seminar do not confirm the thesis of Hernando De Soto, in *The Other Path,* that government bureaucracy stifles the progress of the poor. Instead they confirm another thesis of the same author: that formality is required to get past the level of a subsistence economy. When the poor are obliged and assisted by government to formalize their operations, they gain access to a whole new range of opportunities.

Among these informal traders, 65 percent reportedly earned R 1500 or less per month.[8] Many feared confiscation of their stock-in-trade by the police, reporting that it took three to nine months to replenish their stock to its former level after an arrest. (In what Thomas Kuhn would, or should, call an anomaly, while anti-poverty activists are calling for measures to ease the pain of those who have no option better than hawking on the sidewalks, the solid citizens who have money invested in businesses, pay taxes and insurance premiums and pay employees at least the legal minimum wage are calling on the police to save them from their low-overhead, price-cutting informal competitors.)

Listening to these stories of obstacles encountered in anti-poverty practices on the ground, we can hear throbbing in the background the ongoing drumbeat of the accounting identities of John Maynard Keynes. Total sales equal total purchases. Some purchases are not made because people, businesses and governments prefer liquidity. Again. SF2 shows up as a massive structural obstacle preventing the elimination of poverty with any programmes or policies whatever, as long as our efforts remain confined inside the logic of markets.[9]

A one-word summary of the three-day seminar analysing the Second Economy Study and hearing twenty-nine carefully documented reports would be 'despair'. The goal of eliminating poverty seemed to be receding rather than becoming a more achievable objective.[10] The attendees heard the striking overall statistic that in spite of their efforts between 1995 and 2005, the average monthly income of South African households whose head of household was black had declined from R 7,106 to R 6,979.[11] For the most part, anti-poverty programmes were an order of magnitude too small

---

8. The data showing 65% of street traders (of whom 60% are women) making R 1500 or less per month come from a 2007 South African government labour force survey. This would be, in 2007 numbers, approximately 165 US dollars, 110 British pounds or 128 Euros per month.

9. Keynes observed: 'But we must not conclude that the mean position [i.e., the mean level of unemployment] thus determined by "natural" tendencies, namely by those tendencies which are likely to persist, failing measures expressly designed to correct them, is therefore established by laws of necessity. The unimpeded rule of the above conditions is a fact of observation concerning the world as it is or has been, and not a necessary principle which cannot be changed.' *General Theory*, p. 254.

10. See also Nicoli Nattrass and Jeremy Seekings, 'Democracy and Distribution in Highly Unequal Societies: The Case of South Africa', *The Journal of Modern African Studies*, vol. 39 (2001), pp. 471–498, http://journals.cambridge.org/action/displayAbstract?fromPage=onlineandaid =87361&fileId=S00 22278X01003688, accessed May 2015.

11. This number comes from the report to the seminar by the Development Policy Research Unit of the School of Economics of the University of Cape Town. One presumes that it is adjusted for inflation.

to address the problems they were ostensibly designed to solve.[12] Kate Philip and Ebrahim-Khalil Hassen, in their review of second economy programs, drove home this point with the following numbers:[13]

Number of unemployed seeking work	4,400,000
Number of unemployed discouraged and thus not seeking work	3,218,000
Total unemployed	7,618,000
Number of people employed but earning less than R 1,000 per month	4,025,000
Total either unemployed or earning less than R 1,000 per month	11,643,000

Here the underlying generative structural cause is SF1. The structural reason why there were, and are, millions of South Africans without decent work is that it is not profitable to hire them and pay them decent wages. Employment is generated by investment, which is generated by expectations of profit, which is generated by expectations of sales at prices high enough to cover costs and also provide a margin of profit. When employment so generated did not materialize in the (not atypical) years studied (2006–7), the government's attempts to compensate for market failure were pitifully small.

> The Expanded Public Works Programme (EPWP), the already existing public employment programme in South Africa, had delivered 316,814 'work opportunities'[14] (gigs lasting a few weeks), equivalent to 70,000 full-time jobs.

12. This point emerged implicitly throughout the seminar and was made explicit by Kate Philip in several papers, including her January 2009 research report, 'Second Economy Strategy: Addressing Inequality and Economic Marginalisation', available at www.tips.org.za. The phrase 'second economy' refers, roughly speaking, to the economy of the poor. 'Most national programmes explicitly targeting the second economy are not designed to impact at the scale required to make a difference at a societal level—many have targets of below 50,000 people, with few actually reaching this level' (p. 3).

13. These are 2006 numbers cited in a 2008 paper that served as background for the conclusions of the September 29–October 1 seminar. The total population of South Africa in 2006 was 47.4 million. Kate Philip and Ebrahim-Khalil Hassen, 'The Review of Second Economy Programs: An Overview for the Presidency's Fifteen Year Review,' January 2008, available at www.tips.org.za.

14. As of March 2007; ibid., p. 9.

Number of community care-givers receiving stipends	68,178[15]
Jobs created in environmental conservation programmes	13,800[16]
JOBS database employment intermediation job placements	91[17]
MAFISA pilot phase loans to small farmers	5,170[18]

And so on. The authors conclude: 'While some 12 million people have been identified as broadly within the second economy, many programmes reviewed here struggle to reach 50,000 people; those that reach the 100,000s are the good performers, with only housing delivery exceeding a million.'[19]

While a one-word summary of the three-day seminar would be 'despair', a two-word summary would be 'think again'. Housing provides a place to begin to think again. It was a bright star in the dark night sky, albeit one where much remained to be done. Housing programmes were large enough to address the problems they were designed to solve. The households registered as already beneficiaries of housing programmes numbered 1.9 million, with 2.3 million houses either completed or in process.[20] Notably, government support in the housing sector was preceded and complemented by a massive NGO-supported, self-help grassroots social movement sometimes called the People's Housing Process (PHP).[21]

Although the analogy is not perfect, we suggest that when outcomes depend on market uptake,[22] anti-poverty programmes are more like herding cats, while when outcomes are primarily a function of nonmarket institutions whose objective is getting the job done, anti-poverty programmes are more like herding cattle. Cats go where they want to go. Cattle go more or less where they are driven. In the government-supported housing projects,

---

15. As of the end of August 2007; ibid., p. 9.
16. Ibid., p. 10.
17. Ibid., p. 10.
18. Micro Agricultural Financial Institution of South Africa, figure for year ended March 2007; ibid., p. 14. The default rate on the loans was running at 30 to 40%.
19. Ibid., p. 20.
20. Ibid., p 17.
21. The PHP is discussed in Marie Huchzermeyer, 'Housing the Poor: Negotiated Housing Policy in South Africa', *Habitat International*, vol. 25 (2001), pp. 303–331.
22. 'The Review highlighted that so far, government has not had great success where outcomes depend on a market response, particularly in marginal economic contexts.' Kate Philip, 'Second Economy Strategy: Addressing Inequality and Economic Marginalisation', TIPS January 2009 research report, available at www.tips.org.za, p. 3. The strategy proposed in this report was approved by the South African cabinet in the same month (January 2009).

families joined the PHP, pounded nails and poured cement to build their own and their neighbours' houses because they wanted roofs over their heads; the NGO's donors gave money because they wanted to see roofs over other people's heads; the government's budget processes deliberately delivered capacity to build houses.

During South Africa's first years of democracy the government's blows against poverty, in the form of increasing the supply of qualified labour, goods or services, expecting there would be market demand for them, were ineffective. But when the government acknowledged that providing houses for the poorest of the poor involved partnering with private-sector construction companies and banks, NGOs and the poor themselves—all mobilized around public funding complementing other funding sources—then 2.3 million houses were built. This is thinking again. This is aligning across sectors to serve the common good. This is unbounded organization.

Saying that government programmes often work best when their success does not depend on a desired market response is not saying that markets do nothing to fight poverty. Adam Smith was incomplete but not wrong when he found some causes of the wealth of nations in the division of labour and in capital accumulation. Rather, in the case of South Africa today, markets (in tandem with other institutions) are effective in raising out of poverty perhaps two-thirds of the population. However, when it comes to the remaining third and to those among the two-thirds perched in barely tolerable material insecurity, markets run out of steam and need supplementation by other institutions. As Amartya Sen put the matter, even when markets work well, they need to be regulated and supplemented by other institutions, many of them nonmercantile.

Transitioning to a world that works for everybody is necessarily a participatory process. Its goals include dignity as well as security, the mental health of everybody[23] and social integration that excludes no one. 'No poverty' means all of that. We are confident that unbounded organization

---

23. Building on the biological philosophy of Georges Canguilhem and on the activity theory psychology pioneered by Lev Vygotsky, Yves Clot has brilliantly demonstrated the need for healthy work to lead a healthy life in modern society. Clot makes clear the futility of seeking human happiness through social grants and income guarantees that merely put money in empty pockets. His research has implications not only for the precariat and the jobless, but also and mainly for those who have steady employment, echoing Marx's dream that in an emancipated future, work will support the full and free development of every personality. Yves Clot, *Travail et pouvoir d'agir* (Paris: PUF, 2008); *Fonction psychologique du travail* (Paris: PUF, 1999).

and exponentially increasing technological progress[24] can turn poverty in all its dimensions into a subject children learn about in history classes but do not personally experience.

The kind of thinking[25] done at the September 2008 meetings near Pretoria led to a sea change for the Community Work Programme (CWP), which up to that time had been a pilot programme with donor funding implemented in only three municipalities: Munsieville, Bokfontein and Alfred Nzo.[26] The pilots were under the care of a special projects team in South Africa's Department of Social Development, whose members were Oupa Ramachela, Sidwell Mokgothu (who is also a Methodist pastor and theologian) and Nkere Skosana. The ubiquitous Kate Philip acted as the liaison between the special projects team and the presidency. After the meetings, the CWP became a national flagship programme of the South African government. We quote here most of two slides that were central to Philip's concluding presentation:

> Proposal for three linked national programmes:
> 1. Significantly expand public employment: EPWP 2 [the Expanded Public Works Programme's second phase]. Including the Community Work Programme as an anchor strategy.
> 2. Transform informal settlements into sustainable neighbourhoods and secure well-located urban land for planned new settlement.
> 3. Support a national household food-security programme called 'Let's Get Growing' [proliferating urban gardens]. And focus on subsistence agriculture as subsistence agriculture,[27] and livelihoods, water harvesting, etc.

---

24. Peter Diamandis and Steven Kotler, *Abundance: The Future is Better Than You Think* (New York: Free Press, 2012).

25. Here, 'kind of thinking' is meant to connote the ideas in the TIPS documents we have been citing, other related TIPS documents we have not had occasion to cite, the ideas expressed in the seminar being showcased, and the fact that the 'Second Economy Strategy' published by TIPS and presented at the seminar was three months later endorsed by the Cabinet of the South African government.

26. The pilot programme was funded by the UK's Department for International Development (DfID). The three sites were administered by two NGOs, the first two named by Seriti Institute and the third by Teba Development, headed respectively by Gavin Andersson and by David Cooper. The CWP is now managed by the Department of Cooperative Governance and Traditional Affairs, COGTA.

27. I.e., do not ignore subsistence agriculture or treat it as a practice that should be

These programmes are not dependent on markets to achieve their intended outcomes. But
- they all stimulate local demand and scope for local enterprise activity, i.e., help to 'thicken' local markets;
- they all engage people in economic activity that builds assets and/or incomes, networks and social capital; and
- all three are enabled by existing policy frameworks and can start with little delay.

2. The CWP: A New Kind of Public Employment Programme

The history of public employment programmes goes back at least to June 16, 1817, in Great Britain, when royal assent was given to a British act of Parliament to authorize the issue of Exchequer Bills and the Advance of Money up to a limit of 1.75 million pounds for the employment of the poor in Great Britain by Public Works and Fisheries.[28] Many public employment programmes were motivated by the Great Depression of the 1930s. Many more since then have ranged from temporary work designed to provide hands-on experience and induce an attitude change that would make the unemployed employable, to true employment guarantees, where the government becomes the employer of last resort (e.g., Sweden's employment guarantee, which we discuss in chapter 7). The growth of public employment programmes has been accompanied by a growing academic literature studying them. The current world economic crisis, beginning in 2008, has given rise to new programmes and to innovative approaches.[29] South Africa's Community Work Programme is one of them.

When South Africa's anti-poverty experts decided to emphasize a new kind of public employment programme, the Community Work Programme (CWP),[30] they were aware that many might not agree with or even understand their decision, even though it was based on solid evidence and reasoning. Most voters, most Members of Parliament and some economists tended

eliminated and replaced with commercial agriculture.

28. M.W. Finn, 'The Poor Employment Act of 1817', *Economic History Review*, n.s., vol. 14 (1961), p. 82.

29. E.g., Lieuw-Kie-Song and Kate Philip, 'Mitigating a Job Crisis: Innovations in Public Employment Programmes', *ILO Employment Report No. 6*, July 2010.

30. The name is not new. There are community work programmes in several countries. The story of how the decision came about is told by Rejoice Shumba in *Social Entrepreneurship and South Africa's Community Work Programme: A Critical Reflection on Innovation and Scale*, unpublished PhD thesis, University of Johannesburg, 2014.

to regard a public employment programme as a temporary stopgap until the day when the magic of the market could offer everyone private-sector employment or all the poor had gone to school long enough to qualify for employment. Or they regarded it as relief for people whose disabilities make them unemployable. However, the CWP was intended as, and has become, more than a stopgap measure. As the flagship of South Africa's mix of anti-poverty programmes, the CWP has, so far at least, become acceptable to mainstream common sense while also stretching it. The strategy stated in the wrap-up of the 2008 seminar was to move beyond the old liberal and state-centred paradigms and toward an unbounded organizational paradigm. It was to fight against poverty with weapons that do not require market responses while injecting more money into local grassroots markets.

Singing in the groove of Amartya Sen and illustrating our unbounded idea, the CWP is not about being promarket or anti-market but rather about aligning private-sector and public-sector actors in creative combinations. The CWP also aligns with another, third sector: civil society. The CWP is funded by the national government, but it is run by NGOs that are accountable to local governments and community leaders. The CWP forms alliances with schools, hospitals, water companies, reforestation schemes—with whatever institutions are doing good and could use more hands to help them do more good. This is unbounded alignment. This is 'inter-sectoral collaboration, individuals linking between their own organizations, coalition-building, cross-cultural activities and involvement by all segments of society'.[31] This is Karl Popper's idea of an 'open society' where untrammelled scientific inquiry and democratic processes gradually lead to the improvement of institutions.[32] This is John Dewey's idea of an 'experimental society' where every institution is treated as a hypothesis to be tested and revised in the light of experience.[33]

The concept of unbounded organization suggests that the path to curing the defects of capitalism—notably, the defect of making the lives of the many physically dependent on the profits of the few—is a plural route, like

---

31. Gavin Andersson, 'Looking Back to the Future: Conversations on Unbounded Organisation', Dark Roast Occasional Paper Series Number 12 (Cape Town: Isandla Institute, 2000), p. 4.

32. Karl Popper, *The Open Society and its Enemies* (London: Routledge, 1944). For reservations qualifying Popper's approach see Howard Richards and Joanna Swanger, *Dilemmas of Social Democracies* (Lanham, MD: Rowman and Littlefield), 2006, ch. 9, 'Karl Popper's Vienna'.

33. John Dewey, *The Public and its Problems* (New York: Henry Holt, 1927).

a river with many tributaries and many deltas. The CWP comes on the scene to multiply means of livelihood, not to consolidate them into one or a few. It was started when South Africa learned from bitter experience that jump-starting new private businesses with public money does not solve the problem. But it did not come on the scene to discourage new private business. The CWP is expected to contribute to local economic development.

Say's Law is not true, but it is also not entirely false. The CWP is not either/or; it is both/and. It is really true (as Say said) that when local people have more skills and are more enterprising, they can provide each other with goods and services by exchanging their products in local markets. In poor communities, liquidity preference is low; little money drops out of circulation, leaving few frustrated sellers without buyers. And when a community supports its local businesses and self-employed service providers, the local benefits of the multiplier effect from outside funding are high.

A common consciousness-raising exercise in community development starts by showing, with real, specific numbers, that the day after a large chunk of cash comes into town in the form of government grants to women with children, the same money leaves town. Once this is understood, people start to draw conclusions about how to defend themselves. They become motivated to work together and support one another to become a more self-reliant and resilient community. The capitalist sector of the economy shrinks. The people's sector grows.

To learn more about how and why the CWP is an innovative programme, we turn to one of its three pilots, the one at Bokfontein in North West Province. This settlement was born in trauma. In 2005, people who had been living near Hartbeesport Dam were evicted to clear space for upscale housing. They were relocated to bare land near Bokfontein that did not even have a water supply. They lost everything, even the graves of their ancestors, when their cemetery at Hartbeesport was bulldozed. In 2006, people living at Melodi were also forcibly evicted. They were accused of illegally occupying land designated by the government for building low-cost housing. They too were relocated to Bokfontein, dumped into the same space where the people from Hartbeesport were already living. Those who had arrived first regarded the newcomers as intruders. Violence ensued. It was violence that expressed the deep psychological wounds of people who had been humiliated and denied their human rights. It was also violent competition for scarce resources needed to satisfy basic necessities of life, such as the water that was trucked in by the municipality on an irregular and unreliable schedule.

Gavin Andersson, Owen Stuurman, Leon Mdiya, Langi Malamba and Gwashi Manavhela from the Seriti Institute began community consultations at Bokfontein in early 2008. They started by going around talking and listening. They listened to community leaders. They held weekly public assemblies for three months. In addition to the formal meetings, they did informal interviews, swapped stories, told and listened to jokes and gave talks. They sat on stones, bricks and jam-tins, moving with everyone else to stay in the shade as the sun moved. They heard about the pathologies and the strengths, the dreams and the complaints. They floated ideas as well as questions, and they got deep into dialogues.

They went on 'scoping walks' to see what resources had already been brought in from outside and to think about how resources could be applied more effectively. Taking a cue from *activity theory*, they talked with all those who were part of the *activity system*, including key people at mining houses, in municipal government and in political parties, local churches and charities.

The CWP has its roots in activity theory. Its methods were applied in the Organization Workshops that were the precursors of the CWP and in the CWP pilots at Bokfontein and Munsieville. In many of its versions today, activity theory is called cultural historical activity theory, or CHAT.[34] The following section lays out some of activity theory's main features.

◆ ◆ ◆

> 'It has changed my life in big way. I mean there are STI, HIV and all those diseases; you know sometimes you risk your life and sleep with someone that you don't love just so that he can give you money. Since I started getting a job, knowing that I get something at the end of the month, that stopped. . . . So this job has changed my life. I can go to the bank and withdraw some money.'
>
> — FEMALE CWP PARTICIPANT, RANDFONTEIN CDI

---

34. Gavin Andersson, Raff Carmen, Ivan Labra and Howard Richards, organization workshop, 'Beyond the Workplace: Large Groups, Activity and the Shared Object', *Mind, Culture and Activity*, vol. 25 (2018), pp. 86–99. For some recent research in South Africa using a CHAT approach, see Vivienne Bozalek et al. (eds), *Activity Theory, Authentic Learning and Emerging Technologies* (London: Routledge, 2013).

3. Activity Theory

Activity theory is a research tradition in psychology and allied social sciences begun by the Russian psychologist Lev Vygotsky (1896–1934). Vygotsky disagreed with the then-prevalent positivist and behaviourist approaches to psychology, championed in their Russian versions by Ivan Pavlov. Vygotsky disagreed, to cite an important example, with their claim (or tacit assumption) that words in general, and the terms of a scientific theory in particular, could be defined by reference to the facts they stood for. Instead Vygotsky *saw* words, signs and symbols *as* tools mediating humans' interactions with each other and with the environment. The activities mediated by the tools, called mediating artefacts, precede the facts allegedly mirrored by the words, numbers or logical symbols referring to them. Activities generate events that generate what the facts are *seen as*.

Vygotsky distinguishes a technical tool (such as a hammer) from a psychological tool (such as a word or symbol or, more generally, a sign):

> A technical tool . . . serves as a conductor of humans' influence on the objects of their activity. It is directed toward the external world; it must stimulate some changes in the object; it is a means of humans' external activity, directed toward the subjugation of nature.
>
> A psychological tool . . . changes nothing in the object of a psychological operation. A sign is a means for psychologically influencing behaviour—either the behaviour of another or one's own behaviour; it is a means of internal activity, directed toward the mastery of humans themselves. A sign is inwardly directed.[35]

Here, at the very foundation of practice, thought and science, culture and history come in. The meanings of words and symbols are cultural and historical through and through. They are embedded in activities through and through. An activity system evolves historically. It also evolves biologically and therefore, in a sense, prehistorically. Vygotsky conceived the study of the evolution of life and the study of the human species in particular to be indispensable prerequisites for the study of psychology. The evolution that happened during times prior to the appearance of human beings in

---

35. Lev Vygotsky, quoted by James Wertsch, *The Concept of Activity in Soviet Psychology* (Armonk, NY: M.E. Sharpe, 1981), p. 25.

many ways continued to shape behaviour in historic times and still shapes behaviour today.

The widely applied approach of Yrjö Engeström, a third-generation activity theorist, *sees* an activity system *as* including six key elements:

1. the subject;
2. the mediating artefact (a sign or other tool);
3. the object;
4. the rules;
5. the community;
6. the division of labour.

Each of these is a topic that has been widely discussed. Here we focus briefly on the object. The object may be a physical thing that motivates and structures activity, as a soccer ball motivates and structures play among youths. Or it may be a purpose—the conscious objective of an individual subject or the social function of the activity of which the individual actors may be unaware or only dimly aware. In A. N. Leontiev's famous example of a tribe going on a hunt, some hunters may be beaters while the whole tribe on the hunt is the collective subject, whose object is acquiring food. The animal that is the prey can be regarded as the object of the hunt, but so can eating. In our view, one of the key insights of activity theory is that several such ordinary uses of the word 'object' (or cognate words in other languages) denote intertwined aspects of practices that can usefully be called activities.

This briefest of brief introductions to activity theory is enough to show that it casts a wider net than economics. In CWP's prehistory—and in the minds of the team doing community consultation at Bokfontein—there was a social psychology rooted in culture, history and biology in the broadest sense. Economics, in contrast, can be *seen as* the calculus of a particular social structure and cultural-historical norm. Said differently: activity theory smacks of unboundedness, while economics smacks of boundedness.[36] In its smacking of unboundedness, activity theory lends itself to seeing the ethical dimension of an *act*.

---

36. Here we risk some confusion since there is a tradition in the study of organizations that regards administrative decision-making as necessarily employing a 'bounded rationality' because of limited information, which would make economic models, in contrast, 'unbounded' when they assume an ideal of complete information. See Herbert Simon, *Administrative Behavior: A Study of Decision-Making Processes in Administrative Organizations* (New York: Free Press, 1947).

Seeing sales as acts makes sales more than facts that *cause* economic phenomena. Sales to willing buyers can also become the ethical criterion that determines what ought to be produced. Sale is a juridical act. H. L. A. Hart called it an 'act-in-the-law'.[37] A sale price may be treated as a proxy for 'value', where value is thought of as customer satisfaction and ultimately as welfare.[38] But in terms of operational definitions, it is not someone's enjoyment or any physically beneficial good that counts. What matters is the legal determination that there was a certain kind of act, a sale.[39] Title to the merchandise passed from seller to buyer. Title to consideration for the merchandise (normally money) passed from buyer to seller. Economic statistics count sales. They also count other juridical entities such as debts. Economics can be *seen as* the calculus of an ethic formalized in a particular historically constructed juridical framework.

Activity theory lends itself to unbounded thinking. Partly because cultural and historical evolution is built into its premises, it has become a social psychology of choice for communities of practice devoted to transforming societies dominated by a narrow economic ethic.[40] For example, recently in South Africa, CHAT was applied in designing service learning for architecture students.[41] They built a classroom and landscaped its surroundings for a semi-rural farming community, and they were as happy with their service-learning nonmercantile experience as the schoolchildren were with their new classroom.

◆ ◆ ◆

> 'The people who look after the environment like the CWP volunteers play an important role in our community. They look after our lives. We live in unhealthy conditions. When people are sick, they make sure that we breathe fresh air instead of always breathing dirty air, living around flying plastic bags, and

---

37. H. L. A. Hart, *The Concept of Law* (Oxford: Clarendon Press, 1961).

38. 'Value', however, more properly includes even in strictly economic terms the consumer surplus and producer surplus, defined respectively as the difference between the maximum the consumer was willing to pay and the lower price actually paid, and the difference between the minimum the producer was willing to sell for and the higher price the product actually sold for.

39. For this reason, Robert Solow held that 'value' was a metaphysical concept that should be banished from economics.

40. Peter Hoffman-Kipp, 'Model Activity Systems: Dialogic Teacher Learning for Social Justice Teaching', *Teacher Education Quarterly*, vol. 30 (2003), pp. 27–39.

41. James Garroway and Jolanda Morkel, 'Learning in Sites of Practice Through a CHAT Lens', in Bozalet et al., *Activity Theory*, ch. 2, pp. 22–31.

also the smell of dead dogs. Much as there are those who are polluting our environment, there are those who are doing good by cleaning up the area. Keeping our environment clean, they are trying to do good.'

– CWP PARTICIPANT, RANDFONTEIN CDI

4. Organization Workshops

The team from the Seriti Institute at Bokfontein applied activity theory in their quest for social transformation of a large number of people over a long time span, working from the premise that activity, more than anything else, changes thinking and behaviour. Accordingly, the team planned an organization workshop[42] in Bokfontein. They presented the idea to the community and discussed it in depth with key parties. Everybody in the settlement at Bokfontein was invited, and 180 participated.

The basic idea of an organization workshop is that the subjects (participants) learn organization through activities with the objects (raw materials, tools, equipment) and engagement with mediating artefacts (notably, daily lectures on the theory of organization). Subject, object and mediating artefacts operate like a rotating engine, producing and reproducing new mediational artefacts (new ways to use tools, signs, symbols), small communities working at different levels (such as committees), general assembly meetings, work plans, enterprise by-laws and rules. In the process, the enterprise constructed by the participants itself becomes an object. The psychological process is triggered by changed physical objects. It is mediated by symbolic processes, including the lectures and discussions.[43] Changes in activity change both subjects and objects.

---

42. Organization workshops were first developed by Clodomir Santos de Morais in Brazil in the early 1960s. They have been widely used in Latin America and sub-Saharan Africa. To learn more about organization workshops, see Raff Carmen and Miguel Sobrado (eds.), *A Future for the Excluded: Job Creation and Income Generation by the Poor* (London: ZED Books, 2000), also available as an online book; Gavin Andersson, *The Activity Theory Approach 2000*, available at www.seriti.org.za; and Gavin Andersson and Howard Richards, *Unbounded Organization in Community* (Lake Oswego, OR: Dignity Press, 2015).

43. To learn more about how activity theory relates to organization workshops, see especially the introduction to organization workshops by Iván and Isabel Labra, *The Organization Workshop Method*, 2012, at www.seriti.org, as well as the section on the organization workshops on the Unbounded Organization site www.unboundedorganization.org; and Gavin Andersson, Raff Carmen, Iván Labra and Howard Richards, 'Organisation Workshop. Beyond the Workplace: Large Groups, Activity and the Shared Object', *Mind, Culture, and Activity*, vol. 25 (2018), pp. 86–99.

The three preliminary steps of an organization workshop are as follows:

The first step is an invitation from a community. The organization workshop approach works best when a community knows it has problems to tackle (or major opportunities to respond to), is willing to work to resolve its problems, is united enough to agree on the invitation and has heard enough about organization workshops to want to learn more.

The second step is 'scoping'. The organization workshop planning team observes the site and finds out what people think needs to be done and what could be done. They analyse work activities; identify the required raw materials, tools and equipment; procure and store everything that will be needed on the first day of the organization workshop; and create a comprehensive inventory list.

The third step is to identify, register and assemble the participants.

On the first day of the organization workshop, when the people are gathered together for the opening, the workshop director makes a speech something like this:

- This is not a traditional course. It is a course for adults who can assume responsibility for their actions. *It is a workshop in the true sense: You will work and be able to earn money for your work. The main focus of the workshop is for you to learn about organization, and this means practical work.*
- When we leave you, in five minutes, you must organize yourselves into an enterprise. You can organize any way you like. Draw up your rules for making decisions and for managing money, so these are clear from the start. You will probably have to show these rules to the bank manager if you want to open a bank account.
- When you are organized, we will hand over to you all the tools, machinery, vehicles and offices. We will require the representatives of the newly created enterprise to sign for each item by means of a detailed inventory, and if anything is missing or broken at the end of the organization workshop, you will have to pay for it. Your enterprise will also have access to certain support services, such as a typist, driver, childcare specialist, et cetera.
- We have put up a description of each of the many jobs available for you to work on. Don't do any work unless you have a contract with us. We will pay at market rates for each job, so if you organize well you will be able to carry some money home at the end.

- Participants are expected to work a minimum of six hours a day, and you can work longer if you wish.
- The consumption of alcohol or any kind of intoxicant is prohibited.
- We have organized food for the first three days while you form your organization. After the third day, we will hand over the kitchen to you. You will have to choose some among you to cook, and some of the money you earn will have to be spent on food.
- Our crew will deliver lectures on the theory of organization every day for one and a half hours for the first sixteen days. Attendance is compulsory for all participants, and a register of attendance will be kept. The crew will respond to requests for further training courses that your enterprise deems necessary and asks for in writing.
- Everything that occurs during the workshop needs to be recorded by you in a final document or memoir book. This must be reproduced so each participant can take home a copy at the end of the workshop, along with a copy of *Notes to a Theory of Organization* by Clodomir de Morais, which will be the content for the first lectures.)
- All participants are here on a voluntary basis. Anyone who does not like these conditions of the workshop can leave now. If you don't leave now, then you can only leave the site once your enterprise has established its rules.

5. Success of the Organization Workshop at Bokfontein

In the process of organizing themselves for the organization workshop, the people at Bokfontein bonded as a community. The crowning glory of their deliberations was a decision to sink a borehole to tap into an underground aquifer. A team of specialists drilled the borehole. The participants laid the piping. At last, the community had a reliable supply of water. In the process, they empowered themselves to administer the provision of water for the people of Bokfontein on a daily basis. The water was also used to irrigate a one-hectare community garden established through the organization workshop.

During the organization workshop an old man died because the shacks were huddled so tightly together that an ambulance could not pass between them to get to his. This prompted the settlers to sit down to work out what kind of community they wanted to create. Two realizations emerged: an access road was needed to allow vehicles to enter the settlement, and everyone was craving space. So they designed a new physical layout for the settlement.

Twenty-four shacks were relocated so the participants could create a road. Eleven more shacks were moved to allow space for Polar Park, a large recreation area next to the one-hectare garden. An old farmhouse in the middle of Polar Park was converted into a multipurpose centre, and near it a new thatched house was built as a functions venue that residents could book for gatherings. Then they organized at the multi-purpose venue a day-care centre to free up women so they could seek income-earning activities, as well as an after-school drop-in centre where school children could get a good meal and find a quiet place to do homework.

In addition to these hands-on work projects, the people of Bokfontein analysed the community's main problems—crime, alcohol abuse and divisiveness—and organized themselves to cope with them. The community was divided not only between the first arrivals from Hartbeesport and the second arrivals from Melodi but also between South Africans and foreigners from Zimbabwe, Malawi, Mozambique, Lesotho and other places who had left their homelands hoping for a better life in South Africa. Some had arrived with the people from Hartbeesport, some with the people from Melodi, and some came later.

The prejudices that divided the community were discussed publicly. People were encouraged to reflect on their life histories, which in most cases had fostered deep-seated anger. They also learned to frame their personal stories as parts of a larger and longer story. Specifically, they learned that just over a century earlier, Europeans had divided Africa and created its present national boundaries. They saw the senselessness of infighting over identities created by boundaries so new and so arbitrary. They came to share a vision of working together for peace and prosperity. They built positive identities around communication, collective responsibility, high self-esteem and empowerment.[44] To celebrate their newly forged unity and identity, the participants gave their community a new name: Tshaba di Maketse, 'The Nations Are Amazed'.

As it happened, the night before the workshop's closing ceremony, peace in South Africa was shattered by the first wave of xenophobic violence in

---

44. This high praise for the results of the organization workshop and subsequently the CWP at Bokfontein comes from Malose Langa, in his qualitative study of Bokfontein included in *The Smoke That Calls* (Johannesburg: CSVR, 2017), quoted from ch. 1. See also Malose Langa and Karl von Holdt, 'Bokfontein Amazes the Nations', *New South African Review* (Johannesburg: Wits University Press, 2012).

townships on the outskirts of Johannesburg and elsewhere (which we analysed in chapter 1). However, during the closing ceremony, the community at Bokfontein sang songs from Malawi, Mozambique, Zimbabwe and Lesotho, as well as South Africa.

♦ ♦ ♦

> I stay away from funny things like taverns. In our community the youth is under pressure of getting drunk.'
>
> — CWP PARTICIPANT, JOE MOROLONG LOCAL MUNICIPALITY, NORTHERN CAPE PROVINCE CDI

6. The Second Economy Strategy Discovers Organization Workshops

By mid-2008, the Second Economy Strategy Project was hard at work complying with its mandate: examining why South Africa's economic policies were not having the intended impact on poverty and economic marginalization and what to do about it. The chair of the project, Kate Philip, had attended an international conference on public employment programmes at Addis Ababa, Ethiopia, and had come home thinking particularly about India's Mahatma Gandhi Rural Employment Guarantee Act and about the possibilities for the innovative expansion of public employment in South Africa.

She was very aware of criticisms made of the already existing Expanded Public Works Programme (EPWP)—that it was too state-driven and not enough community-driven.[45] Already in 2007, the concept of the CWP was being incubated at Trade and Industrial Policy Strategies (TIPS), a research organization Philip worked for.[46] It was in this context that Philip visited Munsieville and observed how the organization workshop there worked. She recalls: 'As I sat there, that was the lightbulb moment. . . . What I was struggling with in this nascent CWP concept, like how do you operationalize this thing, how do you organize the work—it just struck me that the Organization Workshop actually offered a tool that could bring

---

45. T. I. Nzimakwe, 'Addressing Unemployment and Poverty through Public Works Programmes in South Africa', *International NGO Journal*, vol. 3 (2008), pp. 207–212.

46. Trade and Industrial Policy Strategies (TIPS) is an independent, nonprofit research institution (see www.tips.org.za). Kate Philip was then the manager of its focus area on inequality and economic inclusion. The initial launch had support from the presidency and the Department of Social Development, and some international funding from the UK government.

communities together and create task management and organizational skills around work that could act as the inception of a community-based public employment programme, where there is a high-level of community direction to that programme.'[47]

One of the problems with organizational workshops was that participants were sometimes left stranded after having learned how to organize themselves effectively to accomplish useful work. Some participants during organization workshops had successfully started co-ops or microenterprises, but many found no buyers for their services when the organization workshop was over. The solution to that problem was the CWP. In our terms, 'sharing the surplus' came together with an effective community development method. Funding the CWP moved resources to where they were needed. They were needed to create dignified livelihoods for those who were structurally unemployed due to the chronic insufficiency of demand for labour power (SF2) in a world where that chronic insufficiency was made worse by advanced technology—in this case, by the mechanization of South Africa's mines.[48]

The organization workshop tradition could deliver to the CWP decades of practical wisdom about combining public employment with community development. These two quickly came together, as the closing ceremonies of the organization workshops at Bokfontein and Munsieville dovetailed with their graduates' initiations as participants in CWP pilot sites.

♦ ♦ ♦

Two ex-convicts who are participants at Ekurluheni hope to use the CWP as a platform to share their experiences. They write:

> 'Since joining the CWP we are now able to use the ATM. Our financial life is changing, and the programme has assisted us to stay away from criminal activities. We even want a platform in the programme to help other participants by sharing the experiences of being in jail and encouraging them to stay away from jail because it is not the right place to be for anyone.'
>
> – CDI

---

47. Kate Philip, quoted in Rejoice Shumba, *Social Entrepreneurship and South Africa's Community Work Programme: A Critical Reflection on Innovation and Scale.* Unpublished PhD thesis, University of Johannesburg, 2014, p. 89. Shumba shows in her thesis that the beginning of the CWP was the fruit of the efforts of a small group properly described as social entrepreneurs.

48. Kate Philip, *Markets on the Margins* (Woodbridge, UK: James Currey, 2018).

7. On the 'Community' in Community Development

The word 'community' came to Bokfontein when the settlement became a pilot site for the *Community* Work Programme. When the word arrived, however, the practice of community development was already present. The people were already running a cooperative water company. They had already relocated shacks to create a road and shared spaces, and their diet of mealy meal (white corn flour, the staple of South Africa's poor) was already complemented with vegetables they grew themselves. Most important, there had been a spiritual change. The spirit of animosity and recrimination had gone; the spirit of alignment for the common good had arrived.

What happened at Bokfontein illustrates what community does in this South African context and what the founders of the CWP expected it to do. Now we resume our discussion of the concept of community (from the section 'Economy and Community: Community as Guiding Star' in chapter 2), which requires us to specify what we mean by 'moral realism' and why we mean it.

Our use of community as a foil to economy is explicitly designed to leverage community to save the biosphere by making capitalism governable. The leveraging we propose aspires to be a tautology: in the universe of social discourse and practice, if community is what economy is not, then community is the place to seek what economy lacks. From this viewpoint, counting volunteering for community service as a plus in staff performance evaluations is readily *seen as* something a socially responsible company should do, as is recycling the social surplus to fund dignity for people whom the economy humiliates. Companies should not be accumulating profits just for the sake of accumulation—or because of some far-fetched utilitarian ethical argument that endless accumulation maximizes the greatest good for the greatest number. They should be creating a surplus that makes it possible to feed the hungry, give drink to the thirsty, clothe the naked, house the homeless, care for the sick, rehabilitate the imprisoned and give a decent burial to the dead.

Writers classified as 'communitarian', such as Amitai Etzioni, Alasdair Macintyre, Michael Walzer and Michael Sandel, do not appear to think of modern society as driven by an overriding imperative to accelerate a chronically weak inducement to invest. The idea that social and ecological objectives are often sacrificed because whatever else a government does, it must please investors is not, or is not yet, part of the communitarian analysis of the problems communitarianism is designed to solve. We want to make it so. On the other hand, Marx's idea that what he called the prehistory[49] of the human species will end and the history of humanity properly so-called will begin when abstract exchange value ceases to dominate concrete use value can be regarded as already present in communitarian thinking. We want to showcase this insight. We also want to marry the physical bottom line—concrete use values like driving down the cost of solar panels to contribute to reversing global warming—to the rising influence today, among mainstream management thought leaders,[50] of thinking that inspires mission-driven organizations and purpose-driven lives.

In David Harvey we find a thinker who resonates with many communitarian values and also *does* think in terms of regimes of accumulation. Economics (unfortunately) drives culture. Neoliberalism did not happen just because the monetarists at Chicago, generously paid by the Olin Foundation, out-talked and out-published the underfunded Keynesians at Cambridge, racking up, at last count, twelve Nobel Memorial Prizes in economics. Nor did it happen, as Robert Reich and Joseph Stiglitz appear to believe,[51] because progressive candidates lost elections, opening the door for lobbyists to rewrite the laws to enrich the few and impoverish the many. Neoliberalism, or something similar under another name and with other prophets, had to happen because the Fordist/Keynesian regime of accumulation no longer worked. Its capacity to induce investment faltered. Its technologies became obsolete. One regime of accumulation went and another one came.

If we look to Harvey for an answer to the question 'What can we do to meet the needs of everyone in harmony with nature?' we find at the end of *The Condition of Postmodernity*[52] a prediction that is also a hope. He predicts that the dull, unending pressure of material necessity will eventually compel humanity to organize itself in a more sensible way. In another, more recent work,[53] Harvey outlines seventeen hopes in the form of seventeen contradictions within capitalism that make it its own enemy. As far as we

---

49. Karl Marx, *A Contribution to the Critique of Political Economy* (Moscow: Progress Publishers, 1977 (1859)), p. 1.

50. For example, the late C. K. Prahalad (1941–2010), who was professor of corporate strategy at the University of Michigan and a member of the board of directors of Hindustan Lever.

51. See Robert Reich's *Saving Capitalism* (New York: Knopf, 2015), and Joseph Stiglitz's *The Great Divide* (New York: W. W. Norton, 2015).

52. Oxford: Blackwell, 1987.

53. David Harvey, *Seventeen Contradictions and the End of Capitalism* (New York: Oxford University Press, 2014).

can tell, community development is not on Harvey's list. It should be. It is a way to help transform the social structures that make necessary one or another regime of accumulation.

We should add that sometimes 'community development' is used in ways not on our list. We are sailing on Neurath's boat, working to remake it plank by plank, but the planks themselves have different meanings for different sailors. We agree with Barthes that every word now in use is part of a dysfunctional system; we agree with Bhaktin that we can only borrow words to work with from a milieu that does not belong to us. Here we are working with the term 'community', and we are touting it as a remedy for economics. While Etzioni's use of the term is on our list of uses we agree with, he did not intend his definition of 'community' (which we quote at the beginning of the next section) to position community as a remedy for the necessity of living under regimes of accumulation. For us, it does serve that purpose.

Many others contribute to what Vygotsky would call the scaffolding for the CWP's strategy for using community to transform the social structure. With moral realism we contribute to the same cause an ethic that is universal because it is firmly grounded in the natural sciences. It does not compete with the diverse moral codes of the diverse religions and cultures of the world. Rather it supports them. It works with them to make them more functional than they already are, treating them as adaptations to the demands of the environment and as treasure-troves of wisdom that have stood the test of time.[54]

The CWP is rebuilding communities that were destroyed by colonialism, destroyed again by apartheid and, since democracy began in 1994, destroyed yet again by neoliberalism. In our view, in all three instances they were destroyed by economics, albeit an economics tempered by many of the teachings of the Christian missionaries who also came to Africa from Europe, and by the cultures of the mosaic of ethnic groups that coexist in Africa today, providing identity and (often) mutual aid for their members.

Michel Aglietta (one of the coiners of the phrase 'regime of accumulation') chimed in with our use of community as a foil for economics when he wrote that capitalism is 'radically opposed to the unification of so many traditional societies by way of myth, custom, and a tight network of

---

54. Howard Richards, 'Moral (and Ethical) Realism', *Journal of Critical Realism*, vol.18 (2019), pp.285–302; David Sloan Wilson, *Darwin's Cathedral* (Chicago: University of Chicago Press, 2011).

interpersonal obligations, by a solidarity of community and neighbourhood. It is because capitalism does not simply utilize in its production workers who still continue to live according to the rules of a traditional community, but penetrates into their whole mode of life, that it necessarily breaks up civil society and recombines it according to the logic of abstract classification and stratification.'[55] The CWP, in contrast (as we document in chapter 9), not only puts money in pockets but also facilitates the revival of the spirit of *ubuntu*: neighbourly bonds, mutual aid and finding meaning in life by doing community service.

Norbert Elias, as well as the formalist economic anthropologists who disagree with the substantivist friends of Polanyi, might be regarded as out of step with the scholarly consensus we allege exists. Elias can be read as claiming that life was perfectly awful in the Middle Ages and has been getting steadily better ever since.[56] Our thesis does not require that we disagree. It requires only asserting that what von Hayek calls the 'extended order' of modernity—whatever may be its virtues—subjects humanity to living under regimes of accumulation. Investors must be pleased, come what may. Even if, for the sake of the argument and without betraying our intellectual friendship with Alasdair Macintyre and Amitai Etzioni, we concede that the masses have never been happier than they are now, eating hamburgers at McDonald's from Delhi to Dakar to Detroit, it still follows from SF1 and SF2 that the system is socially ungovernable and ecologically unsustainable. We will return to the theory of community in the following section on moral values. For now, in place of extending our argument, we offer a short fantasy:

Imagine we are having a beer in a tuck shop[57] in Alexandria, a poor district of Johannesburg where the CWP is doing community development. Imagine that while we drink our beer we are transported in time to the same location four hundred years earlier. We notice that in our new 'now', the human population is quite small, situated in a vast immensity of the natural landscape. Money plays little or no role in the people's lives.

From this perspective, we are able to look at the lives of the people four hundred years later in this very location. We can see that their food consumption in terms of calories per day is comparable to what it is 'now', but they have lost many food-producing and food-gathering skills. They

---

55. Michel Aglietta, *A Theory of Capitalist Regulation* (London: Verso, 2000), p. 70.
56. Norbert Elias, *The Civilizing Process* (Oxford: Blackwell, 1994 (1939)).
57. A small shop where liquor is sold and served, similar to a pub or bar.

spend many more hours a day trying to eke out a living, and they enjoy less leisure.[58] They have also lost the culture and identity handed down among their ancestors for generations.[59] They do not live in extended families and clans where 'children of the same homestead will share even the head of a locust'.[60] They see wealth but cannot touch it. Humiliation is the daily diet of their souls.[61] Drinking, fighting and promiscuity are their constant temptations. They also live far from the lands of their ancestors. They moved to the city to look for work, and many of them have not found it.

'That is a strange concept', say the people of four hundred years earlier, "looking for work and not finding it". How can one not find work when all of nature invites us to do something useful for ourselves and our kin? We cannot grasp the concept, but no doubt the future people will know what it means.'

♦ ♦ ♦

> 'In my area I am assisting and involved in patrolling to stop crime. It is an anti-crime patrol to fight crime.'
>
> — CWP PARTICIPANT, RANDFONTEIN CDI

8. Moral Values

We quote here Amitai Etzioni's influential twenty-first-century definition of community in order to discuss it in some detail, including how it helps us to act here and now to transform the basic structures of the modern world:

> Community is a combination of two elements: A) A web of affect-laden relationships among a group of individuals, relationships that often crisscross and reinforce one another

---

58. This thought is suggested by Marshall Sahlins, *Stone Age Economics* (Chicago: Aldine, 1967), although he wrote of times still longer ago.

59. In the language of Emile Durkheim, they suffer *anomie*, normlessness. Durkheim found that anomie was a typical consequence of the transition from archaic to modern society. Emile Durkheim, *The Division of Labor in Society* (New York: Free Press, 1947 (French original 1893)); and *Suicide* (New York: Free Press, 1951 (French original 1897)). Similarly, Karl Polanyi describes the growth of the modern economy as a 'disembedding' of economic relations from social relations, while Louis Dumont construes the rise of modernity as the rise of the isolated individual. Karl Polanyi, *The Great Transformation* (Boston: Beacon Press, 1944); Louis Dumont, *Essays on Individualism* (Chicago: University of Chicago Press, 1992).

60. '*Bana ba motho ba kgaogana tlhogwana ya tsie.*' A proverb in the Tswana language.

61. See Evelin Lindner, *The Psychology of Humiliation* (Unpublished Ph.D. dissertation, University of Oslo) and other works previously cited, by the same author.

> (rather than merely one-on-one or chainlike individual relationships). B) A measure of commitment to a set of shared values, norms, and meanings, and a shared history and identity in short, to a particular culture. [62]

And again, a few pages later:

> A community, as defined here, is not merely a social entity whose members are bound by a web of crisscrossing affective bonds, but also one in which members share a set of core values, a moral culture. A good society is thus by definition one governed not merely by contracts, voluntary arrangements, and laws freely enacted, but also by a thick layer of mores that are in turn derived from values. This raises the questions: Where do these values emanate from? And are they justifiable? Are they good?[63]

In his definition of community Etzioni echoes Ferdinand Tönnies's nineteenth-century concept of *Gemeinschaft*. He also echoes our view that the centrepiece of the ethics underpinning economic theory is free choice. Tönnies's *Gesellschaft*—and with it, his and our references to Roman law—reappears in Etzioni as three kinds of free choice that describe what community *is not*: contracts, voluntary arrangements and laws freely enacted. In contrast, Etzioni says, community *is* affect-laden. Here Etzioni speaks to the earth's story, to our definition of the human being as a cultural animal, to our sympathy with religion, and to the older layers of the triune brain[64] and our reliance on recent evidence regarding the emotional hard-wiring of bonding and cooperation in the human species.[65]

Etzioni then adds to his definition of community 'thick mores'. He evokes writers who distinguish thin liberal ethics from thick community ethics.[66]

---

62. Amitai Etzioni, 'Creating Good Communities and Good Societies', *Contemporary Sociology*, vol. 29 (2000), p. 188.

63. Ibid., p. 191.

64. Paul McLean, *The Triune Brain in Evolution* (New York: Plenum, 1990).

65. Naomi I. Eisenberger and Matthew D. Lieberman, 'Why It Hurts to Be Left Out: The Neurocognitive Overlap Between Physical Pain and Social Pain', in Kipling Williams et al. (eds.), *The Social Outcast* (New York: Psychology Press, 2005). Social integration is a necessity as basic as air, water or food (p. 110).

66. E.g., Michael Walzer, *Thick and Thin: Moral Argument at Home and Abroad* (Notre Dame, IN: Notre Dame University Press, 1994).

Which thick mores define a community depends on which community is being denoted.[67] In the case of the CWP, the salient communal thick mores are called *ubuntu* in the traditions of the Bantu-speaking peoples. They became ideals for all South Africans, Bantu or not, in the truth and reconciliation process following the end of apartheid.[68]

Etzioni goes on to say that community is defined by its core values, its moral culture. We want to say that too. However, this raises the ethical question: How do you tell the difference between justifiable good values and unjustifiable bad values? We want to answer that question too, which means trespassing into ethical theory. We fear, however, that at this point in intellectual history, moral realism is not commonly seen as an option in ethical history. So, partly as an attempt to join a contemporary conversation where we do not feel welcome, we frame the context by going back to the beginning—to the beginning of the universe. By *seeing* contemporary ethical theory in the context of the long earth story, we hope to illumine and make obvious two points: (1) that ethics ought to be functional, and (2) that ethics ought not to take as its paradigmatic object of study the individual juridical person who coevolved recently with capitalism in Europe and who is authorized to own property, enter into contracts and trade in markets.

It took a very long time for the first photons and light atoms to evolve into heavy atoms, a very long time for our solar system and our earth to form, and on earth a very long time for life to appear. If there is anything to be learned from the study of cosmic epochs longer by several orders of magnitude than geologic ages, it is that whatever forms continue to exist are homeostatic. They remain the same. The only forms now existing have something about them that has enabled them to last. Life lasts by reproducing itself. Since it first came into existence as unicellular organisms, because proteins produce DNA and DNA produces proteins, life has defended itself with mechanisms that work to restore it to its normal state when it is perturbed.[69]

Let us now apply this cosmic context to two fairly recent contributions to ethics by John Searle that on our view have everything to do with replacing

---

67. Alasdair Macintyre, *Whose Justice? Which Rationality?* (Notre Dame, IN: Notre Dame University Press, 1988).

68. Michael Battle, *Reconciliation: The Ubuntu Theology of Desmond Tutu* (Cleveland, OH: Pilgrim Press, 1997); Mfuniswela Bhengu, *African Economic Humanism* (Farnham, UK: Gower Publishing, 2011).

69. Humberto Maturana and Francisco Varela, *The Tree of Knowledge: The Biological Roots of Human Cognition* (Boston: Shambala, 1984); and other works by the same authors. A particularly thorough account of the place of morals in human biological evolution is Richard Joyce, *The Evolution of Morality* (Cambridge, MA: MIT Press, 2006).

standard economic theory with theories of unbounded organization and moral realism congenial to multiple intellectual and practical options. First, he solves a riddle that puzzled David Hume and still puzzles many who (unlike ourselves) find Searle's argument invalid. He shows us how it is possible to derive 'ought' from 'is'. Things that *ought to be*—moral obligations—follow from things that *are* because humans have institutions.[70] Evidently, there *are* institutions. The institutions include languages containing words like *ought* and *should* and *right* and *wrong*. They also include criteria that prescribe when moral obligations arise, for example, in buying and selling, in marriage and in making promises. If we now ask: 'Why do humans have institutions?' our answer is: 'They evolved that way.' Institutions perform functions that have enabled humans to become what they are and to continue to exist as a species. Then when orthodox economists and the new institutionalists tell us that the pinnacle and conclusion of the evolution of human institutions is the doctrine of consumer sovereignty and its corollary, free trade, we feel free to disagree. We also feel free to agree with other philosophers (Dewey, Canguilhem, Bhaskar, Berlin, to name a few) who also find that often ethical conclusions can be drawn from factual premises, for reasons other than Searle's.

Second, Searle elaborates on the idea of constitutive rules, in particular, their *deontic* character. He writes:

> The special feature of reasons [for acting] in institutional reality is that many of these reasons are desire-independent. You will be operating within [the constitutive rules of] marriage, money, private property, or government only if you recognize that in operating within these institutions you have reasons for doing things regardless of whether or not you are otherwise inclined to do them.

We now ask, from our cosmic perspective: Why did humans develop this capacity to do things not because they want to do them but because it is their duty? Searle answers our question in his next sentence:

> Institutional structures enable us to do all sorts of things we could not do without those structures; but this enabling

---

70. John Searle, 'How to Derive "Ought" from "Is"', *Philosophical Review*, vol. 73 (1964), pp. 43–58.

function can be performed only if it is, at least in part, constituted by a deontic system, a system of desire-independent reasons for action.[71]

Embedding ethics in the same earth story with the rest of the sciences helps us to appreciate John Dewey's point that to ask 'Why be ethical?' is like asking 'Why live?' It also helps us make the further point that the successful adaptations of human beings have been favoured not only by *having institutions* but also by *the capacity to modify old institutions and invent new ones.*

Having approved these two major contributions by Searle, we then identify an early article by John Rawls as a turning point where, in our view, mainstream ethical theory went wrong.[72] Rawls proposes to justify and recommend general principles 'that are implicit in the considered judgments of competent judges'.[73] These principles are supposed to reflect accurately each particular judgment that the judges would make in particular cases.[74] The flaw in this approach is that it makes ethics an elaboration of existing morals. Gerald Dworkin, among many others, makes the same methodological error.[75] For Dworkin, legal innovations should present the law as a coherent whole, finding resources for critique within the confines of the law as it already is; the existing normative order is to be criticized not according to external standards outside itself but according to internal standards already implicitly or explicitly contained within itself. Methodologies like those of Rawls (in both his 1951 outline and its subsequent refinements) and Dworkin might make sense if the currently dominant institutions were successfully meeting human needs in harmony with the environment. But in the world as it is, they make no sense at all. Ecology gives us an objective place to stand outside our institutions from where we can employ judgmental rationality to recommend changes.

The ethical realism we propose is two-tiered. At the first tier, it is tolerant. It works with, not against, existing cultures. Ethical realism even tolerates the wrongheaded methodologies of Rawls and Dworkin. Rawls's difference

---

71. John Searle, *Making the Social World* (Oxford: Oxford University Press, 2009), p. 141.
72. John Rawls, 'Outline of a Decision Procedure for Ethics', *Philosophical Review*, vol. 60 (1951), pp. 177–197.
73. Ibid., p. 183.
74. Ibid., p. 184.
75. Gerald Dworkin, *Taking Rights Seriously* (London: Duckworth, 1977).

principle may feed some hungry mouths.[76] Dworkin's passionate advocacy of human rights may save some prisoners from torture.

At the second tier, the ethical realism we propose adjusts culture to physical function. Its criterion for recommending change is meeting needs in harmony with nature. We take from Abraham Maslow's famous list of human needs the idea that for human beings, love, esteem and self-realization are just as real, just as physical, as food and safety. They too contribute to the homeostatic mechanisms that have prolonged our existence and make it possible for us to be here today. Without necessarily agreeing with every word of Maslow, we agree with his proposal to define a good society as a society that meets basic needs and paves the way for individual creative self-realization.

Following Bhaskar, we do not identify the object of scientific study—in this case, human needs—with the vocabulary that any particular scholar or community of scholars uses to describe it. Others besides Maslow have drawn up lists summarizing what science has learned about human needs. Amitai Etzioni is among them. He has drawn up a somewhat different list, and he joins us (actually, we join him) in calling for evaluating institutions using the satisfaction of basic and authentic needs as a criterion. 'Needs' functions as an essentially contested concept. We do not close off debate by saying that we know exactly what human needs are, nor does anybody. Rather, like Amartya Sen, we propose to broaden the criteria for judgment and the range of admissible evidence used in ethical debate.[77] We select 'need' as a convenient word to use to name a rational and empathetically responsive practical conclusion, often supported by hard evidence from the natural sciences, medicine or psychology and reached in the course of humanity's endless philosophical conversations that endlessly question their own assumptions.

We count it as a point in favour of the word 'need' that Carol Gilligan defines a care ethic as 'attending to and responding to need'.[78] To be a caring person one does not have to have all the answers, but it helps to try to ask good questions. We believe that in many contexts good questions are: 'What is needed?' and 'How can I help?'

---

76. Rawls's difference principle holds that only that degree of inequality is just which maximizes benefit for those worst off, for example by providing incentives for people to become doctors because doctors earn more. Brian Barry has shown that in the context of Rawls's system the difference principle does not call for as much redistribution of wealth as at first appears. *The Liberal Theory of Justice* (Oxford: Clarendon Press, 1973).

77. Amartya Sen, *The Idea of Justice* (Cambridge, MA: Harvard University Press, 2009).

78. She said this on several occasions when Howard was present. We have not found these exact words in a published writing.

We count it as a valid argument *against* the word 'need' that so-called 'needs assessments' done by bureaucracies and experts are employed to deprive people of control over their lives. The pretext for this misuse of 'need' is that once the goal, that is, satisfying the need, is known, control of the process should pass to those who have the resources and technical knowledge to reach it.[79] Having given up, like Roland Barthes,[80] on finding a pure word that has not been corrupted in the dysfunctional world we live in, we choose to use 'need' in spite of its drawbacks and its frequent misuse.

---

79. John McKnight, *The Careless Society: Community and its Counterfeits* (New York: Basic Books, 1996).

80. Rolande Barthes, *Sade, Fourier Loyola* (Berkeley: University of California Press, 1989).

CHAPTER SIX
India's Employment Guarantee as an Accumulation of Anomalies

In its origins, South Africa's Community Work Programme, initiated in 2007, was conceived by its inventors as similar to India's National Rural Employment Guarantee Act (NREGA) of 2005, but much better. NREGA was a public employment scheme like any other, paid for by taxes; the CWP was a conceptual revolution. The CWP was inspired by the alignment of people from all sectors of society, achieved in the struggle against apartheid. The feasibility of its community-based approach, drawing on Vygotskyan activity theory, was already being demonstrated in pilots at Munsieville and Bokfontein.

NREGA was simply another item in the government budget. Its size was limited by how much the government was able and willing to pay. The CWP had a mandate from Cabinet *to use public employment to catalyse community development and to mobilize community resources.* Like the Asset-Based Community Development (ABCD) programmes in Chicago, where Barack and Michelle Obama were once trainees, in an age when governments were overwhelmed with more social problems than they could cope with and going ever more deeply into debt, the CWP was going to throw the resources of civil society and, above all the resources already possessed by the poor themselves, into the breach. Unlike Chicago's ABCD, the CWP had the full support of the federal government. Indeed, it was the government's flagship programme. It was going to show the world how to win the war against poverty by making it everybody's war.

At a philosophical level, while making our case for unbounded organization and for the CWP as demonstrating some—unfortunately not fully realized—of its *possibilities*, we must add some qualifications. Unbounded organization is both an ethical science and a neat set of interlocking concepts. It is a design science.[1] It is a management theory superseding economic theory. Its key concepts are valid by definition (sometimes *almost* by definition) once the meanings of the terms are understood. This is the case for the key concepts: sharing of surplus; meeting needs; unbounded organization; the

---

1. Herbert Simon, *The Sciences of the Artificial* (Cambridge, MA; MIT Press, 1969).

intransitive object of economic theory as the basic social structure; functional morals; and community and economy as distinct and complementary, with the latter currently too dominant and the former too weak. But an innovative discourse, internally consistent and correct by definition though it may be, is useful only if it meshes with the facts of experience. This chapter's encounter with the facts of experience in India serves as both a reality test for our tautologies and an indictment of the liberal basic social structure our tautologies aspire to help transform.

OVERVIEW OF THE CHAPTER

1. Community versus Economy in the Thought and Practice of Mahatma Gandhi
2. The Rationale for India's Rural Employment Guarantee
3. Rights Talk
4. What NREGA Does
5. Criticisms from the Left: Failure to Achieve Economic Democracy
6. An Unbounded Alternative: Six Steps
7. Transforming Human Rights by Transforming Possibilities
8. Objections to NREGA: Corruption
9. A Brief Digression on the Philosophy of Social Science
10. Objections to NREGA: 'Crowding Out' Private Enterprise
11. The Suicide of Tapas Soren
12. Common Complaints against NREGA 'in Principle'

1. Community versus Economy in the Thought and Practice of Mahatma Gandhi

In this book's introduction we stated boldly that life needs to be saved from humanity's dominant way of thinking. What we are offering in its place is remarkably aligned with the philosophy of India's Mohandas K. 'Mahatma' Gandhi—with the major difference that while the Mahatma distrusted even locomotives and tractors, we are trusting advanced, sophisticated technology to make satisfying everybody's needs in harmony with nature a real, physical possibility.

Where Gandhi writes that the rich should be trustees, not owners, duty-bound to administer the resources they control for the benefit of the poor, we write that surplus should be shared. Where Gandhi writes that with unity of hearts all things are possible, we write that all sectors—public, private, and all the others—should align to achieve the goals of the societal enterprise. Gandhi's version of *dharma* (with caste excised, retaining the meaning of sacred duty to serve God by serving neighbour) cashes out, at the level of feeding the hungry and healing the sick, as equivalent to our version of moral realism rooted in science (ethics with eighteenth-century European hocus-pocus excised, retaining the adjustment of culture to its physical functions).

Ela Gandhi, a granddaughter of the Mahatma who currently chairs the Gandhi Development Trust, summarizes her grandfather's philosophy as follows:

> Mahatma Gandhi believed that the Truth is God. For Gandhiji, the Truth turns on four fundamental principles: *Sarvodaya*: Work for the benefit of all. *Swadeshi*: Actively participate in constructing the local economy. If we take care of the micro, the macro will take care of itself. *Swaraj*: Liberty, human rights and social justice for all through the practice of self-discipline. *Satyagraha*: Confront evil whenever and wherever you find it with Love.[2]

These principles could hardly be more congruent with sharing and caring and with community as defined in chapter 2.

With regard to guaranteed employment for the poor, Gandhi expected wonderful results from the humble activity of making *khadi* (traditional Indian homespun). In his view, this would provide cash income for the destitute. It would fill with wholesome activity the idle hours of the off-seasons, when agriculture requires little labour. It would instil self-discipline. It would revive the virtue, the *dharma*, that had governed life for centuries in traditional Indian villages until the British imposed modernity by force of arms.[3] With modernity the British imposed cheap, imported, machine-made

---

2. Ela Gandhi, *Valores esenciales de Mahatma Gandhi* (Valparaiso, Chile: Ediciones Chileufu, 2019), pp. 5–6.

3. '[T]he inestimable value of *khadi* consists in its capacity for tremendous mass education, mass uplift and substantial relief from growing starvation.' Mahatma Gandhi, *Young India* 5 October 1928, *Collected Works*, vol. 42, p. 10.

textiles from Birmingham and Manchester, destroying half the livelihood of Indian peasants, who formerly had spun for a living when not tilling the soil. When Indians would once again live by the principles of *swadeshi* (economic self-reliance) and refuse to buy imported goods, the British would no longer find being in India profitable. They would leave.

Gandhi himself made it a practice to sit down every day and spin. He called on his middle- and upper-class followers to do the same, not for the money but to purify their souls and to set a good example for the poor.[4] The symbol on the flag of the party Gandhi led, the Indian National Congress, is even today a spinning wheel.

Gandhi's passion for *khadi* began in 1918, not long after he returned to India from South Africa.[5] It steadily grew. But by 1928, something was clearly amiss. To make ten yards of shirting forty-five inches wide, it was necessary first to acquire the cotton at a cost of nearly three rupees. For their many days of labour it would be unjust for the spinners to earn less than a rupee and a half, or for the weavers to earn less than two rupees. Adding in the cost of moving the *khadi* from the village where it was spun to the shop where it was to be sold, and adding a pittance for unavoidable costs of sale, even when the *khadi* shops were staffed by volunteers it was impossible to sell ten yards of *khadi* shirting for much under seven rupees.[6] At that price, *khadi* was priced out of the market. It could be sold only to buyers who, for humanitarian reasons, were motivated to support the cause. Community was encountering economics, and on the whole economics was winning.

With *khadi*, economics did not win just because we transformers have not yet finished transforming modern social structures. It won at least in part because in a market society goods that cannot be sold for more than their cost of production will not be produced. Any nonmarket or semi-market society humans might construct would, one way or another, have to perform the same functions, e.g., meeting the need for clothing.

Gandhi's initial reaction to such difficulties was to redouble the effort and commitment. He wrote: 'The tendency, however, is to bring down the

---

4. For further details, see Howard Richards and Joanna Swanger, *Gandhi and the Future of Economics* (Lake Oswego, OR: Dignity Press, 2013); and from a neo-Marxist point of view, Lisa Trivedi, *Clothing Gandhi's Nation: Homespun and Modern India* (Bloomington, IN: Indiana University Press, 2007).

5. See Mahatma Gandhi, Letter to Fulch and Shah, 9 August 1918, in *Collected Works*, vol. 17, p. 183.

6. These figures come from the report of Niranjan Patnaik representing the Utkal (Orissa) branch of Gandhi's All-India Spinners' Association, reproduced in Gandhi's *Collected Works*, vol. 42, p. 436.

prices as efficiency and production grow. Meanwhile, appeal must be made to the philanthropy and patriotism of the people to take up this *khadi* and thus help the paupers of Orissa.'[7] Even so, the *khadi* movement still had to cope with the growing surplus stocks of products that could not be sold at prices that would cover the costs of production.

In 1929, Gandhi called for volunteer workers to staff an all-India *khadi* sales exhibition every year, writing: 'If we can get sufficient workers for the purpose, it can become a striking demonstration. It can draw large crowds and it can be a means of selling off all the surplus stock of *khadi* without any difficulty.'[8] Later the same year, he proposed to lower the costs that drove up the sales price by urging villagers to carry out every step of the production process in their own homes, from sowing the cotton seeds to weaving.[9]

Nevertheless, six years later, in 1935, while surpluses of unsold *khadi* continued to mount, benefits to the poor continued to lag. The *Weekly Letter* of Mahadev Desai reported that in Bihar something like 5,000 poor women were walking ten miles a day to receive for their spinning a payment too scanty to survive on. In some parts of Guntur District, people were turning to rice-pounding because it paid more than spinning. For what they were paid, spinners could not be induced to conform to the standards required: yarn of a particular count, a certain evenness and a certain strength.[10] Gandhi had already concluded that the wages of the *khadi* spinners needed to be raised. He had written: 'In trying to commercialize *khadi*, the Association has been hitherto dominated by the ruling prices. Thus, the spinning wage has been the worst of all the wages for any form of labour.'[11]

Gandhi never abandoned his efforts to relieve poverty by promoting the production and sale of homespun cloth, but he never found a way to make his scheme work on the scale he desired with the results he desired. Nevertheless, the Mahatma must be smiling down from heaven today, because the twenty-first century has seen an important revival of *khadi* in India. His granddaughter Ela Gandhi reported to us in 2015 from her home in South Africa:

---

7. Ibid., p. 437.

8. Mahatma Gandhi, Letter to the Secretary, All-India Spinners' Association, 20 January 1929, in *Collected Works*, vol. 44, p. 25.

9. Mahatma Gandhi, Navajivan, 9 December 1929, in *Collected Works*, vol. 45, p. 45. Economists will observe that Gandhi is here recommending the opposite of the division of labour to which in the first pages of *The Wealth of Nations* Adam Smith attributes the superiority of 'civilized' over 'savage' life.

10. Harijan, 8 October 1935, in *Collected Works*, vol. 67, pp. 316–17.

11. Harijan, 7 June 1935, in *Collected Works*, vol. 67, p. 231.

I have just returned from a long journey to India and met many people working in rural areas as well as some who run various NGOs. Yes, *khadi* has had many problems over the years, both in terms of cost of the product as well as in terms of the amount given to the people who produce it. Problems were also experienced in the sale of the product. But from what I was told, the industry is now flourishing with sales going up. More products are on the market. They have improved their skills at spinning as they now have a new better performing spinning wheel. The cloth is therefore of much better quality and they are also modernising their design and colours. Millions are able to earn a livelihood and a unique feature is that even Bollywood stars are now promoting the product. According to the people I interacted with, this was the one strong factor which was able to mobilize people across India.[12]

Some ninety years after the idea had taken shape in Gandhi's mind that India could be saved by spinning, the government rechristened its National Rural Employment Guarantee Act (NREGA), renaming it the Mahatma Gandhi National Rural Employment Guarantee Act (MGNREGA).[13] We refer to it as simply the NREGA in the following discussion.

♦ ♦ ♦

'Everybody sees work as a need; nobody wishes not to work. We all want a job. If someone loses their job today, the next day they will be out there looking for another job. This shows that work is very important.'

— A CWP PARTICIPANT, RANDFONTEIN CDI

---

12. Ela Gandhi, personal email communication, 18 February 2015.

13. The National Rural Employment Guarantee Act was enacted 25 August 2005. After partial implementation in pilot projects in 2006 and 2007, it began to be implemented throughout India in April 2008. Its name was changed to Mahatma Gandhi National Rural Employment Guarantee Act on 2 October 2009.

2. The Rationale for India's Rural Employment Guarantee

The Mahatma Gandhi National Rural Employment Guarantee Act rejects (or at least relaxes) its namesake's implicit yet decisive assumption that the poor can work their way out of poverty, or at least up from the lowest rungs of poverty, by producing merchandise that can be sold at cost-covering prices—in the idiom of contemporary economics and management science, by 'creating value'. Value is often operationally defined as the amount of money customers are willing[14] to pay for the product.[15] As we have seen, it is impossible to 'create value' in this sense without having customers to buy one's products (SF2).[16] It is one thing to fight poverty if there will always be customers. It is quite another to fight poverty if there is a deep-seated and chronic weakness of effective demand.[17]

With NREGA, customers are not needed. Instead, the poor perform public works. The public purse pays for them. Where the public purse gets the money to foot the bill is a matter we discuss in the final chapters of this book.

NREGA has a strong ecological component.[18] The unemployed are employed to build tanks for harvesting rainwater, to change the contours and textures of land so water will sink in instead of evaporating or running off, to reforest areas that deforestation has made prone to drought, and to do the grunt work for small dams and feeder canals so communities of

---

14. If, because of competition among sellers or some other reason, buyers pay less than they are willing to pay, customers get some of the value created in the form of consumer surplus. See, for example, Erik Brynjolfson et. al., 'Consumer Surplus in the Digital Economy: Estimating the Value of Increased Product Variety at Online Booksellers', *Management Science*, vol. 49 (2003), pp. 1580–1596.

15. The production process can be broken down into a chain of activities and transactions where each link in the chain adds value, which becomes manifest when the finished product is sold to a willing buyer. See, for example, A.J. Higgins et al., 'Challenges of Operations Research Practice in Agricultural Value Chains', *Journal of the Operational Research Society*, vol. 16 (2010), pp. 964–973.

16. Historically, the great competitor to a subjective theory of value that makes it depend on people's choices has been a labour theory of value. This history is brilliantly analysed by André Orléan in *L'Empire de la valeur* (Paris: Seuil, 2011).

17. This is why it makes a world of difference to the CWP whether the real world resembles more closely the theoretical constructions of J.B. Say and others whom Joseph Schumpeter called 'no-hitch economists' or those of Thomas Malthus, J. M. Keynes and others whom Schumpeter called 'hitch economists'. Keynes remarked: 'A decreased readiness to spend will be looked on in quite a different light if, instead of being regarded as a factor which will, *cet. par.* increase investment, it is seen as a factor which will, *cet. par.* diminish employment' (*General Theory*, p. 185; *cet. par.* is short for *ceteris paribus*, which means 'other things being equal'. See Joseph Schumpeter, *History of Economic Analysis* (New York: Oxford University Press, 1963), p. 640.

18. Mihir Shah (2007), 'Employment Guarantee, Civil Society, and Indian Democracy', *Economic and Political Weekly*, vol. 42, pp. 43–51.

smallholders can make rational use of what little water there is.[19]

The emphasis on greening complies with the rationale of doing public works to benefit the public. India is a drought-prone nation threatened by climate change. Arguably, what the Indian public most needs is to make its environment sustainable—most immediately to make water supplies larger while making optimal use of existing water supplies.

Notice that now we are talking about producing use value in forms firmly grounded in physical reality. We are jettisoning the conceptual baggage that has accompanied the concepts of production and value in economic science ever since Adam Smith argued that all production was production for sale and then fell into the habit of writing simply *value* when he meant *exchange value*.

♦ ♦ ♦

Agnes Moswale is a coordinator of the Bokfontein CWP.

> 'When I started CWP, I was a participant and couldn't read or write. I used to sign with an X, and I hated it. At our site participants attend ABET [Adult Basic Education and Training] classes. I attended the classes and worked hard and was promoted. As a coordinator I must write a weekly report on the work that is done by my participants. I find that I can do this as well as manage my registers. If it wasn't for CWP I would not be where I am now.'
>
> – COGTA

3. Rights Talk

Although NREGA offers a way around the requirement that products the poor produce must be saleable at cost-covering prices and also serves the public environmentally, the arguments in the Act's favour before its enactment featured rights over either of these benefits. The activists who prepared the early drafts of what would become the National Rural Employment Guarantee Act were human rights activists.[20] Both international human

---

19. NREGA participants do greening work on both public land and private land belonging to poor farmers, but not on the estates of large landholders. One of the complaints against Maharashtra's rural employment guarantee three decades earlier was that sometimes it became a subsidy for the rich to get free labour at government expense to improve their land's fertility.

20. Jean Drèze, 'The Right to Work in Indian Democracy', *Peace Research*, vol. 37 (2005), p. 43.

rights law and the Constitution of India's Directive Principles of State Policy speak of the 'right to an adequate means of livelihood'.[21] This right's near equivalent is the right to food, and experience has shown that public employment with cash wages is superior to other methods of delivering food to the hungry.[22]

The rights talk that propelled the enactment of the NREGA found a home in the operative principles of the Act itself. Any adult living in a rural area who is willing to do unskilled manual work has a right to be employed at minimum wage on public works. There is a limitation, intended to be transitory, that only 100 days of work per year per household are guaranteed. Applicants who are not given work within 15 days of demanding it are entitled to a cash unemployment allowance.

Rights talk has both uses and limitations. In chapter 1 we saw a downside of rights talk: it may lead to absolute conflict. In chapters 3 and 4 we concluded that an economy that honours human social rights will not be a pure market economy (because although there can be a duty to work, there can be no duty to sell, and because a putative right to livelihood is unrealizable if it requires selling). A rights-honouring economy must establish the material basis for a decent life in those cases where there is little or no market demand for what a person has to sell. In chapter 5 we saw one way to do that, namely, South Africa's Community Work Programme, and we also considered an intellectually more inclusive approach, subsuming economics into a broader concept of activity (or organization or culture) called cultural historical activity theory (CHAT).

We have also been claiming that the full flowering of economic and social human rights, made possible in principle by new technologies,[23] faces structural constraints due to the chronic weakness of effective demand and the inducement to invest (SF1 and SF2), both of which are inseparable from the ethical centrepiece of modernity, free choice. Hence the need for a 'paradigm shift' over and above the need for better public policies. (We put 'paradigm shift' in scare quotes because unbounded organization is

---

21. '. . . citizens, men and women equally, have the right to an adequate means of livelihood'. Constitution of India, Article 39.

22. Jean Drèze and Amartya Sen, *Hunger and Public Action* (Oxford: Clarendon Press, 1989); Jean Drèze, 'Democracy and the Right to Food', *Economic and Political Weekly*, vol. 39 (2004), pp. 1723–1731.

23. On the technological possibilities for prosperity, see Peter Diamandis and Stephen Kotler, *Abundance: The Future is Better than You Think* (New York: Free Press, 2012). The argument is not just that new technologies make social justice and environmental sustainability possible, but also that the pace of innovation is accelerating exponentially.

not a paradigm in Kuhn's sense; it is more an open-minded attitude and a commitment to work together for the common good than a model of how to do science.)

Unfortunately, the efforts by lawyers and activists to make legal guarantees of social rights legally binding have usually been unsuccessful. Here are two examples. In 1997, lawyers petitioned South Africa's Constitutional Court to make real the right to emergency medical treatment. They represented Thiagraj Subramoney, who was about to die because the government had deemed it too expensive to continue his renal dialysis. Chief Justice Arthur Chaskalson ruled that 'the obligations imposed on the state by sections 26 and 27 in regard to access to housing, health care, food, water, and social security are dependent on the resources available for such purposes, and that the corresponding rights themselves are limited by reason of lack of resources'. After the ruling, Subramoney's dialysis was discontinued and he died. In 2000, human rights lawyers brought to the South African Constitutional Court the case of Irene Grootboom to try to enforce her constitutional right to housing. While the court found that the then existing housing policy did not meet constitutional standards, it awarded nothing to Grootboom. She died homeless in 2008.[24]

The pattern has been similar in India. The right to food is guaranteed by Article 47 of the Indian Constitution, but it is not a right that a court will enforce.[25]

We wonder in what sense the human rights lawyers themselves believe in rights.[26] Perhaps they invoke the word without believing the historical basis and root of rights: that human rights are natural and imprescriptible; that constitutions, customs and laws acknowledge them but do not create them; that scientific findings cannot add or subtract one jot or tittle from rights because they have always been based on sacred myths (like social contracts and pure reason), not on facts. Perhaps they would, in private or even in public, agree with Jeremy Bentham's comment that natural rights are imaginary[27] and with Alasdair Macintyre's point that we do not believe

---

24. These and other cases are summarized in John Saul and Patrick Bond, *South Africa: The Present as History* (London: James Currey, 2014), ch. 5.

25. Drèze, 'Democracy and the Right to Food', p. 1726.

26. Many authors have recently worked to make sense of rights talk in our sceptical age, including Amartya Sen and Martha Nussbaum, who relate rights talk to capabilities talk.

27. Jeremy Bentham, 'Anarchical Fallacies', in vol. 2 of his *Collected Works* (Edinburgh: Tait, 1843), p 523.

in natural rights for the same reason we do not believe in witches.[28] Perhaps some of them are pro-poor or pro-human or pro–worthy cause first and only secondarily pro–human rights. Perhaps they take advantage of rights clauses in constitutions without giving credence to their natural law rationale or to their timeless and fact-proof rational basis. Or perhaps they invoke them only because they express today's moral consensus; because rights in constitutions can be employed to achieve goals that activists are already convinced, on other grounds, ought to be achieved.

If this last is their view, we agree. From a realist perspective, there are no absolute rights but there are cultures. Cultures have cultural resources that, like natural resources, can be used to meet human needs in harmony with nature. Rights are *cultural* resources.

The origins of the moral consensus that led to enshrining rights talk in the Constitution of India are best explained by B. R. Ambedkar, the man regarded as the author of the Directive Principles, the part of the Constitution where the principal rights language is found, including the right to adequate livelihood. Jean Drèze writes, 'The Directive Principles are chiefly due to B. R. Ambedkar, and they build on his visionary conception of democracy'.[29] He quotes Ambedkar: 'Our object in framing the Constitution is really two-fold: (i) To lay down the form of political democracy, and (ii) To lay down that our ideal is economic democracy and also to prescribe that every government whatever is in power shall strive to bring about economic democracy. The Directive Principles have a great value, for they lay down that our ideal is economic democracy'.[30]

The point of enshrining rights talk in the Constitution of India was to propel India forward from political democracy to economic democracy. The framers must have realized that the entitlement guarantees stated in the Constitution could not possibly be funded without constructing a governable economy—an economy (and hence a social structure) capable of moving resources from where they are surplus to where they are needed and capable of protecting the fragile life of Mother Earth. They must have realized that the economy prescribed by orthodox economic science is not governable.

♦ ♦ ♦

28. Alasdair Macintyre, *After Virtue: A Study in Moral Theory* (London: Duckworth, 1981), p. 67.
29. Drèze, 'Democracy and the Right to Food'.
30. B. R. Ambedkar, as quoted in Drèze, 'Democracy and Right to Food', p. 1723.

'I am also a CWP worker; I am also working at the garden, planting different plants. The vegetables that we plant help a lot, in particular with the people that are sick that need to have the fresh and nutritious foods such as vegetables.'

— CWP PARTICIPANT, UMTHWALUME CDI

4. What NREGA Does

NREGA's purpose, stated on its website, is to enhance 'the livelihood security of people in rural areas by guaranteeing one hundred days of wage-employment in a financial year to a rural household whose adult members volunteer to do unskilled manual work'.[31] That 100 days of employment is to be provided at minimum wage.[32] The minimum wage clause is important because typically India's rural poor are employed at 'market wages', which are lower than the statutory minimum. Because wages are so low, most of the year the rate of unemployment hovers around a low (by South African standards) 7 percent;[33] thus malnutrition and other measures of poverty remain higher than would be expected with low rates of unemployment.

The programme is nationally funded and nationally mandated but state administered. NREGA is expected to protect rural households from hunger, reduce rural-urban migration, increase employment opportunities for rural women, move India toward environmental sustainability, create useful assets generally and increase participation in the local-level town meetings known in India as *panchayati raj* or *gram sabha*.[34]

---

31. www.mgnrega.nic.in.

32. In 2010, the state mandated the minimum daily wage for NREGA work in Bihar to be 100 rupees (2 US dollars or 16 South African rands). Worksite surveys showed wages actually paid from 20 to 125 rupees. Payment in NREGA is usually for work done at piece rates calculated to provide a normal worker who works seven hours with the equivalent of a minimum wage. 'Except in Himachal Pradesh, payment of wages under NREGA is on the basis of piece rate.' D. Narasimha Reddy et al., 'Mahatma Gandhi National Rural Employment Guarantee Scheme (NREGS) as Social Protection in India', available at www.socialprotectionasia.org, p. 14. The state and national laws that prescribe what minimum wage means at a given time and place, and how the minimum wage interacts with piecework rates and with rates of inflation, are complex, and we do not attempt to explain them.

33. The number 'usually unemployed' throughout the year may be as low as 2 percent. 'The number of working poor far outweighs the number who are poor for want of work' (by a factor of approximately 4, i.e., on the order of 7 percent with too little employment and on the order of 28 percent with too little money to live on). K.P. Kannan, 'Linking Guarantee to Human Development', *Economic and Political Weekly* 40 (2005), p. 4518. For more detail see A. Vaidyanathan, 'Employment Guarantee and Decentralisation', *Economic and Political Weekly*, vol. 40 (2005), pp. 1582–1587.

34. Jean Drèze, 'Employment as a Social Responsibility', *The Hindu*, 22 November 2004. The *panchayat*, or *panchayati raj*, stems from a long tradition of local government in

The typical experience of one of NREGA's millions[35] of participants runs like this: First the participant has to learn somehow that she or he has a right to demand employment from the state government at minimum wage. Once the would-be participant knows of the programme, he or she must apply to the local government (the *gram panchayat*) for a job card with an identification number and her or his photograph. The job card is free by law, but it is not uncommon to have to pay a bribe to get it.

With card in hand, the participant can then demand work. The letter of the law says the state must provide work within fifteen days. However, it is common practice to favour and facilitate NREGA work only in agricultural off-seasons, when farmers cannot complain that the government is stealing their workforce. The work, when it is not ecosystem services as described above, is likely to be building rural roads and paths. This is heavy work, digging and lifting earth, and not everyone can stand it. Often the men do the heavier digging while the women do the relatively lighter lifting.

The law requires that at least one-third of the NREGA jobs must go to women. At some times and places, women are the majority. Sometimes the work is scheduled to avoid the midday heat. Sometimes shelter from the heat is provided by canopies. It is important to sign the register, if only with an X, testifying that you were actually present doing the work, or you might not be paid. If you do register and are paid, the pay may be delayed, sometimes for months, and it may be below the promised statutory minimum. Sometimes there have been fictitious registers testifying to the presence of workers who were not really present in order to siphon public funds illicitly into a private purse.[36]

South Asia. The *gram panchayat* is the village (or small area) unit of administration and also the council of ten or so people who administer it. It is supposed to be run democratically in modern India, but often it is not. The *gram sabha* is in principle the assembly of people living in the area. It is supposed to meet at least twice a year to review the work of the gram panchayat and to approve its budget. See the website of the Ministry of Panchati Raj of the Government of India: www.panchayat.gov.in.

35. The programme website www.mgnrega.nic. in keeps a running count of how many person-days of work have been provided in a given fiscal year. As of 1 April 2013, the number for 2012–13 was 4.81 *crore*. A crore is ten million.

36. This short paragraph draws on the longer accounts in Reddy et al., 'Mahatma Gandhi NREGS', and in Reetika Khera and Nandini Nayak, 'Women Workers and Perceptions of the National Rural Employment Guarantee Act', *Economic and Political Weekly*, vol. 44 (2009), pp. 49–57; also Bela Bhatia and Jean Drèze, 'Employment Guarantee in Jharkand: Ground Realities'.

It should be clear that NREGA is not lifting anyone out of poverty.[37] Neither is South Africa's CWP. Both programmes relieve some of the worst of it. They can be regarded as pioneering the principle (capable of further extension) that when one institution (in this case the market) does not succeed in making real a human right (in this case the right to a livelihood) then another institution (in India's case the government) should swing into action.

In answer to author and activist Arundhati Roy's complaint that NREGA pays poor people only about 8,000 rupees (about USD 170) per family per year, Harsh Mander replied:

> I have observed how much NREGA with all its flaws has meant for millions of India's poorest people. Many live on less than one dollar per day, therefore 170 dollars is not a trifle for them. It has enabled them to survive, and that too without doles, but instead with the dignity of (admittedly hard) labour. It has reduced distress, migration and debts, brought more food to their plates and those of their children, and has raised agricultural wages.[38] It is likely that this partly influenced the emphatic vote for the UPA government that had passed the act, in 2009.[39]

NREGA has even had unanticipated desirable results in increasing primary school enrollment and in increasing gender equality.[40] It has demonstrated that it is possible to administer an employment guarantee not just under conditions like those of Sweden (considered in the next chapter) but also under conditions like those of India.[41]

---

37. 'After all, only those really poor or really in need will come forward to do the kind of arduous manual labour to be performed under the programme.' Mihir Shah, 'Employment Guarantee, Civil Society, and Indian Democracy', *Economic and Political Weekly*, vol. 40 (2005), pp. 599–602.

38. Mander's affirmation that NREGA has raised agricultural wages is supported by data provided by C. P. Chandrasekhar and J. Ghosh, 'Public Works and Wages in Rural India', *The Hindu Business Line*, 11 January 2011; and by Jean Drèze and Reetika Khera, 'The Battle for Employment Guarantee', *Frontline*, vol. 26 (2009), p. 10.

39. Harsh Mander, in a book review of Arundathi Roy's *Listening to Grasshoppers: Field Notes on Democracy. India International Centre Quarterly*, vol. 35 (2009), p. 140.

40. The school enrolment result is reported by Reddy et al., 'Mahatma Gandhi NREGS'. The gender equality result is reported by Chandrasekhar and Ghosh, 'Public Works and Wages'.

41. See Shamika Ravi and Monika Engler, *Workfare in Low Income Countries, an Effective Way to Fight Poverty?: The Case of India's NREGS* (Washington, DC: World Bank, 2009); World Bank, *Social Protection for a Changing India* (Washington, DC: World Bank, 2011);

However, India's rights-based employment guarantee escapes some of the main troubles of market-based anti-poverty schemes only to land in troubles of its own. It collides with the political power and intellectual weight of those who oppose, on principle, employing the unemployed to do public work at public expense. It also collides with the entrenched power structures of Indian villages. We examine these collisions in the sections that follow.

♦ ♦ ♦

Lizzie Mankwe is a participant in the Alexandria neighbourhood of Johannesburg.

> Having gotten used to the kind of work we do in the community, I was no longer ashamed to do similar work for money. On the three days of the week when I'm not with the CWP, a friend and I recycle bottles, plastic, paper and so forth. We wheel our dustbins all over Alex. The exercise is good for me, the money pays my bills. I have no shame in doing what I thought were menial tasks.'

– CDI

5. Criticisms from the Left: Failure to Achieve Economic Democracy

Arundhati Roy's complaint is poignant. Working for NREGA is a form of misery that is desirable only because working in rural India without NREGA is worse. It is a far cry from the Keynesian full employment envisioned in the forties, fifties and sixties of the twentieth century, when an adequate livelihood was considered an inalienable human right belonging to all people everywhere. During those decades, when the dominant economic theories were Keynesian, economists believed it was *possible* for public policies to create full employment. Keynes himself apparently believed it.[42] The full employment that was envisioned and largely achieved in social democracies

---

Lalit Mathur, 'Employment Guarantee—Progress So Far', *Economic and Political Weekly*, vol. 42 (2008), pp. 17–20; the paper by Reddy et al., 'Mahatma Gandhi NREGS', and Khera and Nayak, 'Women Workers'.

42. See ch. 24 of Keynes's *General Theory*. He thought, or at least some of the time seemed to think, that full employment (which he defined in a way that allowed for five percent of workers to be unemployed) could be accomplished by low interest rates and by a certain amount of public participation in the planning and implementation of investments, which might today be called industrial policy.

after World War II consisted of 'real'[43] jobs: jobs producing products that could be profitably sold. These jobs yielded for the workers high wages—wages raised above market rates by minimum wage laws and by collective bargaining by strong unions.

In 1943, Michael Kalecki could write that 'a solid majority of economists is now of the opinion that, even in a capitalist system, full employment may be secured by a government spending programme'. The reasons why full employment did not happen were, according to Kalecki, political and not economic. The moneyed classes who held all or most political power threw their weight against full employment because, as employers, it was not in their interest. It was they who decided how much employment there would be. Control over employment gave them 'a powerful indirect control over government policy: everything which may shake the state of confidence must be carefully avoided, because it would cause an economic crisis. But once the government learns the trick of increasing employment by its own purchases, this powerful controlling device loses its effectiveness.'[44] By Kalecki's reasoning, implementing the human right to an adequate livelihood becomes a political problem. The political solution is for the left to win control of the government and then find a way, if it can, to repeal the veto of capital over public policies.

Today, most economists do not believe that governments could create full employment even if they wanted to. Many now agree with Paul Krugman that the series of crises culminating in the economic crisis of 2008 settled once and for all a previously contested theoretical issue: Keynes was right to say that market economies suffer from a chronic weakness of effective demand.[45]

Thus—as in Justice Chaskalson's decision to pull the plug on Thiagraj Subramoney because the South African state could not afford to pay for renal dialysis—questions about human rights turn into questions about economic theory. Ought implies can. Only what is possible can be a moral obligation; what is not possible cannot be a moral obligation.

---

43. We put the word 'real' in quotes because, as good social scientists, we believe in the social construction of reality, but we do not believe any one socially constructed reality is intrinsically more real than any other. While today's dominant ideology counts markets as 'real' and government programmes as artificial, NREGA, with all its faults, often pays higher wages than the market wages its participants would earn working for private farmers. See also footnotes 38 and 42.

44. 'Political Aspects of Full Employment.' This essay was first a talk given to the Marshall Society at Cambridge and then published in *Political Quarterly* in 1943 (http://mrzine.monthlyreview.org/2010/kalecki220510.html). See also Michael Kalecki, *The Last Phase in the Transformation of Capitalism* (New York: Monthly Review Press, 1972).

45. Paul Krugman, *The Return of Depression Economics* (New York: Norton, 2009).

Our reply to those who fault NREGA as well as the CWP for doing so little is that these two programmes are only beginnings. We aspire to move Justice Chaskalson's boundary between what is possible and what is impossible. We propose an unbounded approach in which public employment is part of the mix. A first crucial step is achieving consensus, or close to consensus, that all sectors are working toward the same goal of making real the statement in Section 39 of the Constitution of India that all 'citizens, men and women equally, have the right to an adequate means of livelihood'. Yet achieving a moral consensus and loosening the surly bonds of immovable social structures still get us only halfway to that goal. In the next section, we offer some suggestions on how to complete that transition.

♦ ♦ ♦

> A participant in the CWP at Randfontein said in an interview with researchers: 'It is good to have a job. It protects one from having anger in her heart and . . . thinking bad things like if I can rob someone. When you are working, you become loving. Even at home you can support the kids at home.'
>
> – CDI

6. An Unbounded Alternative: Six Steps

We outline here six steps toward the goal of every person having employment or some other adequate means of livelihood.[46] To those who might disagree with part or all of one of the steps, we point out that being wrong some of the time does not invalidate our unbounded approach; rather, it confirms it. An unbounded approach is Popperian in the sense that every proposal is a conjecture to be examined by unimpeded debate and tested by experiences that might falsify it.[47] Our approach is a combination of imagination, realism and the steady purpose of everyone's needs being met in harmony with nature.

Step One: Discourage speculation. A principle of functional ethics is to move resources from where they are not needed to where they are needed. Today this means moving resources out of a global speculative economy and

---

46. The six steps are also available as a Power Point presentation at www.unbounded-organization.org.

47. Our approach is *not* Popperian in the sense of always agreeing with Karl Popper. See Howard Richards and Joanna Swanger, *Dilemmas of Social Democracies* (Lanham, MD: Rowman and Littlefield, 2006), ch. 9, 'Karl Popper's Vienna'.

into programs like the CWP and NREGA. It also means rescuing India's poor villages, where the employers are almost as poor as their employees, by transfers made possible by growing surpluses of cash that now find no better use than speculating on whether the dollar or the pound will go up or down—or worse, buying up real estate, driving up its price, making housing unaffordable for ordinary people and thus swelling the numbers of homeless.[48] A Tobin tax[49] can be used to discreetly supplement self-help projects that produce livelihoods with dignity. There should be a bias toward low interest rates because high interest rates make speculation more profitable than job creation. Holding land, patents or anything else without using them, or buying them so others cannot while waiting for their prices to rise, should be discouraged.

At this point in history, Step One is difficult for both India and South Africa. Like many other nations, they have largely given up their ability to rein in speculation. They have signed treaties obliging them to refrain from restricting capital flows. These and other surrenders of sovereignty have been greased partly by neoliberal economics' worldwide bewitching of intelligence, but mostly by lenders' keeping borrowers on a short leash by attaching neoliberal conditions to short-term loans that must be frequently refinanced and by enforceable global rules like those of the World Trade Organization. As far as possible, national jurisdiction to stop useless and harmful speculation and restrict capital flows should be reclaimed.

The principle of moving resources to where they are needed applies not only to what the state can do. Individuals and organizations can also choose to be socially responsible, refraining from unproductive speculation, instead devoting their assets to socially useful missions, including employment creation, whether or not the state compels them to do so. Unbounded organization is about aligning all persons and all institutions with the societal enterprise. It involves responsible stewardship of capital by its owners in addition to responsible regulation and prudent redistribution through democratic politics.

Step Two: Directly encourage productive[50] activities that provide

---

48. Michael Hudson, *And Forgive Them Their Debts* (Dresden: ISLET Verlag, 2018); Nick Middleton, *The Global Casino* (London: Routledge, 2013). And other works by the same authors.

49. A Tobin tax is a tax on cross-border currency transactions. An objective is to discourage speculative short-term capital movements that have no productive purposes. Another objective is to raise money for social programs.

50. Here we use 'production' in a common-sense way not limited by Adam Smith's qualification that to be counted as productive, labour must result in a 'vendible' (i.e., saleable) product.

livelihoods and dignity. This can be done in many ways and can include actions to reverse climate change. In Asset-Based Community Development (ABCD) and at some CWP sites, the community's resources are mapped and people brainstorm about how to combine them to meet needs. Entrepreneurs combine the factors of production in new ways to create new enterprises. Entrepreneurs can be motivated by many aims: to enjoy being one's own boss, to create jobs for family members, to combine business with meeting a social need (as in social entrepreneurship—a misnomer because all entrepreneurship is social[51]), to exploit an invention, to create jobs in a poverty-stricken area,[52] to facilitate a professional practice, to do the same things others do more efficiently[53] and to fulfil dreams of glory,[54] among others. Government agencies incubate enterprises and orchestrate joint ventures. When there is market demand, a valid business plan and a credible business team, capital (if it is needed at all) can almost always be raised in capital markets, by local subscription or from public or quasi-public development banks and agencies.[55]

Step Three: Support the people's economy. José Luis Coraggio defines the objective of the people's economy as not profit but making a living and identifies its main resource as not capital but labour.[56] Supporting it means enrolling so-called informal workers to receive health and pension benefits. It means making discreet transfer payments so workers are able to make a good living while maintaining their dignity. It means, as in Holland and Japan, public policies that favour small shops that would fail if exposed to all the rigors of competition with better-capitalized competitors.

In most African and Latin American countries, the people's economy

---

51. Douglas Racionzer, 'All Entrepreneurship is Social', https://www.academia.edu/4219742/ All_entrepreneurship_is_social_entrepreneurship (PowerPoint).

52. This was the stated motive, and we are not cynical enough to say it was absent from the real motives, of the pioneers of the Chilean and Norwegian salmon industries. In the case of Norway, the government assigned to university researchers the task of finding ways to alleviate the poverty of fishing villages in the north of the country. See Alfonso Muena and Howard Richards, 'El Papel de la Empresa en la Eliminación de la Pobreza' on the website www.repensar.cl. (This is an interview with the founder of the Chilean salmon industry.)

53. This is Alfred Marshall's law of substitution. Over time more efficient ways of doing things will replace and supplant less efficient ways.

54. Keynes points out that if business were conducted solely because of rational expectations of profits there would be less of it than there actually is.

55. See Rob Hopkins, *The Power of Just Doing Stuff* (Totnes, UK: Transition Books, 2013); Blake Mycoskie, *Start Something that Matters* (New York: Random House, 2012).

56. José Luis Coraggio, *De la emergencia a la estrategia* (Buenos Aires: Espacio Editores, 2004).

appears to provide more employment than any other sector.[57] As an example, in Rosario, Argentina, behind-the-scenes private and public subsidies make it possible for a family to make a living growing food on urban plots they are usually allowed to farm for free. With community backing, including in some cases training sponsored by the chamber of commerce, free radio spots advertising their organic products and free stalls in the municipal market, they can also develop and sell products like herbs, jam and fruit cookies. The point is that the entire community supports them, yet they enjoy the dignity of paying their own way.

Step Four: Reinvent the public sector. This applies to not only the civil service and state-owned enterprises but also the very concepts of the state and democratic politics.[58] In an open society, the people as a whole constantly improve all institutions and the society's overall functioning in the light of never-ending learning from experience and from ongoing conversations in collaboration with academic researchers.

Public employment is a necessary part of the mix even now—even before we experience the full impact of the technologies of the age of information. It becomes a task of the state and also philanthropical and other institutions to transfer resources from where they are less needed to where they are sorely needed.[59] It becomes a role of the state to act as a supportive partner to local communities and private industry in order to mobilize resources to meet needs on a scale that no single institution can achieve alone.[60]

This step implies and requires adequate funding for the state, a topic we discuss later. However, we are already talking about a plural economy where wealth can be taxed because it no longer holds what Kalecki calls a veto power simply because there is an economic crisis if it refrains from investing. Obviously, taxing surplus to build a society without losers becomes

---

57. Coraggio claims this and it is reasonable to believe it, but it is hard to prove with numbers because the concept of the people's economy is not recognized in official statistics.

58. The reason why the very concepts need to be reinvented is the pervasive influence of neoliberal social philosophies that conceive of certain basic juridical principles of Roman law (seconded by similar principles in Anglo Saxon common law) as an eternal and universal framework of commerce that the sovereign people have no right to modify. See Howard Richards and Joanna Swanger, *The Dilemmas of Social Democracies*.

59. This topic will be further developed later in discussing Alfred Marshall's theories of rents and profits. The Marshallian tradition provides tools for distinguishing what is needed for efficient production from what is surplus that can safely be transferred to the social budget.

60. On the role of the state as partner see the works of Pierre Calame, a civil engineer with a long career in the French civil service who has devoted himself to rethinking economics and especially the state. Most of his works are available only in French but as time goes on more and more of them become available in English.

more feasible when public opinion, including that of the wealthy, holds correctly that public institutions are effective and not corrupt, and when the still small voice of conscience whispers that contributing to the common good is the right thing to do.

Step Five: Fund the development of talent and the doing of good works. No matter how creative entrepreneurs may be in orchestrating enterprises, and no matter how effective states may be in capturing rents to fund public employment, there comes a time when labour is not needed to make things or provide services. At that point, we are reduced to paying people to do something just because society needs a pretext for paying them a wage.[61] We pay people to make music, to scale mountains, to scuba dive, to learn foreign languages, to plant trees to replenish the earth's oxygen, to keep the elderly company and read them poems, and so on.

Mainstream economics has everything backwards when it treats people as resources whose function is to create value demonstrated by selling something. People should be treated as ends in themselves. For example: a visitor to an old church in Alexandra, a poor district of Johannesburg, can observe young CWP participants practicing their song-and-dance routines, which is officially justified as 'useful work' in the CWP Implementation Manual[62] because they put on shows in schools. Schoolchildren see healthy young people on stage who have the self-discipline to learn to dance and sing and who stay off drugs, inspiring the schoolchildren to practice self-discipline and stay off drugs too. The deeper justification is that dancing and singing, like astronomy and rugby, are intrinsically worth doing; they should be funded.

Step Six: Cultivate community development in neighbourhoods. A neighbourhood is a privileged space for implementing *ubuntu, swaraj, ikram*, or the 'fraternity' part of the Enlightenment ideals of liberty, equality and fraternity. In a neighbourhood it is possible to go door to door to be sure there is nobody old, sick and alone. It is possible to check that no orphans are living without adults because both parents left or died. Neighbours can protect each other against crime, especially when they are well organised and their organization works closely with the public authorities. When neighbourhoods are well organized, somebody knows and somebody cares.

---

61. David Graeber, *Bullshit Jobs* (New York: Simon and Schuster, 2018).
62. 'Guidelines on Useful Work', in *Community Work Programme Implementation Manual* (Pretoria: Department of Cooperative Governance, 2011), p. 19.

7. Transforming Human Rights by Transforming Possibilities

Unbounded organization leads to a reconsideration of human rights. As noted above, employment was first declared a human right in the age of Keynes. It was then considered a realizable right because the reigning economic theory held that through fiscal and monetary policies, governments could achieve full employment. During the age of Milton Friedman[63] employment for all ceased to be a human right because it was no longer regarded as possible. Now that we may be entering the age of unbounded organization, we can again say that an adequate livelihood is a human right. It is possible. The resources exist. The ways to organize the resources to meet the needs are plural, indeed innumerable.

Pluralism means redundancy, and redundancy means resilience. Redundancy is a principle ecologists find at work in nature. In a healthy ecosystem, when one way to accomplish a function fails, another takes up the slack. Following Amartya Sen, we can speak similarly of complementarity. Complementarity is a principle underlying our six steps: when one institution does not provide an adequate livelihood for everybody, complement it with another and keep complementing until the problem is solved. We share the dream of Enrique Martinez, the head of Argentina's National Institute of Industrial Technology, that when all else fails, every Argentine will have the option of going home to security in her or his *barrio* (neighbourhood). In every *barrio* people will have housing, food security and primary health care, whether the stock market is booming or crashing.

We turn now to more objections raised in India against NREGA. The plausibility of some of the objections suggests that the true NREGA is still struggling to be born; it is still fighting to come into existence inside a basic social structure that is hostile to the human solidarity that is its rationale and its goal. We arrange the complaints in three categories: (1) corruption; (2) crowding out, exemplified by the complaints of farmers that NREGA is stifling private enterprise by raising wages to a level farmers cannot afford to pay; and (3) complaints that a programme like NREGA is not the best way to spend money to help the poor.

---

63. Andrei Shleifer, 'The Age of Milton Friedman', *Journal of Economic Literature*, vol. 47 (2009), pp. 123–135. Friedman argued, in his lecture accepting the Nobel Memorial Prize in economics, that following Keynesian policies, governments had created intolerable levels of inflation in a vain and unsuccessful attempt to create welfare states with full employment. Milton Friedman, 'Nobel Lecture: Inflation and Unemployment', Journal of Political Economy, vol. 85 (1977), pp 451–472.

8. Objections to NREGA: Corruption

According to Farzana Afridi, 'Public programmes in most developing countries are notorious for being ineffective due to rampant corruption.'[64] K. S. Gopal provides a table showing NREGA funds stolen by fraud between 2006 and 2009 in fifteen villages in just one district, the pilot district of Ananthapur, where NREGA was launched in 2006. The number of rupees stolen was announced in public meetings—'social audits' mandated in the NREGA law, where villagers stand up and speak to control and monitor the expenditures of their local governments. The third column shows the amount of the stolen funds recovered.[65]

NREGA Funds Stolen by Fraud, 2006–2009

Village	Fraud Identified in Public Meetings	Amount Recovered
Chilamathur	3,50,000	20,000
Tanakal	5,00,000	2,00,000
Nalichenuvu	11,27,000	None
Gandlapenta	27,56,000	23,000
Puttaparthi	2,00,000	12,000
Gutti	17,00,000	1,60,000
Kanaganapalli	6,00,000	6,500
Bathalapalli	2,21,900	7,500
Tadimarri	2,00,000	45,000
Dharmavaram	1,50,000	50.000
Midapanakalu	80,000	30,000
Univakonda	50,000	15,000
Raigiri	3,00,000	25,000
Kadiri	2,00,000	20,000
Kalyandurg	3,88,200	None

Although we know of no in-depth quantitative study of the proportion of NREGA funds being lost to corruption nationwide, there is general agreement that the proportion is large.[66]

---

64. Farzana Afridi, 'Can Community Monitoring Improve the Accountability of Public Officials?' *Economic and Political Weekly*, vol. 43 (2008), p. 35. Although there are several kinds of corruption, the one mentioned specifically in this article is 'leakages of funds due to corrupt practices of local officials (such as wage payments to non-existing labourers)', p. 36.

65. K. S. Gopal (2009), 'NREGA Social Audit: Myths and Reality', *Economic and Political Weekly*, vol. 44 (2009), p. 71. The table is based on Afridi's data.

66. A 2007 study by India's Centre for Science and the Environment claims that according

Well before the NREGA legislation was passed by the Indian Parliament in 2005, sceptics were saying that any such ship would inevitably sink, brought to the bottom of the ocean by the pervasive corruption that had doomed all such good intentions in the past. In 1996, two authors wrote concerning an employment guarantee scheme in the state of Maharashtra: 'Finally, by far the greatest problem which plagues the Employment Guarantee Scheme is corruption and leakages at all levels.'[67] In February 2005, before the NREGA was passed, Mihir Shah wrote: 'The major ground for scepticism regarding state-led programmes flows from many years of experience of this money going down the drain.' Shah added, however: 'So what do we do? We certainly cannot take the view that since the attempt has failed in the past, we should not make the attempt again.'[68]

Shah in fact suggests that the legislation about to be enacted might ensure that corruption falls to tolerable levels. In the past, employment guarantees were top-down doles delivered by a welfare state. In contrast, NREGA enshrines work as a right of the people. Priorities are set and projects are planned in local assemblies of villagers. Government responds to the people's demands, and if the people do not prioritize, plan and make demands, nothing happens. Shah comments: 'This is no passivity-inducing dole of a moodily munificent welfare state.'[69] He maintains that the only check to corruption in government is a vigilant people, and that when work starts in response to the people's demands, they will likely be vigilant.

Reasoning like that of Shah led to clauses in the NREGA legislation favouring people power in every possible way, from project inception to monitoring to evaluation, as well as to a complementary Right to Information Act providing transparency to empower grassroots vigilance.[70] Basic

---

to studies by the Government of India itself, after accounting for administrative costs and corruption, only 15 percent of the money appropriated for public programmes in general (without specific reference to NREGA) reaches the intended beneficiaries. *An Ecological Act: Backgrounder to the National Rural Employment Guarantee Act* (Hyderabad: Centre for Science and Environment, 2007). A report filed from India by reporters for *Bloomberg News* claims that as of an unspecified date when 33 billion US dollars had been spent on MGNREGA, 10 billion had been lost to corruption. 'District administrators and village heads have used tactics such as ghost workers, fake projects and over-billing to embezzle about $10 billion [US] from the world's largest workfare initiative.' 'India Jobs Program Scam Pays Wages to Dead Workers', *Bloomberg News*, 4 April 2013.

    67. Meeta Rajivlochan, 'Employment Guarantee Scheme', *Economic and Political Weekly*, vol. 31 (1996), p. 180.

    68. Mihir Shah, 'Saving the Employment Guarantee Act', *Economic and Political Weekly*, vol. 40 (2005), p. 509.

    69. Ibid.

    70. See, for example, L. C. Jain, 'Putting Panchayats in Charge', *Economic and Political Weekly*, vol. 40 (2005), pp. 3649–3650.

data on who is working where for what pay and why money is moving are available to all on the internet. Nevertheless, sceptics replied, caste loyalties rule in Indian villages, and dominant castes will appropriate the gains. The transmission of resources from the centre to the lowest institutional layer, the local *panchayat*, is leaky due to weak governance all along the way.[71]

In fact, studies show that the grassroots vigilance established by NREGA has more positive effects in rooting out corruption under some circumstances than under others.[72] For example, the presence of NGOs supporting the poor in asserting their rights seems to encourage citizen participation in checking corruption.[73] Indeed, intense conflict has occurred throughout India as NREGA's call for the democratization of the countryside collides with vested interests.[74] A most extreme case is the murder of indigenous activist Lalit Mehta in the state of Jharkand in 2008. Mehta had been pushing to realize in practice the social audits the law requires in principle, and it cost him his life.

Those of us who still believe part of the answer to corruption is people power—empowering ordinary citizens to be watchdogs at the grassroots level—need not concede that the data from NREGA refute us.[75] Such a pessimistic conclusion does not take into account reports that the features of NREGA (such as social audits) designed to encourage the growth of a vigilant public have not been properly implemented.[76] What has not been properly implemented cannot be properly evaluated.[77]

---

71. See, for example, Deena Khatkhate, 'Why Employment Guarantee?' *Economic and Political Weekly*, vol. 40 (2005), pp. 2114–2208.

72. See, for example, Aiyar and Samji, 'Improving the Effectiveness of the National Rural Employment Guarantee Act', *Economic and Political Weekly*, vol. 41 (2005), pp. 320–326.

73. See Reddy et al., 'Mahatma Gandhi NREGS', comparing Rajasthan with a strong NGO presence and Andra Pradesh and Bihar without. See also Farzana Afridi , 'Can Community Monitoring'. In several instances, interviewed workers reported *more* abuse in Rajasthan. It could be that there was more abuse in Rajasthan, but it could also be that workers there felt less intimidated and more supported and therefore spoke more freely.

74. Maher Shah, 'Radicalism of NREGA', *Economic and Political Weekly*, vol. 43 (2008), pp. 4, 74.

75. For some references to experiences in several countries see Farzana Afridi, 'Can Community Monitoring'. For a success story where participatory democracy has been associated with virtually zero corruption see Howard Richards, *Solidaridad, participacion, transparencia: Conversaciones sobre el socialismo en Rosario, Argentina* (Rosario, Argentina: Fundacion Estevez Boero, 2008). Some of the chapters have been translated and are available at the Unbounded Organization site, www.unboundedorganization.org.

76. See, for example, an editorial discussing the findings of the Performance Report on the first two years of NREGA by India's comptroller and auditor general: 'Wake-up Call on Rural Employment Guarantee', *Economic and Political Weekly*, vol. 43(2008), pp. 5–6.

77. W. W. Charters and John E. Jones, 'On the Risk of Appraising Non-Events in Program Evaluation', *Educational Researcher*, vol. 2 (1973), pp. 5–7.

By 2007, several places in India had adopted the practice of paying NREGA wages directly into bank accounts (as is done in the CWP). This was followed by a national directive requiring workers to be paid through bank or post office accounts, thereby separating the payment agency from the implementing agency. This directive is supposed to both ensure that the money is paid only to the labourer and reduce the incentive to fudge work registers.[78]

The significance of corruption in India is augmented by its rhetorical role in criticisms of NREGA and of employment guarantees generally. Those who condemn employment guarantees in principle and on general economic grounds tend to highlight corruption by featuring stories about scams and by citing shocking statistics.[79] Our response after considering the ongoing efforts to curb corruption is to return to where we began: the true NREGA, the NREGA as designed and intended, is still struggling to be born.

The structural background of the struggle—the *fonde* against which the details of its *formes* appear—is comprised of Staggering Facts 1 and 2. Given the economic reality of structural exclusion, a proper modernity regulated by proper modern laws is still making limited headway against the illegal survival strategies of many classes of people, including the traditional privileged castes of Indian villages. Modernity has not yet evolved to be a win-win game. A consequence of modernity's basic structure, as often remarked by Michel Foucault, is that illegal practices still govern large flows of money, even when their existence is not acknowledged in the ideal worlds of Economics 101 textbooks.

◆ ◆ ◆

> 'I work at CWP, and on the days that I am not working there, I do door-to-door. I am selling.'
>
> — CWP PARTICIPANT, RANDFONTEIN CDI

9. A Brief Digression on the Philosophy of Social Science

The hypotheses that grassroots people power, transparent records on the internet and direct deposits to bank accounts can diminish corruption are

---

78. Anish Vanaik and Siddhartha, 'Bank Payments—End of Corruption in NREGA?' *Economic and Political Weekly*, vol. 43 (2008), p. 35. The article goes on to answer its title question negatively, in spite of the positive step of paying wages through banks.

79. The *Bloomberg News* article 'India Jobs Program Scam' cited above is an example.

not yet disproven. Nevertheless, even if these three hypotheses are true, nobody believes that they constitute a satisfactory solution to the frustrating *problematique* of Indian rural poverty, of which corruption is an integral part. The absence of any convincing theory linking causes to effects and prescribing corrective actions brings us face to face with the impotence of social science.[80]

The burden of our argument is that making the economy work for the poor requires seeing the economy differently. We cannot prove our case with simple logic like *modus ponens* (if A then B; A, therefore B) or *modus tollens* (if A then B; not B, therefore not A). Simple logic requires starting from premises shared by the parties to the conversation. In our case, the required shared premises are lacking because the people we are trying to persuade do not *see* what we see. Our task, then, is to contribute to persuading the mainstream, both in academia and among the general public, to *see* the world differently. If we can strengthen the arguments of those who tend to agree with us, we may indirectly influence the mainstream, even if few ever read what we write.

To make our case, we need to destabilize some assumptions and motivate people to reread and reinterpret the world. To this end, we count on anomalies arising from the consequences of two general and pervasive principles. One, which we take in the form Marx gave it, is what we call Staggering Fact 1: production depends on profit-making.[81] When there is no profit-making, then (in pure capitalism) there is no production. When there is no production, there is no employment, no consumer goods, no tax base.

The second principle, which we call Staggering Fact 2, we take from Keynes: there is a chronic deficit of aggregate effective demand. In Keynes's own words: 'An intermediate situation which is neither desperate nor satisfactory is our normal lot.'[82] Said more simply: Creating value depends on sales. No sales, no value.

When the full significance of these two principles sinks in, it becomes clear that the real world is not the world of today's prevailing common sense. Nor is it the world protected by the intellectual fortresses at Chicago and other universities where the economics departments are neoliberal. The more these theorists and their computers think in the dominant ways, the

---

80. For valiant efforts see Agata Stachowicz-Stanusch, ed., *Organization Immunity to Corruption: Building Theoretical and Research Foundations* (Charlotte, NC: Information Age Publishing Company, 2010).
81. In Marx's terminology production depends on capital accumulation.
82. Keynes, *General Theory*, p. 250.

more deeply they think themselves and those who follow their advice into holes that are harder and harder to climb out of.

10. Objections to NREGA: 'Crowding Out' Private Enterprise

The doctrine of crowding out—the doctrine that public employment often creates little or no new employment but only or mostly crowds out employment that the private sector would otherwise have created[83]—builds a sophisticated theory on data *as seen by* common sense. Here we consider one baneful practical result of thinking dominated by such ideas: wages in NREGA.

Reddy, Sharma, Tankha and Upendranath of the Institute of Human Development at New Delhi conducted field surveys and focus group discussions to determine how much NREGA workers were being paid. These surveys and discussions occurred at randomly selected worksites in selected villages in six districts, two each in the states of Andhra Pradesh, Bihar and Rajasthan. Part of what they found is represented in the following table:

Range and Averages of Daily Wages Paid under NREGA in Rupees (translated into US dollars at 50 rupees per dollar)[84]

	Andhra Pradesh	Bihar	Rajasthan
Maximum for male workers	125 (USD 2.50)	114 (USD 2.28)	100 (USD 2.00)
Maximum for Female workers	125 (USD 2.50)	114 (USD 2.28)	100 (USD 2.00)
Minimum for Male workers	80 (USD 1.60)	60 (USD 1.20)	20 (USD .40)
Minimum for Female workers	80 (USD 1.60)	68 (USD 1.36)	20 (USD .40)
Average for Male workers	103 (USD 2.06)	104 (USD 2.08)	72 (USD 1.44)
Average for Female workers	102 (USD 2.04)	105 (USD 2.10)	72 (USD 1.44)

The discrepancy between the minimum wage and the wage actually paid is partly due to the use of piece rates. NREGA workers are typically paid not by the day but by how much work they get done, or more precisely, how much work a supervisor certifies that they got done. The piece rate is supposed to be calibrated so that a normal worker working a normal day

---

83. The theory of crowding out was first developed by the Swedish economist Eli Heckscher. We simplify its definition for clarity. Normally the question is not whether all or none of public employment is a net increase in employment. It is *how much* is a net increase and *how much* is offset by a resulting decrease in private employment.

84. This table combines field survey findings at various dates in 2008, 2009 and 2010. More complete wage data can be found in Chandrasekhar and Ghosh, 'Public Works and Wages'.

will earn at least the minimum wage. But the supervisor may make mistakes or be on a power trip or be engaged in a corrupt scheme.[85] Among a group of workers digging a well, it may be hard to tell who is working and who is shirking. Sometimes a worker does not get enough done to earn minimum wage because she or he is weak or impaired or lacks motivation.

Interviews with workers revealed a less obvious explanation for workers' dragging their feet: there is resentment against having to earn their wage through heavy manual labour that could be more effectively and economically done with machines. The same inefficiency cited by critics of the programme who complain that the government is not getting value for its money, translates into feelings among the workers that they are getting neither much money nor much dignity.[86]

The parliamentary majority[87] that enacted NREGA in 2005 did not intend to demean India's rural poor by assigning them useless tasks and making them suffer enough to justify paying them. It *did* intend to give them hard work at low pay. The depth of the hard-work-low-pay intention can be plumbed by reading between the lines of an argument made by T. S. Papola shortly before NREGA was enacted.

One of the debates around the bill's successive drafts pitted those who wanted to restrict eligibility to households below the poverty line against those who wanted the bill to support to the right of every citizen to work stated in the Constitution of India.[88] Papola favoured the latter. He advocated for a right to demand employment with no means test. In doing so he revealed much about the frame of mind of the designers of NREGA.[89]

Papola observes that in rural areas only about 2 percent of the workforce

---

85. It should be noted that Reddy et al. also find that about three-quarters of the time there *is* grassroots participation in deciding what tasks to undertake with NREGA-paid labour. The picture drawn by Deena Khatkhate of the privileged few continuing to dominate the underprivileged many is not the whole picture.

86. We know of no quantitative measures or estimates of how widespread either phenomenon is, i.e., that of use of manual labour where a more capital-intensive technology would be more rational, or that of workers feeling demeaned. We think their apparent existence, in whatever quantity, tells us something about the system and the need for an unbounded approach to transforming it.

87. We speak of the 'majority' involved in the complex politics of getting the act into final form. In its final form it was passed unanimously.

88. T.S. Papola, 'A Universal Programme is Feasible', *Economic and Political Weekly*, vol. 40 (2005), pp. 594–599. The 'universal programme' would of course be only *similar* to a right to work for every citizen, since it presumably would be limited as NREGA is to the countryside, to people able-bodied and over eighteen, and to one worker per household.

89. We assume that Papola also reveals something of the frame of mind of the audience he writes for and hopes to persuade.

falls in the category of 'principal status' unemployed all year. On a typical day about 7 percent are unemployed. He cites evidence that in the Maharashtra state programme started in 1977, self-selection limited the number of participants to levels the government could afford to pay. There was no need to assume the gigantic administrative task of determining who was and was not eligible, thereby inviting corruption by giving officials power to determine who could participate. There were a few 'leakages' in Maharashtra in which nonpoor workers did public work for pay, but those people were not much above the poverty line.

Wages, Papola continues, ought to be fixed so that only the really needy are interested in NREGA and so that labour will not be drawn away from other productive activities, particularly agricultural work. He assumes that India's growing numbers of educated poor will not participate in NREGA because they would rather remain poor while waiting for employment commensurate with their skills than do unskilled manual labour. He uses a standard *crowding out* criticism: if workers choose NREGA over private employment because it pays more, then NREGA 'will only be replacing the existing, and not creating additional employment. At the same time, it will interrupt agricultural operations due to the likely shortage of labour.'[90]

Papola then faces the inevitable conundrum: It is known that farmers customarily (and illegally) pay labourers less than minimum wage. Hence on theoretical grounds any public programme paying minimum wage and available on demand would crowd out private sector labour in agriculture. To this theoretical argument he offers a two-pronged response: First, while in Maharashtra the public employment guarantee tended to raise wages, this tendency was not large. Therefore, whether and how much NREGA might create a shortage of agricultural labour should be monitored empirically and not just assumed on theoretical grounds. Second, if NREGA should have the effect of raising agricultural wages, that should be regarded as a positive impact, not a danger.

Papola then recounts a bit of history: The state of Maharashtra's employment guarantee programme attempted to accommodate the interests of agriculture by paying less than the minimum wage (and less than farmers were paying) at certain times and places. Workers and their activist supporters objected. They sued the state in court. Maharashtra's lawyers made the somewhat contorted argument that the minimum wage law applied

90. Papola, 'A Universal Programme', p. 596.

only to private employment (where, admittedly, it was not enforced), while the state as sovereign could elect to pay less than minimum wage. The case went all the way to the Supreme Court of India. The workers won. It was one thing for a state to be lax in enforcing labour laws, turning a blind eye to employers who were violating them. It was quite another for the state itself to violate both its own laws and national laws.

Papola straddles the fence by agreeing in principle both that NREGA should never take workers away from private sector employment and that it would be a good thing to raise wages. He then makes quantitative projections, seeking to show that, even without a means test, NREGA would be so unattractive that only small numbers of desperately poor people would volunteer for it. It would not threaten farmers with a shortage of workers willing to work for market wages, and it would not threaten the government with a wage bill beyond what the public purse could afford.

We should not read India as a backward country compelled by technical necessity to exact hours of underpaid labour from its semi-starved peasantry to feed the teeming millions of its cities.[91] India is a nation blessed with world-class agricultural scientists. It is dotted with nuclear plants that generate energy used to fix nitrogen from the air for fertilizer. In recent years, the government of India has filled warehouses with food grains deliberately withheld from the market, lest a decline in food prices drive already economically distressed farmers to the wall.[92] There are recurrent waves of suicides of small farmers unable to pay their debts.[93] And if today many farmers cannot sell their harvests at cost-covering prices, leaving a decent margin for themselves, what would happen if tomorrow the government changed its policy, letting food prices fall instead of propping them up? What would happen if farmers were forced to pay minimum wage, and if the minimum wage were raised high enough to lift rural workers out of poverty? How many farmer suicides would occur then? And so the anomalies accumulate.

---

91. However, from an objective if not yet from a subjective point of view, it *is* a technical necessity for India to transform its economy to make life sustainable. This point is well made by the Indian physicist Vandana Shiva in several works. For example, Vandana Shiva, *Staying Alive* (London: ZED Books, 1988).

92. 'The government has been saddled with massive food grain stocks which had built up to 63 million tonnes by the beginning of July 2002.' Prabhat Patnaik, 'On the Need for Providing Employment Guarantee', *Economic and Political Weekly*, vol. 40 (2005), p. 203. Jean Drèze ('Democracy and the Right to Food', p. 1722) writes of 70 million tonnes of surplus grain in government warehouses.

93. Raj Patel, *Stuffed and Starved: Markets, Power and the Hidden Battle for the World Food System* (London: Portobello Books, 2008). See also the Wikipedia article 'Farmer Suicides in India'.

These questions point to anomalies that call for a paradigm shift. They call for an unbounded paradigm that frankly acknowledges that a functional social order must meet needs in harmony with nature. Period. The assumption that the road out of poverty must follow the single route of making business profitable so that business will hire workers, so workers will have money in their pockets, so they can go to stores and buy what they need to live *must be dropped.*

Once again, community, not just economy, is required. Even markets, like other institutions, work only when people are norm-abiding; in Max Weber's terms, there must be community (*Gemeinschaft* and *Gemeinshandeln*) before there can be human social relationships. In John Searle's terms, institutions work only when humans rise to the occasion when duty calls, exercising their remarkable deontic capacity to do the right thing even when it is not what they want to do. People are norm-abiding because they are biologically coded to be culturally coded; they can be socialized to respect the norms of the community, and they can go on to individualize themselves as coherent personalities with moral integrity. From a psychological and physiological perspective, humans can create and operate functional institutions because in most cases their moral development is normal, not pathological. Today's underdose of community and overdose of economy is an underdose of something very real and very promising: ethics. But for millions of poor Indians toiling for NREGA, it is a *pis aller* created by good intentions trapped in bounded thinking.

Amartya Sen and Jean Drèze frequently emphasize, and we agree, that markets are not always the best way to organize human activity, and the prices set by markets are not always the best prices. From our unbounded perspective, it makes no sense to talk, think and act as if market prices were *a priori* the right prices and to talk, think and act as if other institutions become relevant only in cases of market failure.

We find a mentality less enlightened than the minds of Sen and Drèze at work in the public debates that culminated in the approval of NREGA. Private farming tends to be given priority not because of the facts but because of an ideological haze. India's minifarms are in most cases beastly inefficient. On an objective view of the facts, to produce food efficiently, India should eliminate both the work done by many landless labourers and the minifarms of their dirt-poor employers. It should rely on its high-tech, highly capitalized world-class farmers and on future technologies now at the laboratory stage, such as artificial photosynthesis.

But of course in market terms there is no need to produce more food. India already has more food than can be sold without depressing farm prices. It is stored in government warehouses even while the poor go hungry. Here it is appropriate to repeat another opinion of Michel Foucault: the greatest contemporary political problem is *lack of imagination*.

NREGA carries within its constitutive rules the scars of an approval process that deliberately designed the programme to be unattractive and inefficient. Standard arguments against crowding out are partly to blame for this tragic result.

♦ ♦ ♦

> 'We don't sell the vegetables. So you decide that I can see the family is struggling, let me give them some vegetables even though they have not asked for them.'
>
> — CWP PARTICIPANT, UMTHWALUME

11. The Suicide of Tapas Soren

The case of Tapas Soren provides a window on the practical realities we have in mind when we partially blame the economic theory of crowding out for misery that could be avoided.[94] Tapas Soren was a farmer in the village of Birakhap in the state of Jharkand. Birakhap had no road. Soren's business and those of his neighbours might have been stimulated by having a road that connected Birakhap's farms to the world's markets.

Tapas and his brother Dilip owned 4.54 parched acres. Their income from the one crop a year they were able to tease out of the land kept their household afloat for about four months. The remaining eight months of the year, they hired themselves out as labourers on other people's land, often far away. If NREGA had been administered as the letter of the law provides, it would have made their lives easier by employing them at minimum wage within five kilometres of their home.

Tapas's dream was to drill a deep well on his land down twenty feet, where he believed water lay. His dream coincided with the clauses in the NREGA legislation providing funding for labour to create useful infrastructure,

---

94. The following paragraphs are based on Anish Vanaik, 'NREGA and the Death of Tapas Soren', *Economic and Political Weekly*, vol. 43 (2008), pp. 8–10. Vanaik's data on payment delays and number of days worked are fruits of NREGA's transparency policy of putting information online for the entire world to see.

either on public land or on private land belonging to smallholders. Tapas submitted a well-digging proposal to the local authorities.

Tapas was ethnically a tribal person, like most of the villagers in his district. In the district's one nontribal village, twenty-six well-digging projects were funded between 2006, when NREGA began in the area, and mid-2008. Tapas's well was the only one ever authorized in one of the tribal villages. The standard bribe in the district for approval of a well project was 10,000 rupees. Tapas paid 15,000 rupees.

When his well project was approved and in principle funded, Tapas Soren automatically became the responsible leader of ten men digging a well: himself, his brother Dilip, and eight others. His first challenge was to keep his crew working. When the NREGA money to pay their wages was slow in coming, the workers were wont to walk off the job to take employment with local farmers. The farmers paid less, but at least they paid promptly. A farmer like Tapas Soren could really afford to run his project only if he had his own funds to keep his workers on the job while payment from public funds was stalled. Tapas managed to field a big enough crew to keep digging, sometimes three days a week, sometimes four.

The local *panchayat* administering NREGA was paying wages with delays as long as forty or fifty days. Under such circumstances, nobody wanted to work for NREGA. Nobody could wait that long to buy food. Now we know how a local panchayat could make a dead-letter law out of a national law requiring the state to provide NREGA employment on demand in fifteen days or less during an agricultural off-season: by delaying payment. However, in Birakhap that year, the facts were a little different. NREGA projects were minimal, even in the agricultural off-season.[95] The average employment generated for a household participating in NREGA was thirty days. During some parts of the year, there was no NREGA work at all. Needless to say, there was no effort made to build a road.

Work on Tapas's well came to a standstill when it hit a layer of hard rock. Since NREGA had been deliberately designed to provide only manual labour, under the law Tapas had no access to the jackhammers, dynamite or scientific expertise that might have solved the problem. Indeed, proper technical backup might have advised Tapas not to try to dig a well in that particular place at all. Then, on 1 July 2008, when Tapas went to his bank expecting to find NREGA funds there to pay his workers, he was told there

---

95. Ibid., p.8. Part of the explanation might be that, in the Birakhap area, generation of work depended on someone paying a bribe to get a project approved.

was no money in his account. The money had been deposited without his knowledge and then withdrawn without his knowledge. (Evidently the national directive requiring direct deposit of NREGA funds to the participant's account could be circumvented.) Tapas complained to the district block officer and to a headman, the *panchayat sevak*. It is not known what transpired in those conversations. It is known that afterwards, Tapas was heard shouting *aur anyay nahi sahenge*— "I will not tolerate any more injustice."

Tapas was trapped. His workers were demanding their pay. He could not move the rock. Administrators were holding him responsible for failing to complete the project they had authorized and funded. He had spent more than he could afford on bribery and had nothing to show for it. His bank account had been looted. On 2 July, Tapas Soren doused his clothes and his body with kerosene and set himself on fire. Six painful days later, he died in hospital.

There is an obvious chain of causal influences linking his suicide to the general economic theories from which the doctrine of crowding out is derived, to the crowding out theory itself and to the shape the NREGA took under the influence of the crowding out theory.

12. Common Complaints against NREGA 'in Principle'

Expressed in US dollars, the sums per year the government of India has spent on NREGA started out at 2.5 billion dollars a year in 2006–7, grew to 8.91 billion dollars in 2010–11, and remained nearly there. In light of these large state expenditures and the fact that they would be even larger if NREGA paid better and served more people more days per year (recently it has been providing at least some work for more than 50 million households a year), it is not surprising that common neoliberal charges are brought against NREGA. They argue that the amount spent per year and the number of households served should always both be zero.[96] The general arguments in chapters 3 and 4 demonstrating the impossibility of sustainably eliminating poverty with pure free markets already make common neoliberalism a nonstarter. So does our general case for using unbounded thinking to design cultures to meet human needs in harmony with nature. Still, it may be helpful to mention some forms common nonstarters have taken in the Indian context.

---

96. The background for specific complaints about NREGA and general skepticism about alternatives to private investment is typified, e.g., in Frank Zahn, 'A Flow of Funds Analysis of Crowding Out', *Southern Economic Journal*, vol. 45, no. 1 (July 1978), pp. 136–153.

One such objection is that NREGA solves a nonproblem because the proportion of workers who are unemployed most of the year in rural India is only 2 percent.[97] Another generic objection, in principle, to NREGA is that generating employment should be left to the private sector. This is one of many conclusions drawn from the general argument that, with few exceptions, everything is done best when it is motivated by profit-seeking.[98]

A third common objection to public employment in principle agrees to spend public money to help the poor but not through public employment programmes.[99] A common argument supporting this view is that the best way to help the poor rise into prosperity is to raise the value of what they have to sell. This reasoning does not imagine a time when the ex-poor will be prosperous for the same reason the rich are prosperous now, namely, because they capture rents. What the poor have to sell (now) is themselves. They sell their labour power. This reasoning often goes on to recommend raising the market value of the labour power of the poor by concentrating social spending on health and education.[100]

The crowding-out argument and these three related objections to NREGA are visible tips of an invisible iceberg, the iceberg being, once again, Adam Smith's idea of the self-regulating market. Leon Walras declared this idea to be as beautiful as the mechanical perfection of the starry skies. Recent versions of the enchanting visions of Smith and Walras will be considered in chapter 8, where we consider how neoliberal economics is an imaginary world that is holding the real world captive. The following chapter mentions the crowding out argument again in a Swedish context.

---

97. This objection is made, e.g., by Deena Khatkhate in 'Why Employment Guarantee?'

98. Thus Vijay Joshi and Ian Little argue, with respect to the privatization of public sector industries in India and the ensuing dismissal of redundant employees by the new private owners, that the dismissed employees will find real jobs in a private sector revitalized by India's economic reforms. They will then earn their pay by producing goods for which there is market demand. These authors are liberals but not social Darwinists, proposing what they believe to be better ways to serve the poor. They endorse improving the marketable skills of the poor by public expenditures on health and education. See *India's Economic Reforms, 1991–2001* (New York: Clarendon Press, 1996).

99. We here distil what we take to be an underlying premise of many mixed bag criticisms, i.e., that the real way to end poverty is for all poor people to acquire marketable skills, not to separate the duty to work from the necessity to sell. See, for example, the *Wall Street Journal* article, 'India's Boom Bypasses Rural Poor', 29 April 2011.

100. The same or similar reasoning can be used to justify going beyond health and education to support the poor in any number of ways, with the end-in-view of empowering them to compete successfully in markets.

CHAPTER SEVEN
The Swedish Model as Programmed for Failure

OVERVIEW OF THE CHAPTER

1. Introduction
2. Keynes's Problem Revisited
3. Celebrating and Understanding the Swedish Model's Achievements
4. The Seduction of the Swedes by Orthodox Economic Theory
5. The Failure of the Swedish Model: Alice Rivlin
6. The Failure of the Swedish Model: Assar Lindbeck
7. Conclusions: More on Unbounded Organization

1. Introduction

In the thirty glorious years immediately following World War II, the social democracies of western Europe were the inspiration for movements the world over that sought to combine freedom and justice—and Sweden stood out in this regard. Sweden gave us Dag Hammarskjold, the visionary first Secretary General of the United Nations, who led a new world order that avoided what everybody then feared, namely, that the world would fall back into the mass unemployment, fascisms and violence that had prevailed before the war. Sweden also gave us Gunnar Myrdal, a chief architect of what was known as the Swedish Model, who set out how to teach the rest of the world how to achieve similar results with similar methods.[1] And now? In 2021, in many places the long-feared social disintegration and polarization is happening. In Sweden itself the classic post-war Swedish Model is long gone, and the nation is seeking new ideas to prevent the orderly retreat of the welfare state from turning into a rout.

---

1. As a side note, Myrdal's sojourn in India during the 1960s did not shake his faith in the universal applicability of western European social democracy. He and his partner, Alva Myrdal, went to India believing that what had worked in Sweden could be made to work in Asia and worldwide, and they left India nurturing the same belief. Gunnar Myrdal, *Asian Drama* (London: Penguin, 1968). See especially the chapter on Enlightenment ideals.

We choose Sweden as a case study in order to explore this question: Was social democracy inevitably unsustainable and thus programmed for failure, or could social democracy possibly have succeeded and therefore now might be revived? We allege that the failure of the post-war Swedish experiment identifies and demonstrates the causal powers of the deep structures of a global civilizational crisis. It provides evidence for making our case that people and planet can survive only if there are deep culture shifts constituting fundamental transformations of social structures.

Krzysztof Wielecki, a professor of sociology in Warsaw, has devoted himself to studying whether in our times there really is a civilizational crisis. Is the use of the term justified, or is it loose talk that exaggerates or even invents problems? 'Crisis' is a medical term. It refers to the crucial stage in an illness or a recovery from trauma when the patient's life hangs in the balance, when it is determined whether the patient will recover or will die.

Recently Wielicki has summarized his reasons for concluding that today humanity does indeed confront a civilizational crisis. He considers the European social democracies as having been high points of prosocial democratic capitalism, which he calls mature capitalism. Its decline in Europe starting about 1970 is emblematic of a similar decline of hope around the world, and evidence of the reality of a civilizational crisis. Here are seven of his key findings: (1) Powerful social conflicts are increasing as the welfare state, which was an historic social compromise, is invalidated. (2) There are two types of capitalism—a ruthless capitalism that destroys people, environment and culture, and a more communitarian capitalism, best represented by Sweden; the processes of globalization favour the ruthless type. (3) The balance of forces between employers and employees is declining because technology is squeezing out labour. (4) Hence the foundations of democratic liberal states where prosperity is shared are swaying. (5) The dominant global corporations and the global market are not subject to the jurisdiction and control of individual states; hence the state cannot fulfil its role as mediator of the great historical compromise previously reached. (6) The middle class, which was a stabilizing factor, is also being squeezed out. (7) Worldwide, growing numbers of people do not and will not have jobs, and this is becoming hereditary.[2]

We begin this discussion by revisiting, under the heading 'Keynes's

---

2. Krzysztof Wielecki, 'The Contemporary Civilizational Crisis from the Perspective of Critical Realism', *Journal of Critical Realism*, vol. 19 (2020), pp. 269–284.

Problem',[3] some points made in previous chapters. These points connect with Wielecki's points about the role of joblessness in the civilizational crisis. They connect also with why the classic Swedish Model and its subsequent amendments not only did not last but *could not last*. They connect further with why the flexibility and the ethical stance of the unbounded approach offer a way out of the crisis, and with why South Africa's Community Work Programme is a growth point in that possibility.

♦ ♦ ♦

> 'We used to go bed with empty stomachs, but now we are swiping cards like educated people.'
> — FROM A SONG OF CWP PARTICIPANTS IN NONGOMA, KWAZULU-NATAL, COGTA

2. Keynes's Problem Revisited

'Keynes's problem' is the lack of sufficient business activity in a modern market society. It is an economic problem that morphs into any number of crucial political and social problems. People depend on business activity to provide essential goods and to avoid catastrophic bads. The catastrophic bad that weighed most heavily on Keynes's mind was the mass unemployment of the 1930s. Economic activity is important to provide dignified livelihoods in the form of jobs, employment and other honourable and funded ways of being occupied. Part of the civilizational crisis is that conventional jobs are drying up, yet people are culturally programmed to want jobs and to be dependent on them to earn money. We humans now living are being called to invent new livelihoods—as in the Community Work Programme—and to recover old ones. Following Elinor Ostrom, we must notice livelihoods that have been there all the time but have not been acknowledged by conventional economic categories. We denote these livelihoods in all their variety as *slots*.

Keynes's problem can be defined more precisely, using Keynes's own words, as consisting of two complementary parts: (1) 'the drag on prosperity that can be exercised by an insufficiency of effective demand'[4]; and (2) the 'chronic tendency throughout human history for the propensity to save to

---

3. Our thanks to Dean Björn Åstrand of Karlstad University in Sweden for his helpful comments.
4. John Maynard Keynes, *General Theory* (London: Macmillan, 1936), p. 33.

be stronger than the inducement to invest. This weakness of the inducement to invest has been at all times the key to the economic problem.'[5] In other words, (1) lack of sales leads to (2) lack of investment, which leads to no end of troubles.

Investment is often insufficient because there is often reason to doubt that there would be *sufficient sales* of the goods or services whose production the proposed investment would finance. To be *sufficient* to *induce a rational investment*, sales would have to produce revenues that return the original investment, plus cover wage costs and all other costs of production, plus promise an attractive return to the investor with a minimal risk of loss. The attractive return would have to exceed the return the investor could earn without making any contribution to the real economy, for example, by buying up land and waiting for its price to rise.

There are two bottom lines: the modern market economy has more people than slots, and the investors call the shots. In most cases the investors or their agents determine what employment there will be and who will be employed; in Keynes's view, they make these determinations after estimating the size of the market for their products. The size of any market is always limited by what he called liquidity preference. For various reasons, individuals, businesses and public institutions prefer to take money out of circulation, keeping it instead of spending it. We take it to be true that not all money is spent, and consequently there is at least one sufficient reason why not everybody is employed, even though liberals have scored some points in their ceaseless efforts to discredit Keynes's theory.

Troubles endlessly stem partly from the suffering and from the frequently anti-social and/or self-destructive behaviour of people whose work finds no buyers willing to pay a decent price for it. They stem from the violence of gangs and of the police—from the violence of Pol Pot avenging injustice and the violence of General Suharto imposing law and order. Troubles stem also from the subordination of government policies—and of everything about our way of life—to the overriding imperative to please investors.[6]

Keynes found no acceptable solution to Keynes's problem, nor did he claim to have found one. He was of course aware of about a dozen countries that, in his time, *did* achieve full employment in centrally planned

---

5. Ibid., pp. 347–48.
6. See Jeffrey Winters, *Power in Motion: Capital Mobility and the Indonesian State* (Ithaca, NY: Cornell University Press, 1996).

command economies, but he did not consider that route acceptable. If Keynes's problem could be well solved, there would be a future role in society—one providing dignity and security and offering opportunities to satisfy every item in Abraham Maslow's catalogue of human needs—awaiting every newborn child. The message 'Welcome to the world, you are safe and loved here', communicated by satisfaction of the newborn's first desire, to suck milk from its mother's breast, would be a true message.

In outlining our solution to Keynes's problem, we propose that the problem is, at bottom, and contradicting Keynes's own words, not an economic problem. It is a consequence of social structures that are part of what Joseph Schumpeter called the institutional frame of economics, which are a given. It is inevitable, given the individualistic cultural rules that constitute the material positions that comprise Western modernity's standard social structure: buyer and seller, owner, party to contract, and so on. As the European world system became the modern world system, these same material positions morphed into the legal structure of the global economy. The solution we propose to today's civilizational crisis requires a transition from social structures where most people work to social structures where technology does most of the work and most people enjoy what Amartya Sen has called nonmercantile livelihoods and Adam Smith called nonproductive labour because they produce no 'vendible product'.

Keynes glimpsed but did not grasp that his most important discoveries—(1) insufficiency of demand and (2) weakness of the inducement to invest, and hence his (inadequate) explanations for the excess of people over slots—were about consequences of social structures that had been constituted in the course of history by cultural rules. André Orléan has described the central consequences of the currently dominant structure: 'Indeed, the commercial society does not know these bonds of solidarity existing between parents, neighbours or close relations, thanks to which, in traditional societies, each one can directly mobilize the assistance of the others to carry out his projects. To obtain something from others, in the commercial order, there are no "means other than to arouse the others' desire".'[7] Thus in 2011, André Orléan updated Adam Smith's famous words of 1776 asserting that to obtain our daily bread we never appeal to our needs or to our baker's humanity, but always to his desires. Orléan continues: 'Our starting point [i.e., our way of talking about today's dominant social structure] is market

---

7. André Orléan, *L'Empire de la valeur* (Paris: Seuil, 2011), p. 158. Our translation.

separation, that is, a world in which each individual is cut off from their means of existence. Only the power of value, invested in the monetary object, allows the existence of a social life under such auspices. It reunites separated individuals by building for them a common horizon, the desire for money, and a common language, that of accounts.'[8]

Today's dysfunctional structures cannot be transformed into life-affirming win-win structures without transforming the basic cultural structures. To repeat: *the excess of people over slots is a consequence of social structures that have been constituted over the course of history by cultural rules.* As we will see, transforming basic cultural structures was far from the minds of the architects of post–World War II Swedish social democracy.

◆ ◆ ◆

'I am happy for Seriti work. It found me when I was frustrated, and it took away that frustration. I used to drink a lot. But after joining Seriti I realised that God is good and he is alive and he loves me. This is the beginning.'

— CWP PARTICIPANT, RANDFONTEIN CDI

3. Celebrating and Understanding the Swedish Model's Achievements

The Swedish economy today (2021) still looks good when compared to many that are worse, even though the Swedish welfare state continues to decline.[9] However, our topic here is not the Sweden of today but the Sweden that for about thirty years (1945–1975) ended poverty and appeared to demonstrate how the rest of the world could end poverty too.[10] The Swedish Model was taken to show that social democracy worked and that capitalism worked. Its achievements really were remarkable, and both advocates of democratic socialism and advocates of capitalism took credit for them.

---

8. Ibid., p. 227. Our translation.

9. Jeffrey Winters provides an insightful analysis of the ongoing worldwide decline of welfare states with his concept of 'locational revolution'. Today nation-states do not govern capital as much as they attempt to attract capital to their shores and away from the shores of other nation-states. Capital chooses where it wants to go, which *ceteris paribus* is those locations where wages and taxes are lowest while profits are highest. As 'locational revolution', which is still in its beginnings, takes hold, it will further erode welfare states and exacerbate inequality around the world. Winters, *Power in Motion*.

10. See the more complete account given in chs. 5–8 of Howard Richards and Joanna Swanger, *The Dilemmas of Social Democracies* (Lanham, MD: Rowman and Littlefield, 2006).

In a wide sense, the Swedish Model was Keynesian.[11] In a less wide sense, the Swedes arrived at the principles of the model largely on their own, in the thinking of Swedish economists like Hammarskjöld, Myrdal, Alf Johansson and others. In a narrow sense, the Swedish Model was the Rehn-Meidner Model, developed by two economists of Sweden's largest labour confederation (known as the LO), Gösta Rehn and Rudolf Meidner.

Since we interpret the Swedish Model as able to work only temporarily under unusual circumstances and thus doomed to fail,[12] ours is a celebratory yet also cautionary tale addressed to those who do not remember that the neoliberal capitalist revolution was made possible by the failure of 'Keynesian' social democracy[13] and who, now that neoliberalism has also failed, rush to advocate repeating the same policies. (Keynes's diagnosis is still indispensable reading, but so-called Keynesian[14] remedies, while they may sometimes ameliorate, do not cure.)

An integral part of the Swedish Model at its high tide was an employment guarantee. The government became the employer of last resort. Government wages established a floor—a high floor, not a low floor as in NREGA—assuring that there could be no low wages in Sweden (except in the exploitation of immigrants in the country illegally).

The architects of the Swedish Model, in their effort to build a high-wage welfare state[15] with full employment,[16] accepted the constraints that follow when growth is regarded as a logical necessity to bring up the poor

---

11. See Bo Sandelin (ed.), *The History of Swedish Economic Thought* (London: Routledge, 1991).

12. We mean this for any of the senses just discussed. For more on the generically Keynesian solutions to the problems of capitalism here, see Richards and Swanger, *The Dilemmas of Social Democracies*.

13. Nicholas Kaldor, 'Keynesian Economics after Fifty Years', in *Keynes and the Modern World*, compiled by David Warwick and James Trevithick (Cambridge, UK: Cambridge University Press, 1983).

14. 'Keynesian' is not to be confused with Keynes's own nuanced views or with 'post-Keynesian'. Both Steve Keen and Hyman Minsky give details on how Keynes's views were distorted by many of the theories and policies that later became known as 'Keynesian'.

15. We consider together the 'welfare state'—defined as government services, transfers, policies and institutions promoting high wages—and full employment. Both tend to burden profits and high incomes for the sake of promoting social equality. Both also regulate and supplement markets rather than leaving markets to themselves. Hence, they tend to run into similar constraints, i.e., disincentives to production.

16. In the two decades immediately after World War II, unemployment in Sweden fluctuated, according to unemployment insurance statistics, between 1% and 2.5%. These figures count those being paid while being retrained or employed by the government as employer of last resort as employed rather than as unemployed. If they were counted as unemployed the numbers would be about half a percent higher. Assar Lindbeck, 'Period', *American Economic Review*, vol. 58 (1968), pp. 7–8.

while not bringing down the rich. They accepted the necessity of curbing inflation and of subsidizing industries to help them compete in foreign markets. They accepted dependence on exports, ignoring Aristotle's principle that a polis must be self-sufficient to be self-governing. Sweden's initial success seemed to confirm the optimistic thesis the Austrian socialist Karl Renner had advanced in 1904. Renner had argued that the same civil law framework that had been created in Europe in early modernity (drawing heavily on Roman precedents) to make capitalism possible could be used to make socialism possible.[17]

Let us celebrate some of the many ways the Swedish Model succeeded, albeit temporarily.

Given the orthodox premise that profits move the economy, Keynes and his Swedish colleagues reasoned that there are no profits without sales, no sales without customers and no customers without people having money in their pockets. The Swedish Model was designed to put money in the pockets of the people. It spurred growth by assuring investors that they could make profits, first, because their nontradeable products (about two-thirds of all products), i.e., the products that could not be exported, could be sold in domestic markets. Why? Because Swedish consumers had money. Second, Swedish capitalists could make money producing for export, partly because their tradeable products were launched into foreign markets with the backing and often the financing of the state's industrial policy.

Gunnar Myrdal described Swedish social democracy as a 'created harmony'. Conceding to Adam Smith the prerogative of calling free markets, where individual buyers and sellers make deals with each other, *natural*, Myrdal argued that there is a harmony more harmonious than a natural one. Experience has shown, he said, that it is in the interest of workers for economic life to be governed not by separate contracts among individuals but by general rules of labour legislation and for wages to be set by collective bargaining.[18] The result was, as the Swedes proposed even

---

17. Karl Renner, *The Institutions of Private Law and their Social Functions* (London: Routledge, 1976 (German original 1904)). Why a neo-Roman civil law jurisprudence was required to make capitalism possible is discussed extensively by Max Weber in *Economy and Society*. English common law achieved the same goal by a slightly different route and was in fact greatly influenced by Roman law.

18. Gunnar Myrdal, *Beyond the Welfare State* (New Haven, CT: Yale University Press, 1960), pp. 19–29, 62–64. In his Yale lectures published in that book Myrdal attributes Sweden's success to planning (e.g., p. 63). If that were correct, then if other countries learned to plan like Sweden, they could enjoy prosperity like Sweden's. Even as Myrdal spoke, international agencies were running seminars in the capitals of third world countries teaching their governing elites how to plan. Ibid., pp. 228–249.

before they read Keynes, deliberately induced growth stimulated by mass consumption. But after the team of which Myrdal was a key member allayed the great fear that after World War II Sweden would fall back into the depression of the thirties, it became clear that the great danger was not depression but inflation.

Gösta Rehn made an ingenious anti-inflation argument that justified the transfer of corporate profits via the government to fund social programmes. It was a centrepiece of the Rehn-Meidner classic Swedish Model. Profit margins had to be low to force employers to resist wage demands. Somewhat paradoxically, this eminent economist, who was employed by the labour unions, argued that it would be inflationary to give labour everything it asked for. It was not enough to jawbone the unions. It was not effective to keep prices down with price controls and other administrative measures. The supply of money had to be kept reasonably tight and interest rates reasonably high. One way to reduce inflationary pressure was by deducting compulsory contributions from wages for pension funds.[19] As a result, the workers had *less* money to spend, not so much less that they failed to be good consumers, but enough less—thanks to management of the economy by a competent technocracy—to be one component of a created harmony that kept inflation in check.

Further—and here is the key—to stop inflationary wage increases, it had to be really true that employers could not afford wage increases (beyond those justified by productivity increases) because they did not have the money, since the government had taken most of their profits away in taxes. There had to be capital formation, but that did not necessarily mean augmenting the incomes of the fifteen or so families who owned the bulk of Swedish industry. The standard liberal view is that since the rich have incomes exceeding reasonable levels of consumer spending, they are more likely to contribute to capital formation than ordinary people. The rich are seen as the 'saving classes'. But Sweden, like virtually all of Eastern Europe and the Communist Bloc at the time, took a different approach. Capital formation was too important to leave to the capitalists.[20] There were the *löntagarfonder*, union-run pension funds controlling large and growing sums. There were cooperatives.

---

19. Writing in 1968, Lindbeck expected pension fund contributions to be 9.5 percent of wages and salaries in 1969. Lindbeck, 'Period', p. 30.

20. Indeed, public capital formation in socialist countries generally exceeded the rates of capital formation in capitalist countries. Richard Musgrave, *Fiscal Systems* (New Haven, CT: Yale University Press, 1969), p. 35.

The cooperatives and *löntagarfonder* had deep roots in Sweden. They were more likely to invest at home, less likely to roam the world seeking lower wages, lower taxes, more lax environmental regulations and higher profits. Further, they corrected the bias of private capital for short-term profits, being more willing to wait for the payoffs of long-term investments. They could work together with private capital in partnerships that private capital would not undertake on its own.

Meanwhile, Volvo, Saab, Electrolux, Ericsson and other companies, and the fabulously successful musical group ABBA, had plenty of money to invest in winning global technology races and in doing creative marketing. The government made sure they got what they needed. Part of the money that it took away by taxing profits it gave back to subsidize international competitiveness.

A *sine qua non* of the Swedish Model was *export or die*. The tradeable sector had to generate income from sales that could support—in one ingenious way or another—full employment and high wages in all sectors. This implied supporting the Swedish team of companies—Ericsson, Saab, Volvo, Electrolux, ABBA—as they competed in worldwide technological and marketing races. It also implied keeping the prices of Swedish exports low enough—and therefore the value of the Swedish krona relative to other currencies low enough—to be competitive in global markets

Working within the basic cultural rules and basic social structure of modernity in the ways just described and others, the objective of the Swedish Model was to build a welfare state, a *folkhemmet* where the Swedes (the *folks*) would care and be cared for in their home (the *hemmet*). When the government became the employer of last resort, guaranteeing to every Swede dignified and useful employment at high wages—not low wages like those of NREGA and the CWP; and when high-wage public employment available to all built a floor under private wages, since it was virtually impossible to hire anyone paying less than what the government was paying, then one might say that one essential component of a *folkhemmet,* namely, shared prosperity, had been achieved. A pinnacle. It will be instructive to consider some of the details of how that achievement was reached.

As we saw in chapter 3, in a system that resembles Smith's or Walras's theoretical constructions, wages are normally low and full employment rarely happens. Orthodox economic science, and the social structure that science assumes and legitimizes, do not work for the poor. What, then, were the generative causes superimposed upon 'normality' that produced full employment at high wages in Sweden? Our answer has two parts: favourable circumstances and ingenious policies.

The economic circumstances for Sweden in the years immediately following World War II were uniquely favourable. War-torn Europe lay in ruins. Marshall Plan money from the United States flowed into Europe to reconstruct what the war had destroyed. A considerable portion of that money then flowed north to Sweden (which had been neutral during the war) to pay for reconstruction inputs, notably, lumber and iron ore. The automobiles, airplanes, electronic equipment and other products of industrialized countries, such as the United States and Sweden, that had suffered little or no war damage were in demand in countries such as Germany, Japan, Holland and Belgium, whose industries had been devastated.

Swedish workers had work, and the major industries were virtually 100 percent unionized. Wages could not be bid down by playing workers against each other. Swedish workers did not compete with their comrades. They stood in solidarity with their unions. Since Swedish unions controlled a key factor of production (labour) in key industries producing goods that world markets wanted to buy, they were in a position to send wages in those industries through the roof.[21] Although the social democratic government was happy to take credit for the prosperity of the working classes, it was often called upon to dampen wage increases to fight inflation.

Ingenious policies were the other factor in Sweden's achievement of high wages for all workers, no matter where they worked, with rather little inflation.[22] The Swedish economy was conceived as having two parts: a tradeable part and a nontradeable part. The tradeable part—about one-third of the jobs—produced goods for world markets. The tradeable sector was a price taker, since how much the world would buy from Swedish industries and how much it would pay were determined by factors outside Sweden's control. The name of the game was to produce goods efficiently so that costs would sink and quantities sold would rise.[23] When the money rolled

21. A detail highlights how unusual were Sweden's circumstances after the war. Usually, governments are eager to encourage investment, and a chronic shortfall of investment is part of the chronic shortfall of effective demand studied by Keynes. But in the boom years 1952–53 and 1955–57, as an anti-inflation measure the Swedish government imposed a surtax to *discourage* investment (10% in 1952–53 and 12% in 1955–57). The economy already had *too much* effective demand. Lindbeck, 'Period', p. 40.

22. In the period 1950–1965 average yearly inflation was 4.3%. Ibid., p. 8.

23. Erik Lundberg calculated the annual productivity gains in the tradeable sector to be about 4.2% per year in the years 1952–1960 and about 8.2% per year during the years 1960–1968. Erik Lundberg, *Swedish and Keynesian Macroeconomic Theory* (Cambridge, UK: Cambridge University Press, 1996), p. 55.

in—in amounts determined by Sweden's productivity and world market demand[24]—the next question was how to divide it between profits and wages (taking other costs as fixed).

If wages rose too high too fast, inflation would result. There would be too much money chasing too few goods. The rule of thumb came to be that wage increases were tied to productivity increases.[25] If, in a particular industry, productivity, profits and wages all went up 5 percent, there would in principle be no inflation generated by that industry. Consumers would have more money in their pockets, but there would also be more goods (including goods imported with the foreign exchange Sweden had earned by exporting) to buy with it.[26]

This way of dividing Sweden's winnings from playing the international market between capital and labour then set a standard for handling wage increases in the nontradeable sector, which constituted the remaining two-thirds of the work force (the taxi drivers, kindergarten teachers, dental assistants, and so on).[27] The wage pattern was negotiated by the labour unions (the LO previously mentioned, the TCO federation of white-collar unions, and two smaller groupings) and the employers federation (the SAF). In principle, the government did not participate in this collective bargaining. A pattern was set for the whole country in a single bargaining process in which labour negotiated with business.

The rule tying wage increases to productivity increases was supplemented by a rule that when productivity gains made wage increases allowable, the wages of the lowest paid should be raised first. Those whose wages were already high should wait. Later, this rule blended with the rule that the wages of women should be raised to become equal with those of men. These rules were not imposed on business by labour or on labour by business;

---

24. Sweden's winnings in the international game were also augmented after the war by a worldwide increase in the supply of then inexpensive imported commodities such as fuel. Lindbeck, 'Period', p. 11.

25. Historically as well as today, when labour's bargaining power is weak, productivity increases do not generally lead to wage increases. Capping wage increases at the level of productivity growth was a rationale for restraining wage increases at a time when labour was strong.

26. Similar reasoning led Milton Friedman to advocate increasing the money supply just enough to accommodate higher levels of economic activity, i.e., more sales of more goods and services. Milton Friedman, *A Program for Monetary Stability* (New York: Fordham University Press, 1960). During the years 1950–1965, on average prices of consumer goods rose about 4% per year.

27. These ideas were articulated as the EFO model, named after Gösta Edgren, Karl-Olof Faxén and Clos-Erik Odhner, authors of *Wage Formation and the Economy* (London: George Allen and Unwin, 1973 (original Swedish edition 1970)).

they were a negotiated consensus. The labour unions, complying with the negotiated agreement, exercised constraint in raising the wages of the best-paid workers, while they felt free to insist on bringing up to Swedish levels the wages of the lowest-paid workers. That women's wages should be raised to equal men's wages was a principle supported by all sectors and was part of the 'solidaristic wage policy'.

The hapless losers in this process were the owners of marginal businesses, which were often small businesses. Already squeezed by high taxes, they were squeezed again when their workers, who were the lowest-paid workers, achieved pay increases through aggressive unions complying with the solidaristic wage policy. The owners of marginal businesses were being choked by an alliance involving not only big labour and big government but also big business. High-profit, high-productivity businesses—for example, Saab's booming business selling commuter airplanes globally—could afford to pay high wages. They were also winners in the negotiation process because their employees, who were already highly paid, refrained from going on strike to be paid even more, while society was channelling productivity gains to their less-well-paid comrades working elsewhere.

There were two glitches in this situation: First, something had to be done to keep productivity going up, because without its constant rise, there was no growing power to import goods and therefore no way to keep a combination of the same amount of goods and a greater amount of money from producing inflation.[28] Second, less productive businesses could not keep up the pace. The Swedish Model coped with these glitches in several ways. We discuss two of the key ones.

One was to do something—actually, several things—to keep productivity increasing. Productivity growth under the Swedish Model was partly a matter of technical improvements but mainly a matter of altering the mix of Swedish industry. Industries that were already making good profits and paying high wages, such as the paper and paper pulp industry, expanded. Older, declining 'sunset' (*solnedgång*) industries contracted. Swedish shoe factories closed. (Let the Italians make shoes! The Swedes will make high-tech electronics!) When high-productivity industries expanded and low-productivity industries disappeared, average productivity increased.

A second way of coping with the glitches was the application of an active

---

28. We omit the detail that it is theoretically possible to have price stability with more money and the same amount of goods if the velocity of money (i.e., how fast the same money changes hands through sales) declines.

labour market policy. In being active, it marked a departure from public policies designed to have a general impact. Keynes and the Stockholm School economists had often advised boosting consumer purchasing power and boosting incentives to invest through general measures—for example, measures that lowered interest rates. Lower interest rates discouraged leaving money idle in a bank account. They encouraged taking out a loan, hiring people, making something, and selling it—in the whole economy at once.

An active, or positive, policy departs from this pattern by addressing specific bottlenecks. Sweden's active labour market policy shifted the focus out of the comfortable corridors of the *Riksbank* (Sweden's Central Bank) to where the specific problems lay—the ailing businesses and the workers being paid substandard wages, as well as the pockets of unemployment dotting the Swedish landscape—and then addressed those problems where they were. It identified places where employers would hire more qualified employees if they could find them. It helped move people to where the jobs were and away from where the jobs were not, in terms of both geography and education.

Sometimes the policy meant subsidizing marginal businesses so they could meet payroll and stay in business, at least for a while. More characteristically, it assisted the phasing out of *solnedgång* industries. Workers were retrained. They were paid while they were retrained. If all went well, when the workers got their new jobs in *soluppgång* (sunrise) industries, they would be making more money than they had been making in their old jobs. Managers and owners were retrained too. They were provided with credits and technical advice to move into growth industries. They were discouraged from persisting in businesses that could not afford to pay high wages.

Notice, however, that all this optimistic activity pretended that the chronic weakness of effective demand, Staggering Fact 2, is not a fact; it pretended that the basic social structure is not what it is. And when it comes to questions about which way history will go and why, the major causal powers are social structures, not mathematical models or social policies. Notice also that it was nationwide collective bargaining between the labour unions and the employer federation that set solidaristic wage patterns that drove marginal businesses to the wall, but it was government with its active, positive policies that tried to pick up the pieces to put Humpty Dumpty together again.

All would have been well if the rest of the world had cooperated by buying ever larger quantities of capital-intensive, technology-intensive, high-quality Swedish exports at prices high enough to sustain a prosperous and ever-larger tradeable sector that would raise the prosperity of the nontradeable sector and fund transfers to social programmes. And all would have been well if Volvo (for instance) had cooperated by continuing to expand its operations in Sweden, resisting the temptation to make cars and buses in São Paulo and pay Brazilian wages. It was not always so.[29]

But not all went well. Enthusiasm waned in the rest of the world for buying Swedish products, and enthusiasm waned among Swedish industrialists for paying Swedish wages. Let it not be thought that the ability of capital to choose where to site its operations is a law of nature. On the contrary, it is an existentially intransitive, generative mechanism, a social structure.

In the world as it was and is, where global liberal jurisprudence expanded the European world system to form the modern world system, Sweden had to adjust to capital flight. And so the state became appended to the Swedish Model as employer of last resort. When the sun set on a sunset industry and the workers formerly employed there enjoyed all the benefits of unemployment insurance and retraining—but then the sun failed to rise, or to rise fast enough, on a high-productivity growth industry—the state could not renege on its promises of employment for all at good wages. Women (and sometimes men) were put to work for local governments running day-care centres for children. Men (and sometimes women) were funded to work for the same local governments doing construction to overcome Sweden's persistent deficit of social housing. Promises were kept. Everybody who needed work could demand it and get it; no private employer could pay less than the state was paying.

And so it came about that shared prosperity, the crowning glory and pinnacle of the Swedish Model's achievements, the *folkhemmet*, came to exist—temporarily.[30] It came about because promises had to be kept. But given the basic cultural rules and social structures of modernity—in other words, given the institutional frame of orthodox economics—the promises could be kept only temporarily.

---

29. 'Since 1973, a number of industries have been hit by over-capacity breakdowns coupled with demand failures and profitability crises. This has happened to iron ore, steel, shipyards, textiles and to some extent the timber and woodwork industries. We find here a number of interrelated issues: international overinvestment during the boom years of the sixties and seventies, stagnating demand development especially in investment branches, keen international competition from newly industrialized countries.' Erik Lundberg, in his contribution to Ralf Dahrendorf (ed.), *Europe's Economy in Crisis* (New York: Holmes and Meier, 1982), pp. 198–99.

30. See Erik Lundberg, 'The Rise and Fall of the Swedish Economic Model', *Journal of Economic Literature*, vol. 23 (1985): 1–36.

♦ ♦ ♦

> Hartbeespoort Dam is a crucial source of drinking water for Johannesburg and much of the province of Gauteng. In a pilot programme 2,326 CWP participants delivered watershed services, removing litter along the four rivers in the Hartbeespoort catchment area. A purpose of the pilot was to test whether the resulting savings in water purification costs would be sufficient to pay for this kind of clean-up work in the future out of the water company's budget.
>
> — COGTA

4. The Seduction of the Swedes by Orthodox Economic Theory

The reasons why the Swedish Model was programmed for failure exemplify the civilizational crisis that Wielicki analysed. Those reasons are epitomized by the cancellation of the programme that made the government the employer of last resort in 1970. Nevertheless, the main point is not that this particular way of keeping a promise to the people could not work. The main lessons are that it had to come to an end as Sweden's extraordinary post-war good luck in finding buyers for its exports came to an end, and that the global neoliberal capitalist counter-revolution that subsequently took hold in Sweden was no accident; it was another consequence of the same structures that made social democracy unsustainable. These consequences correspond to the second of the seven key lessons we drew earlier from Wielecki's analysis: the cultural rules and social structures that organize the global economy favour ruthless capitalism.

The following two sections of this chapter will deal in detail with the following question: Why did what Myrdal called Sweden's created harmony not work? This section deals with the prior question: Why did anybody ever think it could work? Were the Swedes unaware that by counting on foreign buyers of their exports to deliver the money to fund their welfare state, they were entrusting their future to forces beyond their control? Did they not know from the start that when a high-wage island competes in a global low-wage sea, it will tend to sink into that sea and become low-wage itself?

According to Gunnar Myrdal, experience has shown that it is in the interest of workers for economic life to be governed not by separate contracts among individuals but by general rules of labour legislation, and for wages to be set by collective bargaining. In his Storr Lectures at Yale in 1958,[31] he recounted how this was being learned and acted upon by one nation after another in Europe. Although the United States was a slow learner, it was learning the same lesson, becoming more and more like Sweden at its own pace. Shortly after his lectures at Yale, when he spent time in India studying Asia, Gunnar and his wife, Ava, became close personal friends of Jawaharlal Nehru, the socialist prime minister of India and his wife, Kamala. For this distinguished foursome, and for millions who were less famous but equally sincere in putting into practice the ideals of Enlightenment thinkers, what Wielicki calls the historic compromise of shared prosperity was destined to be humanity's future. But this did not come to pass. Not even in Sweden, the living example of shared prosperity.

Why did it not happen? And why did so many intelligent people think it would happen? A good part of the answer lies in the seductive charm of the holy trinity of orthodox economics: efficiency, free trade and growth. The causal forces that produced the academic hegemony of this trio have been studied by others.[32] Here we comment briefly on how each is seductive—charming and cheating, attractive and dangerous—and superficially plausible yet logically false and ethically dysfunctional.

Efficiency

By definition, an efficient solution is one that achieves its objective at the lowest cost or achieves it to a greater extent at the same cost. Hence, by definition, 'efficiency' has no specific meaning until an objective is specified.

A logical fallacy, endemic among orthodox economists, is to identify the objective with satisfying revealed preferences or free choices or making a product that can be profitably sold. As Alasdair Macintyre, echoed by Martha Nussbaum, Reuel Khoza and other contributors to the contemporary revival of neo-Aristotelian ethics, puts it: It is a fallacy to identify the good with what people want, without going on to ask whether what they want is what they should want.[33]

As to the dysfunctional consequences of efficiency as conceived by orthodox economists, I offer the world as my evidence. The world is awash

---

31. *Beyond the Welfare State,* previously cited.
32. Among many others, Richard Cockett, *Thinking the Unthinkable* (London: Harper Collins, 1994); and the many comprehensive and formidable writings of Immanuel Wallerstein.
33. Alasdair Macintyre, *Ethics in the Conflicts of Modernity* (Cambridge, UK: Cambridge University Press, 2016), as well as his earlier works.

with four-year-old girls who want Barbie dolls and teenage boys who want sports utility vehicles, while, as Wielecki puts it, ruthless capitalism destroys people, environments and culture.

With respect to Sweden, Myrdal admits (although I think his *mea culpa* is overstated) in his Storrs Lectures that the Swedish Model was run by a technocracy that made no effort to mitigate the individualistic and materialistic proclivities of the Swedish people. He fails to mention that raising the cultural level of the people was a high priority for the founder of Sweden's socialist party, Hjalmar Branting (1860–1925).

Free Trade

The logical fallacy of free trade is a category mistake. England specializes in wool. Portugal specializes in wine. Instead of making its own wine, for which its climate is unsuited, England produces more wool, for which its climate is suited, and exchanges some of its wool for some of Portugal's wine. Both win. Portugal gets wool worth more to it than the wine it had a surplus of, while England gets wine worth more to it than the wool it had a surplus of.

This thinking is charming—and dangerous.

In Benedict Anderson's terms, England and Portugal are imagined communities.[34] People salute their flags, sing their anthems, root for their teams, and in other ways identify themselves with something larger than themselves, the nation. A plausible hypothesis is that today imagined communities satisfy emotional needs hard-wired into the human species. They superficially resemble the tribes, clans, or other extended kinship groups humans lived in for thousands of years. Nation was an emotional concept evoked by the idea of *folkhemmet* that Swedish socialists drew on to gather support for a welfare state. But nations produce neither wine nor wool, nor do they consume it.

Modern law, drawing on Roman precedent, counts as the owners of the wine the owners of the enterprises that produce the wine. It is they who sell the wine. The proceeds of the sale go into their bank accounts. Nations do not have bank accounts.

Governments, also sometimes called states, do have a legal existence.

---

34. Benedict Anderson, *Imagined Communities* (London Verso, 1991 (original 1963)). For a more complete critique of comparative advantage see Howard Richards, *Understanding the Global Economy* (Santa Barbara, CA: Peace Education Books, 2004). Cecil Woodham-Smith shows how free trade ideology exacerbated the Irish famine in her *The Great Hunger* (London: Penguin, 1992 (1962)).

They can own property. They have bank accounts. They can make decisions and act on them, most importantly the decision to go to war. (Hegel defined a state as an army plus a means of raising money to pay the army.) But governments should not be confused with the England or Portugal of free trade theory. The fact that the family of English poet John Milton made a good living importing wine from Portugal does not add a single pound to the government of England's treasury nor put a farthing in the pocket of a beggar on the streets of London. Legal persons can occupy material positions, such as owner of a wine-importing business, and government officials can occupy other legal positions, such as tax collector. But it is a feature of modernity, known as the rule of law or the principle of limited government, that the legal powers of states are strictly limited, while the legal rights of property owners are constitutionally protected.

In economic theory, once 'England' has pocketed the gains from free trade with 'Portugal', it can then deliberate on how to spend them, including dividing the winnings from trade among its citizens. This is indeed what the Swedish Model tried to do.

Attributing Volvo's earnings from the export of vehicles to an imagined community named 'Sweden' or regarding those earnings as part of the government of the Swedish state's income partly explains why the Swedish Model did not work. That people expected redistribution of the profits of Volvo and other Swedish firms to be available indefinitely to share prosperity with Sweden's poor was partly due to the category mistake inherent in the doctrine of free trade. The seductive charms of free trade help to explain both why the model did not work and why many intelligent people expected that it would.

Growth

Although this chapter is mainly about Sweden, it is easier to diagnose the attractive but lethal[35] concept of economic growth from a South African point of view. In the chapter 'Power and Principle in South Africa' in our book *The Dilemmas of Social Democracies*,[36] Joanna Swanger and I wrote a summary of the orthodox case for export-led growth with foreign direct investment as the only viable path from poverty to development:

---

35. The classic case for seeing economic growth as lethal is Herman Daly, *Steady-State Economics* (Washington, DC: Island Press, 1991 (1977)). The same point is being driven home today by Greta Thunberg.

36. Richards and Swanger, *The Dilemmas of Social Democracies*.

Premise 1: The only way to overcome poverty is for poor people to get money with which to buy housing, food, medical care and other necessities and conveniences.

Premise 2: The only way (or at least the only desirable way) for a poor person to get money is for that person to find a job.

Premise 3: Jobs come into existence only when investors create jobs.

Premise 4: All human beings, including investors, seek to maximize the satisfaction of their preferences.

Premise 5: In the case of investors, premise 4 mainly means maximizing some combination of high earnings and low risks.

Premise 6: South Africa does not have enough domestic capital to grow its economy fast enough to absorb unemployment and to keep pace with population growth.

Premise 7: Therefore, to overcome poverty, South Africa must seek foreign capital.

Premise 8: Following from premise 5, foreign investors will invest only on terms they will accept, and these will be terms that maximize their confidence that they will achieve their investment objectives.

Conclusion: Consequently, to achieve high growth to end poverty, South Africa must remould itself—as much as possible—to become an environment where potential investors feel confident that they will achieve high rates of profit and run low risks.

If just one of the premises of the chain of reasoning is false, the conclusion does not follow. But in fact, *all eight of the premises are false.* We are reminded of their falsity when we teach a course in the business school of the University of Cape Town every year. There are always some students in the class who spent their youth, as did Nelson Mandela, in a traditional indigenous rural environment. They uniformly report that they were happier in their youth when they had more community and less economy. They find it surprising that what was everyday normal reality when they were growing up is invisible in the university. Nor is it visible when experts and political leaders discuss South Africa's public policies.

The situation is complex. In some ways, the amount of growth depends on factors governments cannot control. In other ways, growth is desirable, which means it competes with other desirable goals. In still other ways, economic success is ecological failure, and vice versa, but sometimes green goals can be combined with economic goals. Whatever the ethical and rational options may be, in the real world, corruption and incompetence are likely to lead to results worse than the results of any rational compromise among competing interest groups.

Further complicating these already complex considerations is the claim that growth is necessary for the stability of democracy, that material gains must be delivered to the have-nots without inflicting material losses on the haves, which is possible only if the total 'pie' is getting larger, making it possible to reward the poor without punishing the rich.[37] Further, given that investment for profit is the *causa causans*[38] of production, more incentives to invest must constantly be followed by still more.[39] Otherwise what is called 'the economy' slows down. Then more people become redundant and have no role in the economy. More debtors cannot pay debts as they come due. The nonpayment of debts generates business failures, leading to more nonpayment of debts, in a downward spiral. Irving Fisher explained the Great Depression of the 1930s as a result of a spiral of sell-offs of assets and dismissals of employees to raise money and cut costs in a desperate effort to balance the books, that is, to come current on payments on debts and stay in business.[40] In this complex picture, saying that, in spite of its many attractions, growth is lethal is a way of calling attention to the unavoidable physical fact that most growth that has actually happened to date, and quite likely most future economic growth, is destroying the delicate balances of nature that have made life possible.

In this complex situation, unbounded organization aspires to propose constructive suggestions and to encourage constructive action. It is not a minor matter that the CWP shows that it is possible to create dignified livelihoods by mobilizing community as well as government resources

---

37. Adam Habib tends to make claims of this sort. However, he might be read as saying that for democracy to be stable in a poor country, people must see their lives as improving *in some way*—not necessarily in a way described by standard economic metrics. Adam Habib, *South Africa's Suspended Revolution* (Johannesburg: Wits University Press, 2013). See also Erik Lundberg, *The Development of Swedish and Keynesian Economic Theory and Its Impact on Economic Policy* (Cambridge, UK: Cambridge University Press, 1996).

38. The phrase *causa causans* refers to the investment for profit that starts production. John Maynard Keynes, 'The General Theory', *The Quarterly Journal of Economics*, vol. 51 (1937), pp 209–223.

39. For example, Paul Samuelson, writing in a Keynesian tradition, postulates in his *Foundations of Economic Analysis* (Cambridge, MA: Harvard University Press, 1947) that the stability of capitalism requires that $Y = C + I$, where Y stands for current national income, C stands for spending on consumption, and I stands for spending on investment (p. 281). Rosa Luxemburg makes a similar argument, explaining European expansion as impelled by its internal instability. *The Accumulation of Capital* (London: Routledge and Kegan Paul, 2008 (1913)).

40. Irving Fisher, 'The Debt-Deflation Theory of Great Depressions', *Econometrica*, vol. 1 (1933), pp 337–357.

without relying on investors to create employment. Somewhat similarly, other forms of community development—including the 'transition towns' of the UK, the Asset-Based Community Development movement that began in Chicago, Local Economy Trading Systems (LETS) in Australia and elsewhere, Abastecimiento Basico Comunitario (ABC) in Argentina and innumerable initiatives, mainly in Latin America, called Economia Social Solidaria—bypass the efforts of big government to jumpstart the economy by offering incentives to big capital. They identify local needs and organize local resources to meet them. In some cases they enjoy the discreet support of surplus brought in from outside by governments and donors who make it a point to encourage local resilience and empowerment.[41] This was the case, for example, with the discreet funding provided by Sibanye Gold and Goldfields for developing innovative alternative livelihoods for their own former employees whose jobs were lost when the mines where they had worked were mechanized.[42] Nor is it a minor matter that unbounded organization underpins a philosophy of peace for the following reason: It sees history as a history of organization, starting with the ways our hunter-gatherer ancestors organized themselves to meet their needs. It understands the rules of the game that currently govern the global economy as outcomes of long historical processes.

Nobody now alive participated in the social construction of the currently prevailing laws of property or contract or any other principal feature of the dominant social structure. We the living are free to align across sectors to serve the common good. Historical understanding of the principal structural causes of our problems frees us to forgive; it frees us to work together for a better world without taking revenge on the descendants of the creators of the structures that oppress us. And—equally important—without feeling that we have no right to deconstruct and reconstruct what the now long-deceased Founding Fathers constructed. We do have a right to build a world that meets the needs of all of us now, in harmony with nature.

Unbounded organization's attitude of peaceful cooperation, aligning across sectors for the common good, is no small matter. It is a breakthrough—precisely because it has become deeply engrained in academic

---

41. Aristotle understood the importance of resilience and local empowerment. In *Politics* he argues that no country can be self-governing in peace or able to defend itself in war if it is not self-sufficient. His ideal is not attainable today, but that is no reason to take the opposite of his ideal to be ideal.

42. For a video of one of the workshops, see *Organising for Good: The Story of Westonaria's Transformation*, https://www.youtube.com/watch?v=BgVF3ODWBv4.

disciplines and in common sense to regard any consensus model in social science as a pretext for keeping the status quo and to regard any movement to radically change the status quo as paired with a conflict model in social science. Nor is it a small matter that unbounded organizing highlights the voluntary sharing of surplus—instead of simply assuming that the have-nots have nothing to share (not even time and affection); that the haves will not voluntarily share (since they allegedly have nothing to gain by it); that the haves are too powerful to be compelled to share against their will; and that therefore any increase in the welfare of the have-nots must come from growth.

The standard definition of growth (i.e., of GDP) is 'a monetary measure of the market value of all the final goods and services produced in a specific time period'. In other words, roughly, it measures sales. We 'grow' when we produce more to sell and then somebody buys it, thus proving that what we produced had market value. Typically GDP is about two-thirds sales to consumers. Much of the rest is made up by sales to government and to foreigners.

To get a handle on what it means in practice to say that today every nation in the world counts on growth to solve Keynes's problem (the shortfall of business activity), we return to South Africa's National Development Plan (NDP). In chapter 1 we observed that the authors of the NDP quietly admitted that on balance the NDP scored at best a net zero on reversing humanity's suicidal rush to environmental catastrophe. Nonetheless they believed that the NDP's pro-growth provisions, if implemented, made it likely that there would be no extreme poverty in South Africa in thirty years. Dani Rodrik, Ricardo Hausmann and Andres Velasco (RHV) coauthored a chapter titled 'Growth Diagnostics' in Rodrik's book *One Economics, Many Recipes* that was cited in the NDP. Let us look more closely at their views to understand better what it means to count on growth to solve a nation's problems.

The chapter starts by asserting that growth is the most direct route to raising a country's scores on social and human indicators. Reform strategies should therefore be growth strategies, principally targeted at raising rates of growth.[43] Development *requires* growth, and growth *requires* getting

---

43. There is a large literature disagreeing with RHV on this point, holding that either (1) there is no clear relationship between economic growth and social welfare, or (2) if there is such a relationship, it is social welfare that causes economic growth, not the other way around. See Richard Wilkinson and Kate Pickett, *The Spirit Level: Why More Equal Societies Almost Always Do Better* (London: Allen Lane, 2009); Krishna Mazumdar, 'Causal Flow between Human Well-Being and Per Capita Real Gross Domestic Product', *Social Indicators*

entrepreneurs 'excited', as Rodrik says,⁴⁴ about doing the investing needed to increase the level of economic activity, that is, to increase sales. (Here we meet again the dependence of economic activity on profit and the dependence of profit on sales, SF1 and SF2).

To design public policies that will get entrepreneurs excited, RHV propose a decision tree to identify the 'binding constraints' that are holding growth back and then, step by step, to create public policies to loosen those constraints. The decision tree begins by identifying possible constraints to growth: 'We start by asking what keeps growth low. Is it inadequate returns to investment, inadequate private appropriability of the returns, or inadequate access to finance?'⁴⁵

Once the most binding of these three constraints is determined, the next step is to analyse how to loosen it. If, for example, the binding constraint in a given nation at a given moment is the second (the difficulty of taking profits they make in South Africa out of South Africa), the decision tree then asks: 'If it is a case of poor appropriability, is it a case of high taxation, poor property rights and contract enforcement, labour-capital conflicts, or learning and coordination externalities?' If, on the other hand, the first constraint (low profits) is the binding constraint, the problem may be inadequate public investment in complementary factors of production, such as human capital, security, access to credit, or infrastructure. Or it may be a case of poor access to imported technologies.

Research, vol. 50 (2000), pp 297–313; and the sources cited by those authors. In Amartya Sen's view, whatever the answers may be, the questions should be better framed. *The Idea of Justice* (Cambridge, MA: Harvard University Press, 2009).

44. The word 'excited' comes from chapter 1 in Dani Rodrik, *One Economics, Many Recipes* (Princeton: Princeton University Press, 2007), written by Rodrik alone.

45. RHV's implicit premise that growth is achieved through investment-for-production-for-sale-for-profit is not idiosyncratic. In general, standard growth models do not consider other ways to mobilize resources to meet needs. That capital accumulation must precede growth is assumed in the concept of a balanced growth path where capital, labour, consumption and output all grow at constant rates. See, for example, Roy Harrod's seminal 'An Essay in Dynamic Theory', *The Economic Journal*, vol. 49 (1939), pp. 14–33; and Robert M. Solow, 'A Contribution to the Theory of Economic Growth', *Quarterly Journal of Economics,* vol. 70, no. 1 (Feb. 1956), pp.65–94. The necessity for capital accumulation, and consequently our first Staggering Fact, remains intact when human capital and endogenous change are considered. Charles Jones, *Introduction to Economic Growth* (New York: Norton, 1998); Paul Romer, 'Endogenous Technological Change', *Journal of Political Economy*, vol. (1990), pp. S71–S102. These last ways of thinking have the real-world consequence of leading to a crusade to protect the profitability of intellectual property rights, rationalized as necessary to keep the growth engine going, by making private investment in research and development profitable. This leads, for example, to pricing needed medicines out of the reach of the poor and to farmers losing control of seeds. Sometimes it leads to a pro-natalist bias against stabilizing population growth. Julian Simon, *The Ultimate Resource 2* (Princeton, NJ: Princeton University Press, 1996).

Let us consider what the mainstream RHV diagnostic of what growth requires *follows from* and what it *leads to*. The RHV diagnostic *follows from* treating SF1, the dependence of the economy on the confidence of investors and entrepreneurs, as a given (rather than as unbounded organization treats it—as a problem to be solved). SF1, in turn, is a consequence of the basic social structure. It is a consequence of the cultural rules that define material relations (as Porpora puts it).

If it is postulated (emphasized as central while not literally declared by RHV) that only profit-driven entrepreneurial decisions generate the activities that produce everybody's daily bread, beer and meat, then the next question must be how to excite the entrepreneurs. The answer to this question need not be precisely the three items on the RHV short list, but it must be something similar.

The RHV diagnostic *leads to* constraining the welfare state. It leads to what, four decades ago, James O'Connor called 'the fiscal crisis of the state'.[46] On one hand, RHV observe that high taxes on profits discourage growth. On the other hand, they observe that growth is discouraged when states fail to provide adequate complementary factors of production in such forms as those listed above. O'Connor (and Jürgen Habermas, citing O'Connor, in *The Legitimation Crisis*) points out that the state loses income because it dares not impose high taxes on the investing classes. Over time, as (in Schumpeter's words) facts hammer logic into the minds of men,[47] the state shifts its tax base to consumption taxes such as a value-added tax. At the same time, state expenses go up because public money must be spent to create the conditions that attract private money, while state income goes down because the same private money cannot be taxed effectively. Further, reading between the lines when RHV observe that a labour-capital conflict is in some cases a binding constraint on growth, we can discern that maximizing growth means tilting the dividing of the revenues of firms to increase the capital shares and decrease the wage shares. And so on.

In brief: SF1 leads to the RHV diagnostic, and the RHV diagnostic leads to a fiscal crisis of the state, favouring capital over labour, and therefore to social disintegration. The original purpose—to bake a larger pie so there would be a larger slice of it for the poor to eat—is undermined (RHV do not

---

46. James O'Connor, *The Fiscal Crisis of the State* (New Brunswick, NJ: Transaction Books, 1973).

47. Joseph Schumpeter, *The Theory of Economic Development* (New Brunswick, NJ: Transaction Books, 2007 (1911)), p.80.

say this) by the measures taken to get entrepreneurs excited about investing in South Africa rather than elsewhere. Meanwhile, the world is awash with excess investment capital circulating the globe in speculations achieved by a few computer strokes while finding no profitable way to participate in any real economy. The diagnosis of this malady, as we suggested in chapter 5, is SF2. While there is a plethora of unmet needs and a plethora of capital, there is a shortage of paying customers who are not already buying whatever they want from well-established firms who have already occupied all the profitable market niches.

At this point, the RHV growth diagnostic drops out of the analysis as an unnecessary middle term. Structural ungovernability follows directly from the constitutive rules of the system—from the constitution of what Charles Taylor has called a bargaining society,[48] that is, from the basic social structure. The basic structure already implies that nobody has to buy anything they do not want to buy, and they are free to set aside and save any income they do not choose to spend.

In South Africa's NDP, the word 'growth' is commonly used to sing a song of *la vie en rose* about growing a larger pie so there will be more pie for all South Africans to share. In grim reality, systemic imperatives demanding growth compel governments to sacrifice other goals (such as raising wages) and to spend more money (on the complementary factors of production RHV mention as well as on the subsidies and outright bribes RHV do not mention) in order to get growth. To make matters worse, multinational corporations are notorious for evading taxes.[49]

The unfortunate conclusions following from this analysis of RHV's version of standard growth theory—which are tragic when translated from abstract terms into the flesh-and-blood suffering of human beings and the heat and wildfires consuming forests of suffering ecosystems—are conclusions that the Swedish Model appeared for a time to have successfully avoided. They are consistent, however, with the expectation that Myrdal, lecturing in New Haven in 1958, expressed and that many educated and intelligent people around the globe already had. Sweden was showing a working model of what was destined to be humanity's future. Experience had shown that the interests of working people were best served by collective

---

48. Charles Taylor, 'Interpretation and the Sciences of Man', *Review of Metaphysics*, vol. 25 (1971), p. 48.

49. See the Mbeki Report: *Report of the High-Level Panel on Illicit Financial Flows from Africa*, www.uneca.org › files › PublicationFiles › iff_main_report_26feb_en.

bargaining and general rules rather than individual contracts. Since in every democracy, the working people were the majority of the voters, what experience had shown to be true would continue to spread from nation to nation, leading to what Wielecki (finding 5) phrased as the great historic compromise between the two great classes of society, the employers and the employees.

Further, in 1958, as is still largely true today, the ideals of efficiency, free trade and growth were regarded as impeccable by the bulk of the economics profession and by educated public opinion around the globe. A student who doubted them was likely to fail Economics 101. A lawyer, doctor or architect who argued against them was likely not to be invited to the next cocktail party. The Swedish Model complied with them. That enhanced its prestige and the prestige of the global trend it led. The orthodox elements of the Swedish Model's philosophy made it appear more likely, not less likely, in 1958, that what Wielecki called mature capitalism, as distinct from ruthless capitalism, was destined to be humanity 's future.

◆ ◆ ◆

> Diangubo in KwaZulu-Natal Province has been ravaged by an HIV/AIDS epidemic that has orphaned many children. The children live either with gogos—grandmothers—or on their own with siblings in child-headed households. CWP built, for example, rondavels for seven orphans. Before CWP these children did not have a place to sleep. They were all sleeping in one mud house battling the rain and cold.
>
> — TIPS

5. The Failure of the Swedish Model: Alice Rivlin

In our view, the principle the Swedish case illustrates is that governability and proper governance cannot be achieved without structural transformation. Transformation involves syntheses and pragmatic compromises combining (a) what modernity has accomplished with a science of self-interest—economics—with (b) a renewed appreciation of moral education transforming the will to live a life of service, and with (c) spirituality, often accomplished by ceremonies, myths and prayer and today sometimes accomplished by secular socio-emotional education; leading to more functional material positions constituted by more functional cultural rules oriented by moral realism.⁵⁰ We want to extrapolate from the failure of the Swedish Model to motivate a general case for unbounded organizing and for the human capacity to adjust humanity's cultures to their physical functions.

To make our case we call two distinguished witnesses to testify. Both witnesses are called to testify (unintentionally) against the discipline they represent. Their conclusions will confirm the finding in chapters 2, 3 and 4 that orthodox economic science does not serve the interests of the poor. Instead, it presupposes and legitimates social structures that do not serve the interests of the poor. The first witness is Alice Rivlin.

Alice Rivlin headed a mission from the Brookings Institution that studied Sweden in the early 1980s. Since she and her institution are both regarded as sympathetic to the cause of working people, she could be expected to draw pro-worker conclusions, insofar as applying economic logic to the facts might allow pro-worker conclusions to be drawn. In her report she finds no such conclusions to draw. Rivlin found, rather, that Sweden suffered from a persistent decline in its competitiveness in world markets. She apparently did not notice the inherent contradiction in advising one country after another that it is not competitive enough, as if the statistical fact that the average basketball team loses half its games were proof that basketball coaches and players do not understand the science of basketball.

Rivlin reports that there were, in mainstream economic circles, two basic explanations of Sweden's decline and, correspondingly, two basic remedies. One emphasized microeconomics: wages, regulations, taxes and other factors that affect the decisions of individuals and businesses to work, produce, save and invest.

The macroeconomic explanation, says Rivlin, is equally valid. It is that the commitments to equality and full employment distorted Swedish economic incentives. The solution, on either approach, would include lowering taxes, reducing transfers and subsidies and generally eliminating interference with market outcomes.

The macroeconomic view, on Rivlin's analysis, emphasized such things as Central Bank monetary policies that affected the overall level of economic activity, wages, prices, interest rates and the exchange value of the krona. Rivlin's macroeconomic hypothesis is that Sweden's macroeconomic policies

---

50. Howard Richards, 'Moral (and Ethical) Realism', *Journal of Critical Realism*, vol. 18 (2019), pp. 285–302. See also vol. 2 of Howard Richards, *Letters from Quebec* (San Francisco and London: International Scholars Press, 1995), titled *Transforming the Basic Cultural Structures of the Modern World*.

fostered consumption at the expense of saving. The results damaged the country's ability to compete in world markets. The remedies would be similar to those prescribed under the microeconomic hypothesis: retreating from the strong commitment to full employment, allowing the krona to float downward to make exports competitive, and so on.[51]

In sum, the recommendations were to lower taxes, reduce the transfers of money from haves to have-nots through the welfare state, reduce public subsidies for social housing and other social goods, and generally revert toward, if not to, pure capitalism, where market outcomes are not 'interfered with' by nonmarket practices. The recommendations were to retreat from full employment and accept unemployment, to combat inflation by taking money out of circulation by reducing wages (thus reducing the purchasing power of workers), and (at the same time) to let the exchange value of the krona fall (further reducing the purchasing power of workers by increasing the cost in kronas of imported goods) in order to make Sweden competitive in world markets.

The cheaper krona would effectively reduce the sales prices of Swedish exports. It would also raise the prices of imports for Swedes. This would effectively lower wages by reducing the purchasing power of workers' pay. In other words, at the same time wages were frozen to fight inflation, inflation would be deliberately induced to promote exports. Such austerity measures, which have been implemented not only in Sweden but in one country after another, perhaps most famously in Greece, are said to be necessary. In the famous words of Margaret Thatcher, *there is no alternative* (TINA).

We take Rivlin's testimony to show that the system works only when social goals are sacrificed, and it does not work well or reliably even then. In one word, it is ungovernable. Without transformation, it will not be capable of adjusting to ecological and medical crises or to technologies' coming online making most human mental and physical labour obsolete. The problems in question do not concern the validity of economic science as much as they concern the functionality of the social structures. The structures, like those of a resistant virus, defeated Gunnar Myrdal and his friends when they tried to build a created harmony, a *folkhemmet*, a home for all Swedes.

Unbounded organizing suggests what is, in principle, a simple remedy.

---

51. Alice Rivlin, in Barry Bosworth and Alice Rivlin (eds.), *The Swedish Economy* (Washington, DC: Brookings Institution, 1987), pp. 10–11.

Put ethics first. Change the goal of economic activity from profit to caring and sharing. Treat competitive markets, like competitive sports, as friendly competition in which the players shake hands before and after the match. Treat economic institutions as ways to harness animal instincts to serve the common good: meet more needs in closer harmony with nature. Once the decision is made to align across sectors to serve the common good, all the rest follows. In Alasdair MacIntyre's terms, we have already decided to follow Plato, Aristotle, Thomas, most Asian wisdom and most indigenous knowledge systems by treating the vagaries of the human will as problems to be solved. We have already declined to regard value as subjective but sovereign—subjective because it has no objective basis in biological or spiritual or social function; sovereign because the agreement of wills that creates a price is accepted in itself as a performative act creating value and defining how much of it there is.[52]

It follows that, to implement unbounded organization, open the mind and let the cobwebs out. As Greta Thunberg says, listen to the scientists. Have open and free dialogue, and remember what Socrates taught by his precepts and by the example of his own conduct: the purpose of dialogue is not to determine who is right but what is right. To engage in dialogue is to purify the will by submitting it to the discipline of the *logos*. It is to participate in a collective effort by friends to determine together where the logos leads the inquiry, for in the direction followed by humans who accept the discipline of the logos lies the truth. More than two thousand years after Socrates, Charles Darwin taught another indispensable lesson: what matters for the survival of a human culture (or for a human moral system, as the evolutionary biologist David Sloan Wilson puts it) is, ultimately, not truth but adaptation.[53]

In short, Alice Rivlin inadvertently proved our case. She correctly applied the logic of her profession, which assumes and legitimizes social structures that do not serve the poor. The practical conclusions of her report shifted wealth from the poor (the workers) to the rich (the investors). She thus certified the failure of the Swedish Model, whose objective was to serve the interests of all the people. She certified Sweden's failure with the logic of a science designed and built, from Adam Smith until today, to protect the interests of property owners.

52. Alasdair MacIntyre, *Ethics in the Conflicts*.
53. David Sloan Wilson, *Darwin's Cathedral* (Chicago: University of Chicago Press, 2011).

6. The Failure of the Swedish Model: Assar Lindbeck

Our other witness is the distinguished Swedish economist Assar Lindbeck, who chaired the Lindbeck Commission, named by the conservative government elected in 1991 to seek a cure for the ills of the Swedish economy. When the socialists were turned out of office by the voters in 1991, they had long since abandoned the Rehn-Meidner Model and its variations. The socialists themselves, without waiting to be voted out, had already implemented neoliberal reforms. When he was named to head the commission, Lindbeck had already been building an impressive CV for several decades. It was studded with academic publications that (in our view) document the incompatibility of the Swedish welfare state with the basic social structure and basic cultural structure that constitute the core of modernity (although not the core of modern ideals of human rights still struggling to pass from promises to realities). We call Lindbeck as a witness against himself. His testimony will show that within his frame of reference the future of humanity is hopeless.[54]

In 1997, after a half century that had seen the Swedish Model's rise and fall, Lindbeck analysed its deterioration with the benefit of hindsight.[55] In his article 'The Swedish Experiment', he provides a mirror image of our own views on what the Swedish Model was, why for a time it worked and why it was not sustainable.[56] Lindbeck points out that already in the late 1970s and early 1980s, Swedish mining, steel, shipbuilding and other industries faced overcapacity, in other words inability to sell what they were equipped to make, in international markets.[57] Gone were the extraordinarily favourable days for Sweden when the few industrial countries that survived World War II intact could sell whatever they could produce.

In our view, with Europe rebuilt and new industrial powers emerging, the world returned to the normality of Staggering Fact 2: a chronic insufficiency of effective demand and more sellers than buyers. As the economy became

---

54. His findings include findings of other researchers he cites.

55. Assar Lindbeck, 'The Swedish Experiment', *Journal of Economic Issues*, vol. 35 (1997), pp. 1273–1319.

56. Lindbeck also emphasizes two dimensions of Sweden's woes that we do not review here: (1) breakdowns in allocative efficiency—for example, rent control discourages private construction, so construction is subsidized with public funds, which diminishes incentives to keep construction costs down; and (2) what might be called a demoralization of the country, leading to Gunnar Myrdal remarking that Sweden had become 'a nation of cheaters' (quoted in Lindbeck, 'Swedish Experiment', p. 1301)—for example, falsely calling in sick and not showing up for work.

57. Ibid., p. 1302.

more internationalized, it became easier for firms based in Sweden (like Volvo) to shift production to places where wages and taxes were lower.[58] A model based on raising productivity (and thus making it possible to raise wages with little inflation) by expanding high-productivity, high-profit exports was no longer feasible.

Lindbeck points out that under the new international conditions, the *soluppgång* (sunrise) industries proved to be few and far between. The idea was to phase out the *solnedgång* (sunset) private industries as painlessly as possible, and then phase in *soluppgång* industries (or expand existing winner industries) where formerly relatively low-paid workers would find jobs in high-productivity industries at high pay. What happened in practice was a staggering increase in the number of workers on the public payroll.[59] Since the private sector had, in fact, few new jobs to offer, the economic returns for the workers who went through retraining turned out to be quite modest.[60]

Paying salaries in the only sector that was growing, the public sector, and providing a generous 'social wage' (benefits from welfare and public services) to complement high wages led to ever-higher taxes.[61] When profits were squeezed between high wages and high taxes, the consequence was sluggish production and investment.[62] By the 1980s, the number of new start-up manufacturing firms had fallen to nearly zero.[63] Private investment fell.[64] The rate of return on physical capital fell.[65] Capital gradually flowed away from the tightly controlled institutions, such as banks and insurance companies

---

58. Ibid., pp. 1293, 1312.

59. Ibid., p. 1292. On p. 1311, Lindbeck writes of 600,000 new public employees, about 15% of Sweden's total labour force.

60. Ibid., p. 1308.

61. Among other data on Swedish taxes, Lindbeck reports that most income earners in Sweden had marginal tax rates of 70–80% in the 1980s. Ibid., p. 1298. High taxes forced most households to have at least two wage earners. Ibid., p. 1300.

62. Ibid., p. 1302, referring to the effect of high wages, with supporting data on several specific aspects of this general point. The authors known as the EFO trio calculate the fall of average yearly profits in Swedish industry during the 1960s as shown below. 'Profit' being a notoriously ambiguous concept, they make their point using three different measures of it.

Year	1960	1961	1962	1963	1964	1965	1966	1966
Profits (1)	10.7	10.5	9.3	9.2	9.9	9.7	7.9	7.5
Profits (2)	7.8	7.5	6.2	6.1	6.9	6.6	4.7	4.3
Profits (3)	6.4	6.1	4.9	4.8	5.4	5.5	4.0	3.8

Source: Gösta Edgren, Karl-Olof Faxén, Clas-Erik Odhner, *Wage Formation and the Economy* (London: George Allen and Unwin, 1973).

63. Lindbeck, 'Swedish Experiment', p. 1294.

64. Ibid., p. 1292.

65. Ibid., p. 1291.

that the government regulated in its attempts to make full employment and a welfare state compatible with price stability.⁶⁶

Faced with high wages that priced many of Sweden's exports out of world markets and motivated Swedish multinational firms to do their manufacturing elsewhere, and faced with strong labour unions that made it impossible to lower wages, Sweden resorted to a series of devaluations of the krona.⁶⁷ In 1992 it decided to begin to let the krona float, or rather, sink.⁶⁸ In this way real wages were lowered to levels comparable to those of Sweden's principal trading partners. Seeking to restore profitability and competitiveness, Sweden carried out a series of neoliberal reforms over the years, similar to those carried out in the rest of the world: deregulating capital markets,⁶⁹ cutting social security benefits,⁷⁰ and making it harder for workers to be absent from work on sick leave, resulting in a drop in average sick days for Swedish workers from 24 to 11 per year.⁷¹ Furthermore, changes in macroeconomic policy made fighting inflation a top priority and put employment on the back burner.⁷² Bank bailouts (the familiar pattern of privatizing profits and socializing losses),⁷³ privatization of public assets,⁷⁴ abandoning the government's commitment to be employer of last resort and cutting public-sector employment followed.⁷⁵ Finally, a general rollback of the welfare state was encapsulated in the abolition of wage-earner funds, which had been a type of pension fund giving organized workers an ownership stake in industry,⁷⁶ and the creation of tax breaks for businesses.⁷⁷

On Lindbeck's spin, Sweden's numerous currency devaluations were a way of honouring the commitment to full employment. Rolling back real

---

66. Ibid., p. 1292. An example of such an attempt would be fixing interest rates at a low level to favour employment and keep down the cost of the government's own borrowing, and then rationing credit to deflate inflationary pressure due to too much lending.

67. Ibid., p. 1293.

68. Ibid., p. 1304.

69. Ibid., pp. 1292–93.

70. Ibid., p. 1301.

71. Ibid., p. 1301. Lindbeck suggests this result may be partly due to not just changes in the rules but also the threat of unemployment making workers more fearful of losing their jobs.

72. Ibid., pp. 1303, 1313. Inflation was of course rising even as fighting it was becoming top priority.

73. Ibid., p. 1305. We add a little editorial comment to the facts Lindbeck cites.

74. Ibid., p. 1306.

75. Ibid., p. 1311. In the early 1990s, public-sector employment was cut back about 10%.

76. Ibid., p. 1313.

77. Ibid., p. 1313.

wages made it profitable to hire more people. From our point of view, there came a time (the early 1990s) when organized labour became so weak that it was no longer necessary to resort to currency devaluations to keep real wage costs down. Lindbeck comments that 'the fact that politicians finally decided that devaluations and further expansion of public employment were not acceptable means of keeping the unemployment rate down means that the previous success of full employment was not sustainable in the long run'.[78]

Lindbeck concluded his analysis by describing the Swedish Model as a brief historical interlude and saying that after the 'radical experiments of the 1960s and 1970s', Sweden has become a more normal country.[79]

But we cannot rest content with a 'normal' that has become dysfunctional and threatens to become fatal. We seek viable alternatives.

♦ ♦ ♦

> 'I was studying towards a chemical engineering degree at Wits University, but I couldn't finish because of financial problems. I joined CWP in 2010 after being tired of doing nothing and being called a crazy person because of the depression I was going through with the frustration of not being able to fulfil my dreams. Thanks to the CWP, I am now a different person with hopes for the future and no longer called a crazy person. I'm able to go to the internet cafés and surf the net for job opportunities and bursary applications. I'm able to help at home because I have something in my pocket. My biggest dream is to go back to school and pursue my career so I can help other people who are in the similar situation as mine.'
>
> – 'VOICES OF CWP' IN A COGTA PAMPHLET INTRODUCING CWP

7. Conclusions: More on Unbounded Organization

In the previous chapter we called India's economy an accumulation of anomalies. That was not quite accurate. An anomaly, as Thomas Kuhn uses the term, either cannot be explained by the reigning theory or can be explained by it only if the data are fudged in implausible ways. But a believer in today's

---

78. Ibid., p. 1311.

79. Ibid., p. 1314. He suggests that nevertheless, the fact that so many Swedes have become dependent on the government may mean that Sweden has passed a point of no return, making its future hard to predict.

reigning theories can regard what we call anomalies—like price supports for agriculture that either limit food production or warehouse food where it cannot be eaten, while paying farmers who are already prosperous—as explainable by the reigning theory and as reasonable choices among the policy options available. These choices are indeed anomalies from our unbounded viewpoint, which widens the options to consider and explore policies better designed to meet human needs in harmony with nature.

Further, alluding to Kuhn might suggest that we advocate a paradigm shift from one paradigm to another. But we propose instead that minds be open to many paradigms, including those of indigenous knowledge systems, including the defeated epistemologies of the global South that colonialism relegated to museums or defined as superstition or simply ignored, and including what Paulo Freire called the new truths that we create as we work together to create a better world. The general concept of community, and with it community development, is the guiding star.

An unbounded approach redefines the problem. For example, the problem is not how to choose between maximizing employment and minimizing inflation. The problem is having to make that choice. It transforms the system that requires the trade-off in the first place. How does it do it?

Our approach to fundamental change is to combine thinking all the time, reading books and talking about them, with, on a practical level, aligning across sectors to solve one problem at a time. This does not exclude many efforts going on simultaneously in the same place or in many places, each focused on a particular problem. Surviving the civilizational crisis, if we do survive it, will most likely result from the summation of many relatively small successes, together with never-ending questioning of our theoretical premises and evaluation of our practical projects.

One way to organize thinking about reversing the failure of the Swedish Model is to list five 'presenting symptoms' of problems the Swedish progressives could not solve—which are also presenting symptoms of the civilizational crisis—and then consider ways to cope with them. They are as follows:

- Capital flight
- Insufficient demand for Swedish exports
- Unbearably high public expenses
- Unpopular high taxes
- As Wielecki put it, the favouring of ruthless capitalism and destruction of mature capitalism by global processes

Capital Flight

An example of capital flight (what Bowles and Gintis call 'the exit power of capital')[80] is when Volvo set up vehicle production in Brazil, where wages were a tenth of Swedish wages. Private investment in manufacturing start-ups in Sweden fell to zero as investors went elsewhere. They preferred lower taxes, lower wages, and less regulation.

Envision ourselves for a moment in *1973* in Sweden. The policy of replacing lost jobs in *solnedgång* industries with new jobs in *soluppgång* industries is not working. The *solnedgång* are too many, and the *soluppgång* are too few (SF2). Swedish industry is turning out to be not so Swedish; it prefers other soils when they are more profitable. What can one do in such a situation?

Suppose we ask the question we recommended in an earlier chapter when trying to facilitate structural changes: 'How can we build (good) community?' Would asking that question make any difference? Yes. It would broaden the choices and deepen the commitments.

An example of building community is the milk industry in Quebec, Canada. In terms of strictly orthodox (and bogus) criteria of efficiency, it would pay Canada to sell something else and import dairy products. But the milk producers are well organised and politically influential.[81] Hence the people who make the decisions are largely the farmers themselves. They want to preserve their livelihoods, their communities, and their way of life. Orthodox economics fails to seduce them, and Quebec remains an exporter, not an importer, of dairy products.

Another example is the 'recovery' of Mil Hojas, a pasta factory in Argentina, after the economic crash of 2001. The factory was and is located in a neighbourhood of the city of Rosario, which has anarchist traditions. When the business failed and the owner left, the employees decided to revive it as a worker-owned cooperative. Extended families, political parties, volunteer professionals and community members (some in organizations, others just friends) rallied around. Family members went door to door lining up advance orders for the forthcoming products. A volunteer accountant reviewed the books and put them in order. She discovered that according to standard economic criteria, Mil Hojas was not viable. The success of the business (it is still running today[82]) in spite of her calculations is an

---

80. Samuel Bowles and Herbert Gintis, *Democracy and Capitalism* (New York: Basic Books, 1986).
81. https://lait.org/en/.
82. For a video on Mil Hojas, see https://www.youtube.com/watch?v=SoEBXVplaI0.

example of what Luis Razeto calls 'Factor C'.[83] The letter C stands for Spanish words naming soft variables that have often spelled success when the hard numbers have predicted failure: *comprensión, compromiso, calor, cariño, compañerismo, comunicación, cooperación, corazón* and of course *comunidad*.

Worldwide, we should not forget the Tobin Tax[84] and its many variations. Sweden itself has been a leader in this field both before and after the decline of its classic model. The Tobin tax deliberately makes short-term capital movements unprofitable by taxing them, since they are typically more about unproductive speculation than about contributing to meeting anybody's needs. The Tobin tax illustrates a larger principle: international institutions should make deliberate efforts to discourage capital flight and thus to encourage the governability of local economies.

Insufficient demand for Swedish exports

The Swedish Model could work when demand for Swedish exports (especially lumber) was abnormally high immediately after World War II. Europe was being reconstructed with aid from the American Marshall Plan, and most other nations were either destroyed by the war or not yet developed. Once industries in other countries began to compete with Swedish exports, however, the demand for Swedish exports dropped and the Swedish Model began to falter.

We know that insufficient demand is a chronic problem in any market economy, international or national. We know that the problem is not so much that sales happen, as that people come to depend on sales. If they cannot sell, either their labour power or something else, they cannot live. Similarly, the problem is not that Sweden exported a lot of lumber to the European mainland after the war. The problem is that Sweden came to depend on high volumes of exports to finance its welfare state, and when exports fell, it had to cut benefits. Similarly, the problem is not that there is economic growth. The problem is that growth becomes a necessity, not a choice. Following Greta Thunberg's sane advice becomes well-nigh impossible because people depend on anti-ecological growth for jobs and for paying debts they have contracted.

83. www.uvirtual.net.

84. James Tobin, 'A Proposal for International Monetary Reform', *Eastern Economic Journal*, vol. 4 (1978), pp. 153–159.

If Sweden had not depended so much on growth to meet human needs in the first place, they would have found it easier to adjust when foreigners lost interest in buying their products. Such considerations and others have led many to adopt a lifestyle culture shift in a narrower sense of the term than we use it.[85] We use culture shift as a general concept naming the necessity of any culture to change to adapt to the challenges of its environment or else go extinct. In the narrower sense, which we also recommend, 'culture shift' means living in a way that is less dependent on 'the system'. One of its benefits is that individuals feel more secure. Another is that governments are in a stronger bargaining position vis-a-vis transnational corporations, because they know their citizens are more resilient. Governments are less desperate to land the growth the transnationals may or may not provide.

Here are some examples of lifestyle changes leading to more personal and national resilience:

- *Reducing, reusing, and recycling.* If I throw away my old shirt and buy a new one, I need money. If I mend my shirt and wear it, my need for cash is less. If I go into debt to buy a fancy new car, instead of riding a bicycle, I am less secure and the bank that financed my car is also less secure because I might default.
- *Family connectivity.* If parents care for their children or ask grandparents to babysit, nothing is contributed to GDP, while if they pay a preschool to care for them, GDP goes up but resilience goes down. The GDP probably goes up twice: once when the nursery is paid and again when the parent goes to work and earns a wage. It is the same if we cook a holiday dinner at home instead of going out to a restaurant, or if we sit around the fire, play instruments and sing songs instead of going out to a nightclub. If I am unemployed and my family is close, I can move in with a relative and make myself useful around the house by washing dishes or planting a garden or building a new bedroom.
- *Many aspects of community development.* The CWP offers an example of multiplying what can be done with public funds by catalysing volunteer time and nonmonetary resources. Hence more needs are met with less money.
- *Home gardening and subsistence farming.*

---

85. Robert Inglehart, *Culture Shift in Advanced Industrial Society* (Princeton: Princeton University Press, 1990).

- *Do-it-yourself projects.*
- *Meeting basic needs for free or at low cost.* When fewer things are free and more things are expensive, there is more need for money, and hence more need to live on the terms the market dictates. As an example, water in Chile has evolved from being a free good to being a commodity so expensive that many cannot afford to plant a garden because they cannot afford to water it. In the health field, many countries get the same or better health care[86] and live as long as or longer than Americans, but they pay less for it or get it free. Hence, they need less money.
- *Leisure.* If people retire or decide to work just one job, they get the health and psychological benefits of more leisure, increasing their resilience.
- *Decent working conditions.* If people take coffee breaks, work an eight-hour day at a pleasant pace and enjoy their work while producing somewhat less, the system may actually be more, not less, efficient, when health and happiness are objectives.[87] Wielicki may have had this point in mind when he contrasted mature capitalism with ruthless capitalism.

None of these 'culture shift' lifestyle items raises GDP. On the contrary, they all lower it.

The Swedish Model was an example of finding useful roles for raising GDP in providing security and well-being to the Swedish population. Lowering GDP and lowering growth, or limiting growth to green growth, can also be designed to increase security and well-being while at the same time reversing humanity's death march to ecological suicide.[88]

---

86. According to the World Health Organization website, in 2012, overall life expectancy was 83 years in Sweden, 81.9 in Norway, 81 in Finland, 79.8 in the United States, and 79.5 in Denmark. In 2010, per capita expenditure on health was USD $3758 in Sweden, $5388 in Norway, $3251 in Finland, $8223 in the USA, and $4464 in Denmark. *Healh Costs—How the US compares with Other Countries*, http://www.pbs.org/ newshour/rundown/health-costs-how-the-us-compares-with-other-countries/ -.

87. Fred Hirsch, *Social Limits to Growth* (Cambridge, MA: Harvard University Press, 1977), p. 16.

88. See the chapters on Vandana Shiva, Arundathi Roy and Manmohan Singh in Howard Richards and Joanna Swanger, *Gandhi and the Future of Economics* (Lake Oswego, OR: World Dignity University Press, 2013), and also Jean Drèze and Amartya Sen, *Hunger and Public Action* (Oxford: Clarendon Press, 1989).

Unbearably high public expenses

If science typically progresses, as Gaston Bachelard suggested, by leaps into abstractions that define the problem more broadly and therefore see more possible solutions, then blurring the distinction between public and private expenses could be considered typical of scientific progress. It would set aside, partially and prudently, one of the great motives for the rise of liberal ethics in early European modernity,[89] namely, to sharply distinguish private from public by constitutionally establishing a sphere of private rights the sovereign was forbidden to violate and commanded to protect—most importantly those private rights that constitute the social structures of market exchange, property and contract.

Blurring the public-private distinction today can be seen as a step back in time from early modern Europe to as far back as prehistoric Africa, where the descendants of Mitochondrial Eve first learned to cooperate to cope.[90] A motive for it today is to reduce unbearably high public expenses through greater social responsibility in the private and civic sectors and at the neighbourhood level.

The social democrats of Sweden saw themselves as practitioners of the true modern ethic, correcting the distortions of capitalism by winning for workers higher wages and a say in working conditions. They did not set out to create a government that would smother individual initiative and undertake its own huge and expensive projects. The Swedish socialists did not nationalize industries. They did not plan the economy. Wages were set by negotiations between associated employers and organized labour from which the government was deliberately and conspicuously absent. Indeed, most of the characteristic features that defined Swedish social democracy, including the Rehn-Meidner model, were initiated by labour, not by government. Nevertheless, programmes such as the employment guarantee, which provided every Swede who could not find high-wage employment in the private sector with high-wage employment in the public sector (usually construction of social housing or staffing preschools and kindergartens), were expensive.

We suggest that the Swedish government becoming what it was not intended to become, not a Leviathan but tending more in that direction than was intended, was in large part due to neglect of SF2, the chronic weakness of demand. The Swedes trusted markets too much. They counted

---

89. John Rawls, *Lectures on the History of Moral Philosophy* (Cambridge, MA: Harvard University Press, 2000), p.7.
90. C. H. Waddington, *The Ethical Animal* (London: George Allen and Unwin, 1960).

on markets to deliver the customers to buy the products, after what they saw as the main problem, the exploitation of labour, had been solved. They also expected markets to continue to perform when subjected to a high degree of government regulation. Markets failed on both counts, and as one strategy after another for achieving full employment at high pay failed, the government was compelled to be the employer of last resort paying high wages. (A 'right to work' guaranteed by the government had existed since 1938, but it did not become crucial, massive and very expensive until a series of efforts to propitiate high-wage employment for all in the private sector failed.)

An unbounded solution requires alignment across sectors to solve the problem. It requires a private sector and a population that regard making human social rights real as everybody's responsibility, not just the government's responsibility. In light of Sweden's experience, and in light of the logical analysis in the section 'Keynes's Problem' above, we must accept two facts: First, markets *do not* provide satisfactory employment for everybody who needs it. Second, governments alone (short of unacceptable command economies) *cannot* pick up the tab for creating dignified slots and decent incomes for everyone markets exclude.

In light of these two facts, we must reconsider what it means to be a human being. Roy Bhaskar indicated the direction toward which the practical necessity of reorganizing economies drives moral education when he wrote in one of his last writings: 'We are no longer Cartesian egos: subjects opposed to an object world which includes other subjects. Rather we approach the thought embodied in some southern African languages by the notion of *ubuntu* which means roughly 'I am because you are.''[91]

Unpopular high taxes

The following considerations on the causes and cures of high taxes elaborate on the reflections on capital flight above and on why governments alone cannot include the excluded. They make constructive suggestions and give examples from an unbounded point of view. The point of view makes a difference, for, as Lev Vygotsky wrote, 'When we learn to see things in other ways, at the same time we acquire other possibilities for acting in relation to them.'[92]

---

91. Roy Bhaskar, 'Critical Realism and the Ontology of Persons', *Journal of Critical Realism*, vol. 19 (2020), p. 119.

92. Lev Vygotsky, *Thought and Language* (Cambridge, MA: MIT Press, 1986 (1934)),

When Volvo chose to build vehicles in Brazil, what the Swedish workers lost, the Brazilian workers labouring in Swedish-owned factories did not gain. The Brazilian economist Paul Singer has stated the operative principle succinctly: 'Neoliberal globalization levels the price of labour downward in all countries.'[93] He could have added that it also shifts the tax burden downward. The Swedes were paying extremely high taxes, sometimes as much as 65 percent of an ordinary person's paycheck,[94] a fact many associate with the high suicide rates in Sweden during the 1960s.

The heavy tax burdens now born by the middle and working classes worldwide are connected with the low or zero taxes paid by large fortunes and powerful corporations. Tax justice depends on governability. Governability depends on how nation-states identified with a certain geographical territory can (or cannot) govern wealthy individuals and corporations that freely move from one territory to another. They choose which laws to obey, which motivates the lawmakers to write laws that will attract them. Such laws tend to impose tax burdens on ordinary people while exempting mobile wealth. As Rexford Tugwell, who in the early 1930s in the United States was a founding member of President Franklin Roosevelt's New Deal Brain Trust, once said, there is a Gresham's Law of laws. As bad money drives out good money (Gresham's Law), so bad laws drive out good laws as nation-states compete to attract investors and wealthy residents.[95] Among the hapless victims are the middle-class and working-class taxpayers.

Singer writes that the global marketplace for labour leaves so many people unemployed, precariously employed, or working for low wages without job security that workers do not dare to stand up for their rights, for there are many ready to take their place if they complain. He adds that in Brazil, labour legislation is not enforced because workers rarely dare to call for its enforcement. When they do, they are routinely met with dismissals and/

quoted by Yves Clot et al., 'Entretiens en autoconfrontation croisée,' *PISTES* 2-1 2000, paragraph 4.2, http://pistes.revues.org/3833.

93. Paul Singer, in his preface to *20 años de economia popular solidaria* (Brasilia: Caritas Brasilera, 2004). Singer headed the Secretariat for Solidarity Economics (Economia Solidaria) in the Brazilian government.

94. The model lost legitimacy, as predicted by Habermas in 1973 in *The Legitimation Crisis* (Boston: Beacon Press, 1975), largely because the expenses of the state exceeded the fiscal resources it could claim in a modern world-system defined by limited governments committed to respecting private law. This led to a combination of unfulfilled social promises, high taxes and debt.

95. See Winters, *Power in Motion*, previously cited. Tugwell suggested that there is a Gresham's Law of laws in conversation in 1965, when he was a senior fellow and I was a junior fellow at the Center for the Study of Democratic Institutions in Santa Barbara, CA.

or plant closings. Workers do not even dare to call for enforcement of the economic and social rights guaranteed to them by the Constitution of Brazil. Thus, there is exploitation of labour in the country the capital flees to (like Brazil), alongside the loss of jobs and the increased burden on ordinary taxpayers in the country the capital flees from (like Sweden).

From an unbounded viewpoint, there are, in principle, an unlimited number of ways to make mobile capital governable and thus ease the tax burden on the middle and lower classes. Here we discuss two: (1) establish trade barriers and (2) tie capital down to social purposes and territories.

Establishing trade barriers is a way to forbid the importation of goods produced in violation of international law, that is, in violation of treaties and covenants guaranteeing (on paper) economic and social human rights. The principle here is the same one that outlaws the buying of stolen goods. Surely enforcing labour rights that have the status of law under treaties and covenants signed and ratified by most countries is a good reason for not buying goods produced by violating those rights.

But one does not need to wait for the legislature of one's country to enact trade barriers. Being part of the solution and not part of the problem often plays out on the ground as simple paths, like donating, recycling, abstaining, volunteering and refusing to buy goods produced through gross violations of human rights. (Mother Teresa titled her autobiography *A Simple Path* to make the point that what she did anybody else could do.)

Experience suggests[96] that eliminating the worst of poverty is not difficult or expensive when approached on a local level by a coalition of the willing. Eliminating the worst includes bringing the excluded into the community and assuring that every resident's basic needs are met, including food, medical attention, and being able to pay utility bills. Assuming that it is a locality where there are at least a few volunteers with a little surplus cash and/or surplus time, and assuming it is in a country like South Africa or Chile where the welfare state, though imperfect, is not nonexistent—the expense of meeting basic material needs of neighbours is not high. This topic will come up again in several forms later. The reason for mentioning it here is to provide background for another suggestion: Meanwhile, most of the prosperous people of the locality can, if they wish, sit back, and do

---

96. We refer to our own experiences, but we could refer to any number of people who have found that making a difference where they are is not expensive, including Mother Teresa just mentioned. *A Simple Path* (New York: Ballantine Books, 1995). We think it likely that the reader knows, or is, such a person.

nothing. There is no need to compel the unwilling when sufficient resources to solve simple, everyday problems are provided by the willing.

Having suggested that there is no reason to wait for government action or structural change or unanimity among one's neighbours to make a difference, and every reason to proceed to make a difference on a small scale, we now return to capital flight, connecting the global with the local. We propose that the *governability of capital*, and hence (for example) more equitable sharing of tax burdens, can be encouraged *by tying capital down to a territory and committing capital to social purposes*. We now give some examples.

One example is the Municipal Bank of Rosario, Argentina. Its social purpose, prescribed by its charter, is to provide credit for micro, small and medium-sized enterprises, which provide nearly all of the city's employment. The bank interprets its purpose to include providing accounting services and seminars on business topics for its clients.[97] It makes operational the ideal of a people's economy whose aim is to provide opportunities for domestic units to make a decent living. The people's economy's aim is not to accumulate capital. The municipal bank's accounting and administrative support for small and micro business does not mean that the world can live in the future without large organizations. It does presuppose that aligning other sectors constructively with big business and big government is partially achieved by building thriving people's economies. And people's economies are tied to territories.

The Municipal Bank is tied to one territory, which is Rosario and its immediate environs. Its capital is not free to roam the globe to seek higher profits elsewhere. Its attachment to its territory was dramatically demonstrated in December 2001 and the following months. On 1 December, during Argentina's ongoing financial crisis, the national government imposed a decree (nicknamed the *corralito*) that froze all bank accounts. Unlike the other banks in Rosario, most of which were branches of multinationals based in other countries, the Municipal Bank bent the rules to serve its purpose. Its board of directors instructed its legal staff to look for loopholes in the decree that would allow the bank's customers access to the funds in their accounts. Juan Carlos Saavedra, the head of the Municipal Bank's legal department, explained: 'We knew that our customers desperately needed access to their funds to stay afloat. We looked for legal alternatives to the

---

97. Howard Richards, *Solidaridad, Participacion, Transparencia* (Rosario: Fundación Estévez Boero, 2008), ch. 7, http://www.humiliationstudies.org/documents/RichardsChapterSevenRosario.pdf (see also Unbounded Organization at www.unboundedorganization.org).

corralito decree of the federal government to find ways to get their money to them. For example, we could make a new loan to them for which they would pledge their frozen funds as collateral. We kept many small businesses open that otherwise would have had to close, and many families fed that otherwise would have gone hungry.'[98]

Although the decision to bend the law to serve a social purpose was mission-driven and not profit-driven, in the long run it proved profitable. Loyalty to purpose attracted depositors and borrowers. The Municipal Bank has since established a foundation dedicated to spending its profits on good and beautiful works. These have included funding engineering studies to further the greening of the city and funding public performances of opera.

Another example of capital chained to a purpose and a territory is India's National Bank for Agriculture and Rural Development (NABARD), established in 1982 by an act of Parliament to 'uplift rural India'. It regards itself as a 100 percent corporate social responsibility (CSR) financial institution. We quote some innovative small farmers whom NABARD has supported:

> The Farmers' Club programme of NABARD attracted us the most. With assistance, we purchased farm machinery and milk animals for our members.[99]

> Hopefully, we will be an example that will encourage other people to participate in organic farming. This is the direction in which WSSS and NABARD are steering this venture.[100]

One of NABARD's projects was to establish simple processing plants to turn the dried fallen sheaths of the areca tree—long added to cow fodder in the Bangalore area—into powder. One farmer reported:

> Previously one cow gave eight litres per day. After I shifted to feeding them Areca sheath, they gave ten litres of milk each. The quality of milk has also improved. It has become

---

98. Ibid. Saavedra has also been an employee-elected member of the bank's board. In the 1990s, he was a leader of resistance against privatizing the Municipal Bank. The neoliberal Carlos Menem, president of Argentina from 1989 to 1999, succeeded in privatizing all the municipal banks in Argentina except 2, the Municipal Bank of Rosario and the Banco Ciudad of Buenos Aires.

99. From *NABARD's Role in Development of Producers' Organisation* (YouTube video).

100. From *Sweet Success a NABARD* (YouTube video). WSSS is Wayanad Social Service Society (see www.wsssindia.com).

thicker. Previously I used to feed them pieces of Areca sheath. But now it is made into powder. So it becomes easier and faster for the cow to digest it.[101]

Even if NABARD's capital could earn higher returns and multiply faster if moved to a tax haven and used to speculate in commodity futures, the bank would not move it one centimetre away from where it is and from what it is doing. The bank knows what that capital is for and where it should be used.

Larger-scale examples of capital tied to purpose and territory are found in China as the Chinese develop what they call 'socialism with Chinese characteristics'.[102] Xi Jinping, Chairman of the Communist Party of China, in a series of speeches studded with exhortations to civic virtue drawn from the Chinese classics, asserted that in China 'the invisible hand' and the 'visible hand' work together for the Chinese Dream.[103] Dani Rodrik observes that China's reforms have not included establishing property rights as understood in the West: 'China's economic policies have violated virtually every rule by which the proselytizers of globalization would like the game to be played.'[104] One can, indeed, question whether Chinese capitalists own their capital in the full Western sense of ownership, since so much of what they can do, including whether they can move it out of China and to where and for what purpose, is governed by public policies. Projects outside China governed by those policies include building railroads in Africa and Asia and building a canal across Nicaragua to link the Atlantic and Pacific oceans.

There are more than 140 city commercial banks in China, most of which have strong ties to local government and are majority or wholly state owned.[105] China's Central Bank supervises all financial institutions. It controls foreign exchange. China's Big Four banks are state-owned and rank among the world's largest.

101. NABARD Online, *The Areca Moment* (YouTube video).

102. In contrast, China's shift away from central planning and toward markets as the decisive means for allocating resources is viewed by many in the West as conversion to pure capitalism. Eamonn Butler, for example, represents contemporary China as a nation converted to Milton Friedman's economic philosophy. Eamonn Butler, *Milton Friedman: A Concise Guide to the Ideas and Influence of the Free-market Economist* (Petersfield, Hampshire: Harriman House, 2011).

103. Xi Jinping, *The Governance of China* (Beijing: Foreign Languages Press, 2014). See especially the seven speeches on the Chinese Dream, the three on core socialist values, and the three on ecology.

104. Dani Rodrik, *One Economics*, ch. 9, Kindle, position 4143. Comments on China are to be found throughout the book.

105. The information is from the Wikipedia article 'Banking in China'. Some details will no doubt have changed by the time this is read.

Our aim is not to praise China. God knows that China, like every country, has characteristics that disqualify it from being the ideal model for the rest of the world to copy. Our aim is to advocate a philosophy of alignment across all sectors for the common good, including the financial services sector. But is the financial sector not the sector where numbers wreak vengeance on humans, where the ruthless capitalist is only the agent of ruthless capital, where there is only one algorithmic imperative leading to only one answer and only one command: 'Accumulate! Accumulate!'? Not necessarily. Yes, we are lived by powers we only pretend to understand, but that is not the whole truth. Capital can also be made a means without being an end in itself. Its accumulation does not have to be the criterion by which everything else is evaluated. Capital's performance can be evaluated using social and ecological criteria. History does not have to be a process without a subject. We human subjects are still here.

As Wielecki put it, the favouring of ruthless capitalism and destruction of mature capitalism by global processes

In 1958 Sweden could be seen as a specimen displaying generic features of humanity's future. Countries that were not yet modern capitalist democracies would become modern capitalist democracies, for reasons Francis Fukuyama would later articulate.[106] Modern capitalist democracies would choose shared prosperity and call it social democracy. The socialists would be happy because the world was socialist. The capitalists would be happy because the world was capitalist.

That history turned out differently was due, *ceteris paribus*, to the basic cultural structure (constitutive rules) and social structure of a market economy. These have been fully in place for about three and a third centuries in the UK,[107] arguably a bit longer in Holland; two and a third in France;[108] and for shorter periods in the rest of the world.[109] Already in 1817 David

---

106. Fukuyama specifically mentions the Scandinavian social democracies as exemplars of what he calls the end of history. Francis Fukuyama, *The End of History and the Last Man* (New York: Macmillan, 1994), p. 294.

107. Counting from the founding of the Bank of England in 1694, although an earlier or later date might be chosen. See, for example, C.B. McPherson, *The Political Theory of Possessive Individualism* (Oxford: Oxford Paperbacks, 1965).

108. Counting from the French Revolution of 1789. See Thomas Piketty, *Capital and Ideology* (Cambridge, MA: Belknap Press, 2020), for an account of how the social structures of France were restructured after the revolution. See also William H. Sewell Jr., 'Historical Events as Transformations of Structures', *Theory and Society*, vol. 25 (1996), pp. 841–881.

109. Maria Mies, *Patriarchy and Accumulation on a World Scale* (London: Zed Books,

Ricardo, in addition to holding that the natural wage of labour, like any commodity bought and sold, was determined by supply and demand (chapter 3, above), also held that capital will naturally move wherever higher profits are to be made. His explanation for the absence of a fully globalized economy in 1817 was that investors felt safer investing close to home. The recovery of countries devastated by World War II, the freeing of former colonies to compete with their former colonizers and with everyone else in a race to the bottom, and a Pax Americana similar to but more extensive than the Pax Britannica prior to World War I triggered the causal powers noticed by Ricardo in 1817 and already present in any market economy.[110] *Ceteris* became more *paribus*. In Wielicki's terms, the processes of globalization made mature capitalism unsustainable—even before recent technological advances made growing numbers of workers redundant.

But some things are new. For more than 90 percent of the time human beings have been on the planet, all human beings were poor. After the Agricultural Revolution, it was technically possible for *some* human beings to escape poverty. The toilers in the fields could produce enough food to feed both themselves and an upper class who did not toil. Now it is technically possible to share prosperity among *all* human beings. (However, although there are some regarded as experts who disagree, it is necessary to check the growth of the sheer numbers of people on the planet.) As Martin Luther King Jr. said in 1968, 'There is nothing new about poverty. What is new is that today we have the resources and the techniques to end poverty. The question is: Do we have the will?'[111]

Something else that is new is that today it no longer serves the interests of the rich and powerful to succeed in winning a war against the poor or against anybody. For many centuries it was in the interest of the winners to win. For example, when the Franks defeated the Gauls, the Franks became the ruling nobility in France, forcing the Gauls to be the peasant toilers. But today humanity is not in a win-lose situation. It is in a lose-lose situation. Fighting among ourselves can only further undermine our already frail capacity to cope with changing physical realities.

1986); and Samir Amin, *Accumulation on a World Scale* (New York: Monthly Review Press, 1974).

110. Ricardo's views and other features of what has come to be called the New International Division of Labour are discussed in Barry Bluestone and Bennet Harrison, *Capital and Communities: Causes and Consequences of Private Disinvestment* (Washington, DC: Progressive Alliance, 1980).

111. Martin Luther King Jr., speech at National Cathedral in Washington, DC, April 1968.

Today we confront an existential physical civilizational crisis. We are, adding a bit to Wielicki's analysis, vulnerable to attacks by a series of viruses that challenge the survival strategy of the cultural animal even as they paralyze 'the economy'. 'The economy' was already incapable of coping with social chaos and ecological disaster before the most recent, and surely not the last, virus attack. The overly rigid basic cultural and social structures of 'the economy' were already increasingly dysfunctional even before COVID-19.

Of 'the economy's' traditional three factors of production—land , labour and capital—one (labour) is every day less relevant as a contributor to production. An unbounded approach is therefore every day more relevant to sharing prosperity with the millions who are redundant in the labour market. This changes everything. Meanwhile two more factors of production have been added—management and knowledge. These also change everything.

In the present situation, nothing would serve the real interests of the rich and powerful more than humans learning to work together as a species to share prosperity in harmony with nature, learning to reverse global warming and other disastrous ecological trends and learning to pursue happiness in a world where technology frees humans from the necessity to make a product to sell in order to live. Nothing would serve the real interests of the downtrodden majority more than a global curriculum of economic solidarity where the poor learn the same lessons just recommended for the rich. Both are fellow victims of inherited cultural rules and social structures, according to which a few play the role of oppressor while the majority play the role of oppressed. This inherited script is part of the problem, not part of the solution.

Do we have the will? On Wielecki's analysis there is no way for humanity to survive its present civilizational crisis without reviving in some form the historic compromise he calls the shared prosperity of mature capitalism. Hence the rational answer to Martin Luther King's question must be that if we do not have the will now, we need to have it soon, for the alternative is game over. If we consult John Locke, the jurists who adapted Roman law and English common law for modern commercial purposes, and the framers of the founding documents of the French and American republics, the early modern official answer to King is clearly no. Ending poverty was not recognized as one of secular society's collective objectives. If we consult more recent official public documents such as the International Declaration of Human Rights of 1948, the Indian Constitution of 1950, South Africa's Freedom Charter of 1955 and the Mandela Constitution of 1996, the answer is that we live in societies whose official public answer is clearly yes.

If the answer, then, is yes, we would add another question to King's: Do we know what we are doing? We attempt to answer this question in the remaining chapters.

CHAPTER EIGHT

Neoliberal Economics as an Imaginary World That Holds the Real World Captive

OVERVIEW OF THE CHAPTER

1. A Note on Method
2. The Astonishment: Regarding Milton Friedman
3. The Stakes: The *Forme* and the *Fond*
4. The *Forme* and *Fond* of Neoliberalism
5. Explaining the Academic Fascination of Neoliberalism
6. The *Forme* and *Fond* of Unbounded Organization
7. Evaluating the Community Work Programme through a Neoliberal Lens
8. An Historical Comment on the Origins of Neoliberalism: Adam Smith
9. The Technification of Hitchlessness: OECD Review Evaluation Criteria
10. Calculating Deadweight
11. Raising the Stakes: Critique of the Tax Wedge and the Unbounded Alternative
12. The Superiority of an Unbounded, Pluralist World
13. Transformative Heterodoxy

1. A Note on Method

We have described our method as doing our best to perform responsible speech acts. Being responsible entails being aware, as best we can, of the consequences of those acts. We have been proposing some ways of talking that are also ways of seeing. For example, we say that needs should be met in harmony with nature. We make a case that the consequences of playing this proposed communities-should-be-constructed-to-meet-needs-in-harmony-with-nature language game are good. For several reasons, they are better than the consequences of playing the language games of natural economics

(Smith) or pure economics (Walras). Indeed, we hold that all economics, even the laudable heterodox economics of Piketty, Varoufakis, the modern monetary theorists and the regulationists is a game poorly played to the extent that it lacks attention to community.[1] In any case, our ethical reasoning is inevitably circular—it is making a responsible choice about what rules to play by; it is not bowing to a logical necessity—because meeting needs in harmony with nature is what we *mean* by good.

In this chapter, we deal mainly (except for another flashback to Adam Smith and one to Jules Dupuit) with contemporary orthodox neoliberal economics. We argue that it is circular too. Ours is a virtuous circle, while the neoliberal economics circle is a vicious circle. Both depend for their meaning on what we choose for them to mean. As Charles Wilber and Robert Harrison have suggested, economics is storytelling. In economic theory, whatever you may want, story is what you get.[2]

Of course, every economist holds his or her own view, different from that of every other economist. With respect to our attacks on views we perceive as more influential than they should be, we say to any particular economist: if the shoe fits, wear it; if it does not fit, you are not the target.

2. The Astonishment: Regarding Milton Friedman

In his famous article 'A Theoretical Framework for Monetary Analysis',[3] Milton Friedman paraphrases 'the first proposition' of Keynes as follows: 'There need not exist, even if all prices are flexible, a long run equilibrium position characterized by "full employment" of resources.' A few paragraphs later, he writes, 'The first proposition can be treated summarily, because it has been demonstrated to be false.'

One wonders what on earth was going on in Friedman's mind. If the proposition that full employment of labour (and other resources) 'need not exist' is false, then it must be true that full employment 'need exist'. And if it must exist, then it must exist all the time. There must always be full

---

1. See Tony Lawson, *The Nature of Social Reality* (London: Routledge, 2019), e.g., pp. 88 and 127. Similarly, for Charles Taylor the community constitutes the individual. *Philosophical Papers*, vol. 2 (Cambridge: Cambridge University Press, 1986), p. 8.

2. 'The use of the term storytelling is not meant pejoratively. Rather, it is an accurate description of most work in the social sciences. To recognize that fact should be helpful to economics.' Charles Wilber and Robert Harrison, 'The Methodological Basis of Institutional Economics', *Journal of Economic Issues*, vol. 12 (1978), p. 70.

3. Milton Friedman, 'A Theoretical Framework for Monetary Analysis', *Journal of Political Economy*, vol. 78 (1970), pp. 193–238.

employment. Yet the empirically observed fact is, as Keynes says, that full employment, or even approximately full employment, rarely happens, and when it does happen, it does not last long.[4]

Friedman must not mean what at first glance he appears to mean, so we must pay more attention to how he qualifies his statement. In fact, he is not saying that full employment necessarily exists and therefore exists all the time. He is saying that a *'long run equilibrium* position' characterized by full employment necessarily exists. (It is false that it need not exist; therefore it is true that it need exist.) He is not saying that there is always full employment; he is saying that there is full employment in the long run and when the economy is in equilibrium.

This meaning is hardly less astonishing. If the economy tends toward equilibrium and in the long run will arrive at full employment, then full employment must be the economy's normal tendency. It must be where the economy tends to go, even if at any given time it is not there, or not there yet. However, if one considers capitalism from its historical beginning around 1700, one must say that in a little over three centuries no such tendency toward full-employment equilibrium has been observed.

The key to Friedman's meaning must lie in his other qualification: 'even if all prices are flexible'. He must believe, contrary to Keynes,[5] that if wages could fall lower and lower without limit (a fall without limit that, as we saw in chapter 2, for David Ricardo implied full employment of all the workers living, since the workers for whom the market did not provide a living wage would die or not be born, for lack of food) and if all other prices were also fully flexible, then there would be full employment in the long run.

Even with this second qualification our astonishment is hardly less. In the real world prices are not fully flexible.[6] They are not now, and they never have been. It seems that for a neoliberal like Friedman, what exists is

---

4. John Maynard Keynes, *The General Theory of Employment, Interest, and Money* (London: Macmillan, 1936), pp. 249–50.

5. 'There is, therefore, no ground for the belief that a flexible wage policy is capable of maintaining a state of continuous full employment; any more than for the belief that an open-market monetary policy is capable, unaided, of achieving this result. The economic system cannot be made self-adjusting along these lines.' Ibid., p. 267.

6. Criticizing Friedman, Paul Davidson argues that the very idea of fully flexible prices is contradictory. Money is by definition and by social function a store of value. It provides socially constructed stability linking past, present and future. An economy can exist only if there is 'continuity over time in contractual commitments in money units'. Paul Davidson, 'A Keynesian View of Friedman's Theoretical Framework for Monetary Analysis', in Robert Gordon (ed.), *Milton Friedman's Monetary Framework* (Chicago: University of Chicago Press, 1974), pp. 90–110.

read as an absence of what ought to be. What actually happens in markets is seen as the absence of fully flexible prices in markets at equilibrium. Our astonishment leads us to the following two questions, which the rest of this chapter is devoted to solving:

1. What is the seductive attraction of a worldview that leads Friedman (and with him, many neoliberal economists who currently make public policy at the global and most national levels) to believe it is useful to declare what would happen in the hypothetical circumstances of equilibrium with fully flexible prices?
2. Why does he (and why do they) think it appropriate to evaluate the real world by comparing it to a hypothetical world that has never existed and (as Joseph Schumpeter[7] and others have shown, and we show in this chapter) could not possibly exist?

3. The Stakes: The *Forme* and the *Fond*

Forme and *fond* are a pair of French words that have proven useful in applying the German psychological term *Gestalt*. Here we apply them to help compare and contrast the worldview we aim to deconstruct (Friedman's) and the worldview we recommend (unbounded organization) by looking at the *forme* and *fond* of each.

Forme, like 'form' in English, means 'shape' or 'figure'. It is what comes into focus and stands out against a background, as the girlfriend of the Nicaraguan poet Ernesto Cardenal came into focus and stood out against the background of the crowd in the stadium.[8]

Consider the well-known line drawing that can be seen as a duck or as a rabbit. That is, its *forme* can be a duck or a rabbit; or it could be something else: it could be lines drawn on a page by a child. As we have noted above, we agree with Heidegger that there is never an uninterpreted sense datum. There is no escape to ground level where pure facts are delivered to the human senses without interpretation. Although one might refer to such a line drawing as ambiguous, it is ambiguous only for people who realize

---

7. Joseph Schumpeter, *The Theory of Economic Development* (New Brunswick, NJ: Transaction Publishers, 2007 (first German edition 1911)). Schumpeter argues that the circular flow *(Kreislauf)* of neoclassical economics could exist only in a static world.

8. From the poem 'Cuando tu no estás en': Ayer estabas en el estadio / en medio de miles de gentes / y te divisé / desde que entré / igual que si hubieras / estado sola / en un estadio vacío. https://arturovasquez.wordpress.com/category/ernesto-cardenal/.

that it can be seen in more than one way. For a person who sees it as a duck and does not realize that it can also be seen as a rabbit, the drawing is not ambiguous. It is a duck. Examples can be found in the documents of the World Trade Organization, where the diminishing of human happiness caused by trade barriers is seen not as ambiguous but as a fact.⁹

The *fond* is the background. A *forme* always comes into focus by emerging from and standing out against a *fond*. The girlfriend comes into focus standing out against a crowd. So also, there is no text without context. The basic idea behind Kurt Gödel's famous incompleteness theorem—that we can never make explicit the complete background of what we mean—applies not just to number theory, not just to mathematics, but to any language. Up to some point, which varies from case to case, we can explain reasonably well the background our ideas are coming out of. But we must eventually surrender to the inevitability that anything we say or write is incomplete. There must be background assumptions that remain unspoken and unwritten. At one level, this must be true because it is impossible to say or write everything at once. At a second level, it must be true because whatever one may say is only an infinitesimal fraction of all the talking going on around one, too vast to record and exhaustively analyse, that gives meaning to the words one uses. As Mikhail Bakhtin points out, words do not belong to us; 'one borrows words from the surrounding milieu and ventriloquizes with them'. At a third level, it must be true because even the totality of human speech depends for its meanings on things outside that speech.

We can to some degree fill in the background to what we say or write by providing more context when people ask us questions, but eventually that effort fades into a vast impossibility. For this reason, while the *fond* is essential for there to be a *forme*, it is also humbling. The *fond* spans an infinite range, starting from what we can pretty easily explain and from there going

---

9. See the seven important objectives of the WTO at http://www.yourarticlelibrary.com/trade-2/world-trade-organization-wto-objectives-and-functions/23529/.

downward and outward, toward the unfathomable beyond the depths and the invisible beyond the horizon. Ludwig Wittgenstein expressed a similar point when he wrote that in mathematics (and with greater reason outside mathematics), communication depends on more than clear definitions; it depends on the wider realities of agreement in action and in judgments.[10] He was neither the first nor the last to observe that it is only because of simplifying cultural conventions ('forms of life', in his terms) that we can communicate at all.

♦ ♦ ♦

While the CWP pays participants, the payment is not high.

> 'Zuma [Jacob Zuma, President of the Republic of South Africa] promised us a better life. But now we are unemployed. We are now engaged in projects where we are not working for anything. You have children, but you earn R520. It does not mean that you are working. It is just a waste of time.'
>
> – CWP PARTICIPANT, JOE MOROLONG LOCAL MUNICIPALITY, NORTHERN CAPE PROVINCE

4. The *Forme* and *Fond* of Neoliberalism

The *forme* of neoliberalism is the set of interconnected ideas we have already characterized as seeing the real world through the lens of an imaginary world where there would be fully flexible prices, markets in equilibrium (which simply means that everything that is brought to market is sold) and all resources fully employed. We have already identified this view with the economics of Milton Friedman, who called himself a liberal. We have also identified the neoliberal view as mainstream, orthodox and dominant while acknowledging that in doing so, we may exaggerate the extent to which the bulk of today's economists and policy makers think alike.

The neoliberal views whose limitations we point out—without, however, wanting to say they are completely mistaken or that there is nothing to be learned from them—overlap with other views that can be called mainstream but are not neoliberal, and with views that are not mainstream but are still not free of the tendency to see the real world as defined by an imaginary perfect market. An extreme example of the latter would be the

---

10. Ludwig Wittgenstein, *Remarks on the Foundations of Mathematics* (Cambridge, MA: MIT Press, 1994), section 39, pp. 342–3.

views of Polish socialist economist Oskar Lange, who defended socialism by arguing that the result of perfect planning would be equivalent to the result of perfect markets.[11]

The closest thing to a single neat and clear idea that ties together and defines the neoliberal (or liberal, or classical) worldview may be Say's Law, which is sometimes summarized as the law that for every seller there is a buyer. Here we get a first glimpse of the *fond* of neoliberalism: a world of individual sellers and buyers, *séparation marchande*.

However, Say's Law—perhaps the most famous and most controversial law in economics—is not fully neat and fully clear, as we discuss in chapter 10. Keynes saw Say's Law as one of three logically equivalent forms of an orthodoxy he had been trained to believe as an economist.[12] Orthodoxy was logically impeccable as an internally coherent pattern of thought. Because he had come to believe that, nevertheless, it did not describe the real world, he wrote his *General Theory*. That book can be described as a book with two main themes: the chronic deficiency of effective demand, and the chronic deficiency of the inducement to invest, corresponding to our SF2 and SF1. For us SF2 and SF1 are consequences of a social structure and the cultural rules that define its positions. Social structures are at bottom legal and ethical norms. (Lawson calls the rules that constitute markets and define property, rights and obligations of social positions[13]).

Here we get a first glimpse of what we are calling the stakes. We propose to see orthodox economic theory as anthropologists: it is the logic of a certain social structure, which is itself a feature of a certain cultural adaptation to physical reality. The true *fond*, as the coronavirus and global warming remind us, is physical reality. What is at stake in the contest between neoliberalism and realism is whether our minds will remain trapped in eighteenth-century European jurisprudence or become free to adjust culture to its physical functions.

To, we hope, make our own discussion in this chapter clearer, we borrow an idea from Jeff Madrick.[14] Madrick shows how one beautiful eighteenth-century idea envisioned by Adam Smith has led to no end of

---

11. Oskar Lange and Fred M. Taylor, *On the Economic Theory of Socialism* (Minneapolis: University of Minnesota Press, 1938). Milton Friedman replied that if the purpose of socialism was to simulate perfect free markets, why not take the more direct route by perfecting the free markets we already have? See Milton Friedman, 'Lerner on the Economics of Control', *Journal of Political Economy*, vol. 55 (1947), pp. 405–416.

12. Keynes, *General Theory*, pp. 21–22.

13. Lawson, *Nature of Social Reality*, passim.

14. Jeff Madrick, *Seven Bad Ideas: How Mainstream Economists Have Damaged America and the World* (New York: Random House, 2014).

trouble. That seductive yet bad idea is the idea of a self-regulating market. Its progeny include austerity economics, government's limited social role, an obsession with keeping inflation under control at all costs, blindness in the face of speculative bubbles, globalization (which Madrick calls Friedman's folly writ large) and the myth that economics is a science.

By helping us to articulate our reasons why neoliberalism is nutty at the level of the *forme*, Madrick leads us to seeing supporting reasons at the level of the *fond*. They supply the missing premises that make it obvious to the educated reader that we need community organizing not only to adjust to the dysfunctional social structures that we are compelled to live with today if we are going to live at all, but also to change social structures, to create win-win green cultures, so that there will be a tomorrow.

♦ ♦ ♦

'There were children who were thieves, but CWP took those people to work.'

— CWP PARTICIPANT, UMTHWALUME

5. Explaining the Academic Fascination of Neoliberalism

Another piece of the puzzle, another approach to another partial explanation of why humanity cannot adjust to the real world because it is trapped in an imaginary one, might be called the 'contribution to the field' approach. According to Karl Popper, every academic field consists, at the print or digital level, of symbols on the pages of books or bits on microchips that preserve what the scholars in the field have learned and, at the human level, of the scholars themselves. Those who are living constitute what Thomas Kuhn called a 'scientific community'. It is in their material interest to add to the knowledge in their field and augment its prestige so they can get more students, more funding and more employment for themselves and their graduates. Another powerful element in the background is the elite of acknowledged leaders in the field who evaluate a new text that appears in the foreground.

An important argument by Milton Friedman and his coauthor L. J. Savage serves as an example. In 1948 and 1952, Friedman and Savage published two articles on utility analysis that turned out to be seminal for Friedman's later works.[15] Part of their argument was that human beings are

---

15. Milton Friedman and L. J. Savage, 'The Utility Analysis of Choices Involving Risks', *Journal of Political Economy*, vol. 56 (1948), pp. 451–472; Milton Friedman and

self-interested individuals seeking to maximize an admittedly abstract entity designated as their utility. More precisely, in the second of the two articles, Friedman and Savage proposed the hypothesis that 'individuals choose among alternatives involving risk as if they were seeking to maximize the expected value of some quantity which has been called utility'.[16]

Friedman and Savage concede that the psychological evidence in favour of this hypothesis is meagre. Nonetheless, they urge its acceptance on two grounds: first, 'its coherence with the body of economic theory'—Popper and Kuhn confirmed! Defending the field (once again) outweighs the facts. And second, convenience. They write, 'Convenience may seem a slender justification; it is in fact an extremely important one.' They go on: 'Aside from inconvenience, need anything be wrong with the use of Roman rather than Arabic numerals; or with dropping numerical nomenclature altogether and replacing it with extemporaneous circumlocutions?' They argue that the justification for articulating a concept named 'utility' measurable in economics is the same as for articulating concepts named 'length and temperature' measurable in physics. In both cases the concept defines interval and ratio scale data to which quantitative techniques can be applied. By choosing to define utility as what human beings maximize, economics claims its right to be regarded as a hard science.

Reading Friedman and Savage's texts against a wider *fond*—a *fond* deeply conscious of the physical functions of cultural-historical stories teaching what it means to be a human being—one arrives at a different judgment. Analysing human behaviour as if it were a matter of calculated rational choices to maximize utility (which in practice tends to mean maximizing utility as measured by money) is *not* convenient. It may be convenient for academics seeking grants, accepted publications, promotion and tenure, but it is not convenient for humanity or Mother Earth. When the *fond* embraces generating social cohesion to meet everybody's needs and to organize sustainable relationships with the environment, then the myth of individual utility maximization reveals itself as not convenient at all.

◆ ◆ ◆

L. J. Savage, 'The Expected-Utility Hypothesis and the Measurability of Utility', *Journal of Political Economy*, vol. 60 (1952), pp. 463–474.

16. Friedman and Savage protect themselves against criticism by formally allowing that a given person's utility might not be selfish at all but pure altruism. Apart from this being a formal precaution rarely if ever carried over into practical applications, it remains within the rhetorical frame of the economic actor. It does not support cultural resources such as, for example, the *imago dei* in the human soul, *ubuntu* or social responsibility.

'We are taught about these things [safe practices] as we are taught about taking care of our people, as we are community workers. So what we have been taught we teach others.'

— CWP PARTICIPANT, RANDFONTEIN CDI

6. The *Forme* and *Fond* of Unbounded Organization

Unbounded organization aspires to be a realist worldview. It cultivates a wide, long and deep consciousness of the best of what the natural sciences currently have to offer. Even though objective reality is never completely known by humans, it is necessarily the real *fond* of any *forme*. Here we repeat a current version of the earth story for the purpose of evoking this realist *fond*:

The universe began about 14 billion years ago as hot, thin gas consisting largely of photons. After about two hundred million years the first stars appeared. They consisted mostly of hydrogen and partly of helium. In the intense heat inside the stars these simple atoms fused to form relatively small quantities of more complex atoms. The heavier atoms persisted in existence because electrical energy bound the protons in their nuclei to the electrons in their peripheries. According to astronomer Mark Whittle, the atoms probably drifted around for one or two billion years before combining into denser clouds. Within such clouds small pockets collapsed to form stars. Around some of these there formed disks of dust and gas, some of which in turn formed into planets.

In the case of the earth about ten to the tenth power atoms ended up in a spherical ball with a barren, cratered surface heaving with volcanism. During the next 4.5 billion years, enabled by atoms' extraordinary ability to combine in complex ways, a selective process took the earth from molecules to life.[17] The selective process selected in favour of life because living cells (and later more complex organisms) reproduce themselves. Cells make DNA, and DNA makes cells. Life is homeostatic. That is to say, it responds to perturbations by defending its structure. It produces descendants of the same kind, that is, of the same DNA code.[18]

The chemistry of life is organic chemistry, that is, the chemistry of carbon compounds. Most of life also depends on nitrogen and oxygen. Life began

---

17. Mark Whittle, *Cosmology: The History and Nature of Our Universe* (Chantilly, VA: The Teaching Company, 2008), p. 126. We recapitulate this previously announced theme to weave it into our text.

18. Francisco Varela, Humberto Maturana and R. Uribe, 'Autopoesis: The Organization of Living Systems, Its Characterization and a Model', *Biosystems*, vol. 5 (1974), pp. 187–196.

when oxygen became abundant in the earth's atmosphere. The processes of life required the favourable conditions of the part of the earth's crust, waters and atmosphere capable of supporting life, that is, of the biosphere. Living beings competed for energy and other vital resources. DNA sometimes mutated. The more successful mutants survived long enough to reproduce and, over time, be 'selected' to continue.

Some 400 thousand to 250 thousand years ago, nature selected in favour of a *cultural* animal. Language, human forms of sexual attraction, stories and rituals gave human groups ethics and therefore coherence.[19] They could cooperate in gathering, hunting, child-rearing and other vital functions. They could pass cultural norms and technologies from generation to generation through education, thus learning faster than species dependent on mutation and natural selection to change behaviour patterns.[20] The set of cultural norms constituting capitalism emerged and persisted because of its productivity (see, e.g., Schumpeter),[21] its homeostatic qualities (see, e.g., Michael Kalecki),[22] and the military advantages of societies driven by capital accumulation (see, e.g., Adam Smith).[23]

Unbounded organization and neoliberalism are not two *formes* with the same *fond*. Unbounded organization aspires to position itself as a logical consequence of a realist worldview and as a conscious continuation of evolution. It is, at an epistemological level, more basic than the worldview of economists who work to fit mathematical models to data provided by social statistics—for example, regressing GDP on average number of years of schooling for all the countries for which data can be found. The simple, unbounded idea that we should align across sectors to accomplish the goals of the societal enterprise does not rest on the clear and distinct ideas of a

---

19. See David Sloan Wilson, *Darwin's Cathedral* (Chicago: University of Chicago Press, 2011); James Boggs, 'The Culture Concept as Theory, in Context', *Current Anthropology*, vol. 45 (2004), pp. 187–209. Boggs shows how the culture concept supersedes the liberal worldview that constitutes the institutions that are currently globally dominant.

20. However, even species dependent on genetics adjust to diverse environments—for example, water plants that assume one form in rapidly flowing water and another in still water.

21. Schumpeter, *Theory of Economic Development*. In this and other works Schumpeter depicts an historical process of creative destruction in which innovation leads to productivity gains.

22. 'Everything which may shake the state of confidence must be carefully avoided because it would cause an economic crisis.' Michael Kalecki, 'Political Aspects of Full Employment', first published in *Political Quarterly* in 1943, http://mrzine.monthlyreview.org/2010/kalecki220510.html, accessed January 23, 2015.

23. Smith, *Wealth of Nations,* bk. 5. The societies Smith calls opulent become militarily superior.

Descartes or on anything Richard Rorty would call foundational.[24] Instead, unbounded efforts to improve the functioning of human institutions are part and parcel of the always-imperfectly-known physical processes that generate matter, life, culture, imagination, stories and all *seeing as*.[25]

◆ ◆ ◆

> CWP even goes into the clinics and helps there as well. They clean the clinics. They plant [food] gardens at the clinics. They also care for those gardens too.'
>
> — CWP PARTICIPANT, RANDFONTEIN CDI

7. Evaluating the Community Work Programme through a Neoliberal Lens

We return to grasping the tree of neoliberalism with the purpose of uprooting it while gently replanting its valid insights in better gardens. We see it as a limited worldview theoretically trapped inside the norms of commercial law that constitute and regulate buying and selling.[26] In today's world, it is out of control in a mad rush to commercialize everything.[27]

Typical of that mad rush is the prescription that all nations ought to be competitive. It skates close to a contradiction; it comes close to insisting that all nations simultaneously must win more competitions than they lose. It is like complaining that, in the century and a quarter since it was invented in Springfield, Massachusetts, in 1891, basketball has made no progress, because the average team still loses half its games. In chapter 4, we noted still other anomalies that arise within the neoliberal view of the world. In chapter 1, we noted the apparently absolute conflict between the seven cardinal pillars

---

24. Richard Rorty, *Philosophy and the Mirror of Nature* (Princeton, NJ: Princeton University Press, 1979). Rorty argues that philosophers have been mistaken to look for foundations of knowledge, and even more mistaken when they claim to have found them.

25. Heidegger's *Geschichtlichkeit* (story-ness) is specifically developed in the 2nd section of ch. 5 in *Sein und Zeit* but implicitly present throughout. See the chapters on Heidegger in Howard Richards, *Letters from Quebec* (San Francisco: International Scholars Press, 1995).

26. Thus Marx writes in his polemic against Proudhon: 'Economic categories are only the theoretical expressions, the abstractions of the social relations of production.' He goes on to say that they are no more eternal than the social relations they express. *The Poverty of Philosophy*, in *Collected Works* (London: Lawrence and Wishart, 1976), pp. 165–66.

27. See the first chapters of Nancy Hartsock's *Money, Sex and Power: Toward a Feminist Historical Materialism* (London: Longman, 1983), where she deconstructs, for example, 'the marriage market'. Consider also Karl Polanyi's historical account of how economic relations became 'disembedded' from social relations and then doubled back to dominate them, in *The Great Transformation* (Boston: Beacon Press, 1944).

of South Africa's Economic Freedom Fighters and its National Development Plan. The preceding discussion of *forme* and *fond,* culminating in a realist vision of culture as part and parcel of physical evolution, was intended to widen our vision so we can see win-win alternatives invisible within the rigid norms of the currently dominant culture.

We begin to uproot the tree of neoliberalism by grasping a leaf on one of its branches. The leaf is the application of neoliberalism to evaluating South Africa's Community Work Programme, and the particular branch on which it hangs is the mental world of contemporary neoliberals.

If the CWP is regarded as a programme using public employment to catalyse community development, and if community development is conceived as transformative, building livelihoods that depend less on sales, then the CWP will be evaluated as a promising step toward a socially and ecologically governable and sustainable future. If, on the other hand, the CWP is evaluated within the scope of neoliberal ideology, we are in the mental world of people like Martin Feldstein, who chaired the council of economic advisors of former USA president Ronald Reagan. Feldstein writes, for instance: 'The primary effect of budget deficits is to reduce capital formation. This is a very serious problem, because a high rate of capital formation is the key to future increases in productivity and economic growth, and therefore to higher real wages and incomes.'[28]

Feldstein goes on to argue that when the government sells bonds on the bond market to finance its deficit, it sucks up money that otherwise would have gone to capital formation in the private sector to fund investments, create jobs and drive productivity increases. Thus deficit-financed public programmes crowd out private-sector jobs and growth. Both NREGA and the CWP are social programmes funded by governments that are running large budget deficits that are likely to worsen as time goes on.[29] Properly funding the two programmes will require not only maintaining but also augmenting current spending.

A similar argument made from within the same bounded worldview holds that, even without a budget deficit, when social programmes are paid for by

---

28. Martin Feldstein, 'Washington: Budget Deficits and Political Choices', *Challenge*, vol. 25 (1983), p. 54.

29. The government of India expects to run a budget deficit for the 2012/13 fiscal year equivalent to 4.9% of gross domestic product (www.tradingeconomics.com/india/government-budget, accessed 25 June 2013). For South Africa in 2012 the government budget deficit was equivalent to 5.1% of gross domestic product (www.tradingeconomics.com/south-africa/government-budget, accessed 25 June 2013).

taxes, a *tax wedge* intervenes between buyers and sellers in the marketplace. Taxes crowd out business. Taxes force buyers to pay more. They leave sellers with smaller proceeds. There are fewer transactions because both buyers and sellers are less motivated. Thus neoliberals allege that the tax wedge kills jobs even when the government is spending tax revenues to create jobs.[30] They engage in endless controversies with economists influenced by Keynes who allege that it is one of the functions of government to increase employment by taxing and spending money that would either remain unspent or be spent in ways that do not create jobs if left in the private sector.

The neoliberal world is the world of the authors of the OECD Territorial Review of Gauteng City-Region (in South Africa). They wrote of the Expanded Public Works Programme (EPWP), of which the CWP is a component, that 'it is far from clear how great a deadweight effect there is (creating jobs that would have been created in any case), or whether it is crowding out commercial private-sector economic activity'. They go on to suggest evaluating the CWP by asking what it contributes to eventual private-sector employment: 'The work readiness of beneficiaries at the end of the programme and the success of individual EPWP beneficiaries in the private sector, has not been evaluated.'[31]

The liberal Swedish economist Assar Lindbeck, whom we called as an expert witness in the preceding chapter, complained that public funding for day care centres for small children in Sweden crowded out the private for-profit day care centre industry.[32] He admitted that in Sweden there was no private for-profit day care industry, but he argued that one might have come into existence in response to market demand if the government had not preempted the field by providing free public day care.

Notice that a private industry in day care would also have been crowded out if Swedish parents had formed nonprofit cooperatives to hire people to take care of their children. It would also have been crowded out if Swedish mothers and fathers had organized themselves to take turns taking care of each other's children themselves. There is indeed a literature about the stifling of private enterprise not by government employment but by volunteering.[33]

30. See Ronald W. Jones, 'Tax Wedges and Mobile Capital', *Scandinavian Journal of Economics*, vol. 89 (1987), pp. 335–346.

31. OECD (2011), *OECD Territorial Reviews, The Gauteng City-Region, South Africa* (OECD: Paris, 2011), p. 176.

32. Assar Lindbeck, 'The Swedish Experiment', *Journal of Economic Literature*, vol. 35 (1997), pp. 1309–10.

33. See Kathleen M. Day and Rose Anne Devlin (1996), 'Volunteerism and Crowding

We and our neoliberal friends look at the same facts but see them through different conceptual lenses. Among the key conceptual lenses that bring our world into focus are the concepts of community, accumulation and effective demand. We take the CWP's mandate to catalyse community development as a call to build resilient communities. The CWP can be an important *solution* to budget deficits because, by mobilizing community resources above and beyond the resources of governments, it can create more welfare at lower cost (from the government's point of view).

More fundamentally and from a wider point of view, a resilient community is one whose high levels of diversity and organization enable it to repair damage quickly, including damage caused by downturns in the national or global economy.[34] The concept of community complements, in theory and practice, the concept of accumulation. The concept of accumulation tells us that in the currently prevailing form of society, most needs are met through production for the sake of selling its product for the purpose of profit. The purpose of profit, in turn, is reinvesting to make more profit. Any other purpose—any deviation from maximizing revenues over and over—implies that the business will not be in business for long.[35] This claim is partly true—which implies that our topic is not only a misleading theory, but also a dysfunctional social structure.

When one acknowledges the fundamental importance of accumulation, one can only agree with Amartya Sen that capitalism leads to disaster unless it is regulated and supplemented by nonmercantile institutions guided by different logics and motivated by different dynamics.[36] Another key concept, the concept of chronically insufficient effective demand (our second Staggering Fact) tells us that markets alone will *never* provide reliable employment for all at good wages. The supply curve and the demand curve *normally* meet at a low-level equilibrium, not at full employment.

Out: Canadian Econometric Evidence', *The Canadian Journal of Economics*, vol. 29, pp. 37–53.

34. Resilience can be defined as 'the capacity of a system, here a human system, to absorb perturbation and to reorganize itself integrating the changes the perturbation brings'. Vincent Liegey et al., *Un projet de décroissance* (Paris: Les Éditions Utopia, 2013), p. 90 (our translation). In homeostasis the system simply stabilizes itself, often at a great social cost, as when General Pinochet restored conditions favourable to capital accumulation in Chile by forcing wages down and profits up. Ricardo Lagos and Oscar Rufatt, 'Military Government and Real Wages in Chile', *Latin American Research Review*, vol. 10 (1975), pp. 139–146. In resilience the system reorganizes itself, integrating changes.

35. Milton Friedman, *Essays in Positive Economics* (Chicago: University of Chicago Press, 1953), p. 13.

36. Amartya Sen, 'Sraffa, Wittgenstein, and Gramsci', *Journal of Economic Literature*, vol. 41 (2003), p. 1247.

The currently dominant neoliberal ideology sees a different world shaped by different conceptual lenses. Among its key concepts are crowding out, deadweight, the Harberger triangle, Pareto optimality, 'real' prices as distinct from unreal or 'distorted' prices, and rent-seeking. One speaks of the constraints imposed by the necessities of capital formation, of currency stability, growth and international competitiveness, as well as the underlying principle that supply creates its own demand (Say's Law). As a result, while through our lens we see everywhere a need to regulate and supplement capitalism, neoliberalism sees everywhere politicians giving in to short-sighted populism leading ultimately to counter-productive consequences.

When we look at CWP participants building a one-room home for a blind ninety-one-year-old widow with building materials donated by people in the area, we see community development. We also see community development in gardens being worked not for profit but for supplementing the diets of people who cannot afford to buy vegetables. We see community growing when thieves find viable ways to live legally. In these and many more examples we will give in the following chapter, we see a process of building resilient communities.

♦ ♦ ♦

> 'CWP helped a lot with the crime in our community. There was too much crime in this community, but all of those people now are at work.'
>
> — CWP PARTICIPANT, UMTHWALUME

8. An Historical Comment on the Origins of Neoliberalism: Adam Smith

We again visit Adam Smith's *An Enquiry into the Nature and Causes of the Wealth of Nations*, in which Smith purports to explain why some nations are wealthy, while other nations are poor. This time, we focus on the word *Causes* in the book's title.

The first sentence of the book identifies as its social objective and its scientific dependent variable the capacity of a nation to supply itself with the 'necessaries and conveniences of life' through the products of its labour. Wealth, for short. [37] A few pages later, at the beginning of book 1, entitled

---

37. Adam Smith, *An Enquiry into the Nature and Causes of the Wealth of Nations* (*Wealth of Nations* for short; first edition 1776). We use the two-volume edition edited by

'Of the Causes of Improvement in the Productive Powers of Labour . . .',[38] Smith writes, 'The greatest improvement in the productive powers of labour, and the greater part of the skill, dexterity, and judgment with which it is anywhere directed or applied, seem to have been the effects of the division of labour.'[39] Thus Smith's first explanation of wealth is that it is mainly caused by the division of labour. He illustrates this point with his famous observation of a pin factory where ten men, each specializing in a particular part of the pin-making process, make upwards of forty-eight thousand pins in a day. But if each had 'wrought separately and independently' without any special education, 'they certainly could not each of them have made twenty, perhaps not one pin in a day'.[40]

Continuing in book 1, Smith compares a civilized nation with a nation of savages.[41] The former practices the division of labour and is wealthy. In the latter (Smith believes), each man tries to do everything, or most things, for himself, and the nation is poor. Smith's reasoning can be diagrammed where it is supposed that what he calls 'civilized' nations practice a high degree of division of labour while 'savage' nations practice it little or not at all.

| Civilized | Wealthy |
| Savage | Poor |

In chapter 2 of book 1, Smith avers that the 'Principle which gives Occasion to the Division of Labour' is contract.[42] The principle of contract is 'Give me that which I want, and you shall have that which you want. . . .'[43] To achieve the cooperation of others that he needs, a civilized person proposes

---

Edwin Cannan, with an introduction by John Chamberlain (New Rochelle, NY: Arlington House, no date). Like many recent editions, it is based on the last edition to be corrected by Smith himself, the 5th edition, published in 1789. We refer to the first sentence of Smith's 'Introduction and Plan of the Work', at p. lix. Throughout, we cite book and chapter (*Wealth of Nations* consists of five books) for the convenience of those using editions where the pagination is different. This first sentence does not appear in early precursors of what was to become *Wealth of Nations*. It shows the influence of the French economists with whom Smith came into contact while in France as tutor to the son of the Duke of Buccleuch in 1774–76.

38. Ibid., p. 1. The complete title of bk. 1 is 'Of the Causes of Improvement in the Productive Powers of Labour, and of the Order according to Which Its Produce Is Naturally Distributed among the Different Ranks of the People'.
39. Ibid.
40. Ibid., p. 3.
41. Ibid., bk. 1, ch. 1, pp. 4, 10-11; bk. 2, introduction, p. 293.
42. Ibid., bk. 1, ch. 2, p. 12.
43. Ibid., bk. 1, ch. 2, p. 13.

to others contracts of exchange, where each gives the other what the other wants, thus contriving to 'interest their self-love in his favour'.[44]

There follows in chapter 2 of book 1 another invidious comparison, which we have glanced at previously, between benevolence[45] and self-interest,[46] in which Smith aligns benevolence with weak motivation and self-interest with strong motivation. This argument of Smith's can be diagrammed as follows:

Benevolence	Weak motivation
Self-interest	Strong motivation

Contrast Smith's arguments here with the opening lines of Karl Marx's *Das Kapital*, which we quoted in chapter 2: 'The wealth of those societies in which capitalist production dominates appears as an enormous collection of commodities (*Waren*). The single commodity appears as its elementary form. Our enquiry begins, therefore, with the analysis of the commodity (*Ware*).'[47]

A commodity is, to be sure, a useful thing, satisfying some human need or want.[48] Making a commodity is useful work. But in a capitalist society, a commodity is more particularly an item produced for sale, and sale is for the purpose of profit. It is implied, therefore, that not all useful work consists of making commodities.

Here we see, once again, the importance of the broad rule established by Parliament that in the CWP participants must do 'useful work'. There is no requirement that during the two days a week they participate in the CWP, the participants produce anything that can be sold for a profit. If they spend their two days caring for a victim of AIDS who has no money

---

44. Ibid.

45. Speaking generally, one can regard Smith's reservations about benevolence and enthusiasm for self-love as part of the gradual transition from a religious worldview to a scientific worldview that took place in early modern Europe. Specifically, it seems likely that Smith targets 'benevolence' because of the then influential views of Francis Hutcheson, who had been Smith's predecessor in the Chair of Moral Philosophy at Glasgow and under whom Smith had been a student. In an earlier work, *The Theory of Moral Sentiments* (1759 and various editions), Smith criticizes the view he attributes to Hutcheson that benevolence was the source and distinctive mark of virtue.

46. *Wealth of Nations*, bk. 1, ch. 2, p. 13.

47. Karl Marx, *Das Kapital* (1867), vol. 1, p. 15. We cite the very beginning of Marx's text after several introductions, where commences the first part, entitled *Ware und Geld*, of the edition published by Alfred Kroner Verlag, Stuttgart, 1957 (our translation). We cite the location of the text as well as the page number for the convenience of those using different editions or translations.

48. Ibid.

to pay them, then they have done *useful work*. On the other hand, if they can start a microenterprise during the remaining days of the week—for instance, pacing the sidewalks selling something at retail for more than they paid for it wholesale—they are encouraged and supported in doing so. If they reach a point where they can raise their standard of living by resigning from working two days a week for the CWP in order to have more time to devote to their business, so much the better.

As Marx's text and Sen's text quoted above imply, there is more than one way to produce what Smith called 'the necessaries and conveniences of life'. The capitalist way—defined here, with due respect for other Marxist definitions of the same term, as production driven by capital accumulation; and elsewhere defined in a more favourable light in this same book as socially responsible service to stakeholders (stakeholder capitalism)—is one among others. This implication chimes in with the contemporary observation of Jean Drèze and Amartya Sen, also previously mentioned, that markets are 'among the instruments that can help to promote human capabilities'.[49]

Adopting from Fernand Braudel the idea of material practices, that is, practices that function to meet the material needs of life,[50] one could draw a Venn diagram showing an outer circle of material practices and an inner circle of 'capitalist material practices' regarded as a subset of all material practices.

This discussion leads to an important dimension of the concept of unbounded organization. The inclusive category (such as all material practices in the Venn diagram, or all societies) is infinite. Nobody knows how many forms of society there are or might be—or how many material practices there are or might be. Unbounded organization allows a logical space for the unknown options as well as a logical space for all the known ones. At a practical level, this unbounded way of thinking lends itself to solutions that are both/and. Liberalism, we are suggesting, as it was classically formulated

---

49. Jean Drèze and Amartya Sen, *India, Economic Development and Social Opportunity* (Delhi: Oxford University Press, 2002), p. 202. Some Marxists and some anti-Marxists will object that Marx would have had no sympathy with the pluralism of Drèze and Sen because Marx was committed to abolishing markets completely, root and branch. Our view is that it will forever remain a mystery what form of socialism Marx would have advocated, since his work is mainly a criticism of capitalism (and in his *Critique of the Gotha Programme* a criticism of a particular socialist proposal). It provides only a few inconclusive hints about what a positive construction of socialism would consist of. See on this point Howard Richards, *Understanding the Global Economy* (Santa Barbara, CA: Peace Education Books, 2004), pp. 100–120. In any event, we comment here only on certain words and ideas expressed by Marx in *Das Kapital*, not on his work as a whole.

50. See Fernand Braudel, *Capitalism and Material Life 1400–1800* (New York: HarperCollins, 1973).

in Adam Smith and as it has continued ever since, manifests a strong tendency to think instead in dichotomies: either/or.

A more recent example of either/or thinking can be found in Ludwig von Mises's *Socialism: An Economic and Sociological Analysis*,[51] where an idealized capitalism with prices that are determined by competitive markets is contrasted with a socialism where there are no markets for producers' goods (i.e., for produced goods that are the means of further production). Since there are no markets for such goods, there are no prices for such goods. Since there are no such prices, there is no rational basis for central planning of an economy. The unfortunate fictitious person von Mises calls 'the Director' is perpetually frustrated because he is unable to plan a socialist economy rationally. He cannot be rational because socialism lacks real prices measuring costs and benefits. Von Mises's central idea is diagrammed below:

| Capitalism | Rational decisions due to the presence of real prices |
| Socialism | Irrational decisions due to the absence of real prices |

We believe that the seductive charm of classic liberalism is enhanced by a deep-seated human tendency to think in binary terms. Claude Levi-Strauss found roots of what he calls binary polarities in deep structures that build dualisms into people's thinking in any given culture at an unconscious and taken-for-granted level.[52] Dualism certainly has roots in common speech. A statement is true or false. An action is right or wrong. 'She loves me; she loves me not.' 'To be, or not to be.' 'Those who are not with us are against us.' And so on. We believe that this innate human tendency toward dualism helps explain why so many people see the world through liberalism's and neoliberalism's conceptual lenses. We also think the real structures of the social and natural worlds are less dual than the mental models (liberal, Marxist or other) that some people employ to represent them. We think the complexity and (on the whole) nonduality of reality provide reasons for regarding an unbounded approach (or any approach that avoids simple dichotomies like civilized/savage, benevolence/self-interest, socialism/capitalism) as superior.

To the obvious objection that the distinction between bounded and unbounded is just one more dualism, we make the obvious reply that unbounded organization—such as Marx's all societies where the capitalist

---

51. Ludwig von Mises, *Socialism: An Economic and Sociological Analysis* (Indianapolis: Liberty Fund, 1981 (first German edition 1922).
52. Claude Levi-Strauss, *Structural Anthropology* (New York: Anchor Books, 1963).

form of production does not prevail, and Drèze and Sen's all instruments other than markets that can be used for promoting human capabilities—is an open category. It is not the second term in a duality. It is a logical space open to considering any number of ways to serve the common good. For example, the Constitution of Ecuador, adopted by a constituent assembly in 2008, defines that nation's economy as a balancing of five principles—production for local use (subsistence), reciprocity, redistribution, markets and planning—but it is not necessary to stop at five, as Jose Luis Coraggio, an Argentine economist influential in Ecuador, has written.[53]

The division of labour is just the beginning of Smith's explanation of the causes of wealth. The principles 'which give occasion to the division of labour'[54] turn out to be those of commercial exchange: contracts, sales and markets. The operation of market principles is assured by the administration of justice; in other words, by civilization; in still other words, by good government. The division of labour is 'limited by the extent of the market'.[55]

Hence, the larger the market the better: the larger the market, the more commercial exchange and the more division of labour; the more division of labour, the more improvement in its productive powers; the more improvement in productive powers, the greater the product and hence the greater the capacity of a society to supply 'all the necessaries and conveniences of life'.[56]

Smith's argument is coherent. Each concept dovetails with its predecessors and its successors. Gliding into Smith's thought world, it is easy to concur that there ought to be as much commercial exchange as possible, on as large a scale as possible. In such a frame of mind, anything other than large-scale commercial exchange appears as a subtraction from the maximum level of wealth (or 'opulence')[57] that must accompany a maximum level of commercial exchange.

---

53. Although it is not necessary to stop at five, these five principles are ones that humans have relied on for their daily bread for thousands of years. They have been tested and found workable. See the chapter by Coraggio in Raul Gonzalez and Howard Richards (eds.), *Hacia otras economias* (Santiago: LOM, 2013).

54. *Wealth of Nations,* bk. 1, ch. 2, p. 12.

55. Ibid., bk. 1, ch. 3, p. 17.

56. Ibid., introduction, p. lix.

57. Although Smith uses the word 'wealth' in the title of his work, in his text he more frequently uses the word 'opulence'. For example, at bk. 1, ch. 1, p. 10 he writes, 'It is the great multiplication of the productions of all the different arts, in consequence of the division of labour, which occasions, in a well-governed society, that universal opulence which extends itself to the lowest ranks of the people.'

But there is an additional layer to Smith's argument. In the introduction to book 2 of *Wealth of Nations* we learn that the accumulation of capital 'must, in the nature of things, be previous to the division of labour, so labour can be more and more subdivided in proportion only as stock is previously more and more accumulated.'[58] In light of this point, everything we thought we knew about Smith's system must be reconsidered. The division of labour at first appeared as the principal cause of wealth. Now it appears not as a cause of wealth but as an effect. It turns out to be an effect[59] of the accumulation of capital. The portion of stock (i.e., useful things) used to produce revenue, Smith calls 'capital'.[60] A notable part of capital is in the form of money.[61]

Capital, in turn, Smith divides into two parts: fixed and circulating. Fixed capital generates revenue for its owners without 'changing masters',[62] that is, without being regularly bought and sold, an example being machinery that is used over and over. 'The intention of the fixed capital is to increase the productive powers of labour.'[63]

The employer's circulating capital, on the other hand, 'is continually going from him in one shape, and returning to him in another, and it is only by means of such circulation, or successive exchanges, that it can yield him any profit'.[64] A key example is the money used to pay the wages of workers, which is continually replenished by revenue from the sale of the products they make.

This key example shows why in Smith's world the accumulation of capital must necessarily *precede* the division of labour. There must be a stock of goods to maintain the workers and to supply them with materials and equipment long enough for two things to happen: first, a saleable (Smith uses the word 'vendible') product must be completed. Second, that

---

58. *Wealth of Nations*, bk. 2, introduction, p.294.

59. The lines just quoted from Smith say only that for there to be division of labour there must be accumulation first. They make the latter a necessary condition of the former. However, it soon appears that the latter is also a *sufficient* condition for the former, because Smith maintains that when capital is accumulated it will inevitably be used to create employment, and to do so efficiently. 'As the accumulation of stock is previously necessary for carrying on this great improvement in the productive powers of labour, so that accumulation naturally leads to this improvement.' Ibid., bk. 2, introduction, p. 294.

60. Ibid., bk. 2, ch. 1, p. 296.

61. Money is the topic of bk. 2, ch. 2, titled 'Of Money Considered as a Particular Branch of the General Stock of Society, or of the Expense of Maintaining the National Capital'.

62. *Wealth of Nations*, bk. 2, ch. 1, p.297.

63. Ibid., bk. 2, ch. 2, p.305.

64. Ibid., bk. 2, ch. 1, p.297.

product must be sold. Until these two things happen, the workers can live and work only by consuming stocks that the capitalists have previously accumulated.[65]

Fixed capital does not by itself generate revenue. 'No fixed capital can yield any revenue but by means of a circulating capital.'[66] It is circulating capital that brings in revenue. Fixed capital is only the supporting cast in a show where circulating capital is the star. The buying-and-selling game is the only game in town, as becomes evident when Smith discusses a third and last way that a capitalist can spend money or consume his stock of goods. He can spend it on houses, servants, grounds, and other forms of personal consumption. Smith—followed by economists from 1776 until now—classifies this third way of spending money as unproductive. It brings in no revenue; it does not generate anything 'vendible'.[67]

Smith does not doubt that more accumulation is better. (In today's terms, where some see injustice and inequality, Smith, like his present-day neoliberal followers, sees capital formation.) More accumulation means more employment and more production. If there is not enough employment and not enough production, it must be because there has not been enough accumulation. Thus, he writes:

> In all countries where there is tolerable security, every man of common understanding will endeavour to employ whatever stock he can command, in procuring either present enjoyment or future profit. If it is employed in procuring present enjoyment, it is a stock reserved for immediate consumption.[68] If it is employed in procuring future profit, it must procure this profit either by staying with him or by going from him. In the one case, it is a fixed, in the other a circulating capital. A man must be perfectly crazy who, where there is tolerable security, does not employ all the stock which he commands, whether it

---

65. Ibid., bk. 2, introduction, p.293.
66. Ibid., bk. 2, ch. 1, p.301.
67. Ibid., bk. 2, ch. 3, titled 'Of the Accumulation of Capital, or of Productive and Unproductive Labour'.
68. Although Smith classifies consumption as 'unproductive', he does not disagree with the famous thesis of Bernard de Mandeville that the luxury consumption of the rich provides employment for the poor. He devotes most of a chapter to de Mandeville in his *Theory of Moral Sentiments*.

be his own or borrowed of other people, in some one or other of those three ways.[69]

And:

> The undertaker of some great manufactory who employs a thousand a year in the maintenance of his machinery, if he can reduce this expense to five hundred, will naturally employ the other five hundred in purchasing an additional quantity of materials to be wrought up by an additional number of workmen.[70]

Smith, like his present-day neoliberal followers, is what Joseph Schumpeter called a *hitchless economist*.[71] That is, Smith sees no inherent hitches (or snags) making the economy normally and usually malfunction. He is not tormented by Keynesian worries about an inevitable and pervasive drag on prosperity generated by a chronic weakness of effective demand. What a hitchless economist like Smith views as capital formation, making possible more investment, more employment, more profit and more economic growth, is seen by a hitchbound economist like Keynes (or Malthus or Minsky)[72] as a liquidity preference not likely to be followed by the profitable investment of the money saved. Keynes remarks: 'A decreased readiness to spend will be looked on in quite a different light if, instead of being regarded as a factor which will *cet. par.* increase investment, it is seen as a factor which will *cet. par.* diminish employment.'[73]

---

69. *Wealth of Nations*, bk. 2, ch. 1, p. 303.
70. Ibid., bk. 2, ch. 2, p.306.
71. 'Economic models differ according to whether they are or are not built on the assumption that the economic engine has or has not an *inherent* tendency to develop hitches (merely by working normally and according to design), which then make it stall or stop working normally or according to design. . . . [F]or example, the strain or stress that—really or supposedly—shows in the impossibility of selling the products it is capable of producing at prices that will cover costs. With apologies, I introduce the term *hitchbound* for models that do recognize the existence in the economic system of such inherent tendencies to stall, and the term *hitchless* for models that do not.' Joseph Schumpeter, *History of Economic Analysis* (New York: Oxford University Press, 1954), p.565. Although Schumpeter's account of the issues involved is comprehensive, he neglects Rosa Luxemburg, who is perhaps the most persuasive hitchbound economist. See Rosa Luxemburg, *The Accumulation of Capital* (London: Routledge, 2003 (German original 1913)).
72. For more on Thomas Malthus or Hyman Minsky, look them up online. I mention them here simply to point out that Keynes is not alone.
73. Keynes, *General Theory*, p. 183. On page 215 of the same work, Keynes points out that the physical capacity to produce something, whether brought about by capital formation or in some other way, is of little consequence if there is no effective demand for it.

♦ ♦ ♦

'I sometimes also help out; especially those who are sickly with all these diseases that are now all over the place. I am able to start the process that will lead to the sick person being put on a treatment program. I have already done this for a number of people. I also go out to get knowledge and information from those who have the expertise in things like how to take care of a person who's chronically ill and is at home. If I am given information, then I take it back to the person who needs it.'

— CWP PARTICIPANT, UMTHWALUME CDI

9. The Technification of Hitchlessness: OECD Review Evaluation Criteria

However much one may disagree with Smith, one must give him credit for making his reasoning clear. His very clarity makes it easy to see that what he is saying is flawed and that the social structure of modern Western society leaves people free to be hitchless or hitchbound. Many choose the latter. A more plural, inclusive, unbounded approach, more deliberately aligned with the common good, would be less flawed. Let us accordingly assume, for now, that it is agreed that a plural economy is needed and that the CWP could contribute to building it. What we want to do next is move from generalities to specifics. One may well be convinced at the level of general principles that there are fundamental misreadings of reality in the liberal tradition and that the contemporary neoliberal consensus is misguided. But one might nevertheless be ensnared by technical calculations that assume hitchlessness. They appear untainted by politics and indifferent to basic economic theory, yet they have the net effect of supporting principles one rejects while failing to implement the principles many of us believe in. We will look at some of today's technical calculations and sketch their history to show that they are rooted in error—in seeing the real world falsely through the distorting lenses of an imaginary world.

The OECD Territorial Review of Gauteng, South Africa, offers an example of specific technical prescriptions for evaluation rooted in a general liberal worldview. The document was written by international technical experts for an audience of national and provincial technical experts. The foreword of the Review declares that it is one of a series of reports sharing a common methodology and conceptual framework.[74] In its text, one quickly recognizes this conceptual framework as expressing the principles of Adam Smith in a contemporary vocabulary without altering their fundamental meanings. While Smith writes of an annual fund that supplies a nation with the 'necessaries and conveniences of life',[75] the OECD Review writes of the GDP.[76] While Smith writes of 'Improvement in the Productive Powers of Labour',[77] the Review writes of 'productivity growth'.[78] Smith writes that the division of labour is limited by the extent of the market; consequently, the larger the market, the more the productive powers of labour are improved.[79] The Review writes of globalization. It writes approvingly of Gauteng's efforts to become more competitive in the global market.[80] Smith writes of capital accumulation.[81] The Review writes of growth.[82]

But at another level the OECD Review offers a sea change relative to Smith's own presentation of his principles. For the Review, what neoliberal economic theory prescribes is what *ought* to be done. Its Territorial Review of Gauteng speaks in a realm of discourse where technical experts prescribe, for example, that 'much effort *should* be made to expand the export-led sector'[83] and 'the functional area *should* include areas surrounded by municipalities which are part of the functional system, and thus Randfontein *should* be

---

74. OECD, *OECD Territorial Reviews: The Gauteng City-Region, South Africa 2011* (Paris: OECD Publishing, 2011), http://dx.doi.org/10.1787/9789264122840-en, p.3. (Cited hereafter as OECD.)

75. *Wealth of Nations,* "Introduction and Plan of the Work", p. lix.

76. OECD, p. 17 and passim. The initials GDP stand for Gross Domestic Product, which can be roughly defined as the market value of the goods and services produced in a country in a year (or in some other time period). For an account of how such indices are calculated see Herman Daly and John Cobb Jr. (1994) *For the Common Good.* Boston, Beacon Press.

77. *Wealth of Nations*, bk. 1, ch. 1, p. 1.

78. OECD, p. 30 and passim.

79. *Wealth of Nations*, bk. 1, ch. 3.

80. OECD pp. 3, 54, 62 and passim. At p. 54 the OECD notes that wage costs in South Africa are competitive when compared to Germany, Japan, the United Kingdom and the United States, being about a fifth of wages in those countries, but not competitive with respect to the developing countries with which South Africa competes to attract foreign investment and with which its exports compete. It notes that South African wages are four times as high as wages in India and three times as high as wages in Indonesia.

81. *Wealth of Nations*, bk. 2, ch. 3.

82. OECD, passim. The OECD (p. 17) praises the Gauteng Region for having had in 1997–2007 a higher average annual growth rate (2.7%) than that of the average metropolitan region in the OECD countries (.96 %). It nevertheless finds that opportunities for growth are not fully exploited (p.3). In its recommendations it writes, 'If properly managed, the city-region's potential for growth could be huge' (p. 17).

83. Ibid., p. 32 (italics added).

included as part of the functional area'.[84] 'Over-emphasis on the public contribution to innovation *should* be avoided'[85] and 'this agenda *should* aim to increase the environmental sustainability and available amenities of the city, which are critical to maintaining Gauteng's competitive edge.'[86] 'Policy makers within Gauteng *should* be supported in their attempts to find more affordable housing solutions.'[87] 'These initiatives indicate a strong commitment to improving the efficiency of the labour market in Gauteng, but *should* nevertheless be subject to objective evaluations.'[88]

Adam Smith's friend the philosopher David Hume was famous in the eighteenth century for promoting the doctrine, still influential today in some circles, that an 'ought' cannot be deduced from an 'is'.[89] Hume observed that authors often proceed 'for some time in the ordinary way of reasoning', in which they make statements about what is and is not, but then they imperceptibly slide into a proposition 'connected with an ought or an ought not' that 'expresses some new relation or affirmation'. It is necessary, Hume says, that some reason or explanation be given 'for what seems altogether inconceivable, how this new relation can be a deduction from others, which are entirely different from it'.[90]

Unlike traditional empiricism and positivism, the OECD Review has no such scruples. It does not hesitate to make value judgments. It does not rely on any ethical theory known to philosophers or theologians. It does not adopt the realist two-tiered approach to moral values that we recommend, following Searle and Dewey in regarding moral language as part and parcel of existing institutions and following Malinowski in wanting institutions to be functional by meeting needs.[91] It assumes that the overall aims of development have already been authoritatively decided, that the path to development is known, that neoliberals know it, and that the details of what provincial and municipal governments ought to do to make development

---

84. Ibid., p. 38 (italics added).
85. Ibid., p. 69 (italics added).
86. Ibid., p. 134 (italics added).
87. Ibid., p. 139 (italics added). The context of this sentence is one where particular attempts the OECD authors look upon favourably have been mentioned: 'To tackle the housing problem, such programmes would need to be supported, replicated and complemented by new initiatives' (ibid.).
88. Ibid., p. 165 (italics added).
89. David Hume, *A Treatise of Human Nature*, first part of first section of third book (Oxford: Clarendon, 2007 (first edition 1739–40)).
90. Ibid., p. 469.
91. Howard Richards, 'Moral and Ethical Realism', *Journal of Critical Realism*, vol. 18 (1919), pp. 285–302.

happen can be prescribed by experts. The invisible hand has become the visible hand, but its *modi operandi* remain the same: capital accumulation, increases in productivity, and more and ever-larger markets.

In a document that is prescriptive throughout, it is not surprising to find standards prescribing how public employment programmes in general, and the CWP in particular, ought to be evaluated. One of the two key standards prescribed is 'the work readiness of beneficiaries at the end of the programme, and the take-up and success' of individual beneficiaries in the private sector.[92] We have already indicated in previous chapters the limitations of this criterion. Sustainable, decent livelihoods for all in the private for-profit sector have not happened in the past, not in the times of Smith and Ricardo, not in South Africa or India, not even in Sweden. They are not going to happen in the future without structural change like that pioneered by the CWP—not in the age of mechanization of mines, robots, 3D printers, artificial photosynthesis, and workers at all skill levels redundant in the labour market.[93]

The other prescribed standard, as the authors of the OECD review state, is that evaluators should calculate 'how great a deadweight effect there is (in creating jobs that would have been created in any case), or whether it is crowding out commercial private-sector activity'.[94] We will consider this criterion by examining how deadweight is calculated as well as the frame of mind required to see a number measuring deadweight as an essential criterion for evaluating the CWP.

◆ ◆ ◆

Agnes Sithole is a CWP coordinator at Bokfontein.

> 'There was a lot of unemployment before, but now there is dignity in the area because people are working. You find people under the bridge, but they have dignity and humanity because they aren't struggling anymore.'
>
> — CDI

---

92. OECD, p. 176. Admittedly this is a composite standard. Following these words of the OECD, which mention its distinguishable elements all in one breath, we propose to treat it as a clump of closely related evaluation criteria.

93. See the publications of Guy Standing, Jeremy Rifkin, the relevant reports of the International Labour Office of the UN, and Diamantis and Kotler for examples documenting this sea change transforming the world we were living in, even before the collapse triggered by the coronavirus.

94. OECD, p. 176.

10. Calculating Deadweight

The calculation of deadweight began with a French engineer named Jules Dupuit. Dupuit defined deadweight loss as the extent to which real total utility is less than the maximum attainable total utility. The crux of this abstract idea is the assumption that we can know what would have happened in circumstances that did not happen. We can then complain about what really happened, subtracting its utility from 'maximum attainable total utility' and calling the difference *deadweight loss*.

In 1844, Dupuit published in the journal *Annales des ponts et chaussèes* an article titled 'De la mesure de l'utilité des travaux publics' (On measuring the utility, or value, of public works).[95] In the article, Dupuit developed the concept of 'deadweight', starting with a diagram of this kind:[96]

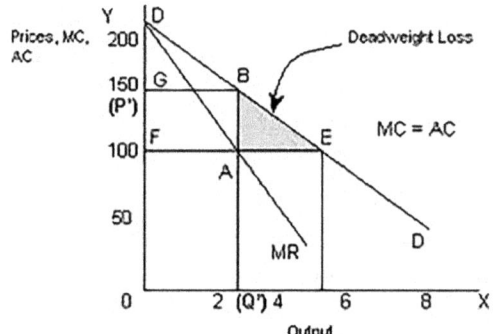

The vertical, or Y, axis measures the prices of a commodity to be sold. The symbol P' stands for Price. (Regarding price formation, here differences between marginal cost and actual cost are ignored, treating MC as equal to AC.) The horizontal, or X, axis represents the quantities offered for sale of the same commodity (meaning simply something to be sold). The symbol Q' stands for Quantity. The X axis is labelled 'Output'. It could also be called 'Supply' or 'Offer'.

The two diagonal lines on the graph both start out high in the upper left-hand corner. This signifies that when the price of, say, sugar is high (like

---

95. Arsène Jules Étienne Juvénal Dupuit, 'De la mesure de la utilité des travaux publics', *Annales des ponts et chaussées*, vol. 8 of second series (1844), translated and reprinted in Kenneth Arrow and Tibor Scitovsky (eds.), *Readings in Welfare Economics* (Homewood, IL: Richard Irwin, 1969), pp. 255–283.

96. This diagram is adapted from Dupuit. The version of the diagram used by Dupuit is more complex, has the axes reversed, and uses a vocabulary we do not now employ.

200 rands, the number of rands written in the upper left-hand corner), then demand is low (in the upper left-hand corner the diagonal lines are at or near zero with respect to the X axis). Not much can be sold at that high price, so Output is low. Q' is low.

Both diagonal lines start out in the upper left-hand corner (high price, low output) and then travel toward the bottom right-hand corner (low price, high output). However, they do not actually reach the bottom right-hand corner. Instead they are left dangling in space. Their failure to intersect the X axis represents the fact that, as the price of sugar falls toward the cost of production, at some point there will no longer be any output. The sugar producers will stop producing because sugar cannot be sold on favourable terms.

Consider the upper diagonal line D–D. It starts with a D in the upper left and ends with a D dangling in empty space toward the lower right. Along the line segment D–D there is a point E. E stands for Excellent! If you buzz a beeline straight left from Excellent to the Y axis, you find the number 100, representing a price of 100 rands. If you drop a plumb line straight down from E to the X axis you hit quantities somewhere between 4 and 6. Say 5.5. Call it 5.5 tonnes of sugar. What this means is that the market has determined an equilibrium price (100 rands) and an equilibrium quantity (5.5 tonnes) at which willing buyers exchange with willing sellers.

Now consider the big triangle with the vertices E, F and D (the D in the upper-left corner). This big triangle represents a lot of happy people. It represents people who would happily have paid 200, 199, 198, . . . 103, 102 or 101 rands for a tonne of sugar but only had to pay 100 rands because the market fixed the equilibrium price at 100. This triangle can be called 'consumer surplus'.[97]

We can, if we want, imagine a similar happy triangle in the bottom right-hand corner. If we imagine a beeline from the point where the another D dangles in space to the Y axis, we see that at a price of 50 rands the sugar producers gave up and there was no output because their product could no longer profitably be sold. On the upside of 50 there were producers who happily would have sold sugar at 99, 98, 97, . . . 53, 52 or 51 rands. They are happy because they were able to sell at the market price of 100 when they would have settled for less. This can be called 'producer's surplus'.

Now consider the letter G three-quarters of the way up the Y axis, beside

---

97. See Alfred Marshall, 'Consumer's Surplus', *Annals of the American Academy of Political and Social Science*, vol. 3, (1983) pp. 90–93.

the number 150, representing a price of 150 rands. Making a straight dash rightward from G, to the first diagonal line at B and from there dropping down from B to the X axis, we find that the Output Q is between 2 and 4, say 2.5. This means that at the higher price of 150 rands, market equilibrium will occur when 2.5 tonnes of sugar are produced and sold. The letter B represents the ordered pair (x=2.5, y=150). Less will be produced. Fewer workers will be hired to produce it. Less will be sold. The happy triangle of consumer surplus at this price will be the smaller triangle with vertices B, G, and the upper left-hand D.

Jules Dupuit considers the situation where the price goes up from 100 to 150 rands because the government imposes a tax, today called a tax wedge. The buyer has to pay the tax, but the seller does not receive it. There are fewer buyers at 150. Meanwhile the sellers still want a price of 100 rands, the same as before. For the sellers, the new equilibrium[98] tells them to produce 2.5 tonnes, as is represented by point A in the hypothetical example depicted in the diagram. At point A (x=2.5, y=100), the quantity is 2.5 tonnes of sugar while the price is 100 (as far as the seller is concerned), but because of the tax wedge the price is 150 for the buyer.

For every tonne of sugar sold the government collects 50 rands, represented by the distance from point F to point G on the Y axis (the difference between the 150 the buyer pays and the 100 the seller receives). The amount sold is the 2.5 tonnes represented by the horizontal distance F to A. Thinking of an area as an image of revenue per item multiplied by number of items taxed, we can think of government revenue as the area of the box with the four vertices G B F A. The consumer surplus shrinks to the smaller triangle BGD.

Here is Dupuit's point: The shaded triangle with vertices B, A and E represents value the consumer loses but the government does not get. The area to the right of the line BA represents transactions that did not happen, output that was not produced, workers who were not hired. It does not represent any government revenue. It is an area past which the second diagonal line (MR, for marginal revenue) represents no revenue for the government because production stopped at the new equilibrium point A,

---

98. To be more exact than in our rough example, it is necessary to give numerical values to the two equilibria and to determine empirically or estimate demand schedules and elasticities (i.e., ratios between change in demand and change in supply). See W. Erwin Diewert, 'The Measurement of Deadweight Loss Revisited', *Econometrica*, vol. 49 (1981), pp. 1225–1244; and Arnold Harberger, 'The Measurement of Waste', *American Economic Review*, vol. 54 (1964), pp. 58–76.

that is, at 2.5 tonnes. The tax wedge eliminated a consumer surplus (and a producer surplus) that was not compensated by an equal amount going to the government as tax revenue.

The difference in (Q) between 2.5 and 5.5 represents economic activity that, because of the tax wedge, did not happen. Since it did not happen, it is of no benefit to anybody. It is a *might have been* that provides neoliberal economists with a criterion for judging *what is*. The deadweight loss is calculated as the area of the triangle with vertices B, A and E (around 75, expressed in units of price x quantity).

Liberal economist James Hines comments on a modern version of Dupuit: 'This simple and straightforward exercise has numerous applications and the virtue of producing answers rather than conjectures.'[99] Gordon Tullock extended Dupuit's analysis by throwing taxes, tariffs on imports, monopolies and theft into the same category as wedges that all restrain trade.[100] Milton Friedman added unions, government regulation of business, and requiring a license to practice a profession.[101] Here we see contemporary neoliberalism reinforcing a tendency already present in Adam Smith: adoration of pure markets.

11. Raising the Stakes: Critique of the Tax Wedge and the Unbounded Alternative

Although neoliberalism is more a worldview than a scientific theory, it is a worldview that supports itself with technical arguments. The one we have just reviewed relies on treating the consumer surplus that is lost when taxes slow down business activity as deadweight not offset by any gain anywhere.

We offer five objections or, to be more precise, qualifications to this argument. Finally, we acknowledge that there is a kernel of truth in the argument that deadweight crowds out tax wedges, and we propose a progressive alternative for coping with that kernel of truth.

---

99. Hines refers to similar contemporary calculations, applying some technical improvements to the basic idea of Dupuit. James Hines, 'Three Sides of Harberger Triangles', in *NBER Working Papers Number 6852* (Cambridge, MA: National Bureau of Economic Research, 1998), p. 1.

100. Gordon Tullock, 'The Welfare Costs of Tariffs, Monopolies, and Theft', *Western Economic Journal*, vol. 5 (1967), pp. 224–232. See also John Kay, 'The Deadweight Loss from a Tax System', *Journal of Public Economics*, vol. 13 (1980), pp. 111–120; and Richard A. Posner, 'The Social Costs of Monopoly and Regulation', *Journal of Political Economy*, vol. 83 (1975), pp. 807–827.

101. Milton Friedman, *Capitalism and Freedom* (Chicago: University of Chicago Press, 1962). Regarding unions and business see ch. 8; regarding licensing of professions, ch. 9.

Objection One: The deadweight argument assumes elasticity of demand. In its absence (or if elasticity is small), instead of less production, there will be the same (or nearly the same) production even though the price is higher. In our example, 5.5 tonnes of sugar will still be produced and sold instead of 2.5. People will pay 150 rands per tonne instead of 100. There will be some redistribution of income when some are favoured and others are disfavoured by the higher price, but there will not be a deadweight loss.

Objection Two: Consider a single mother who has earned 500 rands working in the CWP and then buys maize meal, rice and cooking oil. The value of 500 rands for her may well exceed the value of 5,000 rands lost by a high-income professional because of a tax wedge. Moral: It is not unusual for public spending to satisfy the criterion of creating more real-life value than the real-life value lost by the private sector because of taxes, even when in money terms there is a deadweight loss.

A. C. Pigou and many other economists have established the general principle that when transfers are made from haves to have-nots, as a rule, total welfare goes up. A rand in the pocket of a poor man means more than the same rand in the pocket of a rich man. If the neoliberals are right in affirming a second principle—that tax wedges create deadweight losses—both principles can be true. One does not negate the other.

Objection Three: Suppose that a consumer or taxpayer voluntarily donates to charity. His material spending declines because he can no longer spend on himself the money he donated. But his spiritual welfare goes up, because he has the satisfaction of having donated to charity, which is worth more to him than spending more money on himself. His preference is to give, and he has satisfied it. Now suppose that another taxpayer who is an ardent social democrat derives pleasure from paying taxes because she enjoys helping to pay for public goods. Then consider yet another taxpayer who is also a social democrat but less ardent. He smilingly endures paying taxes because he knows other people are paying taxes too. He derives satisfaction from being part of a collective effort to build a better society. In all these cases, the personal satisfaction and the public good citizenship gained from participating in what Sen and Drèze call 'public action' offset the losses occasioned by a tax wedge.[102]

---

102. In the city of Rosario, Argentina, rate-payers in the city were given the option of paying 10% more on their gas heating bills to create a fund to connect the gas distribution system to poor people living on the outskirts of the city who were not connected. Almost all voluntarily paid the extra 10%. See interview with Hermes Binner (then mayor of Rosario) in Howard Richards, *Solidaridad, participacion, transparencia: Conversaciones sobre el socialismo*

Objection Four: Consumers who lose their consumer surplus but buy anyway lose a bargain, but by definition they still pay a price they are willing to pay. (The definition of consumer surplus is the difference between a lower market price and a higher price a given consumer would be willing to pay.)

Objection Five: In the time of Dupuit, arguably the ethical good might have been as much production and consumption as possible. Today, as we face ecological disaster and social disintegration, the ethical good is living simply, caring and sharing.

To refocus the issues, the larger questions about a public programme are likely to concern corruption, as we saw in the case of NREGA. They are likely to concern effectiveness, as we saw in the case of poultry farms in Limpopo. A larger question about the CWP concerns whether and how it can catalyse community development, as we saw in the case of Bokfontein. The OECD Review's criteria for assessing the CWP reflect a worldview unfriendly to the general idea that public employment catalysing community development should be a permanent part of a mixed economy. They have little application to making the CWP work.

The kernel of truth in deadweight analysis—and in its cousins that object to crowding out: tax wedges, labour unions, environmental regulation, health and safety laws, government regulation of business generally, tariffs and the licensing of professions—is that when costs go up, profits go down, so there is less business. Our conclusion is that we need unbounded organization. We need a plural economy. We do not need a world where all human life depends on one institution and everything else depends on sacrificing other goals so that that one institution will buy and sell at maximal volumes.

The OECD calls deadweight analysis objective. However, even though it looks objective because it leads to a number (75, in our example), the number does not count anything that exists. It is a phenotype of a wider genotype specifying what theoretically *would* happen in a competitive market with fully flexible prices tending toward equilibrium and without tax wedges or other perturbations. We argue in the next section that this theoretical ideal *never* happens. This number lives in an imaginary world that, at this point in history, unfortunately holds the real world captive. It holds the real world captive because it is a myth used to evaluate reality.

en Rosario, Argentina (Rosario: Fundacion Estevez Boero, 2008), ch. 4. Available online at www.lahoradelaetica.wordpress.com. Available in English translation online at www.unboundedorganization.org.

As with any ideology, the myth hides power. The power it hides is revealed in our first Staggering Fact, SF1. To an important extent (disregarding for a moment the great variety of material practices already at work in the world), nothing moves without profit. Hence the kernel of truth: when costs go up, profits go down and there is less business. Costs can go up because of a tax wedge, a wage wedge, an environmental regulation wedge, the costs of complying with health and safety laws, and so on. Costs go up whenever any social or environmental criterion imposes constraints on the accumulation of capital. The solution is not to abolish any and all constraints on the accumulation of capital; the solution is for the lives of the many to become less dependent on the profits of the few.

Imposing constraints on the accumulation of capital should not be seen as negative or as something businesses do not know how to deal with. For the science of management (the science of organizations), constraints are the stuff of everyday life. Managers regularly solve problems that call for choosing among decision variables to achieve objectives subject to constraints. Adding, subtracting or modifying the value of a constraint may add or change the value of a variable, but it does not turn the problem into one that managers do not know how to solve. Managers, lawyers, accountants and judges also know how to deal with an enterprise that has been analysed and shown to be insolvent. They know how to liquidate and pay creditors. They know how to reorganize when reorganization is practicable. They also know how to compensate when a business ceases to exist by setting up a new enterprise. There are many possibilities: corporate, partnership, joint venture, public, cooperative, employee-owned, parastatal, nonprofit, sole proprietor, foundation, to name a few. Today there is a boom in public benefit and other new business forms created by recent European legislation to favour social entrepreneurship.

The neoliberal predilection is for judging the world by the standards of a utopia where all business is private and for profit, all business costs are minimized, and all prices are fully flexible. However, the real world does not need to be judged by comparing it to an ideal state called equilibrium that defines full employment of resources and Pareto optimality.[103] In light of

---

103. A Pareto optimum is defined as a situation in which nobody can be made better off without making someone else worse off. It can also be conceived (similarly to market equilibrium) as a market that has done its work, by facilitating all the transactions in which both parties gain by trade, and has come to rest. Concerning Pareto optimality Amartya Sen has remarked, 'That all competitive market equilibriums are Pareto efficient may not appear to be a terrific trophy for the market mechanism since it is hard to see Pareto efficiency as

the kernel of truth that a tax wedge (or any wedge) will slow down business activity, it is not necessary to surrender down the line, settling also for lower taxes, less public health, less public education, smaller pensions, privatization of the public sector and fewer public goods of all kinds.

There are alternatives to a pure neoliberalism hell-bent on maximizing the size of the private for-profit sector at any cost, a policy that will (as we showed in chapter 3) necessarily fail to produce an economy that works for the poor. One alternative is a private for-profit sector smaller in size, higher in quality and governable. When all private-sector companies do what the best private-sector companies already do (for example, triple-bottom-line accounting: people, planet, profit),[104] there will be fewer of them, but the ones that exist will meet more needs in better harmony with nature. They will be fewer, if only because the marginal enterprises that cannot afford to pay high wages will have to disappear and be replaced, as Sweden unsuccessfully tried to do. The challenge is then to grow other sectors. The CWP represents one of many other sectors.

Achieving livelihoods complying with international standards for economic and social human rights requires other sectors. It cannot be done relying exclusively on the private for-profit sector.[105] The question is not whether to build a plural economy but how.

♦ ♦ ♦

One participant felt that acceptance into the CWP was political.

> **"The other thing is that if you are not an ANC member they won't hire you.'**
>
> — CWP PARTICIPANT, BUSHBUCKRIDGE CDI

---

sufficient for social optimality. Pareto efficiency is completely unconcerned with distribution of utilities (or of incomes or of anything else) and is quite uninterested in equity.' Amartya Sen, 'Markets and Freedoms: Achievements and Limitations of the Market Mechanism in Promoting Individual Freedoms', *Oxford Economic Papers,* vol. 45, p. 521.

104. Triple-bottom-line accounting is now required by law for large companies in Argentina.

105. C. K. Prahalad, who was a great advocate for major private companies (like Hindustan Lever, of which he was a director) throwing their weight behind world-wide efforts to eliminate poverty and achieve environmental sustainability, was very clear in saying that the private sector should not attempt to do it alone. The private sector should work hand-in-hand with other sectors. One of his examples is a campaign to improve personal hygiene in rural India, where major soap manufacturers worked together with state governments, grassroots community groups, university academics and the World Health Organization. *The Fortune at the Bottom of the Pyramid* (Philadelphia: Wharton School, 2004).

12. The Superiority of an Unbounded, Pluralist Worldview

The liberal or neoliberal ideal of a world with fully flexible prices tending toward an equilibrium where all resources are fully employed is behind the technical procedures the OECD Territorial Review of Gauteng recommends for evaluating the CWP. This liberal ideal makes no sense because it ignores economic reality as it has existed historically, ignores economic reality as it exists now, is not ethically defensible and is not a realizable ideal—that is, it does not describe a possible economy. We briefly discuss each of these four points.

Neoliberalism Ignores Historical Economic Reality

The history of capitalism has not been a history of suppliers increasing production until marginal costs of production equal marginal revenue derived from sales. The equilibrium point representing maximum possible consumer satisfaction has existed only in theory. History has been for the most part a history of struggle, not infrequently armed struggle, for more advantageous positions, including the control of profitable enterprises sheltered from intense competition, privileged access to resources and privileged access to markets.[106]

Neoliberalism Ignores Current Economic Reality

Current economic reality has very little to do with a worldview that sees businesses everywhere increasing production and, with it, consumer satisfaction to a point of equilibrium where marginal costs equal marginal revenue. Today, students in business schools study the already classic 'five forces' model of Michael Porter, professor of strategy at Harvard Business School.[107] Based on data derived from hundreds of case studies, his model

---

106. 'Struggle' here refers only indirectly to the struggles of the exploited and dispossessed to raise their living standards; it refers directly to struggles among elites. We do not claim that there is a single unified methodology and/or theoretical structure on which economic historians have reached consensus. We do claim that anyone who studies economic history will realize that struggle for advantageous positions has been central to it, and that general equilibria like those described by theorists like León Walras have been used to justify a system they do not describe. Among the many authors and works that study in detail the struggles of economic history and the dynamics that drive them, we particularly call attention to Immanuel Wallerstein, *The Capitalist World-Economy* (Cambridge, UK: Cambridge University Press, 1979); Fernand Braudel, *Capitalism and Material Life 1400–1800* (London: Weidenfeld and Nicholson, 1973); Samir Amin, *Accumulation on a World Scale* (two volumes) (New York: Monthly Review Press, 1975); and Maria Mies, *Patriarchy and Accumulation on a World Scale* (London: Zed, 1987).

107. Michael Porter: *Competitive Strategy* (New York: Free Press, 1980); *Competitive*

teaches that to achieve sustainable profitability, a firm should position itself in its industry[108] in the light of five causes of competitive advantage:

1. *Competitive rivalry in the industry*. In an industry where there is intense competition on price among many firms, there will be little profit for anybody. Therefore, seek an industry with few major players, free of intense price-cutting.[109]
2. *The threat of new entrants into the industry*. Find a niche, or create one, where there are barriers to entry by new competitors. This can be done, for example, by buying up patents and other intellectual property rights (so others cannot use them even if one does not intend to use them oneself) or by negotiating long-term, exclusive contracts with key suppliers of inputs.
3. *The bargaining power of suppliers*. Seek an advantageous position where the bargaining power of suppliers is weak, so that one can negotiate low prices for inputs. An example would be a company like Cargill trading internationally in soybeans and grains that are most often supplied by farmers with little bargaining power.
4. *The bargaining power of customers*. Similarly, competitive advantage and sustainable profits are caused by the low bargaining power of customers. This can be achieved, for example, by product differentiation such that no other firm sells exactly the same commodity, combined with dependency of the customer on the supplier for post-sale service, spare parts, and technology updates.

Advantage (New York: Free Press, 1985); *Competition in Global Industries* (Boston: Harvard Business School Press, 1986); and *The Competitive Advantage of Nations* (New York: Free Press, 1990). Although Porter remains the single most important writer on business strategy, today his views have been overshadowed by a somewhat different approach known as RBT, the resource-based theory of business strategy. Although one might complain that we cite the classic views of Porter at a time when the zenith of their influence has passed, one cannot say that the RBT writers have provided any data tending to show that businesses naturally and normally behave in ways likely to lead to general equilibrium and welfare maximization as Walras and his followers conceive them. On the contrary, while differing from Porter on certain points, they confirm the main points made here. See Margaret Peteraf and Jay Barney, 'Unraveling the Resource-Based Tangle', *Management and Decision Economics*, Volume 24 (2003), pp. 309–323; and the articles by Margaret Peteraf and others in the October 2003 special issue of *Strategic Management Journal* devoted to the question, 'Why is there a resource-based view?'

108. Porter also points out that quite apart from competitive advantage within a given industry, in some industries (like wholesale trade in grains) all or most firms are profitable, while in others (like automobile tyres) profits are low for everybody.

109. It is often to a firm's advantage that its competitors in the same industry are also profitable. When a major player in the industry is in danger of going under, it may be tempted in its desperation to resort to price-cutting that will make the entire industry unprofitable for all players.

5. *The threat of substitute products.* Profitability is low where customers do not really need the product because they can switch to a different one. For this reason, it is to the interest of all the firms in an industry not only to have a tacit gentleman's agreement (or where it is legal, a cartel) to avoid ferocious price-cutting but also to cooperate within the industry to erect barriers to new entrants. Cooperation among producers, not competition, is often used to promote the public image of the product and develop the technical superiority of their product as distinct from substitutes for it.

In short, the reality of business today is that success is achieved *not* by acting in the ways that liberal theory supposes firms normally act. In contrast, a realist approach seeks to meet human needs in harmony with nature, starting from the world as it is.

Neoliberalism Is Not Ethically Defensible

Although it might be difficult to explain to an extraterrestrial why so many earthling economists classify most, if not all, of the prices that actually exist as 'distortions' and prices that rarely or never exist as 'real',[110] there are several possible explanations.

We will consider one.[111] Prices represented by equilibrium points in graphs like Dupuit's are called true or real not because they represent prices that exist but because they represent prices that *ought to exist.*[112] This is in

---

110. Among the maverick economists who have not adopted this practice are the Latin American structuralists. They have analysed really existing prices as they are shaped by the bargaining power of the parties. See Armando di Filippo, 'Latin American Structuralism and Economic Theory' *Revista CEPAL*, vol. 98 (2009), pp. 175–196.

111. Here we list four other explanations, each of which probably identifies a significant factor explaining the current hegemony of neoliberalism: (1) So-called real prices can be regarded as ideal types, as Max Weber regarded *homo economicus* to be an ideal type, fully aware that in a pure state he does not exist but nevertheless regarding him as conceptually useful as a model for understanding real phenomena by analysing deviations from it. See Donald Macintosh, 'The Objective Basis of Max Weber's Ideal Types', *History and Theory*, vol. 16 (1977), pp. 265–279. (2) Liberal price theory is immune from refutation by evidence, since any prices that might be taken to falsify it can be dismissed as distortions. See Andreas G. Papandreou (1958), *Economics as a Science* (Philadelphia: J. B. Lippincott, 1958). (3) Liberal theory enjoys favour with powerful political and economic interests because it serves as their ideology (see Gunnar Myrdal). (4) Liberal theory's conceptual elegance and mathematical sophistication give it a competitive advantage in the jungle of academic politics. See Herbert A. Simon, *The Sciences of the Artificial* (Cambridge, MA: MIT Press, 1969). Simon argues that the training of professionals in universities has been drawn away both from reality and from practical utility by the academic prestige of the hard sciences.

112. The normative character of the conclusions of mathematical economics was at stake

much the same way one speaks of ideal love as 'true' love or one speaks of a genuine leather sofa as a 'real' leather sofa to distinguish it from the more common imitation leather sofas.

The ethical issue at work here is the bogus identification of what sells with what ought to be. The Nobel Prize–winning liberal economist John Hicks stated succinctly an ethical premise we have mentioned before: 'If an article can be sold at a price which covers its costs of production, it should be produced; if it cannot be sold at a price which covers its cost of production, it should not be produced.' Hicks goes on to say that 'we should accept that the aim of production is to produce the things that consumers want; and that we should accept that the wants of consumers are "revealed" (as Samuelson would say) by their market behaviour'.[113]

From liberal premises it is plausible to conclude that society *ought to be* organized in such a way that competition drives prices down toward, or to, the costs of production. Then also, it might seem plausible to think, consumers who can afford it would get a maximum of what they want. Consumers (i.e., consumers with money) getting a maximum of what they want to buy might seem to be the ethical ideal society should strive to achieve. We hold a different ideal: those who are able should produce a surplus to share with those in need (Acts 20:33–35). This is not an arbitrary ideal. It is biologically functional, adaptive for the species. It is echoed in the values of many cultures.

Notably, these Hicksian premises are a mirror image of the Grenoble School's[114] neo-Marxist concept of regime of accumulation. Hicks says that

---

in the *Methodenstreit* in economics at the end of the 19th century. Those who favoured studying economic phenomena as they are found in society as it is, led by Gustav von Schmoller, used historical methods of research. Others, such as Carl Menger, held that there could be such a thing as pure economics, which did not depend on historical evidence, which could through calculations establish important criteria for rational and therefore optimal decision-making. The issues took on a different focus when Paul Samuelson published his doctoral thesis, *Foundations of Economic Analysis* (Cambridge, MA: Harvard University Press, 1947). Samuelson recast the then mainstream economics of Alfred Marshall in precise mathematical terms. His rationale for doing so was not that pure mathematical economics could establish normative conclusions, but rather that restating the principles of economics with the greater precision mathematics provides would make it possible to formulate more exact research hypotheses and thus to advance the construction of an empirically verified science.

113. John R. Hicks, 'Economic Theory and the Evaluation of Consumers' Wants', *The Journal of Business*, vol. 35 (1962), p. 256. Hicks qualifies his succinct remarks by saying there is more to be said but holds nonetheless that these are the most important points to be made when one is compelled to use few words.

114. We name Hicks's interlocutor after the Grenoble School (generally known as regulationist, whose leading members include Robert Boyer and Michel Aglietta), because that school invented the idea of 'regime of accumulation', even though it has done little to develop its wider implications. See Robert Boyer and Yves Saillard (eds.), *Théorie de la régulation: L'*état des saviors (Paris: La Découverte, 2002). This book includes a short chapter on regimes of

what can be produced and sold at cost-covering prices *should* be produced and sold. Grenoble says that only what can be sold at a profit *will* be produced. Hicks says that society *should* be organized so the profit motive will motivate behaviour that generates a maximum of welfare—welfare being defined as solvent consumers getting what they want. Grenoble says that as long as society is dominated by the imperatives of capitalism, all of its institutions *must* be organized to create more sales, because more sales are required for more accumulation of capital.

What for Hicks seems to satisfy the demands of a utilitarian ethics because it resembles creating the greatest good for the greatest number, on Grenoble principles frustrates ethics because any human project intended to move society closer to achieving inspiring ideals—for example, the ideals of liberty, equality, fraternity and ecology—cannot be implemented. Ethics cannot be implemented because, regardless of what human beings may aspire to do, what they *must* do is obey the imperative of making investment profitable for investors. Social justice must be postponed for the sake of investor confidence. Wages must be kept down to keep profits up. What *must* be done to create the conditions necessary for capital accumulation trumps any and all ethical ideals.

Hicks and Grenoble *look at* the same world, but what they *see* is different. Seeing what Hicks sees, it is reasonable to identify equilibrium prices, even though they are more hypothetical than observed, as true or real prices. We have reasons for believing that the conceptual lenses worn by the likes of Hicks are misleading.[115] We have reasons for believing that the equilibrium they idealize is not ethically defensible. We incorporate by reference here, as if set out in full, the reasons why bare-bones capitalism does not work for the poor, already given in chapter 3. The liberal utopia would not be a desirable utopia.[116] First, purchases made in the market reveal not what

---

accumulation by Michel Juillard at pp. 225–233. Wider implications have been drawn out by David Harvey in *The Condition of Postmodernity* (Oxford: Blackwell, 1987), and even wider ones by Fredric Jameson in *Postmodernism: The Cultural Logic of Late Capitalism* (London: Verso, 1991). The similar idea of 'systemic imperatives of capitalism' is developed in Ellen Meiksins Wood, *Empire of Capital* (London: Verso, 2003). In different ways, numerous writers have made or assumed the general point that where capitalism prevails it is necessary (i.e., not optional) to establish conditions favourable to profit-making. We draw the logical conclusion that to make society governable and widen the range of options available, it is necessary to reduce dependence on capital accumulation as the single or main motor that drives production.

115. Here we refer not just to Hicks but also to similar views of others; but not to all of Hicks, since the few lines we have quoted from him do not reflect the more balanced and nuanced views he expressed on other occasions and indeed on the same occasion when he spelled out his views at greater length. See John Hicks, *Wealth and Welfare* (Oxford: Blackwell, 1981).

116. See Franz Hinkelammert, *Critica de la razón utopica* (Bilbao: Desclee de Brouwer, 2002); Nicholas Georgescu-Roegen, *Energy and Economic Myths: Institutional and Analytical*

consumers want but rather what people with money buy. The market is like a ballot box into which rich people cast many ballots, those with less money cast fewer ballots, and the penniless cast no ballots at all.[117]

Second, the neoliberal ethics that makes what can be sold the criterion for judging what ought to be done is not a proper ethics. For example: A proper medical ethics calls on the doctor to put the life and health of the patient first. Selling the patient whatever she or he will pay for is not ethical medicine. Speaking generally, a proper ethics provides criteria for distinguishing good desires and intentions from bad ones, right from wrong. To say (following Hicks's use of Samuelson's terminology) that people ought to have what their market behaviour indicates they prefer is to beg a question that ethics has historically functioned to answer, namely, whether people ought to desire what they do desire. Aristotle, for instance, holds that a well-educated person finds pleasure in virtue, while a badly educated person finds pleasure in vice.[118] Returning to the medical example, the doctor may prefer to give a bogus treatment and charge a large fee, and the patient may be uninformed enough to prefer the expensive bogus treatment, but that does not make it right, as anybody knows who has ever been caught in the clutches of a venal dentist.

At stake here is whether markets can be evaluated, or whether they cannot be evaluated because they are themselves the standard for evaluating everything else. To be more precise, whether they can be evaluated by any standard other than the extent to which they are perfect (undistorted) or imperfect (distorted) markets. With a proper ethics—even if it is not our ethical realism but some other school of ethical thought—one can judge the market itself. One can evaluate how good or bad a job it is doing in providing health care or preserving endangered species. In general, with a proper ethics, one can use criteria other than those of the market itself to

---

Economic Essays (New York: Pergamon, 1976). Also Michio Morishima, 'General Equilibrium Theory in the Twenty First Century', *The Economic Journal*, vol. 101 (1991), p. 72: 'Once the existence of equilibrium in this fictional world has been proved, GET (General Equilibrium Theory) theorists go crazy. They pursue their model too far, under the illusion that by clarifying its optimum properties they have also clarified the optimality of the modern capitalist economy, in which entrepreneurs and bankers play such an important role, whereas all they have in fact done is clarify the optimality of a hereditary economy.'

117. Amartya Sen has wryly remarked that, because the claim that maximum welfare is produced by minimum 'distortions' would be plausible only if wealth and income were much more equally distributed, those who make that claim should, in order to argue their own viewpoint consistently, become radical revolutionaries. Amartya Sen, 'Markets and Freedoms: Achievements and Limitations of the Market Mechanism in Promoting Individual Freedoms', *Oxford Economic Papers*, vol. 45 (1993), p. 521; see generally Sen, *On Ethics and Economics* (Oxford: Blackwell, 1987).

118. Aristotle, *Nichomachean Ethics* (various versions and translations), 1104b.

evaluate markets. One can ask, for example, whether health care needs are being met, or whether people have old age security or a secure water supply.

The Liberal Utopia Is Not a Realizable Ideal

When many merchants enter the same trade, competition among them drives down prices.[119] This is, of course, what needs to happen to make sense of Dupuit's (or anybody's) deadweight analysis. Adam Smith noticed a point that Alfred Marshall, a little over a century later, made more explicit: when profits fall below a certain point, entrepreneurs tend to close shop because they are no longer motivated to stay in business.[120] To attract investors into hiring workers and producing goods or services, the return must, as a general rule, be at least as high as what the same money would earn if lent out at interest.[121]

From the point of view of an entrepreneur, investing money to produce goods and sell them will become unattractive long before the marginal cost of bringing more goods to market eats up every last ounce of profit. This is not just because profits will be insufficient to motivate entrepreneurs before the point of equilibrium—the imaginary point where marginal cost equals marginal revenue—is reached. The imaginary equilibrium where undistorted markets create a maximum of consumer satisfaction is also in practice impossible because producers strive and connive to make higher profits by selling less at higher prices in less competitive markets.[122]

---

119. *Wealth of Nations*, p. 97, at the beginning of bk. 1, ch. 9: 'When the stocks of many merchants are turned into the same trade, their mutual competition naturally tends to lower profit.'

120. Alfred Marshall, *Principles of Economics* (London: Macmillan, 1920 (first edition 1890)). Marshall develops a concept of 'normal profit' understood as profit high enough to make it worthwhile to be in business.

121. Keynes, *General Theory*, p. 137, and generally ch. 11 and part 4, 'The Inducement to Invest'.

122. The irony that according to the standard economics that serves as an ideology for capitalism in the long run there can be no profits, was noted by Joseph Schumpeter in *Theory of Economic Development* (Cambridge, MA: Harvard University Press), pp. 29–31, 45–46. He elsewhere praises Walras's *entrepreneur ne faisant ni bénéfice ni pert*, explaining why perfect competition would lead to an equilibrium where all firms just break even, as 'the proposition from which starts all clear thinking on profits'. Schumpeter, *History of Economic Analysis* (New York: Oxford University Press, 1956), p. 893. Perhaps the most complete attempt to put such an ideology into practice was that of the Pinochet dictatorship, advised by Chicago-trained economists, in Chile in the years 1974–1981. The economy of Chile crashed in 1981–82. The gross national product fell 14% in 1982 alone, while the major banks collapsed. The dictatorship (which lasted until 1990) then switched to a more pragmatic version of capitalism. See Benny Pollack and Jean Grugel, 'Chile Before and After Monetarism', *Bulletin of Latin American Research*, vol. 3 (1984), pp. 131–143.

'It is well known that the recovery after 1984 was based on a mix of pragmatic and heterodox policies.' Carlos Ominami in Gonzalo Martner and Eugenio Rivera (eds.), *Radiografía crítica al 'modelo chileno'* (Santiago: Ediciones LOM/USACH, 2013), p. 112.

We have been likening the interlocking concepts of neoliberalism to lenses through which the facts are viewed. If our simile is valid, neoliberalism is not just a set of claims about the facts. Other critics have emphasized that the factual claims of neoliberals are, in general, false.[123] For instance, viewing these matters not through the conceptual lenses of an economic theory but in light of what has actually happened in history, the eminent economic historian Immanuel Wallerstein wrote, 'The profitability of [businesses] depends to an important degree on their relative monopolization. That is to say, if a box contains the conditions of perfect competition—multiple small sellers and multiple small buyers, with perfect information—then the rate of profit must inevitably be minimal.'[124]

We are suggesting that liberalism's remarkable capacity for surviving empirical refutation can be explained—and neoliberalism can be more thoroughly refuted—if it is understood less as a set of factual claims and more as a conceptual apparatus. It is a way of viewing the world that provides categories for interpreting what is observed there. In Heideggerian terms, it is less a set of claims about the phenomena observed than it is a predisposition to *read* what *is* in the light of a theory that prescribes what *ought to be*.

13. Transformative Heterodoxy

The foregoing polemic against mainstream neoliberal orthodoxy is not meant to imply that it is always wrong about everything. Nor is it meant to say that there is a single correct heterodoxy. Without seeking to silence any voices, our polemic presupposes an underlying criterion to use like a talisman for distinguishing functional economic theories from dysfunctional ones. This criterion is whether the theory (or approach) in question contributes to transforming the basic social structure.

Applying this criterion to the works of a number of writers, we have already enlisted many in the service of our cause. While they may use different

---

123. Joseph Stiglitz, e.g., points out that in general, markets are not Pareto efficient, that markets may not clear, that in real-world cases markets may be thin or nonexistent, that rents are everywhere, and so on. Joseph Stiglitz, 'Post Marxian and Post Walrasian Economics', *Journal of Economic Perspectives*, vol. 7 (1993), pp. 109–114. Michael Barratt Brown observes that liberal economics does not explain how development historically has happened, remarking caustically that facts do 'not appear to trouble the ideologues of Washington DC'. Book Reviews, *Journal of African Political Economy*, vol. 34 (2007), p. 105.

124. Immanuel Wallerstein, 'Introduction', *Review* (Fernand Braudel Center), vol. 23, no. 1 (2000), p. 8. Wallerstein uses the term 'box' to refer to a category in which he groups a kind of historically existing business.

discursive strategies from ours, they still have the goal of transforming the basic social structure to better meet society's needs in harmony with nature. One example is heterodox economist Jose Luis Coraggio, who has been a major midwife of the plural economies struggling to be born in Ecuador and Bolivia. Coraggio defines economy as follows:

> the system of norms, values, institutions and practices that historically a community or a society has given itself, to organize the metabolism of interchange between human beings and nature; through interdependent activities of production, distribution, circulation and consumption of satisfiers adequate to meet the needs and satisfy the legitimate desires of each and all; defining and mobilizing resources and capacities, in order to achieve their insertion in the overall division of labour; all of this in order to reproduce and amplify the life (*vivir bien*) of society's present and future members, and the life in its territory. For this definition, the economy is part of culture, in a wide sense of the word.[125]

While we contrast economy and community and call for more of the latter, Coraggio recommends resignifying economy to include what we call community. And while we criticize liberalism for assigning too much weight to too simple a concept of freedom, thus undermining community, Amartya Sen redefines freedom.[126] Earlier, against the early modern revolution in ethics that replaced the will of God with free consent as the criterion for distinguishing right from wrong, thus underpinning free markets, St. Ignatius had mounted a counterattack. He defended the moral authority of the will of God. Such counterattacks are still alive and well today, *pace* the global hegemony of liberalism, not only in Christianity but also in Islam and other religions.[127]

---

125. José Luis Coraggio, *Economía social y solidaria* (Quito: Ediciones Abya-Yala, 2011), p. 286. Our translation. The words left in Spanish, meaning 'to live well', refer to indigenous concepts enshrined in the new constitutions of Ecuador and Bolivia. They are intended to replace economic growth as a national goal.

126. In Amartya Sen, *Development as Freedom* (New York: Knopf, 1999) and other works. For an account of how Sen developed his philosophy as a critique of what was at the time mainstream liberal orthodoxy, see the chapter on Sen in Howard Richards and Joanna Swanger, *Gandhi and the Future of Economics* (Lake Oswego, OR: World Dignity University Press, 2011).

127. St. Ignatius Loyola, *The Spiritual Exercises of St. Ignacio Loyola* (Westminster, MD: Newman Press, 1951), pp. 1522–24.

CHAPTER NINE

The Community Work Programme at Orange Farm as Community Development

Coauthored with Malose Langa

OVERVIEW OF THE CHAPTER

1. Where We Have Been and Where We Are Going
2. Community Organizing on the Ground
3. Crime in Orange Farm
4. Crime and Drugs
5. Domestic Violence
6. Local Politics in Orange Farm
7. History and Characteristics of the CWP in Orange Farm
8. Recruitment of CWP Participants
9. A Digression on Public Choice
10. Profile of CWP Participants
11. Work Done by the CWP
12. Gateway: Ex-Offenders against Crime
13. The CWP Multiplies and Strengthens Social Bonds
14. Evidence Supporting an Unbounded Worldview
15. Three Cheers for the Cheerfully Deluded!
16. A Comparison with Asset-Based Community Development

1. Where We Have Been and Where We Are Going

It remains for us to give a more extensive example of community development on the ground in order to illustrate how community meets needs that pure economy does not meet. In this first section of this chapter we make a few general remarks regarding the community principle we have been insisting on. In the rest of the chapter we return to South Africa's Community Work Programme, this time at a specific site, as an example—one among innumerable others—of the practical application of that principle: that community is necessary because pure economy cannot provide dignity for all.

In fact, pure economy without a sufficient dose of community condemns many to humiliation. It causes no end of violence. Many people of good will inadvertently perpetuate the dangerous illusion that pure economy can provide dignity for all. Those people of good will include thousands of successful businesspeople, now comfortably retired, who volunteer to coach young people from disadvantaged backgrounds to become successful too. Sometimes the coaching pays off. The tutee becomes a success. The tutee may, in a few cases, become a 'soprano'—in South Africa, a successful young person from a disadvantaged background who tours slums together with other sopranos on motorcycles, communicating a message of hope: I succeeded; so might you.

Yet even if all the tutees succeed, there remains, barring unusual and temporary circumstances, a population excluded after all the workers the labour market demands are supplied and all the mini-markets that mini-entrepreneurs can supply are supplied. Willing buyers with money in their pockets who are not already customers of companies that have found and occupied the profitable market niches are few.[1]

From this and other fairly complex points we have made in previous chapters some fairly simple practical conclusions follow. One such conclusion is that charitable giving (which sums to around four hundred billion dollars per year in six major donor countries alone) and public social spending (which is over half the budget of many governments) should favor community development, including support for nonprofits and for what in Spanish-speaking countries is called *economia social solidaria*.[2] Why? Because nonprofits, community and other bonding initiatives create dignified livelihoods that bypass the roadblocks that limit employment in the orthodox, mainstream economy, such as the need to find buyers for products.

Sponsor the musicians who are good but not good enough to make a living selling tickets to their performances. Similarly, sponsor sports, scientific research, reforestation—anything that has intrinsic human or ecological value even when it is not a winner in the marketplace. Do not neglect education leading to paying jobs, for paying jobs that require education do exist, and

---

1. International Labor Office, *World Employment and Social Outlook: Trends* 2020 (Geneva: ILO, 20 January 2020). This report is pre-COVID. Reports including effects of the pandemic are available from the same source.
2. Many examples are found at https://caritasespanola.org/economiasolidaria/.

they need to be performed by qualified specialists. But do not expect mainstream paying jobs to solve the social problem. It is not going to happen.

What will solve the problem? A short answer is this: a large series of small wins that move resources from where they are not needed to where they are needed and, once they arrive there, use them wisely. The sum of many small wins complements and facilitates the big wins that are also inevitably needed.

Community development, as we use the term, multiplies the value of those who have surplus sharing it—assuming they are ethical enough to want to share it or they are a public agency or foundation charged with making wise use of public or foundation funds. In community development, the time, intelligence, talents and material resources the poor already have are respected and catalysed through discreet funding provided by outsiders. The outsiders know that the sector of the population that the labour market finds redundant wants dignity as much as they want food, access to medical care and security. They have talents and gifts to share, even if these happen not to be ones the market is currently buying. Nonprofits can create livelihoods above and beyond those the profit sector is able to create. They rely at least partly on gifts. Some rely partly on endowments.

Further, *any* mission-driven organization or purpose-driven life can be devoted to creating value for the common good. The common good simply requires enough love and enough imagination to provide opportunities for everyone to engage in some honourable and worthwhile activity.

Whether the donating organization or the purpose-driven life operates in the public or private sector need not matter. What matters most is moral compass. And today's trend is positive: more enlightenment, more compass. Among many of the world's giant private companies, for example, the same creative efforts that a few decades ago were dedicated to generating profits for shareholders are now regularly made to serve stakeholders, people and planet. Serving the common good is part of their accounting. It is featured in their reports to shareholders.

Are we cynics who believe that today's corporate social and ecological responsibility, private or public, is nothing but show concealing greed? No. Are we unaware that there are still many crooks in business, and that there are still wealthy free riders who benefit from social peace but contribute zero to paying for it? No.[3] Do we expect corporations to transform society

---

3. Andrew Sayer, *Why We Can't Afford the Rich* (Bristol: Polity Press, 2015).

without the involvement of all other sectors, e.g., scholars, labour unions, churches, educators, professionals serving a calling and down-and-outs still cheerful enough to take a shot at becoming up and in? No.

Note also that the cost of employing a participant to do community service—taking the CWP as an example[4]—is on the order of US $900 per year, including the cost of administration of the program. This amount is notoriously low, largely because of morally warped priorities and fiscal constraints. We believe that new technology coming online, intelligent sharing, and stabilizing the size of the human population on the planet can make it possible to comply with International Labour Organization (ILO) global labour standards.[5] Nevertheless, even assuming higher wages for nonmarket livelihoods, the price of discreetly helping people to help themselves is strikingly lower than the investment funds required, typically about $20,000 and often much higher,[6] to create one new job vacancy in the formal sector—even before hiring someone and paying that person a salary.

Meeting people's needs does not have to be expensive. Going the roundabout way—people meeting their needs by spending their salaries after somebody hires them—is expensive. An employer, to be able to hire the unemployed to contribute to making a product, must have identified a market where the product can profitably be sold. This is not easy in a world where most profitable market niches have already been filled. And then—as anybody who has tried to do it knows—numerous and often unpredictable expenses are incurred before the first production workers are hired and long before the product is sold and begins to make a profit.

2. Community Organizing on the Ground

In a South Africa that has run yearly budget deficits of 5 percent or more of GDP with no end in sight[7]; where total indebtedness among the population is approaching twice the money supply; where the economy has been crashing for as long as anybody can remember; and where growth (however it is

---

4. See the figures in section 5 of chapter 10 of this book.
5. See https://www.ilo.org/global/standards/lang--en/index.htm.
6. David Robalino, 'How Much Does It Take to Create a Job?' (Washington, DC: World Bank, 15 February 2018), https://blogs.worldbank.org/jobs/how-much-does-it-cost-create-job.
7. Five percent was the 2015 number. The percentage was higher in 2019 and 2020, especially after the COVID-19 pandemic.

measured) is slowing down, as it is worldwide,[8] achieving social cohesion and community-level resilience becomes a macroeconomic issue.

The general structural question of how to end excessive reliance on capital accumulation to meet human needs, merges with the specific practical question of how to make cooperation in neighbourhoods operational. With this latter question in mind, in this chapter we travel to a township called Orange Farm, about 45 kilometers south of downtown Johannesburg (affectionately called Joburg). To make this journey, we rely on a study of the Community Work Programme at Orange Farm conducted by Malose Langa in 2014.[9] Much of his report is reproduced or paraphrased here.[10]

The CWP works on the ground as a nongovernmental organization, even though it is funded by the government. It was introduced in Orange Farm in 2010 as a subsite of the larger CWP site of Region G, one of the City of Johannesburg's seven administrative regions. Orange Farm was established as an informal settlement in the late 1980s, during the last years of apartheid. At that time, urbanization in South Africa was steadily increasing as the pass laws were being scrapped. New urban migrants to Johannesburg used the open spaces in Orange Farm to build shacks, and by 1989, over 3,000 families had settled there. In the post-apartheid period, after 1994, the population of Orange Farm expanded as people were resettled there from overcrowded, underserviced locations through government social programmes.

Low-cost houses were built through policies related to the Mandela

---

8. Thomas Piketty, in *Capital in the Twenty-First Century* (Cambridge, MA: Belknap Press of Harvard University, 2014), predicts that slow growth will be the norm for the twenty-first century.

9. Malose Langa, *Final Report on Orange Farm* (Johannesburg: Centre for the Study of Violence and Reconciliation, University of the Witwatersrand, 2014). Although much of this report is reproduced here, reading it in its entirety is recommended, as is reading a study of the CWP at Kagiso, another site: Themba Masuko and Malose Langa, *Research on the Community Work Programme (CWP) in Kagiso* (Johannesburg: Centre for the Study of Violence and Reconciliation, Wits University. 2013). See also the studies of the CWP at the Welkom and Bokfontein sites in Rejoice Shumba, *Social Entrepreneurhip and South Africa's Community Work Programme: A Critical Reflection on Innovation and Scale* (unpublished doctoral dissertation, University of Johannesburg, 2013). Profiles of a number of sites can be found at TIPS (www.tips.org.za). Notably, the logic of our argument does not require taking a sum or an average of the CWP over all sites. It is enough to show what is possible by showing what actually happened at one or a few sites.

10. The CWP at Orange Farm is one of several CWP sites that exemplify what the CWP can do when it is well implemented under favourable circumstances. (Others include Bokfontein, discussed in chapter 5, Welkom and Erasmus.) We confine ourselves to describing the CWP at Orange Farm in its first five years, up to 2015. This 'snapshot' shows the CWP operating in its heyday and illustrates the potential of the programme.

government's Reconstruction and Development Programme (RDP). According to the 2011 census, the population of Orange Farm had grown to just under 77,000 people living in an estimated 21,029 households. However, the area covered by the Orange Farm CWP subsite includes the surrounding areas of Stretford, Drieziek and Lakeside, and the population for this larger area is apparently 400,000 people.[11]

Community protests had taken place in the area in 2004 and 2005 due to lack of basic services, such as water, electricity and housing.[12] One of the protest leaders had this to say in his interview with Malose Langa in 2014:

> *There were lots of protests. But before the protests there were awareness campaigns through community meetings, workshops whereby the memorandums were [drawn up]—people were saying enough is enough and they started the protests.*[13]

In response, the ANC (African National Congress) administration of the City of Johannesburg, in partnership with the private sector, rolled out several upliftment initiatives in Orange Farm to accelerate access to basic services. According to a 2008 study of Ward 3 of Orange Farm, 70 percent of the houses in the area were formal structures.[14] In 2011, upliftment initiatives in Orange Farm included 'a modern library, some tarred roads, permanent houses in the central area, additional low cost RDP housing, four clinics, an information and skills development centre with internet access, a multi-purpose community centre and some on-site government offices such as the Department of Health, Social Development, Home Affairs, Housing and Transport, and a police station'.[15] Yet despite these developments, Orange

---

11. The figure of 400,000 is given on one webpage published subsequent to March 2012 (Affordable Land and Housing Data Centre, Suburb Profiles—Orange Farm (http://www.alhdc)) and 350,000 on another undated one: Orange Farm: Beauty in the Land of the Poor.

12. D. McKinley and A. Veriava, *Arresting Dissent: State Repression and Post-apartheid Social Movements* (Johannesburg: Centre for the Study of Violence and Reconciliation Violence and Transition Series, 2005), http://www.csvr.org.za/.

13. Interview with community leader (28/05/2014). All quotations from interviewees are from Malose Langa's interviews conducted as part of the study.

14. T. De Wet, L. Patel, M. Korth and C. Forrester, *Johannesburg Poverty and Livelihoods Study* (Johannesburg: Centre for Social Development Africa, University of Johannesburg, 2008), http://www.ncr.org.za/.

15. City of Johannesburg, 'Change is Coming to Orange Farm', 16 August 2011, http://www.joburg.org.za/.

Farm was still affected by 'extreme levels of poverty and unemployment'.[16] The Anti-Privatisation Forum (APF) had also been active in the Orange Farm area, especially in demanding access to free water.[17]

By 2014, most people in Orange Farm had access to basic services such as water and electricity, as well as social housing. The local ANC leader said during his interview:

> *Fortunately, I am also the head of the ANC in Orange Farm. And we are trying to provide all these basic services such as water, electricity and housing. Also, working hand in hand with the City of Joburg, we are trying to improve our people's lives.*[18]

Community members also now had access to world-class sporting facilities, such as soccer grounds, tennis courts, a rugby field, a public swimming pool and a gym. These facilities were supported by the City of Johannesburg. One of the local leaders was particularly proud of these facilities. Pointing at a well-maintained basketball court, he said:

> *Look at this basketball court; it is one of the things that we must be judged by.*[19]

His statement is an example of G. W. F. Hegel's concept of *Anerkennung* (recognition).[20] Local leaders were also proud of Orange Farm's well-cared-for public parks, maintained by Johannesburg's parks department.[21]

---

16. City of Johannesburg, 2010, Regional SDF2010/11: Region G, Section 2: Regional Analysis, pp. 22–23, http://www.joburg-archive.co.za/2010/pdfs/sdf/regionalsdf/regiong/section2a.pdf, accessed March 2015.

17. For information on the Anti-Privatisation Forum see Wikipedia, 'Anti-Privatisation Forum', http://en.wikipedia.org/wiki/Anti-Privatisation_Forum.

18. Individual interview with an ANC representative (07/05/2014).

19. Individual interview with a second ANC representative (07/05/2014).

20. Hegel regards *Anerkennung* as the characteristic human motive for action and the craving for it a human's deepest desire. It is a foundation for the concept of human rights. It is basic to Hegel's famous master/slave dialectic, where the master also craves recognition from the slave. See Robert R. Williams, *Hegel's Ethics of Recognition* (Berkeley: University of California Press, 1998); and Axel Honneth, *Kampf um Anerkennung* (Frankfurt: Suhrkamp, 2003).

Francis Fukuyama discusses *Anerkennung* extensively in *The End of History and the Last Man* (London: Penguin, 1993). It is Fukuyama's main reason for believing that democracy will be the preferred form of government for the foreseeable future. (Compare this with the economistic tendency to evaluate democratic and authoritarian governments according to which produces the most growth.)

21. Interviews with both the ANC representatives previously mentioned (07/05/2014).

In Orange Farm, middle-class and working-class families live side-by-side, which is not common in South Africa—a big two-storey house sits nextdoor to RDP housing. The area has twelve public and five private high schools. Children of middle-class families mainly go to the private schools.[22]

People in Orange Farm also have access to healthcare facilities. The community has three satellite clinics in addition to the main Community Health Centre, which has a maternity ward, a pediatric ward, an emergency division and an HIV and AIDS unit. Severe medical cases are referred to area hospitals. Neighbourhoods in Orange Farm are interspersed with small shopping complexes that have big popular grocery stores such as Spa, Pick 'n' Pay, and ShopRite. Many interviewees commented that these shops provide job opportunities for some Orange Farm residents.

CWP headquarters in Orange Farm is in the Arekopaneng Skills Centre run by the City of Johannesburg, and CWP participants are allowed to use the Centre's computers. The Skills Centre offers courses in career readiness (3 months), computers (2 months), information technology (9 months) and design (3 months). Among the institutions donating bursary money to help job seekers take these courses are the Reserve Bank of South Africa, Standard Bank and Tiso Foundation.[23]

Many CWP participants (especially young people) regard the CWP as a springboard to better working opportunities. According to one CWP manager, assisting participants in becoming able to access other work opportunities or to establish their own businesses is part of an exit strategy enabling participants to graduate out of the CWP to regular, steady work.[24]

When Malose Langa began interviewing people for this study, a shopping mall was being built in Orange Farm that people hoped would create job opportunities for residents, as the large grocery stores had done.

> *Once opened, the new shopping mall will create permanent and casual jobs.*[25]
>
> *Many people are excited about the new mall. People are thinking about job opportunities.*[26]

---

22. Focus group interview with CWP coordinators (10/04/2014).
23. https://tisofoundation.co.za. The TISO Foundation's motto is 'Enabling Future Leaders'.
24. Interview with a CWP site manager (05/07/2014).
25. Interview with the second ANC representative previously quoted (07/05/2014).
26. Focus group interview with CWP coordinators (10/04/2014).

Accordingly, one of the activities classified as useful community service for which CWP participants were paid was helping other CWP participants prepare CVs to apply for work in the new mall. A local CWP site manager explained:

> *There will be a mall opening, so we [CWP leaders] agreed that the people [CWP participants] must bring their CVs. So they [CWP participants who work as CWP administrators] type them from the Skills Centre. There is that relationship between CWP people and the Skills Centre and the ward councillor and the people who are recruiting for the mall.*[27]

A press report published on 29 October 2014 indicated there had been protests at the opening of the mall by people disappointed at not obtaining jobs. The mall management said they received 10,000 CVs but were looking for only 1,500 people. About 80 residents barricaded roads and burned tyres to express their anger at not receiving jobs.[28]

3. Crime in Orange Farm

In the interviews, crime was mentioned as a major concern:

> *Crime is a big issue in Orange Farm.*[29]
>
> *Yes, we have a problem of crime in Orange Farm.*[30]
>
> *So such crimes, especially common assault and assault GBH* [assault with the intent to do grievous bodily harm], *are the ones reported in high numbers as well as murder.*[31]

Statistics for 2013 on reported crimes from the South African Police Service[32] show changing crime patterns in Orange Farm. As compared to

---

27. Interview (05/07/2014).
28. South African Press Association, 'Orange Farm Residents Protest at Mall Opening', *Times Live*, 29 October 2014, http://www.timeslive.co.za/local/2014/10/29/orange-farm-residents-protest-at-mall-opening, accessed March 2015.
29. Individual interview with Community Policing Forum (CPF) chairperson (07/05/2014).
30. Individual interview with CWP participant (03/04/2014).
31. Interview with police officer (02/04/2014).
32. http://www.crimestatssa.com.

2004 or 2010, some crimes have declined overall (e.g., attempted murder, common assault, sexual crimes) while some have remained stable (e.g., burglary of residential premises). For other crimes (e.g., assault with intent to do grievous bodily harm, robbery with aggravating circumstances, and drug-related crime) there were initial decreases followed by increases. Total sexual crimes, which were already declining before the CWP at Orange Farm began in 2010, declined steadily from 207 in 2010 to 159 in 2013.

We do not have statistics disaggregating crime across South Africa to compare sites where the CWP is present with sites where it is not. Nevertheless, the bulk of CWP participants interviewed perceived crime as decreasing steadily since the tumultuous early days of settlement at Orange Farm. They view the CWP as one of a series of upliftment programmes that have steadily and cumulatively improved their community.

> *This community used to be a terrible place in the past, but things are better now so that you can walk without anything happening to you.*
>
> *This place had so much crime when we were still living in shacks when the community was formed, but now things are much better.*
>
> *Yeah there is crime in the area, but it is not too bad as reported in the media. There are no gangs or professional criminals.*[33]

In sum, the anecdotal evidence indicates that, over time, there has been gradual improvement with respect to crime. This is not clearly supported by quantitative data, nor is it clear that relevant statistical data are available. Nevertheless, the anecdotal evidence fits well with the Durkheimian thesis that higher levels of social integration lead to lower levels of delinquency.[34]

---

33. Interviews with CWP participants (on or about 03/04/2014).

34. Numerous studies from many countries supporting this generalization are reviewed in Clayton Hartjen, 'Delinquency, Development, and Social Integration in India', *Social Problems*, vol. 29 (1982), pp. 464–473. More of the literature is reviewed and nuanced with findings suggesting that self-control theory may be an improvement over social integration theory, in Michael Welch et al., 'Social Integration, Self Control and Conformity', *Journal of Quantitative Criminology*, vol. 24 (2008). Sampson et al. provide data making a case that where communities are more cohesive, there is less crime. Robert J. Sampson et al., 'Neighborhoods and Violent Crime: A Multilevel Study of Collective Efficacy', *Science*, n. s., vol. 277 (1997), pp. 918–924.

Formally, 'high integration means less crime' is a tautology, if the very meaning of social integration implies shared normative standards, conformity to them, communication of them and functional implementation of them in practice.[35] It is, however, a tautology with exceptions, such as cases where integration in a group does not reject delinquency but rather prescribes it.[36]

Durkheim's tautology is illustrated by reports that at the height of the success of social democracy in Austria, when Austrians enjoyed the security of a generous welfare state, people could walk the streets of Vienna at night without fear.[37] If this conceptual approach is valid, then we can predict that when there is employment for all at good wages and the *other components* of social integration are also in place in South Africa, then crime rates will be low. We emphasize *other components* because community development is about more than employment. If Durkheimian assumptions can be made, then the trend remarked upon by interviewees at Orange Farm is corroborated by experience elsewhere: if upliftment continues long enough, intelligently enough, on a large enough scale and with adequate funding, then crime can be confidently expected to decline.

4. Crime and Drugs

Many interviewees who said that violent crime is no longer a major problem in Orange Farm nevertheless raised concerns about the increasing cases of burglary of homes, attributing these break-ins mainly to boys addicted to *nyaope*. Nyaope, or *whoonga*, is a dangerous street drug that has spread like wildfire in South Africa since 2010. It is relatively cheap, and just one hit can produce an addiction. Its ingredients usually include heroin. It is combined with cannabis and smoked.

---

35. Werner Landecker, 'Types of Integration and their Measurement', *American Journal of Sociology*, vol. 56 (1951), pp.332–340.

36. The general proposition that greater social integration means less crime is not inconsistent with the implicit suggestion in Von Holdt et al., *The Smoke That Calls: Insurgent Citizenship, Collective Violence, and the Struggle for a Place in the New South Africa* (Johannesburg: Centre for the Study of Violence and Reconciliation and Society, Work and Development Institute, 2011), frequently cited in ch. 1, that there can be an oppressed community whose community values support violence in protests and perhaps also support thieves like Robin Hood, who steal from the rich. One must, in any case, make an exception to the general principle that high social integration means low crime when one studies social integration within whole groups that are deviant. See Rom Harre et al., *The Rules of Disorder* (London: Routledge, 1980).

37. Barbara Jelavich, *Modern Austria* (Cambridge: Cambridge University Press, 1987), pp. 304–05.

People said that these boys steal household items to sell to buy nyaope and sometimes things they use to make nyaope. The most common item they steal is new flat-screen TVs, which people believe contain a substance used in making nyaope.

> *The crime in the township is mostly committed by young boys who smoke nyaope, and they only steal stuff from their immediate families or do house breakings to sell them to get money to buy nyaope.*[38]

> *Yes, crime is a problem especially on Fridays. It is committed by these boys, especially those who smoke nyaope. . . . You bought a TV for R4000–R5000, but they would just [come and steal it]. They would go and break it (the TV) just to get that substance. . . . They mix [it] with things like Rattex [a rat poison], dagga [marijuana], and ARVs [antiretroviral drugs].*[39]

5. Domestic Violence

Interviewees named domestic violence, especially against women, as a major problem in Orange Farm. According to one police official, at least fifty cases were being reported each month at the Orange Farm police station. A major cause of domestic violence is the disclosure by women to their partners that they have HIV. This confirms the results of a 2003 study showing that many women fear disclosing their HIV status to their partners if they learn that they are infected after being tested at an ante-natal clinic.[40] The study found that men in Soweto often use violence against their partners and accuse their partners of having infected them with the virus.

CWP participants assist both the victims and the police in domestic violence cases. The following comments were made during focus group interviews:

---

38. Focus group with CWP participants (20/05/2014).
39. Interview with CPF chairperson (07/04/2014).
40. Dunkle. K, et al., 'Gender-Based Violence and HIV Infection among Pregnant Women in Soweto', Medical Research Council Technical Report (Medical Research Council, 2003).

We assist with opening of the domestic violence cases. We work with the police and the CPF [Community Policing Forum] and the Youth Desk.[41]

Mostly people who report are women. But we do embark on awareness campaigns to make men aware that they are also welcome to [get help].[42]

[CWP participants] assist victims to open domestic violence cases, refer [them] to courts, and all those things. Mostly they deal with people who are in a state of trauma, whereby a rape victim is always referred to them. They would give them the necessary treatment. The plan is to operate for twenty-four hours, especially during weekends or during festive seasons, because a lot of domestic violence happens during the weekends, month ends and festive seasons.[43]

We do protection order applications. In terms of counselling we have NGOs that we work with.[44]

CWP participants sometimes found it difficult to deal with domestic abuse cases. One person revealed:

Sometimes you encounter things that you also have gone through in life personally. Or maybe at that moment you are facing that similar situation. Sometimes you do not know how to react and you end up crying in front of the victim, which is not correct.[45]

A police officer commented:

We keep statistics of people who come to apply for protection orders and the ones we refer. You can find that within a month we help ninety-six people. Per month, we would

---

41. Focus group interview CWP VEP (Victim Empowerment Programme) members (07/05/2014).
42. Focus group interview with CWP VEP participants (02/04/2014).
43. Ibid.
44. Ibid.
45. Ibid.

> *not get less than fifty people. We always get new people. We embark on awareness programmes for people to come and report domestic violence.*[46]

The incidents of domestic violence often occurred over the weekends, when people are intoxicated. In their study, the South Africa–based nonprofit Sonke Gender Justice found a strong link between alcohol abuse and domestic violence.[47] There is existing literature showing how domestic violence in the new South Africa is linked to men's sense of emasculation[48] and to social practices reflecting patriarchal definitions of what it means to be a man.[49]

> *Yes, you have some men who are just abusing women just to prove he is the head of the house.*[50]

> *Men think it is right to just beat women to prove that they are men.*[51]

6. Local Politics in Orange Farm

The dominant political party in Orange Farm is the African National Congress. In the 2011 local elections, the ANC won in all five wards. The ANC's dominant political position in Orange Farm was also resoundingly confirmed in the May 2014 national and provincial elections, which coincided with the timing of the interviews for this study. Support for the ANC in Guateng Province actually declined from 64 percent to 54 percent, whilst the main opposition party, the Democratic Alliance, increased its share of the vote from 22 percent to 31 percent, and the Economic Freedom Fighters (EFF), contesting a national election for the first time, made a strong showing in the province, obtaining 10 percent of the vote. However, the ANC won

---

46. Individual interview with police officer (02/04/2014).
47. Sonke Gender Justice, *Masculinities, Alcohol and Gender-Based Violence: Bridging the Gaps*, 2006), reviewed at http://menengage.org/resources/masculinities-alcohol-gender-based-violence-bridging-gaps-concept-note-literature-review/, 2015.
48. M. Hunter, 'Cultural Politics and Masculinities: Multiple-partners in Historical Perspective in Kwa-Zulu Natal', in G. Reid and L. Walker (eds.), *Men Behaving Differently* (Cape Town: Double Storey, 2005), pp. 139–160.
49. R. Sathiparsad, 'Developing Alternative Masculinities as a Strategy to Address Gender-based Violence', *International Social Work*, vol. 51, no. 3 (2008), pp. 348–359.
50. Focus group interview with CWP VEP participants (02/04/2014).
51. Individual interview with Nisaa social worker (04/04/2014).

approximately 85 percent of the votes in the Orange Farm area, with the Economic Freedom Fighters (6 percent) and Democratic Alliance (5 percent) together obtaining just over 10 percent of the vote.[52]

Several interviewees commented on the ANC's dominant position in the area. One person said the ANC had obtained its best results for Gauteng Province in Orange Farm. According to ANC members interviewed, the overwhelming support for the ANC was because people were now getting all the necessary basic services, such as water, electricity and houses.

Despite the increasing popularity of the EFF during the elections, ANC members who were interviewed asserted that the EFF will die a natural death, as did the short-lived opposition group COPE (Congress of the People), and that the ANC would remain the ruling party. As one ANC member said:

> *Though the EFF now has the status of the biggest opposition party in Orange Farm, its share of the poll was relatively small and not big as compared to other townships, such as Diepsloot, where it now poses a major threat to the ANC.*[53]

Even so, some interviewees expressed concern that support for the ANC was declining. One ANC member was quick to interpret the challenge to the ANC's dominance as necessary for change to happen.

> *The ANC is stronger than before. . . . Even in Joburg we are the best performing in terms of our percentage and so on and so forth. Well, in terms of the EFF, it's EFF and DA who are sharing this 10 percent. . . . Overall it's a worry a bit that we have declined, but we are optimistic that we are going to regroup as the ANC. I mean even in 2009 our official opposition in Orange Farm was COPE. They are not there anymore. And remember those were tried and tested comrades . . . people who have been there for years and years in terms of the struggle . . . [and] have also served in parliament. They know governance. But I know for a fact they are also*

---

52. These numbers changed in the 2016 elections, when the ANC lost control of Johannesburg. We refrain from updating the electoral statistics, because the relevant numbers for this chapter are those obtained when the study it reports was made.

53. Individual interview with ANC representative 2 (07/05/2014).

going to decline, because in whatever organization, if there is growth, there would be contradictions which are necessary.[54]

EFF members who were interviewed on 7 May 2014 (a National Elections day) were confident about their party's prospects. They were happy about the EFF's growth and looked forward to becoming a dominant political party, especially in the local elections of 2016. One EFF member said:

The ANC is scared of the EFF, and that's why they are harassing us, including our leader, Julius Malema.

The EFF's intention was to mobilize community members to demand better services. Asked about developmental challenges faced by Orange Farm, the EFF leader painted a gloomy picture about the township's current state:

The development is only on the outside, next to highways so that passers-by can think that there is development, but once you are inside the township you will smell stinky sewerage and see unmaintained roads. This place is dirty like Hilbrow in Johannesburg.

He expressed concern that there was corruption in the way budgets for RDP houses were allocated:

For example, each RDP house is allocated a R7000 budget, but some houses have better services than others, although they are all allocated the same amount of money.[55]

He also complained about lack of water. He raised all these complaints even though some of these services were being provided, except in Driezik, which is still a squatter camp area.

7. History and Characteristics of the CWP in Orange Farm

When the CWP, with its roots in the Organization Workshops started by Clodomir de Morais in Brazil and in activity theory social psychology, arrived

54. Individual interview with local government ward councillor 1 (20/04/2014).
55. Interviews with EFF members (07/05/2014).

in Orange Farm it found new soil. Rejoice Shumba has persuasively argued that as the CWP scaled up to become a massive programme, it lost some of the creativity present at its inception.[56] However, it did not lose all of it, as is shown in the interviews.

Before the CWP arrived at Orange Farm, some Orange Farm youth had participated in a campaign called Proud to Serve, which started in the run-up to the 2010 FIFA World Cup. The City of Johannesburg sponsored the campaign in the inner city and eastern suburbs as well as in the neighbouring townships of Soweto, Alexandra and Orange Farm. The initial idea was to clean up the city in preparation for the hundreds of thousands of visitors expected to attend the World Cup, but in the last months of 2009 Johannesburg Executive Mayor Amos Masondo noted the campaign's role in motivating communities to strive for their own betterment.[57] Proud to Serve, with its slogan, 'Youth lend a helping hand', employed seven thousand youth volunteers working across the City of Johannesburg in human rights, HIV/Aids, and drugs and alcohol abuse awareness campaigns, as well as the cleaning up of public spaces and community buildings.[58]

Young people in Orange Farm had joined this campaign and started cleaning streets. Proud to Serve provided volunteers with tools and materials while paying them a R50 stipend per day.[59] One CWP representative commented:

> *The volunteers of the Proud to Serve campaign were getting more money than the CWP participants now.*[60]

Volunteers worked for five days a week, unlike the CWP, which employs people only two days per week, and unlike NREGA, which officially guarantees one hundred days of work a year but may fail to deliver that.

Orange Farm interviewees mentioned that the Seriti Institute, which later brought the CWP to Orange Farm, was involved in the Proud to Serve campaign. Thus while at Bokfontein, Munsieville and some other places the CWP was preceded by an Organization Workshop, at Orange Farm it

---

56. Rejoice Shumba, *Social Entrepreneurship and South Africa's Community Work Programme: A Critical Reflection on Innovation and Scale* (unpublished doctoral dissertation, University of Johannesburg, 2013).
57. 'Proud to Serve' campaign, http://www.publicityupdate.co.za/?idstory=24210.
58. Ibid.
59. Ibid.
60. Individual interview with CWP site manager 2 (05/07/2014).

was Proud to Serve that motivated the youth. When the campaign ended in March 2010, Gavin Andersson of the Seriti Institute said:

> *The Institute hopes that there will be many other opportunities to engage the youth to improve the quality of life in their communities, as is shown by the success of the Proud to Serve campaign.*[61]

As it turned out, within days of that statement a budget was allocated to Seriti to enable it to implement the CWP in Johannesburg's Region G. A Johannesburg city official asserted that this action was in line with the city's plan to develop the area and to create job opportunities for people living there:

> *You see, part of the City of Joburg's plan is to develop all the townships. Yeah, we wanted Orange Farm to also be developed. You see we wanted CWP to also go there [Orange Farm] and help people. We have CWPs in all these townships. We want our people to work.*[62]

All of the CWP representatives interviewed said that Seriti had laid a good foundation for the implementation of the CWP in Orange Farm:

> *Those guys of Seriti were very interested in issues of community development. You know they were working very hard and inspiring us that we can make a change in this community. I really liked their approach of believing in us.*[63]

> *Seriti taught us how to work with people. You know their emphasis was development and people's skills to manage and deal with problems as a leader. I learned from these guys.*[64]

CWP representatives described Seriti's approach in introducing the CWP as consultative in nature.

61. 'Proud to Serve' campaign (http://www.publicityupdate.co.za/?idstory=24210).
62. Individual interview with City of Joburg official (22/05/2014).
63. Individual interview with CWP site manager 1 (20/04/2014).
64. Individual interview with CWP site manager 2 (05/07/2014).

> *We knew CWP through Seriti and it was introduced to the people. There was an open consultation.*[65]

All the key stakeholders, especially local government councillors, were consulted and informed about the implementation of the CWP. Community meetings were held to publicly introduce the CWP before it was actually implemented. Strategies for recruiting potential participants, as well as key community projects to be undertaken, were discussed in these meetings. Seriti encouraged the participants to see the CWP as an employment safety net to use while reskilling themselves to find other work.

Partnerships were created between the CWP and other organizations. For example, Soul City Institute for Health and Development Communication[66] partnered with the CWP in Orange Farm on its campaign against alcohol abuse, called Phuza Wise (drink responsibly). Seriti was also instrumental in facilitating alignment between the CWP and the City of Johannesburg, especially the city's Department of Human Development.

Work within the CWP is generally organized in work teams. Every Friday all the team leaders, also called coordinators, meet to discuss the work done that week and to plan the following week's work. Team members meet with their leader every morning and are assigned their work responsibilities for the day. They sign the attendance register and sign out the tools they need. After work participants sign the register again, and tools are returned to the storeroom.

CWP participants are encouraged to suggest possible projects that can benefit the community, and proposals are shared in the weekly coordinators meeting:

> *I would say we can make suggestions, because usually the coordinators would come and ask, guys do you have any ideas . . . ? And then they would group ourselves and discuss plans that we want to implement and the skills that we would like CWP to provide. So they [coordinators] are giving us the authority to do things.*[67]

---

65. Ibid.
66. Soul City, www.soulcity.org.za.
67. Focus group interviews with CWP participants (06/06/2014).

> Yes, as the participants we suggest plans and . . . we are involved in the planning of projects. . . . Yes, we discuss plans, and then we will say let's do this and this.[68]

In the words of the coordinators:

> We encouraged people to also be innovative. I cannot see at the back of my head. But if you come here and say: Listen, why don't we do this? Yes, we will adopt it.[69]

> Everyone is free to suggest everything that we need to do. It is our project, all of us.[70]

It is evident from the interviews that decision-making processes concerning the CWP activities in Orange Farm are participatory and consultative in nature. Decisions about possible projects to undertake are not left in the hands of the project manager and the implementing nonprofit agency. This approach contributes to building positive social relations between the CWP participants and key actors in the community.

Legal requirements dictate that all CWP work must be approved by the local government. Once the CWP has chosen a project, it is presented to ward councillors, who are expected to sign a letter approving the activity. A citizens advisory committee is also consulted once decisions to implement certain projects have been taken. To date, no councillor has ever refused to approve a project. Indeed, the CWP work helps to give the local government credibility in the eyes of the community.

A CWP senior manager emphasized that the councillors' role is limited to approving projects and to reviewing monthly reports on progress made:

> Every month there is a separate report that goes to councillors about work that has been done in their ward. And they must cosign that report, keep a copy, bring the original to the office. I keep it as part of my portfolio in terms of my stakeholder relations.

---

68. Ibid.
69. Individual interview with CWP site manager 2 (06/04/2014).
70. Focus group with CWP coordinators (10/04/2014).

Councillers can suggest possible projects to the CWP, he said, but as part of a strategy to keep the CWP apolitical, they should not be directly involved in deciding which activities need to be undertaken. Initially, the relationship between the CWP and the ward councillors was conflictual over recruiting potential participants for the programme. The CWP management had to be firm in resisting attempts to politicize the recruitment process and the CWP. Because of taking that firm stance, the CWP is currently seen as purely a community project in which everyone has an equal opportunity to participate, as long as there is available space.

Community members who are not CWP participants, as well as other stakeholders, such as nongovernmental organizations (NGOs) and community-based organizations (CBOs), can suggest possible projects for the CWP to undertake. The manager spoke of one request from the community to clean up a dumping site. When CWP management rejected the request, community members threatened to *toyi-toyi* (protest) against the CWP.

> *I will show you minutes whereby the community called me before the elections and said they will toyi-toyi [because we refused to clean the dumping site as the CWP]. And I said I am going to join you and also toyi-toyi. Let's go toyi-toyi, but I am not going to clean [the dumping site]. They asked why, and I said who wants it clean. They said it is us. Then I said I will bring in tools. I will bring in fifty of my guys [CWP participants] and you bring fifty of your guys [community members] . . . , and then we clean it together so that there must be ownership. After it has been cleaned the residents would never allow anyone to come and dump there. Then there will be a proper monitoring.* [71]

8. Recruitment of CWP Participants

If our economic theory is correct—if major innovative changes are necessary to cope with Staggering Facts 1 and 2—then public employment and community development constitute key sectors that must grow to make capitalism governable. Excessive reliance on the causal chain of investment-production-sale-profit must be balanced by other dynamics. Arguably

---

71. Follow-up individual interview with CWP site manager (08/08/2014).

and as a matter of history, a major reason why neoliberal capitalism is now out of control worldwide is the failure of twentieth-century social democrats to make mixed-economy alternatives work on the ground.[72]

According to some interviewees,[73] in 2010, when the CWP was first implemented, councillors were actively involved in the process of recruiting potential participants. A CWP site manager commented:

> *Some councillors were recruiting their own people. You will find two to four people from the same house all working in the CWP. No, I cannot work like that. This is a poverty alleviation programme. We must assist indigent families for them to have an income.*[74]

> *Councillors would submit a list and say these are the people we want to be part of the programme. Or sometimes, in other wards, I found that there were fifty comrades who come to work and then call a meeting instead of working. They would say we need fifty [people], but they would only choose thirty people, and then say twenty [spaces in the CWP] are going to be reserved for the comrades. So we had to stop that process.... Believe me, we were very unpopular, [but] we stopped it. We suspended sites [wards] which were giving problems.*[75]

Because of these allegations of nepotism against councillors, it was decided that participants would be openly selected by random drawings in public. The same CWP site manager said:

> *You see, the process of recruiting participants was chaotic at the beginning. All people wanted to be in the CWP. Councillors also wanted to put their people. In some wards this of course created serious problems. It was agreed that the*

---

72. This argument is made in Howard Richards and Joanna Swanger, *Dilemmas of Social Democracies* (Lanham, MD: Rowman and Littlefield, 2006), and is implicit in ch. 5 and throughout the present book.

73. Ibid.; individual interview with councillor 1 (20/04/2014); focus group interview with CWP coordinators 1 (10/06/2014).

74. Individual interview with CWP site manager 2 (05/07/2014).

75. Ibid.

selection of participants must be done openly. It was agreed that people must put their IDs in a box, and all people whose IDs are selected should become CWP participants. Yeah, we were not looking at the skill. Then it was an issue of you would invite 500 people [for] fifty jobs, put ID copies in a bucket, and then you choose the fifty.[76]

The CWP manager commented that this method worked very well and that people felt it was fair.

Publicity campaigns were also undertaken to clarify that the CWP was meant to benefit people from indigent households, where there is abject poverty or no one in the family is working, and individuals from such families would be recruited when there was a space.

We now try and look for people that meet the criteria to be in the CWP. For example, when we do a door-to-door campaign, then we go to a house and realize that this family is living in poverty and no one is working. We try and recruit one family [member] if there is a space for them to work in the CWP. If we don't have a space, we wait or put the person on the waiting list and take them in if the space opens.[77]

In fact, other stakeholders in the community, such as NGOs and CBOs, were encouraged by CWP staff and participants to refer people who were in greatest need:

Our stakeholders refer people to us who are indigent to work in the CWP. We also take such people if they are poor and not working. We have people on the waiting list.[78]

Over the years, things have changed [regarding] how we select people into the CWP. We try and recruit who definitely is in need of some financial assistance. We want this programme to become a safety net.[79]

76. Ibid.
77. Ibid.
78. Focus group interviews with CWP coordinators (10/04/2014).
79. Individual interview with CWP site manager 2 (05/07/2014).

> *To eliminate unemployment we would also check households where there are many people [and] we would ensure that they also become participants. . . . Sometimes you'd find that they are a family of eight and no one is working. If there is a space at CWP we would get them in.*[80]

Given the above approach, many interviewees asserted that the CWP at Orange Farm has been working well as a poverty alleviation programme. In 2014 there were lists of people waiting for an opportunity to work in the CWP. CWP management was also working to recruit new people:

> *We do not want to see a participant remaining a CWP participant; we want them to exit the programme and open space for other needy people to benefit from it.*[81]

9. A Digression on Public Choice

In details such as those recounted above, we can observe the CWP pioneering the economic democracy of tomorrow. This is evident in, for example, the consultative processes used to decide who will clean up trash in the streets, what 'useful work' the CWP will do, and the search for a fair way to select participants.

What we are seeing here are community-driven, somewhat homespun and informal, processes of public choice. They lack the formal elegance of mathematical models of public choice, but they work. They get the gardens planted and thus feed the hungry with more healthful food than the standard mealie meal and cooking oil diet of South Africa's poor. They match frail elderly people with victims of HIV and AIDS to take care of them. They help the police and the social work agencies cope with domestic violence. Public goods are produced, while the specious boundary line between public goods and private goods so dear to liberal theory suffers an intelligent blurring. Intelligence itself gets reframed, becoming less a capacity for the rigorous manipulation of abstract symbols and more an ability to cope successfully with the limitlessly variable situations that arise in practice. This is wisdom that is relevant to practical action, known in ancient Greece as *phronesis*, practical virtue.

---

80. Ibid.
81. Focus group interviews with CWP coordinators (10/04/2014).

In 1951, Kenneth Arrow, in his seminal work *Social Choice and Individual Values*,[82] argued that voting is the characteristic alternative adopted by a modern democracy to balance its core choice process, which is the aggregation of consumer preferences as revealed in markets to decide what should be produced and what should be done. Arrow famously showed that neither voting nor buying could justify public choices, regarding what ought to be done, that would satisfy standard criteria derived from liberal ethics—most importantly, the criterion that what individuals choose to do defines what ought to be done. John Dryzek analysed a longer list of ways to make public choices, arranging them into four categories: markets, social norms, legal systems and governments.[83] The standard approach in each of these categories has worrisome limitations.

We have been saying that human life needs liberation from the necessity to promote ever more sales (and ever-higher GDP) simply for the sake of the system's stability. This necessity tends to override social and ecological desiderata when it clashes with them. Our conviction that tomorrow, if there is going to be a tomorrow at all, will be characterized by economic democracy derives from the premise that otherwise capitalism will continue to be ungovernable, which in turn implies the destruction of the biosphere that is the habitat of the human species. The only possible tomorrows are green; therefore, tomorrow's economic processes must be governed to make them comply with green criteria.[84]

What is happening before our eyes at Orange Farm is community-driven social decision-making: public choice at a local level that is working. It exists; therefore it must be possible, and it is more than welcome. Over and above their other merits, participatory practices that empower local communities to organize themselves to meet their own needs have the merit of undermining the TINA (there is no alternative) argument. This argument, voiced

---

82. Kenneth J. Arrow, *Social Choice and Individual Values* (New Haven, CT: Yale University Press, 1963 (1951)). Later, Amartya Sen devoted himself to showing that the alleged impossibility of rational public choices (leaving market outcomes to determine public policy by default) was an artifact of the narrow criteria applied by neoliberal thought. Amartya Sen, *Collective Choice and Social Welfare* (San Francisco: Holden-Day, 1970); see also other works in this vein by the same author.

83. John Dryzek, *Rational Ecology* (New York: Basil Blackwell, 1987).

84. This point is further developed by Howard Richards in 'Unbounded Organization and the Unbounded University Curriculum', which is a chapter in the book edited by Pat Inman and Diana Robinson, *University Development and Environmental Sustainability* (Manchester: Manchester University Press, 2014), included in Manchester Scholarship On Line in 2015. Similar ideas have been popularized by Naomi Klein in *The Shock Doctrine: The Rise of Disaster Capitalism* (New York: Henry Holt Company, 2007).

by Margaret Thatcher, holds that establishing the requisite conditions for large-scale capital accumulation—that is, yielding to the sway of SF1—is the only way to create jobs and incentivize people to do 'useful work' and thereby meet vital human needs.

10. Profile of CWP Participants

In March 2014, there were 433 participants in the CWP in Orange Farm, of whom 72 percent (312) were women, and 28 percent (121) were men,[85] with women over thirty-five years of age accounting for nearly half (48 percent) of participants.

Young people (women and men thirty-five years of age and under) made up about a third (35 percent) of participants in Orange Farm. Although this is roughly half the number of older participants, the young people's view of the CWP is highly positive.[86] They see their involvement in the CWP as a stepping stone to better opportunities—for example, to be able to attend training workshops and get connected to job opportunities. As one CWP coordinator said:

> *If there is training, we involve them [young people]. We want them to get better jobs.*[87]

The popularity of the CWP in Orange Farm among the youth can be partly attributed to the use of cell phones and social media networks, such as WhatsApp, by the CWP itself and by the Skills Centre associated with the CWP in Orange Farm to disseminate information about job opportunities that young people can apply for:

> *We also have a WhatsApp page where we disseminate employment opportunity information. We post information [about job opportunities] on the WhatsApp page and then they apply.*[88]

---

85. In 2013, there were 205,494 participants in the CWP at 140 sites nationwide, of whom 179,700 were still participating at the end of the year, of whom 58% were women and 54% young people, https://pmg.org.za/committee-meeting/16915/).

86. In contrast, young people in Kagiso tended to see CWP work as for people who had failed or who had no aspirations. See Themba Masuko and Malose Langa, *Research on the Community Work Programme (CWP) in Kagiso* (Johannesburg: Centre for the Study of Violence and Reconciliation, Wits University, 2013).

87. Focus group interviews with CWP coordinators (10/04/2014).

88. Ibid.

There are many reasons why women are more actively involved in the CWP than men. Two reasons mentioned by CWP participants (mainly women) in focus groups were that men feared being ridiculed or losing social status if they participated in the CWP, partly because CWP participants receive such a small income, and similarly, that some men feel the CWP is not a 'real job' because it does not involve going to a factory five days per week and working under demanding conditions:

> *Men think a real job is about going to the firms and working the whole week.*[89]

This point is illustrated by Catherine Campbell's study of men working in South African diamond and gold mines, who linked their jobs with constructions of hegemonic masculinity. Masculine identity was developed as an enduring symbol of bravery, strength and hard work, even as the miners also suffered exploitation at the hands of white male bosses.[90]

Another reason voiced by focus-group members was that men viewed the work at the CWP as 'women's work'.

> *Men stay at home. They feel: 'What are people going to say?' if they work here. But women do not care.*[91]

CWP work often involves food gardening, home-based care and early childhood projects—all activities traditionally reserved for women. It is a reasonable hypothesis that more men might participate in the CWP if the nature of the work changed.

Another explanation given was that women are more concerned than men about the welfare of their children and less concerned about the status of the work. Working in the CWP is enough as long it brings some small amount of income.

> *Maybe as women we think for the children and other things. But a man tells himself he won't do it.*[92]

---

89. Individual interview with a male CWP participant (23/05/2014).
90. C. Campbell, 'Learning to Kill? Masculinity, the Family and Violence in Natal', *Journal of Southern African Studies*, vol 18, no 3 (1992), pp. 614–628.
91. Focus group interviews with CWP participants (06/06/2014).
92. Ibid.

> *They [men] are full of pride. I think as a woman you know that. . . . So we do not worry about the money. The little that we get makes a huge difference. But for them [men] it is not a case.*[93]

Women participants who are single parents of children younger than eighteen also receive a child support grant. This supplements their CWP income, so they bring more into the household each month than men do, since few men register for social grants for child support. This lesser earning power may hit hard on the men's sense of masculinity, since men's work is traditionally associated with a particular social status and the ability to earn enough to fully support one's family.[94]

> *The majority of men moved out [of the CWP] because they need other jobs [that pay] more money to feed the family. A woman does not care. As long she supports her children she does not have a problem, she is going to stay there. She [also] gets extra support from the social grants, but a man cannot live on that little money [he only gets from the CWP]. He has to go back to the house and buy groceries for the children.*[95]

One CWP site manager commented that if the CWP could offer training in new technical skills, such as welding and plumbing, more men might interested in the programme, as it would facilitate their employability beyond the CWP once they gained these skills.

> *The men want to get in, [but] they want to be skilled. Most of them are saying: Why you don't take us to school to learn things like welding and plumbing? If I could do such a thing and get a certificate I would be fine [it would be easy to be self-employed or find better-paying job opportunities].*[96]

Both funding technical training through the CWP and increasing CWP wages might attract more male participants. In the end, the issue is how men

---

93. Ibid.
94. M. Hunter, 'Fathers without Amandla: Zulu-speaking Men and Fatherhood', in L. Richter and R. Morrell (eds.), *Baba: Men and Fatherhood in South Africa* (Pretoria: Human Sciences Research Council, 2006), pp. 99–107.
95. Focus group interviews with CWP coordinators (10/04/2014).
96. Follow-up individual interview with CWP site manager 2 (08/08/2014).

and women view 'useful work' and whether they celebrate it, rather than sticking to imaginary categories of men's work and women's work handed down from a previous epoch.

11. Work Done by the CWP

One of the CWP site managers said about the CWP's purpose:

> *CWP is a community project for the community, and CWP people are working for the community.*[97]

The CWP in Orange Farm is involved in various community projects, such as food gardening, home-based care, early childhood learning and adult education. It also engages in prevention work with regard to domestic violence, as well as working to address substance abuse, considered a major cause of crime.

Vegetable gardening is one of the most important projects in Orange Farm. The city of Johannesburg's Department of Human Development has aligned with the CWP in Orange Farm to encourage community members to plant vegetables in their yards, in school yards and in public spaces as part of the poverty alleviation project. The city provides community members with equipment, seeds and sometimes compost. Basic skills training is weak, so Seriti supplements the city's efforts with support from an agriculturalist. Vegetables produced from these gardens are given to indigent families and child-headed households, as well as to elders and to individuals who are HIV-positive and are taking their antiretroviral drugs (ARVs). CWP participants and coordinators commented:

> *We have gardens—and it is also part of a social programme. We help people who are poor. When we go to a home and find that they are poor, we would get some vegetables from the garden and give them.*[98]

> *Our priority is mainly the elderly people, and then the orphans and the child-headed families. . . . And even in households where there is no breadwinner, we would take vegetables to those families.*[99]

---

97. Follow-up individual interview with CWP site manager (22/10/2014).
98. Focus group interviews with CWP participants (06/06/2014).
99. Focus group interviews with CWP coordinators (10/04/2014).

> *They are busy with the food gardens. And then certain produce is given to the crèches [child care centers or preschools] that are struggling and people who are on ARVs.*[100]

Many indigent families benefit significantly from these gardening efforts. Just as ANC leaders are proud for helping to bring world-class sports facilities to Orange Farm and for establishing electricity and water service and constructing RDP social housing, so many CWP participants are proud of being able to assist the needy, including providing them with vegetables.

> *As part of a social programme, I stayed with one lady at my place for three months, because she had no place to stay. She had nothing, so I helped her find a place, and then CWP also helped her by building her a shack. And when there are vegetables we would also give her some.*[101]

CWP participants also help people to establish their own food gardens.

> *If the family has been identified as poor, we will tell them that we are going to give you food, but . . . in three months you must take care of your [own] garden. We set up a garden for you, we give you seeds and everything to make sure that your garden grows. In three months, when we cut you from the [city] food bank, then you are able to feed yourself from your own garden.*
>
> *For the elderly people who need food gardens we are able to go in and assist them with starting gardens. And if she cannot maintain it, we would maintain it and she would just reap.*[102]

Furthermore, the City of Johannesburg encourages Orange Farm community members, especially those interested in generating income by selling their vegetables, to form cooperatives. The city has committed itself

---

100. Ibid.
101. Focus group interviews with CWP coordinators (10/04/2014).
102. Ibid.

to facilitating access to open land (especially city-owned land) for people to grow vegetables for their own livelihood and for commercial purposes. Currently, a hub is being built in Orange Farm to store vegetables grown in community gardens and to sell them to the public (including local hawkers), as well as to the Johannesburg Fresh Produce Market.

The CWP site manager in Orange Farm arranges workshops for CWP participants on different careers and on how to run a small business. Members of a CWP focus group who are selling chickens said their long-term plan is to exit the CWP once their business is fully functional (the business was making more than R5000 per month at the time of the interview).

Home-based care is another important CWP project in Orange Farm. CWP participants clean the houses of the elderly and sick people who live alone without support from relatives. They may also cook for them as well as bathe them. Assistance is also provided to children who do not have parents and to elderly people who stay with their grandchildren but do not receive adequate support from them.

> *I go around checking out children who stay alone, who do not have parents, and then cook for them and do their laundry. And there are elderly women who stay with grandchildren, but they [grandchildren] do not look after her [the elderly woman]. So I would go and check if things are well with her. If things are not going well, I would go back to the coordinators and ask them to get people to go and bathe her.*[103]

> *Sometimes we would be helping an elderly woman from when she is sick until she passes away. So we would go and help with food preparation. We also help with filling the grave. After the funeral, we help with washing the dishes . . . and the family would be thankful that we've helped them.*[104]

CWP participants also offer home support in connection with the three local clinics. Nurses regularly give CWP participants a list of patients who need to be visited in their homes to check if they are following their treatment and taking their medication as prescribed. In addition, they organize health awareness campaigns to encourage parents to bring their children for

---

103. Ibid.
104. Focus group interviews with CWP participants (06/06/2014).

immunization at the clinics. They work with social workers to help people get identity cards and other documents and access social grants. They also work in various crèches in Orange Farm as teachers' assistants. Five former CWP participants decided to open their own crèches using the skills they acquired on the job.

The CWP's adult education project gives people—both CWP participants and general community members—an opportunity to learn basic reading and writing skills. These classes are taught twice a week by CWP participants who have matric and post-matric qualifications. One of these adult students said:

> *Yeah, I'm learning how to read. You see we did not go to school during apartheid.*[105]

12. Gateway: Ex-offenders against Crime

In February 2012, a group of ex-offenders working in the Orange Farm CWP started a crime prevention project called Gateway, whose aim is to raise awareness among the youth in and out of school that crime and drugs are not good. Gateway was established as part of the CWP. The project had twenty-one ex-offenders when it started in February 2012; currently it has eight members still actively involved in the project. It is reported that some members (5) left the project, while others (6) found other job opportunities.

In a focus group interview Gateway members shared:

> *We wanted to spread a message that crime is not good, as well as drugs. So we sat down and then we came up with a decision to form a programme to deal with crime.*[106]

> *With crime prevention programmes in CWP, we have Gateway, whereby we motivate young people not to do crime and drugs.*[107]

Gateway members, as former offenders, use their own experiences to show the youth that crime does not pay, often portrayed through dramas and poems.

105. Ibid.
106. Focus group with Gateway group members (28/04/2014).
107. Group interview with CWP coordinators (2014).

> *We have been there. We know what we are talking about because we served sentence.*[108]
>
> *We do intense motivation through drama and poems. [We] understand the situation in prisons. So [we] do a demonstration through drama from when you are still outside until you get into prison. And we show both sides so that you can see what made a person fall into crime. And then at the end he learns a lesson, he gets his punishment.*[109]
>
> *We have two dramas:* Don't Be a Fool, Crime Is Not Cool *and* Ke Moja (I'm Fine without Crime).[110]

Gateway members go to street corners where nyaope-smoking boys meet and encourage them to seek professional help. Sometimes parents of these boys approach Gateway to ask for assistance in taking their sons to SANCA (South Africa National Council for Alcoholism and Drug Dependence) for rehabilitation. Gateway members are often invited by school principals in Orange Farm and neighbouring communities to perform their dramas for youths both in and out of school.

Gateway has also been invited by the Department of Correctional Services to speak about life after prison to inmates who are close to being released or paroled. The group also planned a tour of correctional centres in Bloemfontein in March 2014, presenting a drama about life outside prison as an ex-convict. Their key message is not to care about insults one receives, such as being called 'jailbird', but to focus on rebuilding one's personal life and resisting temptations to reoffend.

> *Ex-offenders have nothing to do when they come back from jail. Because of their criminal records they cannot get jobs. Because there is a stigma that you are a jailbird, you end up isolating yourself. The challenges ... end up leading one to say it's better I go back to prison.*
>
> *There are people who call us dogs. . . . There are people who [want us] to help them commit crime. And it is a challenge to you, because you have nothing, you are not working*

---

108. Focus group with Gateway group members (28/04/2014).
109. Ibid.
110. Ibid.

and they come to you with money. [They say: Come and join us]. You see we hit a store, so here is R100 for you. The following day when he comes he does not give you R100, but [he still wants] you to be part of the mission. And most of the time we end up in jail [again] because of our situation.

Imagine: You spend seven years in jail, and when you are released, you are lost, you do not know what is happening. Things are no longer the same. Things have changed. There are newer phones, Blackberry and so on. You are still stuck on the past technology.

There are people who've been in prison for fifteen years, and they will plan that 'when we go out we are going to attack Pick n Pay'. So when they go out they do the crime, and that is why you find that a person would be released and then after three months he would be back in jail.[111]

Gateway also works with other CWP participants in helping the elderly and disabled, cleaning streets, painting public buildings and so forth. Gateway members view doing 'public good' as a form of apology.[112] One of Gateway's key objectives is to recruit ex-offenders to work in the CWP as part of their reintegration into society. As ex-offenders acquire skills with which they can start their own businesses, they are less likely to re-offend and return to jail.[113]

13. The CWP Multiplies and Strengthens Social Bonds

The CWP facilitates social cohesion through various processes. Before the inception of the CWP in Orange Farm, many people living in the same ward or neighborhood did not know one another. The inception of the CWP facilitated those who are participants' getting to know one another, a first step toward their working together to assist other community members. Interviewees said that the CWP promotes the spirit of *ubuntu* among participants.

[CWP] does create ubuntu amongst the participants. We did not know each other at first. But right now, as we kept on meeting each other, I ended up knowing her and she ended

111. Ibid.
112. Ibid.
113. Ibid.

up knowing the other one. So if I didn't know this one, then I wouldn't have been able to help this one. So because of the one I know, I am able to help the next person.[114]

So I think [CWP] encourages ubuntu. We help in the community. The other thing is that CWP taught us how to deal with people as leaders. They helped us a lot. We were taught leadership skills. I think we are compassionate.[115]

We are in the same society—we communicate about where we meet. And then if you need advice about something, I would just [ask] for an advice on what to do. We visit each other . . . so friendships develop as colleagues.[116]

We are like a family now because of what CWP taught us. We can work together with the community.[117]

Some of the funerals we attend to help them to fill the graves. Because of CWP we would go and attend, but before, I didn't know them. So now we attend because we are family.[118]

The CWP meetings held once or twice a week to discuss work to be undertaken in the community also enhance social cohesion among the participants, as does the fact that the CWP is generally organized in work teams. The CWP participants in Orange Farm asserted that they work well in teams and that team members support one another. Thus generally, the CWP functions as a social space where social bonding grows as CWP participants work together as a group.

Interviewees also shared that other social networks were formed among the CWP participants, such as *stokvels*, social clubs where members contribute a fixed amount of money monthly. Stokvel members take turns as recipients of the money, which they are free to use for their personal benefit. They often use it for burial society fees or to buy their children's school uniforms.

The projects that the CWP undertakes in Orange Farm arguably

---

114. Follow-up focus group interview with CWP coordinators (18/09/2014).
115. Focus group interviews with CWP coordinators (10/04/2014).
116. Follow-up focus group interview with CWP coordinators (18/09/2014).
117. Ibid.
118. Focus group interviews with CWP coordinators (10/04/2014).

contribute to social cohesion in the community beyond the CWP participants, as well. The CWP participants are seen as an invaluable resource, especially in communities where people lack access to basic social and welfare services. They link people with such services, including making referrals to Home Affairs offices to obtain identification documents and to the Department of Social Development to obtain social grants.

According to one interviewee, the CWP work of assisting the elderly and the sick sometimes motivates community members who are not part of the CWP to also assist these poor households. The CWP appears to be setting precedents of solidarity that become norms, or perhaps reawaken preexisting norms.

> *We find that there are children or older people [who are] suffering. We would go and help, and then the neighbours would see that these people are getting assistance, and then they would also come and offer assistance. [These neighbors] would then tell us: we are helping in bathing her. So the community starts understanding that there are people who are suffering and that, as the community as a whole, we have to support each other.*[119]

14. Evidence Supporting an Unbounded Worldview

Very likely, the creativity of CWP participants at Orange Farm can be linked with the worldview infusing the Seriti Institute at that time, and the television show *Kwanda*[120] and organization workshop methodology it illustrated, as well as with streams of practice going back to the 1970s promoting the message that people learn when they have freedom and responsibility. It seems unlikely that a top-down approach planned in a distant office could have, for instance, produced the Gateway drama *Ke Moja* (I'm Fine without Crime) or Gateway itself. The endless variety of projects, initiatives and alliances we see at the CWP in Orange Farm gives meaning to the word 'unbounded'.

What we see happening with the CWP in Orange Farm also gives meaning to the phrase 'alignment across sectors':

---

119. Follow-up focus group interview with CWP coordinators (18/09/2014).

120. *Kwanda* was a reality-TV show, the world's first community makeover show. Its engine was the organization workshop methodology through Seriti.

> *We work with the department of agriculture, correctional services, safety and security, and SAPS [South African Police Service]. We also have a good relationship with the department of health, governance, sports, arts and culture. We have good relations with [the department] of environment. We work with all entities—for example, your Johannesburg Water regarding water leakage problems. We work with Pikitup [Johannesburg's waste management provider].*[121]

To this list one might add alignment with the private for-profit business sector, an example being Standard Bank's donation of bursaries for students at the Skills Centre with which the CWP is associated.

The functions of the CWP in Orange Farm also provide further evidence (if, at this point in the history of psychology, more were needed[122]) that institutions premised on the myth of *Homo economicus* overlook enormous reservoirs of human motivation. Malose Langa, who did the field work utilized in this chapter, interacting with CWP participants over a period of eight months, says, 'It was evident that the participants were highly happy to work in the CWP. Their happiness may be attributed to the fact that they clearly understood that the CWP was working for the good of the community. It seems the CWP leadership/management in Orange Farm was able to instil this mentality amongst the CWP participants.'

It also seems that the Orange Farm CWP leadership is highly invested in seeing the CWP create other, better opportunities for the participants. This spirit of commitment is also evident among CWP participants. Some were working almost every day and on weekends, including public holidays, although paid for only two days a week. In the interviews many emphasized the importance of having passion for the CWP. It is the participants' passion for the work that makes the CWP in Orange Farm unique.

> *We were here every day. With gardening you can never miss a day. With CWP we were working on alternating days—but then we ended up working every day. And you must remember that we do not get paid for those days, but we are happy to work every day.*[123]

---

121. Focus group interviews with CWP coordinators (10/04/2014).
122. Some of the evidence from psychology and the physiology of the brain is reported in Ian McGilchrist, *The Master and His Emissary* (New Haven, CT: Yale University Press, 2010).
123. Focus group interview with vegetable garden members (27/05/2014).

We have passion for this thing [CWP]. We work Monday to Monday. Weekends do not matter. But then sometimes we do go to church to pray God to bless us.[124]

At CWP we did agriculture out of passion, because everyone has a garden at home. . . . Even when we finished working at CWP at 14:00, we would go to places like Poortjie and help people. We were accompanying the Department of Agriculture. We are always there to assist. We did not expect to get paid. It is just our passion that we want to see our community transformed.[125]

So with CWP we would work eight days in a month, from 8:00 to 14:00. So we realized that it was useless that we'd knock off at 14:00 and you are just going to sit in the location [township] doing nothing. [So] we would work the whole day without eating anything. We had passion.[126]

15. Three Cheers for the Cheerfully Deluded!

A compassionate realist acknowledges the delusions present in the participants' dialogues about the CWP at Orange Farm: Delusions about how many jobs there are. (*Many people are excited about the new mall. People are thinking about job opportunities.*) Delusions about public employment being a temporary stopgap until participants find work and exit. (*We do not want to see a participant remaining a CWP participant—we want them to exit the programme and open space for other needy people to benefit from it.*) Delusions about the power of education and training to guarantee employment. (*Most of them are saying, why you don't take us to school to learn things like welding and plumbing? If I could do such a thing and get a certificate I would be fine.*) And so on.

But delusions often have positive social functions. People whose self-esteem is so high that they overestimate the probability of their success are likely to become optimists. Complete optimists are people who, when in a single day they fail an examination, are dismissed from their employment,

---

124. Ibid.
125. Ibid.
126. Ibid.

and are dumped by their lover, hit the books to study for the next exam that very night. The next day, they are pounding the sidewalks with a CV in their hand, a smile on their face, and their shoes nicely shined. The next evening, they are flirting on Facebook.[127]

People whose self-esteem is so low that their outlook on the likelihood of getting a good job is close to the truth sink into pessimism. They drain the emotional energy of their friends. They swell the ranks of the whiners, the depressed, the alcoholics, the addicts, the delinquents. Pessimists may have truth on their side, but there is little else in their favour.

The CWP in Orange Farm is different things for different people. For the enthusiastic youth, the CWP is *perceived as* a pathway to a career. For the many rejected by the labour market, the CWP means dignity at last. Unlike many other public employment programmes, the CWP provides support for participants as long as they need it. It becomes a way of life for participants who find joy in service. However, for many men, the CWP is not an attractive option because it pays less than they need to get by. Men sometimes join, participate for a while, and then drop out.

Given a world where, year by year, there is a growing precariat[128] whose members, even if well educated and having technical skills, never achieve steady employment, and if they do have steady employment are usually poorly paid,[129] the CWP at Orange Farm addresses two crying needs: (1) to create soft landings for the many enthusiastic youth who will inevitably be disappointed, and (2) to raise wages—both in public employment programmes and for the poorly paid in general. The two are connected. As we saw in the chapters on India and Sweden, public employment guarantees provide a floor under private-sector wages.

This chapter's story about the realities of life on the south side of Johannesburg could be, with variations, a story about the south side of Chicago, the south side of Mexico City, the south side of Cairo, the south side of Mumbai and many other places. In spring 1972, Michel Foucault participated in a panel discussion on life in the public housing projects in the *banlieues* of Paris, during which he described the global trend in which the

---

127. This literary image of the optimist is suggested by the cheerfulness of the young people at Orange Farm who treat the CWP as an opportunity to start on the path of success. Empirical studies tend to show that optimism rewards the optimist only when it is moderate. See, for example, M. Puri and D. T. Robinson, 'Optimism and Economic Choice', *Journal of Financial Economics*, vol. 86, no. 1 (2007), pp. 71–99.

128. Guy Standing, *The Precariat* (London: Bloomsbury Academic, 2011).

129. Guy Standing, 'Economic Insecurity and Global Casualisation', *Social Indicators Research*, vol. 88 (2008), pp. 15–30.

plebeians increasingly outnumber the proletariat.[130] The proletariat are the workers with steady jobs. The plebeians are the excluded. Intelligent policy makers will not waste time imagining a future in which private for-profit employers offer good jobs to every person who needs one. They will accept the reality that in the future there will be dispossessed millions living on transfer payments or worse, somehow subsisting without them.

But there is another reality that is also part of the world as it is. There are millions of optimists who *believe* they can get a good job or successfully run a business of their own. They want that. Their positive attitudes are a big plus for society. If, in the coming years, they are regularly frustrated, many will defect to pessimism, adding to the number of people with bad attitudes that we already have.

Creative, outside-the-box solutions exist that combine social support with private enterprise. One of them is the City of Johannesburg's urban agriculture programme. Discrete subsidies make it possible for minientrepreneurs to enjoy the dignity of earning their own living. Rosario, Argentina, has gone even further than Johannesburg.[131] In Rosario every child development centre[132]—a combination kindergarten, community centre, and drop-in study hall for older children—has an agricultural advisor. Families whose children attend the centre are advised on what food they can produce, even if it is only rabbits kept in a small enclosure and fed on kitchen scraps. Private and public entities lend land for free and give free courses on everything from how to comply with sanitation laws to how to cultivate worms in compost. Free advertising touts the health benefits of the urban farmers' organic products. They get free stalls in the municipal marketplaces. It is their business, but community support makes it possible.

So instead of telling the deluded optimists that their dreams are likely to fail, let's change the world so more of their dreams can come true. Urban agriculture in both Johannesburg and Rosario represents a principle that can be widely amplified: the optimists' belief that they can make it on their own can be gently brought into synch with economic reality through discrete subsidies. What is not possible in pure markets is possible in impure markets. Public policies and public sympathy can rescue not only the bodies of the poor but also their dignity.

---

130. Michel Foucault et al., Table Ronde in *Esprit* for April-May 1972, pp. 678–703. Reprinted in Michel Foucault, *Dits et ecrits* (Paris: Gallimard, 1994), pp. 316–339.

131. Howard Richards, *Solidaridad, participacion, transparencia: Conversaciones sobre el socialismo en Rosario, Argentina* (Rosario: Fundacion Estevez Boero, 2008).

132. *Centro Crecer.*

16. A Comparison with Asset-Based Community Development

Asset-Based Community Development (ABCD), which has become the method of choice for community development worldwide, began in a black church in inner-city Chicago—a setting where, in the considered opinion of investors, there was little profit to be made. The congregation faced a choice: close the church and move or come up with other ways to make a living. They had no employers offering them steady work at good wages. They had no capital they could invest to live off the interest and dividends. They asked themselves: 'What *do* we have?' Answering their own question gave birth to community mapping.[133]

In one of the many versions of ABCD's use of community mapping today, in the first phase people gather in a room and share information about their individual gifts. Guided by a facilitator, each person writes each of his or her gifts on a card—for example, teaching little kids or caring for the elderly or baking or carpentry or appliance repair. The cards are pinned or taped to the walls. Then people walk around the room reading the cards, learning things they never knew before about their neighbours. They can rearrange the cards, putting one asset (say, an unused lot owned by a hospital) next to another that complements it (say, people with green thumbs living in the upper stories of apartment buildings). This is one way to start brainstorming on how to combine existing assets to create solutions that work. ABCD makes it a special point to bring out and affirm everyone's gifts—for instance, the gifts of the elderly man who has a drinking problem but can still put a roof on a building and of the paraplegic woman in a wheelchair who is skilled at bookkeeping.

This inventory of individual skills is followed by an inventory of people's less formal associations (like people who come together to play rugby) and then their connections with more formal organizations, such as businesses, schools, libraries, parks, hospitals and police and fire stations.

Community mapping demonstrates that there are other ways to mobilize resources to meet needs besides persuading entrepreneurs[134] that investing in a given location will yield a surplus. Other approaches include indigenous

---

133. A classic guide to community mapping is Jody Kretzman and John McKnight, *Building Communities from the Inside Out: A Path Toward Finding and Mobilizing a Community's Assets* (Evanston, IL: Institute for Policy Research,1993).

134. Following Keynes, we sometimes use the word 'entrepreneur' generically to include both the investors who put up the money and the Schumpeterian organizer who combines factors of production to create an enterprise.

traditions now no longer practiced, as well as future social innovations that have not yet been invented.

John McKnight, one of the founders of the ABCD approach, never lets us forget another key point: the community development approach has value because *people need community*. Even if people are efficiently fed, clothed, housed and cured of their diseases by formal organizations, if there is no community, they will always carry a community-shaped emptiness in their hearts.

The CWP's approach to community development includes some elements borrowed from ABCD. Whenever the CWP does community development, its lodestar principle is to maximize the potential the community already has. Once it is realized that poor communities are not bottomless pits of unmet needs but are owners of major assets, using public employment to catalyse community development is seen as a brilliant idea. It is also an intelligent approach for a government that is deeply in debt and at the same time striving to address a sea of troubles.

For example, consider the gifts of the ex-offenders who formed Gateway. They had the knowledge and skills to show youth that the straight path is better than the crooked path, through drama and poetry. They gave to the common good many more hours than they were paid for.

The CWP, together with the South African government's Expanded Public Works Program[135] that it is officially part of, represents a breakthrough, in that it is the first instance of community development associated with a massive programme intended to grow into an employment guarantee for a whole nation. As Kate Philip emphasized in the deliberations that led to the launching of the CWP (described in chapter 5), it was necessary to run anti-poverty programmes of a magnitude matching that of South Africa's poverty. The CWP seeks to combine national funding with grassroots control. It was conceived as a programme large enough to have a major impact but still using a human-scale, neighbourhood-by-neighbourhood approach like that of John McKnight and his colleagues in the United States.

As we prepare for the coming era of the robots and adjust to the robots that have already arrived, similar questions become more crucial. On one hand, there is the question of how to get the work on the ground right—how to build communities that work as well as or better than those at

---

135. Although they are not discussed in this book, some parts of the EPWP that are outside the CWP and administered by the Ministry of Public Works engage in community development similar to that in the CWP.

Bokfontein and Orange Farm, how to enhance life-worlds. The myriad life-worlds—primary groups and communities—that dot the planet are, according to Jürgen Habermas and probably everybody who has thought about the subject, the places where people find meaning. They provide the microenvironments where moral values and (for the fortunate) love and happiness flourish. Sometimes the life-worlds are called primary groups; sometimes they are called communities. We want the solution to providing for the basic needs of the majority, who are expected to become redundant in the labour market, to enhance life-worlds. We do not want what McKnight calls counterfeit community or what George Orwell called Big Brother.

On the other hand, there will be no solution at all, not even a reprehensible one, if there is no way to pay for it. As we write this, nations around the world are scrambling to keep their social programmes funded as growth slows and public deficits mount. The CWP itself is threatened by budget cuts made 'inevitable' by 'necessity'. Cost containment is the buzz in South Africa's Union Buildings. A growing minority of intellectual and political leaders are calling into question the concepts that frame the scramble and articulate the buzz, such as debt and GDP and growth. Debt relief is thinkable and sometimes doable.[136] Bolivia and Ecuador, in their new constitutions, have officially replaced 'GDP' with *buen vivir*. Bhutan has replaced 'GDP' with 'gross national happiness'.[137] In Leipzig, thousands of Europeans have gathered to advocate degrowth.[138]

In the final two chapters of this book, we somewhat unwillingly return to our dialogue with the dominant discourse. It is still dominant. New realities have not yet hammered a new logic into the minds of women and men. The reactions of most governments remain trapped in a conceptual box where austerity to please creditors competes with stimulus to please investors. Governability continues to mean government *by* capital, not *of* capital. Reconsidering some currently dominant concepts from various historical and logical perspectives, we will try to contribute, even if only by raising questions, to discussions of more sensible approaches to public-private cooperation, to alignment for the common good, to governing growth and globalization and to paying for social programmes.

---

136. Bartholomew K. Amah, *The Heavily Indebted Poor Country Initiative* (London: Institute of Economic Affairs, 2001).

137. What is Gross National Happiness? (www.gnhbhutan.org/about/).

138. www.leipzig.degrowth.org.

CHAPTER TEN

The Fiscal Crisis of the State as a Philosophical Problem: Part One

OVERVIEW OF THE CHAPTER

1. On the Title of the Chapter
2. On the Concept of Surplus
3. The Conventional Economic View: Alberto Arenas, Minister of Finance, Republic of Chile
4. On the Philosophy of Social Science
5. The State's Fiscal Crisis Defeats the CWP: Marissa Moore, National Treasury, Republic of South Africa
6. A Conversation between Unbounded Organization and Modern Money Theory
7. The Constraints of Fiscal Space: Peter Heller, Senior Economist, International Monetary Fund
8. Raising the Social Status of Use Value

1. On the Title of the Chapter

As the phrase 'the fiscal crisis of the state' in the title indicates, our point of departure for this and the following chapter is certain presenting symptoms of the state's inability to fund its obligations. At this point in the book, the reader knows, or at least suspects, that we will identify the underlying generative causes of these presenting symptoms as two Staggering Facts—a chronic weakness of demand and a chronic weakness of the inducement to invest. We allege that these symptoms are consequences of the modern world's basic social structure, which sets in stone too much separation and not enough cohesion: the *séparation marchande*. The reader already knows that we do not advocate or regard as possible a post-modern social structure completely different from the one now dominant, while we do advocate and regard as necessary sharing the surplus along with more community and less economy.

Having examined in earlier chapters the deep cause (the social structure) of these presenting symptoms, in this chapter we first look at the frustrations of South Africa's Community Work Programme (CWP), whose proximate cause is the fiscal crisis of the state. From there we add to what has been said in earlier chapters about the social and historical construction of today's dominant system, going into more detail about why and how to change it.

Joseph Schumpeter's prediction in his 1918 essay *Die Krise des Steuerstaats* is now coming true. This famous essay anticipated the letter of resignation he wrote shortly afterwards as Minister of Finance of Austria. Its central point is that the constitutions of modern republics and the modern concept of rule of law were designed for self-regulating market economies. They presuppose caretaker states whose main functions are protecting property rights (as John Locke said[1]) and enforcing contracts (as Adam Smith emphasized). Schumpeter anticipated, on the basis of general principles, a point made on the basis of empirical case studies in *The Dilemmas of Social Democracies*:[2] social democracy is incompatible with the basic cultural structure of the modern world. Specifically, a state that relies on taxes as its only or main source of income and at the same time assumes responsibility for putting into practice the latter two of the eighteenth-century ideals *liberté, egalité, fraternité* is unsustainable. To repeat, that state has set in stone too much separation and not enough cohesion.

We have had a lot to say about the successes of the CWP: it shows that community resources, including the available time and the hunger for a meaningful life of the participants, can be combined with discreet and efficient sharing of surplus. Together, grassroots community building and elite surplus sharing can satisfy physical needs, such as planting trees to help to reverse the physical disaster of global warming. It can satisfy psychological needs, such as building self-esteem. If humanity succeeds in changing the course of history, then our descendants will be able to see the CWP in retrospect as an early harbinger of better things to come. But in this and the following chapter we focus on the cause and possible cure of the CWP's failure. The programme was supposed to be the beginning of a true employment guarantee, providing decent work at decent pay for all South Africans who needed it. It wasn't. It was supposed to move from

---

1. 'Government has no other end, but the preservation of property.' John Locke, *The Second Treatise of Civil Government* (Indianapolis, IN: Hackett Publishing, 1980 (first edition 1690)), ch. 7, section 94, p. 51.

2. Joanna Swanger and Howard Richards, *The Dilemmas of Social Democracies* (Lanham, MD: Lexington, 2006).

impossible to possible the words of the Freedom Charter, 'There shall be work and security!' as well as Article 23 of the Universal Declaration of Human Rights (the right to employment) and Article 27 of the Constitution of the Republic of South Africa (social security). It did not.

In official parlance, the reason why the CWP could not become a true employment guarantee, while providing more dignity and getting more useful work done than a universal basic income, was 'fiscal constraints'. It was the gap between the state's obligations and the state's resources. It was the impossibility of moving surplus from where it was not needed to where it was needed. The norms of liberal culture (ethical and legal) overrule a realist definition of 'fiscal constraint' in terms of the limited quantities of real goods and services available for sale,[3] instead defining it in terms of a bogus moral rectitude and a bogus natural law.[4]

Our calling the fiscal crisis of the state a 'philosophical' problem in the title might appear to repeat the mistakes of Fritjof Capra and Charlene Spretnak—to name two of the many who have confused 'philosophical' paradigm shifts, at the level of ideas, with political revolutions, at the level of material reality. It might appear that Capra and Spretnak, in *Green Politics*, propose one impractical worldview, while we propose another. They write: 'The major problems of our time are simply different facets of a single crisis. They are systemic problems, which means they are closely interconnected and interdependent. They cannot be understood through the fragmented approaches pursued by academic disciplines and government agencies. Rather than solving any of our difficulties, such approaches merely shift them around in the complex web of social and ecological relations. Resolution can be found only if the structure of the web itself is changed, and this will involve profound transformations of social and political institutions.'[5]

Capra analyses the deep structures of the mechanical thinking that affects every aspect of our lives, while Spretnak analyses the deep structures of the patriarchal thinking that affects every aspect of our lives. Both analyse the pervasive consequences of seeing nature as a set of resources to exploit for profit. Their synthesis advocates an 'ecological, holistic, and feminist

---

3. For a realist definition of fiscal constraint see William Mitchell, L. Randall Wray and Martin Watts, *Macroeconomics* (London: Red Globe, 2019), Kindle edition, position 7929.

4. On what is bogus in dysfunctional versions of natural law see Hans Kelsen, 'The Natural Law Tradition Before the Tribunal of Science', *The Western Political Quarterly*, vol. 2 (1949), pp. 481–513.

5. Fritjof Capra and Charlene Spretnak, *Green Politics* (New York: E. P. Dutton, 1984), p. xix.

movement that transcends the old political framework of left versus right. It emphasizes interconnectedness and interdependence of all phenomena, as well as the embeddedness of individuals and societies in the cyclical processes of nature. It addresses the unjust and destructive dynamics of patriarchy. It calls for social responsibility and a sound economic system, one that is ecological, decentralized, equitable, and comprised of flexible institutions.'[6]

Nevertheless, when green parties have come to power, for example, in the red-green coalition that ruled Germany from 1998 to 2005, the central issues generated by SF1 and SF2—namely, economic growth, employment, attracting investment, discouraging disinvestment, discouraging capital flight, coping with the dangerous classes marginal to the economy and coping with budget deficits—did not change. In Germany, the greens succeeded in shelving nuclear power, funding research on alternative energy, and placing more women in leadership roles. Materially, economic growth slowed to 2 percent in 2002 and turned negative in 2003, while unemployment soared above 10 percent. In 2005 the red-green coalition was voted out and the long reign of Angela Merkel began.

When we call the fiscal crisis of the state a philosophical problem, we could be accused of idealism along with Capra and Spretnak. That is, it *could* be said that philosophy is about ideas while the problems in question are material; therefore, their solutions must be material, not philosophical. Sure, this could be said. But we recommend saying instead: Ideas are material. They have causal powers. They are among the cultural forces that constitute the rights and duties defining who can do what (as in Porpora's theory of social structure).[7] Therefore, we do not mind being put in the same bag with Capra and Spretnak. Their analyses were incomplete; we propose to complete them. Replacing liberal institutions with green solidarity inevitably requires what Paulo Freire called cultural action, embedded in and part of material realities.[8] Today's material economic reality has been socially and historically constructed; we are happy to join many others who are deconstructing and reconstructing it.

---

6. Ibid., pp. xix–xx.

7. Douglas Porpora, 'Cultural Rules and Material Relations', *Sociological Theory*, vol. 11 (1993), pp. 212–229; and Douglas Porpora, *Reconstructing Sociology* (Cambridge, UK: Cambridge University Press, 2016). See also Roy Bhaskar, *The Possibility of Naturalism*, 4th ed. (London: Routledge, 2014).

8. Howard Richards, *Letters from Quebec* (San Francisco: International Scholars Press, 1995); John Dewey, *The Quest for Certainty* (New York: Putnam, 1929).

2. On the Concept of Surplus

A key aspect of unbounded organization and moral realism[9] is sharing surplus. What is surplus? In this section, we give a simple answer. Along with its subsequent nuances that follow, this answer frames our contributions to answering the practical question: How are dignified livelihoods for all going to be paid for? It revisits the issues John Kenneth Galbraith called private wealth and public squalor. How did humanity get itself trapped in a box where needs are separate from resources, while governments—officially and legally charged to make social rights real—are virtually powerless to move wealth to where it is needed even when they want to? Our historical enquiries into how the fiscal crisis of the state arose support an ethical (neither totalitarian nor libertarian) solution: Give governments less to do and more resources to do it with. Assign the task of making social rights real to *alignments across sectors,* to everybody. End the fiscal crisis of the state by multiplying its sources of income.

The simple answer to the question about surplus is this: your surplus is what you have and do not need. So also, an organization's surplus is what it has and does not need. The concept of surplus is, accordingly, a comment on how the word 'need' functions in language. It functions to prescribe what *should* be done.[10] That needs *should* be met is part of the meaning of 'need'.

Need and surplus are both moral concepts. They are also essentially contested concepts.[11] Conversations about them, like conversations about right and wrong or about good and bad, are never ending. Descartes was wrong when he complained, in his *Discourse on Method*, that before he came along to put philosophy on a firm foundation leading to universal and eternal knowledge, philosophers had wasted century after century discussing virtue and vice without coming to any definite conclusions. Socrates was right to affirm that even when dialogues on ethical issues reach no definite conclusions, we are better persons for having engaged in them.

---

9. Howard Richards, 'Moral and Ethical Realism', *Journal of Critical Realism*, vol. 18 (2019), pp. 385–392.

10. That a person's needs make moral claims on other people is denied by libertarians like Robert Nozick. See Robert Nozick (1973), 'Distributive Justice', *Philosophy and Public Affairs*, vol. 3, pp. 45–126. On his view, when liberty and meeting needs conflict, liberty trumps need. On our view his concept of liberty is dysfunctional.

11. W. B. Gallie, 'Essentially Contested Concepts', *Proceedings of the Aristotelian Society*, n.s., vol. 56 (1956), pp. 167–198. For Gallie, a concept can be contested only if there is at least one uncontested case where its meaning is agreed on by the contesting parties. I believe that medicine provides uncontested cases of need, which helps to make discussions about whether some X is or is not a need meaningful.

Several clusters of ideas from economics and accounting are useful when one is trying to make responsible decisions about what is surplus and how to use surplus to meet needs. These include theories of rent, profit (including excess profit and normal profit), surplus value, earnings, consumer surplus, producer surplus, opportunity cost, internal rate of return and return on investment (ROI). Several clusters of ideas from medicine, psychology, ecology and other fields can be useful also. Some of these ideas can be quantified in standard ways such that two professionals making the same calculations will get the same results. Nevertheless, deciding how to use surplus is ultimately a moral decision, in the sense that customary norms often prescribe how to do it, and also in the sense that it is often a human choice for which no algorithm can define the right answer. It follows, I believe, that better decisions about what is surplus and how to use it flow from improvements in both institutions and moral education. Improving the rules of the game without improving the players is a catastrophic oversight because, as Aristotle taught, a well-educated person finds pleasure in virtue while a poorly educated person finds pleasure in vice.[12] As Schumpeter remarked, institutions are like battleships: they must be properly constructed *and* properly staffed.

The moral education we have in mind supports ethnic identities and cultural codes that already exist, even as it calls attention to the physical facts by which a culture is judged, whatever may be the Habermasian or Rawlsian consensus of speakers and choosers.[13] We are confident, for example, that facilitating conversations about Kohlbergian moral dilemmas, or facilitating role playing where people act out perspectives that are not their own, or organizing group activities inspired by the intellectual tradition of Lev Vygotsky's activity theory will lead toward functional syntheses of solidarity and freedom. Tendencies toward bonding, sharing and caring, and respecting the dignity and autonomy of other people are hard-wired into our biology.[14] The morality needed today to achieve the survival and flourishing of our species and the biosphere will likely emerge from existing best practices in moral education. Humiliating people by challenging their beliefs with authoritarian pedagogies can and should be avoided.

'Power', as opposed to education, echoes the talk of physicists and

---

12. Aristotle, *Nichomachean Ethics*, bk. 2.
13. Richards, 'Moral and Ethical Realism'.
14. A sample of the vast literature supporting this point is Sam Bowles and Herbert Gintis (eds.), *A Cooperative Species* (Princeton, NJ: Princeton University Press, 2011).

engineers and therefore lends itself in the social sciences to being palmed off as a more suitable object of scientific study than morals or ethics. But in social reality, power is normally acquired by winning games that have *rules*. And as society is at present organized, the games have *losers*. Servant leadership to build win-win societies is about the responsible use of power.[15] One of the valid ways to talk about social structure is to say that it is constituted by the morals (or ethics) that define human relationships. They *cause*, for example, the historical emergence of today's global economy[16] and, for another example, the fiscal crisis of the state.[17] And one of the valid ways to talk about social change is to say that it is about education more than it is about force.

For an example of rules and ethics as causes of the evolution of social power, in their classic work *The Modern Corporation and Private Property*, Adolf Berle and Gardiner Means show several ways that control of large corporations tends to pass from shareholders to management, or else to one or a few shareholders identified with management. But control is not naked. It comes clothed in reasons. Management can argue, and often does argue, that retained earnings are *needed*—that it is in the best interest of all concerned not to make a large payout to the nominal owners of the business but rather to invest in acquiring another firm, or in developing a new line of products, or in entering a new market, or some other use of that money.[18] In general, a surplus available to meet needs elsewhere can be decreased by arguments for increased needs nearby. So also, that surplus can be increased by arguments alleging the gravity of needs elsewhere (like reversing global warming) and shrinking needs (like executive compensation) that are nearby. Similar issues arise regarding how much of corporate earnings should be paid as taxes.

When the accounting department of an organization makes a quarterly or annual report, choices must be made concerning what to do with available funds. Should bank debt be paid down? Should executive salaries

---

15. Robert Greenleaf, *Servant Leadership* (New York: Paulist Press, 2002).

16. Howard Richards, *Understanding the Global Economy* (Santa Barbara, CA: Peace Education Books, 2004). There is a PDF digital version online.

17. We think that focussing on the basic ethics of modernity is a valid approach to reading *The Legitimation Crisis* and other early works of Habermas—for example, his point that the market is the primary institution and the state is secondary. Habermas appears to have thought so too, since many of his later works focus on ethics as the place to look for solutions to the systemic problems studied in his early works.

18. Adolf Berle and Gardiner Means, *The Modern Corporation and Private Property* (New York: Macmillan, 1933).

be raised—or lowered? Should wages be raised? Should money be spent to make technology greener (as Coca-Cola spent money to make its vending machines hydrofluorocarbon free)? Should money be spent on social responsibility projects (like Anglo American Corporation's contributions to fighting HIV/AIDS)? The list of questions is in principle endless because money is a general medium of exchange that can be spent in endless ways. All of these questions begin with 'should'.[19] All of them require deliberation and choice. Having served as legal counsel to several businesses, I can testify that even before the accounting department makes its report, choices requiring ethical deliberation and judgment (possibly inviting immoral behaviour) are made concerning how to crunch the numbers and how to present them.

The claim that questions about what is surplus and what to do with surplus are ethical questions implies that a strong ethical case can frequently be made for more than one answer. It implies that education should prepare people to cope with moral dilemmas. It also implies that appropriating surplus for oneself with no ethical justification whatsoever is wrong. Andrew Sayer gives many examples of people who, having the power to do so, take the money for themselves simply 'because they can'.[20] Similar points could be made about family budgets, public budgets and the money in the wallet or bank account of a lone individual.

In all these cases, the simple answer to the question, 'What is surplus?' says surplus is what we do not need and should share. This simple definition serves as a reminder that all of us descendants of Mitochondrial Eve[21] are, as Martin Luther King Jr. put it, members of one human family living in one world house.[22] "Create surplus! Share it!" gives us a principle, although not an algorithm, for deciding what to do day by day until we breathe our last breath.

Following this simple answer, in the subsequent sections and chapter of this book we offer a more complex answer in an attempt to achieve what the historian of science Gaston Bachelard called a *rupture épistémologique*.[23] Bachelard showed that science advances on crucial fronts at key moments by

---

19. They could of course be rephrased to avoid using 'should'. My suggestion is that using 'should' accurately represents what is at stake.

20. Andrew Sayer, Why *We Cannot Afford the Rich* (Bristol: Policy Press, 2015).

21. Mitochondrial Eve is a name given to the common female ancestor of all humans now alive, thought to have lived in Africa more than 180,000 years ago.

22. Martin Luther King Jr., *Where Do We Go from Here: Chaos or Community?* (Boston: Beacon Press, 1967).

23. Gaston Bachelard, *Le nouvel esprit scientifique* (Paris: Presses Universitaires de France, 1937).

waging what Antonio Gramsci might call a war of position against deeply entrenched common sense and its pseudo-scientific rationalizations. The epistemological rupture we propose here breaks with many common sets of assumptions in many fields. It breaks with the liberal worldview that is now so firmly established on such shaky eighteenth-century premises, much as Darwin's work broke with the assumption that the varieties of plants and animals were created with fixed essences, which was then so firmly established on shaky ancient premises.

Once people were persuaded that unbounded organization and moral realism are the way to go, a delicate balancing act would then follow. Those persuaded would (as moral realists) concur with Aristotle that it is not wise to change too many laws (*nomoi*) too often, because laws draw strength from the force of habit.[24] Undermining the habit of obeying the rules makes the consequences of actions less predictable. At the same time, our soulmates would (as unbounded organizers) reform social structures, including the basic rules, in order to adjust culture to its physical functions. Given humanity's dire straits, there is not a moment to lose. At the same time, patience is required to instill immunity to backsliding. Even Karl Popper, famous for the canonical phrase 'open society', backslid.[25]

The following considerations are not an argument that moves from premise to conclusion. They are presented using a rhetorical strategy designed to reinforce the unbounded and realistic attitudes that we believe to be indispensable. Most of them are situated in specific historical times and places. While mostly fictitious and imagined, they are based on published reports and articles. This scenario format saves words by telegraphing tacit assumptions of the speakers. For example, when (in the next chapter) the scene is an interview with Jean-Baptiste Say in Paris in 1803, the reader knows immediately what historical context frames the words spoken.

3. The Conventional Economic View: Alberto Arenas, Minister of Finance, Republic of Chile

We begin our journey with a visit to Santiago, Chile, and a summary of a report by Alberto Arenas, Chile's minister of finance, to the general public on how well the economy was doing in early 2015. Choosing this scene

---

24. Aristotle, *Politics*, bk. 2.
25. Howard Richards and Joanna Swanger, *Dilemmas of Social Democracies* (Lanham, MD: Rowman and Littlefield, 2006), ch. 9.

as representative of conventional economic thinking is not arbitrary. It follows our conversations with several Chilean civil servants who administer anti-poverty programmes. They said, in so many words, that to pay for expanding social programmes it would be necessary to rekindle Chile's sputtering growth.[26] From such a viewpoint the minister of finance reported to the public on what it most needed to know: the prospects for reaccelerating Chile's decelerating economy.

Chile is among the many countries similar to South Africa where slow growth is perceived as clouding the future of social programmes. Worldwide we see what might be called a Bachelet/Piketty paradox. To explain: In 2011, the International Labour Office, supported by the World Health Organization, published the report of a commission chaired by Michelle Bachelet, a former president of Chile, detailing worldwide efforts to establish social safety nets, including public employment programmes like India's NREGA and South Africa's EPWP and CWP.[27] The report explicitly assumes that such programmes are accompanied by efforts to stimulate economic growth, since in the report, the estimated cost of a given social programme is expressed as a percentage of GDP—for example, Rwanda could fund a universal old age pension at a cost between 0.5 percent and 1 percent of its GDP.[28] Two years later, in 2013, Thomas Piketty published his impressively documented study providing weighty reasons for projecting slow GDP growth throughout the twenty-first century.[29] Hence the apparent paradox: big needs, small resources.

We call this paradox 'apparent' because we believe that sharing surplus and building community—not conventional economic thinking—is the way to go. And because we focus on physical facts—the amazingly productive new green technologies, which, in our opinion, will make it easier for unbounded organization and moral realism to be effectively deployed to

26. For an explicit argument that growth is needed to enable redistribution see Anthony Crosland, *The Conservative Enemy* (London: Schocken Books, 1962), p. 24 and passim.

27. Michelle Bachelet et al., *Social Protection Floor for a Fair and Inclusive Globalization* (Geneva: International Labour Organization, 2011). Bachelet chaired the commission during the interim between her two terms as president of Chile, while she was working for the United Nations (http://ilo.org/global /publications/ilo-bookstore/order-online/books/WCMS_165750/lang--en/index.htm).

28. Ibid., p. 44. The figure for Rwanda presumably refers to what the report calls a 'horizontal' old age pension including every old person at a low amount, like the 80,000-peso [about 150 USD] solidarity pension for every senior Chilean who needs it, promulgated by Bachelet herself, leaving pending the 'vertical' challenge of raising the amount.

29. Thomas Piketty, *Capital in the Twenty-First Century* (Cambridge, MA: Harvard University Press, 2014 (original French edition 2013)).

meet needs in harmony with nature. The problem is not small resources. The problem is small minds.

As minister of finance, Alberto Arenas published in Chile's leading newspaper, *El Mercurio*, on 8 February 2015 a short report on the Chilean economy in 2014 and its prospects for 2015. He disregarded, at least for the moment, the question of how to make social programmes more effective with fewer resources. He also disregarded the question how to capture more of the social surplus (however generated and however measured) to transfer it to meeting social needs. He devoted himself entirely to the question of how to accelerate Chile's decelerating growth.[30]

Arenas reported that the Chilean economy decelerated more than expected in 2014, and that Latin America as a whole turned in a poor performance (a *bajo desempeño*). But December 2014 saw a GDP upsurge to a rate of 2.9 percent growth, which lifted GDP growth for the year to 1.8 percent.

Much of the relative dynamism of the last three months of 2014 was due to government spending. (Notice that all the key terms, such as dynamism, spending, decelerated, performance, growth, accelerate, etc., are different ways to talk about how much buying and selling is happening.). Public buying grew 10 percent in the last trimester, completing 2014 with a total 6.5 percent higher than the previous year. The money spent on capital investments (infrastructure), separate from public buying, showed a rate of increase of 22.7 percent for the last three months and 7.4 percent for 2014 as a whole.

The minister encouraged his fellow citizens to look on the bright side. There was more than capital investments by the public sector to justify projecting a better year in 2015. In view of the fall in the price of copper, Chile's largest export, Chile was reassigning resources to selling other products in world markets. This was favoured by a fall of 15 percent in the value of the Chilean peso against the dollar. That made Chilean exports more competitive in manufacturing and in agriculture.

The unemployment variable remained low, which meant that Chileans could expect consumer purchases to recover their dynamism. Recovery

---

30. Arenas cites figures from Chile's own measure of growth, the IMACEC (*Indicador Mensual de Actividad Economica en Chile*), calculated monthly. It is harmonized with GDP and we treat it as equivalent to GDP. See the methodological note, economic study 48 on the web page of the Chilean Central Bank. Let nothing in these pages be taken as implying that Arenas did not do a good job as finance minister. It must be mentioned that he went to jail four times for protesting the Pinochet dictatorship and that he spearheaded a pension reform that made a minimal solidarity pension universal in Chile.

would be aided by another falling variable: lower energy costs due to a fall in the price of oil. Since Chile imports 95 percent of its fuels, a fall in energy costs would translate directly into more money in the pockets of Chilean consumers, which would contribute to stronger sales.

Inflation remained low, which made it possible for the Central Bank to continue its low interest rate policy, which in turn favoured investment. The minister concluded that to project a good year in 2015, Chileans must not let up (*aflojar*, get lazy) in private or public investment. And 'above all [they] must nurture confidence, for confidence is the best ally of investment, employment, and consumption'.[31]

The concluding sentence and indeed the whole report evoke familiar dynamics: Production depends on the confidence of investors. Investor confidence depends on the confidence of consumers, which leads them to spend. Their spending tends to be chronically insufficient. Only when all goes well—when consumers spend more and investors invest more—will there be more good jobs for workers and more revenue from taxes for social programmes.

What Alberto Arenas told the Chilean public is the dominant discourse's standard response to deficits and slow growth—which is to redouble efforts to create conditions (confidence) that elicit more growth (more investment and more sales). This often means cutting public budgets while sweetening offers to private investors.

We take the view that this standard way of thinking reflects economic reality largely (but not entirely) as it is. It is a reality built on a social structure (the exchange relation) that makes it virtually inevitable that over time the machine of investment-for-production-for-sale-for-profit (IPSP) takes hold. When the machine slows down (investment and sales slow down), the dominant discourse calls for cranking it up (stimulating more investment and more sales). The market—erstwhile considered by liberal ethics the authorized expression of the sovereign wills of millions of buyers and sellers—decides that it is time for itself, the market sector of the economy, to stop growing or to shrink. But the dominant discourse refuses to accept the market's decision about itself. It prefers to call on the already impoverished government to finance the restoration of the market sector's former large size. Amartya Sen would advise seizing the opportunity to strengthen complementary nonmarket institutions.

---

31. *Y, por sobre todo, tenemos que cuidar las expectativas, que son las mejores aliadas de la inversión, el empleo, y el consumo.*

4. On the Philosophy of Social Science

The story Minister Arenas tells in *El Mercurio* is a story about variables from beginning to end, beginning with the variable GDP and ending with the variables of investment, employment and consumption.[32] Similarly, Sir Isaac Newton's *Principia Mathematica* is a story about force (*vis*) from beginning to end. The impact of an independent variable on a dependent variable in economics is an analogue of a force in mechanics (as in Newton's formula *force = mass X acceleration*).

However, in mechanics, a formula like $f = ma$ yields an exact prediction once friction, intervening variables and measurement error are accounted for. This is both somewhat different from and somewhat the same as correlations and regressions in the social sciences. In the social sciences, there is typically a trend (regression) line recognizably similar to an equation in Newtonian mechanics, but there are more and larger error terms measuring the difference between the observed data points and the trend. The metaphysical[33] assumption in both cases (more plausible in mechanics, more dubious in economics) is that there are, out there in the world, measurable regularities of the form $y = f(x)$ (the dependent variable is a function of the independent variable) waiting for scientists to measure them.

Economists regularly find themselves constructing models to explain data following a pattern: The models are formally rigorous, because the inferences from the numbers going into the numbers coming out are tautologies. The data are mainly social statistics. The social statistics are mainly

---

32. Irving Fisher: 'The economic system contains innumerable variables—quantities of "goods" (physical wealth, property rights, and services), the prices of these goods, and their values (the quantities multiplied by their prices). Changes in any or all of this vast array of variables may be due to many causes. Only in imagination can all these variables remain constant and be kept in equilibrium by the balanced forces of human desires, as manifested through supply and demand.' *The Debt Deflation Theory of Great Depressions* (Important Books, 2012 (1933)), Kindle edition, position 20. This is the first of 49 conclusions stated at the beginning of the book.

33. The metaphysics of positivism that is still with us in many forms today began at positivism's birth in the writings of its founder, Auguste Comte. Comte's crusade was a now-familiar one in the history of philosophy, 'Away with metaphysics!' Immediately after proclaiming the end of metaphysics he declared that its replacement would be science. Science would be built exclusively from observed facts. In the next breath, however, he unwittingly retracted his denunciation of metaphysics by announcing a metaphysical faith of his own: observing the facts would lead to the discovery of the regular laws governing both nature and society. Scientific sociology would provide new and better principles of authority to replace the authority of the monarchy and the church that had been swept away by the French Revolution. Positivism was born being what other metaphysics are: a synthesis of ontology and ethics, declaring what is (law-like regularity) and what ought to be (technocracy).

defined from accounting categories. The numbers are mainly drawn from accountants' source documents. The source documents mainly record sales. The sales are governed by the constitutive rules of markets. Those rules and their detailed ramifications are specified not by mechanics or by physics but by legal and customary norms.

Seated in offices high in buildings and looking at numbers, economists may be only dimly aware of the normative framework of buying and selling going on in the streets below, which is where the numbers come from. Yet they may also be painfully aware of a certain brooding mushiness infecting their models, like that evoked by Ludwig Wittgenstein in his image of a machine whose motions are supposed to be predictable from its diagram but in reality are unpredictable because the machine's parts melt, break and bend.[34]

Drawing on the contemporary movement in the philosophy of science known as critical realism, as well as on John Searle,[35] Charles Taylor,[36] Wittgenstein and Heidegger, we have been taking the constitutive rules of markets as our *Leitfaden* (guide, thread running through the fabric) for understanding capitalism. Adam Smith called these rules *natural liberty*, and Karl Marx compressed them into the *commodity form*, starting with what he called *simple exchange*. Our two Staggering Facts (the dependence of production on capital accumulation, leading to weakness of the inducement to invest; and the chronic insufficiency of effective demand) are generated by those rules.

Instead of starting by assuming that the world out there consists of variables waiting to be measured, our realist alternative starts by assuming culture to be the ecological niche of the human species. The human activities constantly reorganizing the language games of cultures become sources of scientific explanation.[37] We focus on the basic constitutive rules

---

34. Ludwig Wittgenstein, *Philosophical Investigations* (Oxford: Basil Blackwell, 1958), par. 193.

35. John Searle explains constitutive rules in several works, including *The Construction of Social Reality* (London: Penguin Press, 1995).

36. Charles Taylor begins his seminal essay, 'Interpretation and the Sciences of Man', *The Review of Metaphysics*, vol. 25 (1971), pp. 3–51 (often reprinted) by asking how interpretation (Heidegger's *seeing as*) is essential to causal explanation in the human sciences. Later he contrasts the constitutive rules of our 'bargaining society' with those of a traditional Japanese peasant society.

37. These notions can usefully be compared with Anthony Giddens's notions of 'structuration' and 'double hermeneutic'. Anthony Giddens, *The Structure of Society* (Berkeley: University of California Press, 1984). Social systems are produced and reproduced as a result of the activities of situated actors (p. 25). Andy Blunden has connected the generation of social

of the culture organizing the modern world system. This focus makes it easy to understand why the world as it is presently organized makes plenty of resources available for luxury, for unnecessary goods and services, and for harmful activities but does not provide well-paid work for the poor to plant trees to reforest denuded hills.

Friedrich von Hayek made a methodological point similar to ours in his acceptance speech for the Nobel Memorial Prize in Economics in 1974.[38] In his lecture, titled 'The Pretence of Knowledge', he argued that much of what passes for legitimate quantitative research in economics pretends to know things the researchers could not possibly know. He faulted such bogus research for having led to bad policy advice, which in turn has led to inflation. He advocated instead what he called pattern explanations deployed to understand organized complexity. They start with knowledge of the rules of the games that organize economic life.

We agree with von Hayek on this methodological point. We also agree with both Austrian and Chicago schools of neoliberals, that social democracy is incompatible with the rules of the game that organize economic life. But we draw a different conclusion. We propose that the rules of the game themselves should be changed to make the former, social democracy, possible but in an updated and greener version. We also note that although post–World War II European social democracy proved to be unsustainable, it lasted long enough to prove that the principal thesis of von Hayek's most famous book, *The Road to Serfdom* (1944), was false. The British enjoyed their National Health Service and their council housing without the slightest loss of political freedom. There was no infringement of their freedom of speech or of their right to make decisions about issues they disagreed on by the ballot, not the bullet. In their case, as for the Swedes, the Danes and all the other social democracies, the alleged road to serfdom proved imaginary. Today's road to mass unemployment, social chaos and ecological disaster, in contrast, is not imaginary.

---

structure to the activity theory tradition in social psychology pioneered by Lev Vygotsky. Andy Blunden, *Selected Writings on the Semiotics of Modernity* (Kettering, OH: Erythros Press, 2012).

38. Friedrich von Hayek, *The Pretence of Knowledge* (http://www.nobelprize.org/nobel_prizes/economic-sciences/laureates/ 1974/hayek-lecture.html). Such methodological views are also expressed in other works by the same author. They have historical roots in his Austrian liberal tradition, starting with Carl Menger, who learned something from his opponents in his *Methodenstreit* with the German historicists. See Carl Menger, *Investigations into the Methods of the Social Sciences* (New York: New York University Press, 1985 (1883)). Of the three inventors of marginal utility theory—Jevons, Walras and Menger—Menger was the only one who did not dress it up in a deceptively precise mathematical garb.

5. The State's Fiscal Crisis Defeats the CWP: Marissa Moore, National Treasury, Republic of South Africa

Now, finally, we get to the details of how the fiscal crisis of the state defeated the CWP. We explain this phenomenon, and many others, by the causal powers of rules. The scene shifts from the newspaper stands of Santiago de Chile in early February 2015 to the Union Buildings in Pretoria on 12 February 2014, where an appropriations committee of the South African Parliament met to review funding for the CWP.[39] Liberal economic thinking hung heavily in the air of the meeting room. The difficulty of funding the CWP showed up dressed in the laconic phrase 'fiscal constraints'.

The meeting was confusing. We outline the proceedings as they really happened (*wie es eigentlich gewesen war*) as described in the meeting report in order to be faithful to history, but we forgive the reader who skips the details and goes directly to the general principle at the end of this section.

Before the discussion began, there were two PowerPoint presentations. One was by Tozi Faba of the Department of Cooperative Governance and Traditional Affairs (COGTA), which administers the CWP. The other was by Marissa Moore of the National Treasury, which pays for the CWP. Tozi Faba made the following points:

1. In the fiscal year ending 31 March 2013, the CWP provided work for 204,494 participants.
2. Targets for the current year (2013–14), ending March 2014, have already been surpassed, with work provided for 206,166 participants compared with a target of 172,000.
3. The budget for the current year provides for a total cost of 1,592,268.[40]
4. The target for 2014–2015 is 332,500 participants at a cost of 2,257,480.
5. The target for 2015–16 is 487,500 participants at a cost of 2,505,413.
6. The target for 2016–17 is 1,030,000 participants at a cost of 3,710,368.

---

39. Department of Cooperative Governance and National Treasury on funding model for Community Works Program briefing (/pmg.org.za/committee-meeting/16915/). The committee made no decisions.

40. The cost numbers are in thousands of rands. They can be roughly converted to thousands of US dollars by dividing by ten, that is to say by moving the decimal point one space to the left.

In her presentation Marissa Moore almost agreed with Faba's first point, but from there her data and the points she made differed:

1. In the fiscal year ending 31 March 2013, the CWP provided work for 205,494 participants.
2. The estimated number of participants for the current year (2013–14) is 172,000.
3. The current (2013–14) budget is 1,731,326. (This is 139,058 more than COGTA's figure, being adjusted for actual expenditures.)
4. Unlike COGTA, the Treasury looks back at costs in 2010–11, 2011–12 and 2012–13. The year-by-year cost increases were 39%, 107% and 34%.
5. Regarding future years, Ms. Moore does not give cost numbers or target numbers of participants, but says expenditures are expected to grow at an annual rate of 28.9%.
6. Using words without numbers she concludes: 'Fiscal constraints require CWP to meet employment targets within the current budget allocations, thus emphasis needs to be placed on efficiencies and cost savings.'

The phrase 'current budget allocations' might refer to the current year budget, or it might refer to annual increments no greater than 28.9 percent. It could not refer to the budget COGTA projected to reach 1,030,000 participants, which called for a budget increase in 2016–17 of 67 percent. Further, Moore appeared to suggest that additional participants and new sites might be financed by private-sector funding: 'As the CWP expands, it can make use of the NGOs involved in the non-state sector to run new sites.'[41]

In the ensuing discussion with members of parliament, Moore clarified the Treasury's view that CWP must meet employment targets within

---

41. Our unbounded approach favours both a community-oriented welfare state and contributions from the nonstate sector. See Andrew Crane et al. (eds.), *The Oxford Handbook of Corporate Social Responsibility* (Oxford: Oxford University Press, 2008); Michael Porter and Mark Kramer, 'Creating Shared Value', *Harvard Business Review*, vol. 89 (2006), pages 62–77; Kaspar van Schyndel, 'Redefining Community in the Ecovillage', *Human Ecology Review*, vol. 15 (2008), pp. 12–24; David Bornstein, *How to Change the World: Social Entrepreneurs and the Power of New Ideas* (New York: Oxford University Press, 2007); Frank Adams and Gary Hansen, *Putting Democracy to Work: A Practical Guide to Starting and Managing Worker-Owned Businesses* (San Francisco: Berrett-Koehler, 1993); *ABC Abastecimiento Básico Comunitario* (http://www.inti.gob.ar/abc/); Bill Mollison, *Permaculture: A Designer's Manual* (Tyalgum, Australia: Tagari Publications, 1996) (Mollison's three basic principles are these: Love the earth. Love the people. Share the surplus); Edgar S. Cahn, *No More Throw Away People: The Co-production Imperative* (Washington, DC: Essential Books, 2004); and so on and on.

current budget allocations. She also dropped a bombshell: even the 28.9 percent figure, far under COGTA's 67 percent, needs to decrease. She said that although the CWP budget is expected to grow 28.9 percent per year, in the medium term this is not sustainable. The ballooning expenses must be scaled down. Currently, spending is split 65/35 between wages paid to participants and operational costs, but the Treasury would like to see an even larger portion go to the wages of participants in order to create more job opportunities for less money. (We note here, though it was not noted in the appropriations committee meeting, that more than half of the 35% is due to the CWP, unlike India's NREGA, providing training and proper tools and safety equipment for its workers and putting greater emphasis on doing really useful work.)

Grant Snell MP, representing East London, commented that the participants were doing low-skilled work now, and a way must be found to train them with skills that would enable them to move on to formal jobs. For example, they could be trained to recycle waste. Leonard Ramatlakane MP from Cape Town asked why the number of participants had decreased when the budget had increased. He was referring to the Treasury figure of 172,000 participants for 2013–14 in spite of the increased budget. There were other questions concerning gaps and inconsistencies in the numbers provided.

Aline Mfulo MP spoke from her wheelchair in a different voice. She wanted more involvement by the Department of Social Development. She said participants should be empowered, not merely trained.

Here is a philosophical problem, albeit a comparatively small one: many of the government officials in charge of funding and operating the CWP appear to have known nothing of the philosophy that led to its creation. Apart from Ms. Mfulo's intervention, there are no indications in the meeting report that the committee knew anything about the thinking that had gone into the initiation of the CWP (recounted in chapter 5). The committee members also seemed to know nothing about the proliferation of the CWP's activities on the ground and its alignment with other actors (illustrated in chapter 9 and in the short quotes from participants interspersed in other chapters). Nobody seemed to know that the CWP had a mandate from the Cabinet to use public employment to catalyse community development.

There also seemed to be no awareness that the founders of the CWP back in 2007 had anticipated the problem that confronted the appropriations committee in early 2014: the impossibility of government's singlehandedly solving social problems by taxing and spending, and consequently the necessity of aligning across sectors for the common good. Nobody seemed to know that the CWP was supposed to be part of the solution to public budget deficits, not part of the problem, because it was supposed to use public employment to mobilize complementary resources through partnering and community development.

What general principles does this scenario illustrate? First, governments only marginally allocate the wealth of the countries they are said to govern. 'Fiscal constraint' is a euphemism for facts like these:

- Modern republics were designed to be run by governments with limited powers, dependent on taxes.
- High taxes have an inherent tendency to discourage economic activity, while governments constantly face systemic imperatives (SF2) to encourage economic activity.
- Many voters are reluctant to pay higher taxes to provide funding for social programmes at a scale commensurate with the needs.
- Major businesses and wealthy individuals choose which government they will be taxed by when they choose where to locate, and they tend to choose those governments which tax them least.
- The super-rich for the most part escape taxation for structural reasons like those just mooted, not just because they are greedy or have clever lawyers and friends in high places.
- The finances of a national economy can be eroded by factors beyond national control, such as downturns in global markets and upturns in global interest rates.

Due to 'fiscal constraints', somebody had to be the messenger conveying bad news to the MPs who approve budgets. In this instance, the messenger turned out to be Marissa Moore.

6. A Conversation between Unbounded Organization and Modern Money Theory

On 7 February 2019, Representative Alexandria Ocasio-Cortez of New York introduced in the United States House of Representatives Resolution 109, 'Recognizing the duty of the Federal Government to create a Green New Deal'. It demanded for twenty-first-century Americans benefits that Northwestern Europeans enjoyed back in the 1960s and Americans seemed to be on track toward getting during the Roosevelt years. It demanded high wages, paid vacations, increasing life expectancy and universal access to high-quality health care. Her Green New Deal put special emphasis on cleaning up pollution and reversing global warming. It called for net-zero greenhouse gas emissions by 2050.

'Green New Deal' has become a rallying cry in many countries, including South Africa. Two prominent European movements, T-DEM chaired by Thomas Piketty and DiEM25 chaired by Yanis Varoufakis, made detailed proposals that are also called Green New Deals. One of the authors of DiEM25, Ulf Clerwall, described it as 'basically an investment boom. . . . And yes, the European Deal will be debt-financed, but by a debt to ourselves and that will rapidly pay back with a high rate of return in financial, economic, social and environmental terms.'[42]

The Green New Deal of the Piketty group—similar but more tax-financed—describes its funding as follows: 'This Budget, if the European Assembly so desires, will be financed by **four major European taxes**, the tangible markers of this European solidarity. These will apply to the profits of major firms, the top incomes (over 200,000 Euros per annum), the highest wealth owners (over 1 million Euros)' and carbon emissions.[43]

Randall Wray, a leading exponent of Modern Money Theory[44] and an advocate of a realist definition of fiscal constraint, working with Yeva Nersisyan, a younger coauthor with a bright future, has proposed a better way to pay for Green New Deals[45]. We drop in for a chat with them at Wray's office at the Levy Institute of Bard College, located a hundred miles up the Hudson River from New York City. The words attributed to Wray and Nersisyan are paraphrases of what they write in their plan for funding the Green New Deal, working paper 931 of the Levy Institute, mostly from page one. Their conversation partners are unbounded organization and moral realism (UO and MR).

---

42. Ulf Clerwall in DiEM25, *European New Deal*, Complete Policy Statement, appendix 1, p. 28.
43. Thomas Piketty et al., *Manifesto for the Democratization of Europe*, T-DEM, 2018, p. 3, at www.tdem.eu, accessed December 1, 2019. Boldface in original.
44. L. Randall Wray, *Modern Money Theory* (London: Palgrave Macmillan, 2015).
45. Yeva Nersisyan and L. Randall Wray, 'How to Pay for the Green New Deal', Levy Economics Institute working paper 931 (2019), www.levyinstitute.org/publications/how-to-pay-for-the-green-new-deal.

Wray and Nersisyan: We follow Keynes's method in his famous plan for paying for World War II.[46] *We propose that the Green New Deal can be paid for the same way.*

UO and MR: For the most part, Keynes's approach was similar to the policies actually implemented. It worked. The Allies won the war. The way they paid for it did not set off runaway inflation, either before the war or after it. Prima facie, therefore, following Keynes seems like a good idea.

Wray and Nersisyan: Like Keynes, we estimate the 'costs' of the Green New Deal in terms of real resource requirements. As *Keynes* estimated how many warships Britain could build with the workers, raw materials and machines available, *we* estimate how many doctors and hospital beds it would take to provide universal high-quality health care and how many trained workers with what tools and materials it would take to reverse global warming.

UO and MR: Why (in your article) do you put the word 'costs' in inverted commas?

Wray and Nersisyan: Instead of simply adding up estimates of the government spending that would be required, we assess resource availability that can be devoted to implementing Green New Deal projects. This includes mobilizing unutilized and underutilized resources, as well as shifting resources from current destructive and inefficient uses to Green New Deal projects. We put 'costs' in inverted commas because it is conventional to think first of money. It is conventional to think of natural resources and human resources as if their purpose—that for which they are 'resources'—were capital accumulation.

UO and MR: We agree with your deviation from a conventional economics that places turning money into more money into the conceptual space once occupied by what Plato called the *agathon*

---

46. John Maynard Keynes, *How to Pay for the War* (London: Macmillan, 1940).

(good) and by what Aristotle called *eudaimonia* (happiness or flourishing). Kenneth Arrow provides an example of the current orthodoxy. He says social choice (generally measured, we note, by preferences as expressed in quantities of money), not ethics or needs, defines a key problem to be solved as how to derive a social maximum from individual desires.[47]

Wray and Nersisyan: In our paper on how to pay for the Green New Deal we do not say anything about your 'unbounded' and 'realist' proclivity for reviving appreciation of ancient Western and non-Western ideals. Staying closer to the discourse of professional economics, we do say that governments should and can create and manage money to serve purposes. Accumulating money should not be the purpose.

UO and MR: Would you agree that your approach echoes Abba Lerner's 'functional finance' approach?[48] Lerner says the first and the most fundamental inquiries are about what functions the economy should perform and what real resources are available to perform them with. Money comes second. Money should be managed to perform nonmonetary functions.

Wray and Nersisyan: Yes. And we argue that financial affordability cannot be an issue for the sovereign US government. Rather, the problem will be inflation if sufficient resources cannot be diverted to the Green New Deal. And if inflation is likely, we need to put in place anti-inflationary measures like well-targeted taxes, price controls, rationing and voluntary saving. Deferred consumption is our first choice, should inflation pressures arise.

UO and MR: Howard remembers deferred consumption very well. He experienced part of Keynes's advice on how to pay for the war without inflation as the War Bonds his grandmother gave him every Christmas and every birthday. The working classes

---

47. Kenneth Arrow, *Social Choice and Individual Values* (New Haven, CT: Yale University Press, 1963), pp. 3, 22.
48. Abba Lerner, 'Functional Finance and the Federal Debt', *Social Research*, vol. 10 (1943), pp. 38–51.

worked during the war for wages that partly took the form of bonds that could not be cashed and spent on consumer goods until after the war.

Wray and Nersisyan: So would you agree that the sovereign US government can always pay for anything for sale in its own currency and therefore can afford the Green New Deal, whatever its price in money might be, provided, of course that the real resources—the people and the physical things—are sufficient?

UO and MR: You are saying, then, that if real resources exist that can be mobilized by spending money, then the government, because it can create and spend as much money as it wishes to create and spend—can mobilize them. If the result is 'too much money chasing too few goods' (as Milton Friedman defined inflation), then, after the Green New Deal is paid for, the government has ways of taking money out of circulation. It can also prevent inflation—as it did during the war—by rationing and fixing prices by law.

Keynes did say that a government that controls the currency can always pay.[49] This point may be true by definition, yet it often collides with reality—as happened when the currency authorized by the fledgling US government in 1775 to pay the Revolutionary Army proved to be 'not worth a continental', and as happened again in 1980 when 'stagflation' brought down left-leaning governments, leading to the election of Ronald Reagan, Margaret Thatcher and Helmut Kohl.

Wray and Nersisyan: True enough, but we are claiming that this time we have the theory right. However, we do not expect that our theory that a sovereign government has the tools to control inflation after any amount of public spending will have to be tested by the Green New Deal. On our calculations, the Green New Deal will be a piece of cake. It will probably generate very little inflationary pressure. Its mild inflationary tendency will require only a mild anti-inflationary response.

---

49. Keynes, *How to Pay for the War,* p. 61.

UO and MR: We are generally convinced that the time has come to rethink the financing of governments and to rethink the duties of private wealth holders. Schumpeter was right to prophesy that the *Steuerstaat* would be unsustainable.

Wray and Nersisyan: But do you see the logical coherence of our theory and its close fit with the empirical evidence? Do you believe that a sovereign, currency-issuing government can always purchase anything that is for sale in its own currency?[50]

UO and MR: We take 'logical coherence' to refer to a set of accounting identities[51] (such as 'Total sales must equal total purchases'). These are what make the core of economics true by definition, as do core statements accepted as truths in other sciences (such as 'If an atom has four protons it is carbon', or 'A whale is a mammal'). If so, then 'A sovereign, currency-issuing government can always purchase anything that is for sale in its own currency' would be true by definition—as Thomas Kuhn might say—in the vocabulary of the community of economists. Modern Money Theory, as we understand it, does not propose any new identities; it only asks other economists to be more logical. It asks them to acknowledge important consequences of identities that accountants and economists already employ.

'Close fit with the empirical evidence' we take to refer to building economic models not only with identities (tautologies) but also with equations that express hypotheses that must be empirically tested because they might be true or might be false or—more common in the social sciences—they might be more, less or not at all statistically significant.[52] Thus your methodology, as we read it, is one that employs a fairly standard epistemology and assumes a standard ontology of an empiricist persuasion.

---

50. Mitchell, Wray and Watts, *Macroeconomics*, Kindle edition, position 4929.
51. Ibid., position 4319.
52. Ibid., position 4322. 'Close fit with the evidence' is not a paraphrase of Wray. It is our interpretation of what we think he is thinking.

Our excuse for not directly replying to the last question we attribute to Wray and Nersisyan is that we have been proceeding on the basis of a different ontology. We are sympathetic and appreciative, but we are unable to answer yes or no to questions we would have framed differently. We have been *seeing* economic theory *as* part of the social and historical construction of basic cultural structures; or otherwise put, as the theoretical side of episodes in the history of human organization; or as Marx might put it, as a succession of discourses rooted in the always-changing physical organizations of the human exchange of matter and energy with the environment. We have been reading history as evolutionary biologists, seeing it as selecting ever more adaptive moral systems[53] but as having currently selected a moral system (neoliberalism) so disastrously dysfunctional that history may come to an end.

As we see it, our realist social ontology facilitates some political insights, including these:

- As Keynes himself notes, he wrote *How to Pay for the War* when there was in the UK what we call an *alignment across sectors in pursuit of common goals*, namely, winning the war and social justice. For example, businesspeople voluntarily refrained from raising prices when demand increased but their costs had not increased. Whether similar results can be achieved by applying similar financial measures in today's polarized societies is an open question.
- Social reality existentially depends on how the actors see their roles, and as Tony Lawson has pointed out, there is little reason to believe that today actors see themselves as playing the roles Modern Money Theory assigns to them.[54]
- Social reality, particularly money, also depends on trust. André Orléan gives the telling example of how inflation abated in France when Henri Poincaré was elected president. The money-holding public trusted Poincaré.[55]
- Although many consequences become tautologies when they are predicated on sovereign states, whether there are any sovereign states

---

53. David Sloan Wilson, *Darwin's Cathedral* (Chicago: University of Chicago Press, 2011); and Jared Diamond, *Guns, Germs and Steel* (New York: Norton, 1997).

54. Tony Lawson, "Money's Relation to Debt: Some Problems with MMT's Conception of Money", *Real-World Economics Review*, 89 (1 October 2019), pp. 109–128, http://www.paecon.net/PAEReview/issue89/Lawson89.pdf.

55. André Orléan, *L'Empire de la valeur* (Paris: Seuil, 2011), p. 222. 'La monnaie est, d'abord, une relation entre acteurs économiques que se repose sur de la confiance, des représentations collectives et des attentes stratégiques' (p. 102).

is another open question. The birth of modern republics can be seen as the death of sovereignty. Sovereign control of money can be seen as fatally wounded by historic events like the founding of the Bank of England on 27 July 27 1694. Three bloody civil wars in England in the seventeenth century ended with William and Mary ascending the throne on terms dictated by Parliament. Those terms were similar to the terms of the post–World War I constitution of Austria that prompted Schumpeter to resign as Minister of Finance, since he was being asked to perform tasks that modern constitutional governments were not designed to perform. The Bank of England was an early central bank that became a model for others, as the City of London became in the next two centuries the centre of global finance.[56] It was a privately owned enterprise authorized by its charter to emit legal tender. It promptly funded the national debt at an interest rate of 8 percent, putting the public sector in debt to the private sector.

- We think our realist and unbounded ontology helps us to see more potentials in Modern Money Theory, rather than fewer. From the perspective of unbounded organization and moral realism, Modern Money Theory suggests a thoroughly transformed world. Even imagining the new world's creation requires the idea of an open society where all institutions are tentative—as in the philosophy of science of Karl Popper (who advocated an open society in principle as a young man but shied away from it in practice as an old man), where no theory is ever true; it is at most the survivor of many tests that might have falsified it. In the new world, states, as creators of currency, could employ the financial services industry to generate income for the public purse. Government could make good use of the income that flowed into the public purse because of its monopoly on the creation of money. They could fund community development that would facilitate the grassroots proliferation of dignified livelihoods for the billions whose labour is made redundant by technology. The current world—where states cover their deficits by borrowing money from private institutions, enabling a rentier class to collect interest from the government on something the government itself had authorized private institutions to create—would be history. Students would read about it in school, but they would not experience it.

---

56. Walter Bagehot, *Lombard Street* (London: Henry S. King, 1873).

7. The Constraints of Fiscal Space: Peter Heller, Senior Economist, International Monetary Fund

We are far from exhausting the many meanings of 'fiscal constraint' and, consequently, the many ways of framing the fiscal crisis of the state. In this section we examine the concept of 'fiscal space', beginning with a stop in Geneva in 2011, where a commission chaired by Michelle Bachelet is making a report to the International Labour Organization. That report shows, optimistically, that the nations of the earth have found creative ways to fund social programmes that do not depend on GDP growth. But Geneva is only a stop on the way to Washington, DC, in 2005, and the office of Peter Heller, then Deputy Director of the Fiscal Affairs Department of the International Monetary Fund. There we learn that the proposition that social programmes for the poor must wait until GDP increases, has deep roots in a rigid worldview that tends to see the constitutive rules of markets (property, contract, autonomy of the juridical subject, absence of the duty of solidarity) as required by pure reason and pure morality.

In its report, the Bachelet Commission used the phrase 'creating fiscal space' instead of its equivalent, 'overcoming fiscal constraints', to describe finding the money to pay for a social protection floor. It reported many ways to create fiscal space. In Ghana, debt cancellation provided the fiscal space for its Livelihoods Empowerment Against Poverty Programme.[57] South Africa created fiscal space for social programmes first by giving social spending a special legal status by writing social rights into its Constitution (as Thailand, Costa Rica and Brazil have also done), and then by reprioritizing its budgets, cutting defence spending by 48 percent.[58]

Fiscal space can be created in various ways. Reducing corruption would be one of them. An African Union study estimated that in sub-Saharan Africa in 2002, losses due to corruption were $148 billion USD, approximately half of total tax revenue.[59] Bolivia creates the fiscal space for an annual pension paid to every Bolivian citizen over age sixty with a tax on hydrocarbons.[60] Fiscal space has been created by taxes on airline tickets.[61] There have been many proposals to tax international financial transactions

---

57. Bachelet et al., *Social Protection Floor*, p. 69.
58. Ibid., pp. 69–70.
59. Ibid., p 70.
60. Ibid., p. 69.
61. The UN has sponsored an airline ticket tax to fund basic health care. The scheme was initially adopted by Brazil, Chile, Norway, France and the United Kingdom. Ten African countries, Mauritius and the Republic of Korea later joined. Ibid., p.74.

and earmark the proceeds for social spending.[62] In its examples and lists of ways to fund social programmes the Bachelet Commission does not even mention taking steps to increase GDP growth.

The Commission's report rules out of court the argument that improvement in the lot of the poor must wait until the 'pie' increases sufficiently to pay for it.[63] It does not, however, show, or even claim, that its lists of creative fundraising ideas demonstrate the feasibility of transfers large enough to meet the basic needs that are now unmet. Nor does it consider the many ways rulers have financed themselves through the ages. It treats the modern *Steuerstaat* (the state that lives by taxes)[64] as an unquestioned given, showing no awareness that the revenue of a Tartar chief of old came 'principally from the milk and increase of his own herds and flocks'; or that 'the rent of public lands has been . . . the principal source of revenue of many a great nation';[65] or that ancient states monopolized the right to coin, funding themselves by creating money out of metal and then decreeing that it be accepted, regardless of the value of the metal it was made of, and then collected interest on the money whose making they monopolized; or that they raked in booty from wars and collected tribute from conquered peoples; and so on.[66]

Remarkably, the Commission did not even consider such obvious present-day facts as that the theocratic monarchy of Saudi Arabia can afford to spend money on welfare because of royally owned oil resources.[67] It simply assumed the modern republic as its frame of reference. It did not appear to know that the winners of the revolutions that established modern

---

62. One proposal was made in Bill Gates's report to a Cannes G20 summit. It called for taxing share and bond transactions on the world's stock exchanges to fund basic social protection (ibid., p. 74).

63. On p. 71 of the Bachelet Commission report (ibid.), there is a chart listing ten ways to create fiscal space for social programmes. Economic growth is not on the list. However, economic growth is treated elsewhere in the report as creating possibilities for redistribution—contrary to the implicit argument of James O'Connor in *The Fiscal Crisis of the State* (Milton Park, UK: Routledge, 1973), that the pursuit of economic growth often leads to tax competition and to more regressive taxation (the value-added tax), effectively de-redistributing wealth from the poor to the rich.

64. In 1918, Joseph Schumpeter predicted that the tax state would ultimately go bankrupt, in *Die Krise des Steuerstaats* (Graz, Austria: Leuschner and Lubinsky), 1918.

65. These quotes are from Adam Smith, *An Enquiry into the Nature and Causes of the Wealth of Nations*, edited by Edwin Cannan, with an introduction by John Chamberlain (New Rochelle, NY: Arlington House, n. d.), bk. 5, ch. 2, part 1. Smith gives many more examples of the innumerable ways public expenses have been funded. More can be found in any history of money.

66. M. I. Finley, *The Ancient Economy* (London: Chatto and Windus, 1973), pp. 166–69.

67. Tim Niblock, *The Political Economy of Saudi Arabia* (London: Routledge, 2007).

344 | **Chapter Ten**

governments designed those governments to be poor by, among other things, establishing banking as a private business and making government budgets dependent on taxes voted by parliaments.[68] It is as if Bachelet and her commissioners, like most denizens of modernity, could not see the box they were living in.

Some years earlier, the widespread use of the concept of 'fiscal space' had motivated Peter Heller to pen a discussion paper defining it.[69] Heller's definition of fiscal space in his 2005 paper gives us another opportunity to denounce the rigid thinking that impairs pragmatic solutions to material problems—and unintentionally demonstrates the need for moral realism and unbounded organization. What we are pleading for is remembering the purpose of the game while playing the game. The game is commodity exchange, and its rules are inevitably written in terms of money exchange.[70] The purpose, however, is *serving life*. We are pleading for a pragmatic, realistic worldview that *sees* the rules of the game as flexible and *sees* its purpose of serving life as constant.

Heller writes: 'In its broadest sense, fiscal space can be defined as the availability of budgetary room that allows a government to provide resources for a desired purpose without any prejudice to the sustainability of a government's financial position.'[71] His definition of fiscal space ties finding resources to transfer to the poor (implementing Karl Polanyi's redistribution principle[72]) to a guarantee of doing so 'without any prejudice' (with no danger of default). In other words, it mandates a sustainable

---

68. A key precedent, in important ways following the Netherlands and later followed by most of the rest of the world, was the English Glorious Revolution of 1688–1692 and the ensuing financial revolution. When William and Mary accepted Parliament's invitation to assume the throne on Parliament's terms, the terms included that the Crown would be funded by taxes voted by parliament. In 1694, the Bank of England was founded as a private bank that lent money to the government, starting with a large initial loan at 8% interest.

69. Peter S. Heller, *Understanding Fiscal Space*, IMF Policy Discussion Paper PDP/05/04 (Washington, DC: International Monetary Fund, 2005), http://www.imf.org/external/pubs/ft/pdp/2005/pdp04.pdf, accessed March 2015. Heller retired from the IMF in 2006. Heller was, of course, not responding specifically to the Bachelet Commission, because his paper is older than its report.

70. Karl Marx developed this point in his 'Comments on James Mill', in *Marx Engels Collected Works* (MECW), vol. 3 (1843–1844), p. 211 et seq. MECW was a joint publication of Progress Publishers Moscow, Lawrence and Wishart London, and International Publishers New York. Vol. 3 was published in 1975.

71. Heller, *Understanding Fiscal Space*, p. 3.

72. As mentioned earlier, Polanyi and many historians and anthropologists of the 'substantivist' school find redistribution (as in Exodus, the Pharaoh's granaries redistributed grain to the Egyptians) and reciprocity (social obligation) to be at the heart of many practices that met human needs in precapitalist times and places.

future in which a government must be able to make the payments it owes as they come due.

Playing correctly by the rules of the money game thus becomes, in Kantian terms, a categorical imperative, a command of *reine Vernunft*, or pure reason (though that translation does not express the full moral weight of *reine* in Kant's philosophy). *Reine* also means clean. Continuing in Kantian terms, meeting material human needs is demoted to the impure (unclean) status of the merely material world. Guaranteeing the ability to pay future obligations is promoted to the pure (clean) status of the universal and eternal concepts that frame not just the experiences we happen to have but any possible experiences.

When Heller writes about fiscal space, he speaks softly but carries a big stick: 'Some of the volatility in external assistance experienced by many countries has arisen from the failure to implement agreed macroeconomic policy programs with the IMF. Delays in satisfactory IMF program reviews or cessation of IMF-supported programs can have an adverse multiplier effect in terms of their impact on other donor assistance. Certainly, countries that manage their macroeconomic policies well have far greater potential for creating additional fiscal space.'[73]

Let us look again at the two key parts of Heller's definition of fiscal space. Regarding the first part of Heller's definition—there is fiscal space to fund a social programme only when resources are provided *without prejudice to financial sustainability*: An ordinary human being innocent of economics and finance might well be forgiven for asking why finding resources to meet the vital necessities of the poor should be so complicated. From a physical point of view, moving things from one place to another is simple, as one might think just riding around town on a bicycle, observing the surfeit in the posh suburbs and the shortfall in the bosh townships. However, 'financial sustainability' clouds the picture with a layer of cultural meanings that organize human behaviour and make transferring the surplus complicated. In the sense Heller relies on, it means being able to meet one's financial obligations in the future. Heller cautions against committing to even meritorious social programmes, even when funds are available, if there is no assurance of money to pay for them in the future.[74] Heller's first (but not only) answer to the question of where the government's future revenue will

---

73. Heller, *Understanding Fiscal Space*, pp. 11–12.
74. This thought is further developed in Peter S. Heller, 'Are Governments Overextended?' *World Economics*, vol. 5 (2004), pp. 1–31.

come from is that it will come from production.[75] He says that increased GDP will lead to increased tax revenue due to 'normal buoyancy'.[76]

Regarding the second part of Heller's definition of fiscal space—what governments do with fiscal space is called *providing resources for a desired purpose*: Heller characterizes the desired purpose for which resources are provided as meritorious.[77] His vocabulary suggests that, in his view, financial sustainability is obligatory while other objectives, however desirable or meritorious, are optional. Thus interpreted, Heller echoes Kant: the duty to pay debts is categorically imperative. Any duty to create human happiness or relieve human misery is not categorically imperative; it is merely 'meritorious'.[78] And if the criterion for financial sustainability is without *any* prejudice, as Heller says, then that criterion becomes an absolute duty, like Kant's categorical imperative.

One might ask why we bring Kant into a discussion of how to pay for social programmes. Indeed, there is a remarkable parallel between Heller's principle that the infinite suffering of the poor may be relieved by a social programme only when paying for it does not risk impairing a government's financial position, and Kant's principle that categorical imperatives trump what he calls merely hypothetical imperatives. In fact, a similar moral rigidity impairs pragmatic solutions in other contexts, including the following: cancelling debts, modifying property rights, designing land reform to share land with the descendants of the colonized people from whom it was taken by force, liquidating bankrupt businesses, writing secured debt down to its market value, speculating in junk bonds, taxing accumulated wealth, buying up land or other assets purely to prevent competitors from doing something with them, creating capital controls and other measures against capital flight, and accessing patented pharmaceuticals.

The practical question of why there is so much inequality in the world touches at many points on the theoretical question of whether ethical principles are absolute or are relative to facts. Derek Thompson, Jeremy

---

75. We have been emphasizing that economic growth measured by GDP is essentially about sales. The definition of GDP is the value of production in a given territory in a given time period, which on one of three equivalent approaches is for the most part measured by sales.

76. Heller, *Understanding Fiscal Space*, p. 5.

77. Heller uses the term 'meritorious' in ibid. at pp. 2,4,6,7, and 12.

78. The duty to seek happiness for oneself or others is for Kant a hypothetical imperative, less strict than a categorical imperative, derived from impure facts rather than pure reason. See Mark Timmons, 'Necessitation and Justification in Kant's Ethics', *Canadian Journal of Philosophy*, vol. 22 (1992), pp. 223–261.

Rifkin, Peter Fraser and many others have written books speculating on what humanity might do with the abundance that will be made possible by new technologies now in the pipeline—without paying attention to SF1 or SF2 or to the rigid ethics and jurisprudence installed not just in Washington, DC, at the Deutschebank and in the World Trade Organization rules, but virtually everywhere. Humanity is not free to choose.

We bring in Kant in this connection because he is famous; because his moral authority is often invoked by writers left, centre and right; because his reasoning is clear; and because discussing his views provides a convenient bridge from the specific question of how to pay for social programmes to the general question of why wealth is so badly distributed. But we do not see Kant as a lone genius who used the grey matter between his ears to invent ethical principles that, for unknown reasons, spread like wildfire and became the ethical, legal and accounting principles that organize the modern world system. We see Kant as a spokesperson for deep-seated tendencies in human nature found in *any* culture. Furthermore, we see his writing of philosophical books as part of an historical process that sacralised the basic structure of our culture.

In our view, whether the rules of finance are eternal and rigid or historically created and flexible is not merely a theoretical question. Flexibility and creativity are practical necessities. In order to build diverse, plural, self-reliant economies, democratic processes must be empowered to modify (carefully and prudently) the bedrock of capitalism: property rights and contractual obligations. The alternative, as the above analysis of the rules of the game by a senior IMF economist predicts, is what is in fact observed: gridlock, ungovernability and social disintegration. Said more simply, albeit repetitively: the alternative is an inability to adjust institutions to meet needs in harmony with nature.

As a practical matter, even if minds are cleansed of anti-historical Kantian thinking, democratic polities still have no access to a nation's wealth as long as every attempt to redistribute it causes capital flight and capital flight causes unemployment. Plurality, mission-driven organizations, an ethic of service and a culture of solidarity and community are antidotes to the threat of capital flight. They help to make large-scale capital accumulation governable instead of governing. As a theoretical matter, when the ethics of the Good loses out to an ethics of the priority of the Right over the Good (which cements in place the extremely unequal division of wealth), meeting human needs in harmony with nature loses. It loses because meeting human needs is merely "good", and on an ethics of the priority of right, right trumps good. In terms of IMF policy, meeting needs loses to a definition of fiscal space that requires strict guarantees that future financial obligations will always be met. Form defeats substance. Kant's synthetic *a priori*[79] defeats Dewey's nature.[80]

8. Raising the Social Status of Use Value

Before continuing our discussion of the problem of the fiscal crisis of the state in the next chapter, we suggest a first general solution. Perhaps not surprisingly, our solution is to redefine the problem. As conventionally defined, a fiscal crisis means lack of money. In Smith's terms, it means lack of exchange value, that is, lack of either money or assets that can be exchanged for money. But Smith also recognized that when you get right down to the basics of life, what satisfies your needs is something you can use, something that has use value: water, food, blankets, medicine. When Heller gives absolute priority to being able to pay your bills in the future, he is setting in stone the rules of the game of a dysfunctional world; he is lowering the status of use values that satisfy needs, like a glass of water.

Our first general solution is, as Abba Lerner put it, functional finance. Raise the social status of use value. More community, less economics. More breast-feeding, less formula bought at the store. Where jobs are short, try vocations. Where customers are short, try friends. When the basic cultural structure leads to mass unemployment, crime, drugs, too little oxygen and too much CO^2 in the atmosphere, and the fiscal crisis of the state, try *ubuntu*.[81]

We have already reviewed several times another (besides Kant's moral

---

79. Kant's synthetic *a priori* propositions are supposed to be eternally and universally certain but not mere tautologies. Most famously applied to basic mathematics and science (*Kritik der reinen Vernunft*, 1781), Kant's work also attributed a synthetic *a priori* character to basic norms of morals and jurisprudence (see, for example, *Grundlagen der Metaphysik der Sitten*, 1785; *Rechtslehre*, 1797).

80. For Dewey there are no eternal and universal certainties in science or in ethics. See, for example, John Dewey, *Experience and Nature* (Chicago: Open Court, 1925); and John Dewey, *The Quest for Certainty: A Study of the Relation of Knowledge and Action* (London: George Allen & Unwin, 1929). Enrique Dussel has elaborated an ethics of liberation applying the principle that categories of thought, moral norms, and institutions should all be constructed and reconstructed in the service of life, not the other way about. See, for example, Enrique Dussel, *Ética de la liberación en la edad de la globalizacion y la exclusion* (Madrid: Editorial Trotta, 1998).

81. Catherine Hoppers and Howard Richards, *Rethinking Thinking* (Pretoria: University of South Africa, 2012). *Ubuntu*, or *botho*, has deep roots in Africa: Kemetic wisdom from 6,000 years ago gives us the law of Ma'at, which is essentially about reciprocity.

philosophy) eighteenth-century European historic source of thinking like Heller's: Adam Smith's definition of 'production'. 'Production', as Smith uses it, is a key term needed to understand gross domestic product, which is in turn a key term needed to understand entrenched principles that are leading us nowhere: social budgets are constrained by insufficient GDP growth; therefore, to solve social problems we need more money, and to get more money we need more investors.

In our view, social budgets ought to be constrained by two quite different principles: ecology and justice. Ecology calls for less growth, not more. Justice calls for sharing the enormous surplus that already exists and for building solidarity and self-reliance in neighbourhoods. These two principles go somewhere. They put the physical bottom line, use value, first. Then it makes sense for people to be mission-driven, because they have a mission. Of course, everybody has to find their own mission, their vocation. But whatever it is, it is doing something useful.

The CWP provides many examples of what we mean. In the CWP, people work but do not sell. They do not work for someone else who in turn sells, either. But they do a great deal of production, where production is defined in the physical, down-to-earth sense of making or doing something useful. In June 2015, South Africa's Expanded Public Works Programme, of which the CWP is a component, reported that its working but nonselling participants had erected 33,070 kilometres of fencing, laid down 109,923 kilometres of pipeline, constructed 450 kilometres of storm-water drains, maintained 64,623 kilometres of road, planted 20,045 trees and improved watersheds by clearing 1,366 hectares of eco-unfriendly alien vegetation.[82]

The CWP's predecessor and inspiration, organization workshops, provide more examples. When an organization workshop is over and the participants go home, they invariably leave the host community with tangible assets that did not exist before, such as a building for a crèche or a fence separating grazing land from a residential area. In Bokfontein, it was a deep well that provided—at last!—a reliable supply of water. The final report of every organization workshop lists the tangible assets created. Although the participants are paid for their work, the products of their labour are gifts. In a CWP version of the organization workshop, people are paid for doing community service. They meet needs. They deserve respect. They deserve funding. This is functional finance.

---

82. The list goes on. See *Expanded Public Works Programme Newsletter*, June 2015 (Pretoria: Government of South Africa Department of Public Works), p. 1.

Heller speaks for an outdated and dysfunctional orthodoxy when he identifies programmes for which fiscal space can legitimately be carved out with programmes that will eventually pay for themselves. He clearly prefers to fund projects that pay by making products that sell.[83] But for the sake of the planet and for the sake of humanity, the priorities ought to be the opposite of those of orthodox economics and the orthodoxy at the IMF.[84]

Our proposal for raising the social status of use value has both a general form and a specific form. Generally: Cultivate prosocial, pro-life, mentally healthy, ethically responsible attitudes. Commit to being part of the solution, not part of the problem. Then, joining with others, do what works. A traditional general list of opportunities for service includes the following: Feed the hungry. Give water to the thirsty. Clothe the naked. Shelter the homeless. Care for the sick. Visit the imprisoned. Bury the dead.

Let us be specific: Even now, before the full impact of robotics and information technology is felt, recycle the surplus, making ever more transfer payments. Create surplus to share, as the Apostle Paul, a tent maker, worked with his own hands to make a living for himself and his friends—and then went on to make more tents to be able to share with the weak.[85] Organize ever more useful and dignified paying activities for growing numbers of workers whom economic orthodoxy classifies as out of the labour force or unemployed or underemployed—therefore (by orthodox logic) requiring one thing only: an investor to pay her or him to make something to sell.

Face reality. The problem of chronic precarious employment is often inseparable from addictions, trafficking, cultures of violence, the syndrome named by Nancy Hartsock as the 'negative erotic',[86] ethnic and religious violence, mental illness, gang warfare, sexually transmitted diseases, toxic physical environments and so on, down and down in vicious cycles of deepening misery. Many people fear physical violence more than poverty; many want dignity more than food. Bottlenecks in funding community

---

83. For example, in *Understanding Fiscal Space* at p. 3, Heller writes: 'The incentive for creating fiscal space is strengthened where the resulting fiscal outlays would boost medium-term growth and perhaps even pay for itself in terms of future fiscal revenue.' On p. 2, he favours granting fiscal space to health and education when they will pay for themselves in the long run by upgrading human resources.

84. A friend and college classmate of Howard's was fired by the IMF for pressing unorthodox pro-ecology priorities. He was given a generous pension, a 'golden parachute', on condition that he keep his mouth shut and not say anything in public. We do not give his name, fearing that it might blow his cover and cause him to lose his pension.

85. Acts 20:34.

86. Nancy Hartsock, *Money, Sex and Power* (Boston: Northeastern University Press, 1987).

development coexist with fictitious balance-sheet wealth bringing damage, not benefit, to the real economy: for example, parking enormous surplus funds in real estate, expecting the price of land to rise, driving the price of home ownership, or even rental, out of site for millions, forcing them to sleep in their cars or on sidewalks. [87]

Unbounded organizing is not against investment; the whole point of it is to be open-minded, to align across sectors to do whatever works to accomplish the common good. It advocates investment (private, public or mixed) that produces real social and physical value. It supports social entrepreneurs who create surpluses that flow to where they are needed. It opposes *seeing* investment motivated by money and validated by sales and raising GDP *as* the path to heaven when it is just as likely to be the path to hell.

Whether alignment for the common good happens in the public sector or the private business sector—or in a cooperative, a union, a service club, a church, an NGO or a school—should not be an issue. A major contribution to solving the fiscal crisis of the state is to do useful work, paid or unpaid, whoever you are and whatever your role in life is. Then the state will not have to frantically try to attract investors and offer them subsidies and tax breaks, and run itself deeper and deeper into debt in order to do it. Why? Because it will already be done.

What we have just reemphasized is that, as a matter of history, the dynamic of production-for-sale-for-profit (SF1)—itself a consequence of the constitutive rules of markets—has been conceptually linked to production *defined as* production for sale. This link is not an empirical finding. It is not a discovery about how the world must be. It is a *definition*. It is bounded thinking.

Today when we are told that social programmes should not be 'welfarist' or charitable but should instead be productive, we are being dragged, like it or not, into the worldview of production-for-sale-for-profit. Unfortunately, Smith's limitation of 'production' to 'production for sale' is still so prevalent that it is assumed in the calculation of the official statistics everybody relies on to grasp what is happening in the world.[88] We cannot even cite statistics, such as the unemployment rate, to help us make our point without referring to numbers and concepts that assume that the basic cultural structure is just fine as it is and does not need more servant leaders and volunteer activists, more mission-driven organizations and independent thinkers. We are being

---

87. Michael Hudson, *The Bubble and Beyond* (Dresden: Islet, 2015).
88. Mitchell, Wray and Watts, *Macroeconomics*, chs. 4 and 5.

dragged into an all-consuming conflagration of commodification that burns community solidarity to the ground, leaving in its ashes humiliation for the excluded and fear for the included.

Now let us do a fast-forward from Adam Smith to Francis Fukuyama, who is credited with having written the definitive optimist rebuttal to pessimistic words like those at the end of the preceding paragraph. Fukuyama is often imagined as today's Candide, repeating over and over that all is for the best in this best of all possible worlds.

On a first superficial reading, Fukuyama might be taken to say that the verdict of history is in. If history is defined as competition among different social and economic systems, that competition is over because there is one clear winner that will remain as such until the end of time:[89] Smith was right. Exchange value rules and forevermore will rule Planet Earth. There is and always will be only one social philosophy regarded as legitimate, and it is liberal capitalism, complemented by democracy to satisfy humanity's yearning for *Anerkennung* (recognition).[90]

But from an unbounded organization approach, there are many different solutions to many different problems. For the most part, we do not really know what they are. However, we do know that one of the problems that cry out for a solution is the end of work.[91] And another problem crying out for a solution is global warming. We also know that the *Steuerstaat,* mired in fiscal crisis, with too long a list of things to do and too small a store of resources to do them with, is quite incapable of solving either one. Does all this contradict Fukuyama?

A closer reading of Fukuyama shows, on the contrary, that he is quite aware of the failure of post-historical liberal capitalist democracies to solve their main problems. The claims he actually makes can be scaled down to

---

89. Actually, Fukuyama distinguishes between the liberal capitalist democracies and the rest of the world. The former are post-historical. The rest of the world is 'still in history'; history has not ended there yet. See Francis Fukuyama, *The End of History and the Last Man* (New York, Macmillan, 1992), ch. 26, starting at p. 276.

90. Ibid. It will be remembered from the previous chapter that Hegel's notion of *Anerkennung* builds an ethics on the human need to be recognized and respected by other persons.

91. Karl Popper and John Dewey famously argued that what society needs is not so much solutions to its problems as procedures for systematically looking for solutions and evaluating how well prototype and provisional solutions work. Karl Popper, *The Open Society and Its Enemies* (London: Routledge, 1945); John Dewey, *The Public and Its Problems* (New York: Henry Holt, 1927). Similarly, John Maynard Keynes argued that since economic science does not really know the best way to solve the problems of capitalism, nations should be encouraged to experiment with different solutions. Keynes, 'National Self-sufficiency', *Yale Review*, vol. 22 (1933), pp. 755–769.

saying that, in the future, legitimate problem solving (1) will be done in the context of political democracy; (2) will acknowledge the need for markets and for many autonomous or semi-autonomous institutions, rather than one total institution; and (3) will not see Soviet-style central planning as a viable economic alternative. We agree with all three. We also believe that if we had chosen someone else to speak for capitalist triumphalism, they would agree with us and with Fukuyama that the liberal capitalist democracies have failed to solve their main problems.[92]

Fukuyama acknowledges that we have not yet learned how to reconcile the productivity of a modern economy with the ethical claims of equality and dignity.[93] For Fukuyama, although Soviet Communism is no longer on the agenda as an attractive model, Scandinavian social democracy still is.[94] He also notes that 'no one has solved the problem of creating culture—that is, of regenerating internalized moral values—as a matter of public policy'.[95] In the end, Fukuyama says, life in bourgeois society tends to be *boring*, as it fails to satisfy some of humanity's deepest needs.[96] Liberalism has a corrosive effect on values predating liberalism that are necessary to sustain a community.[97] And so on.[98]

The recognition of the limitations of today's neoliberal dominant ideology by its most famous contemporary proponent encourages us to believe that the triumph of exchange value is not complete.[99] The social status of use value *can* be raised. Indeed, it is being raised.

For example, movements like free-cycling and couch-surfing are bypassing markets through collaborative sharing.[100] Ideas like using public employment to catalyse community development and separating the right to a livelihood

---

92. Robert Paul Wolff notes that in general the left and the right agree that liberal capitalism cannot sustain itself without what Hegel called *Sittlichkeit*, ethical substance, or morality. *The Poverty of Liberalism* (Boston: Beacon Press, 1968).
93. Fukuyama, *End of History*, pp. 289 and following.
94. Ibid., p. 294.
95. Ibid., p. 292.
96. Ibid., p. 314.
97. Ibid., p. 327.
98. See generally parts 4 and 5 of Fukuyama, *End of History*, chs. 20–31.
99. Andy Blunden finds that today's political right is an unstable coalition. It consists of economic neoliberals and social conservatives. But neoliberalism is commodifying family, love, tradition and everything social conservatives hold dear. See Blunden, *Selected Writings on the Semiotics*.
100. These examples are taken from Jeremy Rifkin, *The Zero Marginal Cost Society: The Internet of Things, the Collaborative Commons, and the Eclipse of Capitalism* (New York: Palgrave Macmillan, 2014). See also Arun Sundararajan, *The Sharing Economy* (Cambridge, MA: MIT Press, 2017).

from the necessity to sell have something in common with free-cycling and other movements in civil society that are raising the social status of use value. Use is achieved without a solid and lasting physical product that can be both touched and sold. Social cohesion happens without sales. There are many ways to violate the principle (or better, violate the way of *seeing* the world) that production must or should be for-sale-for-profit. They all give a different meaning to the term 'productive'.

By the old jump-start private business approach, a social programme deserves to be funded only if it helps the recipients break into the market as sellers and earn some money there. Perhaps it also deserves funding if it is a grant that simply gives money.

Once we are talking in terms of use value, we ask different questions when we evaluate, for example, South Africa's Community Work Programme: Are the participants cooking and cleaning house for penniless AIDS victims? Is their gardening improving the diets of prisoners in jails or the unemployed? Are they cleaning up the river and thus making drinking water safer?

Now we can argue that the government gets a bigger bang for its buck when it backs a model that identifies and meets community needs and that builds relationships with partners who provide resources complementary to what the government can provide. Now we have a better rationale for seeking government money, a broader idea of what 'pay for' means and a larger set of potential donors. The community itself helps pay for the programme with everything from the volunteer time of the CWP participant who goes back after hours to change the bandages of an AIDS victim, to the land lent for a community garden by an adjacent hospital that owns it.

What was our method for reconceptualizing the issues? We have dispelled some fog, taken off some blinders. Our method can be described as not just historical but also Wittgensteinian, as when Wittgenstein writes, 'What we are supplying are really remarks on the natural history of human beings; we are not contributing curiosities however, but observations which no one has doubted, but which have escaped remark only because they are always before our eyes.'[101]

---

101. Ludwig Wittgenstein, *Philosophical Investigations* (Oxford: Blackwell, 1958), par. 415 at p. 125e.

CHAPTER ELEVEN

The Fiscal Crisis of the State as a Philosophical Problem: Part Two

OVERVIEW OF THE CHAPTER

1. Setting in Stone the Games People Play: Immanuel Kant
2. Setting in Stone the Games People Play: Jean-Baptiste Say (Say's Law)
3. Structural Transformation: Capturing Rents
4. On Whether a New *Ubuntu* Can Relieve the Fiscal Crisis of the State
5. Structural Transformation: Thomas Piketty's Contributions
6. Cultural Shifts

1. Setting in Stone the Games People Play: Immanuel Kant

After an interlude to consider a first general solution to the fiscal crisis of the state in the final section of chapter 10, we return now to Peter Heller's office at Nineteenth and NW H streets in Washington, DC, to look again at the notion that social programmes must wait until fiscal space is available. Specifically, we want to further elaborate on our point that Heller's rigidity reflects deep-seated rigidities in modern Western culture as classically expressed in the philosophy of Immanuel Kant. We want to nail down this point firmly with respect to ethics before making the same point with respect to economics when we visit Jean-Baptiste Say.

In the deep layers of the mind where philosophy merges with the unconscious assumptions that are sacred to a civilization, Kant succeeds in defining (as obedience to universal legal principles established by his philosophy) a *Weltbürgerliche Standpunkt* (translated into English as a cosmopolitan standpoint, and equivalent to what we call the basic cultural structure of Western modernity) as perpetual and universal peace.[1] Obeying pure reason is equal to respecting natural rights, is equal to peace. As Kant's *Rechtslehre* makes clear,

---

1. Immanuel Kant, 'Idea for a Universal History from a Cosmopolitan [*Weltbürgerliche*] Point of View' (1784), in the collection of his writings, *On History* (Indianapolis: Bobbs-Merrill, 1963).

the *Weltbürger* (world citizen) is none other than the subject of the Roman *jus gentium*, whose powers to do business anywhere in the Empire under the same rules evolve to be defined by eighteenth-century Europeans like Denis Diderot, Adam Smith and Jean-Baptiste Say as natural liberty and natural rights. Later on, anthropologists would choose 'culture' as the concept that best identifies the natural qualities that make our species what it is.[2] Culture explains our capacity to create diverse basic structures that adapt relatively rapidly (compared to mutation) to environmental challenges. In the world of Kant—more precisely, in the metaphysical laws that define any possible world for Kant—ethics never change. Reason commands forever that any person (defined as a *vernünftiger Wille*, a rational will) may go anywhere and take her or his property along. So also, a corporation (legally regarded as having the rights of a person)[3] can choose to go somewhere else and be governed by other laws whenever it wishes to do so.

The modern Western reader of Kant may be charmed and fascinated to read an author who articulates the deepest voice of the reader's unconscious conscience. Hearing his ringing phrases—'dignity above price', 'always as an end, never as a means only'—feels like being lifted above the mud of earth to a realm of pure spiritual duty. For this reason, humanity must not jettison Kant. Without the power of Kant's rhetoric to inspire action based on duty (deontic ethics), the global economy would be worse, not better. Nevertheless, Kant's categorical commands of reason make property ungovernable and democracy unable to fund social rights. Nations compete to lower taxes to attract property, while funding social rights requires redistributing property one way or another (not necessarily by taxes). Kant's unconditional admirers voluntarily swallow the poison that condemns them to live in economic insecurity from birth to death.[4]

Realism and pragmatism, with doses of Aristotle's golden mean and standard psychology, prescribe that human life must balance integrity with flexibility. When a person's behaviour is too rigid, the person is neurotic. When it is not rigid enough, the person is unreliable. Similarly, too much Kant is neurotic. Too little Kant is chaos. We can speak of an overly rigid

---

2. James P. Boggs, 'The Culture Concept as Theory, in Context', *Current Anthropology*, vol. 45 (2004), pp. 187–209.

3. Santa Clara County v. Southern Pacific Railroad Co., 118 U.S. 394 (United States Supreme Court 1886). There are similar judicial decisions in other countries. See the Wikipedia article 'Corporate Personhood'.

4. The shadow side of Kant is further illustrated in Andrew Sayer, *Why Things Matter to People: Social Sciences, Values and Ethical Life* (Cambridge, UK: Cambridge University Press, 2011).

institution, such as a Kant-inspired property law, as a neurotic institution,[5] and of insufficiently rigid institutions, such as the endless gang wars that are part of the survival strategies of the chronically unemployed who deal drugs in the underworld, as unreliable institutions. For individuals and for institutions, it is possible to become dysfunctional by failing to continue established practices and by continuing them when they are not working.

We have claimed that there is a tendency toward excessive rigidity in Peter Heller's discussion paper on fiscal space, in modern Western culture generally, and quite probably in all cultures. If a culture is by definition something that persists and is passed on from generation to generation, then every culture must have a quota of rigidity. Further, every culture tends to see its own basic cultural structure as natural, eternal and universal.[6] Here we extend our previous remarks on Heller and Kant in order to trace, in a little more detail, the historical construction of the dysfunctional liberal ethics that undergird today's global modern world-system.[7]

Heller's definition of fiscal space as 'the availability of budgetary room that allows a government to provide resources for a desired purpose without any prejudice to the sustainability of a government's financial position' does not call for a balance between meeting human needs in the present and preserving capacity to meet them in the future. It does not balance anything with anything. It limits funding for a 'desired purpose' to what can be done without *any* prejudice to financial sustainability.

Further, Heller distinguishes what *must* be done, guaranteeing the government's capacity to pay its bills, from what *may* be done, for which he uses the words 'desired' and 'meritorious'. This distinction parallels Kant's distinction between categorical and hypothetical imperatives.

Heller probably did not consciously have Kant in mind when he wrote. He may have been influenced in his formative years by reading Kant or by reading authors directly or indirectly influenced by Kant—a category that can be stretched to include almost all modern Western authors. However, it seems more likely that the line of influence from Kant to Heller runs not so much through modern Western thought as from an underlying

---

5. For an account of rigidity as neurosis see Jacob Arlow, 'Psychoanalysis as Scientific Method', in Sidney Hook (ed.), *Psychoanalysis, Scientific Method, and Philosophy* (New York: New York University Press, 1959), pp. 206–7.

6. The word 'basic' selects the norms that govern obtaining the basic necessities of life, such as food, water and safety, and on the psychological side, dignity and love.

7. We adopt from Immanuel Wallerstein the idea that the modern world-system is an expansion of the European world-system, and his related idea that today the social sciences have only one object of study and it is the global economy.

sense of the sacredness of basic cultural norms etched into the occident's *conscience collective* to both Kant in the eighteenth century and Heller in the twenty-first.

Kant set forth his categorical/hypothetical imperative distinction in 1785, in his *Groundwork for the Metaphysics of Morals*.[8] He begins the book by saying that he is providing a philosophical defence of the difference between right and wrong as it is already known and understood by ordinary people (i.e., a defence of what we, daring to imitate Durkheim, just called the *conscience collective*). He gives an example of an act ordinary people in eighteenth-century Prussia already know and understand is wrong: incurring a debt without intending to pay it. He works with this example throughout this short book as his paradigm[9] of a categorical imperative. Heller tracks Kant when he says it is wrong to borrow money from the IMF, or from anywhere, or to promise explicitly or implicitly to continue funding social programmes,[10] without guaranteeing the ability to pay in the future. Incurring an obligation without making adequate provision to repay it is seen as tantamount to not intending to pay it.

Having used debt-paying as his example, Kant remarks toward the end of the book that he could have made his point even more distinctly with examples of attacks on the freedom and property of others.[11] Thus Kant assigns the status of categorical imperative to three fundamental features of the constitutive rules of markets: debt-paying (keeping promises, honouring contracts), property rights and the freedom of the juridical subject to choose to buy or not buy. (I regard this last as the structural underpinning of Keynes's liquidity preference.) With his categorical/hypothetical distinction, Kant endorses a fourth constitutive rule of markets: the absence of a strict duty to help others in need.

The duties commanded by categorical imperatives are strict duties.[12]

---

8. Immanuel Kant, *Groundwork for the Metaphysics of Morals* (New Haven: Yale University Press, 2002 (1785)).

9. In the sense of 'paradigm' specified by Kuhn in the second edition of *The Structure of Scientific Revolutions*, i.e., in the sense of the concrete case as opposed to the rule. In this sense, says Kuhn, science can get by without rules, but it cannot get by without paradigms.

10. Peter S. Heller, *Understanding Fiscal Space*, IMF Policy Discussion Paper PDP/05/04 (Washington, DC: International Monetary Fund, 2005), http://www.imf.org/external/pubs/ft/pdp/2005/pdp04.pdf, accessed March 2015, p. 5. Heller often writes 'should' and 'obligation'—e.g., on page 4.

11. Kant, *Groundwork*, p. 48.

12. In addition to strict duties to others there are also strict duties to oneself—for example, a strict duty not to commit suicide. Kant, *Groundwork*, p 47.

There ought to be no exceptions.[13] Their strictness emanates from the pure reason of the free human subject, who, in his freedom, is different from all of nature: 'Everything in nature works in accordance with laws. Only a rational being has the faculty to act *in accordance with the representation of law,* i.e., in accordance with principles, or a *will.*'[14]

This special status of human beings is the source of both the autonomy of the moral subject, which is permitted and required to give itself its own moral commands, and the respect due to other people who are, like oneself, rational beings and therefore ends in themselves. Kant writes: 'But suppose there were something *whose existence in itself had* an absolute worth, something that, as an *end in itself,* could be a ground of determinate laws; then in it and only in it alone would lie the ground of a possible categorical imperative, a practical law.'[15]

A categorical imperative is categorical because it derives from pure reason; it derives from the categories of thought that the mind brings to experience, not from experience itself. In the cases of the categorical imperatives to keep promises and respect property, Kant points out that the very categories of thought employed—promises and property—would dissolve and become meaningless if we made it the law of our actions to break them and steal it, respectively (and as rational beings we are called to give laws[16] to our actions). The putative laws 'Always break promises!' and 'Always steal!' are nonsense because in them the very concepts of contract and property become meaningless. Putting them into practice cannot be imagined.

In this way, one early modern philosopher (we could cite others) bullet-proofed the basic norms of markets, making them immune to empirical refutation. No possible set of facts could invalidate Kant's basic moral principles, because the principles are guaranteed by pure reason.[17]

---

13. Although the strict logic of his argument in *Groundwork* admits no exceptions, in another work, *Critique of Practical Reason*, Kant takes up the question of when, after all, there can be exceptions.

14. Kant, *Groundwork*, p. 29.

15. Ibid., p. 45. Italics added.

16. For simplicity, Kant's distinction between law and maxim is omitted.

17. The link between pure reason in mathematics and science and pure reason in morality and jurisprudence requires, for Kant, not only the notion that there are synthetic a priori truths but also his concept of freedom. The freedom of the rational being is conceived of as independence from the causal laws that govern all experienced phenomena. Armed with freedom conceived as pure independence, Kant is able to deduce from it Ulpian's basic principles of jurisprudence—not surprisingly because in its beginnings Roman law postulated the paterfamilias as absolute ruler of the property of the familia, with nothing to limit his absolute freedom but the equivalent power of another paterfamilias commanding another familia. See Immanuel Kant, *The Metaphysical Elements of Justice* (Rechtslehre), translated by

In contrast, when an imperative is hypothetical, 'the action is commanded not absolutely, but only as a means to another aim'.[18] In the realm of the hypothetical (i.e., not absolute but required only as the means to aims one happens to have) lie what Heller calls desired purposes and social programmes that are 'meritorious'. Kant also uses the word 'meritorious' when he distinguishes between strict (categorical, unremitting) duty and wide (hypothetical, meritorious) duty.[19] A separation is thus established between two realms: a realm of universal and eternal pure reason to which categorical imperatives belong, and a local and contingent realm of empirical reality to which hypothetical imperatives belong. Living things dwell in the latter realm, not the former. Heller echoes Kant when he implies that finance dwells in the former, pure realm and social programmes dwell in the latter, impure realm. In this way, the fiscal crisis of the state is aggravated by concepts set in stone.

There is a parallel here to the dunning letters that collection agencies send to delinquent debtors calling on the debtor to pay 'as agreed'. They demand payment even when the ratio of the debtor's assets to liabilities is one to ten and therefore, in the world of empirical reality, there is no possibility of paying the debts as agreed. Cultural norms prescribing promise-keeping are strong enough that it is worth the while of the collection agency to appeal to the debtor's conscience by writing the phrase 'as agreed', even when everyone knows that the phrase does not refer to a possibility or to a meeting of the minds. In reality, bankruptcies happen all the time and debts are often dissolved over time by inflation, but such concessions to material reality do not prevent august voices from upholding the ideal principle that payment of debts is a sacred duty. Indeed, Heller alluded implicitly to this basic norm in lines quoted above, referring to nations that do not comply with promises that were conditions for receiving IMF assistance.

Although Kant's reasoning is complicated, his assignment of a more-than-empirical status to ethical norms that constitute rules of markets is similar to the simple meaning of 'sacred'. Where the physical existence of a people depends on corn, corn is sacred.[20] Where the physical existence

---

John Ladd (Indianapolis: Hackett Publishing Company, 1999); Juan Iglesias, *Derecho Romano* (Barcelona: Ariel, 2004); Catherine Hoppers and Howard Richards, *Rethinking Thinking* (Pretoria: University of South Africa, 2012), ch. 4.

18. Kant, *Groundwork*, p. 33.

19. Ibid., p. 42.

20. Dennis Wall and Virgil Masayesva, 'People of the Corn: Teachings in Hopi Traditional Agriculture, Spirituality, and Sustainability', *American Indian Quarterly*, vol. 28 (2004), pp. 435–453.

of a people depends on cows, cows are sacred.[21] So too, when the physical existence of a people depends on market exchange, market exchange is sacred. Kant's philosophy sets in stone the basic cultural structure of modernity, just as myths and rituals set in stone the basic cultural structures of Pueblo Native Americans. In modernity, the sacredness of debt-paying reflects the physical fact that without investor confidence the investment-to-produce-for-sale-for-profit machine ceases to turn out food and other necessities of life.

Placing Kant's words in historical context and taking a broader view, the following four points summarize how the current dominant world system looks to us. Although the ideas of Alberto Arenas, Marissa Moore and Peter Heller we presented in chapter 10 do not make these four points explicitly, we submit that everything they say is consistent with them:

1. The system is made up of language-games people play. *It works the way it works*, that is, it is moved mainly by the dynamic of capital accumulation. (We add italics to deflate righteous indignation blaming some now-living person or some group for the way history has turned out.)
2. Until further notice, it is necessary to keep the system going. If the system stops, the vital processes of life stop. In fact, its stability depends on it not only not stopping but growing.
3. The system tolerates meeting vital human needs only within definite limits, even when the resources for meeting those needs are abundantly available. Funding for social programmes is expected to come from taxes, but taxes inhibit growth. Taxes on wealth motivate capital flight.
4. The institutional facts that generate these three points are sold to the public as legitimate and are imposed on practice as unmovable rigidities by clothing them in the garb of science, fiscal constraints and morality.

However, humans *are* capable of organizing themselves in ways different from those now dominant. The CWP is an example. Unbounded organizing is possible: aligning across sectors to serve the common good, making service to life the constant purpose. It *is* possible to make social human rights real by giving the government less to do and more resources to do it with. We say 'less to do' because individuals and nongovernmental institutions can

---

21. Marvin Harris, *Cows, Pigs, Wars, and Witches* (New York: Random House, 2011).

make it more their business to serve the common good. And we say 'more resources to do it with' because taxes do not need to be the only, or almost the only, source of public income.

2. Setting in Stone the Games People Play: Jean-Baptiste Say (Say's Law)

Having shown how Immanuel Kant bulletproofed liberal ethics, we now show how Jean-Baptiste Say bulletproofed liberal economics. To do this, we travel again, this time to early nineteenth-century Paris, where Say lived and worked.

We have mentioned Say's Law before, but we have not yet discussed it in detail. We offer a simple formulation of Say's Law: for every seller there is a buyer. If this were true, then every South African who needs to sell labour power in order to rise out of poverty would sooner or later find a buyer. If it were true, then everybody would already have what today's prevailing ideology assumes everybody already has: an obvious, open path to dignity in the form of a good job. People would need only to offer their services in the labour market. At most, they would need to take a course to become qualified in a field where employers are standing in line to hire employees.

Since Say's Law is false, government policies that try to end poverty by helping would-be sellers of labour power to find buyers and acquire the skills the buyers want to buy are not sufficient. And since it is false, there is a need for stating Staggering Fact 2: there is a chronic shortfall of effective demand.

For many devotees of Say's Law, there is a simple explanation for the millions of young people out of work and the millions more with precarious or miserably paid work around the world, namely, the government got in the way and distorted the natural benevolence of the invisible hand.

A practical consequence of frankly acknowledging that Say's Law is false concerns not *whether* there should be relief for the poor but the *design* of the relief. Because Say's Law is false, sustainable full employment in the private sector will never happen. There is then no point in making the work as miserable as it is in India's NREGA, for example, out of a morbid fear that if it were not thoroughly miserable, it would crowd out private employment.

The neoliberal utopia of everybody earning a good living in market-based employment is never going to happen. The fear that some private jobs might be lost by making livelihoods that are financed by transfer payments attractive, dignified and useful should not morph into a Frankensteinian monster—a towering, roaring absolute principle peremptorily demanding that every last livelihood financed by sales in markets must be squeezed into the economy before even one dignified and meaningful nonmarket livelihood can be squeezed out of the economy by recycling the social surplus.

Unless, of course, Say was right. So let us look now at how the French businessman-turned-politician Jean-Baptiste Say first told the story of what is called Say's Law.

Say's *Traité d'économie politique* was published in 1803[22] and republished repeatedly with revisions during the next several decades. Thomas Jefferson (the third president of the United States) translated it into English. In the book, Say transparently tells a story that claims to be better than other stories because it is scientific and because it is based on the natural order of things.[23] Today the same claim, based on the same story, has become so sophisticated that several years' study of higher mathematics is required before one can even begin to understand the issues. That is all the more reason to go back to 1803, when the story was born naked and undisguised.

On Say's account, there was no science of political economy before Adam Smith. Nevertheless, Say observes, from 1760 onward, even before *The Wealth of Nations* was published in 1776, the opinions of *économistes* dominated the minds of the leading progressive thinkers of France. In spite of their intellectual bungling, he wrote of them: 'What nobody denies to the economists, and what is sufficient to give them a right to recognition and general esteem, is that all of their writings favour the most severe morality and the liberty that every man should have to dispose at will of his person, his talents, and his property, a liberty without which individual happiness and public prosperity are meaningless words. I do not believe that one could find among them a single man of bad faith or a bad citizen.'[24]

These words reveal that, for the leading thinkers of the time, natural liberty came first and the correct elaboration of the science that (according to Say and other proponents) made natural liberty superior to traditional philosophy came second. Now that we know the secret—that at bottom Say was more committed to political effect than to intellectual coherence—we are

---

22. Jean-Baptiste Say, *Traité d'économie politique*, sixth edition (Paris: Guillamin, 1841 (1803)).

23. Of course the same can be said of all the pioneers who first articulated today's dominant ideologies. See, for example, Louis Dumont, *From Mandeville to Marx: The Genesis and Triumph of Economic Ideology* (Chicago: University of Chicago Press, 1977); and Gideon Freudenthal, Atom und Individuum im Zeitalter Newtons. Zur Genese der mechanistischen Natur—und Sozialphilosophie (Frankfurt: Suhrkamp, 1982).

24. Our own translation from Say, *Traité d'économie politique*, in the Discours preliminaire that precedes the beginning of bk. 1.

not surprised that a twentieth-century scholar like W. J. Baumol finds Say's Law subject to at least eight mutually inconsistent interpretations,[25] or that Joseph Schumpeter in his *History of Economic Analysis* finds that the history of debates about Say's Law has been a history of endless confusion, starting with Say himself, who, according to Schumpeter, did not understand his own law.[26] Say wrote with *parti pris*. He was advocating a social philosophy that pre-dated its scientific rationale.

The full title of Say's three-book treatise is *Traité d'économie politique: Ou simple exposition de la manière dont se forment, se distribuent ou se consomment les richesses* (Treatise on political economy: Or a simple explanation of how wealth is formed, distributed or consumed). The first book (*De la production des richesses*) comprises thirty chapters, some of which have long digressions. In the fifteenth chapter, Say considers the common complaint of entrepreneurs that they often produce goods successfully enough but then fail to sell them. They tend to attribute slow sales to a scarcity of money—they wish they could find more buyers.[27] Say writes: 'The entrepreneurs in the several branches of industry are in the habit of saying that the problem is not in producing, but in selling; that one could produce more goods if one could find an outlet for them.'[28] Say at no point denies this as the common experience of entrepreneurs. Nevertheless, he proposes to pursue the analysis, commenting that 'perhaps we will discover new truths, important truths, suitable for enlightening the desires of industrious men, and for securing the actions of governments eager to protect them'.[29]

While the foreground of chapter 15 is a refutation of the entrepreneurs who attribute lack of sales to lack of money, the background is, as always for Say, the desire to persuade the reader that the natural order is the best order. Say describes money as merely the *voiture* (vehicle) that carries value

---

25. William J. Baumol, 'Retrospectives: Say's Law', *Journal of Economic Perspectives*, vol. 13 (1999), pp. 195–204. Diverse interpretations are also discussed in Steven Kates (ed.), *Two Hundred Years of Say's Law: Essays on Economic Theory's Most Controversial Principle* (Cheltenham, UK: Edward Elgar, 2003).

26. Joseph Schumpeter, *History of Economic Analysis* (New York: Oxford University Press, 1954), pp. 621–25.

27. That more could be produced if there were more buyers is of course true in spades today. Most firms in most industries typically operate at a little over half of their productive capacity. Nevertheless, it is common to acquire additional productive capacity, not pursuant to the liberal myth of producing until marginal cost equals marginal revenue, but pursuant to the real-world strategy of erecting barriers to entry to preserve oligopolistic pricing. These matters are elucidated in Yanis Varoufakis et al., *Modern Political Economy: Making Sense of the Post-2008 World* (London: Routledge, 2012).

28. Say, *Traité d'économie politique*, at the beginning of bk. 1, ch. 15.

29. Ibid. Our translations.

from buyer to seller. He claims to refute the common illusion that sometimes there is no buyer for a would-be seller, and he starts by refuting the illusion that scarcity of money is the cause of gluts in markets. Thus begins one of a number of formulations that we call Say's Law or Say's Law of Markets.

Say's reasoning goes like this: A neighbour becomes a buyer because he (or she) produces something useful that has exchange value. This vendible commodity (to use Smith's term) gives him access to the *voiture* that will facilitate exchange of the value of his product for the value of someone else's product. Here is the principle: From the *instant* (the word is the same in French and English) he comes to possess a saleable commodity, the value of his product can be exchanged for the value of someone else's product. Like the transubstantiated host that is not a symbol of the body of Christ but his actual body, the finished goods stored in the manufacturer's warehouse awaiting sale are already effective demand in the marketplace, and not merely potential effective demand.

Having made every producer into a buyer by definition (following Smith in counting as a producer only someone who makes something that can be sold and defining a buyer as someone who possesses a vendible commodity), Say is challenged to reconcile his principle with the real-world experience of entrepreneurs for whom the problem is not in producing but in selling. One can read Say in the balance of the chapter as making a number of sensible observations that are not always consistent with one another or with his principle. Say concedes the facts while in strict logic preserving his principle.

It may be that the merchant cannot sell because the commodity he offers is something people do not want. Thus Say speaks of 'demandes diverses, déterminées par les mœurs, les besoins, l'état des capitaux, de l'industrie, des agents naturels du pays' (diverse demands for goods, determined by custom, needs, the state of development and the natural features of a country).[30] In other words, people's motivations for buying are often independent of someone else's need to sell something to make a living.

Or the merchant may have made something people do want but is already sufficiently supplied. Say writes: 'Car enfin ce n'est que dans les quantités abstraites qu'il y a des progressions infinies, et dans la pratique la nature des choses met des bornes à tous les excès' (Because in the end, consumer demand cannot be infinitely expanded; the nature of things places limits on excess, and there comes a point when markets are satiated).

---

30. These quotations from Say are from bk. 1, ch. 15. The English words following the French are not meant to be exact translations.

Or the would-be seller may live in a backward area where there are no buyers because other people are not producing vendible commodities that could be exchanged with his. Say says: 'Que feraient un actif manufacturier, un habile négociant dans une ville mal peuplée et mal civilisée de certaines portions de l'Espagne ou de la Pologne?' (What can an energetic manufacturer or a skilled businessperson do in a town that is underpopulated and undercivilized, like certain parts of Spain or Poland?) Say advises such entrepreneurs to move to places where there are many other entrepreneurs, so they can buy one another's products.

Or the merchant's costs of production may be so high that he cannot sell at a competitive price. Say writes: 'Alors on peut bien créer une chose utile, mais son utilité ne vaut pas ce qu'elle coûte, et elle ne remplit pas la condition essentielle d'un produit, qui est d'égaler tout au moins en valeur ses frais de production' (One may well create something useful, but the value of its utility is still less than its cost, and one does not fulfil the essential condition of making a product, which is that its value must at least equal the cost of producing it). In other words, one has not really made a product, though if one had made a product there would be a buyer for it. And so on.

Say discusses other reasons why sales do not happen, all the while maintaining his principle, even while conceding all the facts cited by people who believe that in a mercantile system there is a chronic weakness of effective demand. Each reason he offers for why goods are not sold reclassifies entrepreneurs out of the category of producers. By definition, if one's commodity is not vendible, one is not a producer. By definition, every product can be sold, because if it cannot be sold it is not a product. (Similarly, Modern Money Theory can argue that 'a sovereign issuer of currency can always buy whatever is for sale in its currency' is a tautology, true by definition, because if it cannot always buy whatever is for sale, it is not sovereign.) Every seller has a buyer because if there is no buyer, by definition there is no product, and without a product a seller is not a seller.

Meanwhile, the world goes on as before.[31] Say's Law in its first and most transparent version is set in stone because it is true by definition; it is immune to refutation by facts.

Having tracked Say's Law to its source, as well as examined the Kantian

---

31. See also Piero Sraffa, 'The Laws of Returns under Competitive Conditions', *Economic Journal*, vol. 36: 144 (Dec 1926), pp. 535–550. Typically, the chief obstacle to increasing production is the difficulty of selling the product.

roots of the views expressed by Peter Heller, we are now in a better position to see how the veil of cultural meanings that organizes human behaviour complicates what might at first seem a simple process of moving resources from the posh suburbs of surfeit to the bosh townships of despair. First, the resources are *property*, and that is set in stone. Second, legitimate transfers must be *contracts*, and that is set in stone. Third, the juridical subjects who own the property and would be parties to any contract possess *freedom* conceived as independence to do as they may or may not choose, which is also set in stone. Fourth, there is no strict duty for the haves to share with the have-nots, and this is set in stone. Fifth, this state of affairs is supposed to be, in Keynes's words, the best of all possible worlds, provided that we let well enough alone. It is a world where if the poor remain poor, it is their own fault. If they would take the trouble to offer something for sale, they would (in the absence of government or union interference) inevitably find a buyer—and that too is set in stone.[32]

In this chapter and throughout this book we have been suggesting that when you think hard and long about an immediate, pressing problem, such as how to find adequate funding to expand the CWP, you are inexorably led to the conclusion that the fiscal crisis of the state is a symptom of a defective basic social structure. Although in the language of sociology or anthropology it can be called a social or cultural structure, in the language of philosophy it can be called liberal ethics. And in the language of jurisprudence, it can be called private law, or civil law.[33]

3. Structural Transformation: Capturing Rents

To reach our next scene, we fast-forward about a century to the time of Alfred Marshall, which straddled the year 1900, crossing the English Channel and then trekking to Marshall House at Cambridge, arriving there on a chilly, damp and windy day. We can advance our understanding of the theory of economic rent by studying the works of Marshall, who was Keynes's father's teacher. (We believe that Keynes had Marshall's theory of rent in mind when he advocated, in chapter 24 of *General Theory*, the euthanasia of the *rentier* class.) However, before spending time with Marshall's ideas,

---

32. For an important account of how the basic juridical norms listed here organize social life, see Karl Renner, *The Institutions of Private Law and their Social Functions* (New Brunswick, NJ: Transaction Publishers, 2010 (first German edition, 1904)).

33. Ibid.

we need to consider the concept of capturing rents generally, as well as examine its origins.

In this book, we have pinned many hopes on the concept of capturing rent. Guy Standing and others also place many hopes on capturing rent in their proposals for a universal basic income (UBI).[34] Capturing rent is supposed to fund the inclusion of the excluded. It is supposed to make society governable. It is supposed to reduce inequality and withal bring us lower rates of crime, more personal self-esteem, better schools, more united families, better health and so on, down the long list of the benefits research has shown to flow from living in a more equal society.[35] We owe the reader a better explanation of how capturing rent is supposed to work in order to assess the prospects of using it to pay for social programmes. It is a major part, although not all, of what we mean by sharing surplus.

As it happens, during some of the years we have spent writing this book, the prices of minerals South Africa exports have been falling.[36] As prices fall to or near the costs of production experts say that mechanizing the mines is the only way to keep the industry profitable. However, mechanization and mine closures will further swell the already swollen ranks of the unemployed, increasing the number of people who need livelihoods funded by rents even as there appear to be fewer rents to capture. The mining companies will be squeezed between high costs and low prices and thus have less to offer the tax collector. In such situations, if our understanding of the concept of capturing rent is limited to the social surplus derived from the gifts of nature exploited by miners, we will not see much light at the end of the tunnel. All the more reason, then, for us to look more closely at the concept of rent.

We undertake this inquiry presuming that the problem of making the social functions of profit and capital accumulation compatible with dignity for all is a problem everybody wants to solve. Similarly, we presume that the related problems of how to capture rents and recycle the surplus are problems everybody wants to solve. We approach these issues with the

---

34. Guy Standing, *Basic Income: And How We Can Make It Happen* (London: Pelican, 2017).

35. Richard Wilkinson and Kate Pickett, *The Spirit Level: Why More Equal Societies Almost Always Do Better* (London: Allen Lane, 2009).

36. From mid-2014 to mid-2015, the price of platinum fell from around $1500 (USD) per ounce to around $1000. Coal fell from $84 per tonne to $62. From July 2014 to July 2015, the price of an ounce of gold fell from $1364 to $1091. Other minerals followed suit. These numbers can easily be verified by searching on Google for websites providing the prices of these commodities.

expectation that consensus can be reached and absolute conflict avoided. We would never have this expectation if we studied only political science and economics; we get it from psychology.[37]

We believe that the recycling of rents to fund social programmes can be a centrepiece of a policy of social security that makes everyone secure, including the children of the now-euthanized ex-*rentier* dynasties. (We use the word 'recycling' in a general sense.) Moving rents to where the needs are does not have to be done by taxing and spending. It can be done by individuals sharing with their neighbours, by corporations taking on social responsibility, by churches, by charitable organizations, by making pension funds and eleemosynary organizations the owners of shares in corporations and in many other ways.

Many issues around rent and around the potential of rent as a source of funding for social programmes centre on what Alfred Marshall called 'that vague and perhaps misleading sentence—rent does not enter cost of production'.[38] Defined in simple terms, rent is the gravy left over after all the costs of production are paid. In this definition, both normal profit and normal return on capital are counted as costs of production—the former because, in a for-profit private business, without sufficient profit to motivate the entrepreneur there would be no production, and the latter because, also in a for-profit business, without capital (raised in capital markets where one must pay normal rates of return in order to buy its use) there would be no production. In other words, before rent comes into existence, all costs involved in putting production into motion and making it happen must already be paid. Of course, we are not counting as a cost of production paying rent itself, which might be paid to a landlord whose only act is a permissive one—allowing production to occur on his property—and who contributes nothing to production itself.

It follows that if rent is transferred to the government or eleemosynary institutions or used by the *rentier* herself to pay for social programmes, production will not be impaired. By definition, all things needed to supply all the factors of production, including the profit needed to motivate the entrepreneur, will survive that transfer. The entrepreneur whose vocation is to create social surplus to serve society, in the spirit of faithful stewardship and in the spirit of *ubuntu*, will be living his calling, as a medical doctor

---

37. See in general the works of Evelin Lindner. To begin to sample a huge literature, see John Gibbs, *Moral Development and Reality* (Oxford: Oxford University Press, 2013).
38. Alfred Marshall, 'On Rent', *Economic Journal*, vol. 3 (1893), p. 75.

lives her calling by being faithful to her oath to Hippocrates. If a government imposes a tax on rent that causes farms and businesses to fade away into stagnation and bankruptcy because the burden of the tax drives their revenues below what they need to continue, what this proves is that what the government thought was rent was not in fact rent.[39] By Marshall's (and Ricardo's) definition, if it had been rent, the farmers would have continued to farm and the businesspeople would have continued to trade.

A similar point can be made by calling sharing a form of consumption. Once I have my income, however I get it, I can go into shops and spend it. If instead of spending it on a new pair of shoes for myself, I decide to buy noodles for the single mom next door who lost her job, nobody will stop me. I have chosen to recycle my income to where the needs are. Income from any source, not just rents, can be recycled.

Jorge Leiva, a former Minister of the Economy in Chile and a former Chilean representative to the Inter-American Development Bank, provided a succinct list of reasons why rents should be recycled for public purposes in Chile:

1. The private appropriation of rents is the largest source of social inequality in a mining country (*país minero*).
2. Rent-seeking behaviour should be discouraged because it channels resources away from use in the real economy.
3. In the case of rents derived from natural resources, private appropriation of rents diminishes the country's natural capital without making the productive investments needed to prepare the country for the time when the natural resources are exhausted.
4. Financing government with rents is neutral with respect to the efficient allocation of resources and does not affect investment.
5. The public appropriation of rents could finance, among other things, an industrial policy diversifying an economy that is overly specialized.[40]

When ethical realism adjusts morality to physical function, the rest

---

39. This happened in India in the early 19th century, when some disciples of David Ricardo (who pioneered the doctrine of rent) imposed a tax on farmers. The tax was intended to transfer to the public purse a surplus the farmers did not need. In fact, it suffocated agriculture and had to be repealed. Michelle Burge McAlpin, 'Economic Policy and the True Believer', *Journal of Economic History*, vol. 44 (1984), pp. 421–427.

40. Jorge Leiva Lavalle, 'Las rentas del cobre y el desarrollo chileno', in Gonzalo Martner and Jorge Rivera (eds.), *Radiografía crítica del 'Modelo Chileno'* (Santiago: LOM/USACH, 2013), p. 199. We have simplified as well as translated.

follows. It may be simple or it may be complicated, but it follows. In the words of Mahatma Gandhi, 'With unity of hearts, all things are possible; without unity of hearts, all else is futile.'

The history of the economic concept of rent goes back at least to Adam Smith. Smith's answer to the question of how much rent the landlord charges the tenant was this: as much as the landlord can get away with. 'Rent, considered as the price paid for the use of land, is generally the highest which the tenant can afford to pay.'[41] Rent is 'naturally a monopoly price. It is not at all proportioned to what the landlord may have laid out upon the improvement of land, or to what he can afford to take; but to what the farmer can afford to give.'[42]

It should not be forgotten that Smith began to formulate his ideas in *The Wealth of Nations* barely a century after the English Civil War of 1642–48. The social levellers had lost the war. The traditional aristocracy had retained its right to live without working by exacting rent for the use of land. In Smith's language, the landlords 'love to reap where they never sowed'.[43] Smith might not have founded the science of political economy if it had not been for the military victories of Oliver Cromwell and William of Orange, for the social structure that is the object of that science's study might not have existed.

Alfred Marshall similarly observes that economics was late in being developed because the modern industry that is its chief object of study was late in coming into existence.[44] The new science of political economy was, as David Ricardo said, a study of the laws that determine the division of produce among the social classes.[45] The mathematical renaming of social classes as 'factors' or 'variables' came later.

The theory of rent—the ethical and political question of whether some should live in leisure without toil—has, for more than two centuries, been intertwined with the scientific question of whether rent enters into the cost of production. It is sometimes called the theory of Ricardian rent because,

---

41. Adam Smith, *An Enquiry into the Nature and Causes of the Wealth of Nations*, (New Rochelle, NY: Arlington House, n.d.), at the beginning of bk. 1, ch. 11.

42. Ibid.

43. Ibid., ch. 6.

44. Alfred Marshall, *Principles of Economics*, third edition (London: Macmillan, 1895), part 3 of ch. 1, pp. 24–29.

45. David Ricardo, letter to Thomas Malthus of October 9, 1920, quoted by John Maynard Keynes in *The General Theory of Employment, Interest, and Money* (London and New York: Macmillan, 1936), p. 4.

in 1817, David Ricardo gave it its classic formulation.[46] Ricardo thought of rent as primarily rent of land and only secondarily rent of any natural resource. Ricardo asks us to imagine that exactly the same quantities of capital and labour are devoted to raising food on two same-sized plots of land. If the value yielded by the land (i.e., the price times the quantity produced) is greater on one plot than on the other, then the difference between the two values will be rent, not produced by or explained by either capital or labour. If the first plot of land is so marginal that it barely justifies the labour and capital devoted to cultivating it, then that plot pays zero rent. For the second plot, the difference between its yield and the first plot's yield will be its amount of rent. In Ricardo's words: 'Rent is that portion of the produce of the earth, which is paid to the landlord for the use of the original and indestructible powers of the soil.'[47] (Ricardo's critics would later point out that good agricultural land is rarely just these inherent 'powers of the soil'; it is usually also the result of many years of careful cultivation.)

As the population increases, and with it the demand for food and the price of food, more and more land of worse and worse quality is pressed into service. As a result, the rent that can be charged for the use of better land goes up and up. In Ricardo's words, the rent a landlord can charge can be calculated as the difference between the fertility of the land the landlord happens to own and the fertility of 'the least productive land in cultivation'. Ricardo's advice to governments is to tax rents: 'A tax on rent would affect rent only; it would fall wholly on landlords, and could not be shifted to any class of consumers.'[48] It would not affect the wages of the workers, the profits, or the motivations of the farmers.

For Karl Marx, rent is part of the trio of rent, profits and interest, which he mocks as the 'holy trinity'.[49] The three come from a single original source: surplus value. Marx seems to say most of the time that any value generated anywhere, including surplus value, is due to the exploitation of the labour power of the workers. Nevertheless, he begins his 1875 *Critique of the Gotha Programme* with the emphatic words: 'Labour is *not the source* of all wealth. *Nature* is just as much the source of use values (and it is surely of such that

---

46. David Ricardo, *Principles of Political Economy and Taxation*, third edition (London: John Murray, 1821 (1817)).
47. Ibid., ch. 2, first sentence of second paragraph.
48. Ibid., first sentence of ch. 10.
49. Marx develops these ideas in the posthumously published third volume of *Capital*.

material wealth consists!) as labour, which itself is only the manifestation of a force of nature, human labour power.'[50]

Marx did not live long enough to read Joan Robinson's arguments rejecting his labour theory by including private control of capital goods and natural resources as sources of surplus.[51] He is also not alive today to see human labour replaced by robots, while exploitation takes the form of deriving huge rents from financial speculation; charging high interest rates on credit cards; the privatization of water and seeds; and intellectual property such as patents on information technology, alternative fuels and pharmaceuticals.[52]

We believe that if Marx were with us now, he would agree that while we move toward ever more social appropriation of the social product, we must simultaneously take measures to be sure that the social functions performed by profit and interest continue to be performed, one way or another. We think Marx would also agree that rents can and should be transferred to social programmes, provided that we avoid what Marshall calls a violent shock[53] to the productive processes that satisfy (albeit imperfectly so far) the vital needs of the people.

The most famous attack on Ricardo's theory of rent is Leon Walras's 'Exposition and Refutation of the English Theory of Rent' in lesson 39 of *Elements of Pure Economics* (first edition 1874).[54] Walras's critique of Ricardo has been praised by Milton Friedman[55] as an excellent example of using symbolic forms and elementary mathematics to clarify vague statements. What Walras's refutation of Ricardo actually shows is that rent cannot be properly calculated as Ricardo calculated it. The calculation of rent needs to be incorporated into a more complete system of variables, where more quantities are flexible and fewer are fixed and all are related to each other.

Walras specifically separates his scientific inquiry into rent from an ethical inquiry into property rights, which would consider Smith's point that landlords reap where they have not sown.[56] Walras also specifically recognizes that 'to be sure the English school succeeded in demonstrating that rent

50. *Critique of the Gotha Programme*, https://www.marxists.org/archive/marx/works/1875/gotha/ch01.htm. Italics in original.
51. Joan Robinson, *An Essay on Marxian Economics* (London: Macmillan, 1942).
52. See, for example, Vandana Shiva, *Water Wars: Privatization, Pollution, and Profit* (Boston: South End Press, 2002).
53. Marshall, 'On Rent', p. 78.
54. Léon Walras, *Elements of Pure Economics* (London: Routledge, 2003), pp. 404 et seq.
55. Milton Friedman, 'Léon Walras and his Economic System', *Journal of Political Economy*, vol. (1955), p. 906.
56. Walras, *Elements*, lessons 2, 3 and 4.

does not enter into the cost of production'.⁵⁷ He was personally in favour of nationalizing the land and paying public expenses with rents instead of taxes.

We see the contributions of Walras and others to the debates that followed on Ricardo's proposal to tax rents as a prologue to the more sophisticated account of rents provided by Alfred Marshall in his article 'On Rent', first published in 1893. Marshall basically supports Ricardo's concept of rent, extending it and adding his own views, while admitting that Ricardo's critics make some valid points.⁵⁸

Marshall introduces and defines what he calls situation rent. 'It consists of those incomes, or rather those parts of incomes which are the indirect result of the general progress of society rather than the direct result of the investment of capital and labour by individuals for the sake of securing certain gains for themselves.' A good location, for example, gives a business an advantage that can be translated into money. If a small plot of land remains unchanged while a railroad or a port is built nearby, its owner will derive increased rent, because the plot's situation is improved by the general progress of society.

Situation rent is indeed one of the most common kinds of rent. It derives from the fact that there is only so much space on the planet and that some locations are better sites for business than others. Governments have been especially inclined to tax situation rent when the government itself creates a surplus for a landowner by, for example, building a highway that makes the land an ideal site for a business.

Marshall goes on to say that the so-called rent of a building (economists are aware of the difference between the common use of the word 'rent' and 'rent' defined in economics in the Ricardian tradition) is commonly composed of two elements. One is the rent of the ground on which the building is built, which is often chiefly a situation rent. The other part of the rent, generated by the building, may include what Marshall called a quasi-rent, a term he coined to refer to income derived from machines and other man-made sources of income. It refers to income from old investments of capital, as distinct from profits on current investments.

---

57. Ibid., lesson 39, p. 417. Walras goes on to say that 'this proved to be the rock on which the English school foundered', meaning that their reasoning makes their calculations of the amount of rent incorrect. But Walras's reasoning does not deny the point that rents can be transferred from where they are least needed to where they are most needed. See Renato Cirillo, 'Leon Walras and Social Justice', *American Journal of Economics and Sociology*, vol. 43 (1984), pp. 53–60.

58. The bulk of Marshall's views are found in his *Elements*, which went through many editions, and they are largely supported by Stiglitz, Piketty, and others.

With quasi-rent, time enters the picture. Improved agricultural land is scarce, both because a major component of its value consists of gifts of nature, which are limited, and because of improvements like those John Stuart Mill attributed to 'the centuries-long marriage of the peasant and the soil'. Human-made improvements are also limited (hence Ricardo's concept of rent shades into Marshall's concept of quasi-rent), even though human-made improvements are limited less strictly than nature's gifts. While the quantity of human-improved land can be expanded in the course of time, this does not happen quickly.

Much the same can be said of a building or of a complex machine. Both are also scarce. When demand is high, their price will be bid up not only because of what it costs to make them but also because supply is inelastic in the short and medium term. If their price ever descends to their cost of production, it will not be soon. Hence, they fetch a quasi-rent. In other words, the ground on which the building sits generates situation rent, while the business itself and the machinery within it generate quasi-rent.

Marshall comments elsewhere: 'Thus our central doctrine is that interest on free capital and quasi-rent on an old investment of capital shade into one another gradually; even the rent of land being not a thing by itself, but the leading species of a large genus.'[59]

To briefly summarize what Marshall spells out at length in nuanced detail, we have the rent of land, the rent of natural resources, situation rent and quasi-rent. In all four categories of rent, normal profits can often be made and a normal return on capital can often be earned. In other words, the opportunity cost of capital can be paid, leaving rent. The rent is a social surplus.

Critics have made other points that do not really affect Jorge Leiva's and our support for the ethical and rational recycling of surplus to meet vital needs. It is said, for example, that Ricardo was wrong because he expected rent to become an increasing part of national income, when in fact rents have shrunk as a proportion of total national income and wages have become a larger proportion. It is also said that Ricardo's practical problem of the high price of grain in Great Britain was solved by free trade, making all the land in the world available to satisfy the needs of the British consumer. It is further said that Ricardo was wrong because he thought land was unique as a source of rent, while in fact anything can be sold by its owner for more

---

59. Alfred Marshall, *Principles of Economics* (London: Macmillan, 1893), p. 85.

than is necessary to motivate its production (for example, a professional football player who would gladly sell his services for a million dollars might be paid two million because of lucrative contracts to telecast the games he plays in).[60]

None of these points contradicts the principle of paying for social programmes with rents. The last, indeed, augments it, leading to a definition of rent as a payment that is not needed to motivate production (in this example, the production of skilful play by an athlete). Thus, the critics of Marshall and Ricardo pave the way for a contemporary definition of rent: rent is windfall income that performs no social function because it is in excess of the income needed to motivate socially desirable behaviour. As with our example of the football player, whose skills benefit society by entertaining a vast audience, so also soccer aces, rock stars, bankers, real estate speculators and many others can generate rents far in excess of the incentives needed to make their work socially useful, whatever the price of platinum or gold may be in global markets. It can be expected that, in the future, the owners of intellectual property rights to advanced technologies—like the production of lab-grown meat that may one day replace cattle ranches—will be voluntary public benefactors or major taxpayers or the rights will be expropriated, or some combination of the three.

Our opinion remains that of Marshall: 'However untenable may be the so-called "Ricardian dogmas," the analysis, of which Ricardo was the chief builder, has firm if often unseen foundations.'[61] This is also the opinion of Joseph Stiglitz, who has written a series of papers advocating the capture of rents as an integral part of social policies designed to fund social programmes and to reduce inequality.[62]

Thus we see that fiscal constraints imposed by fear that the redistribution of wealth will damage production are constraints that can be lifted to the extent that economic rent can be identified, captured, and transferred to pay for social programmes. However, this is not an area where a simple formula is enough. There are no substitutes for moral integrity, practical

---

60. These criticisms of Ricardo are made in George Stigler, 'Bernard Shaw, Sidney Webb, and the Theory of Fabian Socialism', *Proceedings of the American Philosophical Society*, vol. 103 (1959), pp. 469–475. Stigler nevertheless concedes that there is such a thing as functionless profit. For a view closer to ours see Richard Arnott and Joseph E. Stiglitz, 'Aggregate Land Rents, Expenditure on Public Goods and Optimal City Size', *Quarterly Journal of Economics*, vol. 93 (1979), pp. 471–500.

61. Marshall, 'On Rent', p. 90.

62. See Joseph E. Stiglitz, *The Great Divide: Unequal Societies and What We Can Do about Them* (New York: W. W. Norton, 2015).

judgment, correct and transparent procedures, good will and mutual respect among all concerned in determining the balance between carefully finding the best uses for the golden eggs laid by the goose—the surplus produced by the economy—and properly feeding the goose so she will continue to lay more golden eggs.

4. On Whether a New *Ubuntu* Can Relieve the Fiscal Crisis of the State

In the preceding section, discussing rents, we considered some ways (more will be considered in the following section on Thomas Piketty) that wealth can be shared without seriously impairing the capacity of the golden goose to lay eggs; indeed—invoking in passing one of the least controversial of Keynes' insights—geese lay more eggs when there are more customers who can afford to buy eggs. We thus strengthened our economic defence of our ethical principle that we who have more than we need *should* share; and the economic defence of our psychological principle that the majority of our species *can* reach higher levels of ethical conduct than the currently average levels.

Please notice that these principles welcome but do not require philosophy, religion or cultural consensus. A dual biological adaptation is sufficient: (1) It is *functional* to care and share.[63] (2) Humans are social, or, what amounts to the same thing, spiritual.[64] That is the way evolution has turned out. People evolved to live in cultures where soft emotions contribute to satisfying their spiritual needs and simultaneously help them cope with the hard facts.[65]

Now we ask how such findings from the human sciences—overlooking for now the fact that some people do not agree with them—can help humans evolve beyond the *Steuerstaat*. For that purpose, we visit the avocado-packing house of a scholar turned banker turned business ethics thought-leader, and now turned farmer, in the town of Kiepersol in the province of Mpumalanga, South Africa. In this fictitious interview, for which he should not be held responsible, a fictitious Reuel Khoza offers us a cup of fictitious tea.[66]

---

63. Consider, for example, the arguments of Bronislaw Malinowski, which fell into disgrace for several decades because of the defeat in academic controversies of people who called themselves 'functionalists' but are now being recognized as containing a core of good sense. *A Scientific Theory of Culture* (Chapel Hill: University of North Carolina Press, 1944).

64. Consider the famous arguments of Emile Durkheim in *Les formes elementaires,* and the less famous arguments of Christian Smith.

65. David Sloan Wilson, *Darwin's Cathedral* (Chicago: University of Chicago Press, 2011).

66. Raul Khoza, *Let Africa Lead: African Transformational Leadership for 21st-Century*

He speaks first: 'I think I see what you are trying to accomplish. You are trying to end mass unemployment and at the same time end the fiscal crisis of the state. To accomplish the lifting of these yokes, you are proposing community development made possible by sharing the social surplus, leading to a world where most human behaviour is devoted to intrinsically valuable purposes, instead of to eking out a living *à la recherche de l'argent.*'

We respond: 'Perhaps you understand our purpose because your own purpose has been similar, although until now, at least, you do not seem to have abandoned the illusion that working for wages for someone who makes a profit selling what you make can bring full employment. Perhaps you will soon. Ours would be, like yours, a world guided by what you call moral leadership—the only leadership there is, because if it is immoral or amoral it is by definition misleadership. Sometimes you call your proposal market-oriented communalism carrying on and improving the spirit of social democracy.'[67]

Khoza continues: 'The iron laws of the market, what you call SF1 and SF2—what Keynes and Minsky portray as a perpetual losing battle against perpetually insufficient effective demand and against the perpetual weakness of the inducement to invest—will lose their power to determine a course of history that leaves the majority living from paycheck to paycheck or with no regular paycheck at all. In stressed-out efforts just to get by, they inadvertently kill the biosphere.'

'Yes,' we chime in. 'Your ethical attuned leadership and our ethical unbounded organizing strive to make it possible to take deliberate collective action to reverse global warming and to comply with human social rights. A key to our strategy is discreetly supporting grassroots-led community development. In view of the impossibility of funding employment for all by the sale of what the employee makes, we need a different approach to the 'bad neighbourhood' syndrome of alcohol, drugs, gangs, crime, domestic violence, depression, despair and mental illness. The state should have the capacity to play a role in catalysing basic security for all without relying on conventional economic growth and conventional employment; even when the state is insolvent, compelled to resort, hat in hand, to lenders like the IMF who keep their borrowers on short leashes. As Nelson Mandela used to say, with sports we can achieve dignity for people humiliated by the labour market. But not only with sports. We want to underwrite opportunities to

---

Business, foreword by Nelson Mandela (Cape Town: Vezubuntu Publishing Company, 2006); Raul Khoza, *Attuned Leadership: African Humanism as Compass* (London: Penguin, 2012).

67. Khoza, *Attuned Leadership,* e.g., position 7992 of Kindle edition.

develop talents for art and music and foreign languages and science, and so on; and with them opportunities to develop self-discipline, self-esteem and the good habits that form virtue. We need ways to fund it. We need ways to motivate it. That is where your concept of market-oriented communalism, building on *ubuntu*, comes in.'

'I try to show', says our distinguished host, 'that African ethnic identities, which have so often bedevilled state-building, contributing to violence and nepotism, can strengthen the soul of the state and lighten the burdens of its treasury when the goal is the common good, understood as the expression of our human commonality.'[68]

We add that there is more good news. 'Science is producing hitherto undreamt-of social surplus as we speak. There will be no shortage of material wealth created by green systems kind to the environment. What will be in short supply is what we came to your avocado ranch to talk to you about: wisdom, *phronesis*, *ubuntu*. These are needed to build new human institutions to fit new physical realities.

'Let the CEO of Microsoft, Satya Nadella, brief us: "The confluence of data with massive computational storage and cognitive power will transform industry and society at every level, creating opportunities that were once unimaginable—from health and education to agriculture, manufacturing and services. My company and others are betting on the convergence of several important technology shifts—mixed reality, artificial intelligence and quantum computing. With mixed reality we are building the ultimate computing experience, one in which your field of view becomes a computing surface; your digital world and your physical world become one. . . . Artificial intelligence will power every experience, augmenting human capability with insights and predictive power that would be impossible to achieve on our own." And so on.[69]

'Now, while we would agree that science can save us materially (if we can save ourselves socially and ethically), we must also express our agreement with those who deem it necessary to stabilize or reverse the growth of the human population. And our disagreement with those who applaud the endless multiplication of humans on the planet because growing markets are good for the economy. If economics conflicts with the sustainability of

---

68. Ibid., Kindle edition, position 287.
69. Satya Natella, foreword to Klaus Schwab, *Shaping the Future of the Fourth Industrial Revolution* (Geneva, Switzerland: World Economic Forum, 2018), Kindle edition, p.vii. A vast literature on new technologies on their way can easily be located online.

ecosystems in this way, then economics (and therefore social structure, and therefore ethics) must change.'

Khoza continues: 'Consequently, if your reasoning is right and the unbounded approach to practice that you advocate will work, then the iron laws of the market will have less power to determine the course of history. Since, as Aristotle said,[70] moral choices result not just from following customs but from deliberation leading to voluntary action. Emphasizing ethical leadership and followership with moral purpose when facing the crises that threaten our species today makes the world more governable.'

'Yes,' we add. 'Unbounded organizing, considering everybody's perspective and opinion, seeing for every problem many solutions not seen by conventional economics, makes it possible to take deliberate collective action to save the biosphere and to comply with human social rights.'

He goes on: 'To accomplish these consummations, you propose sharing the surplus. You revoke Ethics 101, defined as a celebration of liberal ethics, and endorse Ethics 102, defined as moral realism, rooted in the natural sciences and finding merit in both older Western traditions (Plato and Aristotle) and newer feminist, ecological and post-colonial philosophies. You are alleging that Ethics 102, but not Ethics 101, adjusts culture to its physical functions (to borrow a phrase from Antonio Gramsci). Orthodox economics, which assumes that most people earn a living by selling their labour power, is a nonstarter. It was an operating manual for the same obsolete basic cultural structure that Ethics 101 rationalized.[71]

'I agree with you that what is needed is not so much what heterodox economists have already given us—better accounts of how the economy really works[72]—but better basic cultural structures. Further and in the same vein, if human rights really are rights and if complying with them really is the law, then Ethics 102 requires every one of us, not just the state, to do what she or he can[73] to make employment, health care, decent pensions and other social rights, as defined in the International Declaration of Human Rights,[74] real and not just empty promises.

---

70. *Nichomachean Ethics*, bk. 3.

71. See, for example, C.B. McPherson, *The Political Philosophy of Possessive Individualism* (Oxford: Clarendon Press, 1962); and Andrew Sayer, *Why Things Matter to People* (Cambridge: Cambridge University Press, 2012), especially Sayer's remarks on Kant.

72. Frederick Lee, *A History of Heterodox Economics* (London: Routledge, 2009).

73. This qualification alludes to the principle 'ought to implies can', i.e., it cannot be your moral duty to do something you cannot do.

74. International Declaration of Human Rights, UN General Assembly Resolution 217A, 1948. Especially Articles 22–26. Many countries, including South Africa, include

'As a practical matter', Khoza goes on, 'the separation between private and public breaks down, because public-private cooperation is the only way to get the job done. If we wait for the state to lift the poor out of misery, we will wait forever. It will never happen. I have often said and written, and I still believe, that entrepreneurship is coupled with moral responsibility.[75] Not just in your sense of Ethics 101, but also in your sense of Ethics 102, which in turn corresponds to how property has been understood in Africa and in most cultures. Leaders and owners are servants of the organization they serve and trustees of the property they own for the common good.[76] Although there is a place for public ownership, and a place for land reform, market-oriented communalism centres on private owners whose identity and resources are inseparable from those of their community. At a political level there is always an awkward fit because law framed in Montesquieu's three-part division of powers is a relatively recent add-on to older traditions. The South African compromise would appear to be that property is private as it is understood in Roman-Dutch law, but the idea that people are expected to share with their ethnic brethren survived colonialism. It became an African precedent for social democracy in the Freedom Charter: "The people shall share."

'Meanwhile, recently, African traditions blend with and enrich the World Economic Forum's view that a leader in a company or in any organization is responsible to all the stakeholders [*alle die Interesse*, in Klaus Schwab's German]. These include the general public and ultimately all of life. The consensus-building words that tie everything together appear to be "ethical", "moral" and "responsible". Where there is ethical consensus, it matters little if one person is black, a second white, a third of some other ethnicity, a fourth a public official, a fifth a private entrepreneur and the sixth a trade union member (the latter three of any ethnicity), and so on, if each person does the same good thing for the same good reason.'

We add: 'If what they each do is align across sectors for the common good, each contributing what they can in light of the several claims their diverse moral obligations make on their resources, then the fiscal crisis of the state will be considerably alleviated.'

We end this section with two general conclusions. But they boil down

---

social rights in their national constitutions.

75. Khoza, *Attuned Leadership*, position 2041 and throughout.
76. Ibid., repeatedly—for example, positions 918, 1524, 2081, 2299, 2355, 2337, 3553, 7521 and appendix I.

to one because they are alternatives to each other. If one is right, the other must be wrong.

Conclusion One: Yes, there is a danger that the logic of accumulation will continue to dominate the world. Indeed, that is what happened in the seventeenth through nineteenth centuries, when accumulation of capital gave Europe military advantages that it used to conquer and colonize Africa, Latin America, Asia and Oceania.[77] It is happening again today under globalized financial neoliberalism.[78] When accumulation runs amok—when the good citizens share while the accumulators accumulate, acting like what economists call free riders, enjoying the benefits of social peace but not helping to pay for it—then the mathematics of compound interest imply what is in fact observed (see the discussion of Piketty's data below): after several generations, the bulk of the nations' and the world's wealth and power tends to end up in the hands of the accumulators.

Conclusion Two: But life does not have to be this way. Societies are open systems, where no set of quasi-Newtonian laws ever determines the final result.[79] As Karl Polanyi points out, the laws of the market are relevant only in the institutional framework of a market economy—and even there they are an extreme simplification of an extremely complex reality.[80] It might just be possible, this time, that Ethics 102 will guide majorities and elites to do what is in their common interest: Use the new technologies for the common good. Share the surplus.

5. Structural Transformation: Thomas Piketty's Contributions

We take the Air France nonstop direct flight back to Paris, leaving Johannesburg at midnight and arriving at Charles de Gaulle airport at 11:15 the next morning. After lunch and a nap, we take a taxi to the Paris School of Economics, 48 Boulevard Jourdan, Building B, where we meet (in our imaginations) the celebrated French economist and historian Thomas Piketty. Piketty and his many collaborators have amassed evidence supporting our claim that it is possible to make the global economy governable, or more governable than it is now, and to redistribute wealth more effectively than

---

77. Adam Smith notes that in modern war the great expense of firearms gives a military advantage to the nation that can best afford that expense. *Wealth of Nations*, Kindle edition at Digireads.com (2012), bk. 5, at the end of part 1, position 11161.
78. Joseph Stiglitz, *Globalization and its Discontents Revisited* (New York: Norton, 2018).
79. Roy Bhaskar, *The Possibility of Naturalism*, 4th ed. (London: Routledge, 2014).
80. Karl Polanyi, *La gran transformación* (Madrid: Quipue, 2007), p. 78.

it is redistributed now and at the same time maintain the golden goose in tip-top good health. They have built up a case for exacting higher taxes from people with high incomes and high wealth. We underscore what we regard as Piketty's most important finding: over time, productive capital tends to become *rentier* capital.[81] Accumulation that starts out as active entrepreneurialism typically becomes, in a few generations, an accumulated fortune that relieves its owners from the necessity of working.

As we noted in chapter 1, sometime in 1992, two years before South Africa's government transitioned to a system of majority rule, Nelson Mandela said to those in his inner circle: 'Chaps, we have to choose. We either keep nationalization and get no investment, or we modify our own attitude and get investment.'[82] However, we suggested, South Africa did not have to choose. It already had a substantial public sector built primarily by Afrikaners, and any challenges it may have faced in accessing international capital were because of the world's moral condemnation of the apartheid system, which in 1992 was soon to end. Brazil's Petrobras stands as an example of a state-run industry that has had no problems raising investment funds in capital markets. Indeed, Brazil's experience has been the opposite of what Mandela implied.[83]

When an enterprise in any sector is profitable enough to pay the cost of capital at market rates, it can acquire capital. This is especially true today, when there are plenty of accumulated funds around the world unable to find productive use in the real economy. We see this in Europe, where there is a shortage of entrepreneurs taking out loans even though central banks have lowered interest rates to zero. An enterprise in any sector with real resources producing real products for real customers with money in their pockets holds the aces when playing poker with global investors.

Walter Bagehot said in 1873 regarding accumulated wealth: 'The briefest and truest way of describing Lombard Street is to say that it is by far the greatest combination of economical power and economical delicacy that the world has even seen. . . . England is the greatest moneyed country in

---

81. Piketty in this respect echoes and updates the 19th-century American economist Henry George. Drawing on his observations in the American West, George observed that inequality increased over time. Some became rentiers able to live from land rents, while others fell into poverty. Henry George, *Progress and Poverty* (Cambridge, UK: Cambridge University Press, 2009 (1879)).

82. Nelson Mandela, quoted in Anthony Sampson, *Mandela: The Authorized Biography* (New York: Alfred A. Knopf, 1999), p. 429.

83. This and other similar experiences are documented in Cheryl Payer, *The World Bank: A Critical Analysis* (New York: Monthly Review Press, 1982).

the world; everyone admits that it has much more immediately disposable and ready cash than any other country. The effect is seen constantly. We are asked to lend, and do lend, vast sums, which it would be impossible to obtain elsewhere. It is sometimes said that any foreign country can borrow in Lombard Street at a price: some countries can borrow much cheaper than others; but all, it is said, can have some money if they choose to pay enough for it. . . . If any nation wants even to make a railway, especially a poor nation, it is sure to come to this country, to the country of banks. In domestic enterprises it is the same. We have entirely lost the idea that any undertaking likely to pay, and seen to be likely, can perish for want of money; yet no idea was more familiar to our ancestors, or is more common now in most countries.'[84]

Piketty makes a related finding that is less important but still significant: increasingly today, *rentiers* who do not have to work nevertheless do work. Piketty and his coauthors comment that 'today, it may be socially unacceptable to live purely off unearned income'.[85] These findings suggest the feasibility of what John Maynard Keynes called the euthanasia of the *rentier* class.[86] They suggest that, in principle, resources could be recycled from the top of the pyramid to the bottom of the pyramid with little or no effect on production.

Consider, for example, the L'Oréal group, founded by Eugène Schueller in 1907. His principal heiress, Liliane Bettencourt, does not need to work for a living, although she can if she wants to. Suppose she gets a bill from the government to pay her share of France's 'solidarity tax on fortunes'. To pay the tax she sells some of her stock in L'Oréal. The stock registrar for the company certifies that she is no longer the owner of these shares and inserts in the registry the name of the new owner. Then everything at L'Oréal goes on as before. Most people in the organization do not even know the transaction happened.

---

84. Walter Bagehot, *Lombard Street* (London: Henry S. King, 1873). A pastiche of words culled from the first few pages.

85. Facundo Alvaredo, Anthony B. Atkinson, Thomas Piketty and Emmanuel Saez, 'The Top 1 Percent in International and Historical Perspective', *Journal of Economic Perspectives*, vol. 27 (2013), p. 18.

86. Paul Mattick argues that so-called Keynesian macroeconomics cannot achieve the necessary transformation of capitalism, in Marx and Keynes, *The Limits of the Mixed Economy* (Boston: Porter Sargent, 1969). We agree with Mattick and we know that Keynes himself would have major reservations about what came to be called Keynesian. We agree with Keynes, with George Stigler in his article cited above and with many others, that there is such a thing as nonfunctional unearned income, but that does not end the story. Whoever has surplus should share it.

As our comments in chapter 1 show, we were already convinced before we read Piketty that capital formation is not the problem. Raising interest rates and raising profits will not solve the nonproblem we do not have. The problem is SF2. Transferring surplus to pay people who are redundant or precarious in the labour market to plant trees and to develop their musical talents will solve it.

Keynes suggested that the amazing productivity and decentralized decision-making of capitalism could be preserved in governable and equitable social democracies, where they could help those democracies achieve—not completely but more than formerly—the social appropriation of the social product that socialists have always advocated and enlightened capitalists have always attempted to deliver.[87] Keynes wrote: 'I see, therefore, the *rentier* aspect of capitalism as a transitional phase which will disappear when it has done its work. And with the disappearance of its *rentier* aspect much else in it besides will suffer a sea-change. It will be, moreover, a great advantage of the order of events which I am advocating, that the euthanasia of the *rentier*, of the functionless investor, will be nothing sudden, merely a gradual but prolonged continuance of what we have seen recently in Great Britain, and will need no revolution.'[88]

To Keynes's proposal-cum-expectation of a transformed capitalism without its *rentier* aspects one might add other transformations that, some people say, indicate we are now living in a time of post-capitalism. These include what Peter Drucker calls a 'society of organizations'; a shift in the locus of control from shareholders to management; retained earnings as the principal source of capital; knowledge as the principal factor of production; creating shared value and other forms of ethical responsibility; capital made available due to the discounting of notes, creation of money by lending, the rise of pension funds, mutual funds, insurance companies, charitable endowments and other institutional investors; and, more recently, the reliance of stock markets on public funding through the emissions of central

---

87. Another approach to social appropriation of the product is the concept of social market economy. Ludwig Erhard, *The Economics of Success* (London: Thames and Hudson, 1963). Erhard advocates a *soziale Markwirtschaft* that in principle harnesses efficiency fostered by competition to fund meeting social needs generally, and specifically a welfare state. Many other books promote variations on this theme. Given a wide consensus on the soziale objectives, there is room for many views on how to achieve them, including our view that an unbounded mixed economy aligned toward the common good achieves them better than a pure Markwirtschaft. A wealthy person like Andrew Carnegie can imagine himself achieving the social appropriation of the social product by his own personal decision to donate money to build libraries in small towns across America.

88. Keynes, *General Theory*, p. 376.

banks. In short, the ink had hardly dried on Marx's scathing critique of Mr. Moneybags in the first volume of *Capital* when modern finance and modern management gave him a pink slip and politely suggested that he devote himself to philanthropy; industry did not need him.

Piketty shows that the accumulated wealth in the hands of 'functionless investors' is quite large. In Europe it is something on the order of six times Europe's annual national income.[89] We put 'functionless investors' in quotation marks for several reasons. Two of them are: (1) much accumulated wealth takes the form of intact capital goods (for example, a pharmaceutical factory), where it is functional to leave the wealth intact since it cannot be divided and put in the form of consumer goods without grave damage to society; and (2) many of the *rentiers* who are collecting unearned income from accumulated wealth are pensioners, hospital endowments, museum endowments, and eleemosynary institutions of other kinds.[90] When the revenue pie is divided between capital and labour, and when capital over the years accumulates and becomes enormous wealth that generates enormous unearned income, not all of capital's share goes to the idle rich. Nevertheless, Piketty's findings show that, in most countries, the scope for redistributing resources from where they are not needed to where they are needed, while doing little or no sapping of the incentives that motivate socially useful activity, is quite large.

We already knew that structural transformation can be accomplished by transfers of a particular kind of *income*: rents, defined as revenue that is not a cost of production. From Piketty we now know that structural transformation can be accomplished by transfers of a particular kind of *wealth*: fortunes that have accumulated over the years and no longer play an active role in supplying 'the wants and conveniences of life'.

Recent decades have seen, particularly in the United States and the United Kingdom, the tendency to tax top incomes and the inheritance of wealth less, not more. Piketty and his colleagues find that the much-touted benefits predicted by proponents of cutting taxes on high incomes have not materialized. Inequality has increased as taxes on the rich have decreased,

---

89. Thomas Piketty, *Capital in the Twenty-First Century* (Cambridge, MA: Harvard University Press, 2014). 'The current per capita national income in Britain and France is on the order of 30,000 euros per year, and national capital is about 6 times national income, or roughly 180,000 euros per head.' From position 2108 of the Kindle edition.

90. Piketty estimates that about 7% of private wealth in the countries he studies is held by nonprofit foundations. Public wealth is a wash, the total value of all public assets being roughly equivalent to total public debt.

but the rich have not worked harder or been more creative in ways that have boosted general prosperity. Here is their proof: The advanced industrial countries have all grown at approximately the same rates—both those, like the United States and the United Kingdom, that have tried to stimulate growth by lowering the taxes of the rich, and those, like Germany and Switzerland, that have continued the tax rates of the post–World War II years. 'The regression analysis... using the complete time-series data since 1960, shows that the absence of correlation between economic growth and top tax rates is quite robust. By and large, the bottom line is that rich countries have all grown at roughly the same rate over the past 40 years—in spite of huge variations in tax policies.'[91]

Piketty and his coauthors estimate that recent astronomical pay increases of top executives in some countries have been at least three-fifths due to factors not related to performance. In fact, their evidence suggests that percentage should be closer to five-fifths. They find no reason to believe that these executives actually did their jobs any better than their peers. Plugging the three-fifths estimates into a model designed to optimize tax rates, they conclude that the tax rate on the highest incomes could potentially be set as high as 83 percent.[92]

Piketty and his colleague Emmanuel Saez propose an econometric model for calculating optimal inheritance tax rates. Considering equity-efficiency trade-offs and social preferences for redistribution, they conclude: 'We find that, for realistic parameters, the optimal inheritance tax rate might be as large as 50 percent to 60 percent, or even higher for top bequests, in line with historical experience.'[93]

In part 4 of *Capital in the Twenty-First Century*, Piketty sets out his proposals for funding a social state. For him, the issue of paying for social programmes dovetails with a broader goal that we have also emphasized and cannot emphasize enough: 'regaining control over the dynamics of capital accumulation'.[94] With those words Piketty states, though slightly differently, our Staggering Fact One. As long as the need of keeping up the rate of profit trumps any social or ecological objective that comes into conflict

---

91. Alvaredo, Atkinson, Piketty and Saez, 'The Top 1 Percent', p. 12.

92. Ibid., pp. 11 & 12.

93. Thomas Piketty and Emmanuel Saez, 'A Theory of Optimal Inheritance Taxation', *Econometrica*, vol. 81 (2013), pp. 1851–1886. The quoted text is the last sentence of the abstract.

94. Piketty, *Capital in the Twenty-First Century*, p. 471 (position 8171 in the Kindle edition). This key sentence was omitted in the Spanish edition.

with it, nations will not be governable. Our species, in spite of occasional victories for environmentalism, will remain on a path toward destroying itself and the biosphere.

Before World War I, the tax share of national income was in the neighbourhood of 7 or 8 percent, making it impossible to fund a social state. Between 1920 and 1980, the tax share of national income dramatically increased. After 1980, it stabilized around 25 percent in South Africa, 30 percent in the United States, 40 percent in the United Kingdom, 45 percent in Germany, 50 percent in France, and 55 percent in Sweden.[95] Piketty sees some room for income tax increases, but he does not see anything on the scale of the 1920–1980 increases happening again.

Public spending on education and health consumes 10 to 15 percent of the national income in developed countries today. Other transfer payments[96] consume the same proportion or somewhat more, up to 20 percent. Spending on these two social categories accounts for most of the now-stabilized 1920–1980 tax increases.

Mainly, the new taxes have gone to fund a social state. Piketty regards it as an open question whether anything of the sort will happen in the developing world. On one hand, the developing world has taken the social states of the developed world as the definition of modernization. On the other hand, the ideological and economic pressures of a global economy promoted by the developed world make it hard for developing countries to raise the tax share of national income above 10 to 15 percent, which is insufficient to fund health, education, and pensions on the scale enjoyed in the developed world. He adds that in the developed world itself there is danger that the pattern of rise followed by stabilization will turn into a pattern of rise followed by stabilization followed by decline: 'But progressive taxation today is under serious threat, both intellectually (because its various functions have never been debated) and politically (because tax competition is allowing entire categories of income to gain exemption from the common rules).'[97]

We would add that social benefits have already been reduced in the developed world. The aging of the population, structural unemployment

---

95. Ibid., position 8254 of Kindle edition. The South Africa figure is from Wikipedia and is for 2012 and 2013.

96. Piketty counts as transfer payments family allowances, guaranteed income, etc., and as income replacement, pensions and unemployment insurance. We lump more than he lumps into the category of transfers.

97. Piketty, *Capital in the Twenty-First Century*, p. 497.

and other factors have driven up the numbers of people receiving those reduced benefits. There are cutbacks—the welfare state is not as generous as it used to be—but in spite of the cutbacks the total costs and the total tax-take needed to pay those costs have so far remained approximately stable (and governments have gotten deeper in debt). Although the benefits are smaller, a larger proportion of the population is receiving them.

Piketty's breakthrough proposal is 'a progressive annual tax on individual wealth—that is, on the net value of assets each person controls'.[98] He imagines a tax rate of 0 percent on fortunes worth less than 1 million euros, 1 percent on fortunes between 1 and 5 million, and 2 percent for those above 5 million.[99] Piketty's proposal commands attention because it is advanced by a scholar who, with the help of many colleagues, has marshalled an enormous quantity of statistical data that demonstrates that most wealth—and an increasing proportion of wealth—is in a few private hands and only rarely in the hands of active entrepreneurs. Although they are riddled with exemptions, progressive taxes on total wealth are already used in some European countries (including France, Switzerland and Spain). Ideally, Piketty's tax would be worldwide, levied on everyone whose fortune is large enough to be taxed more than 0 percent. He regards such an ideal as worth retaining as an ultimate goal, even though it is not realizable anytime soon.

Piketty goes on: 'The primary purpose of the capital tax is not to finance the social state but to regulate capitalism.'[100] With these words he underlines again a key point we underlined earlier: the first step toward regulating global capitalism is transparency. At this point in history, global capitalism cannot be regulated because it is opaque to begin with. Reducing opacity by putting in place appropriate information-gathering systems regarding financial transactions and income flows as well as taxation of accumulated wealth itself would be a major step toward making effective taxation possible.

An example of opacity is when transfer pricing occurs. Transfer pricing refers to the numbers that transnational corporations make up when they sell things to themselves by having a branch in one nation 'sell' to another branch in another nation. Transfer prices are routinely manipulated to

---

98. Ibid., p. 516.

99. Ibid. On page 542, Piketty makes a different but related proposal: a one-time tax on large fortunes at a rate of 15% in order to pay down the national debt to zero. He appears to have in mind a typical country where accumulated private wealth held by a few people is equivalent to about six times one year's national income, and where public wealth is zero because the amount of public debt is equal to the value of all public assets.

100. Ibid., p. 518 (italics added).

minimize taxes.¹⁰¹ Joseph Stiglitz gives an example: 'Apple has become the prime example of how a clever firm can use its ingenuity to avoid paying its fair share of taxes by attributing profits to corporations that are essentially stateless, existing only in cyberspace, and which pay taxes to no jurisdiction.'¹⁰² An African Union study led by a committee chaired by Thabo Mbeki found that illicit financial flows out of Africa dwarf the foreign aid coming into Africa. Transfer pricing by multinational corporations is by far the largest culprit, followed at some distance by laundered drug money and organized crime.¹⁰³

A second purpose of Piketty's proposed capital tax is to reverse the process of ever-increasing inequality. If nothing is done to counter it, inequality will tend to continue increasing because of an empirical trend Piketty documents and expresses as r > g. The rate of growth (r) of large fortunes is around 6 or 7 percent per year, while most of the time, for most economies, the overall rate of growth (g) is around 2 percent in a typical year and around 5 percent in a very good year, thus, by simple arithmetic, leading to increasing inequality.¹⁰⁴

A third purpose for the capital tax, not to be sneezed at, is to pay for social programmes. At the tax rates Piketty imagines for Europe alone (0 percent under a million, 1percent from 1 to 5 million, 2 percent on total wealth exceeding 5 million euros), the tax would be paid by about 2.5 percent of the population and would bring in revenues on the order of 2 percent of Europe's GDP.¹⁰⁵

Piketty struggles with the practical barrier to enacting this tax: without almost inconceivable levels of international cooperation, significant taxes

---

101. Messaoud Mehafdi, 'The Ethics of International Transfer Pricing', *Journal of Business Ethics*, vol. 28 (2000), pp. 365–381.

102. 'Reforming Taxation to Promote Growth and Equity', http://rooseveltinstitute.org/sites/all/files/Stiglitz_Reforming_Taxation_White_Paper_Roosevelt_Institute.pdf, p. 9.

103. 'Report of the High Level Panel on Illicit Financial Flows from Africa', commissioned by the 4th Joint AUC/ECA Conference of Ministers of Finance, Planning and Economic Development; https://www.uneca.org/archive/publications/illicit-financial-flows.

104. Piketty cautions against taking r>g as a general explanation of inequality, in his article 'About Capital in the Twenty-First Century', *American Economic Review: Papers and Proceedings*, vol. 105 (2015), pp. 1–6. Robert Reich observes that although Piketty documents the high recent growth rates of large fortunes, he does not explain why today's enormous supply of capital has not led to a lower price of capital (as both Adam Smith and J.M. Keynes expected). Reich's explanation is (in brief and approximately) that economic power and political power combine to enable the wealthy to bend the rules of the game of capitalism in their favour. Robert Reich, *Saving Capitalism: For the Many, Not the Few* (New York: Knopf Doubleday, 2015), Kindle edition, locations 1604–1610.

105. Piketty, *Capital in the Twenty-First Century*, p. 528.

on wealth worldwide will be almost impossible to collect. He gives the example of a failed attempt to impose a similar tax in Italy. Faced with an exceptionally high public debt and an exceptionally high concentration of private wealth, Italy in 2012 enacted what was supposed to be a progressive annual tax on individual wealth. For fear that financial wealth would simply flee the country, the tax rate on wealth was set at 0.1 percent. Since real estate is harder to move, its tax rate was 0.8 percent. Nevertheless, the tax could not withstand the political opposition mobilized against it and was abandoned in 2013.[106]

Piketty concludes his discussion of the capital tax by reaffirming that a global progressive annual tax on individual wealth would be ideal. There is no technical reason why it would not be possible. But he does not convince himself, let alone the reader, that his ideal is realizable as the world is now organized. Our view is that Piketty's proposals and the similar proposals of Joseph Stiglitz are good ideas, but without cultural shifts that move hearts, minds, norms and laws to positions more aligned across sectors with the common good, they are not likely to be successfully implemented.

Before leaving Piketty, we want to examine a different topic he discusses that has particular bearing on the fiscal crisis of the state. In his 2020 book *Capital and Ideology*,[107] Piketty argues that, throughout history, the course of events had many 'switch points' when it could have taken a turn other than the turn it did take—the point being that choices you and I make now could indeed determine a different future. We agree. However, our interest is in a different theme from the same book: fiscal limitations on the powers of the government were built into the foundations of the first modern republics, and since those republics became models for others that followed, today's governments are deeply in debt. England, the Netherlands, the United States of America and France were the foundries where the constitutive rules that define the material positions of people who live in modern republics were forged. Piketty, in his book, provides details regarding France.[108]

---

106. Ibid. Piketty believes that if bank information were automatically shared internationally and if authorities had accurate information on who owns what, then a single country like Italy could impose a substantial wealth tax acting on its own. Ibid., p. 529.

107. Thomas Piketty, *Capital and Ideology* (Cambridge, MA: Harvard University Press, 2020 (2014)). Both in 2014 and 2020 and for citations to Habermas, the dates are for English editions, while the original French and German editions were a little earlier.

108. Regarding other countries see, among many, C. B. Macpherson, preface to John Locke's *Second Treatise of Government* (Indianapolis: Hackett, 1980); Howard Zinn, *A People's History of the United States* (New York: Harper and Row, 1980); and Costas Douzinas, *The End of Human Rights* (Oxford: Hart Publishing, 2000).

After the Revolution of 1789, when the victors set out to rebuild France as a modern republic, they contributed to defining what property *is* and what the modern rule of law *is*. 'The general philosophy was that the state—one and indivisible—would finance itself in the future through annual taxes duly approved by representatives of the citizenry, whereas the exploitation of perpetual property would henceforth be left to private individuals.'[109] The general rule (we would call it a cultural constitutive rule establishing material positions of the social structure) was that income-producing property would become the property of the victorious class. Church property was classified as feudal and was confiscated and sold at auction. The property of the monarchy, the property of the hereditary military aristocracy and the assets of numerous other dignitaries in the complex pattern of French customary life were also confiscated and auctioned. The buyers at the auctions were members of the class that was making the new (now old) rules.

Let there be no mistake about who the victors were. The victors who claimed the spoils that the philosophers conceptually set in stone were property owners. Everyone else, as Keynes and Kalecki later put it, depended on capital's confidence for their livelihoods. To be sure, the poor people and some of the peasantry had fought on the revolutionary side. To be sure, the Revolution's slogan, and self-image, was *liberté egalité fraternité*. But shortly after August 4, 1789, when the Assembly decreed the abolition of all feudal privileges, the same Assembly decreed that the only active citizens would be property-owning males. Anyone who was a servant or in any way employed by someone else was not qualified to vote or hold office. (Women did not get the vote in France until 1944.)

Property owners held the reins. Everyone else was on a short leash. The government became a *Steuerstaat* controlled by a parliament of property-owning males. Workers lost their status as lowly servants on the feudal totem pole because there was no longer a totem pole topped by a lord who was supposed to protect them. The abolition of the compulsory tithe and of church-owned property ended most of the church's capacity to run hospitals, schools and homes for the aged, leaving the workers with no social safety net until the rise of the social state in the twentieth century. Not surprisingly, in 1914, more than a century after *liberté egalité fraternité* became

---

109. Piketty, *Capital and Ideology*, Kindle edition, p. 101. See generally pages 99–105, titled '. . . The Invention of Modern Property'. This refers to 'the great demarcation' of 1789. It was never fully implemented and there were many subsequent variations.

modernity's official unkept promise, France was, by objective measures, *less* equal, not more equal. [110]

The European world-system became a collection of what Piketty calls ownership societies that dominated slave and colonial societies in the rest of the world. Ownership societies prevailed in the modern West until efforts to create social democratic societies began to have some success in the early twentieth century.

6. Culture Shifts

We have no one left to interview. We just need a place to sit and think. Since we are already in Paris, and since we have long daydreamed of sitting in chairs where Jean-Paul Sartre and Simone de Beauvoir used to sit, we take the subway to Saint-Germain-des-Prés and walk to Café Les Deux Magots. It is full of tourists and expensive—much different from the way it must have been during dark, dreary winters in German-occupied Paris, when Jean-Paul and Simone came here to shiver, drink cheap coffee and smoke cheap cigarettes. We order our coffees and sit in silence for a moment before starting to talk.

What we need to think about are culture shifts. So much depends on the discreet funding of programs like South Africa's Community Work Program. We use the word 'discreet' because for human dignity it is important to do community development in a way that builds community. Local resources—especially but not only people's time—should be mobilized; local personalities should be playing leadership roles. It is bad news when the funders—public or private—insist on taking charge and running the show. It is worse when they keep the local people busy filling out one form after another. There are more humane ways to evaluate what is really happening that do not humiliate anybody.[111]

If it were not for the fiscal crisis of the state—what Marissa Moore of the South African treasury called 'fiscal constraints'—the CWP could pay good wages. A wide variety of programmes like the CWP, offering activities for different folks with different interests and talents, could provide every citizen with a dignified livelihood doing something useful while developing their talents and practicing the good habits that lead to virtue. Moore suggested that since the state had run out of money, additional CWP sites

---

110. Piketty, *Capital and Ideology*, Kindle edition, pp 131–2.
111. Howard Richards, *The Evaluation of Cultural Action* (London: Macmillan, 1985).

could be funded by the private sector. She might have added that the day Adam Smith anticipated long ago, and many others anticipated since, has arrived. The world is awash with excess capital unable to find profitable investments in the real economy.

We suggest a simple solution, anticipated long ago by Thomas Aquinas and many others and practiced by some people since the beginning of time: channel the surplus to where it is needed. And this idea is beginning to take off under names like social entrepreneurship, impact investment and philanthropy. It may become the new normal. Indeed, something of the sort seems to have happened for the town of Westonaria, South Africa. It was funded mainly by two mining firms.[112]

Thomas Piketty and Joseph Stiglitz, as we have seen, are among the highly educated activists with good ideas for ending the fiscal crisis of the state. We have commented that their good ideas are unlikely to come to fruition without a culture shift. One might say the same thing of many good ideas now being advocated by the World Economic Forum, the World Social Forum and countless other organizations and individuals. This raises two questions that we address through the rest of this section: First, what is it about the phrase 'culture shift' that commends it to be the name of causal powers that, as we allege, can help to make the fiscal crisis of the state past history and the seeming impossible a possibility? Second, how does one go about making a culture shift toward aligning across sectors for the common good?

To begin responding to the first question, we need a working definition of 'culture'. For this we turn to James P. Boggs, who is both an academic anthropologist and a practicing professional who collaborates regularly with the indigenous peoples of the Great Plains of the United States. Boggs is one of the scholars who have made a thorough study of the history and current uses of the word 'culture' and of recent controversies surrounding it. On page 189 of his article 'The Culture Concept as Theory, in Context',[113] he defines theory—and therefore culture, since his thesis is that culture is a theory—as 'an abstraction from and representation of the ordering principles that govern a class of concrete systems or a realm of systemic order'.

Boggs's concept of ordering principles that govern is a wide net. Ordering principles govern every culture, just as they govern physical, chemical

---

112. See the YouTube video 'Organising for Good: The Story of Westonaria's Transformation', https://www.youtube.com/watch?v=BgVF3ODWBv4.

113. James P. Boggs, 'The Culture Concept as Theory, in Context', *Current Anthropology*, vol. 45 (2004), pp. 187–209.

and biological systems, most of which are open systems. As applied to the particular culture that now holds us captive in what Weber called the iron cage of modernity, economic theory represents the organizing principles of a particular culture that in the past—but no more—got away with calling itself civilization, while everyone else had merely 'culture'.

A culture shift is a shift of the ordering principles. And the ordering principles of the dominant culture now being shifted include the principles we have been naming with phrases like 'basic cultural structure', 'market society' (K. Polanyi), 'deep structures of capitalism' (Bhaskar), 'séparation marchande' (Orléan) and 'the institutions of private law and their social functions' (Renner).

In previous chapters and in previous sections of this chapter we have concluded that coping with physical necessities—like funding dignified livelihoods for the accelerating numbers of humans whose services are redundant in the labour market and decelerating the parts per million (ppm) of CO_2 in the atmosphere (currently over 400,000; higher than it has been in the last 800,000 years)—depends on terminating the fiscal crisis of the state. The state is virtually powerless as long as it is underfunded, deeply in debt, obliged to obey its creditors and compelled to woo potential investors.

And Boggs's definition of culture is relevant here too. His definition of culture is not arbitrary. It represents a corpus of scientific theory carefully built up by empirical research—facts all the way. The findings of anthropologists, centred on their flagship concept of culture, mesh with the findings of biologists and physical scientists. In contrast, the liberal ethics that dominates jurisprudence, politics and economics rests on, in Michel Foucault's terms, the social contract and natural liberty ideologies of the winners of Europe's civil wars in the seventeenth and eighteenth centuries. That is why anthropology is under attack today. Its scientific findings threaten the mythical and at times bogus philosophical foundations of our present crumbling and dysfunctional social order.

Invoking the word 'culture' to name both the present (the dominant culture) and the goal (a culture shift to a mosaic of functional cultures) gives us priceless advantages that recall and reinforce points made previously:

1. Culture shift is the 'once upon a time' that begins the history of a series of basic cultural structures invented by humans and judged worthy, either of survival or of death, by nature over the course of

thousands of years. This parade of living forms is not of individuals, or nations, or tribes or groups of any kind, and not DNA codes either, but rather moral systems.[114] These organizational codes have been passed from generation to generation by education through activity and ceremony. They survive or disappear by either meeting or failing to meet the test of satisfying the vital needs of the people, including the need for the cohesion that gives a form of life the power to survive among its competitors.

2. Culture shift demurs to the claim that no ruling class ever gave up power voluntarily with the counter-claim that no ruling class ever held power. The power has always been in the constitutive rules of the basic cultural structures, never in the hands of a bourgeoisie or other ruling class living by powers it pretended to understand. Thus unbounded organization comes out *engagé* on the side of life, on the side of everybody, including the living plant and animal forms that share with humans the earth as our common habitat. In a world where unbounded organization shapes the constitutive rules, the wealthy will no longer enjoy the power and the privileges they have now, but they and their grandchildren will enjoy living in a more equal society—a safer, healthier, more loving and sustainable society.

3. Humans survived, evolved, prospered and became the dominant species because culture shifts made it possible to adjust to a changing environment more rapidly than species that changed behaviour very slowly by mutating and waiting for nature to select the most adapted mutant. It can be argued that before capitalism and in the previous phases of capitalism, it was adaptive for an upper class or race or gender to keep others down so they could be up. Today there is ample evidence that it is to the interest of everybody to work together across sectors for the common good.[115] The present unjust distribution of property and unethical use of it does not benefit one single person—no, not one; and it certainly does not benefit even one single person's grandchildren. It is sinking all of us deeper and deeper into chaos. It is taking down the plants and animals that share

---

114. David Sloan Wilson, *Darwin's Cathedral* (Chicago: University of Chicago Press, 2011). An evolutionary biologist, Wilson takes the view that with respect to humans, what Darwinian selection mostly selects are adaptive moral systems.

115. Martin Luther King, Jr., *Where Do We Go from Here? Chaos or Community* (Boston: Beacon Press, 1967); Kate Pickett and Richard Wilkinson, *The Spirit Level: Why Equality is Better for Everyone* (London: Allen Lane, 2009).

the earth with us as it destroys the physical and biological equilibria that make life possible. Practicing the ancient capacity for culture shift that gave our hunter-gatherer ancestors a competitive advantage will save us from ecological disaster and social chaos.

4. Charles Darwin explained the competitive advantages of cultures that live by inventing adaptive ethical norms and passing them on to their children through education this way: 'Selfish and contentious people will not cohere, and without coherence nothing can be effected. A tribe rich in the above [cooperative] qualities would spread and be victorious over other tribes; but in the course of time it would, judging from all past history, be in its turn overcome by some other tribe still more highly endowed. Thus the social and moral qualities would tend slowly to advance and be diffused throughout the world.'[116]

5. A culture shift we need, as we have emphasized throughout this book, is a shift away from accumulation for its own sake and toward sharing the surplus; toward community, vocation, mission-driven organizations; toward service and purposeful living. We can plausibly say that if every country in the world was economically unprepared for the COVID-19 pandemic, it was because of bounded thinking. Governments and most people can think only 'inside the box'. They can think only of creating employment by creating incentives for investors to invest, by boosting sales and profits. Few seem to know about the principles of the CWP that some of its participants called 'bringing back *ubuntu*' or about the good but ultimately unsustainable start made by the Swedish Model, which could be refuelled by unbounded thinking and moral realism.

A common argument against the idea that pro-social emotions were hardwired into the human body by the requirements of survival during the millennia of human evolution that transpired before the agricultural revolution, patriarchy, empires, militarism and modern economies—is that it proves too much. It proves that humans tend to behave better than the evidence shows that we actually do tend to behave. In our view, as we have emphasized throughout this book, the modern world has not been ruled by normal moral development, and by a normal diversity of cultures multiplying

---

116. Charles Darwin, *The Descent of Man* (London: John Murray, 1871), p. 362 (quoted from the Luarna ebook reprint found on Google).

the options of moral systems for achieving cohesion and meeting needs,[117] for one big reason: accumulation has ruled the world. There is a reason why after a century of struggle most of humanity ended up in the year 2000 dominated by the same free-market ideology that was dominant in 1900. It is that accumulation (also called the free market, or simply freedom, or capitalism, or economic rationality, or the rule of law, or investor confidence) has a homeostatic quality. When accumulation is perturbed, compensatory mechanisms are set in motion (e.g., capital flight, tax competition attracting business by cutting taxes, inflation and unemployment). These mechanisms force the imposition of one or another regime of accumulation (in other words, one or another set of institutions that motivates investors to invest) by the ballot or by the bullet.

But there is reason to believe that the necessary culture shift is underway. For several decades now there has been a growing movement among business leaders themselves, explicitly rejecting accumulation for its own sake and increasingly contributing with deeds, not just words, to solving social and ecological problems and to a more equal distribution of wealth and income. Recently, pro-social values were solemnly reaffirmed by the world's most prominent business leaders, gathered at Davos in Switzerland. If accumulation was the story of the past, responsibility may be the story of the future.[118]

Time will tell whether the Davos Manifesto of the World Economic Forum declared on March 20, 2020, is a turning point of history—leading to honest dialogue, with the World Social Forum, for example, and to practical cooperation across sectors—or a great disappointment.

The problems are not simple. Here are five examples:

1. Many business owners are poor. As we saw in the chapter on India, many are nearly as poor as their impoverished workers. No doubt the majority of people in business could not possibly meet the Davos standards even with the best intentions.
2. What about the free riders, the prosperous businesspeople who are happy to enjoy the social peace other businesspeople devote their fortunes to funding, but have no intention of helping to pay for it

---

117. John Maynard Keynes, 'National Self-Sufficiency', *Yale Review*, vol. 22 (1933), pp. 755–769.

118. The full Davos text can be read at https://www.weforum.org/the-davos-manifesto/manifesto.

and, to boot, are perfectly capable of hiding their assets where tax collectors cannot find them?
3. Piketty's data show that the bulk of the world's wealth is held not by people who are active in business but by *rentiers* whose ancestors were active in business. Much of it cannot be traced.
4. Higher social expectations mean many ordinary businesses cannot meet them and still turn what Alfred Marshall called a normal profit. Decent employment for all will mean a plural economy with diverse enterprises taking up the slack, somehow providing quality employment where others dropped out because they could no longer comply with ethical and legal expectations and still earn sufficient profit.
5. What will become of the superprofits earned by the owners of intellectual property of the new supertechnologies coming online? Will nations compete to attract them by offering patent protection that lasts forever?

Perhaps we will know whether the culture shift is for real or just for show when we see whether the people apparently committed to the responsible sharing of wealth give up in the face of such wicked problems or make serious efforts to solve them.

As for our second question—how does one go about facilitating a culture shift toward aligning across sectors for the common good? —one possible method is called the growth-point method. A growth point is a point where needed structural transformation is already happening, or can easily be made to start happening, like low-hanging fruit that can easily be picked. It consists of four steps:[119]

First, the growth point should be expressed in communicable themes. If a growth point does not make sense to people, it cannot be a code for social interactions that construct new norms (or revive old norms). Growth-point themes can be music as well as lyrics; they can be symbolic acts like dying your hair red, getting a tattoo or wearing a coat and tie. Paulo Freire often used what he called 'hinge themes' to connect what people already understood with what they could easily understand. A bounced check was a hinge theme used by Martin Luther King, Jr.: 'Instead of honoring this

---

119. For more detail, see Howard Richards and Joanna Swanger, 'Culture Change: A Practical Method with a Theoretical Basis', in Joe de Rivera (ed.), *Handbook on Building Cultures of Peace* (New York: Springer, 2008).

sacred obligation, *America has given the Negro* people a bad *check,* a *check* which has come back marked "insufficient *funds*".'[120]

Second, the growth point must attract energy and resources. It can be either a bandwagon already moving that people can jump on or an idea that moves people to start a new bandwagon. If it is just someone's personal passion, it is not a growth point. Furthermore, constructing the four legs of the table of peace is not a fight of them against us. In this light, it is disappointing to see that, while in the economic justice area there are multiple reform movements powered by the energy of the privileged (such as impact investing—investing to achieve measurable social good), in the criminal justice area there is comparatively little energy, for instance, powering voluntary self-reform among the police. Here 'comparatively little' does not mean 'none'. I know there are policemen and -women working day and night for social justice, because my nephew, Tim McGraw, is one of them.

Third, to count as a growth point, a movement must possess potential for structural transformation. For example, Ernesto Laclau and Chantal Mouffe propose 'democracy' as a theme that has energy with potential for structural transformation. Political democracy morphs to economic democracy and then onward to democracy in other human relationships.[121] In the realm of religious beliefs and practices, some make a similar case for the potential for structural transformation of faithfulness.

Finally, the growth point must contribute to transforming the deep structures of modern society. These structures include capitalism, racism, sexism, markets, domination over instead of harmony with nature, and don't forget individualism. Because anything that might be said about society's deep structures can be said in many ways and from many perspectives, and because anything that might be said could also be wrong, implementing unbounded organization with the growth-point method (or any social-change method) implies ongoing study, reflection, and conversations that include sharing perspectives with others whose points of view differ from one's own.

---

120. Martin Luther King, Jr., 'I Have a Dream' (speech, Washington DC, August 28, 1963).

121. Ernesto Laclau and Chantal Mouffe, *Hegemony and Socialist Strategy* (London: Verso, 1985).

Index

absolute conflict, 24, 26, 28–29, 39
accumulation. *See* capital accumulation
act-in-the-law, 124
activity theory, 122–125; CWP in Orange Farm, 288–289; roots of CWP community development, 121; using surplus to meet needs, 321
adaptation, 94, 207, 396
adharmic way of life, 84, 84(n70)
African National Congress (ANC), 20, 24–25, 29–30, 279, 286–288
Afridi, Farzana, 164(n64), 166(n73), 166(n75)
agathon (good), 336–337
Aglietta, Michel, 133–134, 134(n55)
agriculture: Bokfontein's Organization Workshop, 127–129; capturing rent, 370–372; Chile's exports, 326–327; culture shifts to benefit the community, 216; Gandhi's cash income plan, 144; India's tax on farmers, 370(n39); inefficiency of India's private farms, 173–174; NABARD commitment to rural development, 222–223; NREGA crowding out private enterprise, 171; quasi-rent, 375; South Africa's public employment figures, 115; the suicide of Tapas Soren, 174–176; vegetable gardening in Orange Farm, 301–303
ahimsa, 96
alcohol abuse: domestic violence in Orange Farm, 286
Aldous, Jean, 55(n31)
Alesina, Alberto, 37(n55)
alignment across sectors: an unbounded worldview in Orange Farm, 308–309; fiscal crisis of the state challenging, 334, 381–382; freedom to create, 199–200, 207; growth-point method, 399–400; making culture shifts, 394–400; paying for World War II, 340; prioritizing service to life, 361; redefining the problem, 212–213; South Africa's housing construction, 116. *See also* unbounded organization
Alvaredo, Facundo, 384(n85), 387(n91)
Amah, Bartholomew K., 315(n136)
Ambedkar, B.R., 152, 152(n30)
ambiguity between form and meaning, 231–233
Amin, Samir, 66(n22), 224–225(n109), 264(n106)
Anderson, Benedict, 21(n20), 195(n34)
Andersson, Gavin, 4–5, 4(n12), 5, 5(n15), 98(n29), 119(n31), 121(n34), 125(n42), 290
Anerkennung (recognition), 279–280

402 | Index

anomalies, 172–173, 211–212
anomie, 6
anthropology: the importance of culture, 93–94
anti-apartheid struggles (South Africa): continuing violence in South Africa's townships, 20; Economic Freedom Fighters, 21–29
anti-poverty programs. *See* poverty alleviation and elimination
Apple corporation, 390
Aquinas, Thomas, 47(n14), 394
Archer, Margaret, 6(n19), 11, 11(n38), 51, 56(n34), 64–65, 64(n12)
Arenas, Alberto, 326–328, 361
Argentina: Mil Holas pasta factory, 213–214; Municipal Bank of Rosario, 221–222; National Institute of Industrial Technology, 163
Aristotle, 6, 269(n118), 321(n12), 324(n24)
Arlow, Jacob, 357(n5)
Arnott, Richard, 376(n60)
Arrow, Kenneth, 73(n42), 297, 297(n82), 337(n47)
arts: Gateway performances, 304–305; music, 99–100, 162, 274–275; as useful work, 162
Asset-Based Community Development (ABCD) programmes, 142, 160, 313–315
Atkinson, Anthony B., 384(n85), 387(n91)
Austria: lower crime associated with social democracy, 283
Azania Township, South Africa, 21

Bachelard, Gaston, 323(n23)
Bachelet, Michelle, 325(n27), 342(n57)
Bachelet Commission, 342–344, 343(n63)
Bagehot, Walter, 341(n56), 383–384, 384(n84)
Bakhtin, Mikhail, 52–53, 232
bank bailouts: decline and failure of the Swedish Model, 210
banking: China's city commercial banks, 223–224; Municipal Bank of Rosario, Argentina, 221–222; Organization Workshop, 126; sovereign control of money, 341; Sweden's labour market policy, 191; tying capital to a purpose and a territory, 221–224
bankism, 10–11
bargaining power, 265
bargaining society, 203
Barry, Brian, 140(n76)
Barthes, Roland, 57–58
basic cultural structures. *See* basic social structures
basic needs, 5–6; the basic social structure, 45–46; defining community and economy, 55–56; economic theory addressing, 26; including emotional needs, 47–48, 47–48(n16); lowering the cost of, 216; meeting in harmony with nature, 68; NREGA's purpose and activities, 153–156;

reassigning the social status of need, 46–47; self-esteem, 100; South Africa's EFF Manifesto, 24. *See also* human needs
basic services, Orange Farm's access to, 278–279
basic social structures, 7, 88; colonial roots, 45–46; cultural element of, 45–46; culture shift, 395–396; decline of social democracy, 58; economy and community, 50–51; fiscal crisis of the state, 367; lowering wages to raise profit, 78–79; rebuilding the system of mainstream economic theory, 16–17; self-evaluation, 357; South Africa's poultry program, 111; structural humiliation, 89–92; underlying the Staggering Facts, 88–89; unsustainability of social democracy, 14; vocabulary of, 9–10
Battle, Michael, 137(n68)
Bauman, Zygmunt, 55, 55(n32)
Baumol, William J., 364(n25)
Beck, Ulrich, 34(n52)
benevolence, 245, 245(n45)
Bentham, Jeremy, 63, 151, 151(n27)
Berle, Adolf, 75, 322, 322(n18)
Bettencourt, Liliane, 384
Bhaskar, Roy, 7, 7(n25), 8, 8(n26), 11, 11(n37), 18, 18(n9), 46, 58, 81, 81(n62), 90(n10), 99, 218, 218(n91), 319(n7), 382(n79)
Bhatia, Bela, 154(n36)
Bhengu, Mfuniselwa J., 25(n32)
Bhengu, Mfuniswela, 137(n68)
binary polarities, 247–248
Binner, Hermes, 260(n102)
biosphere, 1–2, 32, 35–36, 97, 131, 238, 297, 321, 378, 380, 388
Blanchot, Maurice, 56, 56(n40)
Blunden, Andy, 329(n37), 353(n99)
Boggs, John, 93–94, 93(n18), 238(n19), 356(n2), 394–395, 394(n113)
Böhm-Bawerk, Eugen von, 10
Bokfontein, South Africa, 50, 117; activity theory, 123; innovation of CWP, 120; Organization Workshop, 125–129; the role and significance of community, 131
Bolivia, 272, 315, 342
Bombo, Phumi, 54
Bond, Patrick, 31(n46), 66(n22), 108(n1), 151(n24)
Bornstein, David, 332(n41)
Boulding, Kenneth, 32
bounded thinking, 92–93, 124, 173, 176, 351, 397
Bourdieu, Pierre, 64–65
Bowles, Samuel, 56–57, 57(n41), 80(n60), 213(n80), 321(n14)
Boyd, Keith, 37(n57)
Boyer, Robert, 267(n114)
Bozalek, Vivienne, 121(n34)

Branting, Hjalmar, 195
Braudel, Fernand, 88(n5), 246, 246(n50), 264(n106)
Brazil: exploitation of labour, 219–220; investment in state-run industry, 383; nationalization of industry, 29
Britain: combining economical power and delicacy, 383–384; destruction of India's textiles industry, 144–145; English Glorious Revolution, 344(n68). *See also* colonialism
Brown, Michael Barratt, 271(n123)
brute facts, 15–18, 46–47, 80–81
Buchanan, James, 103(n37)
budget deficits, 241–242, 276–277
Butler, Eamonn, 223(n102)
buying. *See* free choice; Say's Law
buying: defining, 9–10

Cahn, Edgar S., 332(n41)
Calvin, Jean, 52
Campbell, Catherine, 299, 299(n90)
Cannan, Edwin, 244(n37), 343(n65)
capital: defining, 249; the exit power of, 80; fixed and circulating, 249–251; tying to a purpose and a territory, 221–224
capital accumulation, 4; the causes of wealth, 63; the circular path of production and accumulation, 65–67; decline and failure of the Swedish Model, 209–210; defining, 10; Grenoble School's regime of, 267–268; making a culture shift away from, 397–398; making the global economy governable, 382–393; markets and poverty alleviation, 116; the origins of life, 238; origins of neoliberalism, 249–250; persistent world domination, 382; rentier capital, 383; resilient communities, 242–243; social and environmental costs, 262; South Africa's CWP tenets, 41–42; structural frustration, 97–98; as systemic imperative, 7; taking a balanced growth path, 201(n45); violence in South African townships, 20
capital flight: connecting the global with the local, 221; the Swedish Model, 192, 212–214
capital formation: deficit-financed public programmes, 240; hitchless economists' view of, 251; in planned economies, 84–85; as requirement for employment and production, 250–251; the Swedish Model, 186
capital tax, 388–393
capitalism: elements of basic social structure, 46; homeostasis, 49–50; leveraging the poor to make it governable, 131; making socialism possible, 185; Marx on the wealth of nations, 245; persistence and resilience, 64–65; pluralism as cure for, 119–120; ruthless and communitarian, 179, 195, 204, 212, 216, 224–225; sharing surpluses, 3; Wielicki's mature capitalism, 179. *See also* neoliberalism
Capro, Fritjof, 318–319, 318(n5)

carbon emissions: South Africa's goal, 34–35
caretaker states, 317
caring and sharing: collaborative sharing, 353–354; as consumption, 370; defining community, 52–54; as the ethical good, 261; moving surplus to address need, 75–76; public choice processes in CWP, 296–298; using surplus for, 131–132. *See also* community building; surplus, sharing and productive use of
Carmen, Raff, 121(n34), 125(nn42,43)
casino economy, 30, 66(n23), 97
caste, 144, 166–167
Castro, Fidel, 21–22
categorical imperatives, 345–346, 358–360
causa causans, 198, 198(n38)
causality, 7–8; causal powers of the Swedish Model, 191; market exchange driving down wages, 76–77; the questions answered by economic theory, 28–29; South Africa's NDP balancing economic growth and poverty alleviation, 43–45
central banks: liquidity trap, 30
central planning: China's policy shift away from, 223(n102); either/or thinking on markets, 247; failure to work to plan, 84–85; full employment, 3–4, 181–182; as nonviable alternative to neoliberalism, 32; plausibility, successes, and failures, 84–86
Ceres corporation, 112
Chamberlain, John, 244(n37)
Chandrasekhar, C.P., 155(n38), 169–170(n84)
charitable giving, 260, 274–275
Charters, W.W., 166(n77)
Chaskalson, Arthur, 151, 157–158
children: Bokfontein day-care, 128; home-based care in Orange Farm, 303–304; public funding for, 120
Chile, 29, 342(n61); commodification of water, 216; economic collapse, 270(n122); economic homeostasis, 242(n34); recycling rents, 370; rekindling economic growth, 324–327; salmon fishing industry, 160(n52)
China: tying capital to purpose and territory, 223–224
Chitonge, Horman, 66(n22)
chronic insufficiency of demand. *See* Staggering Fact 2
circulating capital, 249–251
Cirillo, Renato, 374(n57)
civil society: CWP alignment, 119
civilizational crisis, 179–182, 193, 212–227
civilizations, shared values in, 49
civilized nations, 244–245
classical economics. *See* orthodox liberal economics
Clerwall, Ulf, 335, 335(n42)

climate change, 160; CWP community building successes, 317; ending the fiscal crisis of the state, 395; Green New Deal, 334–340; India's NREGA public works, 149; unbounded organization providing different solutions, 352
Clot, Yves, 116(n23)
Cobb, John, Jr., 253(n76)
Cockett, Richard, 194(n32)
collaborative sharing, 353–354
collective bargaining: the Swedish Model, 185–186, 189, 193–194, 203–204
collective intentions, 47
colonialism: Africa's social and cultural friction, 128; CWP rebuilding destroyed communities, 133; defeating indigenous knowledge systems, 212; effect on India's culture and economy, 144–145; roots of basic social structure, 45–46; South Africa's legacy of land ownership and modernization, 24–25
commodities: calculating deadweight, 256–259; changing capitalism, 65; defining community in terms of, 52; Marx on the wealth of nations, 245; metamorphosis of forms of value, 10; natural economics of, 61–62; the natural price of labour, 77–79
commodity form, 329
commodity hell, 75
Commons (England), 77
communitarian capitalism, 179
community: combining economy with, 54–57; the concept of, 6–7; defining, 52–57, 133, 135–137; economy and community, 50–54; as essential unit of human action and institutions, 93–94; evolutionary view of moral system selection, 48–50; human action presupposing, 93; resignifying economy to include, 272; Smith's argument for self-interest, 91–92; talking up versus talking down, 57–59; tying capital to purpose and territory, 221–223
community building: avoiding capital flight, 213; building good community, 51–52; CWP creating *ubuntu* in Orange Farm, 306–308; CWP success, 317; economic growth versus, 197–198; as foil for economics, 133–134; NREGA's purpose and activities, 153–154; reducing dependence on investment and growth, 83–86
community development: CWP labour mandate, 99–100; CWP Organization Workshop, 129; discreet funding, 393; distinction between public and private expenses, 217–218; form of Organization Workshops, 125–127; government institutions creating and supplying funding, 341; identifying with caring and sharing, 53; meeting more needs with less money, 215–216; mobilizing community to create employment without investors, 198–199; the neoliberal view of CWP, 240; organization and planning at Bokfontein, 127–128; public ignorance of CWP philosophy, 333; pure economy and, 273–274; the role of community, 131–135; as a step towards full employment, 162; *ubuntu* relieving the fiscal crisis, 378; unbounded organization and, 33–34. *See also* Community Work Programme

community mapping, 313–315
community service, costs of, 276
community versus economy: Gandhi's philosophy and practice, 143–147
Community Work Programme (CWP; South Africa), 12, 14, 76, 131; ABCD and, 313–315; activity theory, 123; alternatives to neoliberalism, 40–42; benefits for orphaned children, 204; building good community, 51; creating employment without investors, 198–199; developing talent, 162; exemplifying social change strategy, 99–100; financing and functioning, 4; the fiscal crisis of the state, 331–334, 393–394; labour, production, sales and value, 349; a neoliberal evaluation of, 239–2423; OECD Review Evaluation, 252–257; Organization Workshop, 125–130; pilot programs, 117; the poor sharing surplus, 47; program failures and frustrations, 317–318; providing basic and emotional needs, 47–48, 68–69; public choice processes, 296–298; as public employment program, 118–121; rebuilding communities, 133; requirements for "useful work," 245–246; similarities to NREGA, 142; thick mores of *ubuntu*, 137; unbounded organization, 41–42. *See also* Orange Farm township
competition: achievements of the Swedish model, 207; commodity hell, 75; cooperation versus, 266; creating insufficient demand for Swedish products, 214; creating overproduction, 85–86; decline and failure of the Swedish Model, 205–206; effect on profitability, 264–265, 265(nn108,109); general equilibrium without profits, 73–75; lowering the price of commodities, 61–62; a neoliberal evaluation of CWP, 239–240; success of adaptive cultures, 397; Sweden's subsidies, 187
complementarity, 163
Comte, Auguste, 328(n33)
conflict: consensus and, 95; the downside of rights talk, 150; interests challenging NREGA's call for democratization, 166
conscience collective, 358
consciousness-raising exercises, 120
constant conjunctions, 8
Constitution of India, 152, 158
constitutive rules, 60; achievable change in, 47; basic social structures, 61; connecting natural sciences with market rules, 94; the deontic character of, 138–139; the existence of economic losers, 81–82; form and functions, 15–18; the freedom to buy or not buy, 81–82; understanding capitalism through, 329–330
consumption: decline and failure of the Swedish Model, 205–206; sharing as, 370; Smith's view of spending, 250–251; the Swedish Model of economic growth, 185–186
convenience justifying utility, 236
cooperation defining community, 136
Cooperative Governance and Traditional Affairs Department (COGTA), 331–332

cooperatives: capital formation in the Swedish model, 186–187; vegetable gardening in Orange Farm, 302–303
Coraggio, José Luis, 67(n25), 160, 160(n56), 161(n57), 248(n53), 272, 272(n125)
corporate social responsibility (CSR), 222–223, 275–276
corruption: bribes for India's well projects, 175–176; creating fiscal space through reduction of, 342; CWO nepotism in Orange Farm, 294–295; local politics in Orange Farm, 288; NREGA activities, 164–167, 170; South Africa's EFF Manifesto, 24; South Africa's townships, 19–20
Coser, Lewis, 24, 24(n31)
cosmology, 137–138, 237–238
cosmopolitan standpoint, 355–365
Crane, Andrew, 332(n41)
created harmony, social democracy as, 185–186, 193, 206
creating value, 148–149, 148(n14), 168, 207, 275
credit: instability hypothesis, 82
crime in Orange Farm, 281–286, 304–306
critical realism, 7–9, 11–12, 18, 329
Crockett, Richard, 8(n28)
Crossland, Anthony, 325(n26)
crowding out, 169–176, 243
cultural capital: South Africa's poultry program, 109–110
cultural historical activity theory (CHAT), 121, 150, 152
cultural structures, 183; failure of the Swedish Model, 224–225; incompatibility of social democracy with, 317. *See also* constitutive rules
culture: activity theory, 122–123; basic social structure, 45–46; cosmology and the origins of life, 237–238; creating, 353; defining, 356, 394–396; defining community, 136–137; as ecological niche of humans, 93; economics driving, 132; as essential unit of human action and institutions, 93–94; rigidity, 357; using surplus to meet needs, 321–324
culture shift, 215–216, 393–400
culture wars: talking community down, 57–59
currency valuation: the Swedish Model, 187, 189, 206, 210–211

Dahrendorf, Ralf, 192(n29)
Daly, Herman, 253(n76)
dance, 99–100
Darwin, Charles, 207, 397, 397(n116)
Davidson, Paul, 230(n5)
Davos Manifesto, 398
Day, Kathleen M., 241(n33)
day-care: Bokfontein community planning, 128; CWP activities in Orange Farm, 304; the Swedish economic model, 192, 241
de Morais, Clodomir, 125(n42), 127, 288–289

De Soto, Hernando, 112(n6)
De Wet, T., 278(n14)
deadweight effect, 241, 243, 255–260, 270
debt: categorical imperative to pay, 358, 360–361; as economic necessity, 82; overproduction and lagging sales, 85–86; South Africa's increase, 276–277
debt cancellation, 342
deferred consumption, 337
deficit-financed public programs, 240–241
demand: calculating deadweight, 256–259; the freedom to buy or not buy, 81–83; poverty alleviation relying on Say's Law, 362–363; Say's Law, 364–366; South Africa's poultry program, 108–112. *See also* insufficiency of effective demand; Staggering Fact 2
democracy and democratization: economic growth as necessity for stability, 198; interests challenging NREGA's call for, 166; NREGA's failure to achieve economic democracy, 156–158; South Africa's Economic Freedom Fighters, 21–29; South Africa's housing programs, 116; South Africa's National Development Plan, 37; as theme from structural transformation, 400; violence in South Africa's townships, 19–21
deontic systems, 48, 138–139, 173, 356
Descartes, Réné, 320
despair over poverty reduction, 113–114
determination of current prices, 69–70
Devlin, Rose Anne, 241(n33)
Dewey, John, 6(n21), 93, 93(n16), 119(n33), 319(n8), 348(n80), 352(n91)
dharma (serving God by serving neighbour), 144
di Filippo, Armando, 70(n34)
Diamond, Jared, 340(n53)
Diamondis, Peter, 51(n22), 117(n24), 150(n23)
DiEM25 movement, 335
Diewert, W. Erwin, 258(n98)
dignifying dialogues (dignilogues), 97–98
dignity, ethic of, 5, 131; discreet funding, 393; effects of capturing rent, 368–369; NREGA providing, 155; participatory processes, 116–117; self-esteem as a basic need, 100; sharing surplus, 320; structural humiliation, 89–92; supplementing self-help projects, 159
The Dilemmas of Social Democracies (Schumpeter), 317
Discourse on Method (Descartes), 320
discreet funding, 393
distant markets, 112
distortions, market, 269–270
division of labour, 62–63; causes of wealth, 244–245; extent of the market, 253; markets and poverty alleviation, 116; Smith on the causes of wealth, 248–250
Dlamini, Jacob, 19(n10), 20–21

DNA, 137–138, 237–238
domestic violence in Orange Farm, 284–286
dominant economic model. *See* neoliberalism; orthodox liberal economics
dominant social structures, 83–86
dominium concept, 25
Donati, Pierpaolo, 56(n34)
Dornbusch, Rudiger, 38(n61)
Douzinas, Costas, 55(n30), 72, 83, 391(n107)
Drèze, Jean, 33, 149(n20), 150(n22), 151(n25), 152, 152(n29), 153–154(n34), 154(n36), 155(n38), 172(n92), 173, 216(n88), 246, 246(n49), 248
drought, India's, 148–149
Drucker, Peter, 95, 95(n21), 385
drug use and trafficking in Orange Farm, 283–284
Dryzek, John, 297, 297(n83)
dualism in classic liberalism, 247–248
Dummont, Louis, 363(n23)
Dunkle, K., 284(n40)
Dupuit, Juvénal, 256(n95)
Durkheim, Emile, 6, 55, 55(n31), 135(n59), 283, 377(n64)
Dussel, Enrique, 348(n80)
Dworkin, Gerald, 139(n75)

earth, origins of, 237–238
ecology, 32; constraints on social budgets, 349; dependence of economic growth on anti-ecological practices, 214–215; NREGA prioritizing rights over, 149–153; NREGA's public works employment, 148–149; realist worldview of culture, 93
economia solidaria, 51, 94–95, 274
economic crisis (2008), 36, 118
economic development: OECD Review of the CWP, 253–255; South Africa's EFF Manifesto, 24; South Africa's tension between property rights and absolute conflict, 27–28
Economic Freedom Fighters (EFF; South Africa), 21–29, 240, 287–288
economic growth: an unbounded approach to the Swedish Model, 214–215; defining production, 349; effect on employment and poverty, 37; ending unemployment, 4; global and national slowing, 276–277; governable growth as alternative, 38; loosening the constraints on, 201–202; OECD Review of the CWP, 253; orthodox economic theory, 196–197; social programmes' dependence on, 342–343; South Africa's NDP, 37–38; spurring Chile's, 325–327; the Swedish Model, 185, 214–215
economic reality: neoliberalism versus unbounded organization, 264–266; South Africa's economic and environmental policies, 34–36
economic society, defining community and, 54

economics: combining community with, 54–57; community as other, 6–7; moral and political history, 16–17; as social structure, 60–86. *See also* orthodox liberal economics

Ecuador, 272

Edgren, Gösta, 189(n27)

education: the illusion of education as the solution for poverty, 82; NREGA increasing school enrollment, 155; Organization Workshop, 126–127; public spending levels, 388; South Africa's EFF Manifesto, 24; South Africa's poultry program, 109–112; sponsorship for, 274–275; training CWP workers, 300–301, 333; using surplus to meet needs, 321–324

Edwards, Sebastian, 37(n55), 38(n61)

efficiency, 194–195; India's private farms, 173–174; Quebec's milk industry, 213

Einstein, Albert, 28

Eisenberger, Naomi, 136(n65)

elderly individuals: CWP creating *ubuntu* in Orange Farm, 296, 301–303, 306, 308, 313

Elements of Pure Economics (Walras), 69

Elias, Norbert, 134(n56)

Ellerman, David, 47(n13)

emissions control, 34–35

employment: CWP figures, 331–332; effect of economic growth on, 37; effect of lagging sales on, 87–88; effect of the tax wedge on jobs, 241; effects of modernity, 135; job creation in Orange Farm, 280–281; Keynes's problem and lack of full employment, 181; lowering wages to increase, 79; metamorphosis of forms of value, 10; neoliberal claims on increases in, 31; NREGA's purpose and activities, 153–156; Organization Workshop, 126–127; in planned economies, 84–85; problem of chronic precarious employment, 350; Smith's view of accumulation, 250–251; South Africa's housing programs, 115–116; South Africa's poultry program, 108–112; work readiness of CWP participants, 255; youth campaign in Orange Farm, 289–290. *See also* Community Work Programme; National Rural Employment Guarantee Act; public employment plans

employment guarantee, 118; CWP program failures and frustrations, 317–318; dependence on sales, 87–88; Gandhi's philosophy and practice, 144; Swedish Model, 184–185. *See also* Community Work Programme; National Rural Employment Guarantee Act

energy production: effect of falling prices on Chile's economy, 327; Saudi Arabia's welfare spending, 343–344; South Africa's environmental policy and economic plan, 34–35

Engels, Friedrich, 54(n28), 64(n10)

Engeström, Yrjö, 123

Engler, Monika, 155(n41)

English Civil War, 371

English Glorious Revolution, 344(n68)
entrepreneurs: the dependence of the economy on the confidence of investors, 65–66; lowering wages to increase production and profit, 78–79; moving towards more productive actions, 160; the nature of profits, 73(n45); Say's Law, 364–366; South Africa's poultry program, 110
environmental policy: public-private cooperation, 263(n105); South Africa's planning commissioners, 34–35
epistemicological rupture, 323–324
equilibrium, economic, 229–231, 233–235; calculating deadweight, 256–258; theoretical nature of, 264; true prices, 266–270
Erhard, Ludwig, 385(n87)
ethical realism, 84; capturing rents, 371; economic growth and absolute conflict, 27; indefensibility of neoliberalism, 266–270; rebuilding basic social structures, 17–18; structural humiliation, 91. *See also* caring and sharing; unbounded organization
ethical theory, 137–138
ethics: achievements of the Swedish model, 207; activity theory, 123–124; building community not economy, 55–56; defining community in terms of surplus sharing, 52–53; distinction between public and private expenses in Sweden, 217–218; explaining the failure of the Swedish Model, 207; Gandhi's philosophy and practice, 144; government support of social programmes, 347–348; grounding in natural science, 133; human evolution and deontic ethics, 48; as requirement for human action and human institutions, 93–94; separating pure economics from, 70; sharing surplus, 2–4; Smith's argument for self-interest over sharing, 91–92; Smith's natural economics, 62; the transition from tribal market to feudal market ethics, 84–85; unbounded organization, 4–5; the unchanging nature of, 356; Walras's pure economics, 70–71. *See also* caring and sharing; moral realism; unbounded organization
Étienne, Arsène Jules, 256(n95)
Etzioni, Amitai, 133, 135–137, 136(n62)
eudaimonia (flourishing), 336–337
evolution, 137–138; of a deontic system, 138–139; organization for the common good, 48–50; Vygotsky's activity theory, 122–123
exchange: defining, 9–10; forms of value, 10; Walras's theory of pure economics, 69–70. *See also* Say's Law
exchange value, 103, 132, 149, 206, 348, 352–353, 365
exemplars, 53
Expanded Public Works Programme (EPWP; South Africa), 41, 314; failure to reduce unemployment, 114–115; the neoliberal view of, 241; nonmercantile work, 349; proposed expansion, 117
experimental society, 119
export trade. *See* trade
expropriation of land: South Africa's EFF Manifesto, 23–26

Index | 413

extended order of modernity, 134
extended social order, 83

Faba, Tozi, 331–332
family connectivity, effect on GDP and community resilience, 215
famine: constitutive rules of the right to eat, 16; effect of basic social structure, 9–10
Fanon, Frantz, 23
Favero, Carlo, 37(n55)
Faxén, Karl-Olof, 189(n27)
Feldstein, Martin, 240, 240(n28)
feudal market ethics, 84–85
fictitious capital, 10–11
FIFA World Cup, 289
Finley, M.I., 343(n66)
Finn, M.W., 118(n28)
first wave critical realism, 18
fiscal constraints, 318, 342; on capital accumulation, 262; cost containment in the CWP, 315; defective basic social structures, 367; euphemisms contained in, 334; rent capturing, 376
fiscal crisis of the state, 202–203; culture shifts, 393–400; defeat of the CWP, 331–334; defining, 348; *ubuntu* as relief, 377–382
fiscal space: creating for social programming, 342–348; defining, 344–346, 357
Fisher, Irving, 198, 198(n40), 328(n32)
fixed capital, 249–251
flexible prices and economic equilibrium, 229–231, 233–235, 264
folkshemmet (Swedish welfare state), 187, 192, 195, 206
food: as basic need, 47–48; the hunt as social activity, 123; India's support of small farmers, 172–173; loss of production and gathering skills, 134–135; in a mercantile economy, 65; the natural price of labour, 77–79; Organization Workshop, 127; the right to, 151; vegetable gardening in Orange Farm, 301–303. *See also* agriculture
foreign direct investment: the lethal concept of economic growth, 196–197
formality: transacting business across distances, 112
forme and *fond*, 167, 231–233, 236–239
Forrester, C., 278(n14)
Forrester, Viviane, 65, 65(n18), 82(n65)
Foucault, Michel, 16(n3), 17, 77(n53), 167, 174, 312(n130)
fragile economies, 33–34
France: taxing income-producing property, 392–393
Francis I, 25, 25(n36)
free choice: to buy and not buy, 81–83, 90–91, 358; defining community, 136; the downside of rights talk, 150–151; efficiency and orthodox economics, 194–195; Walras's pure economics, 70–71

free markets: the global hegemony of liberalism, 31, 272; poverty alleviation, 176–177; Smith's natural economics, 62, 185; socialism and, 234(n11)
free riders, 275–276, 398–399
free trade: human institutions and, 138; imperial Britain, 375–376; orthodox economic systems, 195–196, 204
freedom: as a basic social structure, 71–72; defining, 272; of the rational being, 359(n17); strict duties associated with, 358–359; the Swedish model combining justice and, 178–179
Freedom Charter (South Africa), 22, 30, 227
Freire, Paulo, 6, 50, 399–400
French Revolution, 392–393
Freudenthal, Gideon, 363(n23)
Friedman, Milton, 31(n47), 72, 79, 79(n56), 101–107, 105(n42), 106(nn43,44), 163, 163(n63), 189(n26), 229, 229(n3), 231, 234(n11), 235(n15), 236(n16), 242(n35), 259, 259(n101), 373, 373(n55)
Frost, Robert, 40
Fukuyama, Francis, 23, 23(n28), 49, 49(n19), 224(n106), 279(n20), 352–353, 352(n89), 353(n93), 353(n98)
full employment: an unbounded approach to the Swedish Model, 212–213; centrally planned economies, 181–182; decline and failure of the Swedish Model, 210–211, 217–218; Keynes's problem, 181; NREGA's failure, 156–157; the paradox of, 229–230; production, profit, sales requirements, 87; six steps towards, 158–162; the Swedish Model's employment guarantee and wage floor, 184–185, 187–188; unsustainability of, 362. *See also* employment guarantee
functional ethics, 158–159
functional finance, 337, 348–349
functionless investors, 386

Gallie, W.B., 52–53, 53(n25), 320(n11)
Gandhi, Ela, 144, 144(n2), 146
Gandhi, Mohandas K. 'Mahatma,' 142–147, 145(n5), 146(nn7,8)
Garroway, James, 124(n41)
Gateway (ex-offenders program), 304–306
Gemeinhandel, 93
Gemeinschaft (community), 54–56, 136
gender equality, NREGA increasing, 155
genetics, 237–238
George, Henry, 383(n81)
Georgescu-Roegen, Nicholas, 268(n116)
Gesellschaft (economy), 54–56
Ghana: creating fiscal space for social programmes, 342
Ghosh, J., 155(n38), 169–170(n84)
Giavazzi, Francesco, 37(n55)

Giddens, Anthony, 43(n1), 64–65, 64(n13), 329(n37)
Gilligan, Carol, 5, 140–141
Gini coefficient: South Africa, 21
Gintis, Herbert, 56–57, 57(n41), 80(n60), 321(n14)
global casino economy, 30
global economy as moral system, 49
globalization: effect on social democracy, 179; leveling the price of labour downward, 219; making mature capitalism unsustainable, 225; OECD Review of the CWP, 253; persistent world domination, 382
Gödel, Kurt, 232
good works, public funding for, 162
Gopal, K.S., 164(n65)
Gordon, Robert, 230(n5)
governability, structural, 134; committing capital to social purposes, 221; making the global economy governable, 382–393; of mobile capital, 220; the Swedish Model, 204–205; tax justice, 219
governance: Smith on the causes of wealth, 248; South Africa's EFF Manifesto, 24; tension between rights and absolute conflict, 28
government support: achieving full employment, 157; creating fiscal space for social programming, 342–343; South Africa's housing programs, 115–116. *See also* Community Work Programme; fiscal crisis of the state; National Rural Employment Guarantee Act
Graeber, David, 82(nn65,66), 162(n61)
Gramsci, Antonio, 50
grassroots activities: rooting out NREGA's corruption, 166
Great Depression, 85, 90, 118, 180, 198
Green New Deal, 334–340
green political parties, 319
Green Politics (Capra and Spretnak), 318–319
Greenleaf, Robert, 56(n36), 322(n15)
Greer, Scott, 56(n39)
Grenoble School, 267–268
Gresham's Law, 219
Grootboom, Irene, 151
Groundwork for the Metaphysics of Morals (Kant), 358
growth-points, 399
guaranteed employment. *See* employment guarantee
Gurr, Ted Robert, 21(n20)
Gutierrez, Gustavo, 25(n35)

Habermas, Jürgen, 11, 202, 219(n93)
Habib, Adam, 37, 37(n56), 198(n37)
Hammarskjold, Dag, 178
Hansen, Alvin, 104(n38)

Harberger, Arnold, 258(n98)
harmony with nature, 77; adjusting culture to function, 140; decline and failure of the Swedish Model, 206; economic development, 28–29; effective social change strategies, 96–97; government support of social programmes, 347–348; investors and entrepreneurs, 63–68; meeting needs, 228–229; moral realism and, 5, 98–99; relationship between economy and community, 51–55, 77, 96–97, 132–133, 143–144; serving the interests of the rich, 226; unbounded organization, 158–163; using surplus, 38. *See also* unbounded organization
Harre, Rom, 283(n36)
Harris, Marvin, 361(n21)
Harrison, Robert, 229(n2)
Harrod, Roy, 201(n45)
Hart, H.L.A., 124(n37)
Hartjen, Clayton, 282(n34)
Hartsock, Nancy, 65(n19), 239(n27), 350, 350(n86)
Harvey, David, 64(n15), 132–133, 132(n53), 268(n114)
Hassen, Ebrahim-Khalil, 114, 114(n13)
Hausmann, Ricardo, 36, 44, 200
hawkers: South Africa, 109, 112–113
Hayek, Friedrich von, 83, 84(n72), 330, 330(n38)
health care and medicine, 216(n86); indefensibility of neoliberalism, 269–270; lowering the cost of basic needs, 216; Orange Farm access, 280, 303–304; public spending levels, 388; South Africa prioritizing the right to emergency medical treatment, 151; using surplus to meet needs, 321; workers in the people's economy, 160–161
Heckscher, Eli, 169(83)
Hegel, G.W.E., 28, 279(n20)
Heidegger, Martin, 18, 18(n8), 25, 25(n37), 60, 239(n25)
Heller, Peter, 342, 344–346, 344(n69), 344(n71), 345(nn73,74), 346(n76), 350, 355–358, 358(n10), 360–361
Hempel, Carl, 8
heterodoxy, transformative, 271–272
Hicks, John, 267, 267(n113), 268(n115)
Hines, James, 259, 259(n99)
hinge themes, 399–400
Hinkelammert, Franz, 268(n116)
Hirsch, Fred, 216(n87)
historic compromise of shared prosperity, 194
history: activity theory, 122–123
hitchbound economists, 85–86, 148(n17), 251(n71)
hitchless economists, 148(n17), 251–252, 251(n71)
HIV/AIDS epidemic, 204, 280, 284, 289, 301, 323
Hobson, J.A., 81

Hoffmann-Kipp, Peter, 124(n40)
home-based care: CWP in Orange Farm, 303
homeostasis: cosmology, 137–138, 237–238
homeostatic mechanisms of capitalism, 64–65, 88, 242(n34)
homespun cloth, India's, 144–147
Homo economicus, 56–57, 62–63, 82, 266(n111)
Honneth, Alex, 54, 54(n29), 279(n20)
Hook, Sidney, 357(n5)
Hopfmann, Arndt, 66(n22)
Hopkins, Rob, 160(n55)
Hoppers, Catherine, 1(n1), 6(n20), 25(n33), 348(n81), 360(n17)
housing: Orange Farm settlement, 277–278, 288; organization and planning at Bokfontein, 128; the right to, 151; six steps towards full employment, 159; success of South Africa's programs, 115–116
Huchzermeyer, Marie, 115(n21)
Hudson, Michael, 159(n48), 351(n87)
human emancipation, 11–12; ethics, economics, and environmentalism, 36; South Africa's EFF Manifesto, 22–23
human needs: connecting social programs to economic growth, 325–327; effective social change strategies, 94–95; meeting in harmony with nature, 71–72; the moral duty to help those in need, 358; raising the social status of use value, 348–354; solving Keynes's problem, 182; using surplus to meet, 320–324. *See also* basic needs
human rights, 150–152, 157, 163, 165, 220
Hume, David, 254, 254(n89)
humiliation: combining pure economy with community, 174; countering, 321; effects of modernity, 135; structural, 89–92; violence in South Africa's townships, 120–121
Hunter, M., 286(n48), 300(n94)
Hutcheson, Francis, 245(n45)

Iglesias, Juan, 360(n17)
ikram, 162
income: capturing rent, 367–377; Keynes on the insufficiency of effective demand, 90–91; Keynes's identification of structural humiliation, 90–91; South African levels, 113–114; South Africa's unemployment figures, 114–115; the Swedish Model, 186. *See also* wages
incompleteness theorem (Gödel), 232
India: agriculture tax, 370(n39); Gandhi's philosophy and practice, 143–147; reining in speculation, 159; the suicide of Tapas Soren, 174–176; tying capital to a purpose and a territory, 222–223. *See also* National Rural Employment Guarantee Act
indigenous knowledge systems, 14, 313–314, 381
indigenous peoples: murder of Lalit Mehta, 166; the suicide of Tapas Soran, 174–176

individual experience, 18
individualism: successes and failures of planned economies, 84–86
induction, canons of, 7–8
industrialization: the model for successful development, 28–29; South Africa's EFF Manifesto, 24
inequality, 346–347; capital tax reversing, 390; capturing rent as reduction method, 368–370; governable growth under South Africa's NDP, 38; lower taxes for the wealthy, 386–387; shifting power from the wealthy, 396; South Africa, 21
inflation: the fiscal crisis of the state, 330; funding the Green New Deal, 336–339; increasing Chilean investment, 327; self-regulating market, 235; social reality and trust, 340; the Swedish model, 185–186, 188–190, 206, 209–210, 212–213
Inglehart, Robert, 215(n85)
inheritance taxes, 387–388
Inman, Pat, 297(n84)
innovation creating overproduction, 85–86
instability, the structural sources of, 80–83
instability hypothesis, 82
institutional facts, 15–18
institutional frame of economics, 32, 182
institutions, function and evolution of, 138–139
insufficiency of effective demand, 87–89, 88(n2); the choice not to buy or sell countering Say's Law, 82–83; the effect on full employment, 242; as a function of basic social structures, 60; the inevitability of structural humiliation, 90–92; Keynes's problem, 180, 182; South Africa's poultry program, 111; structural instability, 80–83; the Swedish Model, 212, 214–218. *See also* Staggering Fact 2
insufficient investment, 181
integrity, flexibility and, 356–357
intellectual property, 265, 376
intellectual reform, 14
interest rates: Sweden's labour market policy, 191
International Declaration of Human Rights (1948), 226–227, 380(n74)
International Labour Organization (ILO), 274(n1), 276, 325, 342
International Monetary Fund (IMF), 37, 345, 348, 350(n84), 358, 360
inter-sectoral collaboration, 119. *See also* alignment across sectors
intransitive objects, 11, 99
investment, 87; changing the perspective on economic growth, 202–203; control of large corporations, 322–323; dependence of production on profits, 87–88; the dependence of the economy on the confidence of investors, 65–68; economic dependence on capital accumulation, 63–68; economic growth as necessity for democratic stability, 198; effect of rent capturing, 370; ending poverty through economic growth, 197; freedom not to

invest, 60; Friedman's view of Keynes's predictions, 101–107; Keynes's problem, 180–182; mainstream development theory, 44–46; as obstacle to poverty alleviation, 114; South Africa's economic choice, 383; South Africa's poultry program, 108–112; unbounded organizing supporting, 351
investment-for-production-for-sale-for-profit (IPSP), 327
Italy: capital tax, 391

Jain, L.C., 165(n70)
Jameson, Fredric, 268(n114)
Jameson, Kenneth, 100(n33)
Jefferson, Thomas, 93
Jelavich, Barbara, 283(n37)
John Deere company, 75
Jones, Charles, 201(n45)
Jones, John E., 166(n77)
Jones, Ronald W., 241(n30)
Joshi, Vijay, 177(n98)
Joyce, Richard, 48(n18)
justice: constraints on social budgets, 349; freedom of the rational being, 359(n17)

Kaldor, Nicholas, 184(n13)
Kalecki, Michael, 157, 157(n44), 238(n22)
Kant, Immanuel, 56(n33), 72, 93, 130(n18), 346–347, 348(n79), 355–362, 358(nn8,11,12), 359(n17)
Kay, John, 259(n100)
Keen, Steve, 2(n2), 74(n47), 184(n14)
Kelsen, Hans, 318(n4)
Kentridge, Matthew, 28(n40)
Keynes, John Maynard, 44(n3), 45(n6), 79(n58), 81(n63), 83(n67), 83(nn64,67,68),87(n1), 97(n26), 101–107, 101(n34), 104(n39), 105(n40), 112(n5), 113(n9), 156(n42), 168(n82), 180(n4), 198(n38), 230(n4), 234(n12), 251(n73), 270(n121), 336(n46), 338(n49), 352(n91), 367–368, 371(n45), 384(n86), 398(n117); belief in full employment, 156–157; connection between investment and economic development, 44–45; creation of value depending on sales, 168; defining community, 52; economic overproduction, 85; ending unemployment, 3; funding World War II, 336–337; the inevitability of structural humiliation, 90–91; the Keynesian nature of the Swedish model, 183–184; lack of inducement to invest, 97; liquidity trap, 30; lowering wages to raise profit, 79–80; rational expectation of profits, 160(n54); rentier capital, 385; the structural sources of instability, 80–83. *See also* Staggering Fact 2
Keynes's problem, 179–183, 200–201. *See also* insufficiency of effective demand; Staggering Fact 2

khadi (traditional Indian homespun), 144–147, 144(n3)
Khatkhate, Deena, 166(n71), 170(n85), 177(n97)
Khera, Reetika, 154(n36), 155(n38)
Khoza, Reuel, 377–378, 377(n66), 378, 378(n67), 379–382
King, Martin Luther, Jr., 51, 51(n23), 95, 225, 306(n115), 323(n22), 399–400, 400(n120)
Kirsten, Adèle, 19(n10)
Klein, Naomi, 297(n84)
Kornai, Janos, 84–85, 84(n71)
Korth, M., 278(n14)
Kotler, Stephen, 117(n24), 150(n23)
Kramer, Mark, 332(n41)
Kretzman, Jody, 313(n133)
Krugman, Paul, 36, 37(n54), 101(n35), 157, 157–158(n45)
Kuhn, Thomas, 211–212, 235–236, 358(n9)
Kwanda (television show), 308

labour: CWP labour mandate for community building, 99–100; declining relevance in production, 226; employment guarantees serving the rich, 149(n19); failure of the Swedish Model, 193–194; globalization leveling the price of labour downward, 219; the productive power of, 244; as resource of the people's economy, 160; structural humiliation, 89–92. *See also* division of labour; employment; wages; *specific programs*
labour market policy: the Swedish Model, 190–191
labour theory of value, 148(n16)
Labra, Isabel, 125(n43)
Labra, Iván, 121(n34), 125(n43)
Laclau, Ernesto, 400, 400(n121)
Ladd, John, 360(n17)
Lagos, Ricardo, 242(n34)
land ownership: France taxing income-producing property, 392–393; landlords extracting the hardest bargain from tenant farmers, 51; rent, 375–376; South Africa's EFF Manifesto, 23–26; vegetable gardening in Orange Farm, 302–303
Landecker, Werner, 283(n35)
Langa, Malose, 19(n10), 277, 277(n9), 278, 280–281, 309
Lange, Oskar, 3–4, 4(n10), 103(n37), 234, 234(n11)
language: the origins and evolution of life, 238
Lawson, Tony, 8(n28), 9(n31), 229(n1), 234(n13), 340(n54)
Lee, Frederick, 2(n3), 8(n28), 380(n72)
leisure activities, 216
Leiva Lavalle, Jorge, 370, 370(n40), 375
Lenin, Vladimir, 23
Leontiev, A.N., 123

Lerner, Abba, 337(n48), 348
Levi-Strauss, Claude, 247, 247(n52)
l'horreur économique, 65
liberal institutions, unbounded organization rejecting, 93
liberal price theory, 266(n111)
liberté, egalité, and *fraternité,* 317, 392–393
Lider (Chilean supermarket chain), 29
Lieberman, Matthew, 136(n65)
life, the origins of, 137–138, 237–238
life-world *(Lebenswelt),* 11
limited government, 77
Lindbeck, Assar, 31(n44), 186(n19), 188(n21), 189(n24), 208–211, 209(n61), 241, 241(n32)
Lindner, Evelin, 89(n8), 135(n61), 369(n37)
liquidity preference, 181; effect in poor communities, 120; hitchbound view, 251; Kant's categorical imperatives, 358; psychological basis, 104–107; structural humiliation, 90–92
liquidity trap, 30
Little, Ian, 177(n98)
livelihood: nonmercantile, 182; NREGA prioritizing rights, 150–153; slots, 180–181
local government, elites co-opting South Africa's, 20
locational revolution, 183(n9)
Locke, John, 391(n107)
Lockwood, David, 64(n15)
logical coherence, 339
long earth story, 136–137
long run equilibrium position, 229–230
long-term investments: the Swedish model, 187
löntagarfonder (Swedish union-run pension funds), 186–187
L'Oréal group, 384
lose-lose situation, humanity's, 226–227
losers, economic, 81–82
Loyola, Ignatius, 272(n127)
Lundberg, Erik, 188(n23), 192(nn29,30), 198(n37)
Luther, Martin, 95
Luxemburg, Rosa, 66(n22), 85, 88(n2), 198(n39), 251(n71)

Maccarini, Andrea, 6(n19)
MacIntyre, Alasdair, 137(n67), 151–152, 152(n28), 194(n33), 207(n52)
Mackey, John, 97(n26)
Macpherson, C.B., 391(n107)
macroeconomics: decline and failure of the Swedish Model, 205–206
Madrick, Jeff, 234–235, 234(n14)

Magapi, Nomfundo, 19(n10)
Mahatma Gandhi Rural Employment Guarantee Act (India), 12, 47, 129. *See also* National Rural Employment Guarantee Act
mainstream empirical studies, 36
mainstream philosophy of economics (MPE), 8. *See also* neoliberalism; orthodox liberal economics
Malinowski, Bronislaw, 377(n63)
Malthus, Thomas, 85
Mandela, Nelson, 29–32, 30(n43), 378–379, 378(n66), 383, 383(n82)
Mandela Constitution, 227
Mander, Harsh, 155, 155(nn38,39)
manufacturing industry: capital flight, 213–214; Chile's exports, 326–327; Swedish production, 188, 214–216
Marais, Hein, 28(n40), 31(n47)
marginal businesses: failure of the Swedish Model, 190–191
market as an institution: buyers and sellers as decision makers, 72–73; defining welfare state, 184(n15); limiting the division of labour, 248
market economy, China's policy shift towards, 223(n102)
market equilibrium, 70; structural instability, 81; theorizing market equilibrium with unemployment, 90–91
Marques, Gustavo, 8, 8(n27)
Marshall, Alfred, 10, 52, 81, 257(n97), 270(n120), 367–369, 369(n38), 371, 371(n44), 373(n53), 374, 374(n58), 375, 375(n59), 376(n61)
Martinez, Enrique, 163
Martner, Gonzalo, 270(n122)
marula oil exports, 112
Marx, Karl, 3, 10–11, 23, 25(n35), 50–51, 54, 54(n28), 56(n33), 63–68, 64(n10), 66(n22), 76–77, 101, 132(n49), 239(n26), 245(n47), 344(n70), 372–373, 372(n49), 384(n86)
Masayesva, Virgil, 360(n20)
masculine identity, 299–300
Maslow, Abraham, 5, 5(n16), 47–48, 47(n16), 100, 100(n32), 192
Maslow's hierarchy of needs, 11–12, 140, 182
Masondo, Amos, 289
mass unemployment: Keynes's problem, 180–181
Masuko, Themba, 277(n9)
material practices, 246
mathematical value of pure economics, 69–70
Mathieu, Frederic, 6(n21)
Mattick, Paul, 384(n86)
Maturana, Humberto, 137(n69), 237(n18)
mature capitalism, 179, 204; increasing efficiency and productivity, 216; presenting symptoms of the Swedish Model, 212; reviving the shared prosperity of, 226–227
Mbeki, Thabo, 390

McAlpin, Michelle Burge, 370(n39)
McGilchrist, Ian, 309(n122)
McKinley, D., 278(n12)
McKnight, John, 53, 53(n26), 59, 313(n133), 314
McLean, Paul, 136(n64)
McPherson, C.B., 224(n107), 380(n71)
Means, Gardiner, 75, 322, 322(n18)
Medicare, 53
medicine. *See* health care and medicine
Mehafdi, Messaoud, 390(n101)
Mehta, Lalit, 166
Meidner, Rudolf, 184
Menger, Carl, 330(n38)
metaphysics, 328, 328(n33)
methodology: constitutive rules, 15–18
Mfulo, Aline, 333
middle class: decline of, 179; Gresham's Law of bad driving out good, 219; heavy tax burdens, 219
Middleton, Nick, 159(n48)
Mies, Maria, 18(n6), 25(n34), 66(n22), 224–225(n109), 264(n106)
Mil Hojas pasta factory, 213–214
milk industry: NABARD commitment to rural development, 222–223; Quebec, 213
Mill, John Stuart: canons of induction, 7–8
Milton, John, 196
Minar, David, 56(n39)
mineral prices, 368–369
minimum wage: informal sectors, 113; NREGA workers, 169–173; work as human right, 150, 153–154
Minsky, Hyman, 80–83, 82(n65), 184(n14)
Mises, Ludwig von, 247, 247(n51)
missionaries, 133
Mitchell, William, 318(n3), 339(n50), 351(n88)
Mitochondrial Eve, 323, 323(n21)
mixed-economy alternatives, 294
Modern Money Theory, 334–335, 339–341, 366
modern world-system, 83
modernity: defining community, 54–57; effect on India's culture and economy, 144–145; incompatibility of the Swedish Model, 208; loss of community and identity, 134–135; sacredness of debt-paying, 361
Molapo, Sepetla, 19(n10)
Mollison, Bill, 332(n41)
Monares, Andres, 91(n13)
monetary policies: decline and failure of the Swedish Model, 205–206
money management: Organization Workshop, 126

money: the purpose of investment in the economy, 66–67
moneyed classes challenging full employment, 157
Moore, Marissa, 331–334, 361, 393
moral codes and systems: a biologist's view of, 48–50; defining community, 136–137; global consensus on social responsibility, 6; Kant's categorical/hypothetical imperatives, 336–338; moral growth in the life-world, 11; as requirement for human action and human institutions, 93–94
moral compass, 275
moral culture, 136–137
moral realism: addressing structural humiliation, 91; defining community, 137; the failure of the Swedish Model, 204–205; Gandhi's philosophy and practice, 144; Green New Deal, 335–340; grounding ethics in natural science, 133; importance of community, 131; the importance to unbounded thinking, 92–98; needs creating community, 47–48; principles and tenets, 5–6; realist theory of science, 11–12; using surplus to meet needs, 320–324. *See also* unbounded organization
moral reform, 14
moralism, 6(n21)
Morishima, Michio, 269(n116)
Morkel, Jolanda, 124(n41)
Moswale, Agnes, 149
Mother Teresa, 220, 220(n96)
motivation: benevolence and self-interest, 245
Mouffe, Chantal, 400, 400(n121)
Municipal Bank of Rosario, Argentina, 221–222
Musgrave, Richard, 85(n73), 186(n20)
music and musicians, 99–100, 162, 274–275
Mycoskie, Blake, 160(n55)
Myrdal, Gunnar, 62, 178, 178(n1), 185, 185(n18), 193–194, 206

Nadella, Satya, 379, 379(n69)
nation states: the fallacy of free trade, 195–196; generating income for the public purse, 341
National Bank for Agriculture and Rural Development (NABARD), 222–223
National Development Plan (NDP; South Africa): economic growth and absolute conflict, 27; economic growth and poverty alleviation, 43–45; economic reality and sentimental solidarity, 33–39; pro-growth provisions, 200; standard economic growth theory, 203
National Institute of Industrial Technology (Argentina), 163
National Planning Commission (South Africa), 33
National Rural Employment Guarantee Act (India), 147(n13); budget deficit, 240; corrupt behavior, 164–167; crowding out private enterprise, 169–174; failure to achieve economic democracy, 156–158; minimum

daily wage, 153(n32); origins, 142; prioritizing rights, 149–153; purpose and activities, 153–156; rationale for, 148–149; state expenditures, 176–177; the suicide of Tapas Soren, 174–176; wage floor, 184
nationalization: Mandela's choice between liberalism and, 29–32; South Africa's EFF Manifesto, 24
Nattrass, Nicoli, 113(n10)
natural economics, 60–63, 70–71, 83
natural law: status of the world citizen, 356
natural liberty, 16–17, 59, 329, 363–364
natural markets, 185
natural price, 61–62. *See also* wages
natural resource, rent as, 370, 372, 375
natural rights, 151–152, 355–356
natural selection: evolution of moral systems, 48–50
natural wage, 61–62
naturalist moral realism. *See* moral realism
nature: empiricism, truth, and, 8
Nayak, Nandini, 154(n36)
necessaries and convenience of life, 9–10, 246, 253
needs. *See* basic needs; human needs
needs assessments, 140–141
negative erotic, 350
negotiation, the purposes of, 96
Nehru, Jawaharlal, 194
neoliberalism: the academic fascination of, 235–237; alternatives to regimes of accumulation, 132; criticism of South Africa's NDP, 40; decline and failure of the Swedish Model, 208, 210; ethical indefensibility of, 266–270; evaluating the CWP, 239–2423; explaining the current hegemony, 266(n111); false claims, 270–271; *forme* and *fond*, 233–235; global entrenchment, 31; ignoring historical and current economic realities, 264–266; lowering wages to raise profit, 79; nonviable alternatives, 32, 40; the origins of, 243–252; the origins of life, 238–239; reining in speculation, 159; successes and failures of planned and capitalist economies, 85–86; the tax wedge and unbounded alternatives, 259–263; transformative heterodoxy transforming, 271–272. *See also* orthodox liberal economics
Nersisyan, Yeva, 335–340, 335(n45)
Neumark, David, 37(n55)
Neurath's boat, 16–17, 43–59, 133
neurotic institutions, 357
Newton, Isaac, 328
Ngubeni, Kindeza, 19(n10)
Niblock, Tim, 343(n66)

Nobel Prizes, 31
Noddings, Nel, 53(n26)
nonmercantile livelihoods, 182; CWP music and dance, 99–100; CWP participants in Orange Farm livelihoods, 299; raising the social status of use value, 349; regulation of capital, 242; Sweden's nontradeable sector, 189–190; wage levels, 276
nonproductive labour, 182
nontradeable part of the Swedish economy, 188–189
Norway: salmon fishing industry, 160(n52)
Nozick, Robert, 320(n10)
Ntshangase, Phindile, 89
nuclear wear, prevention of, 1–2
Nussbaum, Martha, 33, 100, 194
nyaope (street drug), 283–284, 305
Nzimakwe, T.I., 129(n45)

Ocasio-Cortez, Alexandria, 334–340
O'Connor, Elizabeth, 56(n38)
O'Connor, James, 202, 202(n46), 343(n63)
Odhner, Clos-Erik, 189(n27)
OECD Review of the CWP, 252–257, 253(n74), 261–262, 264
oil resources: effect of falling prices on Chile's economy, 327; Saudi Arabia's welfare spending, 343–344
Ominami, Carlos, 270(n122)
One Economics, Many Recipes (Rodrik), 35–36, 44, 200–201
ontology, 61, 90, 328(n33), 339–340
open society, 119, 161, 324, 341
optimism of economic theory, 81–83
opulent society, 248, 248(n57)
Orange Farm township, South Africa: ABCD and, 313–315; crime, 281–283; CWP history and characteristics, 288–293; CWP participant profiles, 298–301; CWP participants and activities, 280–281; domestic violence, 284–286; evidence of an unbounded worldview, 308–310; ex-offenders against crime, 304–306; local politics, 286–288; migration and expansion, 277–279; multiplying and strengthening social bonds, 306–308; optimism and enthusiasm, 310–312; Proud to Serve campaign, 289; purpose and work of the CWP, 301–304; recruitment of CWP participants, 293–296; socioeconomic diversity, 280
ordering principles, 394–395
organic chemistry, 237–238
Organization Workshop, 121, 288–289; Bokfontein, 127–129; form and mechanics of, 125–127; raising the social status of use value, 349; Second Economy Strategy, 129–130
Orléan, André, 2, 2(n4), 7, 65, 65(n17), 84(n69), 148(n16), 182, 182(n7), 340(n55)

orthodox liberal economics, 43–45, 194–195; the basic cultural structure of modernity, 55; failure to work for the poor, 187–188; free trade, 195–196; importance of investments, 44–45; incompatibility with human survival, 1–2; the lethal concept of economic growth, 196–204; rebuilding basic social structures, 16–17; South Africa's Community Work Programme challenging, 40–42; South Africa's tension between property rights and absolute conflict, 27–28; the stakes of, 234–235; the structural sources of economic instability, 81–83. *See also* neoliberalism
overproduction, 85–86

Panayatou, Theodore, 27(n38)
Papandreou, Andreas G., 266(n111)
Papola, T.S., 170–171, 170(n88), 171–172, 171(n90), 172
paradigm shifts: community in NREGA's programs, 173; the downside of rights talk, 150–151; fiscal crisis of the state, 318; including indigenous knowledge systems, 212
Pareto optimum, 72, 243, 262–263(n103)
Parsons, Talcott, 6, 7(n23)
past factory, 213–214
Patel, L., 278(n14)
Patel, Raj, 172(n93)
Patnaik, Prabhat, 172(n92)
patriarchal thinking and institutions, 286, 318–319
patriotism, South Africa's NDP appealing to, 37
Payer, Cheryl, 29(n42), 383(n83)
peace, universal, 355–356
pension funds: cost of social programmes, 325, 325(n28); inflationary pressure of the Swedish Model, 186; workers in the people's economy, 160–161
people's economy, 160–161
perfect liberty, 59, 62
permaculture, 4–5
Peron, Eva, 46
philanthropy: India's *khadi* industry, 145–146
Philip, Kate, 111–112, 111(n4), 114, 114(nn12,13), 115(n21), 117, 118(n29), 129, 130(nn47,48)
philosophy: the fiscal crisis as a philosophical problem, 319; Say's observations on early economists, 363–364; of social science, 167–169
phronesis (practical wisdom), 96, 296
Pickett, Kate, 27(n39), 306(n115), 368(n35)
piece rate, NREGA wage payments, 169–170
Piketty, Thomas, 37–38, 38(n59), 68, 224(n108), 277(n8), 325, 325(n29), 335, 335(n43), 374(n58), 382–393, 383(n81), 384(n85), 386(n89), 387(nn93,94), 389(n99), 390(n105), 391(n107), 392(n109), 393(n110)

pin factor, Smith's observations on, 244
planned economies, 234. *See also* central planning
Plato, 47(n15), 96
pluralism, 33, 252; curing the defects of capitalism, 119–120; organizing for full employment, 163; taxing wealth, 161–162
Poincaré, Henri, 340
Polanyi, Karl, 83, 91–92, 92(n14), 135(n59), 239(n27), 344(n72), 382(n80)
Polar Park (Bokfontein), 128
police forces: violence in South Africa's townships, 19–21
policymaking: loosening the constraints on economic growth, 201–202; moneyed classes' control of employment, 157; the Swedish Model's high wages and full employment, 188–189
political economy, science of, 363–364
political institutions. *See also* fiscal crisis of the state
political institutions of Orange Farm, 286–288, 292–293
political movements: South Africa's Economic Freedom Fighters, 21–29, 287–288
Popper, Karl, 88–89, 119(n32), 235, 341, 352(n91)
populism, 38–39, 243
Porpora, Douglas, 9(nn30,32), 16(n2), 45(n7), 46(n8), 60, 319(n7)
Porter, Michael, 74(n47), 75(n48), 264–265, 264(n107), 332(n41)
positivism, 8, 254, 328(n33)
Posner, Richard A., 259(n100)
poultry program (South Africa), 109–112
poverty: chronic precarious employment, 350; as a consequence of market exchange, 76–79; Davos standards, 398–399; effect of economic growth on, 37; history of, 225; the illusion of education as the solution for, 82; the lethal concept of economic growth, 197; neoliberal claims on reduction of, 31; NREGA and CWP function, 155; six steps towards full employment, 158–159; Smith's 'civilized' nations observations, 244–245; South Africa's NDP balancing economic growth and, 43–45; South Africa's unemployment figures, 114–115; triggering South African violence, 21
poverty alleviation and elimination: creating value, 148; failure of orthodox economic constructs, 187–188; reliance on Say's Law, 362–363; restarting Chile's economic growth, 325–327; reviving the shared prosperity of mature capitalism, 226–227; simple measures leading to, 220–221; South Africa's housing programs, 115–116; South Africa's poultry program, 108–112; South Africa's Second Economy Study, 108–118; success of the Swedish model, 183–184. *See also* Community Work Programme; National Rural Employment Guarantee Act
power: making a culture shift, 396; the responsible use of, 321–322
practical law, 359
Prahalad, C.K., 263(n105)

prehistory of the human species, 132
presenting symptoms of the civilization crisis, 212–227
Prinsloo, Melani, 14
private enterprise: effect of public funding on, 241; NREGA crowding out, 169–174; public employment evaluations, 255
private expenses, 217
private sector: Orange Farm upliftment initiatives, 278; protecting and serving, 76; South Africa's housing programs, 115–116
privatization: decline and failure of the Swedish Model, 210
production: application to profit, 101–102; declining relevance of labour towards, 226; defining, 349; dependence on expectation of profit, 87–89; effective social change strategies, 96; increasing productive capacity, 364(n27); South Africa's poultry program, 111; successes and failures of planned economies, 85–86. *See also* Staggering Fact 1
production, cost of: India's *khadi* industry outpricing the market, 144–147; lowering wages to increase production and profit, 78–79; market demand for labour, 77–79; rent, 369–372, 374; sale price and, 267–268; Say's Law, 366
production-for-sale-for-profit, 87–88, 351. *See also* Staggering Fact 1
productivity: dominant social structures motivating, 83–86; ethical claims of equality and dignity, 353; fixed and circulating capital, 249–251; six steps towards full employment, 159–160; social programmes as production-for-sale-for-profit, 351; Sweden's export trade, 188–191
productivity growth, 253
profit: dependence of production on, 87–89; disposal of corporate earnings, 322–323; driving to the cost of production, 73–74; loosening the constraints on economic growth, 201–202; as obstacle to poverty alleviation, 114; South Africa's economic activity, 34; South Africa's poultry program, 108–112; Sweden's tradeable economic sector, 188–189; the Swedish Model of economic growth, 185, 209(n62). *See also* capital accumulation; Staggering Fact 1; surplus, sharing and productive use of
profits, expectation of, 96–97. *See also* Staggering Fact 1
property owners: failure of the Swedish Model, 207
property rights, 15–16; categorical imperatives, 359; China, 223; conditions for economic growth, 39; the design of modern republics, 317; Kant's categorical imperatives, 358; South Africa's EFF Manifesto, 23–28; Walras's inquiries into rents, 373–374; Walras's pure economics, 70–71
protest. *See* social protest
Proud to Serve campaign (Orange Farm), 289–290
provisioning, economic theory addressing, 26
psychology: activity theory, 122–124
public choice, 296–298
public employment plans: proper evaluation, 255; reinventing the public sector to support, 161–162; South Africa's CWC, 118–121; South Africa's

poultry program, 109–112; the Swedish Model, 187. *See also* Community Work Programme; National Rural Employment Guarantee Act
public expenses: Swedish Model, 212, 217–218
public funding: effect on private industry, 241; funding talent and good works, 162
public ownership of resources: South Africa's EFF Manifesto, 22–23
public works: deadweight loss, 256; NREGA employment, 148–149
public-private cooperation: CWP alignment, 119; CWP in Orange Farm, 290–292; environmental policy, 263(n105)
pure capitalism: decline and failure of the Swedish Model, 206
pure economy and pure economics: community and, 273–274; dependence on markets, 63–69; Keynesian economics, 80; mathematical creation, 267(n112); Smith's natural economics, 60–63; viability of a high-wage economy, 80; Walras's ideal economy, 69–76, 229
pure markets, 259
pure reason, 345, 359, 359(n17)
Puri, M., 311(n127)
Putnam, Hilary, 2(n7)

quantitative predictions, 101–102
quasi-rent, 374–375
Quine, Willard van Orman, 16(n4), 88–89

Racionzer, Douglas, 160(n51)
Rajivlochan, Meeta, 165(n67)
Ramachela, Oupa, 117
Ramatlakane, Leonard, 333
Ravi, Shamika, 155(n41)
Rawls, John, 139, 139(n72), 140(n76), 217(n89)
real prices, 266–270, 266(n111)
A Realist Theory of Science (Bhaskar), 7
reason and pure economics, 70–71
reciprocity and redistribution, 91–92, 344(n72)
recyling rents, 370, 375
Reddy, D. Narasimha, 154(n36), 155(n40), 166(n73), 170(n85)
reducing, reusing, and recycling, 215
redundancy, 163
regimes of accumulation, 132, 267–268
regulation: decline and failure of the Swedish Model, 205
Rehn, Gösta, 184, 186
Rehn-Meidner economic model, 184, 208, 217–218
Reich, Robert, 58, 132(n51), 390(n104)
Reid, G., 286(n48)
reine Vernunft (pure reason), 345
relation marchande, 7

religious ideals and values, 272; sharing surpluses, 3
Renner, Karl, 185, 185(n17), 367(n32)
rentier capital, 383–386
rents: capturing, 367–377; defining, 376; landlords extracting the hardest bargain, 51; sharing surpluses, 3; structural transformation, 386
resilience: culture shifts decreasing dependence on the system, 215–216; defining, 242(n34); defining a resilient community, 242
resource-based theory of business strategy (RBT), 265(n107)
resources, ownership and exploitation of: connecting social programs to economic growth, 325–327; full employment of labour, 229–230; funding the Green New Deal, 336–340; medical rights, 151; nature as a set of resources, 318–319; the poor sharing surplus, 47; redistribution as social problem solution, 274–275; rent as natural resource, 370, 372, 375; South Africa's EFF Manifesto, 23–25; South Africa's NDP, 38; steps towards full employment, 158–159; using surplus to meet needs, 320–324
The Return of Depression Economics (Krugman), 36
revealed preference as a measure of value, 73
Ricardo, David, 78–79, 78(n55), 225(n110), 370(n39), 371(n45), 372, 372(n46), 374–375
Richards, Howard, 1(n1), 4(n12), 5(n18), 6(nn20,21), 9(n29), 25(n33), 25(n35), 40(n63), 45(n4), 46(n9), 50(n21), 56(n35), 64(n11), 79(n57), 81, 84(n70), 88(n3), 89(n6), 92(n15), 94(n20), 97(n27), 99(n30), 121(n34), 125(nn42,43), 133(n54), 145(n4), 158(n47), 161(n58), 183(n10), 184(n12), 195(n34), 196(n36), 205(n50), 216(n88), 221(n97), 239(n25), 248(n53), 254(n91), 260(n102), 294(n72), 297(n84), 312(n131), 317(n2), 319(n8), 320(n9), 321(n13), 322(n16), 324(n25), 348(n81), 360(n17), 393(n111)
Richardson, George, 74(n46)
Rifkin, Jeremy, 32(n49), 346–347, 353(n100)
rights, NREGA prioritizing, 149–153
rigid institutions, 357
Rivera, Eugenio, 270(n122)
Rivlin, Alice, 205–207
Robbins, Lionel, 6, 6(n22)
Robinson, Diana, 297(n84)
Robinson, D.T., 311(n127)
Robinson, Joan, 373, 373(n51)
Rodrik, Dani, 18, 35–36, 36(n53), 44, 44(n2), 200–201, 201(n44), 223, 223(n104)
Rodrik-Hausmann-Velasco (RHV) mainstream theory of development, 44; centrality of GNP growth to development, 73; connecting economic development theory and investment, 45–46; understanding economic growth and reform strategies, 200–203

Roman law, 17, 61, 161(n58); absolute rule as absolute freedom, 359(n17); colonialism in Africa, 25; defining community, 54–55, 136; freedom as the main principle of liberal justice, 72; status of the world citizen, 356
Romer, Paul, 201(n45)
Rorty, Richard, 239(n24)
Rosario, Argentina, 161, 221–222, 260(n102), 312
Roy, Arundhati, 155–156
Royce, Josiah, 51
Rufatt, Oscar, 242(n34)
ruthless capitalism, 204; communitarian capitalism and, 179; dysfunctional nature of, 195; increasing efficiency and productivity, 216; the Swedish Model, 212, 224–225

Saab company, 187, 190
Saavedra, Juan Carlos, 221–222, 222(n98)
sacredness, 360–361
Saez, Emmanuel, 384(n85), 387, 387(n93)
Sahlins, Marshall, 135(n58)
Saillard, Yves, 267(n114)
sales: as acts causing economic phenomena, 124; the dependence of capitalism on, 67–68; Keynes's problem, 180–181; regimes of capital accumulation, 267–268; Say's Law, 364–366
salmon fishing industry, 160(n52)
Sampson, Anthony, 29(n41), 31(n45), 383(n82)
Sampson, Robert J., 282(n34)
Samuelson, Paul, 103(n37), 198(n39), 267(n112)
Sandelin, Bo, 184(n11)
sarvodaya (work for the benefit of all) principle, 144
Sathiparsad, R., 286(n48)
satyagraha (confronting evil with love), 144
Saudi Arabia: welfare spending, 343–344
Saul, John S., 31(n46), 108(n1), 151(n24)
Savage, L.J., 235(n15), 236(n16)
savages, 244–245
saving: decline and failure of the Swedish Model, 205–206; Keynes's liquidity preference theory, 104–107
Say, Jean-Baptiste, 85, 355, 363–364, 363(n22), 364(n28), 365(n30)
Sayer, Andrew, 100(n31), 275(n2), 323, 323(n20), 356(n4)
Say's Law, 81(n63); the choice not to buy or sell countering, 81; CWP's social and economic contribution, 120; defining the neoliberal worldview, 234; falseness of, 362–367; Keynes on the insufficiency of effective demand, 90–91; structural instability, 81–82
scaling up production: South Africa's poultry program, 111
scarcity value of a utility, 70

Schumpeter, Joseph, 32, 32(n48), 148(n17), 202(n47), 231(n7), 238(n21), 251(n71), 270(n122), 317, 341, 343(n64), 364, 364(n26)
Schwab, Klaus, 379(n69)
Schyndel, Kaspar van, 332(n41)
science and scientific knowledge: the academic field, 235; activity theory, 122–124; culture linking human sciences and natural sciences, 94; defining culture, 395; the epistemicological rupture, 323–324; moral realism and, 11–12; Neurath's boat, 16–17
scoping walks, 121, 126
Searle, John, 9(n33), 15(n1), 17, 46, 46(n10), 47(n2), 48, 137–139, 138(n70), 139(n71), 173, 329(n35)
Second Economy Strategy, 111–112, 129–130
Second Economy Study (South Africa), 108–118
Seekings, Jeremy, 113(n10)
self-esteem as a basic need, 100, 317
self-interest, 204; accumulation following from, 84; appropriation of surplus, 323; benevolence, motivation, and, 245–248; concealing preferences, 96; optimizing utility, 236; Smith's moral and economic views, 61(n3), 91
self-regulating markets, 235; constitutions of modern republics, 317; criticisms against NREGA, 177
selling: defining, 9–10; finding buyers and increasing production, 364. *See also* Say's Law
Sen, Amartya, 2, 2(n6), 9–10, 10(n35), 16, 33, 33(n51), 45(n7), 65, 65(n16), 97(n26), 140(n77), 150(n22), 173, 216(n88), 242(n36), 246, 246(n49), 262–263(n103), 269(n117), 272(n126), 297(n82)
séparation marchande, 7, 65, 84–86, 234, 316, 395
serfdom, 330
Seriti Institute, 121, 289–290, 308
Sewell, William H., Jr., 224(n108)
Shah, Mahir, 148(n18), 155(n37), 165, 165(n68), 166(n74)
shared prosperity, 187, 192, 194, 224, 226
sharing. *See* caring and sharing; surplus, sharing and productive use of
Shiva, Vandana, 172(n91), 373(n52)
Shleifer, Andrei, 163(n63)
short-term profits: the Swedish model, 187
Shumba, Rejoice, 118(n30), 130(n47), 277(n9), 289, 289(n56)
Simon, Herbert, 40(n62), 123(n36), 142(n1), 266(n111)
Simon, Julian, 201(n45)
simple exchange, 329
A Simple Path (Mother Teresa), 220, 220(n96)
Singer, Paul, 219, 219(n93)
Sisodia, Rajendra, 97(n26)
situation rent, 374–375
Skinner, Caroline, 112–113

Skosana, Nkere, 117
slots, 180–181, 183
Smith, Adam, 62(nn4,5), 63(nn6,7,8), 76(n51), 78(n54), 91, 91(nn12,13), 146(n7), 238(n23), 243(n37), 245(n45), 270(n119), 343(n65), 371(n41), 382(n77); advocating the market way of life as a natural way of life, 70–71; arguing against humanity and ethics of individuals, 91; capturing rents, 371; defining economics, 7; natural economics and pure economics, 60–63; natural liberty, 16–17; natural liberty and perfect liberty, 59; poverty as a consequence of market exchange, 76–77; use of surplus, 2–4
Snell, Grant, 333
Sobrado, Miguel, 125(n42)
social audits: NREGA corruption, 166
social change strategy, 92–100. *See also* unbounded organization
social chaos, 1
social cohesion: CWP multiplying and strengthening in Orange Farm, 306–308; individual utility maximization, 236; NDP tenets, 37, 42; the origins of life, 238; productivity without sales, 353–354; reliance on capital accumulation, 276–277
social compact: conditions for economic growth, 39
social construction of reality: construction through economic theories, 16–17, 46; Modern Money Theory, 340. *See also* moral realism
social democracy, 353; achieving full employment, 156–157; effects of public actions, 260; the exit power of capital, 80; incompatibility with modern cultural structures, 317, 330; lower crime associated with, 282–283; Myrdal defining, 185; as nonviable alternative to neoliberalism, 32, 40; sustainability of the Swedish model, 179; talking community down, 58; unsustainability of, 14
social disintegration, 178, 202–203
social integration: effect on crime, 282–283, 283(n36)
social market economy, 385(n87)
social media networks: CWP participants in Orange Farm, 298
social peace, economic theory addressing, 26
social progress, business investment in, 30
social protest: Orange Farm's lack of basic services, 278; South Africa's peaceful protest, 20; violence in South Africa's townships, 19–21
social science, the philosophy of, 328–330
social security: CWP program failures and frustrations, 318
social statistics, 328–329
social status: brute facts, 15–16; raising the social status of use value, 348–354; structural humiliation, 89–92
social structures: causal powers of the Swedish Model, 191; the dependence of the economy on the confidence of investors, 65–66; economics as, 60–86; environmental policy and, 36–37; the excess of people over

livelihood slots, 183; as legal and ethical norms, 234; motivating immense productivity, 83–86; natural economics and pure economics, 60–61; the responsible use of power, 321–322; solving Keynes's problem, 182; Staggering Facts, 8

social values. *See* values

social welfare, re-examining economic growth in terms of, 200–204, 260

socialism, 234; ANC ideals, 29; capitalism making socialism possible, 185; either/or thinking on markets, 247; Mandela's ideals and choices, 29–32; sharing surpluses, 3

socially constructed reality: full employment, 156–157, 157(n43)

society of organizations, 385

Socrates, 320

solidaristic wage policy (Sweden), 189–190

solidarity: defining community, 58; ethic of, 5; Sweden's union labour, 186, 188

solnedgång (sunset) industries, 191–192, 209, 213

Solow, Robert M., 61, 201(n45)

soluppgång (sunrise) industries, 191–192, 209, 213

Somers, Margaret, 57–58, 57(n42)

Song, Lieuw-Kie, 118(n29)

Soren, Dilip, 174–176

Soren, Tapas, 174–176

South Africa: achieving social cohesion, 276–277; anger and violence, 19–21, 120–121, 128–129; creating fiscal space for social programmes, 342; Economic Freedom Fighters, 21–29; falling mineral prices, 368–369; Green New Deal, 335; Mandela's choice between liberalism and socialism, 29–32; opportunities to rethink basic economic theory, 40–42; reining in speculation, 159; the right to emergency medical treatment, 151; Second Economy Study, 108–118; talking community up, 58. *See also* Community Work Programme; National Development Plan; Orange Farm township

South African Charter, 24–25

sovereign control of money, 138, 159, 172, 207, 217, 337–338, 341

spiritual welfare, 260

Spretnak, Charlene, 318–319, 318(n5)

Stachowicz-Stanusch, Agata, 168(n80)

Staggering Fact 1: connection to unbounded thinking, 92–98; creation of NREGA, 167; critical realism origins, 329; the downside of rights talk, 150–151; effective social change strategies, 94–97; fiscal crisis of the state, 316; inadequate progress of green parties, 319; loosening constraints on economic growth, 201–203; South Africa's unemployment figures, 114–115; ungovernability of capital, 134

Staggering Fact 2: connection to unbounded thinking, 92–98; creation of NREGA, 167; critical realism origins, 329; CWP Organization Workshop, 130; decline of the Swedish Model, 208–209; the downside of rights talk, 150–151; effective social change strategies, 96–97; failure

of the Swedish Model, 217–218; fiscal crisis of the state, 316; inadequate progress of green parties, 319; loosening the constraints on economic growth, 203; NREGA's public works, 148–149; preventing poverty alleviation, 113–114; rentier capital, 385; Say's Law, 362; ungovernability of capital, 134
stakeholder capitalism, 246
Standing, Guy, 311(n128,129), 368(n34)
Steurstaat (the state that lives by taxes), 317, 339, 343, 352, 377, 392
Stiegler, Bernard, 32(n49)
Stigler, George, 376(n60)
Stiglitz, Joseph, 2(n5), 58, 73, 73(n44), 132(n51), 271(n123), 374(n58), 376, 376(nn60,62), 382(n78), 390–391
storytelling: Bokfontein community planning, 128
Straffa, Piero, 85, 366(n31)
Strange, Susan, 66(n23)
Strawson, Peter, 45(n5)
strict duties, 358–369
structural facts, 81–82
structural frustration, 97–98
structural humiliation, 80–81, 89–92
structural instability, 80–83
structural transformation, 382–393; capturing rents, 367–377; culture shifts, 393–400; growth points, 399
subjective theory of value, 148(n16)
Subramoney, Thiagraj, 151, 157
subsidies: Argentinian agriculture, 161; contribution to dignity and optimism, 312; as economic anomalies, 211–212; NREGA activities, 149(n19); South Africa's NDP, 203, 206; the Swedish Model, 185, 191, 208(n56)
subsistence-oriented agriculture: South Africa, 109
substitution, the law of, 10, 160(n53)
suicides of India's small farmers, 172–176
Sundararajan, Arun, 353(n100)
sunrise industries (Sweden), 191–192, 209, 213
sunset industries (Sweden), 191–192, 209, 213
supply: calculating deadweight, 256–259; Say's Law, 365–366; South Africa's poultry program, 108–112. *See also* Say's Law
surplus, sharing and productive use of, 2–4; achievable change in constitutive rules, 47; calculating deadweight, 257–258; capturing rent as strategy, 368–370; connecting social programs to economic growth, 325–327; culture shifts, 394; CWP community development method, 130; CWP success, 317; defining, 75–76, 320–324; defining community, 52–53; effective social change strategies, 95–96; effects of tax wedges, 261; Gandhi's philosophy and practice, 144; improving South Africa's economic enterprises, 34–35; the logical fallacy of free trade, 195–196; moving to address need, 75–76; rent as, 375; South Africa's NDP, 38;

taxing wealth in a plural economy, 161–162; use for caring and sharing, 131–132; using surplus to meet needs, 320–324
swadeshi (constructing the local economy), 144–145
Swanger, Joanna, 25(n35), 40(n63), 45(n4), 56(n35), 64(n11), 79(n57), 84(n70), 88(n3), 94(n20), 97(n27), 145(n4), 158(n47), 161(n58), 183(n10), 184(n12), 196(n36), 216(n88), 294(n72), 317(n2), 324(n25)
swaraj (social justice for all through self-discipline), 144, 162
Swedish Model: the achievements of, 183–193; economic efficiency, 195; effect of public funding on private industry, 241; the failure of, 204–211; the logical fallacy of free trade, 196; macroeconomic explanations for the failure of, 204–207; orthodox economic theory and, 193–204; presenting symptoms, 212–227; standard economic growth theory, 203–204
switch points, historical, 391
Switzerland: full employment, 88

talent, development of, 162
Tambo, Oliver, 19–20
tax wedge, 241, 258–263
taxation: of corporate earnings, 322–323; creating fiscal space, 342–343, 343(n62); euphemisms contained in fiscal constraints, 334; financing a Green New Deal, 335; funding a social state, 387–389; India's tax on farmers, 370(n39); loosening constraints on economic growth, 202; lower taxes for the wealthy, 386–387; of rent, 372; the Swedish Model, 186, 205–206, 209–210, 212, 219; taxing wealth in a plural economy, 161–162; Tobin tax, 159, 159(n49); of total personal wealth, 388–393; the unbounded view of the Swedish Model, 218
Taylor, Charles, 203(n48), 329(n36)
Taylor, Fred, 103(n37), 234(n11)
T-DEM movement, 335
technology and technological innovation: effect on unemployment, 32; Gandhi's distrust of, 143; replacing human labour, 97; squeezing out labour, 179; Sweden's export trade, 190–192
tenants, landlords extracting the hardest bargain from, 51
territorial capital commitment, 221–222
textiles industry: India's *khadi,* 144–147, 144(n3)
Thatcher, Margaret, 206, 297–298
there is no alternative (TINA) argument, 297–298
thick mores, 136–137
Third Estate (France), 77
Thompson, Derek, 346–347
Thunberg, Greta, 207, 214
Timmons, Mark, 346(n78)
Tobin, James, 214(n84)
Tobin tax, 159, 159(n49)

Tönnies, Ferdinand, 54–55, 55(n31), 136
toyi toyi (South African protest), 20
Toynbee, Arnold, 49
trade: Chile's shift to agriculture and manufacturing, 326–327; effect of trade barriers on labour rights, 220; insufficient demand for Swedish products, 214–216; Pareto optimum, 72; the Swedish Model, 187–189, 191–193, 205–206, 208–210
Trade and Industrial Policy Strategies (TIPS), 129, 129(n46)
tradeable part of the Swedish economy, 188–189, 191–192
Traité d'économie politique (Say), 363–364
transfer pricing, 389–390
tribal market ethics, 84–85
triune brain, 136
Trivedi, Lisa, 145(n4)
trust: broken trust triggering violence, 19–20; social reality depending on, 340
truth: Gandhi's philosophy and practice, 144–147
Tufts, James, 6(n21)
Tugwell, Rexford, 219
Tullock, Gordon, 259, 259(n100)
Turner, Victor, 46(n8)

ubuntu: capturing rent, 370; CWP creation in Orange Farm, 306–308; CWP reviving the spirit of, 134; raising the social status of use value, 348–349; a relief for the fiscal crisis, 377–382; thick mores, 137; use of community and neighborhood for implementing, 162
unbounded organization (UO), 4–5, 231; absolute conflict and property rights, 26–27; activity theory, 123–124; aligning human needs with economics, 64–65; alternative to the tax wedge, 259–263; arguments for superiority over neoliberalism, 264–266; averting absolute conflict, 28; capitalism as a homeostatic system, 49–50; creating employment without investors, 198–199; definition and concepts, 142–143; employment as a human right, 163; evidence of Orange Farm's unbounded worldview, 308–310; the *forme* and *fond* of, 237–239; Green New Deal, 335–340; Modern Money Theory, 341; pluralism and, 33–34; private-public expenses, 218; providing different solutions, 352; rebuilding basic social structures, 17–18; redefining the concept of economic growth, 199–204; replacing capital accumulation with ethical activities, 68; sharing surplus, 320–324; shifting power from the wealthy, 396; six steps towards full employment, 158–162; as social change strategy, 92–98; social integration, 116–117; solutions for known and unknown possibilities, 246–248; South Africa's CWP, 41–42, 119; South Africa's NDP modeling, 39; the Swedish Model, 206–207, 211–227. *See also* Community Work Programme
unemployment: challenging the global economy, 49; destructive actions leading to, 97; ending, 3; increasing Chile's economic dynamism, 326–327;

post-war Sweden, 184(n15); South Africa's falling mineral prices, 368–369; South Africa's figures, 114–115; theorizing market equilibrium with unemployment, 90–91. *See also* Community Work Programme; employment guarantee; full employment; National Rural Employment Guarantee Act

ungovernability: structural frustration, 97–98; the Swedish Model, 206–207

union labour: Sweden's solidarity, 186, 188

universal basic income (UBI), 3, 368

Universal Declaration of Human Rights (1948), 47, 47(n2)

universe, the origins and evolution of, 137–138

Uribe, R., 237(n18)

use values, 103, 132, 149, 348–354, 372–373

utility, maximizing, 236, 236(n16); deadweight loss, 256–259; propositions of Walras's pure economics, 71–72. *See also* harmony with nature

utility analysis, 235–236

value: achievements of the Swedish model, 207; acts causing economic phenomena, 124; community development as multiplier, 275; constitutive rules, 15–16; defining, 124(n38); forms of, 10; operational definition, 148(n14); raising the social status of use value, 348–354; redefining the concept of economic growth, 200; revealed preference as a measure of value, 73; Say's Law, 364–366; Smith's natural price, 62; the value of people, 162

values: communitarianism, 131–132; defining community, 136–137; South Africa's NDP appealing to patriotism, 37. *See also* ethical realism; ethics

Vanaik, Anish, 167(n78), 174(n94)

Vandenberghe, Frédéric, 6(n19)

Varela, Francisco, 137(n69), 237(n18)

Varoufakis, Yanis, 335, 364(n27)

Vawda, Shamima, 14(n40)

Velasco, Andres, 36, 44, 200

vendible products, 159(n50); capital and division of labour, 249–250; fixed and circulating capital, 249–250; post-war full employment, 156–157; Say's Law, 365–366; transition from full employment to including nonproductive labour, 182

Veriava, A., 278(n12)

Vhemba poultry program (South Africa), 109–112

violence: chronic precarious employment, 350–351; combining pure economy with community, 174; Keynes's problem and the consequences of unemployment, 181; South Africa's townships, 19–21, 120–121, 128–129

volunteering, 131; India's *khadi* industry, 145–146; Orange Farm campaign, 289–290; Organization Workshop, 127

volunteerism, 241

Volvo, 187, 192, 196, 209, 213, 219

von Holdt, Karl, 19(n10), 20
Voortrekker township, South Africa, 19–20
voting as public choice, 297
Vygotsky, Lev, 122, 122(n35), 218(n92)

Waddington, C.H., 48(n18), 93(n19), 217(n90)
wages: circulating capital, 249; competitive level of South Africa's, 253(n80); fighting corruption in NREGA, 166–167; flexible prices and economic equilibrium, 229–231; India's *khadi* industry, 145–147; in a mercantile economy, 66–67; for nonmarket livelihoods, 276; NREGA, 153(n32), 155, 169–174; poverty as a consequence of market exchange, 76–79; Say's Law, 81; South Africa's hawkers, 113; South Africa's poultry program, 109–110; Sweden's tradeable economic sector, 188–189; the Swedish Model, 184, 190–192, 205, 209–210
Walker, L., 286(n48)
Wall, Dennis, 360(n20)
Wallerstein, Immanuel, 49, 83, 94, 264(n106), 271, 271(n124)
Walmart, 29
Walras, Leon, 60–63, 69–76, 69(nn31,32,33), 70(n35), 71(n38), 73(n42), 112(n5), 177, 264(n106), 270(n122), 373–374, 373(nn54,56), 374(n57)
Walsh, Vivian, 2(n7)
Walzer, Michael, 136(n66)
wares: role in capitalism, 65, 245
water resources: Bokfontein's Organization Workshop, 127; lowering the cost of basic needs, 216; NREGA public works, 148–149; Orange Farm's access, 278–279
Watts, Martin, 318(n3), 339(n50), 351(n88)
wealth: Gresham's Law of bad driving out good, 219; the origins of neoliberalism, 243–252; Smith on consumption and, 250–251; Smith's exploration of the nature and causes, 62–63; structural transformation through transfer of accumulation, 385–386; taxing, 388–389
Wealth of Nations (Smith), 243–252
Weber, Max, 66(n20), 67(n26), 93, 266(n111)
Welch, Michael, 282(n34)
welfare dependency, 57
welfare economics: maximizing utility, 71–72; revealed preference as a measure of value, 73
welfare state, 385(n87); affordability of poverty elimination, 220–221; correlation with crime, 283; CWP as alternative, 40; decline and failure of the Swedish Model, 183–184, 187, 193–195, 208, 210, 214; defining, 184(n15); effect of decline on social democracy, 179; the fiscal crisis of the state, 202, 206; India's employment guarantees, 165; as a lost cause, 57–58; making the global economy governable, 382–393; populist promises, 38–39; unbounded approach, 332(n41)

well-digging projects, 174–176
Weltbürgerliche Standpunkt (cosmopolitan standpoint), 355–365
Wertsch, James, 122(n35)
Westonaria, South Africa, 394
Whittle, Mark, 237(n17)
Wielecki, Krzysztof, 179, 179(n2), 193, 195, 204, 224–225
Wilber, Charles, 100(n33), 229(n2)
Wilkinson, Richard, 27(n39), 306(n115), 368(n35)
Williams, Robert R., 279(n20)
Wilson, David Sloan, 48–50, 133(n54), 207, 207(n53), 238(n19), 306(n114), 340(n53), 377(n65)
Winters, Jeffrey, 181(n6), 183(n9), 219(n95)
Wittgenstein, Ludwig, 38(n60), 233, 233(n10), 329, 329(n34), 354(n101)
Wolff, Robert Paul, 353(n92)
women: CWP participants in Orange Farm, 298–301; domestic violence in Orange Farm, 284–286; India's *khadi* industry, 146; NREGA's purpose and activities, 153–154; public funding for, 120; Sweden's nontradeable sector, 189–190
Wood, Ellen Meiksins, 7, 7(n24), 268(n114)
Woodham-Smith, Cecil, 195(n34)
Woodward, Susan, 4(n11)
working conditions: increasing efficiency and productivity, 216
World Economic Forum, 394, 398
World Health Organization (WHO), 325
World Social Forum, 394, 398
World Trade Organization (WTO), 31, 49, 159, 232
world-system, modern, 357(n7)
Wray, L. Randall, 318(n3), 335–340, 335(nn44,45), 339(n50), 351(n88)
Wright, Robert, 48(n17)

xenophobic violence, 19–21, 128–129
Xi Jinping, 223, 223(n103)

youth: CWP participants in Orange Farm, 298; motivation in Orange Farm, 289–290

Zahn, Frank, 176(n96)
Zinn, Howard, 391(n107)
Zuma, Jacob: National Development Plan, 33

About the Authors

Howard Richards was born in Pasadena, California, in 1938. He holds a doctorate in education with mention in moral education from the University of Toronto, a doctorate in philosophy from the University of California at Santa Barbara, a law degree from Stanford and an advanced certificate in education (with honours) from Oxford. As an undergraduate at Yale, he won the New York Yale Club prize for outstanding scholarship.

Howard served as a volunteer attorney for Cesar Chavez and Dolores Huerta when they organized farm workers in California's Central Valley in the 1960s. Later he worked in popular education at the Centro de Investigacion y Desarrollo de la Educacion in Santiago, Chile. He taught for thirty years (1974–2004) at Earlham College. His many earlier works include *The Evaluation of Cultural Action* (1985) and, with Joanna Swanger, *The Dilemmas of Social Democracies* (2006). He and his wife, Caroline, now live in Chile. He continues to teach one course a year at the Graduate Business School at the University of Cape Town.

Gavin Andersson grew up in Botswana. While studying in Johannesburg he became active in restarting the black trade union movement and was banned by the Apartheid government in 1976. After five years working as a carpenter, he returned to Botswana and cofounded CORDE, which strengthened cooperatives and grassroots business enterprises.

In South Africa, after it became a democratic country, he led organizations focused on community development and multi-stakeholder development initiatives. His use of the Moraisean Organization Workshop (OW) has enabled community actors to tackle social, environmental and economic issues collectively. Gavin was cocreator of *Kwanda*, a reality TV show on community transformation. He was a pioneer of the Community Work Programme, facilitating development processes at its earliest sites. He holds a doctorate in Development Studies from the Open University in the UK, writes on unbounded organizing and teaches in the Executive MBA programme at the University of Cape Town.

www.ingramcontent.com/pod-product-compliance
Lightning Source LLC
Chambersburg PA
CBHW050417170426
43201CB00008B/438